COMPARATIVE POLITICS

Notes and Readings

THE DORSEY SERIES IN POLITICAL SCIENCE

COMPARATIVE POLITICS
Notes and Readings

Edited by
ROY C. MACRIDIS
Professor of Politics
Brandeis University

and

BERNARD E. BROWN
Professor of Political Science
City University of New York (Brooklyn)

Fourth Edition 1972
THE DORSEY PRESS Homewood, Illinois 60430
IRWIN-DORSEY LIMITED Georgetown, Ontario

Fourth Edition

First Printing, January, 1972

Library of Congress Catalog Card No. 74-172968

Printed in the United States of America

PREFACE

To paraphrase Emile Durkheim, comparative politics is not a branch of political science; it *is* political science insofar as the discipline ceases to be purely descriptive and seeks to make sense of reality. All inquiry is comparative in that hypotheses are tested or appraised in as many different situations as possible. We have conceived of this volume, therefore, as a broad introduction to the study of political science. The general analytic categories used for presentation of the materials—political analysis, legitimacy and consensus, dynamics, institutions, and change—cover the entire field of political science and most special interests of students and teachers.

In bringing out this fourth edition, we have tried to adhere to our original purpose: to furnish the student both tools of political analysis and substantive studies that illustrate their utility. But, as we wrote in the preface to the first edition over a decade ago: "The study of politics is also an unrelenting quest (in Aristotle's terms) for the highest good. The student should attempt to relate his knowledge about the functioning of political systems to the issues of our time." Today, more than ever, it is necessary to view our institutions and our discontents in a critical perspective.

Regretfully, we had to eliminate many of our original selections in order to keep this book down to a reasonable size. In making final choices, our primary concern was to offer representative selections of readings, rather than favor one approach to the exclusion of all others. We are, of course, grateful to the publishers or authors for granting their kind permission to reprint. Our thanks go to many friends and colleagues for their advice and encouragement, and to Jacklyn Macridis and Eleanor J. Brown for their sympathetic support. Eleanor J. Brown again gave us the benefit of her invaluable editorial talents.

December, 1971   R. C. M.
                                                         B. E. B.

LIST OF AUTHORS

(Note: Pages in brackets refer to contributions in this volume.)

Gabriel Almond. Professor of Political Science, Stanford University. Author, *The American People and Foreign Policy* (1950); *The Appeals of Communism* (1954). Coauthor, *The Politics of Developing Areas* (1960); *The Civic Culture* (1963); and *Comparative Politics: A Developmental Approach* (1966).
[35–49, 198–205]

Raymond Aron. Professor Emeritus of Sociology, University of Paris. His works available in English translation include: *The Century of Total War* (1955); *German Sociology* (1957); *Peace and War* (1962); *The Industrial Society* (1967); and *Main Currents in Sociological Thought* (1967). [23–35]

Karl Dietrich Bracher. Professor of Political Science and Modern History, University of Bonn (Germany). Author, *The German Dictatorship* (1970), and numerous other works in German. [311–328]

Crane Brinton (1898–1968). Late Professor of Ancient and Modern History, Harvard University. Author, *The Jacobins* (1930); *Nietzsche* (1941); *The United States and Britain* (1948); *English Political Thought in the Nineteenth Century* (1949); *Ideas and Men* (1950); and *The Americans and the French* (1968).
[480–494]

Bernard E. Brown. Professor of Political Science, City University of New York (Brooklyn). Author, *American Conservatives* (1951); and *New Directions in Comparative Politics* (1962). Coauthor, *The De Gaulle Republic* (1960, 1963); and *Cases in Comparative Politics* (rev. ed., 1969). Coeditor, *The American Political System* (rev. ed., 1971). [274–289, 442–461]

Robert A. Dahl. Sterling Professor of Political Science, Yale University. Author, *A Preface to Democratic Theory* (1956); *Who Governs?* (1961); *Modern Political Analysis* (1963); *Pluralist Democracy in the United States* (1967); and *After the Revolution* (1970). Coauthor, *Politics, Economics, and Welfare* (1953).
[142–155]

Karl W. Deutsch. Professor of Government, Harvard University. Author, *Nationalism and Social Communication* (1953); *The Nerves of Government* (1963); *Arms Control and the Atlantic Alliance* (1967); and *Nationalism and Its Alternatives* (1969). Coauthor, *Political Community and the North Atlantic Area* (1957); and *Germany Rejoins the Powers* (1959). Coeditor, *Nation-Building* (1966).   [400–407]

Ivo D. Duchacek. Professor of Political Science, City College of the City University of New York. Author, *Nations and Men* (rev. ed., 1970); and *Comparative Federalism* (1970).   [328–340]

Emile Durkheim (1858–1917). French sociologist. His works in English translation include: *The Rules of the Sociological Method* (1938); *The Division of Labor in Society* (1965); and *The Elementary Forms of the Religious Life* (1965).   [504–512]

David Easton. Professor of Political Science, University of Chicago. Author, *The Political System* (1953); *A Framework for Political Analysis* (1965); and *A Systems Analysis of Political Life* (1965). Coauthor, *Children in the Political System* (1969).   [72–85]

Samuel P. Huntington. Frank G. Thomson Professor of Government, Harvard University. Author, *The Soldier and the State* (1957); *The Common Defense* (1961); and *Political Order in Changing Societies* (1968). Coauthor, *Authoritarian Politics in Modern Society* (1970). Editor, *Changing Patterns of Military Politics* (1962).   [407–425]

Alex Inkeles. Professor of Sociology, Harvard University. Author, *Public Opinion in Soviet Russia* (1950); *What is Sociology?* (1964); and *Social Change in Soviet Society* (1968). Coauthor, *The Soviet Citizen, Daily Life in a Totalitarian Society* (1959).   [13–22]

Anthony King. Professor of Government, University of Essex (Colchester, England). Coauthor, with David E. Butler, of *The British General Election of 1964* and *The British General Election of 1966*.   [233–251]

Otto Kirchheimer (1905–65). Late Professor of Government, Columbia University. Author, *A Constitution for the Fourth Republic* (1947); and *Political Justice* (1961). Also, *Politics, Law, and Social Change, Selected Essays of Otto Kirchheimer,* edited by F. S. Burin and K. L. Shell (1969).   [221–233]

Joseph G. LaPalombara. Professor of Political Science, Yale University. Author, *The Italian Labor Movement* (1959); *Interest Groups in Italian Politics* (1964); and *Italy, the Politics of Planning* (1966). Coauthor, *Bureaucracy and Political Development* (1963); and *Political Parties and Political Development* (1966).   [262–274]

Marion J. Levy, Jr. Professor of Sociology, Princeton University. Author, *The Family Revolution in Modern China* (1949); *The Structure of Society* (1952); and *Modernization and the Structure of Societies* (2 vols., 1966).
                                                                                            [61–72]

Seymour M. Lipset. Professor of Sociology, Harvard University. Author, *Agrarian Socialism* (1950); *Political Man* (1960); *The First New Nation* (1963); and *Revolution and Counterrevolution* (1968). Coauthor, *Union Democracy* (1956); and *The Politics of Unreason* (1970). Editor, *Elites in Latin America* (1967); *Party Systems and Voter Alignments* (1967); and *Student Politics* (1967).   [124–142]

Val R. Lorwin. Professor of History, University of Oregon. Author, *The French Labor Movement* (1954).   [253–262]

Richard Lowenthal. Professor of Political Science, Free University of Berlin. His works in English include: *World Communism, The Disintegration of a Secular Faith* (1966).   [517–534]

Robert M. MacIver (1882–1970). Late Professor of Political Philosophy and Sociology, Columbia University. Author, *The Modern State* (1926); *Community* (1931); *Leviathan and the People* (1939); *Social Causation* (1942); *Society* (rev. ed., 1949); *The Ramparts We Guard* (1950); *The Pursuit of Happiness* (1955); *Power Transformed* (1964); and numerous other works.   [115–122]

C. B. MacPherson. Professor of Political Economy, University of Toronto. Author, *The Political Theory of Possessive Individualism* (1962); and *The Real World of Democracy* (1966).   [362–373]

Roy C. Macridis. Professor of Politics, Brandeis University. Author, *The Study of Comparative Government* (1955). Coauthor, *The De Gaulle Republic* (1960, 1963); *Foreign Policy in World Politics* (rev. ed., 1961); *France, Germany, and the Western Alliance* (1967); *Modern Political Systems: Europe* (rev. ed., 1968); and *Modern European Governments, Cases in Comparative Policy Making* (1968). Editor, *De Gaulle, Implacable Ally* (1966); and *Political Parties* (1967).
[85–97, 206–211]

Herbert Marcuse. Professor of Philosophy, University of California at San Diego. Author, *Reason and Revolution* (1941, 1954); *Eros and Civilization* (1955, 1966); *Soviet Marxism, A Critical Analysis* (1958); *One-Dimensional Man* (1964); *Negations, Essays in Critical Theory* (1968); and *An Essay on Liberation* (1969).   [512–517]

Karl Marx (1818–83). Useful one-volume collections include *Capital and Other Writings,* edited by Max Eastman (Modern Library edition, 1932); and *Marx and Engels: Basic Writings on Politics and Philosophy,* edited by Lewis S. Feuer (1959).   [477–479]

Robert Michels (1876–1946). Italian economist and sociologist. Author of *Political Parties* (1914), and numerous other works in Italian and German.
[213–220]

John Stuart Mill (1806–73). Noted English philosopher and essayist. A convenient collection of his political writings is the Everyman edition of *Utilitarianism, Liberty, and Representative Government.*   [304–311]

x LIST OF AUTHORS

Gaetano Mosca (1858–1941). Italian historian and political scientist. Author, *Elementi di Scienza Politica* (1947); *Storia delle Dottrine Politiche* (1937); and *Partiti e Sindacati nella Crisi del Regime Parlamentare* (1949).   [107–115]

Franz L. Neumann (1900–54). Late Professor of Government, Columbia University. Author, *Behemoth: The Structure and Practice of National Socialism* (1944); and *The Democratic and the Authoritarian State* (1957).
[49–59, 157–170]

Donald C. Rowat. Professor of Political Science, Carleton University (Ottawa). Editor, *Basic Issues in Public Administration* (1961); and *The Ombudsman* (1965).   [374–382]

Dankwart A. Rustow. Professor of Political Science, City University of New York (Brooklyn). Author, *The Politics of Compromise, A Study of Parties and Cabinet Government in Sweden* (1955); *A World of Nations* (1967). Coauthor, *Political Modernization in Japan and Turkey* (1964).   [461–475]

Wallace S. Sayre. Eaton Professor of Public Administration, Columbia University. Coauthor, *Governing New York City* (1960).   [350–359]

Robert C. Tucker. Professor of Politics, Princeton University. Author, *Philosophy and Myth in Karl Marx* (1961); *The Soviet Political Mind* (1963); and *The Marxian Revolutionary Idea* (1969).   [170–182]

Thorstein Veblen (1857–1929). American economist and sociologist. Among his works are: *The Theory of the Leisure Class* (1899); *The Instinct of Workmanship and the State of the Industrial Arts* (1914); *Imperial Germany and the Industrial Revolution* (1915); and *The Engineers and the Price System* (1921).
[395–399]

Robert E. Ward. Professor of Political Science, University of Michigan. Author, *Japanese Political Science* (1961); and *Japan's Political System* (1967). Coauthor, *Village Japan* (1959); *Political Modernization in Japan and Turkey* (1962); and *Studying Politics Abroad* (1964). Editor, *Five Studies in Japanese Politics* (1957).   [427–442]

Max Weber (1864–1920). German sociologist and political scientist. Among his works in English translation are: *The Protestant Ethic and the Spirit of Capitalism* (1930); *The Theory of Social and Economic Organization* (1947); and *From Max Weber,* edited by H. H. Gerth and C. W. Mills (1952).
[342–350]

Eric R. Wolf. Professor of Anthropology, University of Michigan. Author, *Sons of the Shaking Earth* (1959); *Anthropology* (1964); *Peasant Wars of the 20th Century* (1969).   [495–502]

CONTENTS

part ONE
Political Analysis

I. POLITICAL SYSTEMS

This volume is prepared on the basis of a general conception: a political system is, above all, a mechanism for the making of decisions. It is endowed with legitimacy, that is, the decisions made by the various organs of government are expected to be widely obeyed.

Decisions involve compromises among many conflicting points of view held by social groups, parties, associations, interest organizations, and regions. On the one hand, we have the governmental organs that make decisions—the legislature, the executive, the courts, and the bureaucracy. On the other hand, there are the social and economic forces and groupings, and the beliefs and values held by the members of the society about their political system. This suggests a threefold distinction: (1) the government; (2) the "social and cultural configuration," that is, social classes, economic groups, ethnic groups, regions, interest groups and their mode of action; and (3) the pattern of values and ideologies relating specifically to political authority, permissive areas of governmental action, and the role and position of individuals and associations.

It is the interplay between social configuration, ideology, and the governmental organs that constitutes the dynamics of politics—the making of decisions. Social and economic groups, molded and patterned in accordance with the ideas men hold, press their claims upon the government. Interest groups and political parties function as conveyor belts between interest claims and governmental decisions. Political leadership sifts these claims, often provides for compromise, and articulates them in the form of pledges or decisions. It is not impossible, especially when conflicts assume a high level of intensity and when opposing sides are evenly balanced, for a political system to find itself in a situation where no decision can be made. The system is at a state of stalemate, or to use the expression often employed to characterize the French parliamentary system under the Third and Fourth Republics, "immobility."

1

The efficiency of a political system can be gauged in terms of its ability to make decisions that are widely accepted. In a democratic system this can be determined by the response such decisions elicit among the social groups, interest groups, and voluntary associations. In authoritarian systems the electoral process is not a reliable indicator of legitimacy; nonetheless, there is ultimately a comparable test of effectiveness.

An efficient system maintains a balance between change and stability. Change is the result of constant claims that arise from the social groups because of evolving technical and economic conditions. Emerging social groups inevitably put forward demands as they gain access to positions of influence and power. Throughout the 19th century, for instance, the general theme of political change was associated with the claims of the lower middle classes and the workers (in some cases the slaves and serfs) for suffrage and political participation. As societies industrialize, these same groups organize in order to facilitate the translation of their newly acquired political influence into immediate socio-economic benefits. Efficiency therefore depends upon the nature of governmental response to the demands from groups. If existing institutions prove incapable of meeting these demands, the new groups may attempt to gain power by revolutionary means, which has disruptive effects upon the whole system.

From this point of view there is no guarantee that a democratic system is more efficient than a totalitarian one. The latter must provide some way (for example, through the ruling party) for significant groups to be heard. The former may find that its representative institutions no longer adequately translate claims of equally strong and competing groups into decisions or provide a satisfactory synthesis. In both systems leadership plays an important role. Basically, a leader decides in favor of certain groups and at the expense of other groups. But he cannot impose a policy which is out of line with the existing balance of forces. In fact a democratic society may become the victim of its own philosophy. By creating organs that register accurately the demands of all groups and by attempting to satisfy all of them, it may give to each a "veto power" over decisions and thus founder in stalemate.

The most persistent challenges to a political system derive from economic and technological modernization. In underdeveloped countries modernization involves literally the restructuring of society—the inculcation of new norms of behavior, the training of skilled bureaucrats, and drastic action on the basis of newly established goals. Modernization at the political level involves the identification of the masses of the people with these goals. Disciplined effort is indispensable because of the lack of available resources. These societies must rely upon their most plentiful and therefore cheapest commodity—human labor—whose effective utilization requires sacrifice and unremitting toil. In Western Europe, the Protestant religion, it has been suggested by Max Weber, provided the philosophy that broke down the barriers of feudal and medieval society, secularized human motivation, and supplied incentive that made possible the Industrial Revolution. Ideologies and values in the underdeveloped societies are now undergoing similar transformations. Will these nations follow the European pattern of economic individualism, or the Communist type of collective effort with emphasis on coercion and indoctrination? Their choice will largely determine the nature of their emerging political institutions.

Problems of modernization are naturally different for the societies that have already attained a high level of industrialization. The crucial problem in economically advanced systems is to maintain a constant rate of economic growth, to develop technology rapidly and effectively in order to increase the productivity of labor, and to make the benefits of increased productivity available to all in the form of better living conditions and welfare. The government is compelled to provide a wide range of services and to enforce social justice by means of income distribution.

To summarize: We have suggested that in a political system conflicting claims and demands are translated into accepted decisions. The claims are made by social groups. The manner in which conflicts are expressed depends to a great degree upon the nature of ideologies and values concerning political authority. The links between the social structure and the governmental organs are political parties, interest groups, and other associations. It is the role of political leadership to articulate interests and conflicts, achieve a synthesis in the form of policy, and carry it out through the governmental organs. An efficient government is able to provide for change in a stable fashion—that is, without response to violence on the part of important groups. It must also be able to survive as a system in the midst of competing nation-states.

An examination of all these propositions requires comparative analysis and study.

II. THE COMPARATIVE APPROACH

The study of comparative government is in a state of flux. Traditionally, it has been preponderantly descriptive rather than problem-solving, explanatory, or analytic in its method. It did not lend itself to the development of theories and the testing of hypotheses and the compilation of significant data. It was limited to the description of the forms of government of foreign political systems.

Recently there has been an increasing awareness of the shortcomings of the traditional approach, leading to an attempt to develop a more systematic orientation. The need has been felt to broaden our approach both horizontally (by including as many political systems—Western and non-Western—as possible) and vertically (by attempting to relate the political process to broad scale and economic conditions). There has been a growing concern to be more "scientific." Science aspires to the establishment of universal patterns of behavior and requires the testing of hypothetical propositions. This means that the testing should be made against as many systems as possible in the light of common analytical categories.[1]

[1] See Roy C. Macridis, *The Study of Comparative Government* (New York: Random House, 1955), especially pp. 15–17; and Bernard E. Brown, *New Directions in Comparative Politics* (London: Asia Publishers, 1962), chap. 1.

The new approach is more probing and systematic. It is probing in that it attempts to go behind the facade of political institutions; it is primarily concerned with the social configuration, the interest-group universe, political parties, ideological attitudes as they shape and condition political behavior, and elite structure. It is systematic in seeking to discover "relations" between politics and the contextual elements of a system.

But a systematic approach requires an overall view or theory of politics. Political science has therefore borrowed extensively from sociological theory. For example, politics has been viewed by some analysts as a system of interaction between actors (individuals and groups) for the purpose of realizing specific goals. A political system must perform certain indispensable (or requisite) functions in order to survive. Certain institutions are also indispensable (or requisite) structures for the performance of these functions. Structures differ from one system to another and undergo profound modifications under the impact of diverse factors—war, industrialization, economic changes, new aspirations, and new demands.

The study of politics (as for Aristotle) becomes the study of a "system" linked organically with social structure, traditions and ideologies, culture, and the environment within which it operates. It may then be possible to discern significant similarities and differences which mere description of the legal forms of a state does not suggest. Establishment of *correlations* between political, economic, cultural, and social phenomena provides a perspective in terms of which the dynamics of change may be understood and broad generalizations made. In essence, this is the application of scientific method to the study of political phenomena. Hypotheses and theories about the political process are elaborated into a rational system and then examined critically in the light of available evidence.

The analytical approach, then, strives toward a definition of a political system, identifies the most important structures through which a system functions, and studies differences and similarities. It purports to establish general propositions about political behavior. As in natural science, generalizations are stated in the form of hypotheses involving a series of conditions. For instance, it could be posited that if there are no serious ideological conflicts in a society and if there is a majority electoral system, then two parties will develop. It can be posited that industrialization and prosperity will, all other conditions being held in check, lead to a decrease in conflict about issues and the development of a political system concerned with the solution of concrete problems. It may be posited that economic policies endangering the status of certain social groups will provoke a strong movement of protest on the part of the threatened groups, who will seek to protect themselves even by violence—or that groups denied participation in the political system will, all other things being equal, seek to gain status and influence also by violence.

These hypotheses can be tested against reality and accordingly qualified, modified, or rejected. Field work and empirical observation are therefore indispensable for comparative study as for all forms of scientific inquiry. This kind of analysis will add to our knowledge of the conditioning factors whose presence or absence accounts for the validation or the rejection of our hypothesis. For instance, if we propose that wherever there is A (for example, a majority electoral system) then B (a two-party system) will follow and find that in one system this obtains but in another it does not, then we have to seek the reasons for this disparity. We do so by finding a series of other factors $(X, X_1, X_2, X_3, X_4, X_5,$ etc.). Our hypothesis then will be qualified to read A will follow B provided factors X_2 (religious differences), X_3 (regionalism) or X_4 (ethnic groups) or others, depending upon field observation, obtain. In this manner a comprehensive explanation accounting for the differences between two systems may be given.

It is at this point that comparative analysis becomes both challenging and at the same time frustrating for the student. Rarely if ever can we provide a coherent and satisfactory generalization explaining the differences between systems. Historical and other factors give nations characteristics that are unique, that is to say, cannot be duplicated. In fact we shall find it virtually impossible to verify any hypothesis or to develop any generalization that is valid for *all* political systems. It is necessary to lengthen the chain of conditioning factors (X's) for each political system in order to take into account individual and idiosyncratic factors. The proposal to develop general laws seems to bog down in a never-ending explanation for unique situations. Some observers contend that there are no universally valid laws. In despair they conclude that the indeterminacy and uniqueness of political behavior does not permit generalization.

It would be a serious mistake to accept this point of view. Comparative analysis can at the very least identify and perhaps explain uniqueness, which is of crucial importance. Unless we start with general concepts and hypotheses, we are not able even to draw distinctions let alone account for them. How can we tell what is unique without knowing what is general? Power, for instance, is manifested in many ways and contains many elements—religion, property, birth, administration, and so on. But these different manifestations can be distinguished, related, and understood only in terms of some general concept of power.

The Range of Comparison

The range of comparison will usually be determined by the theoretical scheme, by the formulation of a *problem* or the study of *a given area.* In all cases two crucial questions must be confronted: How do we compare? What do we compare?

Comparison may be attempted between segments of the political process in various systems, or between certain institutions, or between political systems as such, in order to clarify issues which preoccupy us. Let us take the multiparty system in France. The historian of French political institutions will describe the origin, development, ideologies, and characteristics of the French multiparty system. The student of comparative politics faced with the same problem would ask rather: What are the conditions for the existence of a multiparty system? Are they institutional?—social?—sectional?—ideological? Once the conditions have been identified, then comparison with other multiparty systems will show the relevance of some but not others, that is, comparative study may disprove the relationship between certain conditions and multipartism. We find, for instance, that analogous sectional conditions in the United States have not produced a multiparty system—or that similar electoral systems exist in both two-party and multiparty systems.

Through comparison it is possible to explain the nature of a phenomenon like a multiparty system in the light of a chain of conditioning factors, such as sectionalism, proportional representation, the cabinet's inability to dissolve parliament, and so on. The chain of conditioning factors that we find in France cannot be reproduced historically or experimentally in any other country. But this in no way lessens the need for suggesting relationships among conditioning factors for the purpose of analysis and empirical investigation. Nor does it mean that because France and Country X or Y are unique they cannot be the subject of comparison. France is indeed unique, but in an analytical sense the conditions of multipartism are general categories permitting comparison of France with other political systems. Every suicide is unique. But as Emile Durkheim demonstrated, the conditions under which people commit suicide can be analytically identified in terms of a number of broad categories.

We compare, therefore, in order to discover the conditions under which certain phenomena take place. Conditions or, more precisely, a series of conditions are hypothetically related to the phenomenon we study. The task of empirical observation is to test the validity of such hypothetical formulations. By so doing we enrich our knowledge of the factors that account for a given phenomenon until we are able to generalize about them. The presence or absence of some or others will enable us to make tentative judgments about political developments and occurrences.

Comparison may be either *static* or *dynamic.* In the first instance, we undertake an anatomy, so to speak, of political systems. Structures are described and related. In this connection classificatory tables are useful in that they suggest analogies and differences. Structures, however, must be identified in terms of the particular function they perform in a system. This is much more difficult than it may seem to be. It is essential to discern the *overt* from the *covert,* and the *manifest* from the *latent* functions. For instance, though there are striking structural analogies between the electoral system of the Soviet Union and that of the United States, their functions are wholly dissimilar. Elections in the United States are an integral part of the process of arriving at decisions over which the body politic is divided. In the Soviet Union, on the other hand, elections are used to express loyalty to the regime, and to rally the people around the policy of their leaders. Their function is roughly that of a patriotic celebration.

Dynamic comparison is the study of the performance of various systems. We not only identify structures through which certain functions are performed but also account for the structural variations between systems. Ultimately an effort may be made to trace out consequences of alternative courses of action, or predict in the light of a chain of conditioning factors. This last stage is indeed the most significant but at the same time the most difficult to reach.

The Problem Approach in Comparative Studies

The study of a problem in comparative terms may be conducted at several different levels of abstraction. For instance, the study of political instability as a "problem" would be at a high level of generalization. On the other hand, the study of political instability in parliamentary systems would involve less sweeping concepts and a more limited range of observation and variables. Finally, the study of cabinet instability in its relation to electoral systems would deal with even narrower concepts and more strictly defined variables.

Three types of problem approaches may be distinguished:
1. The "middle-range theory problem" approach.
2. The "policy-oriented problem" approach.
3. The "narrow-gauge theory problem" approach.

The Middle-Range Approach.   This approach requires a theoretical scheme involving a fairly high degree of generalization and abstraction but remains below the level of a comprehensive scheme of politics. In the words of Robert K. Merton, theories of the middle range are "theories intermediate to the minor working hypotheses evolved in abundance during the day-to-day routines of research, and the all-inclusive speculations comprising a master conceptual scheme from which it is hoped to derive a very large number of empirically observed uniformities of social behavior."[2] The problem is significant and not trivial or narrow, yet is "researchable." It is possible, that is, to test out the theory by examining relevant data. Its flexibility and adaptability to modest levels of empirical research at manageable levels is its greatest merit. Many of the selections in this volume are illustrative of the "middle-range" approach, for example, Otto Kirchheimer on ideological trends in industrialized societies or Dankwart Rustow on the social conditions under which democracy emerges.

A Policy-Oriented Approach.   A second type of approach, put forward recently by a number of authors, is the presentation and selection of problems for policy purposes.[3] Both in their selection and in their study, problems are related to the requirements of policy making. They are chosen because of a "conflict situation" or a "high degree of tension." They are studied for the purpose of suggesting "solutions" through which the causes of tensions may be removed and conflict lessened. An examination of racial relations in major urban centers in the United States, for instance, is in a sense comparative and attempts to elicit information and data that may guide policy makers. Insecurity

[2] Robert K. Merton, *Social Theory and Social Structure* (Glencoe, Ill.; Free Press, 1949), p. 5.

[3] See Daniel Lerner and Harold Lasswell, eds., *The Policy Sciences* (Stanford, Calif.: Stanford University Press, 1951).

and its manifestations under various political and economic systems is a problem that can also be studied comparatively and again is formulated because of the observable signs of tension. Studies of revolution undertaken comparatively may shed light upon the relevant factors that bring about violent action on the part of certain groups. They may be undertaken either for the purpose of studying this phenomenon as such or for the purpose of working out a policy to prevent its recurrence.

The problem approach has the great advantage of orienting research empirically along multiple avenues without being tied down to premature theoretical schemes. Also, it is perhaps inevitable that political scientists should concern themselves with contemporary crises. But one of the dangers is oversimplification. Conflict and tensions are the result of many factors situated in a time dimension. Suggested policies may provoke new tensions or have unanticipated consequences unless they are carefully thought out in the light of the many existing factors.

Narrow-Gauge Theory Approach.   Narrow-gauge theory involves the selection of a problem that has a limited range of variables. It fulfills some of the same functions as middle-range theory but can be used only for the study of phenomena in similar social contexts. For this reason narrow-gauge hypotheses are fruitful mainly in suggesting broader theories.

The most familiar narrow-gauge hypotheses are those used for the study of Western political systems. Invariably they are "disproved" and as a result abandoned. To give an illustration: Does the power of dissolution create well-disciplined parties which in turn account for cabinet stability? The question as formulated obviously relates to the parliamentary systems of Great Britain and Western Europe. Observation reveals that there is a missing link—the electoral system. Hence, the question may be rephrased in the following terms: Does the power of dissolution in a single-member district system bring about party discipline and cabinet stability? On the basis of comparative study an affirmative or negative answer is unwarranted. No two parliamentary systems of Western Europe satisfy the requirements of this proposition. Even if they did, stability or instability might still be caused by other factors.

Nonetheless, the narrow-gauge theory approach is extremely useful. Through a process of disproof rather than proof it trains students to think in terms of hypotheses and their verification. By eliminating irrelevant causes, students learn how to relate politics to social, economic, and cultural factors.

The most fruitful work in the field of comparative politics in recent years has resulted from analysis of middle-range theory problems. It should be emphasized, however, that the study of the issues and crises of our century is not necessarily to be shunted aside in favor of an exclusive preoccupation with theoretical constructs and model building. It would be unfortunate, indeed self-defeating, if students of politics confined their attention only to problems which can be formulated on a low or middle level of abstraction, or if all lines of political inquiry were to be dictated by the research tools at our disposal. The political scientist should be concerned not only with predictability but also desirability and the social conditions under which desired goals can be realized. The examination of such goals in terms of ethical postulates is part of the task of the political scientist. Unless we resign ourselves to acceptance of any state which happens to exist, and to any goals sought by a group, then ethics will always constitute a legitimate subject of political inquiry. In this volume, however, we are deliberately focusing our interest on the political process and system.

III. THE SEARCH FOR NEW DEFINITIONS

Awareness of the need for a more systematic approach to the study of politics, coupled with a new appreciation of the interrelationship between social and political structures, has played havoc with the old descriptive definitions and classifications. Traditionally, a state has been described as a community of people living in a given territory with a government. Wherever there is a stable relationship between governors and governed there is a state. Thus, both Ecuador and the United States are examples of "states." But the classic definition does not tell us what to look for and where to look in order to find out how and why these two states are different. The use of categories like ideology, social configuration, and government as a decision-making mechanism aids the student to understand similarities and differences.

The United States is an industrial society; Ecuador is agrarian. In the one, effective participation in politics is widespread; in the other, it is extremely limited. In the one, there is a clear differentiation between the bureaucrat, the soldier, the priest, or the producer; in the other, the differentiation is blurred. In the one, literacy is very high; in the other, literacy is low. In the one, people constantly made demands through a number of clearly discernible institutions—interest groups, parties, and legislatures; in the other, emerging aspirations are not clearly channeled in an orderly way. All these differences constitute the real "stuff" of politics.

Most scholars writing in the field of comparative politics today have abandoned the traditional classification of governments—as put forth by Aristotle and Montesquieu, for example—in terms of monarchy, aristocracy, democracy, mixed governments, and separation of powers. Even the distinction between totalitarian systems and constitutional democracies is not wholly satisfactory. The structure of political power is only one of many interrelated factors.

A profusion of new schemes for classifying governments has been suggested in recent years. Many stem from Max Weber's distinction between three types of authority: traditional, rational, and charismatic. Gabriel Almond in his article "Comparative Political Systems" distinguishes between four major kinds of systems: consensual (primarily Anglo-American), fragmented (continental Europe), totalitarian (communist and fascist), and preindustrial. David Apter refers to political systems as dictatorial, indirectly and directly representational, and oligarchical. A group of authors from the Massachusetts Institute of Technology, in a report prepared for the Senate Committee on Foreign Policy, identify the following types among the erstwhile colonies: traditional oligarchies, modernizing oligarchies, and potentially democratic societies. James Coleman refers to "terminal colonial democracy" and "colonial or racial oligarchy." In addition, he describes "stable and unstable" systems, and "underdeveloped and developing" societies. There are "transitional" societies in which Daniel Lerner tells us that we must look for a cluster of interrelated phenomena—industrialization, urbanization, literacy, participation in mass media, role differentiation, and empathy. Karl W. Deutsch develops an impressive listing of variables in order to differentiate systems on the basis of diverse combinations. Finally, the terms "Western" and "non-Western" are on everybody's lips today.

The "boundaries" of the field of politics have become blurred. In identifying the component elements of a system, Gabriel Almond lists the following "input" (primarily political) functions: political socialization and recruitment, interest articulation, interest aggregation, and political communication. The "output" (or governmental) functions are more familiar even if the terms appear to be new. They are rule making, rule application, and rule adjudication. Professor Lasswell goes a step further in describing the functions of a political system as follows: intelligence, recommendation, prescription, invocation, application, appraisal, and termination. David Easton is more parsimonious. He holds that the main functions of a political system are demands, supports, and authoritative decisions—the latter determining the proper boundaries of politics. Samuel Beer discusses a political system with reference to its "political culture," the "pattern of power," the "pattern of interests," and the "pattern of policy."[4]

We are, therefore, as was said at the outset, in a state of flux. We are uncertain of the boundaries of political science in its relation to other social sciences and in disagreement over the significant components of political systems. But a state of flux is not necessarily a state of confusion. It may rather be an indication of healthy curiosity and intellectual ferment. The discipline is maturing as it attempts to relate political and social factors, explain behavior, and clarify problems. Description of the institutions and policies of states continues to be of crucial importance. But they are properly viewed only as parts of the "political system."

[4] The works referred to include: Max Weber, *The Theory of Social and Economic Organization* (New York: Oxford University Press, 1947), pp. 324–91; Gabriel A. Almond, "Comparative Political Systems," *Journal of Politics*, August 1956 (reproduced below); David Apter, "A Comparative Method for the Study of Politics," *American Journal of Sociology* (November, 1958), pp. 221–37; Gabriel A. Almond and James S. Coleman, *The Politics of Developing Areas* (Princeton, N.J.: Princeton University Press, 1960); Daniel Lerner, *The Passing of Traditional Society* (Glencoe, Ill.: Free Press, 1958); Karl W. Deutsch, "Towards an Inventory of Basic Trends and Patterns in Comparative and International Politics," *American Political Science Review*, March, 1960; Harold D. Lasswell, *The Decision Process* (Bureau of Governmental Research, University of Maryland, 1956); David Easton, "An Approach to an Analysis of Political Systems," *World Politics* (April, 1957) (reproduced below); and Samuel Beer, *Patterns of Government* (New York: Random House, 1958), pp. 3–51.

chapter 1

CONCEPTS AND THEORIES

The role of a "concept" is to suggest a special analytical category in terms of which a political system can be studied. Some writers consider a political system to be a state of conflict and competition between influential groups; they are prone, as a result, to emphasize the concept of power and study political manifestations as power phenomena. Others study the personality structure and the actors and gauge the functioning of the system in terms of its outlets or its inhibitions. Some emphasize what might be called a cultural configurative approach—in which personality, satisfactions of economic needs, ideals, and symbols are interwoven and patterned to form different structural types of government and authority. Still others study those who control the instrumentalities of power—formal and informal—and concentrate on *elites.* Attention may also be focused upon *role*—the particular positions individuals hold in the social and political system and the perception they have of their positions, or upon *political culture*—a complex of attitudes and orientations through which the individual comprehends his political environment and acts within it. Related research has dealt with problems and processes of the assimilation or socialization of the individual within a given political culture.

Concepts, when related to each other, lead to the development of a theory. Theory purports to isolate and connect the most significant variables of political dynamics. A scientific theory can be readily related to social variables and tested by observation and comparison. For example, Marx developed theories that are cast readily in the form of causal relations. The given modes of production determined the total political and ideological configurations of a society. This interpretation became and, to some extent, continues to remain, despite its many errors and contradictions, one of the most prevalent modes of thinking not only in Europe but also in the United States and England. In the United States, Charles A. Beard (1874–1948) in a number of his works—notably in his *Economic Interpretation of the Constitution* (1913)—stressed the economic basis of politics. Harold Laski's *Parliamentary Government in England* (1938) reflects the same influence.

11

In contrast, Max Weber was more concerned with the development of a comprehensive analytical scheme rather than the establishment of causal hypotheses. His work, particularly with reference to the nature of political systems, the modes of economic organization, types of authority and legitimacy, and the nature of bureaucracy, is typological rather than explanatory. He has had a great impact upon contemporary sociological and political theory in the United States. The Weberian influence is evident in the writings of Talcott Parsons, notably *Essays on Sociological Theory, Pure and Applied* (1949), *Social Systems* (1951), and *Toward a General Theory of Action* (1958); and also in Robert K. Merton's *Social Theory and Social Structure* (1949); and Marion Levy's *The Structure of Society* (1952), to mention only a few. An excellent critical evaluation may be found in Reinhard Bendix, *Max Weber, An Intellectual Portrait* (1960).

Political scientists have become increasingly concerned with the use of concepts. In studying the types of political authority, the changing character of traditional societies, the characteristics of bureaucracy and "ideologies," they found a number of the Weberian categories useful and fruitful. Works by Gabriel A. Almond—notably his *The Politics of the Developing Areas* (1960); David Easton, *The Political System* (1953); David Apter, *Ghana in Transition* (1963), and Harry Eckstein, *Pressure Group Politics* (1960)—reflect this great concern with conceptualization and the influence of Weber in particular.

In the readings included here are only a sample of the most significant concepts that have been advanced for comparative study of political systems. Mention, therefore, might be made of some other trends which, regretfully, had to be omitted for lack of space. Professor Richard Snyder's studies of decision making, for example, have proved fruitful for the comparative study of foreign policy making. Examples of the utility of historical analysis in understanding the development of political systems are Louis Hartz, *The Liberal Tradition in America* (1955), and R. R. Palmer, *The Age of the Democratic Revolution* (1959). A comprehensive treatment of political culture and socialization may be found in Gabriel Almond and Sidney Verba, *The Civic Culture* (1963). For a fine synthesis see also Robert Dahl, *Political Analysis* (1963).

A. Personality

1. National Character*

ALEX INKELES

The method of analysis which yields studies in "culture and personality" when applied to "primitive" peoples has its analogue among studies of large-scale societies in a varied assortment of investigations on what is called national character. If, under this heading, we allow impressionistic, introspective, and loosely evaluative works to qualify, then for the United States alone—from De Tocqueville to Brogan and Gorer—the articles and books depicting the American character will be numbered in the hundreds. Were we to extend our coverage to the major nations of Europe and Asia, the number of relevant studies would be in the thousands. To view even the most important of these would strain the limits of our alloted space even while permitting only the driest catalogue of their contents. Yet if we were to insist on the more rigorous standards of empirical social science, and were to consider only more systematic investigations based on representative samples and utilizing standard psychological tests, then not more than two or three studies in the relevant literature could qualify. There is a third alternative. By selecting a specific problem focus we may simultaneously escape the boundlessness of a general review and the confining restrictions forced on us through the adoption of a rigorous methodological canon. A topic suitable to our purpose, one of interest and importance, is the relation of national character to the political systems found in modern national states, and more specifically, to the establishment and maintenance of democracy. Before we examine this relationship, we must clarify the meaning of our concepts.

WHAT IS NATIONAL CHARACTER AND HOW CAN IT BE MEASURED?

Problems of Definition

The confusion about the term *national character* is pervasive and enduring. Yet arguing about what a concept *should* mean can be utterly sterile. What is important is that we designate some empirical phenomenon which has concrete reference, which can be effectively distinguished from other phenomena, and which can conceivably be investigated by standard replicable, reliable, and valid

---

*From "National Character and Modern Political Systems," in Francis L. Hsu, ed., *Psychological Anthropology: Approaches to Culture and Personality* (Homewood, Ill.: Dorsey Press, 1961), pp. 172–202. Reprinted by permission of the publisher and the author. Essay and footnotes abridged by the editors. An abridged list of sources cited by the author appears at the end.

methods. For purposes of this discussion I will adopt the definition of national character presented in the *Handbook of Social-Psychology* (Inkeles and Levinson 1954) which, I believe, is now widely accepted: "National character refers to relatively enduring personality characteristics and patterns that are modal among the adult members of a society."

The other meanings given to national character, and related terms such as people's character, folk character, national (or "racial" or popular) psychology, are almost as numerous as the roster of political essayists from Plato to Pareto and from Pareto to Potter. Some treat national character as simply "the sum total" of all the values, institutions, cultural traditions, ways of acting, and history of a people. However useful this idea may be for popular discourse, it is sadly lacking for purposes of scientific analysis, since the failure to differentiate the elements of the phenomenon makes an impossible task of measurement, obfuscates issues of cause and effect, and precludes systematic study of the relations between elements. With most other definitions we have no quarrel, so long as those using the different terms are appropriately aware that each has a special and restricted meaning, and that no one of these concepts exhaustively describes the phenomenon under investigation.

*   *   *

If progress is to be made in the field, we need to make our investigations more systematic. There is no one line of development which can do full justice to the complexities of the problem. We feel, however, that great advantages inhere in the concentration on *modal adult personality* characteristics as a central problem in national character study. We therefore pose the question: whether produced by common heritage, common upbringing, the sharing of common culture, the exposure to common institutional pressures, or other causes, are there in fact any clearly demonstrated important differences in the psychological character-istics of the populations who make up modern national states? The question is more difficult to answer with confidence than many imagine it to be.

The Problem of Measurement

No matter how we conceive of national character, a scientific approach to it must face the problem of its assessment—or to use a less evasive word, its measurement. This subject generates as much confusion and malaise as does the issue of definition. The different approaches to national character based on institutional structure, and on national action or behavior, involve virtually no common understanding, standard techniques, regular procedures, or canons of reliability and validity. The situation is only slightly less variable in the racial psychology and the culture-pattern approaches. Each study proceeds almost entirely independently of all others, utilizes unique perspectives, draws on dis-tinctive materials, follows idiosyncratic rules of evidence, and observes only its own standards of reliability and validity. The result is, if not intellectual chaos or anarchy, at least a great buzzing, blooming confusion which defies representation. Under the circumstances, a systematic comparative perspective is almost impossible.

It is argued by some, not without cogency, that institutional arrangements are so varied, culture patterns so unique, national psychologies so distinctive, that no common or standard language can hope to encompass this infinite diversity. Under these circumstances, it is said, we cannot do justice to the unique character of any people unless we develop a special battery of concepts and a new glossary of terms to describe them. This claim may be somewhat exaggerated. In any event it suggests that systematic analysis of national character as a field of scientific investigation is blocked. The same basic difficulty does not, at least in equal degree, attend efforts to deal with national character as modal personality patterns. There is good reason to believe that the range of variation in human personality, however great, can be adequately encompassed by a conceptual scheme, with a sufficiently limited set of terms to make for manageable research designs without sacrifice of essential richness or variety. We also maintain that, despite the many methodological and conceptual problems involved, this scheme and its measuring instruments can be developed so as to permit reliable and valid applications across national lines.

*   *   *

TOWARD THE DELINEATION OF THE DEMOCRATIC CHARACTER

It is apparent that we have made at least a modest beginning in studying the relation of personality patterns to the development and maintenance of political systems. There is substantial and rather compelling evidence of a regular and intimate connection between personality and the mode of political participation by individuals and groups within any one political system. In many different institutional settings and in many parts of the world, those who adhere to the more extreme political positions have distinctive personality traits separating them from those taking more moderate positions in the same setting. The formal or explicit "content" of one's political orientation—left or right, conservative or radical, pro- or antilabor—may be determined mainly by more "extrinsic" characteristics such as education and social class; but the form or style of political expression—favoring force or persuasion, compromise or arbitrary dictation, being tolerant or narrowly prejudiced, flexible in policy or rigidly dogmatic—is apparently largely determined by personality. At least this seems clear with regard to the political extremes. It is not yet certain whether the same characteristics make for extremism in all national groups and institutional settings, but that also seems highly likely.

Prominent among the traits which make for extremism appear to be the following: exaggerated faith in powerful leaders and insistence on absolute obedience to them; hatred of outsiders and deviates; excessive projection of guilt and hostility; extreme cynicism; a sense of powerlessness and ineffectiveness (alienation and anomie); suspicion and distrust of others; and dogmatism and rigidity. Some of these terms have been or will be shown to be merely alternative designations of the same phenomenon, but some such general syndrome of authoritarianism, dogmatism, and alienation undoubtedly is the psychological root of that political extremism which makes this type actively or potentially disruptive to democratic systems.

If political extremism is indeed an accompaniment—and even more a product —of a certain personality syndrome, and if this syndrome produces the equivalent extremism in all national populations and subgroups, that fact poses a considerable challenge to the student of national character in its relation to political systems. At once we face this question: Are the societies which have a long history of democracy peopled by a majority of individuals who possess a personality conducive to democracy? Alternatively, are societies which have experienced recurrent or prolonged authoritarian, dictatorial, or totalitarian government inhabited by a proportionately large number of individuals with the personality traits we have seen to be associated with extremism? In other words, can we move from the individual and group level, to generalize about the relations of personality and political system at the societal level?

Almost all the modern students of national character are convinced that the answer to this question is in the affirmative. Systematic empirical evidence for this faith is unfortunately lacking. To prove the point we would be required to show that the qualities of personality presumably supportive or less destructive of democracy are more widely prevalent in stable democracies such as the United States, England, Switzerland, or Sweden than in Germany, Japan, Italy, or Russia. At the present time we cannot offer such proof. We will continue to be unable to settle this question until we undertake nation-wide studies of modal personality patterns—such as we do of literacy or per capita income—and test their relation to the forms of political organization in various countries. Before we undertake such studies we must have some conception of the character types for which we are looking.

The problem of defining anything as broad as "the democratic character" may be much like the problem of locating the Manchester economists' "economic man" who Unamuno somewhere described as "a man neither of here nor there, neither this age nor another, who has neither sex nor country, who is, in brief, merely an idea—that is to say, a 'no-man.'"

The danger of excessive generality in defining the democratic character is not greater than the danger of "misplaced concreteness," that is, defining the characterological requirements of *any* democracy as identical with those of some particular people who have a strong democratic tradition. For example, it has been true of the great majority of commentaries on the people of the United States, going back to its earliest days, that "practicality" and "emphasis on religion" have been consistently cited as American traits (Coleman 1941). Yet it would be difficult to argue that either quality is a sufficient or even a necessary requirement for effective citizenship in a democracy. The same may be said of other traits frequently cited as characterizing the American people, such as valuing success and achievement, which are also strongly emphasized in Japanese culture, or the marked emphasis on activity and work, which is also commonly cited as typifying the German character.

. . . What specific qualities do we then require in a people as a necessary condition for the maintenance of a democratic political order? Even a casual content analysis of any sampling of opinion on the democratic society reveals an extraordinary degree of agreement about the values, attitudes, opinion and traits of character which are important to its maintenance. The various formulations may be summed up by reference to conceptions about others, about the self, about authority, and about community and society.

Values about the Self.   All authorities are agreed that democratic societies require widespread belief in what Maritain calls the "inalienable rights of the person," and Hook "the belief that every individual should be regarded as possessing intrinsic worth or dignity." "Where low estimates of the self are permitted to develop," says Harold Lasswell, "there the democratic character cannot develop."

Orientation toward Others.   The basic dignity not only of the self but of all others is an essential ingredient cited by virtually every theory on the democratic character. This particularly manifests itself in the concept of equality, under which Hook includes recognition "that equal opportunities of development should be provided for the realization of individual talents and capacities." To hold this view one must have a basic acceptance of other people. In Lasswell's words: "The democratic attitude toward other human beings is warm rather than frigid, inclusive and expanding rather than exclusive and constricting . . . an underlying personality structure which is capable of 'friendship' as Aristotle put it, and which is unalienated from humanity." Underlying these attitudes is a fundamental conception of the perfectibility of man, which De Tocqueville phrased as the belief "that man will be led to do what is just and good by following his own interest rightly understood."

Orientation toward Authority.   At the core of the democratic personality lies a stress on personal autonomy and a certain distance from, if not distrust of, powerful authority, or, to put it negatively, an absence of the need to dominate or submit such as is found in the authoritarian personality. As Sidney Hook phrased it: "a positive requirement of a working democracy is an intelligent distrust of its leadership, a skepticism stubborn but not blind, of all demands for the enlargement of power, and an emphasis upon critical method in every phase of social life . . . . Where skepticism is replaced by uncritical enthusiasm . . . a fertile soil for dictatorship has been prepared." Almost identical language is used by Maritain. Maritain described the democratic philosophy as one insisting on the "political rights of the people whose consent is implied by any political regime, and whose rulers rule as vicars of the people . . . it denies to the rulers the right to consider themselves and be considered a superior race and wills nevertheless that their authority be respected on a juridical basis. It does not admit that the state is a transcendent power incorporating within itself all authority and imposed from above upon human life . . . ." The same idea is stressed by Lasswell who says: "the democratic character is multi-valued rather than single-valued . . . disposed to share rather than to monopolize. In particular, little significance is attached to the exercise of power as a scope value . . . [for] when the demand for respect is the consuming passion, other values are sacrificed for the sake of receiving symbolic acknowledgments of eminence."

Attitudes toward the Community. Although overweaning authority may be controlled, there is always the danger of that tyranny of the majority which De Tocqueville early warned might undo democracy. This realization has repeatedly led those who sought to define the democratic character to stress the importance of openness, ready acceptance of differences, and willingness to compromise and change. De Tocqueville early anticipated this point, as he did so many others. Stressing the belief "that every man is born of the right of self-government, and that no one has the right of constraining his fellow creatures to be happy," he went on to say we must recognize "society as a body in a state of improvement, [and] humanity as a changing scene in which nothing is or ought to be permanent." Hook also speaks of the importance of "a belief in the value of differences, variety, and uniqueness in a democracy [where] differences of interest and achievement must not be merely suffered, they must be encouraged." According to Hook this requires that the ultimate commitment of a democracy must be in some method by which value conflicts are to be resolved, which in turn means that policies must be treated as hypotheses, not dogmas, and customary practices as generalizations rather than as God-given truths.

It will be apparent from this extremely brief review that there is substantial agreement about the core personal beliefs and values which have been frequently identified as important to the maintenance of a democratic order. The relevant "themes" can, of course, be integrated into the personality at different levels. They may reflect opinions publicly held, but not vitally important to the person. They may represent basic attitudes or central values in the belief system, typical "ideologies" to which the individual has deep allegiance. Or they may be even more "deeply" embedded in the personality at the level of character traits and modes of psychodynamic functioning. Most of the outstanding writers on the democratic character do not trouble to distinguish these "levels." I have not attempted above to sort them out, and merely note here that most of the characterizations given above are statements at the level of ideology. We can, however, translate or transform the classic portrait of the democratic character to present it in the language of clinical psychology, expressed in terms of character traits, defenses, ways of dealing with wishes and feelings, and the like. In those terms, the democratic character emerges at the opposite pole from the authoritarian personality syndrome. The citizen of a democracy should be accepting of others rather than alienated and harshly rejecting; open to new experience, to ideas and impulses rather than excessively timid, fearful, or extremely conventional with regard to new ideas and ways of acting; able to be responsible with constituted authority even though always watchful, rather than blindly submissive to or hostilely rejecting of all authority; tolerant of differences and of ambiguity, rather than rigid and inflexible; able to recognize, control, and channel his emotions, rather than immaturely projecting hostility and other impulses on to others.

This model of the democratic personality represents only a very rough first approximation. Although it is based on a great deal of philosophical wisdom and historical experience, by the standards of modern social science it rests on an extremely narrow and uncertain base of empirical research. Indeed, it might be argued that at the present moment there is no relevant evidence which meets the standards set by contemporary social science research. It is largely to the future that we must look for refinement of the model, and for testing of its actual relevance for political systems and popular participation in them. No doubt some elements in the model will be discarded, others added. It may even by discovered that some one element is critical, all the others incidental or even irrelevant. In the present stage of our work it is important to avoid premature closure through the exclusive concentration on one conceptual scheme for analyzing personality. It is true that earlier efforts which accepted publicly offered opinions, attitudes, and values as guides to the individual's probable political action were often naive and misleading. Nevertheless, an analysis couched exclusively in terms of psychodynamic depth psychology, of defenses, projective tendencies, and the like may also leave out much which is of great significance in shaping the pattern of political life. . . .

Whatever the defects of the available scheme, the use of some explicit model is essential to focus our studies in this area. It is also a necessary condition for the meaningful comparison of different studies, and particularly for our efforts to cumulate the results in ever firmer generalizations or conclusions. We must particularly regret, therefore, that so few of the empirical investigations into the relations of character and political systems have sought systematically to test the model of the democratic character presented above, or, for that matter, any other explicit model.

SOME PROBLEMS AND PROSPECTS

With very few exceptions, the available studies of modal or group personality unfortunately suffer from several defects which make them poor evidence in support of *any* systematic proposition. As a rule they are not designed to test any theory or validate any model. They are usually based on very small and haphazardly selected samples, making it extremely difficult to generalize with any confidence beyond the sample itself or the narrow circle from which it is drawn. In addition, the analysis is usually based on the total sample, without basic differentiation of the characteristics of subgroups, whether deviant or merely variant. More serious for our purposes is the fact that the description of personality is generally cast in clinical or psychodynamic terms which are difficult to relate to social structure. Even in the rare cases when a study has given attention to the more politically relevant realms of personality such as attitude toward authority, tolerance of ambiguity, acceptance of differences, and the need for power, it generally fails to record information on the political attitudes and opinions, the party affiliation, or other political characteristics of the subjects. Most of these studies, therefore, are obviously of limited usefulness to the student of politics. Only in the last few years have we attained the first, limited personality inventory of a representative sample of the national population of the United States. . . . There are apparently no comparable results on these or any other dimensions for any other modern nation, and it will undoubtedly be many years before we have such results for a number of major nations simultaneously.

Even when we attain good data on the distribution of personality traits in a number of national populations, a great many questions will remain. For example, we will need to understand better the relation between personality dispositions in the rank and file of a population, and their orientation to different kinds of leadership. The decisive factor affecting the chances of preserving democracy may not be the prevalence of one or another undemocratic personality type, but rather the relation between the typical or average personality and that of the leaders. It is highly unlikely that any character type will be found to be invariably associated with a single form of political system. Nevertheless, certain personality types may indeed be more responsive to one than to another form of government. Their character, then, may be an important determinant of their susceptibility to certain kinds of influence. Thus, Dicks does not argue for the propensity toward authoritarian government *per se* in the German character. The typical German character delineated by Dicks was a type highly susceptible to the style of leadership the Hitler movement offered and extremely vulnerable to the kind of propaganda appeals it utilized. Much the same conclusion is suggested by Erikson's analysis of the German character and Hitler's appeal to it. Neither analysis should be interpreted as suggesting that the German character, as described, could not under any circumstances adjust to or function in *any* democratic political order. McClelland's analysis (1958) of the distinctive structure of obligations to self and society in Germany and the United States is particularly interesting for the light it throws on this question.

Whatever the distribution of personality types, including leaders, in any population, we will want to know what produces the types. This enormously complex problem is one I have been obliged by limits of space to ignore almost entirely, although it is one of the most fundamental facing the field. The predominant opinion among students of national character is that these types arise mainly out of the socialization process, and that in democratic societies the family structure is one which generates individuals adapted to life in a democracy. The typical argument was forcefully stated by Ralph Linton when he declared: "Nations with authoritarian family structure inevitably seem to develop authoritarian governments, no matter what the official government forms may be. Latin American countries with their excellent democratic constitutions and actual dictatorships would be a case in point."

Linton's opinion is not uniformly held. On the basis of a thorough review of a great deal of relevant empirical research, Herbert Hyman poses a formidable challenge to this assumption and suggests a number of other factors—particularly experiences in adulthood—which may account for the political orientations we observe in certain groups. Even after we secure data on the distribution of personality characteristics in large populations, there will be much work to be done in discovering what produces the propensity to extremism, how it operates, and what—if anything—changes or modifies it.

Another problem we must face is the relation between personality factors and other forces which affect the political process (*cf.* Levinson 1958). To analyze political participation and political structures through a study of personality and its statistical distribution is, of course, only one of the possible avenues of approach to the problem. Clearly, political institutions and political action can not be comprehended exclusively or even predominantly by reference to attitudes and values. The history of a people obviously plays a major role in shaping the basic structure of their political institutions. And institutional frameworks, once established, may have an endurance much greater than the formal allegiance to their principles would have indicated. Indeed, once firmly established, institutions have the capacity to develop or generate support among those whose early disposition would hardly have led them to move spontaneously in that direction.

A recent extensive comparative study by S. M. Lipset (1959) of the relation between a complex of factors including industrialization, urbanization, literacy, education, and wealth, reveals that they are highly correlated not only with each other, but also with the existence of stable democratic systems. None of these factors cited by Lipset is at all psychological or attitudinal, but it is interesting to note that in seeking to understand why these factors play such a role, Lipset had to fall back from these more "objective" to more subjective causes, in particular to such concepts as the "effectiveness" and the "legitimacy" of a political system in the eyes of its constituents. By effectiveness he means the capacity to satisfy the basic interests of most members of society, or of the most important groups in it, and by legitimacy "the capacity of a political system to engender and maintain the belief that existing political institutions are the most appropriate or proper ones for the society." . . . Surely the tolerance of ambiguity, the readiness for compromise, the level of projectivity characteristic of a people or important subgroups, will play a major role in shaping the "effectiveness" of the political system and even its freedom of action *to be* effective. The value placed on autonomy versus control and direction, the strength of needs for power or achievement, the wish for dominance or subordination; the orientation toward authority figures, will all clearly play an important part in determining whether a particular political system is felt by people to be legitimate or not.

Although further refinements are needed, it is not likely that we will make any further unusual leaps along the line of analysis which Lipset has so diligently pursued. By contrast, the role of psychological factors—of attitudes, values, and character traits—in influencing the political process is an almost virgin field which promises a rich harvest. To secure it we must overcome imposing but by no means insuperable obstacles. We need to clarify our concepts, isolating or delineating those personal characteristics which, on theoretical grounds, seem to have the greatest relevance for the development and functioning of the political system. We must also refine our analysis of the political system, so that our descriptive categories are maximally analytical and conducive to comparative study. Our next step must be to assess systematically the distribution of these qualities in different national populations and in important subgroups of those populations. This poses one of the most difficult methodological problems, since the meaning of important terms, the pattern of response to tests, and the interpretation of those responses are highly variable as we move from country to country. On this base we can then proceed to correlational and causal analyses of the relations between opinions, values, and personality on the one hand, and the quality of political participation and the stability of political structures on the other. We may thus develop a comparative social psychology of the political process to support and supplement our traditional study of politics.

SOURCES CITED BY AUTHOR

Adorno, T. W., E. Frenkel-Brunswick, D. J. Levinson and R. N. Sanford
   1950 The authoritarian personality. New York, Harper and Bros.
Coleman, Lee
   1941 What is American: a study of alleged American traits. Social Forces
         19:492–499.
Dicks, Henry V.
   1950 Personality traits and national socialist ideology, a war-time study
         of German prisoners of war. Human Relations 3:111–154.
   1952 Observations on contemporary Russian behavior. Human Relations
         5:111–175.
Hook, Sidney
   1950 Reason, social myths, and democracy. New York, Humanities Press.
Inkeles, Alex and D. J. Levinson
   1954 National character: the study of modal personality and sociocultural
         systems. *In* Handbook of social psychology, vol. II, G. Lindzey, ed.
         Cambridge, Addison-Wesley.
Lasswell, Harold D.
   1930 Psychopathology and politics. *In* The political writings of Harold D.
         Lasswell. Glencoe, Ill., Free Press, 1951.
   1951 Democratic character. *In* The political writings of Harold D. Lass-
         well. Glencoe, Ill., Free Press.
   1959 Political constitution and character. Psychoanalysis and the Psycho-
         analytic Review 46:3–18.
Levinson, Daniel J.
   1957 Authoritarian personality and foreign policy. Conflict Resolution 1:
         37–47.
   1958 The relevance of personality for political participation. Public Opin-
         ion Quarterly 22:3–10.
Maritain, Jacques
   1944 Christianity and democracy. New York, Scribners.
McClelland, David, J. F. Sturr, R. H. Knapp and H. W. Wendt
   1958 Obligations to self and society in the United States and Germany.
         Journal of Abnormal and Social Psychology 56:245–255.
Tocqueville, Alexis de
   1947 Democracy in America. New York and London, Oxford University
         Press.

B. Elites

2. Social Structure and the Ruling Class*

RAYMOND ARON

The object of this article is to try to combine in a synthesis the sociology which is based on Marxist ideas and that which derives from Pareto and, from that starting point, to outline a few general ideas on the evolution of modern societies.

Why, it may be asked, should I choose Marx and Pareto, whose works were, in one case, written nearly a century, and in the other, several decades ago? Does recent literature offer nothing more scientific? I have no doubt that more accurate empirical studies could be found than those scattered through Marx's books or concentrated in the *General Treatise on Sociology*, but I do not think that any theory has been elaborated which can take the place of either of those doctrines.

For a Marxist, the determining factor is the opposition between the owners of the means of production and workers who hire out their labour. The "alienation" of the workers is the origin of all social ills, the opposition between the classes the root of all human conflicts. History is a dialectical process by which, from contradiction to contradiction, we are brought to a classless society and a self-reconciled humanity.

For Pareto and his followers, on the other hand, the exercise of power by a minority is a constant factor in any social order. The constitution and character of governing minorities, or, to use the usual term, the "elites", change; the privileged are replaced by others. But there is always a minority, holding the key posts in society, which appropriates to itself a more or less disproportionate share of the national income.

These two views of historical philosophy—on the one hand a dialectical process tending towards a classless society and, on the other, a permanent division between the masses and the elite—are reflected in the two most influential political ideologies of our time, Communism and Fascism. The Marxists justify the revolutionary desires of the proletariat by the need to put a stop to the alienation of labour by overcoming class struggles. The followers of Pareto have often justified the revolutionary spirit of a nonproletarian party by the need to replace weak, degenerate, democratic elites by strong and ruthless elites. On the one hand, there is revolution to eradicate the class system; on the other,

*From *The British Journal of Sociology*, vol. I (March 1950 and June 1950), by permission of the publisher, Routledge & Kegan Paul Ltd. Article abridged by the editors.

23

revolution to restore to communities that strength and prosperity which are always dependent on the virtue, in the Machiavellian sense, of the few who rule the multitude.

Our study will, therefore, be concentrated on that delicate point where the analytical method touches political ideology. The problem of combining in a synthesis "class" sociology and "elite" sociology is a scientific one. It can be reduced to the following question: "What is the relation between social differentiation and political hierarchy in modern societies?" We shall find the answer by considering the facts, i.e. by comparing the various types of society. The consideration of the facts, however, does not by itself lead to a political ideology. Whether policy should work towards the elimination of classes or towards replacing the elite, will depend on one's estimate of values and of the future course of history. All that scientific analysis can give us is a criticism of political ideologies in so far as they pervert or distort reality. The refusal of the Marxists to take into account the political hierarchy which existed before, and survives, the division of society into classes is an attempt to mystify, and is disclosed as such by sociological analysis. The refusal of the Fascists to take into account social differentiation is a similar or contrasting attempt to mystify, and is also so discovered by scientific analysis. When the true nature of the ideologies have thus been disclosed, however, there is still ground for the two conflicting revolutionary desires. Sociology shows men what they truly desire and what will be the probable results of their actions; it never indicates to them what they ought to desire.

The word "class" is in daily use, still more on the continent probably than in Britain, but a definition of it is seldom given. We shall try to show, from the writings of Marx, that such a definition is not very easy.

Everyone knows Marx's famous words in the *Communist Manifesto:*

> The history of all hitherto existing society is the history of class struggles. In previous eras we see that practically everywhere society was organized in a complicated system of separate classes and that there was a hierarchy of many social ranks. In ancient Rome there were Patricians, Knights, Plebeians and Slaves; in the Middle Ages, Barons, Vassals, Guildmasters, Journeymen and Serfs. Such antagonisms still survive in modern bourgeois society, which has merely substituted new classes, new opportunities for oppression and new types of struggle for the earlier ones. The special characteristic of our age is that it has simplified the antagonisms between the classes and the whole of society is becoming increasingly divided into two great classes in direct opposition to one another—the bourgeoisie and the proletariat.

In this quotation the term "class" is taken in its most extensive sense, applying equally to patricians as distinct from plebeians or slaves, as to barons as distinct from craftsmen or serfs. The connotation of the word "class" in this general sense is necessarily scantily defined. We might say that a class is a secondary grouping within a community, characterized by the fact that it fulfills certain functions and has a distinct place in the social hierarchy in relation to other groups. We can hardly go further than that, because the basis of differentiation varies with different societies. We might say, in a symbolic sense, that the proletarian is the slave of modern societies, but the legal status of the slave and proletarian have nothing in common. The proletarian is subject to the same law as the bourgeois, which was not true of the plebeian or slave in comparison with the patrician, or of the serf in comparison with the baron. Although men were once born nobles or burghers and generally kept that status all their life, today they are born the sons of bourgeois or workers but with opportunities of improving their positions which are, in law, unlimited and, in practice, limited but real.

I therefore think it wiser not to take the word "class" in its general meaning but to give an historical definition of it applicable to modern industrial societies. Classes in modern societies are not based on religion, kinship, blood or land. On what are they based?

We find in Marx three concepts of classes which are not identical but are also not incompatible. I shall call them the historical, economic and philosophical concepts. If we refer to Marx's historical works, such as *The Eighteenth Brumaire of Louis Bonaparte,* we realize that he does not keep to the theoretical opposition of the bourgeoisie and the proletariat, but distinguishes social groups as they are seen in reality in any particular historical circumstances. The actors in the drama, between the February Revolution and Louis Napoleon's *coup d'état,* are the industrial workers in the towns, the lower middle class, made up of craftsmen and tradesmen, the peasants, land-owning capitalists and financial capitalists. The July Monarchy had represented the victory of the bankers over the great landowners and of the new bourgeoisie over the old aristocracy. The French peasantry supported the great emperor's nephew because of the obsessive fear of socialists among landowners who, to some extent, held their lands as a result of the great revolution.

That is how the idea of class is generally used in the historical and sociological analyses of the Marxists. A class appears as a social group distinguished by certain common interests, by the fulfillment of a certain function or the holding of certain positions, but it is not possible to specify precisely the number of classes into which a society is divided or what are the distinguishing characteristics of a class. Depending upon the circumstances, landowners, industrialists and bankers may be considered as separate classes or as individual groups within a single class. Similarly, the peasantry may be considered as a single class or as divided into ground landlords, smallholders and agricultural workers. There may, of course, be good reasons for the different views; in one respect we see a moral unity among the peasantry; in another, conflict between the different groups included in the peasantry may arise from the vertical class struggle. What we want to show is that the idea of class, in its empirical connotation, is comparatively loose and can be determined only by considering each society individually. In his theory Marx tried to furnish a double, economic and philosophical, basis for this historical concept.

At the end of *Capital* Marx states that he will develop a theory of classes on the basis of the economic analysis of the various categories of income. "Social categories" may, in fact, be distinguished by their type of income: ground landlords receiving rents; owners of the means of production, industrialists, who appropriate surplus value or profit; workers receiving wages. These social categories are of course never found in unadulterated form, simply because mixed incomes exist; the craftsman employing a few assistants, the working garage proprietor who also employs a few mechanics, make no distinction in their incomes between the wage paid for their own work and the surplus value they derive from their employees. Furthermore, these categories are not necessarily conscious of their own identity. For example, from the point of view of the source of their income, the unskilled worker and the engineer at the *Miles* factories are both wage-earners, i.e., in the economic sense, proletarians. They do not, for that reason, however, feel themselves to be members of one group, nor are they conscious of any community of interests in opposition to the owners of the means of production. In other words, the conversion of an income category into a coherent social group is hindered by two obstacles: the combination in certain individuals of different economic types of income and the fact that the boundaries of the income categories and the psychological or intellectual boundaries of groups do not coincide.

Marx was clearly not unaware of these difficulties. He thought they could be overcome in two ways. Firstly, he considered, as he said in the quotation I gave before, that society is becoming increasingly divided into two large classes directly opposed to one another—the bourgeoisie and the proletariat. Secondly, in his view, a class was not so much an objective reality—as it were a stone or an animal to be studied by the pure scientific observer—as a human reality, which creates itself when it becomes conscious of its identity. I should like to dwell on these two points for a few moments.

Marx witnessed social developments in the first part of the nineteenth century, in the period of economic history which I shall call the first stage of capitalist equipment (the stage through which Soviet Russia has been passing since its Five-Year Plans began). This stage is characterized by the large-scale transfer of workers from the country to the towns, by the absorption of independent workers (craftsmen and journeymen) into the industrial proletariat. Furthermore, he considered mainly the textile industry which employed a large number of unskilled workers, women and children. The conclusions he drew were accurate but incomplete; he thought there was a constant and fundamental tendency towards uniformity within the proletariat, he thought that the elimination of independent workers would proceed to its logical conclusion, he thought that as a result of industrial concentration alone the ruthless conflict required by his theory, between a tiny minority of privileged persons and a vast mass of exploited workers, would come into being. Today, with the experience of a century of capitalism behind us, we know that this is not so. Against the law of proletarization and pauperization I shall set what I shall call the law of social differentiation.

In the latter part of his life, Marx probably realized that that might be the case. If he had, he would not therefore necessarily have changed his doctrine, for it was not merely an empirical interpretation of events, but a philosophy of history. When we look at Marx's early writings—before the *Communist Manifesto* —some of which were not published until after the first World War (in particular the so-called Economic and Philosophical Manuscript and *The German Ideology),* we realize that the desire for social revolution preceded the study of contemporary society in the development of his thought. The proletarian is alienated because he does not belong to himself, because he works for an employer who appropriates the product of his labour, because his employer himself, being subject to the market, is in the grip of impersonal and mysterious forces. The abolition of private property aims at putting a stop to such alienation, at restoring to societies the control of their economy, at protecting the liberty of the individual by giving him a direct share in the community life. The proletariat as such only exists when it is conscious of its historic mission. We might also say that the wage-earners constitute a proletariat when they realize that they are being exploited and join together in the determination to break the wage system.

It is true that Marx believed that the force of events would incline the proletariat to that historic mission. Because the proletariat would be reduced to the barest minimum of human existence, because, in its misery, it would be deprived of every mark of distinction, it would be the universal class and would bring about the universal revolution, in the name of the majority, for the benefit of all mankind. The Marxists, however, find no difficulty in maintaining that this is the mission of the proletariat, in spite of the growing divergence between the proletariat as conceived in the philosophy of Marx as a young man, and the real proletariat resulting from a century of capitalism.

That, then, is the Marxist conception of classes, including three different ideas: that of the historical social group distinguished by common interests and psychological similarity; that of the social category distinguished by a certain type of income; and lastly that of the social class distinguished by its consciousness of a certain place in the process of production and the desire to overthrow the existing system. Everyone is free to choose his own vocabulary according to the requirements of research and clarity, provided that he explains the precise meaning of his vocabulary. For my part, I shall observe the distinction which I have just outlined between the social group in empirical sociology, the social category in economic analysis, and the social class in the philosophy of history.

The analysis of the structure of a society aims at distinguishing its various groups. Such an analysis is infinitely more complex and more subtle than that which is generally made by merely applying a scheme drawn from some philosophy of history. Indeed, the distinction between these groups can be made on many different criteria, which do not give the same results.

This is what I mean. A group may be characterized by a particular standard of life, a particular type of life, the nature of its professional activities, its legal status or by the degree of unity recognized in it by society or of which it is conscious.

Let us take as our starting point the standard of life. Individuals enjoying a similar standard of life are not by any means uniform in the way they live or in their mental outlook. A clerk does not necessarily earn more than a skilled workman; a "stiff-collared" proletarian, as the Germans say, does not consider himself a member of the same group as the horny-handed working man. Comparative surveys of family budgets have shown that the clerk does not spend his income in the same way and that he allows more for housing and keeping up his position and less for food. There is a still greater difference in psychology and the outlook on life when the town worker is compared with the country worker or the skilled worker with the smallholder, even when their real incomes are the same.

We may also consider professional activities or occupations. The differences within the industrial proletariat have been increased by technical developments. In 1940, out of 51,000,000 persons actively employed in the United States, there were less than 9,000,000 unskilled workers, i.e. workers without any real professional training, including 3,530,000 agricultural workers, 1,193,000 of whom were members of the farmers' own families. The proportion of absolute proletarians was therefore down to 18 per cent in 1940, whereas in 1910 it had been over 25 per cent.

What is even more important is the division of the workers between the various sectors of economic activity. Colin Clark, in his book on the *Conditions of Economic Progress,* has taught us to distinguish between three basic sectors: that of primary activities (agricultural production and raw materials); that of secondary activities (the manufacture of goods); and that of tertiary activities (the public services, commerce and administration). We know that in modern industrial societies there is an initial phase in which the secondary activities expand at the expense of the primary activities; then in their turn the tertiary activities develop at the expense of the secondary. In the United States at the present day more than half the working population is employed in tertiary activities and about 35 per cent in secondary activities. In other words, the Marxist type of industrial worker will not represent the bulk of society for the future but a decreasing fraction of the population.

No doubt we might pursue the analysis of professional differentiation. In the tertiary group of activities there are some manual workers, in the secondary group some clerical workers. The tendency is, however, very clear. We are moving towards a civilization made up of clerical workers rather than towards a civilization of manual workers. Planning, organization, administration and distribution are becoming increasingly complicated and absorbing an increasing number of men. We are living in the administrative age no less than in the machine age.

It is evident that this distinction between the three sectors cannot claim to correspond to the dividing lines between the conscious social groups. The psychological boundaries, which are in any case indeterminate, are based in essence on three types of influence: horizontal economic community of interests, i.e. interests of agriculture in opposition to industry, or of grain producers in opposition to producers of dairy products, or of industries working for the internal market in opposition to export industries; the social status of an occupation according to public opinion or in the eyes of the persons involved (in European societies there is still a prejudice against manual work, and the son of a middle-class or lower middle-class family feels that he loses less prestige if he finds a post as a clerk than if he has to work with his hands, even when he earns the same amount); and lastly a person's legal status as a wage-earner or independent worker. The opposition of certain liberal professions, such as the medical profession, to schemes for a National Service, is partly due to the loss of prestige which they consider would be involved in giving up their independent position to become salaried officials.

We could easily continue such analyses, which are only intended to illustrate what I call the law of social differentiation and to support the following proposition: if it is the standard or type of life, the nature of the profession, the legal status or collective psychological outlook which is considered, the social groups will be defined differently in each case. The structure of contemporary society is characterized, firstly, by the elimination of the barriers between the "Orders", founded on birth or the traditional hierarchy and, secondly, by the numerous distinctions maintained by differences between professions and standards of life, and in prestige.

This elementary analysis marks the first stage of a sociological study. Should we stop there and be content with merely listing the groups? Certainly not. After the microscopic examination comes what we might call the macroscopic examination, that is, an endeavour to find new embracing wholes. Which groups have a common destiny? Which groups are conscious of that community? The communities which exist are discovered by economic analysis and the consciousness of community is discovered by sociological and political analysis.

It is easy to show that such a community and consciousness of community do not necessarily coincide. When the market mechanism is unhampered, the workers' remuneration varies with the prosperity of the branch of industry in which they are employed. A community of practical interests frequently links together the employers and employees of one branch of industry rather than the employees in competing branches. Similarly, it is to the advantage of skilled workers that there should be increasing differentiation of wages and consequently that independent trade unions should be set up to protect the higher wage scales. The idea of working-class solidarity, however, generally transcends conflicts between divergent interests.

It is usual to divide society into three wholes: the industrial workers or wage-earners, the middle class, and the bourgeoisie or upper class. This division might be useful politically, but has little scientific value, because none of these so-called classes possesses a real unity. The middle class consists of those who receive salaries rather than wages, but this distinction is more one of psychology than of economics. At the same time the middle class includes men from professional occupations (what we call *les professions libérales*) like physicians, who are (or were), in an economic sense, independent; and it also contains small industrialists or shopkeepers, who belong to the category of the owners of means of production. It would perhaps not be impossible to observe a few tendencies which seem common to all the intermediary groups: medium income, liking for independence, in some cases leaning towards intellectual tastes. But it is not enough to bring about economic solidarity. In the same way, the upper class possesses neither a unity of interests nor of ideology.

It is not a criticism of Marxism to say that the community of interest of wage-earners is often a fiction, for Marxism defines the common interests of wage-earners or proletarians less as existing within the present organizations, than in opposition to it. Their common interest, or rather their historical mission, is to destroy the wage system. Once more the proletariat as such comes into existence only when it refuses to accept its position. Class, in the philosophic sense which Marxism gives to the word, is defined only in relation to a classless society. But what can a classless society be?

According to the analysis which we have just made, a classless society is obviously not a society without social groups. The differences in types of life, standards of life and sectors of activity still remain. The distinctions founded on barriers associated with the social value of occupations and the survival of traditional prestige could be reduced. Admittedly the differences in legal status will disappear. When the means of production are nationalized, the economic and social category of the owners of the means of production is automatically destroyed; there is no longer any entrepreneur's profit or ground rent. All workers become the employees of a single employer—the State. In this sense, it is perfectly true that there are no classes in a society of the Soviet type. But it does not follow that economic inequalities therefore disappear. It all depends on the hierarchy of remuneration established, nominally to meet the requirements of production, by those in power in the State.

In a society where there are no classes, as in one where there are, there are unskilled workers, clerks, engineers and managers; there is one part of the national income for current consumption and another for capital investment. The distribution of the national resources between consumption and investment and between the various grades in the hierarchy is theoretically decided by the planning office. Differences in fortune are necessarily lessened by the fact that the means of production are not held as private property and that the saving necessary for investment is largely achieved by the State's own action and not through the medium of private incomes. Individual incomes, may, however, remain as unequal as in a society with numerous classes, if the rulers think it desirable for the community or for their own interests.

Indeed the first discovery which the Soviet rulers made was that nothing can take the place of self-interest as an incentive. Piece wages are more general than in any capitalist country. The managers receive a large share of the profits of any undertaking, so that it is to their personal advantage to improve production. The economic inequality which was eliminated by the abolition of acquired fortunes is coming back through the hierarchy of social functions and in order to encourage production.

Inequality in political power is in no way eliminated or diminished by the abolition of classes, for it is quite impossible for the government of a society to be in the hands of any but a few. In a society where there are no classes, as in one where there are, all do not share to the same extent in the administration and government of the society. When people speak of the proletariat's seizing power, they are using a metaphor or symbol. Power never can be in the hands of millions of men. There is government *for* the people; there is no government *by* the people.

There may be two types of changes in the society: one type affects the constitution of the elite (let me explain once for all that by "elite" I mean the minority which, in any society, performs the function of ruling the community), the other, recruitment to the elite.

In my opinion, the elite in a modern society is subdivided into five groups: political leaders, government administrators, economic directors, leaders of the masses and military chiefs. In the British, American or French democracy, everyone distinguishes between Parliamentary Members, civil servants, business managers or proprietors, trade union secretaries and Generals or Admirals. I pass over the question of how far this scheme could be applied to the societies before capitalism or what alterations would be necessary to make it generally applicable. There seems to me to be no doubt at all that it fits modern societies.

In all modern societies these five groups correspond to essential functions. The differences lie in the degree of separation between the groups and their relative strength. For example, in France the principal officials are seldom drawn from the ranks of the directors of private industry; public opinion would immediately rise against the annexation of the State by the two hundred families. In the United States, on the other hand, the chief administrators are appointed for specific tasks and frequently come from private business and return to it after their service to the State. Similarly, the Parliamentary representatives come, to a varying degree in different countries, from business and the trade unions. There were many personal links between Members of Parliament and economic leaders in the Conservative party in Britain and there are also many personal links between Members of Parliament and trade union leaders in the Labour party. In France before the war the Parliamentary representatives were not so much associated either with the capitalist or with the trade unionist but were drawn from the middle classes and particularly from the liberal professions. With regard to the military leaders, in Great Britain their part in politics is no greater than that of other officials. In Spain and the South American Republics they are still an essential and active part of the ruling class.

For the first time I have used the words the ruling class. My reason for avoiding it till now is that in classic sociological theory the ruling class is always considered more or less as a unity. For example, Pareto tended to characterize every ruling class by the psycho-social type to which it belonged and the means it used to remain in power. He distinguished between cunning and violent elites, between elites who prefer to use artifice, argument, ideology, and financial manipulation, and those who are more ready to resort to force and constraint.

The former speak of democracy, peace and humanitarianism, the latter of national greatness and conquest. James Burnham, who in *The Managerial Revolution* has also outlined a synthesis of the theory of classes and that of elites, contrasts the managerial society with the capitalist society, as that in which the managers instead of the owners of the means of production control those means.

The analysis of the groups included in the elite is, in my view, more useful because the structure of the elite is as characteristic of the society as the structure of the social groups. By structure of the elite I mean the relation between the various groups in the elite which is peculiar to each society. Indeed, although there are everywhere business managers, government officials, trade union secretaries and ministers, they are not everywhere recruited in the same way and they may either form one coherent whole or remain comparatively distinct from one another. The fundamental difference between a society of the Soviet type and one of the Western type is that the former has a unified elite and the latter a divided elite.

In the U.S.S.R. the trade union secretaries, the business managers and the higher officials generally belong to the Communist party. If they do not belong to the party they are nonpolitical technicians, working in isolation and with little opportunity of organizing as an independent body. The Generals were the only people who might have been able to constitute a power more or less independent of the Party-State. Stalin appointed himself a Marshal, a party member was made Minister of War and the Generals who were too popular were scattered through the vast spaces of the Union; the unity of the elite has been entirely restored.

This unity obviously does not prevent competition between administrative departments or rivalry between individuals, which are inherent in the organization of every human society, but this competition and rivalry is not openly declared and does not take the form of a struggle between independent bodies; they can hardly operate except through plots. This explains how, in mass societies, we find recurring personal struggles around the inner sanctum.

On the other hand democratic societies, which I would rather call pluralistic societies, are full of the noise of public strife between the owners of the means of production, trade union leaders and politicians. As all are entitled to form associations, professional and political organizations abound, each one defending its members' interests with passionate ardour. Government becomes a business of compromises. Those in power are well aware of their precarious position. They are considerate of the opposition because they themselves have been, and will one day again be, in opposition.

The foregoing analyses are to be used for three possible functions. First, in order to study the structures of the social group and of the elite in a particular society. Secondly, in order to determine different types of social events or of societies—as example, one could try to differentiate between various revolutions, in showing to what extent each one has brought about a change, either in the relations between the social groups, or in the relations between the sub-groups of the elite, or in the way in which an elite maintains its power. The 1830 revolution, in France, has given to industrialists and bankers a stronger position, weakened the landlords' influence, partly renewed the political personnel, but it remained almost without action upon the social structure. On the contrary, a revolution like the 1917 revolution, in Russia, has suppressed the whole aristocracy, given power to a wholly new set of individuals, modified the method of government and upset the social structure. Thirdly and lastly, one could try to distinguish the successive moments of the evolution of a civilization. In other words, this system of concepts could be the instruments of a synthesis between analytical sociology, the sociology of social types and the interpretation of history. . . .

[Professor Aron's analysis of social structure in postwar France is omitted.]

. . . I hope I have shown you a method of analysis, combining familiar methods which are seldom used in conjunction: analysis of the economic structure, the social structure, the structure of the groups within the elite, and, it should be added, the structure of the constitutional system; all these elements are of equal importance in any theory of sociology which wishes to understand society as a whole.

Secondly, I hope I have convinced you that one of the most characteristic features of any society's structure is the structure of the elite, that is, the relationship between the groups exercising power, the degree of unity or division between these groups, the system of recruiting the elite and the ease or difficulty of entering it. No doubt its constitutional system is characteristic of any society. The real nature of a constitutional system, however, can only be understood when the men who in fact operate the system are taken into account. The aristocratic parliaments of the nineteenth century were fundamentally different from the popular parliaments of our own century, even when no point in the constitution has been altered. The parliaments elected by proportional representation on the continent, the battlefield on which communists and anti-communists carry on their wordy fight before they fight on another field, are profoundly unlike the British and American parliaments, in which the representatives of the various interests try to arrive at practicable compromises and observe the rules of the game.

Thirdly, I hope I have shown you the significance of the classless society in history. The unified elite deriving from the proletariat offers to fulfill the office which should have been fulfilled by capitalism, in cases where a weak or degenerate elite fails to eliminate the surviving traces of feudalism and to provide its country with industrial equipment. It offers to carry out the task which sometimes seems beyond the strength of socialistic democracies in countries which have been rich and are today impoverished; the adherents of the classless society would unhesitatingly impose all those measures which democratic socialism is unwilling to impose—compulsory saving, investment, discipline, incentives—because they would have the material and moral means necessary: unlimited power in the State and an ideology to justify them.

Thus, through many different channels, we come to a synthesis of Marxist ideas with those of Pareto. A society cannot be characterized only by the class which owns the means of production or by the psychological and social nature of the elite. The power and influence in the State of the industrial and financial leaders varies between different capitalistic countries with the constitutional machinery and the power of the political rulers. The distribution of power changed radically in Germany between the time of the Kaiser's Empire, the Weimar Republic and the Third Reich, even although the owners of the means of production remained in their places. Changes in the relative strength of the groups included in the elites are a typical sign of political and social evolution. The definition of the post-capitalist organization as the replacement of the owners of the means of production by the new class of managers, is inadequate, for the character of the society is entirely different if those managers come to power within a pluralistic society or if they do so through the seizure of power by a unified elite. The managers are one of the groups in any modern elite. They are never, as managers, the ruling group. In both capitalism and socialism there are, above the managers, mass leaders or politicians who fix the targets for the managers and hold the secret of securing obedience from the masses.

Neither does the idea of an elite working by force or guile, or that of the substitution of an elite using force for an elite using guile represent reality in all its complexity. It is true that both the fascist and communist revolutions are a sign of the strengthening of the means of compulsion and the abandonment of slow and more subtle methods by which men are convinced, for the adoption of ruthless methods of policing and propaganda by which they are compelled. Pareto was therefore certainly right in his interpretation of one aspect of contemporary history, but when we say that an elite decays it is a fact more than an explanation. There are many ways by which elites may be renewed, transformed or disintegrated. A typical form of disintegration at the present day is paralysis due to internal strife. The democratic method of elections to parliament and free trade unions means that representatives of the mass of the people come to take part in the work of administration. This phenomenon, which is comparatively recent in history, gives a new meaning to the law of the succession of elites. It offers a hope that fortunate societies may succeed, renewing their elite gradually, without a revolutionary upheaval. It involves the danger to which unfortunate societies and nations who prefer ideology to wisdom fall victim, that there may be fatal conflicts which only the dictatorship of one group can succeed in overcoming. The substitution of one elite for another, which is an essential point in Pareto's treatise, can be explained to a large extent by phenomena of economic and social change which Marxism has accustomed us to consider of primary importance. The Marxist type of revolution, involving the seizure of power by the party deriving from the proletariat, can be fitted into both Pareto's scheme and that of Marx, being, as it is, the victory of one elite and the elimination of the owners of the means of production. Those who see in it only the elimination of the capitalists and teach that a State in control of the whole economy will wither away, whereas in fact it grows stronger, and that a classless society knows no master, when in fact it has a single omnipotent master, are deliberately trying to mystify the people. But those who see only the substitution of one master for another and forget that the disappearance of the private owners of the means of production involves a far-reaching change in the social atmosphere and the hierarchy of men and values, also try to mystify.

I told you at the beginning that sociology helps us to know what is at stake in political struggles but never provides us with a judgment. I am afraid that my own convictions may have become apparent. I should merely like to add that the choice cannot be decided by the mere analysis of the social machinery which I have tried in this study. A single factor never decides the whole nature of society, but the consequences of the fact that an elite is united or divided, and of the question whether the rulers of the State also control the economy or not, and whether the hierarchy is based on technical skill, a single party or numerous groups, are tremendous.

A classless society may be efficient and imposing, it may give millions of men, who feel sure that they are building the future, joy and pride and even the feeling of fulfilling themselves in their activity, which may be called a sense of freedom. Such a society breeds soldiers, workers, devotees, but I am afraid it may stifle the individual man, responsible to his conscience and master of his own fate. Leaving out of account this argument, which is above politics, the theory of divided and united elites brings us back to the old idea that freedom depends on a system of checks and balances. That theory must, however, be transferred from the constitutional organization to society as a whole. A unified elite means the end of freedom. But when the groups of the elite are not only distinct but become a disunity, it means the end of the State. Freedom survives in those intermediate regions, which are continually threatened when there is moral unity of the elite, where men and groups preserve the secret of single and eternal wisdom and have learned how to combine autonomy with cooperation.

C. Political Culture

3. Comparative Political Systems*

GABRIEL A. ALMOND

What I propose to do in this brief paper is to suggest how the application of certain sociological and anthropological concepts may facilitate systematic comparison among the major types of political systems operative in the world today.

*From *The Journal of Politics*, vol. XVIII (1956), pp. 391–409. By permission of the journal and the author.

At the risk of saying the obvious, I am not suggesting to my colleagues in the field of comparative government that social theory is a conceptual cure-all for the ailments of the discipline. There are many ways of laboring in the vineyard of the Lord, and I am quite prepared to concede that there are more musical forms of psalmody than sociological jargon. I suppose the test of the sociological approach that is discussed here is whether or not it enables us to solve certain persistent problems in the field more effectively than we now are able to solve them.

Our expectations of the field of comparative government have changed in at least two ways in the last decades. In the first place, as American interests have broadened to include literally the whole world, our course offerings have expanded to include the many areas outside of Western Europe—Asia, the Middle East, Africa, and Latin America. Secondly, as our international interests have expanded and become more urgent, our requirements in knowledge have become more exacting. We can no longer view political crises in France with detached curiosity or view countries such as Indo-China and Indonesia as interesting political pathologies. We are led to extend our discipline and intensify it simultaneously.

It would simply be untrue to say that the discipline of comparative government has not begun to meet both of these challenges. As rapidly as it has been possible to train the personnel, new areas have opened up to teaching and research; and there has been substantial encouragement to those who have been tempted to explore new aspects of the political process both here and abroad and to employ new methods in such research. It is precisely because of the eagerness and energy with which these challenges have been met that the field is now confronted with the problem of systematic cumulation and comparison. What appears to be required in view of the rapid expansion of the field are more comparative efforts in the tradition of Finer and Friedrich, if we are to gain the maximum in insight and knowledge from this large-scale research effort.

The problem to which this paper is a tentative and provisional answer is the following. With the proliferation of courses and special studies of specific "governments" and groupings of governments on an area or other bases, is it possible to set up and justify a preliminary classification into which most of the political systems which we study today can be assigned? The classifications which we now employ are particularistic (e.g., American Government, British Government, the Soviet Union, and the like); regional (e.g., Government and Politics of the Far East, Latin America, and the like); or political (e.g., the British Commonwealth, Colonial Government, and the like); or functional (e.g., the comprehensive comparative efforts limited to the European-American area, such as Finer and Friedrich, and the specific institutional comparisons such as comparative parties, and comparative administration).

Anyone concerned with this general problem of classification of political systems will find that all of the existing bases of classification leave something to be desired. Dealing with governments particularistically is no classification at all. A regional classification is based not on the properties of the political systems, but on the contiguity in space. The existing structural classifications, such as democracy-dictatorship, parliamentary-presidential systems, two-party and multi-party systems, often turn out to miss the point, particularly when they are used in the strikingly different political systems of the pre-industrial areas. There may be a certain use therefore in exploring the possibilities of other ways of classifying political systems. What is proposed here is just one of these ways, and because of the uneven state of our knowledge is necessarily crude and provisional.

In my own efforts to stand far off, so to speak, and make the grossest discriminations between types of empirical political systems operative in the world today, I have found a fourfold classification to be most useful: the Anglo-American (including some members of the Commonwealth), the Continental European (exclusive of the Scandinavian and Low Countries, which combine some of the features of the Continental European and the Anglo-American), the pre-industrial, or partially industrial, political systems outside the European-American area, and the totalitarian political systems. This classification will not include all the political systems in existence today, but it comes close to doing so. It will serve the purpose of our discussion, which is not that of testing the inconclusiveness of this classification but rather the usefulness of sociological concepts in bringing out the essential differences between these political systems.

The terms which I shall use in discriminating the essential properties of these classes have emerged out of the Weber-Parsons tradition in social theory.[1] I shall try to suggest why I find some of these concepts useful. First, a political system is a system of *action*. What this means is that the student of political systems is concerned with empirically observable behavior. He is concerned with norms or institutions in so far as they affect behavior. Emphasizing "action" merely means that the description of a political system can never be satisfied by a simple description of its legal or ethical norms. In other words, political institutions or persons performing political roles are viewed in terms of what it is that they do, why they do it, and how what they do is related to and affects what others do. The term *system*[2] satisfies the need for an inclusive concept which covers all of the patterned actions relevant to the making of political decisions. Most political scientists use the term *political process* for these purposes. The difficulty with the term *process* is that it means any patterning of action through time. In contrast to *process,* the concept of *system* implies a *totality* of relevant units, an interdependence between the interactions of units, and a certain stability in the interaction of these units (perhaps best described as a changing equilibrium).

The unit of the political system is the role. The role, according to Parsons and Shils, ". . . is that organized sector of an actor's orientation which constitutes and defines his participation in an interactive process."[3] It involves a set of com-

---

[1] See in particular Max Weber, *The Theory of Social and Economic Organization,* trans. by A. M. Henderson and Talcott Parsons (New York: Oxford University Press, 1947), pp. 87 ff.

[2] See David Easton, *The Political System: An Inquiry into the State of Political Science* (New York: Alfred Knopf, 1953), pp. 90 ff.

[3] Talcott Parsons and Edward A. Shils, eds., *Towards a General Theory of Action* (Cambridge: Harvard University Press, 1951), p. 23.

plementary expectations concerning his own actions and those of others with whom he interacts. Thus a political system may be defined as a set of interacting roles, or as a structure of roles, if we understand by *structure* a patterning of interactions. The advantage of the concept of *role* as compared with such terms as *institutions, organizations,* or *groups,* is that it is a more inclusive and more open concept. It can include formal offices, informal offices, families, electorates, mobs, casual as well as persistent groupings, and the like, in so far as they enter into and affect the political system. The use of other concepts such as those indicated above involves ambiguity, forced definitions (such as groups), or residual categories. Like the concept of system it does not prejudice our choice of units but rather enables us to nominate them on the basis of empirical investigation.

While there appear to be certain advantages in these concepts of political system and role for our purposes, they confront the political scientist with a serious problem. While he intends the concept to have a general application, Parsons appears to have had before him in elaborating the concept the model of the primary group—family, friendship, and the like—and not complex social systems, the units of which are collectivities and not individual actors. In this sense the sociological concept of system and of role can only be a beginning of a conceptual model of the political system. The job of developing additional concepts necessary to handle macrocosmic social systems such as political systems—national and international—is still to be done.

My own conception of the distinguishing properties of the political system proceeds from Weber's definition—the legitimate monopoly of physical coercion over a given territory and population.[4] The political systems with which most political scientists concern themselves all are characterized by a specialized apparatus which possesses this legitimate monopoly, and the political system consists of those interacting roles which affect its employment. There are, of course, simpler societies in which this function of maintenance of order through coercion is diffuse and unspecialized; it is combined with other functions in the family and other groupings. While these systems are also properly the subject matter of political science, there are few political scientists indeed with the specialized equipment necessary to study them.

It may be useful to add a few comments about this definition of politics and the political order to avoid misunderstanding. To define politics as having this distinguishing property of monopolizing legitimate coercion in a given territory is not the same thing as saying that this is *all* that government does. It is the thing that government does and that other social systems ordinarily may not do legitimately. Other social systems may employ other forms of compulsion than physical coercion. Some indeed may legitimately employ physical coercion on a limited scale. But the employment of *ultimate, comprehensive,* and *legitimate* physical coercion is the monopoly of states, and the political system is uniquely concerned with the scope, the direction, and the conditions affecting the em-

---

4 From Max Weber, *Essays in Sociology,* trans. by H. H. Gerth and C. Wright Mills (New York: Oxford University Press, 1946), p. 78.

ployment of this physical coercion. It is, of course, clear that political systems protect freedoms and provide welfare, as well as impose order backed up by physical compulsion, but even their protection of freedom and their provision of welfare is characteristically backed up by the threat of physical compulsion. Hence it seems appropriate to define the political system as the patterned interaction of roles affecting decisions backed up by the threat of physical compulsion.

The task of describing a political system consists in characterizing all the patterned interactions which take place within it. It takes us beyond the legal system into all the roles which occur and involves our defining these roles in action or behavioral terms. The concept of system implies that these roles are interdependent and that a significant change in any one role affects changes in the others, and thereby changes the system as a whole. Thus the emergence of pressure groups in the present century produced certain changes in the party system and in the administrative and legislative processes. The rapid expansion of executive bureaucracy was one of the factors that triggered off the development of legislative bureaucracy and pressure group bureaucracy. Changes in the role of political communication have transformed the electoral process, the behavior of parties, the legislature, the executive. The concepts of system and of interdependence lead us to look for these changes when any specific role changes significantly. It suggests the usefulness of thinking at the level of the system and and its interdependence rather than in terms of discrete phenomena or only limited bilateral relationships, or relationships occurring only within the formal-legal role structure.

The fourth concept is *orientation to political action.* Every political system is embedded in a set of meanings and purposes. We speak of "attitudes toward politics," "political values," "ideologies," "national character," "cultural ethos." The difficulty with all these terms is that their meanings are diffuse and ambiguous. The concepts of orientation to action and of the pattern variables are useful since they at least attempt logical distinctness and comprehensiveness. It is not essential for my purposes to go into the modes of orientation of action, or into the "pattern variables" in detail. Parsons and Shils tell us that any orientation to politics involves three components: the first is perception, or *cognition;* the second is preference, involvement, or affect (*cathexis*); the third is evaluation or choice through the application of standards or values to the cognitive and affective components. By *cognition* is meant the knowledge and discrimination of the objects, events, actions, issues, and the like. By *cathexis* is meant the investment of objects, issues, etc., with emotional significance, or affect. By *evaluation* is meant the manner in which individuals organize and select their perceptions, preferences, and values in the process of establishing a position *vis-à-vis political action.* [5]

Every political system is embedded in a particular pattern of orientations to political action. I have found it useful to refer to this as the *political culture.* There are two points to be made regarding the concept of political culture. First,

5 Parsons and Shils, *op. cit.,* pp. 58 ff.

it does not coincide with a given political system or society. Patterns of orientation to politics may, and usually do, extend beyond the boundaries of political systems. The second point is that the political culture is not the same thing as the general culture, although it is related to it. Because political orientation involves cognition, intellection, and adaptation to external situations, as well as the standards and values of the general culture, it is a differentiated part of the culture and has a certain autonomy. Indeed, it is the failure to give proper weight to the cognitive and evaluative factors, and to the consequent autonomy of political culture, that has been responsible for the exaggerations and over-simplifications of the "national character" literature of recent years.

The usefulness of the concept of political culture and its meaning may perhaps be conveyed more effectively through illustration. I would argue that the United States, England, and several of the Commonwealth countries have a common political culture, but are separate and different kinds of political systems. And I would argue that the typical countries of continental Western Europe, while constituting individual political systems, include several different political cultures which extend beyond their borders. In other words, they are political systems with fragmented political cultures.

In an effort to overcome understandable resistances to the introduction of a new term, I should like to suggest why I find the concept of political culture more useful than the terms we now employ, such as *ideology* or *political party*. As I understand the term *ideology*, it means the systematic and explicit formulation of a general orientation to politics. We need this term to describe such political phenomena as these and should not reduce its specificity by broadening it to include not only the explicit doctrinal structure characteristically borne by a minority of *militants*, but also the vaguer and more implicit orientations which generally characterize political followings. The term *political party* also cannot serve our purpose, for we are here dealing with a formal organization which may or may not be a manifestation of a political culture. Indeed, we will be gravely misled if we try to force the concept of party to mean political culture. Thus the commonly used distinctions between one-party, two-party, and multi-party systems simply get nowhere in distinguishing the essential properties of the totalitarian, the Anglo-American, and the Continental European political systems. For the structure we call *party* in the totalitarian system is not a party at all; the two parties of the Anglo-American system are organized manifestations of a homogeneous political culture; and the multi-parties of Continental European political systems in some cases are and in some cases are not the organized manifestations of different political cultures.

But the actual test of the usefulness of this conceptual scheme can only come from a more detailed application of it in developing the special properties of the classes of political systems to which we earlier referred.

THE ANGLO-AMERICAN POLITICAL SYSTEMS

The Anglo-American political systems are characterized by a *homogeneous, secular* political culture. By a secular political culture I mean a multi-valued political culture, a rational-calculating, bargaining, and experimental political culture. It is a homogeneous culture in the sense that there is a sharing of political ends and means. The great majority of the actors in the political system accept as the ultimate goals of the political system some combination of the values of freedom, mass welfare, and security. There are groups which stress one value at the expense of the others; there are times when one value is stressed by all groups; but by and large the tendency is for all these values to be shared, and for no one of them to be completely repressed. To a Continental European this kind of political culture often looks sloppy. It has no logic, no clarity. This is probably correct in an intellectual sense, since this balancing of competing values occurs below the surface among most people and is not explicated in any very elegant way. Actually the logic is complex and is constantly referred to reality in an inductive process. It avoids the kind of logical simplism which characterizes much of the Continental European ideological polemic.

A secularized political system involves an individuation of and a measure of autonomy among the various roles. Each one of the roles sets itself up autonomously in political business, so to speak. There tends to be an arms-length bargaining relationship among the roles. The political system is saturated with the atmosphere of the market. Groups of electors come to the political market with votes to sell in exchange for policies. Holders of offices in the formal-legal role structure tend to be viewed as agents and instrumentalities, or as brokers occupying points in the bargaining process. The secularized political process has some of the characteristics of a laboratory; that is, policies offered by candidates are viewed as hypotheses, and the consequences of legislation are rapidly communicated within the system and constitute a crude form of testing hypotheses. Finally, because the political culture tends to be homogeneous and pragmatic, it takes some of the atmosphere of a game. A game is a good game when the outcome is in doubt and when the stakes are not too high. When the stakes are too high, the tone changes from excitement to anxiety. While "fun" is frequently an aspect of Anglo-American politics, it is rarely a manifestation of Continental European politics; and, unless one stretches the definition, it never occurs at all in totalitarian politics.

ROLE STRUCTURE IN THE ANGLO-AMERICAN POLITICAL SYSTEMS

The role structure in this group of political systems is (1) highly differentiated, (2) manifest, organized, and bureaucratized, (3) characterized by a high degree of stability in the function of the roles, and (4) likely to have a diffusion of power and influence within the political system as a whole.

With regard to the first point, each one of the units—formal government agencies, political parties, pressure groups and other kinds of voluntary associations, the media of communication, and "publics" of various kinds—pursues specialized purposes and performs specialized functions in the system. As was already pointed out, each one of these entities is more or less autonomous—interdependent, but autonomous. Certainly there are striking differences in this respect as between the United States and the United Kingdom, but their similarity becomes clear in contrast to the other major types of systems which will be described below. Secondly, this role structure is manifest and on the surface. Most of the potential "interests" have been organized and possess bureaucracies. Thirdly, there is in contrast to some of the other systems a relatively high degree of stability of function in the various parts of the structure. Bureaucracies function as bureaucracies, armies as armies, parliaments as parliaments. The functions are not ordinarily substitutable as among these various institutions and organizations, in contrast to some of the other systems. This is another way of saying that the political division of labor is more complex, more explicit, and more stable. There are, of course, striking differences between the British and American versions in these respects. For the American system is at the same time more complex and less stable than the British. There are, for example, many more pressure groups and types of pressure groups in the United States for reasons of size, economic complexity, and ethnic and religious heterogeneity. Furthermore there is more substitutability of function in the American system, more policy-making by pressure groups and the media of communication, more intervention in policy-making through the transient impact of "public moods." But again if we are comparing the Anglo-American system with, for example, the pre-industrial or partially industrial systems, the British and American systems will stand out by virtue of their similarities on the score of complexity, manifestness, and stability of role structure.

Finally the Anglo-American type of political system is one in which there is diffusion of power and influence. This is only partially expressed in the formal legal phraseology of a democratic suffrage and representative government. There is an effective as well as a legal diffusion of power, resulting from a system of mass communications, mass education, and representation by interest groups. Here again the British and American versions differ sharply in terms of formal governmental structure, the relations between parties and pressure groups, and the system of communication and education. The net result is a more centralized, predictable role structure in Britain than in the United States.

THE PRE-INDUSTRIAL POLITICAL SYSTEMS

The political systems which fall under this very general category are the least well-known of all four of the classes discussed here. But despite our relative ignorance in this area and our inability to elaborate the many sub-types which no doubt exist, a discussion of this kind of political system is analytically useful since it presents such a striking contrast to the homogeneous, secular political culture, and the complex and relatively stable role structure of the Anglo-American political system.

The pre-industrial—or partially industrialized and Westernized—political systems may be best described as mixed political cultures and mixed political systems. Nowhere does the need for additional vocabulary become clearer than in the analysis of these systems; for here parliaments tend to be something other than parliaments, parties and pressure groups behave in unusual ways, bureaucracies and armies often dominate the political system, and there is an atmosphere of unpredictability and gunpowder surrounding the political system as a whole.

Some clarity is introduced into the understanding of these systems if one recognizes that they are embedded in mixed political cultures. What this means is that as a minimum we have two political cultures, the Western system with its parliaments, its electoral system, its bureaucracy and the like, and the pre-Western system or systems. In countries such as India there are many traditional political cultures which intermingle with the Western system. What kind of amalgam emerges from this impingement of different political cultures will depend on at least five factors: (1) the type of traditional cultures which are involved; (2) the auspices under which Westernization has been introduced (e.g., Western colonial powers, or native elites); (3) the functions of the society which have been Westernized; (4) the tempo and tactics of the Westernization process; (5) the type of Western cultural products which have been introduced. As a consequence of this impingement of the Western and traditional political cultures, there is a third type of political culture which frequently emerges in this type of system; what in Max Weber's language may be called a charismatic political culture. It often happens as a consequence of the erosion of a traditional political culture that powerful forces are released—anxieties over the violation of sacred customs and relationships, feelings of rootlessness and directionlessness because of the rejection of habitual routines. The impact of the Western rational system on the traditional system or systems often creates a large potential for violence. One of the typical manifestations of this conflict of political cultures is the charismatic nationalism which occurs so frequently in these areas and which may be in part understood as being a movement toward accepting a new system of political norms, or a movement toward reaffirming the older traditional ones, often both in peculiar combinations. To overcome the resistance of habitual routines backed up by supernatural sanctions, the new form of legitimacy must represent a powerful affirmation capable of breaking up deeply ingrained habits and replacing earlier loyalties. Thus, at the minimum, we must have in these political systems the old or the traditional political culture, or cultures, the new or the Western-rational political culture, and transitional or resultant political phenomena of one kind or another. Needless to say, this typical mixture of political cultures presents the most serious problems of communication and coordination. We are dealing with a political system in which large groups have fundamentally different "cognitive maps" of politics and apply different norms to political action. Instability and unpredictability are not to be viewed as inescapable consequences of this type of mixture of political cultures.

ROLE STRUCTURE IN THE PRE-INDUSTRIAL POLITICAL SYSTEMS

These characteristics of the pre-industrial political systems may be brought out more clearly and systematically in an analysis of the political role structure which is more or less characteristic.

There is first a relatively low degree of structural differentiation. Political interest often tends to be latent and when it emerges into politics often takes the form of spontaneous, violent action. Political parties are unstable; they fragment and consolidate, appear and disappear. There is ordinarily only a rudimentary specialized system of communication. Unless there is a bureaucracy left by a Western colonial power, the bureaucratic structure may be only partially developed.

Secondly, because of the absence of a stable and explicit role structure, there is likely to be a high degree of *substitutability* of roles. Thus bureaucracies may take over the legislative function, and armies may and often do the same. A political party may pre-empt the policy-making function, or a mob may emerge and take the center of the policy-making stage for a brief interval. In other words, in contrast to the Anglo-American political systems, there is no stable division of political labor.

A third and most important aspect of these political systems is the mixing of political role structures. Thus there may be a parliament formally based on a set of legal norms and regulations; but operating within it may be a powerful family, a religious sect, a group of tribal chieftains, or some combination of these. These are elements of the traditional role structure operating according to their own traditional norms. The student of these political systems would be greatly misled if he followed Western norms and expectations in describing such a decision-making system. What would be corruption in a Western parliament would be normatively oriented conduct in a "mixed parliament" of the kind often found in the regions outside of the Western-European American area.

Thus such concepts as mixed political culture and mixed political role structures may prepare the field researcher more adequately than the accepted political science theory and terminology; for in going to Indonesia or Thailand he will not only have in mind the Western conception of political process and system and a conception of the appropriate roles of legislatures, bureaucracies, parties, pressure groups, and public opinion, but will rather look for the particular pattern of amalgamation of these roles with the traditional roles. His intellectual apparatus would enable him to grapple more quickly and more adequately with political phenomena which he might otherwise overlook, or treat as pathologies.

TOTALITARIAN POLITICAL SYSTEMS

The totalitarian political culture gives the appearance of being homogeneous, but the homogeneity is synthetic. Since there are no voluntary associations, and political communication is controlled from the center, it is impossible to judge in any accurate way the extent to which there is a positive acceptance of the totalitarian order. One can only say that in view of the thorough-going penetration of the society by a centrally controlled system of organizations and communications, and the special way in which coercion or its threat is applied, the totalitarian system, in contrast to the others, tends to be non-consensual. This is not to say that it is completely non-consensual. A completely coercive political system is unthinkable. But if one were to place the totalitarian system on a continuum of consensual–non-consensual it would be located rather more at the non-consensual end of the continuum than the others described here. Unlike the other systems where some form of legitimacy—whether traditional, rational-legal, or charismatic—underlies the acquiescence of the individual in the political system, in the totalitarian order the characteristic orientation to authority tends to be some combination of conformity and apathy. This type of political system has become possible only in modern times, since it depends on the modern technology of communication, on modern types of organization, and on the modern technology of violence. Historic tyrannies have no doubt sought this kind of dominion but were limited in the effectiveness of their means. Totalitarianism is tyranny with a rational bureaucracy, a monopoly of the modern technology of communication, and a monopoly of the modern technology of violence.

ROLE STRUCTURE IN TOTALITARIAN POLITICAL SYSTEMS

I believe Franz Neumann in his *Behemoth*[6] was one of the first students of totalitarianism who rejected the *monocratic* model as being useful in understanding these systems. He spoke of the peculiar shapelessness of the Nazi regime, of the fact that there was no stable delegation of power among the bureaucracy, party, the army, the organizations of big business, and the like. He concluded, as you recall, that there was no state under the Nazis. I believe what he meant to say was that there was no *legitimate* state. Later students of totalitarianism such as Hannah Arendt,[7] Merle Fainsod,[8] Carl Friedrich,[9] Alex Inkeles,[10] and Barrington Moore, Jr.,[11] have been led to similar conclusions about totalitarianism in general, or about Soviet totalitarianism. Hannah Arendt has painted the most extreme picture, which, while an exaggeration, is useful analytically. She urges that the "isolation of atomized individuals provides not only the mass basis for totalitarian rule, but is carried through at the very top of the whole structure." The aim of this process of atomization is to destroy solidarity at any point in the system and to avoid all stable delegations of power which might reduce the freedom of maneuver of those at the very center of the system. "As techniques of government, the totalitarian devices appear simple and ingeniously effective. They assure not only an absolute power monopoly, but unparalleled certainty that all commands will always be carried out; the multi-

---

[6] Franz Neumann, *Behemoth: The Structure and Practice of National Socialism* (New York: Oxford University Press, 1942), pp. 459 ff.

[7] Hannah Arendt, *The Origins of Totalitarianism* (New York: Harcourt, Brace and Company, 1951), p. 388.

[8] Merle Fainsod, *How Russia Is Ruled* (Cambridge: Harvard University Press, 1953), pp. 354 ff.

[9] Carl J. Friedrich, ed., *Totalitarianism* (Cambridge: Harvard University Press, 1954), pp. 47 ff.

[10] Alex Inkeles in *ibid.,* pp. 88 ff.

[11] Barrington Moore, Jr., *Terror and Progress USSR: Some Sources of Change and Stability in the Soviet Dictatorship* (Cambridge: Harvard University Press, 1954), pp. 154 ff.

plicity of the transmission belts, the confusion of the hierarchy, secure the dictator's complete independence of all his inferiors and make possible the swift and surprising changes in policy for which totalitarianism has become famous."[12]

There are thus at least two distinctive characteristics of the totalitarian role structure: (1) the predominance of the coercive roles, and (2) the functional instability of the power roles—bureaucracy, party, army, and secret police. The predominance of the coercive role structure is reflected in its penetration of all of the other role structures. Thus all forms of organization and communication become saturated with a coercive flavor. This predominance of coercion is reflected in the celebrated definition of the state as "bodies of armed men" in Lenin's *State and Revolution.* It is also reflected in the doctrine of the "potential enemy of the state," a conception under which almost any behavior may be arbitrarily defined as disloyal behavior. This eliminates the predictability of the impact of coercion and renders it an omnipresent force, however limited its application may be in a quantitative sense.

The functional instability among the power roles has as its main purpose the prevention of any stable delegation of power, and the consequent diffusion of power and creation of other power centers. This pattern was apparently quite marked in the development of the Nazi regime and has been observable in the uneasy balance established in the Soviet Union between party, bureaucracy, army, and secret police. In the nature of the case there must be a stabler delegation of power among the economic allocative roles, but even these roles are penetrated by the coercive role structure and manipulated within limits. A third class of roles is illustrated by the electoral process and the representative system, as well as the practice of "self-criticism" in the party. While there is a set of norms under which these activities are supposed to influence power and policy-making, they are rather to be understood as mobilizing devices, as devices intended to create a facade of consent.

THE CONTINENTAL EUROPEAN POLITICAL SYSTEMS

We refer here primarily to France, Germany, and Italy. The Scandinavian and Low Countries stand somewhere in between the Continental pattern and the Anglo-American. What is most marked about the Continental European systems is the fragmentation of political culture; but this fragmentation is rather different from that of the non-Western systems. For in the non-Western systems we are dealing with mixed political cultures involving the most striking contrasts. The Western political culture arising out of a very different development pattern is introduced bodily, so to speak, from the outside. In the Continental European systems we are dealing with a pattern of political culture characterized by an uneven pattern of development. There are significant survivals, "outcroppings," of older cultures and their political manifestations. But all of the cultural variations have common roots and share a common heritage.

[12] Arendt, *op. cit.,* p. 389.

In view of this developmental pattern it may be appropriate to speak of the Continental European systems as having political sub-cultures. There is indeed in all the examples of this type of system a surviving pre-industrial sub-culture (e.g., the Catholic *Ancien Régime* areas in France, Southern Italy, and the Islands, and parts of Bavaria). The historical background of all three of these systems is characterized by a failure on the part of the middle classes in the nineteenth century to carry through a thorough-going secularization of the political culture. Thus another political sub-culture in these political systems constitutes remnants of the older middle classes who are still primarily concerned with the secularization of the political system itself. A third group of political sub-cultures is associated with the modernized and industrialized parts of these societies. But because they emerged in an only partially secularized political culture, their potentialities for "political market" behavior were thwarted. As major political sub-cultures there are thus these three: (1) the pre-industrial, primarily Catholic components, (2) the older middle-class components, and (3) the industrial components proper. But the political culture is more complex than this. Since in the last century the political issues have involved the very survival of these sub-cultures, and the basic form of the political system itself, the political actors have not come to politics with specific bargainable differences but rather with conflicting and mutually exclusive designs for the political culture and political system. This has involved a further fragmentation at the level of ideology and political organizations. Thus the pre-industrial, primarily Catholic element has both an adaptive, semi-secular wing and an anti-secular wing. The middle classes are divided into conservative wings in an uneasy alliance with clerical pre-republican elements, and left-wings in uneasy friendship with socialists. Finally, the industrial workers are divided according to the degree of their alienation from the political system as a whole. The organized political manifestations of this fragmented political culture take the form of "movements" or sects, rather than of political parties. This means that political affiliation is more of an act of faith than of agency.

Perhaps the most pronounced characteristic of the political role structure in these areas is what one might call a general alienation from the political market. The political culture pattern is not adapted to the political system. For while these countries have adopted parliaments and popular elections, they are not appropriately oriented to these institutions. The political actors come to the market not to exchange, compromise, and adapt, but to preach, exhort, convert, and transform the political system into something other than a bargaining agency. What bargaining and exchanging does occur tends to take the form of under-the-counter transactions. Thus demoralization (*"transformism"*) is an almost inescapable consequence of this combination of political culture and system. In contrast, the normatively consistent, morally confident actor in this type of political system is the *militant* who remains within the confines of his political sub-culture, continually reaffirms his special norms, and scolds his parliamentarians.

This suggests another essential characteristic of this type of role structure, which places it in contrast to the Anglo-American. There is not an individuation of the political roles, but rather the roles are embedded in the sub-cultures and tend to constitute separate sub-systems of roles. Thus the Catholic sub-culture has the Church itself, the Catholic schools, propaganda organizations such as Catholic Action, Catholic trade unions, or worker organizations, a Catholic party or parties, and a Catholic press. The Communist sub-culture—the sub-culture of the political "alienates"—similarly has a complete and separate system of roles. The socialist and "liberal" sub-cultures tend in the same direction but are less fully organized and less exclusive. Thus one would have to say that the center of gravity in these political systems is not in the formal legal role structure but in the political sub-cultures. Thus "immobilism" would appear to be a normal property of this kind of political system, and it is not so much an "immobilism" of formal-legal institutions as a consequence of the condition of the political culture. Needless to say, this portrayal of the Continental European political system has been exaggerated for purposes of contrast and comparison.

Two other general aspects of the role structure of these countries call for comment. First, there is a higher degree of substitutability of roles than in the Anglo-American political systems and a lesser degree than in the non-Western systems. Thus parties may manipulate pressure groups in the sense of making their decisions for them (the Communist case); interest groups such as the Church and Catholic Action may manipulate parties and trade unions; and interest groups may operate directly in the legislative process, although this last pattern occurs in the Anglo-American system as well. The "immobilism" of the formally political organs often leads to a predominance of the bureaucracy in policy-making.

A second general characteristic, which is a consequence of the immobilism of the political system as a whole, is the ever-present threat of what is often called the "Caesaristic" breakthrough. As in the non-Western area, although the situations and causes are different, these systems tend always to be threatened by, and sometimes to be swept away by, movements of charismatic nationalism which break through the boundaries of the political sub-cultures and overcome immobilism through coercive action and organization. In other words these systems have a totalitarian potentiality in them. The fragmented political culture may be transformed into a synthetically homogeneous one and the stalemated role structure mobilized by the introduction of the coercive pattern already described.

*   *   *

In conclusion perhaps the point might be made that conceptual and terminological growth in the sciences is as inevitable as the growth of language itself. But just as all the slang and neologisms of the moment do not find a permanent place in the language, so also all of the conceptual jargon which the restless minds of scholars invent—sometimes to facilitate communication with their colleagues and sometimes to confound them—will not find its permanent place in the vocabulary of the disciplines. The ultimate criterion of admission or rejection is the facilitation of understanding, and this, fortunately enough, is not in the hands of the restless and inventive scholar, but in the hands of the future scholarly generations who will try them out for "fit." If I may be permitted to conclude with a minor note of blasphemy, it may be said of new concepts as it was said of the salvation of souls . . . "there shall be weeping and gnashing of teeth, for many are called but few are chosen."

D. Power

4. Approaches to the Study of Political Power*

FRANZ L. NEUMANN

POLITICAL POWER AND PSYCHOLOGY

Political power is an elusive concept. It embraces two radically different relations: control of nature, and control of man. Power over nature is mere intellectual power. It consists in man's understanding of the lawfulness of external nature for the ultimate purpose of subjecting external nature to man's needs. It is this accumulated knowledge which is the basis of the productivity of any given society. This power is powerless. It does not involve control of other men.

Political power is social power focused on the state. It involves control of other men for the purpose of influencing the behavior of the state, its legislative, administrative and judicial activities. Since political power is control of other men, political power (as contrasted with power over external nature) is always a two-sided relationship. Man is not simply a piece of external nature; he is an organism endowed with reason, although frequently not capable of, or prevented from, acting rationally. Consequently, those who wield political power are compelled to create emotional and rational responses in those whom they rule, inducing them to accept, implicitly or explicitly, the commands of the rulers. Failure to evoke emotional or intellectual responses in the ruled compels the ruler to resort to simple violence, ultimately to liquidation.

The two-sided character of political power already marks political science off from natural science. It makes it impossible (even if it were desirable) to measure power relationships as one measures the behavior of external nature. The varia-

*From *Political Science Quarterly,* vol. LXV, no. 2 (June 1950), pp. 161–80. By permission.

tions of the power relationships are numberless. One may classify and describe them, but one cannot measure them.

Political power is not comparable to the category of energy in physics. Nor is power the sole category of political science. Politics is not merely the art of getting something in a certain way regardless of the what and of the how. The trend to equate politics with power politics goes back to Machiavelli and appears to have become the predominant trait of American and, perhaps, of modern political science in general. Politics is viewed as a purely technical concern. "Values" (the term is used only provisionally) are then mere personal preferences; valid if they work, invalid if they fail. History is then quite meaningless. It is an indifferent repetition of the endless struggle of "in-groups" versus "out-groups." It is thus reduced to mere chronology, a file of illustrative materials for so-called hypotheses or, at best, is governed by what Machiavelli called Fortuna, the luck of the participants in the struggle.

The theoretical basis of this approach to politics and political science is usually psychological, as Machiavelli has already developed it. Men are the same throughout history. They have certain stable traits, and all, or almost all, are equipped with "power drive," an uncontrollable and irrational impulse for power. From this assertion are then derived such facile half-true generalizations as the famous statement of Lord Acton: "Power tends to corrupt, absolute power corrupts absolutely."

This is not to imply that the psychology of power has no place in political science. Its significance is great, but not decisive. Its contribution is twofold. First, it leads to the realization that the optimistic theories of human nature are one-sided and thus false. Man, although endowed with reason, frequently knows not—or is not permitted to know—what his true interests are. This rediscovery of ancient truths is particularly the merit of the materialistic psychology of Freud. Secondly, psychological techniques permit us to describe in concrete and convincing terms the personality structures most capable of exerting or of suffering power. But psychology cannot go beyond concretization and description. It cannot supply a theory of political power. The action of each man is as much the result of the environment as it is the manifestation of a personality structure. Indeed, personality itself is historically conditioned. To the psychologist, the environment is a mere "stimulus" of the individual act. To the political scientist, it is one element in the total setting of political power.

The present orientation of psychology, besides, tends to make it simply a technique of rule, of maintaining and strengthening power relationships, an instrument of manipulation of the masses by the elite.

The rejection of the psychological approach involves in its positive aspect the view that politics (and thus history) is not simply a struggle of power groups for power, but an attempt to mold the world according to one's image, to impress one's view upon it. The historical process has a meaning. Provisionally, we may accept the traditional pre-positivistic formulation that politics is the struggle of ideas as well as of force. . . .

THE SIGNIFICANCE OF POLITICAL POWER

No society in recorded history has ever been able to dispense with political power. This is as true of liberalism as of absolutism, as true of laissez-faire as of an interventionist state. No greater disservice has been rendered to political science than the statement that the liberal state was a "weak" state. It was precisely as strong as it needed to be in the circumstances. It acquired substantial colonial empires, waged wars, held down internal disorders, and stabilized itself over long periods of time.

But the methods applied by those who wield power and the scope of its application vary, of course. And it is precisely this problem that is of major significance for the political scientist. Formally, the methods range from the marginal case of killing to the marginal case of education. Three basic methods are at the disposal of the power group: persuasion, material benefits, violence. Violence is probably most effective as a short-range method, but little effective as the principal method of maintaining power over long periods since it compels the group (particularly under modern conditions) to intensify the methods of violence and to extend it to larger sections of the ruled. The most efficient (that is, cheapest form) is, of course, persuasion. Yet all three, persuasion, benefits, violence, are always present in all forms of government. And it is precisely the mixture of the three elements which constitutes another major problem for the political scientist. I shall attempt to clarify the meaning by the formulation of some sociological generalizations.

Sociological Generalization 1

The significance of persuasion grows with the growing complexity of society. It is, perhaps, legitimate to consider persuasion, as a rule, to be merely a form of violence, "violence committed against the soul" as the French historian of Catholic England under Henry VIII formulated it. Through persuasion, the rulers achieve a marked degree of habituation of the ruled so that their reactions assume an almost automatic character. The success of persuasion will, however, depend upon the scope and duration of the propaganda and the skills by which stereotypes are produced. There is little doubt that persuasion is a more efficient and cheaper exercise of political power than the employment of large police forces, armies and militias.

Sociological Generalization 2

The increasing complexity of society requires that the rulers increasingly utilize arcane, secret techniques of rule. The struggle for power is a real struggle aiming at the control of the state machine. In any struggle, however, tactical decisions can be effectively made only in secret. Secrecy, in turn, can be preserved only by small numbers. It is this very fact that necessitates the rise of oligarchies within mass movements. Max Weber and Robert Michels (and probably many others) have drawn attention to this phenomenon, and Max Weber, besides, correctly stressed the superiority of small over large numbers because of the significance of secrecy for any rule designed to be more than temporary. It is precisely for this reason that the rule of the few becomes particularly marked in those mass organizations which, more than other movements, are essentially devoted to democracy: the trade unions and the social democratic (labor) parties. The reason is obvious. The opponents of these movements are usually numerically few, but individually powerful, subjects who are thus able to keep their strategic and tactical decisions secret. The mass organization, faced with such opposition, must, in turn, resort to the construction of forms of rule which also permit secrecy. Aristocratic rule thus becomes a sociologically necessary implementation of democratic movements.[1] It is, therefore, no accident that the growth of oligarchies within mass movements was first studied in the example of the German Social Democratic party.

Lenin made a virtue of this necessity. His vanguard theory of leadership frankly replaces the traditional democratic conception of social democracy by an aristocratic one.

Sociological Generalization 3

The higher the state of technological development, the greater the concentration of political power. The legal conception of ownership is quite irrelevant for an analysis of this phenomenon. It matters not who owns a technical unit: an individual, a corporation, a state, any other organized society. The social organization of large technical units may, of course, be a cooperative one. In every social group which is based on struggle, however, the organization will, of necessity, be hierarchic. The larger the size, the more hierarchic it becomes. Growing hierarchic trends lead to concentration of power at the top. The relation between social and political power will be analyzed at a later place.

Sociological Generalization 4

With the growing complexity of society and its increasing industrialization, the significance of political power in the social process grows. Concentration of power (in the economy, in society, in culture) makes for more rigidity. A process of social petrifaction sets in and prevents the system from achieving a semiautomatic balance. The equilibrium, once disturbed, can be restored only through active intervention of the political power. Control of the state then becomes more precious than ever before.

Sociological Generalization 5

The same trend also produces a greater separation of political power from social power—a phenomenon that shall concern us later.

[1] That it may become, not its implementation, but its negation should be kept in mind.

Some or all of these generalizations are subject to challenge. They are not meant to be exhaustive, but merely point the direction to a proper study of political power. That they produce uneasiness is to be expected. At first sight it seems difficult to reconcile them with the theory of democracy. If by democracy is understood that mixture of diverse elements, of Locke and Rousseau, St. Augustine and St. Thomas, which is usually called "democratic theory," a reconciliation of those realistic trends with the doctrine is, indeed, impossible. We are not now concerned with the problem of democratic theory. For the present it suffices to say that an adequate democratic theory will have to deal with these problems.

ROOTS OF POLITICAL POWER

Three questions have to be faced in the analysis of the roots of political power: the conceptual framework has to be established; the institutional setting to be clarified; and the historical process to be understood which leads to a change in institutions and different attitudes toward power and to a different political behavior. For the ancient historians, this was no problem. Political power derived squarely from economic power, particularly from the control of land. Changes in ownership, the emergence of new modes of production, and so on, created new sources of political power and thus made for conflicts. Modern historians dealing with this period of history have not hesitated to restate the problem in the same way as the ancients stated it.

As we shall directly show, modern capitalist economy has rendered this whole subject problematical. And, despite the fact that the issue is so crucial, analysis has been hindered by senseless taboos. The older insights have been lost or hidden and are rarely brought fully into the open. Thus, the classical approach has been restated in modern times by Marx's interpretation of history (that this did not originate with him—and is not "Marxist"—he himself admitted). Yet since it is fashionable to reject Marxism root and branch—sight unseen so to speak—the student precludes himself from a clear understanding of the relationship between economic power and political power.

The approach is facilitated by the establishment of certain categories of relationships.

1. The ancient conception. Here—and this follows already from what has been said—although the source of political power is economic power, political power permeates all social activities and all spheres of life. The economic power position merely provides the motor of political power which then includes all power relationships.

2. The feudal conception. In the ideal-typical form, political power does not exist. It is merely a function of an economic power position: the ownership of land. From it flow judicial, military, religious, legislative and administrative powers.

3. The capitalist conception. It is only in this period that a real problem arises: the independence of political power and yet its interconnection with

economic power. Political power (the theoretical construction has been per-fected by Hobbes) is a separate activity, carried out in a separate institution: the state. The state has the monopoly of coercive power which it exercises in a separate institutional framework. At the same time, however, this separate insti-tution is intrinsically connected with society in the service of which it operates. It is this conception of political power that unites Locke and Hobbes, and distinguishes both from Rousseau. Both separate political power from social power; both connect them. Hobbes believes it necessary to maximize political power in order to serve society; Locke maintains that only by its minimizations can society be served. Both, however, admit of exceptions. In Hobbes's theory, political power will be destroyed if it fails to serve its social function (the social contract lapses); Locke, through the institution of the prerogative and federative power, maximizes political power if it is necessary for the good of the common-wealth. What Hobbes and Locke did not clearly state is that the two are not only functionally but genetically connected; that is, economic power is the root of political power. The first systematic analysis of this relationship stems from St. Simon's analysis of the French Revolution and then spreads rapidly into French and English historiography and sociology.

From this general view of Hobbes and Locke it follows that whatever freedom society, and particularly economic activity, is to have, it has for the sake of maintaining a stable political order. There is thus no "pure" economic power and no "pure" political activity. Economics is as much an instrument of politics as politics is a tool of economics. The mythological conception of the laissez-faire state ought finally to be destroyed.

If this general view is accepted, the translation of economic power into social power and thence into political power becomes the crucial concern of the political scientist.

The Political Party

The single most important instrument for the translation of social power into political power is the political party. The reason for the supreme position of the party lies in the vary nature of democracy. The party permits the presentation of particular and, quite frequently, very egoistic interests as national interests. At the same time, however, it prevents the total domination of national interests by particular interests. The function of the political party in democracy is thus ambiguous. The democratic process compels each social group to strive for mass support. Each group, therefore, must present its egoistic interests as universal. Politics in a democracy, the struggle for political power, thus becomes far more ideological than in any previous period in history. What was obvious for the ancients, and clear to the feudal system, becomes hidden in the democratic process. But the valuable side of this process must equally not be forgotten. The very need to appeal to social groups larger than the immediate interest group compels adjustment of various interests. Politics becomes more democratic.[2]

---

[2] It is this fact that Marxists usually overlook.

Private Property

Social power, in turn, either is derived from private property or is against it. The legal meaning of private property comprises two radically different conceptions: power over an external piece of nature (or an absolute right) and power over other men derived from power over nature. It is only the second meaning of private property with which the political scientist is concerned: with proprietorship in the means of production. This type of property gives power—power in the labor market, in the commodity market, and in the political market of the state.

The three power functions of property are usually (and particularly in Europe where political and social life is more petrified than in the United States) institutionalized in three types of organization: for the labor market, the employer's association; for the commodity market, the cartel; for the political market, the territorial form of the chambers of commerce and the functional form of the trade associations.

As against property, the trade unions (in Europe) attempt to organize the labor markets and the political markets by the collective power of organized labor, sometimes in one organization, sometimes in several. Consumers' and producers' cooperatives, however, affect only slightly the power of property in the commodity market.

Studies of these organizations and the devices by which their power is translated into political power are vital to the political scientist. Large numbers of individual studies of pressure groups exist, but a really sophisticated, comparative analysis is still lacking. The translation of these economic power positions differs from country to country and from historical situation to historical situation. The relative strength of the competing economic groups is far more important for the analysis of political power than the study of the political institutions proper. There are countries (like Germany and England) where the agents and managers of the economic organizations enter parliaments directly; there are others (like the United States) where the influence is more indirect. There are countries (like Germany and England) where trade unions are political as well as industrial bodies; there are others (like France and the United States in certain situations) where they apparently abstain from politics.

The devices and forms for the translation of economic power into political power thus vary considerably and yet patterns are discernible which ought to be more sharply defined on a comparative basis. A high degree of knowledge of problems of social stratification and economic organization is thus indispensable for the political scientist.

The Ascendance of Politics and of Bureaucracies

The classical relationship between economics and politics changes. It now appears as if political power has begun to emancipate itself from its economic roots and, indeed, tends to become a base for the acquisition of economic power.

In general, bureaucratization is believed to be the manifestation of that trend which culminates in doctrines of managerial rule: private and public managers eliminating property owners and parliaments. The trend toward bureaucratization has unquestionably two roots: the transformation of parliamentary democracy into mass democracy; and the transition of a predominantly competitive economy into a predominantly organized economy. While these trends are known and progress under our very eyes, they do not necessarily involve an assumption of political power by bureaucracies. The growth of the scope and number of bureaucratic structures may merely indicate that the social groups which rule now need more and more bureaucracies in order to cope with the exercise of political power. But the equation of a larger number of bureaucrats with increase of their power is due to the inability (or unwillingness) to distinguish sharply three different problems involved in what is called "bureaucratization"; namely, bureaucratic behavior, bureaucratic structure, and bureaucratic power.

Bureaucratic behavior (roughly equated here with routine performance as against initiative or creative performance) is, of course, spreading. No sphere of activity is exempted from it. Whether it is beneficial or not shall not be discussed here. We should merely remember the tremendous extent to which our comforts depend on routine performances. Moreover, it is untrue that the decisions of the bureaucrats (public or private) are exclusively routine decisions. Many, indeed, are creative ones, not derived from precedent or standing rules, but highly discretionary and thus essentially lawmaking in character. Finally, bureaucratic organization, that is, hierarchies where commands are channeled from above to below and responsibility goes from below to above, is not confined to public life. The facts are obvious.

Though the growth of bureaucratic behavior, with the increase in the number of bureaucratic structures, is a continuous process, it does not thereby follow that power (private or public) has shifted to the bureaucracies. No abstract answer can be given; only empirical investigations can reveal whether shifts in power have taken place. Such investigations are, unfortunately, rare.

The Soviet Union presents a clear-cut marginal case where political power not only has made itself supreme but has become the fount of whatever economic power positions exist. Nazi Germany, on the other hand, exhibited a transitional case. It is undisputed that the Nazi party rose to power with the financial and political assistance of German big-business leaders who doubtless hoped to use the party for the promotion of their own interests. But the party, once having achieved power, emancipated itself from business control, and its political power became autonomous. The party then went further and attempted to create economic power positions for itself. Clearly the new political power was seeking to give itself an economic power base. This, indeed, is the significance of the Goering combine, the expanding enterprises of the Labor Front and the S.S., and the acquisitions resulting from Aryanization and Germanization. The war, which made it inadvisable to carry out sweeping institutional changes, interrupted the process. But it is quite safe to assume that, had there been no war or had the Nazis been victorious, the Soviet pattern would have prevailed.

The reactions to the ascendant role of political power are, as a rule, hostile. Most notable is the attempt to ascribe this phenomenon to democracy. This is, of course, essentially correct. For, as we have indicated, the attitude of democracy toward political power is undoubtedly positive. Yet more is meant by that statement which by no means is a mere scientific one but has definite political undertones. It is implied that the growing political power will, by its inner dynamics, be abused and will ultimately lead to a totalitarian system. In this, modern criticism resumes the traditionalist critique not of political power but of democracy. Maistre and Bonald are resurrected. Proceeding from the shaky psychology of the essential evilness of man, they assert the inevitable transformation of democracy into mob rule, which, in conjunction with the modern trend of state interventionism, must culminate in totalitarianism. The remedy is some kind of aristocratic rule. A second reaction believes bureaucracy to be inimical to liberty and attempts to protect democracy by identifying it with individual liberty against the state.

Both reactions base themselves on what they call the tradition of Western civilization, the kernel of which is allegedly hostility to political power as expressed in constitutionalism. This is only a partial truth and, therefore, false. The tradition of Western civilization is more complex. . . . Certainly, one may say that Rousseauism is a more important element in the political tradition of democracy than the essentially self-contradictory and arbitrary doctrines of Locke and of the natural law. That political power (whether democratic, aristocratic, or monarchic) can be abused is beyond doubt; but it is doubtful that abuses can be effectively checked by constitutionalism. The problem of modern democracy is much less the fencing of political power than its rational utilization and provision for effective mass participation in its exercise.

IDENTIFICATION OF POLITICAL POWER

In the Soviet Union, there is little doubt where political power resides. In Nazi Germany, after June 1934, it was equally clear that the monopolistic party concentrated all political power. In a liberal democracy (and in constitutional systems generally) the identification of political power is extremely difficult. Our contention that political power has its roots in economic power can merely provide a frame within which the analyses have to be made; for we deliberately stated: "Social power . . . is derived from private property or is against it." Since the distribution of the "for" and "against" varies, the empirical sociological analyses of this interrelationship are the crucial concern of the political scientist.

Constitutional law helps but little. The form of government may or may not truly express the distribution of power. The doctrine of separate powers may or may not express the fact that social forces are as balanced as are the political institutions. As a rule, they are not. Constitutional law merely supplies the frame for the exercise of political power but does not indicate its holder or its functions. All traditional legal conceptions are negative ones. They limit activities but do not shape them. It is this very character of law which grants to the citizen a minimum of protection. This applies specifically to the conception of external sovereignty, a term which we have so far avoided. It does not indicate the owner of sovereign power nor the use to which this power may or can be put; it merely delimits the power of one territorial unit from any other. The conception of property is fashioned in exactly the same way. It does not reveal the object of property nor its social function; it merely protects man's control of an external piece of nature. Constitutional law, secondly, indicates the form in which political power may be legitimately exercised. While the significance of both aspects of constitutional law may not be underestimated, empirical sociological studies of the locus of political power are indispensable.

There are, however, situations which may reveal in a flash, so to speak, where political power resides. There are emergency situations such as stages of siege, martial law, and so on. It is for this reason that Carl Schmitt, the famous Nazi constitutional lawyer, stated in his pre-Nazi period: "Sovereign is he who decides the emergency situation." While not accepting the implications of Schmitt's doctrine of sovereignty, it is clear that the study of such emergency situations will yield valuable hints as to where political power actually resides in "normal" periods. Such a marginal situation existed in Nazi Germany on June 30, 1934. Up to that date, it could be very doubtful whether political power rested with the party alone, or with a combination of party, army, business, and so on. The liquidation of the Rohm group, of the generals, and of others made it, however, abundantly clear that the party had succeeded in monopolizing political power.

Such studies have been neglected. They are carried out mostly in terms of constitutional law, but rarely in political-sociological categories.

POLITICAL POWER AND FREEDOM

I stressed initially that political power is neither comparable to the concept of energy in physics nor the sole conception of political science. Yet the original formulation, power vs. idea, is too ideological. If history were a conflict between power groups and ideas, ideas would be invariably defeated. Politics is certainly the conflict between power groups, and the conflicts may be resolved by victory and defeat or by conciliation, that is, compromise. But one group may, in its struggle for power, represent more than a particular interest; it may indeed represent the idea of freedom, the idea crucial to political theory. If, for example, you analyze immigration legislation and come to the conclusion that business groups pressured for its liberalization in order to secure cheaper labor power, you have indeed done part of your tasks as political scientists, but only part of it. Of equal importance is the analysis of the role of immigration legislation in the historical development of the United States. The task of political theory is thus the determination of the degree to which a power group transcends its particular interest and advocates (in Hegelian terms) universal interests.

This determination is by no means easy. In fact, the distinction between ideology and truth becomes increasingly difficult. Some of the difficulty lies in the ideological character of politics in a democracy (discussed above), but, in the last resort, it results from the tremendous weight of power on what is called public opinion. Every political system impresses the mores of the ruling group upon the population. The greater the tensions, the more stringent the impositions become. The individual then resorts to many forms of dissimulation; and, in certain periods of history, it is the liar who becomes the hero. The lie (in its many forms) becomes the protection of the individual against a universalized system of propaganda. It is for this reason that I am skeptical of the value of the various highly developed techniques of measuring attitudes, particularly attitudes which may challenge the basic foundation of a contemporary society. George Orwell, in his otherwise brilliant performance, *1984,* overlooks the fact that compulsion operates wherever political power exists. . . .

chapter II

COMPARISON OF POLITICAL SYSTEMS

Basic concepts—like personality, elites, political culture, and power—are attempts to interpret a political system from a specific and significant point of view. But emphasis on one or another of the manifold characteristics of political behavior does not constitute a general theory—or a "model" of political behavior. In his *Study of Comparative Government* (1955), one of the editors of the present volume suggested four categories that could be useful for comparative study: the deliberative process and decision making; the power configuration—with particular reference to group conflict; the ideology—traditions, ideas, etc., about political authority; and the organization of political authority (that is, the structure of government). Professor Samuel H. Beer has proposed a somewhat similar scheme in his *Patterns of Government* (1958). A political system is characterized by a political culture—a "pattern" of ideas and traditions about the nature and purpose of authority; a "pattern" of power with primary emphasis on political power; an interest "configuration"—with groups being of major importance; and, finally, a "pattern" of policy—that is, the flow and character of decisions made by a political system. In the essay by five sociologists, reproduced below, a "system" is viewed as a pattern of interrelations in which functions and the structures through which they are performed are clearly distinguished.

The utility of beginning with any systematic theory is that it helps direct research along more significant lines and enables us to see interrelations more readily. Instead of putting together odd bits of research in the hope that they will somehow add up to a perspective view of politics, we begin with a comprehensive theory in terms of which the various aspects of the political process may then be investigated. Among the influential works pointing toward a systematic theory of politics are: Emile Durkheim, *The Social Division of Labor in Society* (1933); Max Weber, *A Theory of Social and Economic Organization* (1947); Talcott Parsons, *The Social System* (1951); and David Easton, *A Systems Analysis of Political Life* (1965).

In order to provide an empirical basis for comparison, a number of observers have collected and attempted to correlate information on social, economic, and cultural as well as political variables. See, for example, B. M. Russett, H. R. Alker, K. W. Deutsch, and H. Lasswell, *World Handbook of Political and Social Indicators* (1964), and A. Banks and R. Textor, *A Cross-Polity Survey* (1963). Recent works on problems of method in comparing political systems include: H. A. Scarrow, *Comparative Political Analysis* (1969); R. L. Merritt, *Systematic Approaches to Comparative Politics* (1969); H. Teune and A. Przeworski, *The Logic of Comparative Social Inquiry* (1970); and R. T. Holt and J. E. Turner, eds., *The Methodology of Comparative Research* (1970). The reader is also referred to the special issue of the journal, *Comparative Politics,* vol. 1, no. 1 (October 1968) on the comparative method.

5. The Functional Prerequisites of a Society*

D. F. ABERLE, A. K. COHEN, A. K. DAVIS, M. J. LEVY, JR., and F. X. SUTTON

A comparative social science requires a generalized system of concepts which will enable the scientific observer to compare and contrast large bodies of concretely different social phenomena in consistent terms. A promising step in furthering the development of systematic social analysis is a tentative formulation of the functional prerequisites of a society. Functional prerequisites refer broadly to the things that must get done in any society if it is to continue as a going concern, i.e., the generalized conditions necessary for the maintenance of the system concerned. The specific structural arrangements for meeting the functional prerequisites differ, of course, from one society to another and, in the course of time, change in any given society.[1]

*Reprinted from "The Functional Prerequisites of a Society," in *Ethics,* vol. LX, no. 2 (January 1950), pp. 100–111. By permission of the University of Chicago Press. Copyright 1950 by the University of Chicago Press.

[1] Thus all societies must allocate goods and services somehow. A particular society may change from one method, say business enterprise, to another, say a centrally planned economy, without the destruction of the society as a society but merely with a change in its concrete structures.

We seek to avoid the limitation inherent in defining the function of a social element solely in terms of its contributions to the survival or maintenance of the particular system of which it is a component. Structure analysis, which has recently undergone notable development, is prone to focus attention on static equilibriums. We consider *what* must be done in *any* society and hope our effort may be of use in considering the alterations that take place in *how* things are done in a society while that society persists.

This paper offers (1) a definition of a society on the most general level; (2) a statement of four generalized conditions, the complete realization of any one of which would terminate the existence of a society as defined; (3) a list of the functional prerequisites of a society. It seeks to justify the inclusion of each prerequisite by the demonstration that in its hypothetical absence the society could not survive, since at least one of the four conditions terminating a society would occur. There is no reason to believe that the list of functional prerequisites offered here is definitive. It is subject to revision with the growth of general theory and with experience in its application to concrete situations.

Any formulation of functional prerequisites depends for its categories on the theory of action employed. Our theory of action uses the concept of an actor whose orientation to his situation is threefold: cognitive, affective, and goal-directed. The actor is an abstraction from the total human being. Many of the qualities of the human being constitute part of the situation, the set of means and conditions, within which the actor operates.

Though the definition of the functional prerequisites of a society logically precedes the development of a scheme of structural prerequisites—which tell *how* the functional prerequisites may be met—in actuality the theoretic development of the two approaches is indivisible.

I. A DEFINITION OF A SOCIETY

The unit we have selected for analysis is a *society,* such as a nation, tribe, or band, and not any social system in general. The statement of the functional prerequisites of *any social system*—a monastery, a church, or a town, for example—would be on too general a level for the present discussion, though it may be an important task. Furthermore, once the functional prerequisites of a society are outlined, it becomes easier to state those of other types of social systems, often by dropping certain prerequisites from the list, since most of these other types of systems are parts of a society (or result from the interrelations of two or more societies) and depend for their perpetuation on the existence of a society.

A society is a group of human beings sharing a self-sufficient system of action which is capable of existing longer than the life-span of an individual, the group being recruited at least in part by the sexual reproduction of the members.

The identity and continuity of a society inhere in the persistence of the system of action in which the actors participate rather than in the particular set of actors themselves. There may be a complete turnover of individuals, but the society may survive. The individuals may survive, but the society may disintegrate. A system may persist in a situation while its component relationships change. Its persistence inheres in the fact that it maintains its separation from the situation, i.e., it inheres in the *integrity* of the organism, not in its fixity or unalterable character.

A system of action always exists in a situation. In the case of a society this situation includes the nonhuman environment and, in almost every case, it includes other societies. The viability of a social system and its recognition as a society within the terms of this definition depend upon the particular set of conditions in which it functions. Study of the system itself cannot alone determine whether the system meets the criteria of the definition. What is crucial is that a social system contain successful arrangements for meeting the chronic and recurrent features of its milieu.[2]

"Longer than the life-span of an individual" reminds us that a society must be able to replace its members with effectively socialized individuals from the maturing generation. The requirement of sexual reproduction excludes from consideration such groups (monasteries, cliques) as depend *solely* on types of recruitment other than sexual. But a society may be recruited in part by nonsexual means, e.g., by immigration and conquest.

The heart of the definition is "self-sufficient system of action."[3] Its full meaning will be developed in the exposition of the functional prerequisites and in the next paragraphs.

A number of questions are bound to arise in the reader's mind as to the application of the definition to particular social systems and as to the basis on which the decision is to be made as to whether such systems fall within the definition of a society. We emphasize that the definition is an ideal type. *A concrete aggregate is a society in so far as it approaches the generalized model.* The following examples, though not definitive, suggest the way in which the definition may be applied.

A society is not a culture. Culture is socially transmitted behavior conceived as an abstraction from concrete social groups. Two or more *societies* may have the same *culture* or similar cultures. Though the Greek city-states shared similar culture patterns, each possessed a self-sufficient structure of action and is hence to be considered a separate society. One society may be composed of groups with some marked differences in culture. The union of agricultural, industrial, and pastoral groups in a single structure of action is an example. We discuss below the limits as to the amount of diversity possible and the conditions under which such diversity may occur without the disintegration of the society.

To some degree two different societies may possess overlapping personnel and even structural elements without losing their identity as distinct societies. The fact that Englishmen live in the United States as diplomats and traders and function, in effect, as actors in both systems, does not destroy the identity or the self-sufficiency of the United States or of Great Britain as action-systems.

To be considered a society, a group need not be self-sufficient with respect to

---

[2] This point receives further treatment below. A social system need not be copper-plated to meet the definition of a society. Natural catastrophe may terminate a concrete society. Such an event does not represent a failure to meet the functional prerequisites but is rather to be considered the result of a change in the nonhuman environment beyond the limits assumed here as the setting of a society. Many concrete societies have been assimilated by the expansion of groups with which these societies had had little or no previous contact. This, too, represents an alteration in the situation of the society beyond the limits within which it had been meeting its functional prerequisites.

[3] "System" and "structure" will be used interchangeably throughout the remainder of this treatment.

resources. It is the structure of action that must be self-sufficient. Thus, the United States is a society. While imports and exports are necessary to its maintenance, arrangements for foreign trade are part of its self-sufficient structure of action. It is this, and not the group of individuals, that is self-sufficient. Hence Chinese-American trade does not make China and America parts of a larger society. Trade relationships are limited and relatively unstable. Their existence does not involve the two aggregates in the same self-sufficient structure of action. For parallel reasons the British Empire and the United Nations are not societies but associations.

A series of difficult decisions about the relationships of various social systems can be resolved by the introduction of a point of crucial differentiation. When a social aggregate is not capable of providing a structure, structures, or parts of structures which can meet the functional prerequisites in question, it is not to be considered a society. Thus, occupied Japan does not constitute part of American society, since in the absence of American forces Japan would seem to be able to continue control and the legitimized use of force. A group of American Indians governed by the United States for a sufficient length of time may lack the crucial structures necessary for continued existence as an independent entity and therefore be considered part of American society, in spite of an important cultural variation. An American town does not constitute a society because of its thorough participation in American political, economic, value, and other structures. The early Mormon settlement in Utah, however, did constitute a society. . . .

We assume that social change characterizes all societies. Change may be gradual and peaceful or characterized by severe conflicts. In either case there may be profound structural changes. Societies may split or merge peacefully or violently. In all these instances a society of some sort exists. Whether it is considered the same society or a new one depends on the relation between the level of the structural change and the level of analysis. The changes in question may be analyzed in terms of this frame of reference. We may examine the way in which a society meets its functional prerequisites, the points of tension (those functional prerequisites least effectively met), and the responses to those strains. We do not assume the perfect integration of any society.

We have omitted from our definition any statements regarding territoriality. Action, it has been pointed out, always takes place in a situation, one feature of which is a spatial dimension. The existence of two societies intermingled during a civil war, or any such example, does not negate considerations of spatiality, which are always an essential background feature of any society.

II. FOUR CONDITIONS TERMINATING THE EXISTENCE OF A SOCIETY

The realization of any of the following conditions terminates the existence of a society—the existence of the structure of action, though not necessarily of the members.

A. *The biological extinction or dispersion of the members.*—To arrive at this condition, a society need not lose all its members but need only suffer such losses as to make inoperative its structure of action. Analyses of such conditions may be made at this level in terms of fertility, morbidity, and migration rates, without reference to the highly complex factors underlying them.

B. *Apathy of the members.*—Apathy means the cessation of individual motivation. This condition affects some individuals to some extent in all societies and large numbers in a few societies. That migrant Polynesian laborers have died of nostalgia is well known. It is claimed that whole societies in Melanesia have withered away from ennui. In these cases, physical extinction is merely an extreme consequence of the cessation of motivation.

C. *The war of all against all.*—This condition appears if the members of an aggregate pursue their ends by means selected only on the basis of instrumental efficiency. Though the choice of means on this basis may result at times in cooperative combinations, these combinations are by definition subject to immediate dissolution if, for example, exploitation or annihilation becomes more advantageous for any one member. Hence a state of indeterminate flux, rather than a system of action, exists. The use of force is efficient only for limited purposes. Force is a sanction, but never the essence, of a society. A society based solely on force is a contradiction in terms that raises the classical question, *Quis custodiet ipsos custodes?*

D. *The absorption of the society into another society.*—This entails the partial loss of identity and self-sufficiency of the total action-system but not necessarily the extinction of the members.

The more fully these four conditions are realized, the more indeterminate is the structure of action, a condition also induced when the rate of social change is very rapid. Hence we may hypothesize that fluctuations in the vital indices, in apathy, and in coercion are to some extent functions of the rate of social change. In fact, revolutions (extreme social change) are characterized by increases in mortality, morbidity, apathy, force, and fraud. The faster the change, the greater the stress, two manifestations of which are force and/or apathy. Viewing coercion as a response to stress should help us to put the discussion of the role of force in social systems on a nonideological basis.

III. THE FUNCTIONAL PREREQUISITES OF A SOCIETY

The performance of a given function is prerequisite to a society if in its absence one or more of the four conditions dissolving a society results. This can be demonstrated clearly in some cases. Less clearly, but still convincingly, the nonfulfillment of certain other functions can be shown at least to foster one or more of the conditions negating a society. No specific action-pattern is prerequisite to the existence of our ideal-typical society. We are concerned with *what* must get done in a society, not with *how* it is done.

A. *Provision for adequate relationship to the environment and for sexual recruitment.*—This includes modes of adapting to, manipulating, and altering the environment in such a way as (*a*) to maintain a sufficient number and kind of members of the society at an adequate level of functioning; (b) to deal with the existence of other societies in a manner which permits the persistence of the system of action; and (c) to pattern heterosexual relationships to insure opportunities and motivation for a sufficient rate of reproduction. In the absence of these provisions, the group will suffer biological extinction through the death of the members or failure to reproduce or it will suffer absorption into another social system. . . .

A society must adapt to, manipulate, and alter its situation. Among the features thus dealt with may be chronically threatening aspects of the situation. In a dry region a society may employ techniques of food storage, irrigation, or nomadic migration. If neighboring societies are hostile, an army may be essential and the society thus dependent on the deliberate hazarding of some of its members' lives. The existence of Murngin society depends partly on the destruction of a portion of its adult males by chronic warfare. Resistance is only one possible response to hostile neighbors. Certain "men-o-bush" tribes of New Guinea make but little resistance to raids. These raids, however, do not threaten to extinguish the society. Only if they do can such a passive adaptation be said to be inadequate to meet the functional prerequisite.

The inclusion of such apparently disparate features as maintenance of the organism, defense, and provision for sexual reproduction under one heading is by no means arbitrary. From the point of view of a social system, the nonhuman environment, the biological nature of man, and the existence of other societies are all part of the situation of action. To none of these aspects of the situation is passive adaptation the only mode of adequate relationship. Thus the biological basis of society itself is molded. Individuals have constitutional differences, but the latter are variously evaluated and dealt with by societies. The biological birth-growth-death cycle is a dynamic process in its own right, yet societies both adapt to it and modify it in a number of ways. In noting the necessity for a society to meet certain biological prerequisites, we remark also upon the great plasticity of individuals. It is scarcely necessary to remark that, concretely, societies alter their modes of relationship to their situations; that technological changes occur, sometimes through loss, more often by invention and diffusion.

B. *Role differentiation and role assignment.*—This signifies the systematic and stable division of activities. We will treat under other headings role-learning and the sanctions perpetuating the role structure.

In any society there are activities which must be regularly performed if the society is to persist. If they are to be done dependably, these extensive and varied activities must be broken down and assigned to capable individuals trained and motivated to carry them out. Otherwise everyone would be doing everything or nothing—a state of indeterminacy which is the antithesis of a society and which precludes getting essential activities carried out. The universal problems of scarcity and order are insoluble without legitimized allocation of property rights and authority, and these, in turn, are unattainable without reasonably integrated role-differentiation. While a given individual is often the locus of several roles, he can never combine all the roles of his society in himself. Age and sex differences impose a degree of role-differentiation everywhere; in some societies class and occupation are additional bases of differentiation. Arguments for specialization based on differential ability, while of great force in complex societies, have no clear bearing on societies so simple that any technique can be learned by any individual who is not feeble-minded. Whatever the society, activities necessary to its survival must be worked out in predictable, determinate ways, or else apathy or the war of each against all must prevail. Without reliable provision for child-rearing activities and without their assignment to specific persons or groups, the society invites extinction, since children at birth are helpless. The absence of role-differentiation and of role-assignment thus makes for three of the conditions negating a society. A system of role-differentiation alone is useless without a system of selection for assigning individuals to those roles.

Mention should be made of one particular type of role-differentiation that is a requirement for any society, namely, stratification. Stratification is that particular type of role-differentiation which discriminates between higher and lower standings in terms of one or more criteria. Given the universality of scarcity, some system of differential allocation of the scarce values of a society is essential. These values may consist of such desiderata as wealth, power, magic, women and ceremonial precedence. That conflict over scarce values may destroy a society will be shown in another connection below. Our present point is that the rank order must be legitimized and accepted by most of the members—at least by the important ones—of a society if stability is to be attained. Allocation of ranks may be on the basis of ascribed or achieved qualities or both.

Role-differentiation implies organization. Precedence in specialized activities must be correlated to some extent with rank order. Coercive sanctions and initiative must be vested in specified status-positions. Some individuals will thus receive more than others. These privileges are usually made acceptable to the rank and file by joining to the greater rights of the elite a larger share of responsibilities. The Brahmins stand closer to other-worldly nonexistence than do the members of any other Hindu caste, but they also have to observe the most elaborate ritual obligations. The Trobriand chief enjoys a multiple share of wealth and wives; he must also finance community enterprises and exhibit at all times more generosity than anyone else. . . .

C. *Communication.*—Evidence from deaf-mutes, "wolf children," and bilinguals shows that speech, the basic form of communication, is learned and that only rudimentary communication is possible in the absence of shared, learned linguistic symbols. Without learned symbolic communication only a few highly general emotional states—e.g., anger, sexual passion—in one individual can evoke an appropriate response in another; only a few skills may be conveyed by imitation.

No society, however simple, can exist without shared, learned symbolic modes of communication, because without them it cannot maintain the common-value structure or the protective sanctions which hold back the war of each against all. Communication is indispensable if socialization and role-differentiation are to function effectively. That each functional prerequisite thus depends in part on other functional prerequisites does not vitiate our argument so long as the functional prerequisites are logically separable. But they need not be empirically distinct activities, since any action-system may contribute to several functional prerequisites.

In a simple society, where relationships are exclusively face-to-face, shared speech forms suffice. In complex societies, other than oral communication is necessary for the system as a whole, though not for subsystems. Thus, in China, writing facilitates the survival of the society despite local dialect differences too great to permit oral communication without bilingual intermediaries. Clearly, no modern society could survive without writing. Thus, communication requires language, a medium of communication, and channels.

D. *Shared cognitive orientations.*—In any society the members must share a body of cognitive orientations which (*a*) make possible adaptation to and manipulation of the situation; (*b*) make stable, meaningful, and predictable the social situations in which they are engaged; and (*c*) account for those significant aspects of the situation over which they do not have adequate prediction and control in such a way as to sustain and not to destroy motivation.

If the first criterion were not met, biological existence would be impossible. If the second were not, interpersonal and intergroup relations could not exist. Private definitions of social situations or the absence of such definitions could lead only to mutually incompatible actions and the war of each against all. In no society are all conditions predictable and controllable; so the frustration of expectations is a chronic feature of social life. Without a reasonably determinate explanation of such areas of existence, the individual would exist in an unstructured world and could not avoid psychological disorganization. In the absence of shared orientations, serious clashes would ensue.

Cognitive orientations must be shared, but only in so far as the actors are involved in the same situation of action. A housewife may not distinguish a colonel from a corporal; a soldier may not appreciate that he is using his hostess' "wedding silver." They must agree, however, that a foot is "so long" and that that gentleman is a "policeman." But though a farmer may pray for rain and an aviator rub a rabbit's foot for good weather with no resultant difficulties between them, both must define the American political system in a roughly similar fashion if they are to vote.

E. *A shared, articulated set of goals.*—To phrase this prerequisite in terms of action produces a vague and not very useful formulation. . . . It is equally difficult to operate in terms of motivations, since these are exceedingly diverse and are intricately articulated with the social structure. Our statement in terms of goals seeks a middle ground and is couched in the terms most suitable for considering a system of action.

Because there is role-differentiation in every society, we must consider a set of goals rather than a common goal. The facts of scarcity and of differential individual endowment, features of all societies, also make it necessary to speak of a set of goals. It is the range of goals, however narrow, that provides alternatives for individuals and thus reduces one serious source of conflict in societies. (The possibility of universally sought goals in a society is not ruled out.)

The goals must be sufficiently articulated to insure the performance of socially necessary activities. They must not include too much action which threatens the existence of a society. A cult of sexual abstinence, if universalized, would terminate the society. The goals must be shared to some degree, though this will vary with the differentiation of the society. Finally, the goals of one individual must be meaningful to another in so far as they share a common structure of action.

There will be both empirical and nonempirical goals. Some goals may be mutually incompatible without being destructive to the society. Without an articulated set of goals the society would invite extinction, apathy, or the war of all against all.

F. *The normative regulation of means.*—This functional prerequisite is the prescription of means for attaining the socially formulated goals of a society and its subsystems. It complements but does not overlap the functional prerequisite of "effective control of disruptive behavior." The "normative regulation of means" defines positively the means (mostly noncoercive) to the society's goals.

That these means must be stated clearly for the sake of order and the effective functioning of the society follows from (*a*) the nature of other functional prerequisites and (*b*) the *anomie* that must result from the lack of recognized legitimized means. First, role-differentiation specifies *who* is to act, while the common articulated set of goals defines *what* is to be done. The normative regulation of means tells *how* these goals may be won. Second, the absence of normative regulation of means invites apathy or the war of each against all. Without socially prescribed means, a goal must be either devalued or forcibly seized. As the loss of a bolt may cause a great machine to beat itself to pieces, so the absence of normatively regulated means operates cumulatively to destroy the social structure.

Especially in ritual and initiatory activities must procedures be normatively specified. The content of prescriptions may vary greatly among societies; what is indispensable is simply that socially accepted directives for ceremonial and symbolic action exist. This point emphasizes the necessity for the category of normative regulation of means, in addition to the effective control of disruptive behavior. Moreover, there are often alternative, noncoercive ways of realizing goals, and they must be differentially evaluated for the sake of order, or else some must be ruled out.

G. *The regulation of affective expression.*—In any society the affective states of the members must be mutually communicable and comprehensible. Furthermore, not every affect can be expressed in every situation. Some must be suppressed or repressed. Lastly, there are affects which must be produced in the members if the social structure is to survive. All these aspects are included in the regulation of affective expression.

In the absence of the first of these conditions, stability of expectations between individuals is destroyed, and apathetic or destructive reactions will occur. This is true alike of states of anger and of affection, of love, lust and the like. Without comprehensibility and communicability, mutually inappropriate responses in affectively charged situations can only result in the destruction of the relationship. In a love affair, if one member's expression of affection has the intended meaning of a flirtation, while to the other it signifies willingness to consummate the affair, the relationship is headed for a crisis. The same state of affairs with respect to the expression of affect in an entire society is clearly incompatible with the continuation of that society. This is not a matter of a lack of a shared cognitive frame of reference; rather, the conflicts are potentially explosive because of the emotional involvement. The cues that make affective expression comprehensible range from obvious and subtle linguistic behavior to posture, facial expression, gesture, and tone of voice. Many of these cues are not consciously recognized by the actors themselves.

In the face of regulated competitive, cooperative, and authority relationships, some of which are entailed in any conceivable system of role-allocation, taken together with disturbances of expectation and scarcity situations, no society can survive if it permits complete latitude of affective expression in all situations. The ungoverned expression of lust and rage leads to the disruption of relationships and ultimately to the war of all against all.

Finally, a society must not only structure the way in which affects are expressed and restrict certain forms of emotional expression; it must actively foster some affects. Unless we adopt the view that all relationships in all societies can be rational and contractual in character, we must take the position that some relationships depend on regulated affects for their perpetuation. In the absence of the production of appropriate affects, the family, for example, would not survive. The question of what affects must regularly be produced in any society is closely related to the way other functional prerequisites are fulfilled. In American society the urban middle-class conjugal family depends heavily on the establishment of strong affective ties between spouses. The American family system in meeting the demands of a highly mobile society is deprived of certain bases of stability which other family systems possess, and the mutual affection of spouses becomes of correspondingly greater importance.

H. *Socialization.*—A problem is posed for any society by the fact that its structure of action must be learned by new members. To each individual must be transmitted so much of the modes of dealing with the total situation—the modes of communication, the shared cognitive frame of reference, goal-system, attitudes involved in the regulation of means, modes of expression, and the like—as will render him capable of adequate performance in his several roles throughout life, both as respects skills and as respects attitudes. Socialization thus is a different concept from the maintenance of the child in a state of biological well-being.

Furthermore, socialization includes both the development of new adult members from infants and the induction of an individual of any age into any role of the society or its subsystems where new learning is required.

A society cannot persist unless it perpetuates a self-sufficient system of action—whether in changed or traditional form—through the socialization of new members, drawn, in part, from the maturing generation. Whatever the defects of any particular mode of socialization, a universal failure of socialization means the extinction of the society, through a combination of all four of the terminating conditions mentioned previously.

One individual cannot become equally familiar with all aspects of his society; indeed, he may remain completely ignorant of some. But he must acquire a working knowledge of the behavior and attitudes relevant to his various roles and identify to some degree with such values as are shared by the whole society or segments thereof wherever his behavior articulates with that of other members of the society. A Brahmin and an Untouchable learn some skills and attitudes unknown to each other. Both, however, must learn that the Hindu world is made up of castes and that this is the way things should be.

I. *The effective control of disruptive forms of behavior.*—Prominent among disruptive modes of behavior are force and fraud. The extent to which such behavior will occur is dependent on the way that various other functional prerequisites are met: role-allocation, goal-system, regulation of means and of expression, and socialization being the more obvious cases in point. All these functional prerequisites, it is clear from the preceding argument, tend to prevent the occurrence of disruptive behavior. In addition to, and separate from, these is the effective control of such behavior when it occurs. To understand why this functional prerequisite is necessary, we must ask: Why would not a perfectly integrated society exist in its absence?

The answer lies in three conditions inherent in any society: scarcity of means, frustrations of expectations, and imperfections of socialization. That many of the desiderata of life are ultimately scarce needs no emphasis. Since sexual objects are differentially evaluated by a society, those few at the top of the scale tend to be sought by a large number of the opposite sex. Wealth, however defined, is basically scarce for the mass of individuals everywhere. Force and fraud are often the most efficient methods of acquiring scarce values. Indeed, only scarce values can be objects of rationally directed coercive effort. To argue that society without coercion and deceit can exist, one must first demonstrate the absence of scarcity. Frustration of expectations is inevitable for many individuals in any society so long as there are such universal realities as unexpected consequences of purposive behavior, scarcity, and uncertainty.

Imperfect socialization results, among other things, in evasions of the normatively prescribed paths of action. Together with frustrations of expectations, it results in explosive outbursts of anger and violence. Thus, both rationally directed exercise of force and fraud and less rational outbursts of emotion continually press to disrupt stable social relationships. If resort to these disruptive behaviors is restricted only by opportunity, the war of all against all will ultimately result. (Some disruptive action may also tend in the direction of an apathetic breakdown. This does not alter the nature of the argument.)

The system of goals tells *what* must be done; the normative regulation of means prescribes *how*. It also includes pre- and proscriptions regarding the use of force and fraud. In addition, however, the society must have techniques for handling those who, for reasons outlined, use these disruptive means or are subject to these outbreaks. The form of control and the degree of efficiency may vary greatly. What type of action is directly destructive of a society depends on the nature of the society: patricide in a society founded on patriarchal clans, violation of property rights in a property-emphasizing society, and so on.

Conversely, some societies can tolerate forms of these behaviors that others cannot. Chuckchee social structure, for example, withstands a high homicide rate.

IV. CONCLUSION

This treatment makes no claim to be final. Our list of functional prerequisites can be elaborated and altered by the reader by making explicit the elements we have left implicit. At present, a statement of the functional prerequisites of a society is primarily useful as a contribution to general social theory rather than as a tool for analyzing individual societies. It should be especially useful for constructing a general system of structural prerequisites that will tell us how the functional prerequisites may be met, and this in turn may lead to a more comprehensive and precise comparative sociology.

Even at the present stage, however, the authors have found this approach useful as a point of reference for analyses of societies and their subsystems, and for suggesting inadequacies in the analysis of given societies and in the empirical data available. It directs attention to features of social systems, relationships among institutional structures, and implications for social change which might otherwise be overlooked.

6. The Analysis of Political Systems*

DAVID EASTON

I. SOME ATTRIBUTES OF POLITICAL SYSTEMS

In an earlier work I have argued for the need to develop general, empirically oriented theory as the most economical way in the long run to understand political life. Here I propose to indicate a point of view that, at the least, might serve as a springboard for discussion of alternative approaches and, at most, as a small step in the direction of a general political theory. I wish to stress that what I have to say is a mere orientation to the problem of theory; outside of economics and perhaps psychology, it would be presumptuous to call very much in social science "theory," in the strict sense of the term.

Furthermore, I shall offer only a Gestalt of my point of view, so that it will

*From "An Approach to the Analysis of Political Systems," *World Politics*, vol. IX, no. 3 (April 1957), pp. 383–400. By permission.

be possible to evaluate, in the light of the whole, those parts that I do stress. In doing this, I know I can run the definite risk that the meaning and implications of this point of view may be only superficially communicated; but it is a risk I shall have to undertake since I do not know how to avoid it sensibly.

The study of politics is concerned with understanding how authoritative decisions are made and executed for a society. We can try to understand political life by viewing each of its aspects piecemeal. We can examine the operation of such institutions as political parties, interest groups, government, and voting; we can study the nature and consequences of such political practices as manipulation, propaganda, and violence; we can seek to reveal the structure within which these practices occur. By combining the results we can obtain a rough picture of what happens in any self-contained political unit.

In combining these results, however, there is already implicit the notion that each part of the larger political canvas does not stand alone but is related to each other part; or, to put it positively, that the operation of no one part can be fully understood without reference to the way in which the whole itself operates. I have suggested in my book, *The Political System,*[1] that it is valuable to adopt this implicit assumption as an articulate premise for research and to view political life as a system of interrelated activities. These activities derive their relatedness or systemic ties from the fact that they all more or less influence the way in which authoritative decisions are formulated and executed for a society.

Once we begin to speak of political life as a system of activity, certain consequences follow for the way in which we can undertake to analyze the working of a system. The very idea of a system suggests that we can separate political life from the rest of social activity, at least for analytical purposes, and examine it as though for the moment it were a self-contained entity surrounded by, but clearly distinguishable from, the environment or setting in which it operates. In much the same way, astronomers consider the solar system a complex of events isolated for certain purposes from the rest of the universe.

Furthermore, if we hold the system of political actions as a unit before our mind's eye, as it were, we can see that what keeps the system going are inputs of various kinds. These inputs are converted by the processes of the system into outputs and these, in turn, have consequences both for the system and for the environment in which the system exists. The formula here is very simple but, as I hope to show, also very illuminating: inputs—political system or processes—outputs. These relationships are shown diagrammatically in Figure 1. This diagram represents a very primitive "model"—to dignify it with a fashionable name—for approaching the study of political life.

Political systems have certain properties because they are systems. To present an over-all view of the whole approach, let me identify the major attributes, say a little about each, and then treat one of these properties at somewhat greater length, even though still inadequately.

(1) Properties of identification. To distinguish a political system from other

[1] New York, 1953.

social systems, we must be able to identify it by describing its fundamental units and establishing the boundaries that demarcate it from units outside the system.

(a) Units of a political system. The units are the elements of which we say a system is composed. In the case of a political system, they are political actions. Normally it is useful to look at these as they structure themselves in political roles and political groups.

(b) Boundaries. Some of the most significant questions with regard to the operation of political systems can be answered only if we bear in mind the obvious fact that a system does not exist in a vacuum. It is always immersed in a specific setting or environment. The way in which a system works will be in part a function of its response to the total social, biological, and physical environment.

The special problem with which we are confronted is how to distinguish systematically between a political system and its setting. Does it even make sense to say that a political system has a boundary dividing it from its setting? If so, how are we to identify the line of demarcation?

Without pausing to argue the matter, I would suggest that it is useful to conceive of a political system as having a boundary in the same sense as a physical system. The boundary of a political system is defined by all those actions more or less directly related to the making of binding decisions for a society; every social action that does not partake of this characteristic will be excluded from the system and thereby will automatically be viewed as an external variable in the environment.

FIGURE 1

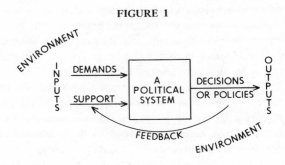

(2) Inputs and outputs. Presumably, if we select political systems for special study, we do so because we believe that they have characteristically important consequences for society, namely, authoritative decisions. These consequences I shall call the outputs. If we judged that political systems did not have important outputs for society, we would probably not be interested in them.

Unless a system is approaching a state of entropy—and we can assume that this is not true of most political systems—it must have continuing inputs to keep it going. Without inputs the system can do no work; without outputs we cannot

identify the work done by the system. The specific research tasks in this connection would be to identify the inputs and the forces that shape and change them,
to trace the processes through which they are transformed into outputs, to
describe the general conditions under which such processes can be maintained,
and to establish the relationship between outputs and succeeding inputs of the
system.

From this point of view, much light can be shed on the working of a political
system if we take into account the fact that much of what happens within a
system has its birth in the efforts of the members of the system to cope with the
changing environment. We can appreciate this point if we consider a familiar
biological system such as the human organism. It is subject to constant stress
from its surroundings to which it must adapt in one way or another if it is not
to be completely destroyed. In part, of course, the way in which the body works
represents responses to needs that are generated by the very organization of its
anatomy and functions; but in large part, in order to understand both the
structure and the working of the body, we must also be very sensitive to the
inputs from the environment.

In the same way, the behavior of every political system is to some degree
imposed upon it by the kind of system it is, that is, by its own structure and
internal needs. But its behavior also reflects the strains occasioned by the
specific setting within which the system operates. It may be argued that most of
the significant changes within a political system have their origin in shifts among
the external variables. Since I shall be devoting the bulk of this article to
examining some of the problems related to the exchange between political
systems and their environments, I shall move on to a rapid description of other
properties of political systems.

(3) Differentiation within a system. As we shall see in a moment, from the
environment come both energy to activate a system and information with regard
to which the system uses this energy. In this way a system is able to do work. It
has some sort of output that is different from the input that enters from the
environment. We can take it as a useful hypothesis that if a political system is to
perform some work for anything but a limited interval of time, a minimal
amount of differentiation in its structure must occur. In fact, empirically it is
impossible to find a significant political system in which the same units all perform the same activities at the same time. The members of a system engage in at
least some minimal division of labor that provides a structure within which
action takes place.

(4) Integration of a system. This fact of differentiation opens up a major
area of inquiry with regard to political systems. Structural differentiation sets in
motion forces that are potentially disintegrative in their results for the system.
If two or more units are performing different kinds of activity at the same time,
how are these activities to be brought into the minimal degree of articulation
necessary if the members of the system are not to end up in utter disorganization
with regard to the production of the outputs of interest to us? We can hypothesize that if a structured system is to maintain itself, it must provide mechanisms

whereby its members are integrated or induced to cooperate in some minimal degree so that they make authoritative decisions.

II. INPUTS: DEMANDS

Now that I have mentioned some major attributes of political systems that I suggest require special attention if we are to develop a generalized approach, I want to consider in greater detail the way in which an examination of inputs and outputs will shed some light on the working of these systems.

Among inputs of a political system there are two basic kinds: demands and support. These inputs give a political system its dynamic character. They furnish it both with the raw material or information that the system is called upon to process and with the energy to keep it going.

The reason why a political system emerges in a society at all—that is, why men engage in political activity—is that demands are being made by persons or groups in the society that cannot all be fully satisfied. In all societies one fact dominates political life: scarcity prevails with regard to most of the valued things. Some of the claims for these relatively scarce things never find their way into the political system but are satisfied through the private negotiations of or settlements by the persons involved. Demands for prestige may find satisfaction through the status relations of society; claims for wealth are met in part through the economic system; aspirations for power find expression in educational, fraternal, labor, and similar private organizations. Only where wants require some special organized effort on the part of society to settle them authoritatively may we say that they have become inputs of the political system.

Systematic research would require us to address ourselves to several key questions with regard to these demands.

(1) How do demands arise and assume their particular character in a society? In answer to this question, we can point out that demands have their birth in two sectors of experience: either in the environment of a system or within the system itself. We shall call these the external and internal demands, respectively.

Let us look at the external demands first. I find it useful to see the environment not as an undifferentiated mass of events but rather as systems clearly distinguishable from one another and from the political system. In the environment we have such systems as the ecology, economy, culture, personality, social structure, and demography. Each of these constitutes a major set of variables in the setting that helps to shape the kind of demands entering a political system. For purposes of illustrating what I mean, I shall say a few words about culture.

The members of every society act within the framework of an ongoing culture that shapes their general goals, specific objectives, and the procedures that the members feel ought to be used. Every culture derives part of its unique quality from the fact that it emphasizes one or more special aspects of behavior and this strategic emphasis serves to differentiate it from other cultures with respect to the demands that it generates. As far as the mass of the people is concerned, some cultures, such as our own, are weighted heavily on the side of economic wants, success, privacy, leisure activity, and rational efficiency. Others, such as that of the Fox Indians, strive toward the maintenance of harmony, even if in the process the goals of efficiency and rationality may be sacrificed. Still others, such as the Kachins of highland Burma, stress the pursuit of power and prestige. The culture embodies the standards of value in a society and thereby marks out areas of potential conflict, if the valued things are in short supply relative to demand. The typical demands that will find their way into the political process will concern the matters in conflict that are labeled important by the culture. For this reason we cannot hope to understand the nature of the demands presenting themselves for political settlement unless we are ready to explore systematically and intensively their connection with the culture. And what I have said about culture applies, with suitable modifications, to other parts of the setting of a political system.

But not all demands originate or have their major locus in the environment. Important types stem from situations occurring within a political system itself. Typically, in every ongoing system, demands may emerge for alterations in the political relationships of the members themselves, as the result of dissatisfaction stemming from these relationships. For example, in a political system based upon representation, in which equal representation is an important political norm, demands may arise for equalizing representation between urban and rural voting districts. Similarly, demands for changes in the process of recruitment of formal political leaders, for modifications of the way in which constitutions are amended, and the like may all be internally inspired demands.

I find it useful and necessary to distinguish these from external demands because they are, strictly speaking, not inputs of the system but something that we can call "withinputs," if we can tolerate a cumbersome neologism, and because their consequences for the character of a political system are more direct than in the case of external demands. Furthermore, if we were not aware of this difference in classes of demands, we might search in vain for an explanation of the emergence of a given set of internal demands if we turned only to the environment.

(2) How are demands transformed into issues? What determines whether a demand becomes a matter for serious political discussion or remains something to be resolved privately among the members of society? The occurence of a demand, whether internal or external, does not thereby automatically convert it into a political *issue*. Many demands die at birth or linger on with the support of an insignificant fraction of the society and are never raised to the level of possible political decision. Others become issues, an issue being a demand that the members of a political system are prepared to deal with as a significant item for discussion through the recognized channels in the system.

The distinction between demands and issues raises a number of questions about which we need data if we are to understand the processes through which claims typically become transformed into issues. For example, we would need to know something about the relationship between a demand and the location of its initiators or supporters in the power structures of the society, the importance of secrecy as compared with publicity in presenting demands, the matter of timing of demands, the possession of political skills or know-how, access to channels of communication, the attitudes and states of mind of possible publics, and the images held by the initiators of demands with regard to the way in which things get done in the particular political system. Answers to matters such as these would possibly yield a conversion index reflecting the probability of a set of demands being converted into live political issues.

If we assume that political science is primarily concerned with the way in which authoritative decisions are made for a society, demands require special attention as a major type of input of political systems. I have suggested that demands influence the behavior of a system in a number of ways. They constitute a significant part of the material upon which the system operates. They are also one of the sources of change in political systems, since as the environment fluctuates it generates new types of demand-inputs for the system. Accordingly, without this attention to the origin and determinants of demands we would be at a loss to be able to treat rigorously not only the operation of a system at a moment of time but also its change over a specified interval. Both the statics and historical dynamics of a political system depend upon a detailed understanding of demands, particularly of the impact of the setting on them.

III. INPUTS: SUPPORT

Inputs of demands alone are not enough to keep a political system operating. They are only the raw material out of which finished products called decisions are manufactured. Energy in the form of actions or orientations promoting and resisting a political system, the demands arising in it, and the decisions issuing from it must also be put into the system to keep it running. This input I shall call support. Without support, demands could not be satisfied or conflicts in goals composed. If demands are to be acted upon, the members of a system undertaking to pilot the demands through to their transformation into binding decisions and those who seek to influence the relevant processes in any way must be able to count on support from others in the system. Just how much support, from how many and which members of a political system, are separate and important questions that I shall touch on shortly.

What do we mean by support? We can say that A supports B either when A acts on behalf of or when he orients himself favorably toward B's goals, interests, and actions. Supportive behavior may thus be of two kinds. It may consist of actions promoting the goals, interests, and actions of another person. We may vote for a political candidate, or defend a decision by the highest court of the land. In these cases, support manifests itself through overt action.

On the other hand, supportive behavior may involve not external observable acts, but those internal forms of behavior we call orientations or states of mind. As I use the phrase, a supportive state of mind is a deep-seated set of attitudes or predispositions, or a readiness to act on behalf of some other person. It exists when we say that a man is loyal to his party, attached to democracy, or infused with patriotism. What such phrases as these have in common is the fact that they refer to a state of feelings on the part of a person. No overt action is involved at this level of description, although the implication is that the individual will pursue a course of action consistent with his attitudes. Where the anticipated action does not flow from our perception of the state of mind, we assume that we have not penetrated deeply enough into the true feelings of the person but have merely skimmed off his surface attitudes.

Supportive states of mind are vital inputs for the operation and maintenance of a political system. For example, it is often said that the struggle in the international sphere concerns mastery over men's minds. To a certain extent this is true. If the members of a political system are deeply attached to a system or its ideals, the likelihood of their participating in either domestic or foreign politics in such a way as to undermine the system is reduced by a large factor. Presumably, even in the face of considerable provocation, ingrained supportive feelings of loyalty may be expected to prevail.

We shall need to identify the typical mechanisms through which supportive attitudes are inculcated and continuously reinforced within a political system. But our prior task is to specify and examine the political objects in relation to which support is extended.

(1) The Domain of Support

Support is fed into the political system in relation to three objects: the community, the regime, and the government. There must be convergence of attitude and opinion as well as some willingness to act with regard to each of these objects. Let us examine each in turn.

(a) The political community. No political system can continue to operate unless its members are willing to support the existence of a group that seeks to settle differences or promote decisions through peaceful action in common. The point is so obvious—being dealt with usually under the heading of the growth of national unity—that it may well be overlooked; and yet it is a premise upon which the continuation of any political system depends. To refer to this phenomenon we can speak of the political community. At this level of support we are not concerned with whether a government exists or whether there is loyalty to a constitutional order. For the moment we only ask whether the members of the group that we are examining are sufficiently oriented toward each other to want to contribute their collective energies toward pacific settlement of their varying demands. . . .

(b) The regime. Support for a second major part of a political system helps to supply the energy to keep the system running. This aspect of the system I shall call the regime. It consists of all those arrangements that regulate the way in which the demands put into the system are settled and the way in which decisions are put into effect. They are the so-called rules of the game, in the light of which actions by members of the system are legitimated and accepted by the bulk of the members as authoritative. Unless there is a minimum convergence of attitudes in support of these fundamental rules—the constitutional principles, as we call them in Western society—there would be insufficient harmony in the actions of the members of a system to meet the problems generated by their support of a political community. The fact of trying to settle demands in common means that there must be known principles governing the way in which resolutions of differences of claims are to take place.

(c) The government. If a political system is going to be able to handle the conflicting demands put into it, not only must the members of the system be prepared to support the settlement of these conflicts in common and possess some consensus with regard to the rules governing the mode of settlement; they must also be ready to support a government as it undertakes the concrete tasks involved in negotiating such settlements. When we come to the outputs of a system, we shall see the rewards that are available to a government for mobilizing support. At this point, I just wish to draw attention to this need on the part of a government for support if it is going to be able to make decisions with regard to demands. Of course, a government may elicit support in many ways: through persuasion, consent, or manipulation. It may also impose unsupported settlements of demands through threats of force. But it is a familiar axiom of political science that a government based upon force alone is not long for this world; it must buttress its position by inducing a favorable state of mind in its subjects through fair or foul means.

The fact that support directed to a political system can be broken down conceptually into three elements—support for the community, regime, and government—does not mean, of course, that in the concrete case support for each of these three objects is independent. In fact we might and normally do find all three kinds of support very closely intertwined, so that the presence of one is a function of the presence of one or both of the other types. . . .

(2) Quantity and Scope of Support

How much support needs to be put into a system and how many of its members need to contribute such support if the system is to be able to do the job of converting demands to decisions? No ready answer can be offered. The actual situation in each case would determine the amount and scope required. We can, however, visualize a number of situations that will be helpful in directing our attention to possible generalizations.

Under certain circumstances very few members need to support a system at any level. The members might be dull and apathetic, indifferent to the general operations of the system, its progress or decisions. In a loosely connected system such as India has had, this might well be the state of mind of by far the largest segment of the membership. Either in fact they have not been affected by national decisions or they have not perceived that they were so affected. They may have little sense of identification with the present regime and government and yet, with regard to the input of demands, the system may be able to act on the basis of the support offered by the known 3 per cent of the Western-oriented politicians and intellectuals who are politically active. In other words, we can have a small minority putting in quantitatively sufficient supportive energy to keep the system going. However, we can venture the hypothesis that where members of a system are putting in numerous demands, there is a strong probability that they will actively offer support or hostility at one of the three levels of the system, depending upon the degree to which these demands are being met through appropriate decisions.

Alternatively, we may find that all the members of a system are putting in support, but the amount may be so low as to place one or all aspects of the system in jeopardy. Modern France is perhaps a classic illustration. The input of support at the level of the political community is probably adequate for the maintenance of France as a national political unit. But for a variety of historical and contemporary reasons, there is considerable doubt as to whether the members of the French political system are putting in anything but a low order of support to the regime or any particular government. This low amount of support, even though spread over a relatively large segment of the population, leaves the French political system on somewhat less secure foundations than is the case with India. There support is less widespread but more active—that is, quantitatively greater—on the part of a minority. As this illustration indicates, the amount of support is not necessarily proportional to its scope.

It may seem from the above discussion as though the members of a political system either put in support or withhold it—that is, demonstrate hostility or apathy. In fact, members may and normally do simultaneously engage in supportive and hostile behavior. What we must be interested in is the net balance of support.

IV. MECHANISMS OF SUPPORT

To this point I have suggested that no political system can yield the important outputs we call authoritative decisions unless, in addition to demands, support finds its way into the system. I have discussed the possible object to which support may be directed, and some problems with regard to the domain, quantity, and scope of support. We are now ready to turn to the main question raised by our attention to support as a crucial input: how do systems typically manage to maintain a steady flow of support? Without it a system will not absorb sufficient energy from its members to be able to convert demands to decisions.

In theory, there might be an infinite variety of means through which members could be induced to support a system; in practice, certain well-established classes of mechanisms are used. Research in this area needs to be directed to exploring the precise way in which a particular system utilizes these mechanisms and to refining our understanding of the way in which they contribute to the making of authoritative policy.

A society generates support for a political system in two ways: through outputs that meet the demands of the members of society; and through the processes of politicization. Let us look at outputs first.

(1) Outputs as a Mechanism of Support

An output of a political system, it will be recalled, is a political decision or policy. One of the major ways of strengthening the ties of the members to their system is through providing decisions that tend to satisfy the day-to-day demands of these members. Fundamentally this is the truth that lies in the aphorism that one can fool some of the people some of the time but not all of them all of the time. Without some minimal satisfaction of demands, the ardor of all but the most fanatical patriot is sure to cool. The outputs, consisting of political decisions, constitute a body of specific inducements for the members of a system to support that system.

Inducements of this kind may be positive or negative. Where negative, they threaten the members of the system with various kinds of sanctions ranging from a small monetary fine to physical detention, ostracism, or loss of life, as in our own system with regard to the case of legally defined treason. In every system support stems in part from fear of sanctions or compulsion; in autocratic systems the proportion of coerced support is at a maximum. For want of space I shall confine myself to those cases where positive incentives loom largest.

Since the specific outputs of a system are policy decisions, it is upon the government that the final responsibility falls for matching or balancing outputs of decisions against input of demand. But it is clear that to obtain the support of the members of a system through positive incentives, a government need not meet all the demands of even its most influential and ardent supporters. Most governments, or groups such as political parties that seek to control governments, succeed in building up a reserve of support. This reserve will carry the government along even though it offends its followers, so long as over the extended short run these followers perceive the particular government as one that is in general favorable to their interests. One form that this reserve support takes in Western society is that of party loyalty, since the party is the typical instrument in a mass industrialized society for mobilizing and maintaining support for a government. However, continuous lack of specific rewards through policy decisions ultimately leads to the danger that even the deepest party loyalty may be shaken. . . .

Thus a system need not meet *all the demands* of its members so long as it has stored up a reserve of support over the years. Nor need it satisfy even *some of the demands* of all its members. Just whose demands a system must seek to meet, how much of their demands, at what time, and under what conditions are questions for special research. We can say in advance that at least the demands of the most influential members require satisfaction. But this tells us little unless we know how to discover the influentials in a political system and how new sets of members rise to positions of influence.

The critical significance of the decisions of governments for the support of the other two aspects of a system—namely, the political community and the regime—is clear from what I have said above. Not all withdrawal of support from a government has consequences for the success or failure of a regime or community. But persistent inability of a government to produce satisfactory outputs for the members of a system may well lead to demands for changing of the regime or for dissolution of the political community. It is for this reason that the input-output balance is a vital mechanism in the life of a political system.

(2) Politicization as a Mechanism of Support

It would be wrong to consider that the level of support available to a system is a function exclusively of the outputs in the form of either sanctions or rewards. If we did so conclude, we could scarcely account for the maintenance of numerous political systems in which satisfaction of demands has been manifestly low, in which public coercion is limited, and yet which have endured for epochs. Alternately, it might be difficult to explain how political systems could endure and yet manage to flout or thwart urgent demands, failing thereby to render sufficient *quid pro quo* for the input of support. The fact is that whatever reserve of support has been accumulated through past decisions is increased and reinforced by a complicated method for steadily manufacturing support through what I shall call the process of politicization. It is an awkward term, but nevertheless an appropriately descriptive one.

As each person grows up in a society, through a network of rewards and punishments the other members of society communicate to and instill in him the various institutionalized goals and norms of that society. This is well known in social research as the process of socialization. Through its operation a person learns to play his various social roles. Part of these goals and norms relate to to what the society considers desirable in political life. The ways in which these political patterns are learned by the members of society constitute what I call the process of politicization. Through it a person learns to play his political roles, which include the absorption of the proper political attitudes.

Let us examine a little more closely something of what happens during the process of politicization. As members of a society mature, they must absorb the various orientations toward political matters that one is expected to have in that society. If the expectations of the members of society with regard to the way each should behave in specific political situations diverged beyond a certain range, it would be impossible to get common action with regard to the making of binding decisions. It is essential for the viability of an orderly political system that the members of the system have some common basic expectations with regard to the standards that are to be used in making political evaluations, to the way people will feel about various political matters, and to the way members of the system will perceive and interpret political phenomena.

The mechanism through which this learning takes place is of considerable significance in understanding how a political system generates and accumulates a strong reserve of support. Although we cannot pursue the details, we can mention a few of the relevant dimensions. In the first place, of course, the learning or politicization process does not stop at any particular period for the individual; it starts with the child and, in the light of our knowledge of learning, may have its deepest impact through the teen age. . . .

In the second place, the actual process of politicization at its most general level brings into operation a complex network of rewards and punishments. For adopting the correct political attitudes and performing the right political acts, for conforming to the generally accepted interpretations of political goals, and for undertaking the institutionalized obligations of a member of the given system, we are variously rewarded or punished. For conforming we are made to feel worthy, wanted, and respected and often obtain material advantages such as wealth, influence, improved opportunities. For deviating beyond the permissible range, we are made to feel unworthy, rejected, dishonored, and often suffer material losses. . . .

In the third place, the means used for communicating the goals and norms to others tend to be repetitive in all societies. The various political myths, doctrines, and philosophies transmit to each generation a particular interpretation of the goals and norms. The decisive links in this chain of transmission are parents, siblings, peers, teachers, organizations, and social leaders, as well as physical symbols such as flags or totems, ceremonies, and rituals freighted with political meaning.

These processes through which attachments to a political system become built into the maturing member of a society I have lumped together under the rubric of politicization. . . .

When the basic political attachments become deeply rooted or institutionalized, we say that the system has become accepted as legitimate. Politicization therefore effectively sums up the way in which legitimacy is created and transmitted in a political system. And it is an empirical observation that in those instances where political systems have survived the longest, support has been nourished by an ingrained belief in the legitimacy of the relevant governments and regimes.

What I am suggesting here is that support resting on a sense of the legitimacy of a government and regime provides a necessary reserve if the system is to weather those frequent storms when the more obvious outputs of the system seem to impose greater hardships than rewards. Answers to questions concerning the formation, maintenance, transmission, and change of standards of legitimacy will contribute generously to an understanding of the way in which support is sufficiently institutionalized so that a system may regularly and without excessive expenditure of effort transform inputs of demand into outputs of decision.

That there is a need for general theory in the study of political life is apparent. The only question is how best to proceed. There is no one royal road that can be said to be either the correct one or the best. It is only a matter of what appears as the given level of available knowledge to be the most useful. At this stage it appears that system theory, with its sensitivity to the input-output exchange between a system and its setting offers a fruitful approach. It is an economical way of organizing presently disconnected political data and promises interesting dividends.

7. The Search for Focus*

ROY C. MACRIDIS

Years ago, it seems now decades ago, I outlined in a little book some of the most widespread dissatisfactions with what was at the time the study of comparative government—the way it was taught, the kinds of preoccupations and research it inspired, and more generally its place in the discipline.[1] I concluded, not unjustifiably it seems to me in retrospect, that the traditional approach was essentially parochial, monographic, descriptive, bound to the West and particularly to Western Europe, excessively formalistic and legalistic, and insensitive to theory-building and theory-testing. I suggested at the time a crude conceptual outline in terms of which individual systems could be studied and compared. It comprised the following three categories: interests and interest configuration, ideology, and governmental structures. The first corresponded to what are generally referred to today as the "input" factors. I defined interest in a broad sense. It encompassed primarily manifested and articulated interests rather than "latent" interests. My definition had, therefore, a concrete and direct relevance to the political process. Ideology was a loose term I gave to all the relevant political attitudes as they manifest themselves and as they have crystallized in various political systems over a period of time. I think it corresponds to what some call today the political culture. Finally, by "government" I understood the structures through which public officials, selected in one manner or another, make decisions. I viewed a political system in terms of its capacity to translate interests and aspirations into policy and to resolve conflicts[2]

*From "Comparative Politics and the Study of Government: The Search for Focus," *Comparative Politics,* vol. 1, no. 1 (October 1968), pp. 79–90. Reprinted by permission of the journal.

[1] The *Study of Comparative Government* (New York, 1955). For a discussion of the evolution and later state of the field, see Harry Eckstein and David E. Apter, eds., *Comparative Politics: A Reader* (New York, 1963), particularly the excellent general introduction by Harry Eckstein.

[2] The term "authoritative allocation of values," suggested by David Easton to define a political system, is misleading unless the words convey only what the author understands. There are many "values" that are not "authoritatively allocated" in a social system.

by transforming both interests and aspirations into decisions that are widely accepted. In this view, stability and consensus correlate directly with performance and responsivness.

I did not go beyond this crude formulation. Perhaps I lacked the appropriate theoretical sophistication. But I also felt, and continue to feel, that given the state of our discipline, an attempt to develop a well-knit and broad-gauge theoretical scheme was, and remains, not only premature but downright unproductive. I felt, and continue to feel, that the major task of comparative politics was, and remains, that of raising political questions, illuminating through parallel studies aspects of political behavior and decision-making, providing us gradually with a body of experience and data and sharpening our evaluation of governmental structures and policies. Only in the long run could hypotheses be developed and tested, and only then could a scientific outlook in the proper sense of the term be discerned at least as a distant promise. Finally, I pointed out that one of the major functions of the study of comparative government was to broaden the horizons of the students of American politics and help them shed their parochialism. I argued the obvious: that the study of foreign governmental forms, policies, and political predicaments helps us step out of our system and look at it from outside. Plato's allegory of the cave may be used to illustrate the plight of the scholars of American politics who have consistently and persistently failed to take this obvious advice.[3]

Much has happened since my little book appeared and the study of comparative politics—rather than of comparative governments—has been greatly modified. Many of my suggestions have now become part of the field—not, of course, because I made them, but because many factors have converged to fashion a new outlook and a new approach. The "behavioral revolution" or the "successful protest" to which Robert Dahl wrote an elegant epitaph came down upon us with a crash.[4] It is my purpose here not to judge this revolution as a whole,[5] but rather to evaluate some of its most serious contributions—not all of them beneficial—to the study of comparative politics.

I

Behavioralism provided, to begin with, a salutary emphasis upon political factors other than the governmental forms. Although their discovery was not entirely original, it opened up the study of what we may call the contextual factors within which political structures and forms develop and political roles flourish. Borrowing in great part from sociology and anthropology, behavior-

[3] Students of American political institutions, after paying tribute to the "genius," the "pragmatism," and the "consensual nature" of the polity, are now beginning to ask questions they should have raised long ago.

[4] Robert A. Dahl, "The Behavioral Approach in Political Science: Epitaph for a Monument to a Successful Protest," *American Political Science Review*, LV (December 1961), 763–772.

[5] See Heinz Eulau, *The Behavioral Persuasion in Politics* (New York, 1963); and Eulau, ed., *Political Behavior in America: New Directions* (New York, 1966).

alism put a stress upon careful definitions of the empirical problems to be investigated and upon the formulation of hypotheses and their testing. It sharpened the tools of our analysis by introducing new techniques—surveys, interviewing, the compilation of aggregate data—in an effort to provide correlations between various socioeconomic and psychological factors and political behavior. Weighing, measuring, and correlating are among the most positive aspects of the behavioral revolution in politics. When applied to a political scene, American or foreign, of which the observers had adequate knowledge, the emphasis was most beneficial.[6] The students were picking dark or shadowy areas and throwing light upon them. Their findings, or at least their observations, added to the picture we had and helped us refine it. The findings, in other words, made sense and produced new data about the system being studied because we already had a great deal of information about the system.

Where the behavioral revolution went wrong was at its two extremes—in its efforts to build "grand theory" or "system theory," at the one extreme, and in its study of what may well be called political trivia, at the other. In between the two lay a fertile field for study and exploration. But it is to the extremes that most of the work was directed, generally with disappointing results. This will become abundantly clear, I hope, when I discuss the following points that exemplify the state of the discipline today: its failure to establish criteria of relevance and its gross neglect of the study of governmental structures and forms.

II

The search for relevance and the criteria of relevance has bedeviled political thought and inquiry. It is an issue that cannot be easily resolved. Society as an overall system, i.e., a set of interrelations, roles, and structures, consists of a number of subsystems for which no hard and fast boundaries can be drawn. In a sense, all that is social is also political, firmly rooted in history. What is social can be broken down analytically into subsystems, but again, the lower we move in identifying subsystems, the harder it becomes to set boundaries. The "web" is there.

Conceivably then every manifestation, every attitude or relationship, every motivation or idea in society has a relevance to politics. It may engender aspirations; it may shape interests; it may evoke demands; it may call for decisions; it may lead to conflicts about values and interests which necessitate arbitration. Child-rearing, the school curriculum, modes of entertainment, sex relations, to say nothing of economic interests and activities, are all *potentially* related to politics. Yet what is potential is not actual in empirical terms. In most cases and for most of the time, the great host of social, economic, and interpersonal relations has no actual relevance to politics and therefore to the discipline. Yet each and all *may* at a given time and place, and under a set of

---

[6] For instance, Angus Campbell, Philip E. Converse, Warren E. Miller, and Donald E. Stokes, *The American Voter* (New York, 1960). Also, E. Deutsch, D. Lindon, and P. Weill, *Les Familles politiques aujourd'hui en France* (Paris, 1966).

conditions that is impossible to foresee, assume a political relevance, only to subside again into an apolitical stance.

The dilemma is obvious. Should we study everything that is *potentially* political?[7] Should we narrow our definition and, if so, how? Behavioralism provides the worst possible answer—study everything. It postulates that every aspect of political behavior relates to every aspect of social behavior. Hence we may finish by studying manifestations and attitudes and relationships that have no discernible political relevance.

To be sure, there are no *a priori* grounds on the strength of which one can discard this holistic approach. The element of potentiality is ever present, and our inability to develop any rules about the intricate phenomenon that accounts for the actualization of what is potential makes it impossible to condemn potentiality as a criterion of relevance. Only two closely related grounds for its rejection can be suggested. The first is what Professor LaPalombara has called the rule of parsimony,[8] and the second is what I call the concern with focus. Parsimony suggests the choice of those categories and concepts on the basis of which we are as sure as we can be that what we are studying is politically relevant. Concern with focus simply suggests the most direct way to get at politically relevant phenomena.

Relevance and Focus: A Set of Priorities

First and above all, I think it is our obligation to study all those organized manifestations, attitudes, and movements that press directly for state action or oppose state action. No matter what terms we use—decision-making, authoritative allocation of values, regulation, adjudication, enforcement—we are concerned with the same old thing, the state. What is it asked to do? And what is it that people in a community do not want to see it do? To deny this pervasive empirical phenomenon, in the name of a given theory, is to deny our art or, for those who prefer, our science. The demand for state action or the demand that a given action cease is the very guts of politics. No science of politics—or for that matter, no science—can be built upon concepts and theories that disregard or avoid empirical phenomena. Why do the French farmers throw their peaches in the river and their beets on the highway? Why do the American students leave their comfortable homes to demonstrate in the streets? Why have American workers patterned their political demands in one way, but French workers in another? Obviously, to control, to influence, or to oppose state action.

Thus, my second priority also relates to what I have called the state, resurrecting what may appear to many graduate students to be an ancient term. I mean by it, of course, what we have always understood the term to mean,

---

[7] The pitfalls are obvious in David Truman's *The Governmental Process* (New York, 1951). For a criticism of the latent-group theory, see my "Interest Groups in Comparative Analysis," *Journal of Politics*, XXIII (February 1961), 25–45 (reproduced below).

[8] Joseph LaPalombara, "Macrotheories and Microapplications in Comparative Politics: A Widening Chasm," *Comparative Politics*, vol. 1, no. 1 (October 1968).

stripped of all its metaphysical trimmings. It means all the structures and organizations that make decisions and resolve conflicts with the expectation that their decisions will be obeyed: the civil service, the legislature, the executive, the judiciary, the host of public or semipublic corporations and organizations that are called upon to resolve differences and to make decisions. I include also the agencies whose function is to study facts, to deliberate about them, to identify areas of conflict, and to suggest policy decisions. The most relevant issue here is not the one that David Easton discusses, or rather suggests, i.e., a theory of likely problems and predicaments—especially when the theory is pitched at a very high level of generalization.[9] I think that what is instead important is to study the preparedness of the state to discern predicaments or problems. Potential problems can be theorized about. The actual political phenomenon, however, is the existing machinery through which problems are perceived—the agencies, the research, the flow of information, the manner in which individual values and constituency considerations enter into the minds of the men and women who work for the state—and finally includes that happy or fatal moment when the state copes with, ignores, or is simply unable to perceive the problem. The state can also, while perceiving the problem, either alleviate the predicament or suggest solutions utterly unrelated to it. It was not only the Queen of France who showed a gross lack of discernment when she suggested that they eat cakes. In what is reputed to be the most enlightened and modern political system, the President and the Congress acted in the best tradition of Marie Antoinette by declaring, "Let them have open housing. . . ."

It is this second priority—the study of the state and all state agencies; their organization and performance; the scope of their decision-making; the attitudes of the men and women who perform within their structures the roles of informing, studying, consulting, and deciding; and the major constituencies they serve—that has been so sadly neglected in the last decade or so. Few are the studies that focus on the state as an agency of deliberation, problem identification, and problem-solving. Few are the studies of the institutions of the state in the modern developed systems.[10] This is no accident at all. After the state was ostracized from the vocabulary of politics, we found it far more fashionable to study the systems in which there was no state, i.e., the so-called developing, emerging, or new systems. The result was to eschew the urgent and nagging empirical situations in the modern and highly industrialized societies where our fate is to be decided—in order to study political phenomena and especially political development in the societies where there was no state. No wonder Professor Huntington began to despair of studying the process of development in any terms other than "institutionalization," i.e., the building of institutions with authority and legitimacy, such as the state and the party.[11]

[9] *A Systems Analysis of Political Life* (New York, 1955), esp. chaps. 4, 14, and 15.

[10] See, however, among others, Kenneth Waltz, *Foreign Policy and Democratic Politics* (Boston, 1967); Andrew Shonfield, *Modern Capitalism* (London, 1965); and Richard F. Fenno, *The President's Cabinet* (Cambridge, Mass., 1959).

[11] Samuel P. Huntington, "Political Development and Political Decay," *World Politics,* XVII (April 1965), 386–430.

My third priority is the study of political attitudes—the "civic culture," as Professor Almond puts it, or what Professor Beer calls "the structure of norms and beliefs,"[12] and what others have very loosely called ideology. But whatever name we give to them, the phenomena to be studied must point directly to the beliefs, norms, and orientations about the state (authority, scope of action, legitimacy, sense of participation, and involvement). If we are to remain strictly within the confines of relevance we must narrow our scope to those manifestations and attitudes that directly link the personal, economic, or psychological phenomena with the political. The linkage between "micro" and "macro" so well developed by Professor Almond in his *Civic Culture* in order to identify meaningful political orientations needs to be carried a step forward. This can be done only when we reintroduce the state and its agencies and link them directly to political orientations. Unless we take this step, we shall remain at the "micro" level. We shall not link attitudes to structures and forms, to decisions and policies. The specifics about governmental decisions and performance will elude us.

Finally, my fourth priority—which in a real sense is no priority at all—relates to the study of what may be called the infrastructure of the political world: attitudes and ideas; social, economic, and cultural institutions; norms and values that are prevalent in any given society, national or international. There is no reason why we shouldn't study child-rearing, the patterns of socialization, the degree of concentration of economic power, the identification of personality types and traits, family life patterns, small groups and private associations, religious attitudes, and so on. All of these, as I indicated, *may* have a relevance to politics. In a number of cases—and they are the ones that count—the relevance is only too clear. It suggests itself by the very nature of the empirical phenomenon we are studying. It links a given organized political manifestation with a contextual factor that may explain it. It would be difficult to understand the role of the French military up until the Dreyfus case without knowing something about the education they received in Jesuit schools. But in this case we study education because we begin with the army as a political force operating within the government and the state. We go deeper into contextual factors in order to find an explanation of a manifest political phenomenon.

What I am trying to suggest by these priorities, then, is primarily a change of focus. My concern is simply to pinpoint what is political. We begin with the political; we catch it, so to speak, in its most visible, open, and raw manifestation; we begin with the top of the iceberg before we go deep to search for its submerged base. We focus on the state and its agencies, on its types of action or inaction, and on all those organized manifestations that call for action or inaction on its part. We study the forms of decision-making and analyze and evaluate its substance. We explore its impact upon groups, interests, and power elites within the system; we study in turn their reactions to state actions and

---

[12] Gabriel A. Almond and Sidney Verba, *The Civic Culture* (Boston, 1965); Samuel H. Beer and Adam B. Ulam, eds., *Patterns of Government,* 2d ed. (New York, 1962), Introduction by Samuel H. Beer.

their counterdemands as they are manifested through various media from political parties down to voting.

The Fallacy of Inputism

Two terms that have gained wide currency in the last decade are "input" and "output." The system converts demands into decisions. Through the feedback mechanism, output factors influence the input side. Emphasis is placed upon the input factors, but the state is given a degree of autonomy and independence, and through a process that is by no means clear, it can influence supports and demands.[13] The difficulty comes with the selection of the input factors, i.e., with the same problem of relevance that we have discussed. Do we study again all societal manifestations on the assumption that they all make inputs? Do we consider attitudinal data, aggregate data, hard and soft data ranging from the number of hospital beds to child-father relations? Where and in what manner do we define the subject matter for study, and what is our cutoff point? Political scientists are often like thirsty men who go looking for water in a contextual Sahara when more often than not it is right there fresh from the spring—or at least from a well-chlorinated reservoir. Their search in the contextual wasteland brings only further difficulties upon them, for there is no theory, no conceptual scheme that links—in any form that is testable—the amassed socioeconomic and psychological data with the political. In fact, emphasis upon the input factors very often not only neglects the political but sometimes explicitly avoids it.

I am inclined to define what I call "inputism" as the study of society by political scientists without a political focus and very often without a political question. The job is enticingly easy. All that is needed is a questionnaire, interviewers, a pool of respondents, the *UN Statistical Yearbook,* and a countersorter or, even better, a computer. I wish to reemphasize the phrase "without a political focus and very often without a political question." When the empirical political situation and the empirical political phenomenon we are investigating make it necessary—as often happens—to study the socioeconomic or psychological factors on the input side, then such study is focused and relevant, for the input factors are analyzed to "explain" the situation we are investigating. We hypothesize that the attitude of the French military with regard to a series of political decisions or with regard to the process of decision-making was, among other things, shaped by the education they received at the Jesuit schools. The linkage between the two, I believe, can be made. It will not fully explain the attitude of the military. But I think it may provide one of the first steps leading to explanation. We start with the concrete political problem. Inputism would reverse the priorities, advocating the study of the socialization of the elite groups in the French educational system, with the unwarranted expectation that such

---

[13] David Easton, "An Approach to the Analysis of Political Systems," *World Politics,* IX (April 1957), 383–400.

study would clarify "politics" in general and help us explain political behavior. What behavior? With regard to what problem? At what time?

Inputism tends to lead to three fallacies: that of determinism, that of scientism, and that of superficiality. All three fallacies are related.

According to determinism, it is the input factors that shape political action. The political phenomenon is almost invariably reduced either to a number of nonpolitical determinants, in which case we have a multiple kind of reductionism, or to one factor, in which case we have a single-factor reductionism. In either case, the state can play virtually no independent problem-solving or attitude-forming role. It is only through a process of feedback—not clearly understood and not easily demonstrated—that governmental action may influence the determinants that then in turn will act upon the governmental decision-making process. Politics constantly remains a dependent variable. It is, to use Bentley's expression, the parallelogram of interest action and interaction, that is, the parallelogram of all socioeconomic and psychological determinants that will shape the decision-making machinery and will determine its output. The famous "black box," as the graduate students have come to know the government, is at its best a filter mechanism through which interests express themselves and at its worst a simple transmission mechanism. The role of the state is reduced to the narrow confines of an organization that channels, reflects, and expresses commands and instructions that come from "elsewhere." The hint to political scientists is obvious: study everything but the machinery of the state and its organizational structures; study the "elsewhere."

Scientism constitutes the effort to measure as accurately as possible the weight, scope, and persistence of the input factors, on the purely gratuitous assumption that they are or can be linked causally to political phenomena. The assumption is gratuitous because we have failed as yet to establish any such causal links and because it is doubtful that we ever will. The assumption is confounded when the political phenomena with which the input factors are to be linked are not clearly stated. Sometimes system theory suggests the broadest possible relationship among "concepts," rather than variables—consensus, stability, performance; sometimes it offers a very narrow-gauge hypothesis linking some political manifestation to one nonpolitical variable (for example, voting with income or race). The first attempt obviously bogs down into analytical exercise rather than empirical testing, while the second one will never attain the level of testability on the basis of which higher-level propositions can be made. Even when system theory establishes clear-cut concepts linked to empirical phenomena from which testable propositions can emerge, it is impossible to move back from the propositions to the concepts and to the overall theory through a series of verifiable tests that exclude all alternative propositions, concepts and theories. Scientism therefore leads us from hyperfactualism to hypertheorizing—the latter becoming progressively an exercise (often brilliant) in intellectual virtuosity. It lacks, however, the only thing that really counts—empirical relevance.

Since no theory as yet offered has shown its worth in causally linking determinants with political phenomena, our efforts very often end with the superficial juxtaposition of a given determinant with a given political phenomenon—that is to say, with correlations. Since no adequate theory has been offered, however, and since we therefore have no explanation, correlational findings are a somewhat more sophisticated version of the "sun spot" theory. Martin Lipset's book *Political Man* is an illustration of this.[14] At the end of this excellent study, the reader is not sure whether open democratic societies are affluent because they are open and democratic or whether it is the other way round.

III

Determinism, scientism, and correlational studies that have a distinct trait of superficiality typify the state of a discipline that has consistently eschewed the hard and persistent empirical phenomena that ought to concern it in the name of theory-building and theory-testing. Structures and processes and the manifestly political institutions through which decisions are made have been relegated to the level of epiphenomena. The examination and evaluation of policies have been handed over to the journalists and politicians, and the formulation of a judgment *in the name of knowledge* is considered incompatible with the canons of a self-imposed scientific objectivity. It is these trends that account for the state of the discipline as a whole, and they affect particularly the study of comparative politics, or the comparative study of politics. The state of the discipline can be summed up in one phrase: the gradual disappearance of the political. To repeat, if government is viewed as the reflection of the parallelogram of socioeconomic and psychological and other determinants, the prescription for political science becomes a proscription of the study of government.

Yet the behavioral revolution has also had, as I have noted, beneficial effects. We shall never return exclusively to normative speculation, and we shall never be satisfied with judgments about political phenomena without the benefit of careful measurement. We shall continue to distinguish sharply between "facts" and "values," and we shall subject our postulates to a critical examination, demanding always clarity of definitions and terms. Where the propositions about behavior can be tested, we shall test them under all the canons of controlled inquiry that the social sciences have developed. We shall continue to seek to build theory, i.e., a set of interrelated and interconnected propositions, each of which has direct empirical meaning and relevance, and we shall continue to develop narrow hypotheses that can be tested, i.e., invariably falsified. We shall use the many tools of empirical inquiry available to us—survey opinion data, aggregate data—and in both the construction of our research and our search for the explanation of political phenomena, we shall feel free to borrow, when the occasion demands, from the theoretical sophistication of many disciplines—sociology, anthropology, economics, and psychology—and, of course, to use the empirical data that history provides. But the time has come to qualify and

[14] Seymour Martin Lipset, *Political Man* (New York, 1960).

reconsider our quest for a science of politics in the full sense of the term. But in the last analysis this may be a contradiction in terms. There can be no science where the element of human will and purpose predominates. Politics is a problem-solving mechanism; its study must deal with it and not with the laws surrounding behavior. The ultimate irony is that even if laws could be discovered, then our discipline would be primarily concerned with an effort to explain why they are not obeyed—why the laws are really non-laws. Natural sciences began by addressing themselves to empirical phenomena in order to understand them, explain them, and control them. The ultimate goal of the natural sciences has been to control nature. The higher the level of generalization that subsumes a number of measurable relationships, the higher the potentiality of control. It is the other way around with politics. The study of politics explicitly divorces knowledge from action and understanding from control. The laws that we constantly seek will tell us little about our political problems and what to do about them. Our concern becomes scholastic. [15]

I therefore suggest that we reconcile ourselves to the fact that while we can have an understanding of some political phenomena, a history of politics and political movements, an understanding of the functioning of governmental forms and structures, a concern and indeed a focus on major concepts such as power, decision-making, interest, organization, control, political norms and beliefs, obedience, equality, development, consensus, performance, and the like, we do not and cannot have a science of politics. We can have, at most, an art. Second, and this is the sign of the art, we may manage to arrive at some inductive generalizations based upon fragmentary empirical evidence. An inductive generalization is at best a statement about behavior. It can be derived from identical action and interaction under generally similar conditions over a long period of time in as many different contexts as possible. The behavior is not explained, but the weight of evidence allows us to anticipate and often predict it. A series of solidly supported inductive generalizations may in the last analysis be the most fruitful way to move gradually to a scientific approach, as it provides us with a rudimentary form of behavioral patterns. Our knowledge of politics is then at most an understanding of our accumulated experience. It is in this area that comparative politics has an important role to play. By carefully identifying a given behavior or structure or movement and by attempting to study it in as many settings as possible and over as long a period of time as possible, we can provide generalizations backed by evidence.

If we view our discipline as an art and if we limit its goals to inductive generalizations about politics, i.e., a well-ordered and catalogued table or listing of accumulated experience, then two or three imperatives for research emerge, providing focus and satisfying the need for parsimony. First, we must study the practitioners of the art, the political leaders who hold office and, more generally, the governing elites that aspire to or possess political power. Second, we must

---

[15] Barrington Moore, Jr., "The New Scholasticism and the Study of Politics," *World Politics,* VI (October 1953), 122–38.

study the structures and organizations and mechanisms through which the elites gain political power and exercise it, that is, the parties and other political associations. Third, we must be concerned with the governmental institutions through which demands are channeled or, just as often, by which they are generated. These imperatives do not exhaust our immediate task, but give us a starting point.

In studying the governmental elites and the institutions through which they gain and exercise power, we ought to consider the art of government as a problem-solving and goal-oriented activity. This kind of activity characterizes any art. The task of government is to identify problems (or to anticipate them) and provide for solutions. Our study then is constantly to ask ourselves, How well is the art performed? Who within the government listens, who foresees, who advises and suggests policy? What are the skills of the practitioners, and what are their objective capabilities? Finally, what is the impact of a decision upon the problem or the predicament it was designed to alleviate or to remove? The practitioner is not strictly bound by determinants. Communal life suggests and often sets goals of performance and achievement that become more than normative goals. They become in a way the "operative goals" that give direction to political action. The governing elite plays an independent role in seeking out the goals and in implementing them. Shonfield in his book on planning refers to the French planning as the result of an "elitist conspiracy."[16] More often than not decision-making is an elitist conspiracy whose study and assessment would be far more rewarding than the survey and elaboration of all the input factors or the nonpolitical determinants.

But in the last analysis government is an act of will that can shuffle and reshuffle many of the determinants. Government involves choice, and the parameters are often wider than we are inclined to think. Any government will begin by surveying the conditions that appear to indicate the limits of freedom and choice; a government must always ask "what it has." But any government must also be in a position to assess what it wills. To say this is not to return to metaphysical speculation about the "will" of the state or the government. It is simply to reintroduce as integral parts of our discipline the state's performance and choices and the institutions through which they are implemented.

IV

The central focus of politics, therefore, and of the study of comparative politics is, in my opinion, the governmental institutions and political elites, their role, their levels of performance and nonperformance. Stating this in such blunt terms appears to be utterly naïve. Shall we return then to the descriptive study of governmental institutions? Far from it. What I am suggesting is a starting point and a focus of investigation. Any such investigation, we know today, will inevitably lead us, as it should, far and wide in search of the contextual factors

---

[16] Shonfield, *op. cit.*

(rather than determinants) within the framework of which a government operates and to which its action, its performance, and its policies may often be attributed. We shall have to probe the infrastructure, but without losing sight of either our focus or the relevant question we began our investigation with.

I can think, in the manner of Machiavelli and Montesquieu and Tocqueville, of a number of relevant questions, all of which we tend to evade either because they are "difficult" or because they are not amenable to "scientific inquiry" or because they involve "value judgments": What accounts for a well organized civil service? What is the impact of large-scale organizations—parties, bureaucracy, and so on—upon the citizen? Under what conditions does public opinion exercise its influence on the government? What accounts for political instability? Is an executive who is responsible to the people more restrained than one responsible to the legislature? How and under what conditions does representation degenerate into an expression of particular interests? Under what conditions do the young people maintain political attitudes different from those of their fathers, and at what point do they revolt? Why does a ruling class become amenable to reform? Under what conditions do ruling groups become responsive to popular demands?

I can multiply these questions, but I think these illustrate my point. None of them can lead to hard hypotheses and proof (or disproof). Some cannot be easily answered. But this is not too important unless we are to accept that only those questions that can lead to testing in the rigorous, and therefore impossible, meaning of the term have the freedom of the market. In fact, the questions I suggest lead to a comparative survey, both historical and contemporaneous, of some of the most crucial political phenomena: responsiveness, performance, change, development, and a host of others. Such a survey will inevitably produce inductive generalizations, perhaps in the manner of Machiavelli, but with far more sophisticated tools and greater access to data than was ever the case before. It will inevitably help us to qualify our questions and to reformulate them as hypotheses that will suggest other qualifications—new variables, if you wish—and lead to further investigation—testing if you wish—and the reformulation of the questions—the gradual development of theory, if you like.

Through the study of governmental institutions and political elites, we shall be concerned with fundamental problems of politics. The first symptoms and indicators of all pervasive political phenomena—revolution, authority and stability, legitimacy, participation—are registered in the composition, organization, and performance of the government. I suggest that we begin with these and broaden our horizon as our study goes on. The policies pursued, their consistency, their congruence with the existing social and economic problems, the governors' awareness of such problems—all constitute good indicators of stability or instability.

My second suggestion, therefore, for the study of comparative politics is to concentrate on the policies pursued by various governments in differing political systems—to highlight the conditions of performance or nonperformance, as the case may be. Here one of the cardinal tasks of political science is not to study all the integrative factors, as has been the case, but to identify problems that may lead to conflict—not when conflict erupts, but when the society is at the threshold, so to speak, of a conflict situation. The study of the impact of the decisions made by the government can provide us with an excellent laboratory for comparative analysis. *Conflict-policies-decisions-consequences,* this is the heart of the political life. If the political scientists and particularly the students of comparative politics were to concentrate on these central manifestations, they would liberate themselves from the shackles that bind them today, according to which the "determinants" come first and the political questions second. Problems and questions about economic planning, the decay of the representative institutions fashioned in the nineteenth century, the impact of the expanding population upon individual freedoms or of "bigness" upon the individual citizen as a participant member of the body politic, the handling of the new instruments of violence and the growth of the power and status of those who command them, the military, these are the basic problems that affect us. To evade them in the name of science is to abandon our vocation to understand, to explain, to point to dangers, and to draw from our accumulated experience both suggestions and warnings.

Last, we must be prepared in the light of the experience we have studied and accumulated to move forward and offer policies. In doing so we do not enter the forbidden territory of "political action" nor, as it is so naïvely argued so often, do we simply leave our scientific hat in the office to don the activist hat. We do not move from "fact" to "value"—to repeat the facile distinction made by Max Weber, as if the dichotomy between the two did not involve a value judgment. We remain at the level of problem identification and problem-solving, and we suggest remedies to the policy-makers. The more detached our suggestions, the better based upon political experience (in the broad sense), the more plausible they are likely to be. And if we evaluate the same problem differently and suggest different solutions and reach different conclusions, this is only an indication, provided all canons of objectivity and reasoning are respected, that ours is an art. The body of accumulated experience must still be refined and studied if we are to gain an understanding that we can all share alike.

part TWO

Legitimacy and Consensus

In every political system, we have noted, individuals and groups seek to influence the state and thereby translate their interests into authoritative political decisions. An indispensable condition for the efficient functioning of political systems is widespread acceptance of the decision-making process—which we shall call "consensus." Wherever this kind of consensus exists, the state itself becomes legitimized. Legitimacy and consensus are key indicators of the effectiveness and performance of the system and conversely of the existence of basic instabilities that may undermine it. Ultimately, the phenomenon of government—what Mosca calls "the political fact"—is a matter of will as well as force; that is, political relations are willed relations.

CONCEPTS AND THEORIES

One aspect of legitimacy is the use of the power of the state by officials in accordance with prearranged and agreed upon rules. A legitimate act is also legal, but a lawful command is not always legitimate. For example, the commands issued by the Nazi government in Germany were legal, and presumably subordinate officials down to the private soldier or individual citizen had to obey them. But at the same time, these orders violated a code of civilized behavior and morality that brought into question their legitimacy. Legality refers to the letter of the law as decreed by a state organ, while legitimacy involves the very character of the state and the substance and purpose of a legal enactment. But who will decide when there is a difference between legality and legitimacy? No clear answer can be given. On the one hand, the state always claims legitimacy for its legal commands. "What is pleasing to the prince has the force of law," according to an old axiom of the Romans. On the other hand, many individuals see a higher law beyond the formal law of the state. Ultimately, they obey their own conscience and consider some acts of the state as illegitimate. This is the justification of civil disobedience, as advocated by Thoreau, Tolstoy, and Gandhi.

But these extreme formulations are hypothetical. In actual political life, legality, legitimacy, and consent *tend* to converge. Consensus is more than agreement; it denotes acceptance of a given political system. Acceptance may be due to individual consent stemming from recognition of the beneficent purposes of the state; acceptance is also the product of tradition and habit. Consensus is generally addressed to the basic rules that establish, define, limit, and channel political power—that is, to the constitution. It is not limited to specific laws or specific acts of the government, or even to governmental forms. Consensus transforms power into authority, and the legal enactments emanating from the government into legitimate orders.

Democratic theory postulates canons of legitimacy that clarify the distinctions we are trying to make. Force can be used only in accordance with certain previously agreed upon procedures. There is an elaborate setting of limitations upon the exercise of power, which can be used only by persons elevated to office through elections. Individuals agree to the basic rules so long as they are not violated. The government derives its authority from these basic rules; whenever disagreements about the government and its policies erupt, they are resolved through popular choice. The substance of political life, therefore, is the consensus—or "agreement on fundamentals"—that binds the citizens into an organized common political life.

The contract theory as developed by John Locke is a classic formulation of this consensual model. According to it, the formation of a political community is an act of will embodying the cardinal rule that the majority of the people, acting through their legislature, govern. However, property rights and individual freedoms may not be infringed upon by the majority, and there must be periodic free elections of the legislative body. In such a political community, a minority can be coerced only in order to implement the basic agreement entered into by the whole community. But such coercion cannot be used to destroy or silence the minority. The consensus on a free and open society gives the majority the right to act, while allowing the minority the right to protest peacefully and ultimately to appeal to the community at large in favor of its positions—in other words, the right to become the majority. This model, then, incorporates the obligation to obey and the right to protest, criticize, and oppose. It allows the force of the state to be transformed into authority, deriving its legitimacy from the basic agreement. Individual dissent is expressed not in disobedience, but through organized opposition seeking to present alternative policies. Thus, opposition in the democratic scheme is harnessed to the total political system, which is strengthened, not weakened, by dissent.

The model helps us to see clearly the distinctions between force and authority, consensus and legitimacy. It also has analytic value in calling our attention to the conditions under which consensus is likely to emerge, or be disrupted. But most political systems at present are not based on the Lockean model. Force rather than authority is frequently the rule, and this is an indication of a lack of consensus binding the citizens together. More important, values other than free elections, including national or ethnic identity, may serve to legitimize the state.

Political decisions may be accepted by a population for a variety of reasons. Freely given consent is only one basis of legitimacy, and in the modern world is becoming increasingly precarious.

CONSENSUS BUILDING

The contract theory that Locke used to illustrate the formation of a political community—all citizens agreeing to form it through a solemn compact—is at best a fiction or simply an illustration with no historical foundation. It holds that, under certain conditions, a state of mind develops among a given people to establish a set of fundamental rules about the manner in which they would cooperate and live peacefully together. But what accounts for such a state of mind? And why was it reached in some societies and not in others? When and under what conditions does a community become a political one accepting a common agreement?

There are no simple answers to these questions, but some general indications may be given. First, there must be a fairly extensive acceptance of common norms of social conduct. Customs must begin to develop—even everyday habits—before we can begin to talk of a community. Second, social behavior must be predictable, at least to the extent that makes human intercourse possible. If all parishioners spied upon one another, while celebrating mass, for fear that each might carry a gun, a functioning community would hardly be likely. Third, a political community requires common expectations of material benefits for all members. The utilitarian argument was put forward by Thomas Hobbes and, later, more persuasively by James Mill and John Stuart Mill. Put simply, this means that the chances for achieving consensus are greater in political communities that enjoy economic prosperity.

Finally, the role of elites is crucial in the formation of consensus. It is axiomatic that leadership is always lodged in the hands of a few. In all countries that have experienced the Industrial Revolution, rule by a relatively small traditional elite was challenged by new groups, in particular the bourgeoisie and the working class. This was a momentous period in the evolution of political systems, since claims to political leadership had to be subordinated to the requirements of popular participation and support. Two developments can be discerned. In some cases, the ruling groups became restrictive and negative, attempting to thwart participation and to maintain themselves in a position of control and leadership through the use of repressive measures. In other cases, they became permissive and supportive, allowing their claims to leadership to be qualified and indeed ultimately subverted by new symbols, forms, and practices deriving from popular participation. The greater the degree of permissiveness on the part of the traditional elites, the smoother was the transition to a consensual and participant society; the greater their tendency to reject newcomers, the more difficult and the less likely was the emergence of consensus.

In Britain, for example, ever increasing participation and influence was offered to the citizenry at large throughout the nineteenth century. But in

Russia, despite some half-hearted reforms, autocratic rule was maintained. The result was that in Britain the people began to value and accept their system as an instrument for the satisfaction of their wants, while the rising groups in Russia either rejected their government or remained apathetic to it. In the one case, consensus was built; in the other, its very preconditions were denied. Thus, we may postulate that the congruence between mass demands for participation and influence and a positive elite response to these demands is a fundamental condition for the development of consensus.

This hypothesis is equally relevant for the developing societies today. Throughout Asia and Africa many of the preconditions of consensus—the sense of national identity, compatibility of values, and predictability of behavior—are lacking. In all these societies demands for material progress have been stimulated through exposure to more advanced societies. The role of the elites then becomes critical for the development of political consensus. Rejection of new groups may lead to sharp conflict between the few and the many, and a state of virtual civil war. Complete permissiveness, on the other hand, may thrust unprepared and unqualified groups into power prematurely. Inability to forward industrialization produces popular disenchantment and apathy.

Under these circumstances the only force in society capable of maintaining discipline is the army. The politicians who promise what cannot be delivered are overthrown, and military rulers then scale down the original goals. In many instances, the new military regimes revert to the political relationships that existed under colonial rule, with the native military assuming the role of the former colonial power. Consensual regimes may still emerge. A balance between demands and concessions, supports and restraints, expectations and satisfaction, may produce a gradually evolving consensus. But such a balance is exceedingly difficult to achieve.

In the last analysis, it is the interplay between a great number of factors that accounts for the development of a consensual society, or for the failure of consensus to emerge. We have emphasized the relationship between mass and elite under conditions of economic modernization in order to illustrate the complexity of the phenomenon rather than to identify it as a single causal factor. For the very attitude of the elite—whether it is permissive and open or restrictive and negative—in turn depends upon many other historical and social factors. Common linguistic or religious bonds; prolonged community life behind natural barriers that deter attack or invasion; feelings of ethnic or racial identity; continuing economic progress; and the impact of technology and science upon the society are all factors that we subsumed earlier under the general terms of common values, predictability of behavior, and perception of common material benefits. It is only when these factors materialize at the proper time that the conditions for consensus also emerge, and that the Lockean model is relevant.

Consensus is always under stress, even in systems with a long tradition of legitimacy. Efforts to create an independent Quebec, the conflict between the Flemish and Walloons in Belgium, the appearance of a black power movement in the United States, are all threats to the basic consensus in previously stable systems. In these cases, dissidence stems from the conditions we have discussed—repressive or rejective measures by the elite and a relative inability to fulfill the demands for economic well-being aroused by the elites themselves and the ideology prevalent in the whole system. A theory of consensus therefore can be used to assess and to measure degrees of alienation, including the emergence of revolutionary situations.

The processes of socialization and politicization—whereby individuals are conditioned to accept their society and government—are of special importance in consensus building. No society can exist for long unless its norms are transmitted to the young. In early childhood the pattern of transmission is sheer habit. The young simply accept the behavior of their parents, on pain of discipline, identifying with their symbols and values. There can be no rational inquiry into the fundamental rules of the system. Within the entire educational establishment an overt effort is made to inculcate favorable attitudes toward the state. Through ceremony, ritual, and outright indoctrination, the young learn to cherish their national community and their political system. The manner in which national history is taught and the emphasis upon the unique and superior traits of the national culture are calculated to create an emotional acceptance of the political system.

Generally, the young begin to assume a critical attitude toward authority in secondary schools and universities. In many societies there is a tradition of unrest and political alienation among university students, though frequently radical students of middle class backgrounds tend to be absorbed readily into the system once they complete their studies and enter the job market. But revolutions can rarely, if ever, be traced to intergenerational strife. They stem rather from discontinuities in historical development, and basic divisions with the society that split the generations internally. In revolutionary situations consensus is already undermined. Disagreement about norms and symbols of authority is sharp, and the young are inducted into a system that is embroiled in conflict. The agencies of socialization, including the family, school, and church, speak with different tongues and cultivate contradictory ideas, involving the very nature and character of the system itself.

EFFECTIVENESS AND PERFORMANCE

All social groups have goals or purposes in terms of which their discipline is justified. The effectiveness of the organization—be it church, trade union, corporation, or state—must be appraised in relation to its success in achieving stated goals. An army, for example, has well defined goals: the application of superior firepower at a given point or, more broadly, defense of the country. An army is disciplined—command and obedience relations are established in unequivocal fashion, and criticism of its code is severely limited. It is an organization geared to performance, so that an order by a single chief moves masses of men and equipment. The efficiency of the "army model" accounts for widespread admiration of autocratic and authoritarian political systems, and constantly feeds the antidemocratic schools of thought. Lenin fashioned his theory of the Communist party after the army model, calling for rigorous discipline and total commitment of its members. His works are strewn with Napoleonic aphorisms. Many of the symbols of fascist and other authoritarian parties are borrowed from the military. Order, discipline, and unquestioning obedience are equated with performance and effectiveness.

The army is a single or limited purpose organization. Politics, on the other hand, entails regulation and control of a society that contains many organizations, each striving to attain unique and frequently divergent goals. The family, school, church, corporation, and university are concerned with such distinctly different activities as reproduction of the species, rearing of the young, education, religion, industrial production, and the acquisition of scientific knowledge. The state is not only a relationship of command and obedience; it also involves conciliation and supports. For example, throughout Europe in the nineteenth century new groups were being created in the course of industrialization, and sought entry into the political system. Complex societies are participant societies. The "army model" is relevant only to the coercive aspect of a political system.

As Karl Deutsch suggests, in his *Nerves of Government*,[1] a political system may be viewed as complex sets of messages within a communication system that has been learned and internalized by all members of the society. A structured and learned communication system makes the government a sensitive instrument for the satisfaction of demands and interests of the citizens, and also makes the citizens receptive to the needs and directives of the government. The government and citizens are mutually supportive.

The "communications model" is useful in analyzing performance. It points to the following: that obedience to commands is learned and willed; that the government is constantly listening to the messages that come from all social groups and individuals; that so long as official directives are generally consonant with demands and expectations they are likely to be obeyed—indeed, obedience is taken for granted; that if such a pattern of relations is established over a period of time the relationship between government and citizens will become intimate and positive, characterized by marked interdependence and mutual trust. The capabilities of the government to act are immense since it can count on popular support. It can mobilize the citizenry for common purposes.

But what are these common purposes? In terms of what criteria is the effectiveness of a political system to be appraised? Every political society sets for itself varying goals, both specific (such as the creation of the infrastructure of a modern economy) and broad (the realization of values like equality or freedom). Comparison of political systems in terms of performance is difficult. What is considered success in one society may be failure in another, since the goals or values may be entirely different. There are, however, some generally accepted ends to which all political systems are committed—the survival of their societies in a hostile world; the maintenance of order; the resolution of conflict-

---

[1] New York: The Free Press, 1966 (rev. ed.).

ing demands and the allocation of goods in a manner that provides maximum satisfaction for all. The system must be able to maintain itself as it adjusts to constantly changing environmental factors. It must resolve problems as they arise and provide mechanisms for settling them.

A consensual democratic system derives its strength from the open communication between state and society. It contains a responsive mechanism that permits the articulation of interests and demands on the part of the governed, gears its decisions to those demands, and, by so doing, elicits supports that can again be converted into a resource for the achievement of common ends. Emerging conflicts engage the attention of government and citizens so that the way is paved for their resolution. Broad participation in the system and the open nature of communications guarantee acceptance of policy, and help legitimize the state. A consensual system does not hesitate to arm the citizens, to draft them into the army, and to decree stringent measures calling for individual restraints in order to safeguard collective ends.

But, as we noted earlier, consensus is never universal in complex societies. The very openness of communications in democratic regimes permits dissident elements ample opportunity to clash with each other, and with the government. Indeed, dissidence may be so widespread that no majority can form, and the ability of the political system to formulate public policy is reduced. Nonconsensual democracies will tend to be ineffective in achieving socially accepted goals, or may even collapse altogether—as in Russia in October, 1917, Italy in 1922, and Germany in 1933.

Authoritarian regimes do not enjoy the advantages of an open communication system between leaders and the people. Since the citizens do not have the right to express their criticism, it is difficult for those in power to understand the nature of popular expectations, and to assess the effectiveness of policy. There is always a danger of solving political problems by violence, which includes popular uprisings as well as repression by the state. But some dictatorships have demonstrated a remarkable ability to mobilize popular energies and resources, and to promulgate effective policy. This requires exceptional dynamism and perspicacity on the part of the leaders, who in effect give the people what they want without going through the bother of inquiring beforehand or afterward. The citizens may be reasonably content, even if they have no opportunity to criticize, under conditions of full employment and material progress, and especially if the regime succeeds in embodying nationalistic sentiment. Military victory is also a good way of arousing popular enthusiasm for any regime, democratic or authoritarian. Popular support for authoritarian regimes is most likely in countries which have been governed previously by ineffective parliamentary democracies. It is noteworthy that the most important dictatorships in modern Europe—Bolshevism in Russia, fascism in Italy, and Nazism in Germany—all replaced nonconsensual and ineffective democracies.

The student will find that his analysis of any aspect of a given political system—such as the interest groups, parties, political institutions, administration, and ideologies—always leads him back to the critical question of consensus.

chapter III

THEORIES OF AUTHORITY

As has already been pointed out, every political system provides for the making of decisions which are widely obeyed. In order to inculcate obedience—which is essential to the maintenance of the state—authority is reinforced by a network of symbols, beliefs, and ideologies. In primitive societies the myth of supernatural right to rule is propagated by priests, medicine men, and other interpreters of tribal customs. Modern systems universally make use of symbols which evoke a favorable emotional response—flags, seals of office, uniforms, anthems, and so on. They also disseminate beliefs, through the schools and other institutions, which unify the society. Fundamentally, these beliefs *justify* the existing power structure. They legitimize the system.

Although all political systems seek to bring about universal acceptance of the values they embody, perhaps only those in very primitive societies are wholly successful. As societies evolve, the consensus upon which the regime rests becomes more complex. In industrial societies such groups as the capitalists, managers, workers, and scientists may begin to question the political values of the traditional system. Inevitably the pattern of legitimacy, or as Mosca puts it, the "political formula," is transformed. Myths of divine right and rule by heredity lose their hold upon intellectuals and ultimately the masses as well; they must be replaced by new values that accord a greater place (at least in principle) to the people. In the new scheme legitimacy derives from the electorate, or the class, or the nation, rather than from divinely ordained chiefs.

For analytic purposes it is useful to distinguish at least three levels of consensus or acceptance of the legitimating values of the political system. The most fundamental level is that of the national community itself. Are the major groups in the population agreed on the fact that they constitute a single political entity? All modern political systems have gone through, and some are still going through, a crisis of legitimacy regarding the nature of the national community. The process of nation building everywhere has been marked by controversy and violence. A second level of consensus concerns the regime, that is to say,

106

acceptance of the basic political institutions and the values they embody. This is quite different from the third level, or acceptance of the individuals who happen to be wielding power at any given time. In parliamentary democracies it is normal that a large minority, and occasionally even a majority of the electorate should oppose the government of the day. For example, in the general election of June 1970 the British Conservative party won a comfortable majority in the House of Commons with only 46 percent of the popular vote. Those who voted for the Labor and Liberal parties actually outnumbered the supporters of the victorious Conservative party. In authoritarian systems opposition to governments is expressed usually through apathy, occasionally through underground conspiracies. The important question is whether the opponents of a specific government also oppose the regime, or even the national community. This question should be posed at the very outset in the study of any political system. In parliamentary regimes the most reliable indicators of consensus are elections and public opinion surveys; in authoritarian regimes it is especially useful to focus attention on problems of succession, but the task of the student is far more difficult.

Thus, the values serving to legitimize a regime are a component part of that political system. It is necessary for the student first to understand the nature of these values, and then to determine to what extent the pattern of legitimacy is accepted by the population. For a general treatment of legitimacy the student is referred to the works of Gaetano Mosca and Robert M. MacIver, reproduced below, and to Charles E. Merriam, *Systematic Politics* (1945); Karl Loewenstein, *Political Power and the Governmental Process* (1957); Carl J. Friedrich, ed., *Authority* (1958); David Easton, *A Systems Analysis of Political Life* (1965); and Hannah Arendt, "Authority in the Twentieth Century," *Review of Politics* (October 1956).

8. The Political Formula*

GAETANO MOSCA

THE RULING CLASS

Among the constant facts and tendencies that are to be found in all political organisms, one is so obvious that it is apparent to the most casual eye. In all societies—from societies that are very meagerly developed and have barely attained the dawnings of civilization, down to the most advanced and powerful societies—

two classes of people appear—a class that rules and a class that is ruled. The first class, always the less numerous, performs all political functions, monopolizes power and enjoys the advantages that power brings, whereas the second, the more numerous class, is directed and controlled by the first, in a manner that is now more or less legal, now more or less arbitrary and violent, and supplies the first, in appearance at least, with material means of subsistence and with the instrumentalities that are essential to the vitality of the political organism.

In practical life we all recognize the existence of this ruling class (or political class, as we have elsewhere chosen to define it).[1] We all know that, in our own country, whichever it may be, the management of public affairs is in the hands of a minority of influential persons, to which management, willingly or unwillingly, the majority defer. We know that the same thing goes on in neighboring countries, and in fact we should be put to it to conceive of a real world otherwise organized—a world in which all men would be directly subject to a single person without relationships of superiority or subordination, or in which all men would share equally in the direction of political affairs. If we reason otherwise in theory, that is due partly to inveterate habits that we follow in our thinking and partly to the exaggerated importance that we attach to two political facts that loom far larger in appearance than they are in reality.

The first of these facts—and one has only to open one's eyes to see it—is that in every political organism there is one individual who is chief among the leaders of the ruling class as a whole and stands, as we say, at the helm of the state. That person is not always the person who holds supreme power according to law. At times, alongside of the hereditary king or emperor there is a prime minister or a major-domo who wields an actual power that is greater than the sovereign's. At other times, in place of the elected president the influential politician who has procured the president's election will govern. Under special circumstances there may be, instead of a single person, two or three who discharge the functions of supreme control.

The second fact, too, is readily discernible. Whatever the type of political organization, pressures arising from the discontent of the masses who are governed, from the passions by which they are swayed, exert a certain amount of influence on the policies of the ruling, the political, class.

But the man who is at the head of the state would certainly not be able to govern without the support of a numerous class to enforce respect for his orders and to have them carried out; and granting that he can make one individual, or indeed many individuals, in the ruling class feel the weight of his power, he certainly cannot be at odds with the class as a whole or do away with it. Even if that were possible, he would at once be forced to create another class, without the support of which action on his part would be completely paralyzed. On the other hand, granting that the discontent of the masses might succeed in deposing a ruling class, inevitably, as we shall later show, there would have to be another organized minority within the masses themselves to discharge the functions of a

[1] Mosca, *Teorica dei governi e governo parlamentare*, chap. I.

rūling class. Otherwise all organization, and the whole social structure would be destroyed.

*   *   *

THE POLITICAL FORMULA

. . . In fairly populous societies that have attained a certain level of civilization, ruling classes do not justify their power exclusively by de facto possession of it, but try to find a moral and legal basis for it, representing it as the logical and necessary consequence of doctrines and beliefs that are generally recognized and accepted. So if a society is deeply imbued with the Christian spirit the political class will govern by the will of the sovereign, who, in turn, will reign because he is God's anointed. So too in Mohammedan societies political authority is exercised directly in the name of the caliph, or vicar, of the Prophet, or in the name of someone who has received investiture, tacit or explicit, from the caliph. The Chinese mandarins ruled the state because they were supposed to be interpreters of the will of the Son of Heaven, who had received from heaven the mandate to govern paternally, and in accordance with the rules of the Confucian ethic, "the people of the hundred families." The complicated hierarchy of civil and military functionaries in the Roman Empire rested upon the will of the emperor, who, at least down to Diocletian's time, was assumed by a legal fiction to have received from the people a mandate to rule the commonwealth. The powers of all lawmakers, magistrates and government officials in the United States emanate directly or indirectly from the vote of the voters, which is held to be the expression of the sovereign will of the whole American people.

This legal and moral basis, or principle, on which the power of the political class rests, is what we have elsewhere called, and shall continue here to call, the "political formula." (Writers on the philosophy of law generally call it the "principle of sovereignty."[2]) The political formula can hardly be the same in two or more different societies; and fundamental or even notable similarities between two or more political formulas appear only where the peoples professing them have the same type of civilization (or—to use an expression which we shall shortly define—belong to the same social type). According to the level of civilization in the peoples among whom they are current, the various political formulas may be based either upon supernatural beliefs or upon concepts which, if they do not correspond to positive realities, at least appear to be rational. We shall not say that they correspond in either case to scientific truths. A conscientious observer would be obliged to confess that, if no one has ever seen the authentic document by which the Lord empowered certain privileged persons or families to rule his people on his behalf, neither can it be maintained that a popular election, however liberal the suffrage may be, is ordinarily the expression of the will of a people, or even of the will of the majority of a people.

---

[2] Mosca, *Teorica dei governi e governo parlamentare,* chap. I; see also Mosca, *Le costituzioni moderne.*

And yet that does not mean that political formulas are mere quackeries aptly invented to trick the masses into obedience. Anyone who viewed them in that light would fall into grave error. The truth is that they answer a real need in man's social nature; and this need, so universally felt, of governing and knowing that one is governed not on the basis of mere material or intellectual force, but on the basis of a moral principle, has beyond any doubt a practical and a real importance.

Spencer wrote that the divine right of kings was the great superstition of past ages, and that the divine right of elected assemblies is the great superstition of our present age. The idea cannot be called wholly mistaken, but certainly it does not consider or exhaust all aspects of the question. It is further necessary to see whether a society can hold together without one of these "great superstitions"— whether a universal illusion is not a social force that contributes powerfully to consolidating political organization and unifying peoples or even whole civilizations.

Mankind is divided into social groups each of which is set apart from other groups by beliefs, sentiments, habits and interests that are peculiar to it. The individuals who belong to one such group are held together by a consciousness of common brotherhood and held apart from other groups by passions and tendencies that are more or less antagonistic and mutually repellent. As we have already indicated, the political formula must be based upon the special beliefs and the strongest sentiments of the social group in which it is current, or at least upon the beliefs and sentiments of the particular portion of that group which holds political preeminence.

This phenomenon—the existence of social groups each of which has characteristics peculiar to itself and often presumes absolute superiority over other groups (the *boria nazionale,* the national conceit, that Vico talks about!)—has been recognized and studied by many writers, and particularly by modern scholars, in dealing with the principle of nationality. Gumplowicz, for instance, pointed to its importance in political science, or in sociology if you will. We should be quite ready to adopt the word that Gumplowicz uses to designate it— syngenism—did the term not imply, in conformity with the fundamental ideas of that writer, an almost absolute preponderance of the ethnological element, of community of blood and race, in the formation of each separate social group.[3] We do think that, in a number of primitive civilizations, not so much community of blood as a belief that such community existed—belief in a common ancestor, often arising, as Gumplowicz himself admits, after the social type had been formed—may have helped to cement group unities. But we also think that certain modern anthropological and philological doctrines have served to awaken between social groups and between fractions within one group antipathies that use racial differences as mere pretexts. Actually, moreover, in the formation of the group, or social type, many other elements besides a more or less certain racial affinity figure—for example, community of language, of religion, of interests,

[3] Gumplowicz, *Der Rassenkampf,* book II, chap. XXXVII.

and the recurring relationships that result from geographical situation. It is not necessary that all these factors be present at one and the same time, for community of history—a life that is lived for centuries in common, with identical or similar experiences, engendering similar moral and intellectual habits, similar passions and memories—often become the chief element in the development of a conscious social type.

Once such a type is formed, we get, to return to a metaphor which we have earlier used, a sort of crucible that fuses all individuals who enter it into a single alloy. Call it suggestion, call it imitation or mimetism, call it education pure and simple, it nevertheless comes about that a man feels, believes, loves, hates, according to the environment in which he lives. With exceedingly rare exceptions, we are Christians or Jews, Mohammedans or Buddhists, Frenchmen or Italians, for the simple reason that such were the people among whom we were born and bred.

*   *   *

UNITY AND SOCIAL CLASSES

Now we come to a social phenomenon that is less apparent to the eye but is perhaps more important. The case where several social types coexist in guises more or less masked within a single political organism may be noted in countries that present all the appearances of strong social unity. This situation arises whenever the political formula, on which the ruling class in a given society bases its dominion, is not accessible to the lower classes, or when the complex of beliefs and moral and philosophical principles that underlie the formula have not sunk deeply enough into the consciousness of the more populous and less well educated strata of society. The same thing occurs when there is any considerable difference between the customs, culture and habits of the ruling class and those of the governed classes. . . .

As a rule it is the very ancient political formulas, complexes of beliefs and sentiments which have the sanction of the ages, that succeed in making their way into the lowest strata of human societies. On the other hand, when rapid flows of ideas agitate the higher classes, or the more active intellectual centers, which are generally located in large cities, the lower classes and the outlying districts of a state are likely to be left behind, and differing social types tend to form inside the society.

Greater or lesser spiritual unity among all social classes explains the strength or weakness that political organisms exhibit at certain moments. However grievously the governing class in Turkey may have sinned on the side of corruption, inefficiency and negligence—army, navy, and finance were completely disorganized in the domains of the Sublime Porte—nevertheless, at certain definite moments, when the Crescent seemed to be in danger, the Turkish people displayed a fierce energy that gave pause to Europe's strongest military states. The reason was that the poor nizam, ragged and barefoot, who fearlessly went to his death in a trench, the redif who left his hut at the sultan's summons, really felt the political formula which they were called upon to serve and stood ready to give their last para and even their lives to support it. The Turkish peasants in Rumelia and Anatolia believed sincerely and deeply in Islam, in the Prophet, in the sultan as the Prophet's vicar, and the beliefs for which they were asked to make the utmost sacrifices were the beliefs that ordinarily filled their lives and made up their moral and intellectual worlds.

This analysis bears on events prior to 1895, yet we cannot see that they require any great modification in the light of the events of 1912–1913, or the events connected with the World War or the rise of Kemal Atatürk. The Turkish disasters in the Balkan and World Wars were due to the disorganization and incapacity of the Turkish ruling class, intensified by thirty years of Hamidian despotism and by four years of rule by the Young Turks. But in the World War, Kut-el-Amara showed that the Turkish soldier could fight and die for the faith that was in him; and we say nothing of the tremendous Turkish uprising of 1920 that overthrew the Treaty of Sèvres, [and] swept the Greeks from Asia Minor. . . .

In spite of the talents of men like Kutuzov, Barcley de Tolly, Benningsen, Doktorov and Bagration, no one can deny that the average training and capacity of the Russian generals with whom Napoleon had to deal was decidedly inferior to Austrian or Prussian standards. The famous Suvarov knew his Russian soldier well and had a way of leading him to the most daring enterprise. But Suvarov was after all a courageous leader rather than an able one. The Russian soldier was the adversary that Napoleon most feared. In the famous Moscow campaign the failure of the invading army was caused not so much by cold, hunger or desertion as by the hatred that gathered about the French and harried them from Vitebsk on—in other words, from the time they entered strictly Russian territory. It was this hatred that inspired the sinister fury of the Russians to the point of destroying all provisions along the path of the enemy and burning all towns and villages between Smolensk and Moscow. It gave Rostopchin the courage to burn Moscow itself. For the Russian muzhik God, the czar, Holy Russia, formed an integral unit in the beliefs and sentiments that he had begun to absorb on the day of his birth and which he had learned by home tradition to revere.

This same moral unity holds the secret of other successful and quasi-miraculous cases of resistance, just as lack of it yields the secret of certain shameful demonstrations of weakness. The Vendée was strong in the wars of the Revolution because nobles, priests and peasants had the same beliefs, the same desires, the same passions. Spain was strong in 1808 because the Spanish grandee and the lowliest Spanish shepherd were alike filled with hatred for the French invader (whom they regarded as a godless unbeliever), with loyalty to their sovereign, with pride in being a self-respecting, independent nation. This unanimity of sentiment, in spite of the incapacity of the Spanish generals and the utter worthlessness of the Spanish regular armies, accounts for the miracles of Saragossa and Tarragona and for the final victory that crowned the Spanish wars for independence. Never would the most ragged peasant consent, under whatever threat, to show the roads to the French. The regular Spanish army was composed largely of raw recruits and it had no experienced officers. Its ineffectualness is attested not only by French writers but by letters of the Duke of Wellington and other English officers. On the other hand, Spain showed the utmost weakness during the French Legitimist invasion of 1822. At that time only a small portion of the upper classes had any comprehension of, or devotion to, the principle of constitutional monarchy which was at issue. That principle was incomprehensible to the majority of the upper classes and to the vast bulk of the nation.

*   *   *

Class Isolation

Psychological and intellectual isolation on the part of the lower classes, as well as too noticeable differences in beliefs and education between the various social classes, give rise to social phenomena that are very interesting to the student of the political sciences, dangerous as they may be to the societies in which they occur.

In the first place, as a consequence of their isolation, within the lower classes another ruling class, or directing minority, necessarily forms, and often this new class is antagonistic to the class that holds possession of the legal government. When this class of plebeian leaders is well organized it may seriously embarrass an official government. In many Catholic countries the clergy is still the only authority that exerts any moral influence over the peasantry, and the peasants extend to the parish priest all the confidence that they withhold from the government official. In other countries, where the people look upon the public functionary and the nobleman if not exactly as enemies certainly as utter strangers, the more resolute and aggressive of the plebeians sometimes succeed in organizing widespread and fairly permanent associations, which levy assessments, administer a special justice of their own and have their own hierarchies of officials, their own leaders, their own recognized institutions. So a real state within the state comes into being, a government that is clandestine but often more feared, better obeyed, and if not better loved certainly better understood, than the legal government.

In the second place, whenever and wherever a section of the ruling class tries to overthrow the legal government, whether because of conversion to a new political formula or for some other reason, it always seeks the support of the lower classes, and these readily follow its lead when they are hostile or indifferent to the established order. This alliance is so often struck that the plebs becomes an essential instrument in almost all upheavals and revolutions, and to the same alliance also is due the fact that we so often find men from the higher social levels leading popular movements. Yet the opposite phenomenon also appears at times. The portion of the ruling class that is holding power and resisting the revolutionary current may find its main support in the lower classes, which still cling loyally to old ideas and to the old social type. That was the situation in Spain in 1822 and down to 1830, and so it was with the Kingdom of Naples in 1799 and more or less down to 1860. In such cases there may be periods of government by an ignorant, inept and vulgar demagoguery which someone thought of defining as "the negation of God."

But the most dangerous among the consequences that may result from differences in social type between the various social classes, and from the reciprocal isolation of classes that necessarily follows in their wake, is a decline in energy in the upper classes, which grow poorer and poorer in bold and aggressive characters and richer and richer in "soft," remissive individuals. We have seen that that development is practically impossible in a state of the feudal type. In a society that is broken up into virtually independent fragments the heads of the individual groups have to be energetic, resourceful men. Their supremacy in large measure depends on their own physical or moral strength, which, moreover, they are continually exercising in struggles with their immediate neighbors. As social organization progresses and the governing class begins to reap the benefits of an improved bureaucratic machine, its superiority in culture and wealth, and especially its better organization and firmer cohesion, may compensate to some extent for the lack of individual energy; and so it may come about that considerable portions of the governing class, especially the circles that give the society its intellectual tone and direction, lose the habit of dealing with people of the lower classes and commanding them directly. This state of affairs generally enables frivolousness, and a sort of culture that is wholly abstract and conventional, to supplant a vivid sense of realities and a sound and accurate knowledge of human nature. Thinking loses virility. Sentimental and exaggeratedly humanitarian theories come to the fore, theories that proclaim the innate goodness of men, especially when they are not spoiled by civilization, or theories that uphold the absolute preferableness, in the arts of government, of gentle and persuasive means to severe authoritarian measures. . . .

. . . In the course of the last two centuries, many philosophers have raised paeans to the holiness of savage morals and to the rustic simplicity of the plain, untutored man. It would seem therefore that there is a frequent, if not a universal, tendency in very mature civilizations, where ruling classes have acquired highly refined literary cultures, to wax enthusiastic, by a sort of antithesis, over the simple ways of savages, barbarians and peasants (the case of Arcadia!), and to clothe them with all sorts of virtues and sentiments that are as stereotyped as they are imaginary. Invariably underlying all such tendencies is the concept that was so aptly phrased by Rousseau, that man is good by nature but spoiled by society and civilization. This notion has had a very great influence on political thinking during the past hundred years.

A ruling class is the more prone to fall into errors of this kind the more closed it is, actually if not legally, to elements rising from the lower classes. In the lower classes the hard necessities of life, the unending and carking scramble for bread, the lack of literary culture, keep the primordial instincts of struggle and the unfailing ruggedness of human nature, alive. In any case, whether or not the factor of intellectual and moral isolation is reinforced by this factor of, so to say, personal isolation, certain it is that when the ruling class has degenerated in the manner described, it loses its ability to provide against its own dangers and against those of the society that has the misfortune to be guided by it. So the state crashes at the first appreciable shock from the outside foe. Those who govern are unable to deal with the least flurry; and the changes that a strong and intelligent ruling class would have carried out at a negligible cost in wealth, blood and human dignity take on the proportions of a social cataclysm. . . .

9. The Myth of Authority*

ROBERT M. MAC IVER

MYTH AND SOCIETY

We have pointed out that all social relations—the whole texture and the very being of society—are myth-sustained, and that all changes of the social structure are mothered and nurtured by appropriate new myths. Myth is the all-pervading atmosphere of society, the air it breathes. One great function of myth is to turn valuations into propositions about the nature of things. These propositions range from cosmogonies interpreting the whole universe to statements about what will happen to an individual if he violates the tribal code. The forms and kinds of myth are endless, but at the core of every myth-structure lies the myth of authority.

Myth always postulates a fact relative to a value. In this way it ratifies values, attaching them to reality. The kind of attachment depends on the cultural level of the folk and on the extent of the knowledge of the evidential linkage between phenomena that we call science.

Thus we find myth at every level of rationality. On the lowest level the myth is, in a sense, without content. The nexus between value and postulated fact is unrationalized. This is the character of taboo. If before the start of a trading expedition you have sexual relations with a woman the voyage will end in disaster. If you eat of the totem animal of your group you will go mad or your flesh will break out into boils, or something else dreadful will happen to you. Often the consequence of violating the taboo is unspecified, but there is always a hazard, none the less formidable for being undefined. Sometimes there is a technique for avoiding the curse, sometimes there is not. This is the field of the medicine man. There are no intermediary links offered between the act and the doom. We are in the realm of *magic*. This form of myth, unrationalized by any reference to a causal principle, whether natural or supernatural, includes the belief in sorcery, witchcraft, the "evil eye," and numerous other occult operations bringing sometimes good but more frequently evil upon those at whom they are directed. It is the level of childhood belief. And it is the level upon which in turn children are so often instructed, when they are told this is right and that is wrong, this is proper and that is improper, without any explanation of the grounds that justify the admonition.

The myth still remains on the primitive level, essentially without content, when the ground offered is the mere alleged will or interposition of some supernatural power. This is right because God says so. This is wrong because God forbids it. If you do this God will punish you. And so forth. Such pronouncements are only one step beyond the magical formula: if you do this something dreadful will happen. It is still unrationalized prescription and so far has no ethical content. It prepares the way, however, for the transition from magic to religion, because the appeal to God has implicit in it the conception of an ethical scheme.

*   *   *

To pursue this theme would carry us beyond our present intention, which is to show that social myth, the myth that presides over human relationships, pervades every type and stage of society, gaining more content and more rationalization in the more advanced forms. Social myth at every level enjoins some kind of order among men, and enshrines that order in a context of value-impregnated lore and legend, in tradition and in philosophy. With the aid of authority the myth-conveyed scheme of values determines the social order. Hence the central myth in the maintenance of any social system is the myth of authority.

INSTITUTIONALIZATION OF THE CENTRAL MYTH

The sense of the social order as controlling the behavior of human beings, since it is not fully instinct-governed as with the ants and bees, requires the establishment of social sanctions to secure it against the strains and pulls of contrary impulses. In the very simplest societies, where the community is a group of nearly autonomous, nearly self-sufficient families and where the conduct of each is within the perspective of all, there may be no need for any further sanctions than those that depend on the immediate reaction of the folk against the violator of custom, of the "customary law." But the further we move from the simplicity of this situation the more do we find the confirmation of authority by institutional devices of increasing formality.

The routinized respect for age or ancestry or skill or prowess confers authority on individuals so that they are presumed to speak for or to represent the folk, to embody its spirit or its virtue. This personal authority may have little or no paraphernalia of office. But when the person becomes the instituted chief, especially when the line of chieftainship is established by heredity or otherwise, authority gains a new dimension. Now the person in authority is set further apart from his fellow men. He undergoes the equivalent of sanctification. He cannot be approached as a person among other persons, differing perhaps in degree. Now as the embodiment of authority he differs in kind. Some peoples carry the process further than do others. But the tendency exists everywhere. Authority is thus safeguarded, stabilized, removed in a measure from the competition for power.

This result, this sanctification of authority, is attained in two closely related ways, through the elaboration of the lore, the accredited body of myths, and through the elaboration of the institutional structure.

The lore takes endlessly variant shape with different peoples, but in all shapes it tends to magnify the office of chief or king. Obviously the lore has greater opportunity when the governing head is a single person than when there is a ruling council with no markedly pre-eminent suzerain. In the latter case authority cannot enjoy the same sanctity of apartness and cannot be endowed with the simpler magic. It must depend more largely instead on institutional devices. With the single chief, the "monarch," the process is very different, especially if he is hereditary. Then he becomes of other clay than his fellows. He is cast in a higher mold. He is, like the Homeric chief, the offspring of heroes or of Gods; or, like the Japanese emperor, the veritable son of heaven. The history of the folk revolves about the glorious deeds of his ancestors. All the virtues of these ancestors are again incarnated in him. The "divinity" that "doth hedge a king" pervades the lore not only of many primitive peoples but also of higher cultures, such as those of Babylonia, Persia, and ancient Egypt, and it was accepted still in seventeenth-century Europe, in nineteenth-century Russia, and in twentieth-century Japan. These attributions seemed to give the rulers a completely tyrannical power over their peoples, but there were in the last resort various safety devices that limited this danger.

The lore promotes and is in turn corroborated by the development of appropriate institutions. The ruler becomes the center of a ceremonial order, inculcating the difference between him and other men. He is addressed in a special way, under honorific titles. Ceremony maintains his apartness, draws invisible lines of sanctity before his presence. He becomes the bestower of title and dignity on other men, the fountainhead of honor. He is thus the apex of a class system as well as of a power system. Wealth also goes with honor, so that it becomes the strong interest of all dominant groups and classes to enhance established authority. Thus all the social forces that are, as we shall see, the historical bulwarks of authority, status and power, converge to ratify and stabilize the pre-eminent position of the headship of the state. They all contribute to the elaboration of the institutional devices that promote this end.

We may pause here to consider the peculiar efficacy of the institutional props of authority. Let us take, for example, the influence of ceremonial forms, at first appearance the most merely ornamental and the least utilitarian elements of an institutional scheme. Ceremony conveys, under appropriate conditions, an almost ineluctable impression of the high and enduring worth of that which it enshrines. It does so by suggesting the superior dignity of the person and the order of things that cannot be treated in the casual manner of everyday behavior, that demand the formality of the stiff back and the bended knee. It is all very well for a satiric writer, like Thomas Carlyle, to make fun of the "philosophy of clothes," the dress and pomp of ceremonial occasion, but there remains an element of truth in the maxim of his Teufelsdröckh, that "society is founded upon cloth." The investiture and the insignia of authority are characteristic of society at all stages and in all civilizations. Symbols may be more convincing than any logic, for they cannot be refuted. Contrary doctrines can arise against the lore, against the established indoctrinations, but they cannot control the minds of the mass of men, the many whose beliefs are determined not by speculation but by habituation, until they clothe themselves in new insignia, in symbols accessible to all.

Ceremony has another no less important aspect. It keeps ordinary men at a respectful distance from authority. To approach anything—or anyone—in a ceremonial way is to treat that thing as though it occupied a level higher than yours. However near you approach you still stand below it. Hence every solemn occasion employs ceremony, and every religion has its rites; the more ceremonious it is, the more it inculcates the majesty of God. Likewise the state is a great dispenser of ceremony, in the treatment of its flag and other symbols, in its law courts, in its elaboration of a "protocol" system, and above all in the usages designed for all events and activities in which the head of the state participates. The intention and broadly the effect of these ceremonial observances is to inculcate attitudes congenial to the prevailing myth of authority.

But ceremony is merely the sign attached to institutions, intimating that authority resides in them. It is not attached to all institutions, and perhaps least to the immediately operative institutions of the political order. All institutions, whether dignified by ceremony or not, tend to implant in men a sense of the authority that maintains them. Since the state is the guardian and maintainer, at least in a formal sense, of all social institutions the might of its authority is omnipresent. Whatever men do, whatever they strive for, predicates under normal conditions the existing frame of institutions. Our dependence on institutions becomes identified with our dependence on authority, and the value we attach to institutions is reflected in our respect for authority.

In the more sophisticated society we may distinguish between respect for the personal qualities of the ruling group and respect for the large body of institutions they preside over. We may, at times, have little regard for "politicians" and much regard for the system, including the form of government. But for the less sophisticated, and especially in the simpler societies, no such distinction is easily drawn. And even the most abstract philosopher is apt to confound the two.

*　　　*　　　*

The whole institutional order tends to confirm the authority of those who rule within it, not only because the value attached to institutions is reflected upon the authority-holder but also because the authority-holder is concerned to guard the myth that elevates his own power and accordingly operates the institutions themselves so as to check any assault upon them, to subordinate or discourage all opposing claims, and to assure the favorable indoctrination of those who are schooled under the prevailing system. The rigor of this control is mitigated under democratic conditions, since democracy rests on the premises that opinions shall have free vogue and that authority is derived from the people. In this way it achieves for men one important liberation—it enables them to dissociate, in degree at least, the value of the institution from the judgment they may pass on the functionaries of that institution. The extreme opposite holds under modern dictatorship, which maintains the most rigorous monopoly of the expression of opinion, sheltering its particular myth of authority against all overt criticism. Under these conditions the institution and the authority are so ultimately bound together that their fate must be a common one. If either fails, the other fails with it.

Here we reach an issue that demands special consideration. Not only under democratic conditions, but wherever modern industrial civilization extends, the nature of authority undergoes a transformation. A modern society, with its complexity of organization, becomes a multi-group society. It possesses no longer the homogeneity of culture that has pervaded former types of society, even when they were sharply divided by class and caste. There is no longer one religion, one scale of values, one pervasive indoctrination. A multi-group society is a multi-myth society. Its appropriate form of government can be based only on some form of myth that accommodates conflicting myths, and as we shall later see that condition is met by the myth of democracy. What kind of authority is consistent with this development? How can essential authority, the guardian of ordered society, be still assured?

TRANSFORMATION OF THE CENTRAL MYTH

In the simpler societies, where the socio-economic organization is less complex, the institutions of a community, so long as they are not imposed from without, are in broad accord with its *mores.* There is one pervasive and relatively coherent system of *mores* and there is a corresponding system of institutional controls. There is one system of beliefs, one system of values, and whatever divergencies arise are merely in the form of special cults or of heresies, special developments or variant interpretations of the established myths. The prevailing *mores* are reaffirmed in every aspect of life, in the arts and crafts, in the modes of economic behavior, in family relationships, in the rites and recreations of the folk. The religious aura that surrounds the *mores* gives them a finality, a supremacy, that imposes its inexorable compulsion upon the members of the folk. Even if the community has a rigid separation of classes or castes it does not mean that the separate orders have separate mythologies. On the contrary, the caste system is possible only on the assumption that there is a universally accepted code of values, but one that assigns grades of sanctity, of participation and of exclusion, to the different categories of the total folk, as prescribed by the central myth itself.

This community-wide synthesis of doctrines and institutions is broken in the complex civilization, especially in the modern multi-group society with its numerous specializations of interest and of cultural affiliation. The mobility of individuals and groups and the increased facility of communications within and beyond the large-scale national unities combine with the increased specialization of function to promote diversities of loyalty that are not attached to the communal institution and may be alien to or at strife with the traditional and originally universal loyalties that the communal institutions maintain.

These diverse loyalties compete and fight for control of the communal institutions. For example, the institutional establishment protects and inculcates a particular religion. But new religions and new sects gain hold and there is war between them and the establishment. In modern western society this strife of religious groups drove the first great wedge into the cracking unity of community and culture.

The next breach in the traditional and spontaneous "totalitarianism" of earlier society was made by the forces of economic specialization. Industrial and technological advances created many foci of opposing interests, competing or bargaining for advantage one against the other, and at the same time many relatively detached centers of economic and political power. Here was something utterly uncongenial to the feudalistic condition in which land was the only economic attribute conferring—locally, regionally, and nationally—power and status. The surge and thrust of these new forces brought about the open market for success in which, and later for dominance over which, the opposing interests fought. No authority, it was claimed, was needed to regulate the open market— the only business of authority was to leave it alone, to refrain from meddling with an order that regulated itself by the very nature of things, or at most to ensure that it remained open and free. . . .

Our purpose here is to show the crumbling, in many areas of modern industrial civilization, of the old bases of authority. We do not imply that under other conditions such as those of late fifth-century Athens or of first-century (B.C.) Rome an equally drastic transformation did not occur. Still less do we imply that the transformation precluded the re-establishment of authority on new bases or that it signified in the longer run any inevitable dissolution of society itself. We are concerned with the process as revealing a change of values, not as an eclipse of values. When old values are lost new values may be in the making. How to establish an ethical scale, to assess the one against the other, is not here the question. That some new values were achieved can hardly be disputed. In this upthrust of individualism and rationalism there was a dislodgement of old abuses and exploitations of authority, hitherto sheltered by tradition. There was a purification of dogmatic and irrational elements in the former myths. There was a challenge to the sheerly extrinsic and superficial titles to superiority inherent in old class systems. There was a release from the cheap unscientific ideas, alike of human nature and of the world it inhabited, inherent in many old orthodoxies. Most of all, there was some liberation of the human mind from the taboos against its search for what truth it can discover, against free inquiry in the realm of values as well as in the realm of knowledge.

At the same time the need for a new basis of authority was evident enough, and there were many social phenomena that gave ground for the fears of the conservatives. The fragmentation ethics of group interests could not bind a society together. The detachment of individuals and of groups in the competitive struggle and the preoccupation with the means of material success weakened the sense of the larger and more universal relationships between men. The marvelous advances of technology led many to devote themselves to it to the exclusion of more cultural devotions, and thus also the unifying influences of society were diminished. For technology lives on the thin edge of the contemporary, without contemplation of future or of past. The loss of the sense of integrating relationships was evidenced in the rise of theories of the state that interpreted it either as a mere mechanism of protection or insurance or as a mere instrument of class exploitation or as a neutral apparatus of control for the possession of which organized interests fought an eternally fluctuating fight or as itself one of a plurality of diverse vast organizations, one syndicate among many in a world of final "anomie." These otherwise most dissimilar doctrines were alike in this, that they denied or rejected the integrating function of the state. It may not be fanciful to see a reflection of the same attitude, the denial of the unity in things, in various philosophical expressions of recent times, for example in psychological and sociological positivism, with its dislike of synthesis, its emphasis on the person as detached organism, its insistence on specific measurable "facts," the atomic components of knowledge, and its disregard of the relationships between them, which are neither, in that sense, "facts" nor yet measurable by its techniques of research.

In the realm of practical politics the dissolution of the bases of authority was evidenced by a phenomenon that had appeared on previous occasions, from the time of the Greek "tyrants," when old values were challenged and new values were confused—the rise to the highest power of men neither sanctified by tradition nor dignified by principle, but ruthless or cunning opportunists who violently seized their hour, men without scruples and without goals. To this category Napoleon belonged, and various lesser Caesars who flourished briefly after the First World War. On another level the same phenomenon manifested itself in the United States, in the dominance of city bosses, in the revival of Ku Klux Klan leadership in Indiana and in the South, and in the ascendancy of Huey Long in Louisiana, perhaps the most threatening of a number of similar occurrences.

It seems, however, that the people must always seek some unity, some whole to which they belong. If the old bases of authority were challenged or destroyed, there were many who yearned to find new ones and there were still many who sought to re-establish the old ones. The conservative reaction could scarcely by itself succeed against the currents of social change, though in the turmoils and grave unsettlements that followed the First World War it was able to regain ascendancy in some countries, such as Spain, certain East European countries, and Japan. In countries where the ferment of socio-economic change had worked more deeply, where traditional authority had suffered more complete eclipse the prophets of the people envisioned other goals. Some forsook the cultural ground of unity and found the answer in a politico-economic transformation. They would destroy division and recreate unity by reclaiming the economic arena, abolishing capitalism with its exploitations and its warring interests, and setting in its place some system of collectivism. Others, taking more primitive ground, wanted to rebuild the old authoritarianism by the ruthless suppression of differences, making the myth of nationality supreme, holding the indoctrinated masses by monopolistic control over all the means of communication and converting all the agencies of the community into the instruments of the dictatorial state. This was the line of fascism in all its forms.

. . . [These developments] had in their various forms of realization the mortal defect that they rejected the difference-breeding processes inherent in modern civilization and found no source of authority except through the usurping and precarious power that arrogated to itself the supreme right to crush what it would not reconcile. None of them met or faced the genuine problem, the old problem with which on another level philosophy had always wrestled, the problem which presented itself wherever society expanded, and above all wherever men gained new freedoms or new horizons, the problem of unity in diversity. Whatever triumphs they might achieve, taking the opportunities offered in times of crisis or of despair, they could not be expected to endure. The myths they proclaimed were hastily developed and crudely magnified; tested by time they gave a hollow sound. Beneath the imposed surface of unity differences grew again and waited their turn. If a lasting solution were to be found it had to meet the conditions and the needs of the age. A new ground of authority was indeed imperative, but it had to be sought along another road.

chapter IV

MODERN DEMOCRACY

In all political systems there is an attempt to justify rule in terms of political values. One of these pervasive values in the modern world is parliamentary democracy. That is, regimes are considered legitimate because they derive their powers from the consent of the governed. Although the exact meaning of democracy has always been a matter of controversy, there is a large area of agreement among such commentators as Max Weber, A. D. Lindsay, Robert MacIver, Joseph Schumpeter, and Walter Lippmann. The distinctiveness of democracy is that the people can choose and change their government. The role of the public is to intervene from time to time in order to decide which set of leaders shall be vested with the state power. Democracy cannot exist unless it establishes basic civil liberties (freedom of speech, freedom of the press, freedom of criticism) through which the people are able to express their views for or against policies and leaders. The right to criticize, if it is to be effective, must include the right to *organize* opposition. The dominant Western view of democracy is thus *procedural*. It is characterized by free elections, free expression, and free parties. The existence of these procedures serves to legitimize the actions of the state in the eyes of the citizenry.

As in all political systems, whether traditional or modern, democratic or authoritarian, one question to be asked by the student is to what extent democratic values are accepted by the population. Some parliamentary democracies have been stable for a long period of time, and the values of parliamentarism are held in high repute. All major political parties in such countries as Great Britain, the United States, Holland, Sweden, Denmark, Switzerland, and Australia accept the principles of parliamentarism. This does not mean that consensus is perfect or universal. One task of the analyst is to assess the importance of such groups as Irish nationalists in Britain, Black Panthers in the United States, and Communists and Fascists everywhere. In many other parliamentary democracies the values of free discussion, free criticism, and representative government are widely questioned. In such countries as France, Italy, and Finland, political parties that

123

repudiate fundamental tenets of parliamentary democracy are able to win massive popular support. The student of legitimacy in modern democracies should first distinguish among the stable and unstable political systems, and then seek to identify the factors which might account for lack of consensus on democratic values. Is acceptance of the democratic pattern of legitimacy correlated with economic prosperity, high rates of literacy, and rapid economic development? What other factors might be relevant?

Among the leading works on democratic theory are: A. D. Lindsay, *The Modern Democratic State* (1943); Robert M. MacIver, *The Web of Government* (1947); Joseph A. Schumpeter, *Capitalism, Socialism and Democracy* (1947); Walter Lippmann, *The Public Philosophy* (1955); Carl J. Friedrich, *Constitutional Government and Democracy* (1950); Giovanni Sartori, *Democratic Theory* (1965); and Robert A. Dahl, *Political Oppositions in Western Democracies* (1966).

10. Some Social Requisites of Democracy*

SEYMOUR M. LIPSET

The conditions associated with the existence and stability of democratic society have been a leading concern of political philosophy. In this paper the problem is attacked from a sociological and behavioral standpoint, by presenting a number of hypotheses concerning some social requisites for democracy, and by discussing some of the data available to test these hypotheses. In its concern with conditions—values, social institutions, historical events—external to the political system itself which sustain different general types of political systems, the paper moves outside the generally recognized province of political sociology. This growing field has dealt largely with the internal analysis of organizations with political goals, or with the determinants of action *within* various political institutions, such as parties, government agencies, or the electoral process. It has in the main left to the political philosopher the larger concern with the relations of the total political system to society as a whole.

INTRODUCTION

A sociological analysis of any pattern of behavior, whether referring to a small or a large social system, must result in specific hypotheses, empirically

*From "Some Social Requisites of Democracy: Economic Development and Political Legitimacy," *American Political Science Review,* vol. LIII, no. 1 (March 1959). By permission.

testable statements. Thus, in dealing with democracy, one must be able to point to a set of conditions that have actually existed in a number of countries, and say: democracy has emerged out of these conditions, and has become stabilized because of certain supporting institutions and values, as well as because of its own internal self-maintaining processes. The conditions listed must be ones which differentiate most democratic states from most others. . . .

Clearly in order to discuss democracy, or any other phenomenon, it is first necessary to define it. For the purposes of this paper, democracy (in a complex society) is defined as a political system which supplies regular constitutional opportunities for changing the governing officials. It is a social mechanism for the resolution of the problem of societal decision-making among conflicting interest groups which permits the largest possible part of the population to influence these decisions through their ability to choose among alternative contenders for political office. In large measure abstracted from the work of Joseph Schumpeter and Max Weber,[1] this definition implies a number of specific conditions: (a) a "political formula," a system of beliefs, legitimizing the democratic system and specifying the institutions—parties, a free press, and so forth—which are legitimized, i.e., accepted as proper by all; (b) one set of political leaders in office; and (c) one or more sets of leaders, out of office, who act as a legitimate opposition attempting to gain office.

The need for these conditions is clear. *First,* if a political system is not characterized by a value system allowing the peaceful "play" of power—the adherence by the "outs" to decisions made by "ins" and the recognition by "ins" of the rights of the "outs"—there can be no stable democracy. This has been the problem faced by many Latin American states. *Second,* if the outcome of the political game is not the periodic awarding of effective authority to one group, a party or stable coalition, then unstable and irresponsible government rather than democracy will result. This state of affairs existed in pre-Fascist Italy, and for much, though not all of the history of the Third and Fourth French Republics, which were characterized by weak coalition governments, often formed among parties which had major interest and value conflicts with each other. *Third,* if the conditions facilitating the perpetuation of an effective opposition do not exist, then the authority of officials will be maximized, and popular influence on policy will be at a minimum. This is the situation in all one-party states; and by general agreement, at least in the West, these are dictatorships. . . .

No detailed examination of the political history of individual countries will be undertaken in accordance with the generic definition, since the relative degree or social content of democracy in different countries is not the real problem of this paper. Certain problems of method in the handling of relationships between complex characteristics of total societies do merit brief discussion, however.

An extremely high correlation between aspects of social structure, such as income, education, religion, on the one hand, and democracy, on the other, is

[1] Joseph Schumpeter, *Capitalism, Socialism and Democracy* (New York: Harper and Bros., 1947), pp. 232–302, esp. 269; Max Weber, *Essays in Sociology* (New York: Oxford University Press, 1946), p. 226.

not to be anticipated even on theoretical grounds, because to the extent that the political subsystem of the society operates autonomously, a particular political form may persist under conditions normally adverse to the *emergence* of that form. Or, a political form may develop because of a syndrome of fairly unique historical factors, even though major social characteristics favor another form. Germany is an example of a nation in which the structural changes—growing industrialization, urbanization, wealth, and education—all favored the establishment of a democratic system, but in which a series of adverse historical events prevented democracy from securing legitimacy in the eyes of many important segments of society, and thus weakened German democracy's ability to withstand crisis.

The high correlations which appear in the data to be presented between democracy and other institutional characteristics of societies must not be overly stressed, since unique events may account for *either* the persistence *or* the failure of democracy in any particular society. Max Weber argued strongly that differences in national patterns often reflect key historical events which set one process in motion in one country, and a second process in another. To illustrate his point, he used the analogy of a dice game in which each time the dice came up with a certain number they were increasingly loaded in the direction of coming up with that number again.[2] To Weber, an event predisposing a country toward democracy sets a process in motion which increases the likelihood that at the next critical point in the country's history democracy will win out again. This process can only have meaning if we assume that once established, a democratic political system gathers some momentum, and creates some social supports (institutions) to ensure its continued existence. Thus a "premature" democracy which survives will do so by (among other things) facilitating the growth of other conditions conducive to democracy, such as universal literacy, or autonomous private associations. This paper is primarily concerned with explicating the social conditions which serve to *support* a democratic political system, such as education or legitimacy; it will not deal in detail with the kinds of internal mechanisms which serve to *maintain* democratic systems such as the specific rules of the political game.

Comparative generalizations dealing with complex social systems must necessarily deal rather summarily with particular historical features of any one society within the scope of the investigation. In order to test these generalizations bearing on the differences between countries which rank high or low in possession of the attributes associated with democracy, it is necessary to establish some empirical measures of the type of political system. Individual deviations from a particular aspect of democracy are not too important, as long as the definitions unambiguously cover the great majority of nations which are located as democratic or undemocratic. The precise dividing line between "more democratic" and "less democratic" is also not a basic problem, since presumably

<hr/>

[2] Max Weber, *The Methodology of the Social Sciences* (Glencoe, Ill.: The Free Press, 1949), pp. 182–85; see also S. M. Lipset, "A Sociologist Looks at History," *Pacific Sociological Review*, vol. 1 (Spring 1958), pp. 13–17.

democracy is *not* a quality of a social system which either does or does not exist, but is rather a complex of characteristics which may be ranked in many different ways. For this reason it was decided to divide the countries under consideration into two groups, rather than to attempt to rank them from highest to lowest. Ranking *individual* countries from the most to the least democratic is much more difficult than splitting the countries into two classes, "more" or "less" democratic, although even here borderline cases such as Mexico pose problems.

Efforts to classify all countries raise a number of problems. Most countries which lack an enduring tradition of political democracy lie in the traditionally underdeveloped sections of the world. It is possible that Max Weber was right when he suggested that modern democracy in its clearest forms can only occur under the unique conditions of capitalist industrialization. Some of the complications introduced by the sharp variations in political practices in different parts of the earth can be reduced by dealing with differences among countries within political culture areas. The two best areas for such internal comparison are Latin America as one, and Europe and the English-speaking countries as the other. More limited comparisons may be made among the Asian states, and among the Arab countries.

The main criteria used in this paper to locate European democracies are the uninterrupted continuation of political democracy since World War I, *and* the absence over the past 25 years of a major political movement opposed to the democratic "rules of the game."[3] The somewhat less stringent criterion employed for Latin America is whether a given country has had a history of more or less free elections for most of the post-World War I period. Where in Europe we look for stable democracies, in South America we look for countries which have not had fairly constant dictatorial rule (See Table 1). No detailed analysis of the political history of either Europe or Latin America has been made with an eye toward more specific criteria of differentiation; at this point in the examination of the requisites of democracy, election results are sufficient to locate the European countries, and the judgments of experts and impressionistic assessments based on fairly well-known facts of political history will suffice for Latin America. . . .[4]

---

[3] The latter requirement means that no totalitarian movement, either Fascist or Communist, received 20 per cent of the vote during this time. Actually all the European nations falling on the democratic side of the continuum had totalitarian movements which secured less than seven per cent of the vote.

[4] The historian Arthur P. Whitaker, for example, has summarized the judgments of experts on Latin America to be that "the countries which have approximated most closely to the democratic ideal have been . . . Argentina, Brazil, Chile, Colombia, Costa Rica, and Uruguay." See "The Pathology of Democracy in Latin America: A Historian's Point of View," *American Political Science Review,* vol. 44 (1950), pp. 101–18. To this group I have added Mexico. Mexico has allowed freedom of the press, of assembly and of organization, to opposition parties, although there is good evidence that it does not allow them the opportunity to win elections, since ballots are counted by the incumbents. The existence of opposition groups, contested elections, and adjustments among the various factions of the governing *Partido Revolucionario Institucional* does introduce a considerable element of popular influence in the system. . . .

TABLE 1

**Classification of European, English-Speaking and Latin American Nations
by Degree of Stable Democracy**

European and English-Speaking Nations		Latin American Nations	
Stable Democracies	*Unstable Democracies and Dictatorships*	*Democracies and Unstable Dictatorships*	*Stable Dictatorships*
Australia	Austria	Argentina	Bolivia
Belgium	Bulgaria	Brazil	Cuba
Canada	Czechoslovakia	Chile	Dominican Republic
Denmark	Finland	Columbia	Ecuador
Ireland	France	Costa Rica	El Salvador
Luxemburg	Germany (West)	Mexico	Guatemala
Netherlands	Greece	Uruguay	Haiti
New Zealand	Hungary		Honduras
Norway	Iceland		Nicaragua
Sweden	Italy		Panama
Switzerland	Poland		Paraguay
United Kingdom	Portugal		Peru
United States	Rumania		Venezuela
	Spain		
	Yugoslavia		

[Professor Lipset's discussion of economic development and democracy is omitted—Eds.]

It is obvious that democracy and the conditions related to stable democracy are essentially located in the countries of northwest Europe and their English-speaking offspring in America and Australasia. It has been argued by Max Weber among others that the factors making for democracy in this area are a historically unique concatenation of elements, part of the complex which also produced capitalism in this area. The basic argument runs that capitalist economic development (facilitated and most developed in Protestant areas) created the burgher class whose existence was both a catalyst and a necessary condition for democracy. The emphasis within Protestantism on individual responsibility furthered the emergence of democratic values. The greater initial strength of the middle classes in these countries resulted in an alignment between burghers and throne, an alignment which preserved the monarchy, and thus facilitated the legitimation of democracy among the conservative strata. Thus we have an interrelated cluster of economic development, Protestantism, monarchy, gradual political change, legitimacy and democracy. Men may argue as to whether any aspect of this cluster is primary, but the cluster of factors and forces hangs together.

LEGITIMACY AND DEMOCRACY

In this section I turn to an examination of some of the requisites of democracy which are derived from specifically historical elements in this complex, particularly those which relate to the need of a democratic political system for legitimacy, and for mechanisms which reduce the intensity of political cleavage. These requisites are correlated with economic development, but are also distinct from it since they are elements in the political system itself.

Legitimacy and Effectiveness.   In the modern world . . . economic development involving industrialization, urbanization, high educational standards, and a steady increase in the overall wealth of the society, is a basic condition sustaining democracy; it is a mark of the efficiency of the total system.

But the stability of a given democratic system depends not only on the system's efficiency in modernization, but also upon the *effectiveness* and *legitimacy* of the political system. By effectiveness is meant the actual performance of a political system, the extent to which it satisfies the basic functions of government as defined by the expectations of most members of a society, and the expectations of powerful groups within it which might threaten the system, such as the armed forces. The effectiveness of a democratic political system, marked by an efficient bureaucracy and decision-making system, which is able to resolve political problems, can be distinguished from the efficiency of the total system, although breakdown in the functioning of the society as a whole will, of course, affect the political sub-system. Legitimacy involves the capacity of a political system to engender and maintain the belief that existing political institutions are the most appropriate or proper ones for the society. The extent to which contemporary democratic political systems are legitimate depends in large measure upon the ways in which the key issues which have historically divided the society have been resolved. It is the task of these sections of the paper to show *first,* how the degree of legitimacy of a democratic system may affect its capacity to survive the crises of effectiveness, such as depressions or lost wars and *second,* to indicate the ways in which the different resolutions of basic historical cleavages—which determine the legitimacy of various systems— also strengthen or weaken democracy through their effect on contemporary party struggles.

While effectiveness is primarily an instrumental dimension, legitimacy is more affective and evaluative. Groups will regard a political system as legitimate or illegitimate according to the way in which its values fit in with their primary values. Important segments of the German army, civil service, and aristocratic classes rejected the Weimar Republic not because it was ineffective, but because its symbolism and basic values negated their own. Legitimacy, in and of itself, may be associated with many forms of political organization, including oppressive ones. Feudal societies, before the advent of industrialism, undoubtedly enjoyed the basic loyalty of most of their members. Crises of legitimacy are primarily a recent historical phenomenon, following the rise of sharp cleavages among groups which have been able, because of mass communication resources, to organize around different values than those previously considered to be the only legitimate ones for the total society.

A crisis of legitimacy is a crisis of change, and therefore its roots, as a factor affecting the stability of democratic systems, must be sought in the character of change in modern society. It may be hypothesized that crises of legitimacy occur during a transition to a new social structure, if (a) all major groups do not secure access to the political system early in the transitional period, or at least as soon as they develop political demands; or, if (b) the *status* of major conservative institutions is threatened during the period of structural change. After a new social structure is established, if the new system is unable to sustain the expectations of major groups (on the grounds of "effectiveness") for a long enough period to develop legitimacy upon the new basis, a new crisis may develop.

Tocqueville gave a graphic description of the first general type of loss of legitimacy, referring mainly to countries which had moved from aristocratic monarchies to democratic republics: ". . . epochs sometimes occur in the life of a nation when the old customs of a people are changed, public morality is destroyed, religious belief shaken, and the spell of tradition broken. . . ." The citizens then have "neither the instinctive patriotism of a monarchy nor the reflecting patriotism of a republic; . . . they have stopped between the two in the midst of confusion and distress."

If, however, the status of major conservative groups and symbols is not threatened during this transitional period even though they lose most of their power, democracy seems to be much more secure. Striking evidence of the link between the preserved legitimacy of conservative institutions and democracy is the relationship between monarchy and democracy. Given the role of the American and French republican revolutions as the initiators of modern democratic political movements, the fact that 10 out of 12 of the stable European and English-speaking democracies are monarchies seems a rather ludicrous correlation. Great Britain, Sweden, Norway, Denmark, the Netherlands, Belgium, Luxemburg, Australia, Canada, and New Zealand are kingdoms; while the only republics which meet the twin conditions, of stable democratic procedures since democracy was instituted, and the absence of major totalitarian movement in the past 25 years, are the United States, Switzerland and Uruguay. Nations which have moved from absolutism and oligarchy (linked to a state church) to a democratic welfare state, while retaining the forms of monarchy, more frequently seem able to make changes while sustaining a continuous thread of legitimacy for their political institutions.[5]

The preservation of the monarchy has apparently retained for the system the loyalty of the aristocratic, traditionalist, and clerical sectors of the population which resented increased democratization and equalitarianism. And, by more graciously accepting the lower strata, by not resisting to the point that revolution might be necessary, the conservative orders won or retained the loyalty of the new "citizens." Where monarchy was overthrown by revolution, and orderly succession was broken, those forces aligned with monarchy have sometimes continued to refuse legitimacy to republican successors down to the fifth generation or more.

[5] Walter Lippmann, referring to the seemingly greater capacity of the constitutional monarchies than the republics of Europe to "preserve order with freedom," suggests that this may be because "in a republic the governing power, being wholly secularized, loses much of its prestige; it is stripped, if one prefers, of all the illusions of intrinsic majesty." See his *The Public Philosophy* (New York: Mentor Books, 1956), p. 50.

The one constitutional monarchy which became a Fascist dictatorship, Italy, was, like the French Republic, relatively new and still illegitimate for major groups in the society. The House of Savoy alienated the Catholics by destroying the temporal power of the Poles, and was also not a legitimate successor in the old Kingdom of the Two Sicilies. Catholics, in fact, were forbidden by the church to participate in Italian politics until close to World War I, and the church rescinded its original ban only because of its fear of the Socialists. A similar attitude was taken by French Catholics to the Third Republic during the same period. Both Italian and French democracy have had to operate for much of their histories without loyal support from important groups in their society, both on the left and on the right. Thus, one main source of legitimacy lies in the continuity of primary conservative and integrative institutions during a transitional period in which new social institutions are emerging.

The second general type of loss of legitimacy is, as indicated above, related to the way in which societies handle the "entry into politics" problem. The determination of when new social groups shall obtain access to the political process affects the legitimacy of the political system, either for conservative or for emerging groups. In the 19th century these new groups were primarily industrial workers; the "entry into politics" crisis of the 20th century typically involves colonial elites, and peasant peoples. Whenever new groups become politically active (e.g., when the workers first seek access to economic and political power through economic organization and the suffrage, when the bourgeoisie demanded access to and participation in government, when colonial elites demand control over their own system), comparatively easy access to the legitimate political institutions tends to win the loyalty of the new groups to the system, and they in turn can permit the old dominating strata to maintain their own status integrity. In nations such as Germany, where access was denied for prolonged periods, first to the bourgeoisie and later to the workers, and where force was used to restrict access, the lower strata were alienated from the system, and were led to adopt extremist ideologies which, in turn, alienated the more established groups from an acceptance of the workers' political movement as a legitimate alternative.

Political systems which denied new strata access to power except through revolutionary means also inhibited the growth of legitimacy by introducing millenial hopes into the political arena. Groups which feel obligated to push their way into the body politic through forceful means tend to overexaggerate the possibilities which political participation affords. Their hopes are for far more than the inherent limitations of political stability permit. Consequently, democratic regimes born under such stress will not only face the difficulty of being regarded as illegitimate by those groups loyal to the ancien regime, but may be also rejected by those whose millenial hopes were not fulfilled by the change. France seems to offer an example of such a phenomenon. Right-wing clericalists have viewed the Republic as illegitimate, while sections of the lower strata still impatiently await millenial fulfillment. Many of the newly independent nations of Asia and Africa face the problem of winning the loyalties of the masses to democratic states which can do little to fulfill the utopian objectives set by nationalist movements during the period of colonialism, and the transitional struggle to independence.

We have discussed several conditions bearing upon the maintenance, or the initial securing of legitimacy by a political system. Assuming reasonable effectiveness, if the status of major conservative groups is threatened, or if access to the political system is denied at crucial periods, the legitimacy of the system will remain in question. Even in legitimate systems, a breakdown of effectiveness, repeatedly or for a long period, will endanger its stability.

A major test of legitimacy is the extent to which given nations have developed a common "secular political culture," national rituals and holidays which serve to maintain the legitimacy of various democratic practices.[6] The United States has developed a common homogeneous secular political culture as reflected in the veneration and consensus surrounding the Founding Fathers, Jefferson, Lincoln, Theodore Roosevelt and their principles. These common elements to which all American politicians appeal are not present in all democratic societies. In some European countries, the Left and the Right have a different set of symbols, and different historical political heroes. France offers the clearest example of a nation which has not developed such a common heritage. Thus many of the battles involving use of different symbols between the left and the right from 1789 down through much of the 19th century are "still in progress, and the issue is still open; everyone of these dates [of major political controversy] still divides left and right, clerical and anti-clerical, progressive and reactionary, in all their historically determined constellations."[7]

As we have seen, nations may vary in the extent to which their political institutions are viewed as legitimate by different strata. And knowledge concerning the relative degree of legitimacy of a nation's political institutions is of key importance in every effort to analyze the stability of these institutions when faced with a crisis of effectiveness. The relationship between different degrees of legitimacy and effectiveness in specific political systems may be more graphically presented in the form of a fourfold table, with examples of countries characterized by the various possible combinations.

EFFECTIVENESS

	+	−
+	A	B
−	C	D

LEGITIMACY

Societies which fall in box A, those which are high on the scales of both legitimacy and effectiveness, will clearly have stable political systems. Nations like the United States, Sweden, and Britain satisfy the basic political needs of

---

[6] See Gabriel Almond, "Comparative Political Systems," *Journal of Politics* (1956) [reproduced above, chap. I, reading 3].

[7] Herbert Luethy, *The State of France* (London: Secker and Warburg, 1955), p. 29.

their citizens, have efficient bureaucracies and political decision-making systems, possess traditional legitimacy through long-term continuity of the key symbols of sovereignty, the monarchy or constitution, and do not contain any important minorities whose basic values run counter to those of the system.[8] Ineffective and illegitimate regimes, those which would be found in box D, must, of course, by definition be unstable and break down, unless they are dictatorships main- raining themselves by force such as the governments of Hungary and eastern Germany today. The political experiences of different countries in the early 1930's illustrate the effect of varying combinations of legitimacy and effective- ness. In the late 1920's, neither the German nor the Austrian republics were held legitimate by large and powerful segments of their populations, but never- theless remained reasonably effective. In the fourfold table, they fell in box C.

When the effectiveness of the governments of the various countries broke down in the 1930's, those societies which were high on the scale of legitimacy remained democratic, while countries which were low such as Germany, Austria, and Spain, lost their freedom, and France narrowly escaped a similar fate. Or to put the changes in terms of location in the fourfold table, countries which shifted from A to B remained democratic, while the political systems of those which shifted from C to D broke down. It remained for the military defeat in 1940 to prove conclusively the low position of French democracy on the scale of legitimacy. It was the sole defeated democracy which furnished large-scale support for a Quisling regime.[9]

Situations such as those discussed above in which either legitimacy or effec- tiveness is high while the other is low demonstrate the utility of this type of analysis. From a short-range point of view, a highly effective but illegitimate system, such as a well governed colony, is more unstable than regimes which are relatively low in effectiveness and high in legitimacy. The social stability of a nation such as Thailand—even with its occasional *coups d'états*—stands out in sharp contrast to the situation in the neighboring former colonial nations of Southeast Asia. The link between the analysis of legitimacy and the earlier dis- cussion of the contribution of economic development to democracy is evident in the processes through which regimes low in legitimacy may gain it, and con-

[8] The race problem in the American South does constitute one basic challenge to the legitimacy of the system, and at one time did cause a breakdown of the national order. The conflict reduces the commitment of many white Southerners to the democratic rules down to the present. Great Britain had a comparable problem as long as Catholic Ireland remained part of the United Kingdom. Effective government could not satisfy Ireland. Political prac- tices by both sides in Northern Ireland, Ulster, also illustrate the problem of a regime which is not legitimate to a large segment of its population.

[9] The French legitimacy problem is well described by Katherine Munro: "The Right wing parties never quite forgot the possibility of a counter revolution while the Left wing parties revived the Revolution militant in their Marxism or Communism; each side suspected the other of using the Republic to achieve its own ends and of being loyal only so far as it suited it. This suspicion threatened time and time again to make the Republic unworkable, since it led to obstruction in both the political and the economic sphere, and difficulties of govern- ment in turn undermined confidence in the regime and its rulers." Quoted in Charles A. Micaud, "French Political Parties: Ideological Myths and Social Realities," in Sigmund Neumann, ed., *Modern Political Parties* (Chicago: University of Chicago Press, 1956), p. 108.

versely in those which are related to the collapse of a legitimate system. Prolonged effectiveness which lasts over a number of generations may give legitimacy to a political system; in the modern world, such effectiveness mainly means constant economic development. Thus those nations which adapted most successfully to the requirements of an industrial system had the fewest internal political strains, and either preserved their traditional legitimacy, the monarchy, or developed new strong symbols of legitimacy.

The social and economic structure which Latin America inherited from the Iberian peninsula prevented it from following the lead of the former English colonies, and its republics never developed the symbols and aura of legitimacy. In large measure, the survival of the new political democracies of Asia and Africa is related to their ability to sustain a prolonged period of effectiveness, of being able to meet the defined instrumental needs of their populations.

Legitimacy and Cleavage.   Prolonged effectiveness of the system as a whole may, as in the cases of the United States and Switzerland, eventually legitimate the democratic political system. Inherent, however, in all democratic systems is the constant threat that the conflicts among different groups which are the life-blood of the system may crystallize to the point where societal disintegration is threatened. Hence, conditions which serve to moderate the intensity of partisan battle, in addition to effectiveness, are among the key requisites for a democratic political system.

Since the existence of a moderate state of conflict is an inherent aspect of a legitimate democratic system, and is in fact another way of defining it, we should not be surprised that the principal factors determining such an optimum state are closely linked to those which produce legitimacy viewed in terms of continuities of symbols and status. Essentially the character and content of the major cleavages affecting the political stability of a society are largely determined by historical factors which have affected the way in which major issues dividing society have been solved or left unresolved over time.

In modern times, three major issues have emerged in western states. The first was the religious issue: the place of the church and/or various religions within the nation. The second has been the problem of the admission of the lower strata, particularly the workers, to "citizenship," the establishment of access to power through universal suffrage, and the legitimate right to bargain collectively in the economic sphere. The third has been the continual struggle over the distribution of the national income.

The significant general question here is this: were these major issues dealt with one by one, and each one more or less solved before the next arose, or did the problems accumulate, so that historical issues and sources of cleavage mixed with newer ones? Resolving tensions one at a time contributes toward a stable political system; carrying over issues from one historical period to another makes for a political atmosphere characterized by bitterness and frustration rather than by tolerance and compromise. Men and parties come to differ with each other, not simply on ways of settling current problems, but rather by fundamental and opposed *weltanschauungen.* They come to see the political victory of their opponents as a major moral threat; and the total system, as a result, lacks effective value-integration.

The religious issue, the place of the church in the society, was fought through and solved in most of the Protestant nations in the 18th and 19th centuries, and ceased to be a matter for serious political controversy. In some states, such as the United States, the church was disestablished and it accepted this result. In others, such as Britain, Scandinavia, and Switzerland, religion remains state-supported, but the state churches, like constitutional monarchs, have only nominal sway and have ceased to be major sources of controversy. It remains for the Catholic countries of Europe to provide us with examples of situations in which the historic controversy between clerical and anti-clerical forces, sparked by the French Revolution, has continued to divide men politically down to the present day. Thus in countries such as France, Italy, Spain, and Austria, being Catholic has meant being allied with rightist or conservative groups in politics; while being anti-clerical (or a member of a minority religion) has most often meant alliance with the left. In a number of these countries, newer issues, when they emerged, became superimposed on the religious question; and for conservative Catholics, the fight against Socialists was not simply an economic struggle, or a controversy over social institutions, but a deep-rooted conflict between God and Satan, between good and evil.[10] For many secular intellectuals in contemporary Italy, opposition to the church legitimates alliance with the Communists. As long as religious ties reinforce secular political alignments, the chances for democratic give-and-take, and compromise, are weak.

The "citizenship" or "political equality" issue has also been resolved in various ways. Thus the United States and Britain gave citizenship to the workers in the early or mid-nineteenth century. Sweden and a number of European nations resisted through the beginning of the 20th century, and the struggle for citizenship became combined in these countries with socialism as a *political* movement, thereby producing a revolutionary socialism. Or to put this in other terms, where the workers were denied economic and political citizenship rights, their struggle for redistribution of income and status was superimposed on a

---

[10] The linkage between democratic instability and Catholicism may also be accounted for by elements inherent in Catholicism as a religious system. Democracy requires a universalistic political belief system in the sense that it legitimates different ideologies. And it might be assumed that religious value systems which are more universalistic in the sense of placing less stress on being the only true church will be more compatible with democracy than those which assume that they have the only truth. The latter belief, held much more strongly by the Catholic than by most other Christian churches, makes it difficult for the religious value system to help legitimate a political system which requires, as part of its basic value system, the belief that "good" is served best through conflict among opposing beliefs.

Kingsley Davis has argued that a Catholic state church tends to be irreconcilable with democracy since "Catholicism attempts to control so many aspects of life, to encourage so much fixity of status and submission to authority, and to remain so independent of secular authority that it invariably clashes with the liberalism, individualism, freedom, mobility and sovereignty of the democratic nation." See his "Political Ambivalence in Latin America," *Journal of Legal and Political Sociology,* vol. 1 (1943), reprinted in Christensen, *The Evolution of Latin American Government* (New York, 1951), p. 240.

revolutionary ideology. Where the economic and status struggle developed outside this context, the ideology with which it was linked tended to be that of gradualist reformism. In Hohenzollern Germany, for example, the workers were denied a free and equal suffrage in Prussia until the revolution of 1918. This denial of "citizenship" facilitated the retention of revolutionary Marxism in those parts of Germany where equal suffrage did not exist. In Southern Germany, where full citizenship rights were granted in the late 19th century, reformist, democratic, and nonrevolutionary socialism was dominant. The perpetuation of revolutionary dogmas in much of the Social Democratic party served to give ultra-leftists a voice in party leadership, enabled the Communists to win strength after the military defeat, and perhaps even more important historically, served to frighten large sections of the German middle classes. The latter feared that a Socialist victory would really mean an end to all their privileges and status.

In France, the workers won the suffrage but were refused basic economic rights until after World War II. Major groups of French employers denied legitimacy to the French trade unions, and sought to weaken or destroy them following every trade-union victory. The inability of the French unions, their constant need to preserve worker militancy to survive, gave access to the workers to the more revolutionary and extremist political groups. Communist domination of the French labor movement can in large part be traced to the tactics of the French business classes.

The examples presented above do not explain why different countries varied in the way they handled basic national cleavages. They should suffice, however, to illustrate the worth of a hypothesis relating the conditions for stable democratic government to the bases of diversity. Where a number of historic cleavages intermix and create the basis for *weltanschauung* politics, the democracy will be unstable and weak, for by definition such political views do not include the concept of tolerance. . . .

The intense forms of cleavage developed by that cumulation of unresolved issues which creates *weltanschauung* politics is sustained by the systematic segregation of different strata of the population in organized political or religious enclaves. Conversely, however, it should be noted that wherever the social structure operates so as naturally to "isolate" individuals or groups with the same political disposition characteristics from contact with differing views, those so isolated tend to back political extremists.

It has been repeatedly remarked, for example, that workers in so-called "isolated" industries, miners, sailors, fishermen, lumbermen, sheeptenders, and longshoremen, tend to give overwhelming support to the more left-wing tendencies. Such districts tend to vote Communist or Socialist by large majorities, sometimes to the point of having what is essentially a "one-party" system in the areas concerned. Isolation is created by the fact that the requirements of the job make workers in these industries live in communities which are predominantly inhabited by others in the same occupation. And this very isolation seems to reduce the pressures on such workers to be tolerant of other points of view, to contain among themselves diverse strains of thought; and makes them receptive to extremist versions of the doctrine generally held by other less isolated members of their class. One should expect that the least "cosmopolitan" (the most isolated) of every political predisposition, or stratum, will be the ones most likely to accept extremism. The political intolerance of farm-based groups in times of crisis may be another illustration of this pattern, since farmers, like workers in isolated industries, tend to have a more homogeneous political environment than do those employed in most urban occupations. . . .

A stable democracy requires relatively moderate tension among the contending political forces. And political moderation is facilitated by the capacity of a system to resolve key dividing issues before new ones arise. To the extent that the cleavages of religion, citizenship, and "collective bargaining" have been allowed to cumulate and reinforce each other as stimulants of partisan hostility, the system is weakened. The more reinforced and correlated the sources of cleavage, the less the likelihood for political tolerance. Similarly, on the level of group and individual behavior, the greater the isolation from heterogeneous political stimuli, the more that background factors "pile up" in one direction, the greater the chances that the group or individual will have an extremist perspective. These two relationships, one on the level of partisan issues, the other on the nature of party support, are linked together by the fact that parties reflecting accumulated unresolved issues will seek to isolate their followers from conflicting stimuli, to prevent exposure to "error," while isolated individuals and groups will strengthen the intolerant tendencies in the political party system. The conditions maximizing political cosmopolitanism among the electorate are the growth of urbanization, education, communications media, and increased wealth. Most of the obvious isolated occupations, mining, lumbering, agriculture, belong to the category of "primary" occupations, occupations whose relative share of the labor force declines sharply with economic development.

Thus, we see again how the factors involved in modernization or economic development are linked closely to those involved in the historic institutionalization of the values of legitimacy and tolerance. But it should always be noted that correlations are only statements concerning relative degrees of congruence, and that another condition for political action is that the correlation never be so clear-cut that men cannot feel that they can change the direction of affairs by their actions. And this fact of low correlation means also that it is important for analytic purposes to keep variables distinct even if they intercorrelate. For example, the analysis of cleavage presented here suggests specific propositions concerning the ways in which different electoral and constitutional arrangements may affect the chances for democracy. These generalizations are presented in the following section.

SYSTEMS OF GOVERNMENT AND DEMOCRACY

From the hypothesis that cross-cutting bases of cleavage are better for the vitality of democracy, it follows that two-party systems are better than multiparty systems, that electoral systems involving the election of officials on a territorial basis are preferable to systems of proportional representation, and that federalism is superior to a unitary state. In evaluating these propositions, it is important to note again that they are made with the assumption of all other factors being held constant. Clearly, stable democracies are compatible with multi-party systems, with proportional representation, and with a unitary state. And in fact, I would argue that such variations in systems of government, while significant, are much less important than those derived from basic differences in social structure of the sort discussed in the previous sections.

The argument for the two-party system rests on the assumptions that in a complex society, such parties must necessarily be broad coalitions; that they cannot seek to serve only the interests of one major group; that they cannot be parties of integration; and that in building electoral coalitions, they necessarily antagonize support among those most committed to them, and conversely must seek to win support among groups which are preponderantly allied to the opposition party. Thus, the British Conservative or American Republican parties must not so act as to antagonize basically the manual workers, since a large part of the vote must come from them. The Democratic and Labor parties are faced with a similar problem *vis-à-vis* the middle strata. Parties which are never oriented toward gaining a majority seek to maximize their electoral support from a limited base. Thus a peasant-oriented party will accentuate peasant group interest consciousness, and a party appealing primarily to small businessmen will do the same for its group. Elections, instead of being occasions on which parties seek to find the broadest possible base of support, and so to bring divergent groups to see their common interests, become events in which parties stress the cleavages separating their principal supporters from other groupings.

The proposition that proportional representation weakens rather than strengthens democracy rests on the analysis of the differences between multi-party and majority party situations. If it is true, as is suggested above, that "multi-partyness" serves to sharpen differences and reduce consensus, then any electoral system which increases the chance for more rather than fewer parties serves democracy badly.

Further, . . . the system of electing members of parliament to represent territorial constituencies, as contrasted with systems which encourage direct group representation (such as proportional representation), is preferable, since territorial representation helps to stabilize the political systems by forcing interest groups to secure their ends only within an electoral framework that involves some concern with many interests and the need for compromise.

Federalism serves to strengthen democracy by increasing the opportunity for multiple sources of cleavage. It adds regional interests and values to the others such as class, religion and ethnicity which cross-cut the social structure.

A major exception to this generalization occurs when federalism divides the country according to lines of basic cleavage, *e.g.,* between different ethnic, religious, or linguistic areas. In such cases, as in India or in Canada, federalism may then serve to accentuate and reinforce cleavages. Cleavage is desirable within linguistic or religious groups, not between them. But where such divisions do not exist, then federalism seems to serve democracy well. Besides creating a further source of cruss-cutting cleavage, it also serves various functions which Tocqueville noted it shared with strong voluntary associations. Among these, it is the source of resistance to centralization of power and a source of training of new political leaders; and it gives the "out" party a stake in the system as a whole, since national "out" parties usually continue to control some units of the system.

Let me repeat that I do not suggest that these aspects of the political structure as such are key conditions for democratic systems. If the underlying social conditions are such as to facilitate democracy, as seems true for Sweden, then the combination of multi-partyness, proportional representation, and a unitary state, do not seriously weaken it. At most they serve to permit irresponsible minorities to gain a foothold in parliament. On the other hand, where a low level of effectiveness and of legitimacy has operated to weaken the foundations of democracy as occurred in Weimar Germany, or in France, then constitutional factors encouraging multi-partyness serve to reduce the chances that the system will survive.

PROBLEMS OF CONTEMPORARY DEMOCRACY

The characteristic pattern of the stable western democracies in the mid-20th century is that of a "post-politics" phase—there is relatively little difference between the democratic left and right, the socialists are moderates, and the conservatives accept the welfare state. In large measure this reflects the fact that in these countries the workers have won their fight for citizenship and for political access, i.e., the right to take part in all decisions of the body politic on an equal level with others.[11]

The struggle for citizenship had two aspects, political (access to power through the suffrage) and economic (institutionalization of trade union rights to share in the decisions affecting work rewards and conditions). The representatives of the lower strata are now part of the governing classes, members of the club. Political controversy has declined in the wealthier stable democracies because the basic political issue of the industrial revolution, the incorporation of the workers into the legitimate body politic, has been settled. The only key domestic issue today is collective bargaining over differences in the division of the total product within the framework of a Keynesian welfare state; and such issues do not require or precipitate extremism on either side.

In most of Latin and Eastern Europe, the struggle for working-class integration

[11] T. H. Marshall has analyzed the gradual process of incorporation of the working class into the body politic in the 19th century, and has seen that process as the achievement of a "basic human equality, associated with full community membership, which is not inconsistent with a superstructure of economic inequality." See his brief but brilliant book, *Citizenship and Social Class* (Cambridge University Press, 1950), p. 77. Even though universal citizenship opens the way for the challenging of remaining social inequalities, it also provides a basis for believing that the process of social change toward equality will remain within the boundaries of allowable conflict in a democratic system.

into the body politic was not settled before the Communists appeared on the scene to take over leadership of the workers. This fact drastically changed the political game, since inherently the Communists could not be absorbed within the system in the way that the Socialists have been. Communist workers, their parties and trade unions, cannot possibly be accorded the right of access by a democratic society. The Communists' self-image and more particularly their ties to the Soviet Union lead them to accept a self-confirming prophecy. Their self-definition prevents them from being allowed access and this in turn reinforces the sense of alienation from the system (of not being accepted by the other strata) which workers in nations with large Communist parties have. And the more conservative strata are reinforced in their belief that giving increased rights to the workers or their representatives threatens all that is good in life. Thus, the presence of Communists precludes an easy prediction that economic development will stabilize democracy in these European countries.

In the newly independent nations of Asia, the situation is somewhat different. In Europe at the beginning of modern politics, the workers were faced with the problem of winning citizenship, the right to take part in the political game, from the dominant aristocratic and business strata who controlled politics. In Asia, the long-term presence of colonial rulers has identified conservatism as an ideology and the more well-to-do classes with subservience to colonialism; while leftist ideologies, usually of a Marxist variety, have been dominant, being identified with nationalism. The trade unions and the workers' parties of Asia have been part of the political process from the beginning of the democratic system. Conceivably such a situation could mean a stable democracy, except for the fact that these lower-strata rights pre-date the development of a stable economy with a large middle class and an industrial society.

The whole system stands on its head. The left in the European stable democracies grew gradually in a fight for more democracy, and gave expression to the discontents involved in early industrialization, while the right retained the support of traditionalist elements in the society, until eventually the system came into an easy balance between a modified left and right. In Asia, the left is in power during the period of population explosion and early industrialization, and must accept responsibility for all the consequent miseries. As in the poorer areas of Europe, the Communists exist to capitalize on all these discontents in completely irresponsible fashion, and currently are a major party, usually the second largest in most Asian states.

Given the existence of poverty-stricken masses, low levels of education, an elongated pyramid class structure, and the "premature" triumph of the democratic left, the prognosis for the perpetuation of political democracy in Asia and Africa is bleak. The nations which have the best prospects, Israel, Japan, Lebanon, the Philippines and Turkey, tend to resemble Europe in one or more major factors, high educational level (all except Turkey), substantial and growing middle class, and the retention of political legitimacy by non-leftist groups. The other emerging national states in Asia and Africa are committed more deeply to a certain tempo and pattern of economic development and to national independence, under whatever political form, than they are to the pattern of party politics and free elections which exemplify our model of democracy. It seems likely that in countries which avoid Communist or military dictatorship political developments will follow the pattern developing in countries such as Ghana, Tunisia or Mexico, where an educated minority uses a mass movement expressing leftist slogans to exercise effective control, and holds elections as a gesture toward ultimate democratic objectives, and as a means of estimating public opinion, not as effective instruments for legitimate turnover in office of governing parties. Given the pressure for rapid industrialization and for the immediate solution of chronic problems of poverty and famine through political agencies, it is unlikely that many of the new governments of Asia and Africa will be characterized by an open party system representing basically different class positions and values.

Latin America, underdeveloped economically like Asia, is, however, politically more like Europe in the early 19th century than like Asia today. Most Latin American countries became independent states before the rise of industrialism and Marxist ideologies, and contain strongholds of traditional conservatism. The countryside is often apolitical or traditional, and the leftist movements secure support primarily from the industrial proletariat. Latin American communists, for example, have chosen the European Marxist path of organizing urban workers, rather than the "Yenan way" of Mao, seeking a peasant base. If Latin America is allowed to develop on its own, and is able to increase its productivity and middle classes, there is a good chance that many Latin American countries will follow in the European direction. Recent developments, including the overthrowal of a number of dictatorships, in large measure reflect the effects of an increased middle class, growing wealth, and increased education. There is, however, also the possibility that these countries may yet follow in the French and Italian direction rather than that of northern Europe, that the communists will seize the leadership of the workers, and that the middle class will be alienated from democracy.

The analysis of the social requisites for democracy contained in this paper has sought to identify some, though obviously far from all, of the structural conditions which are linked to this political system. It has been possible in a very limited fashion to attempt some tests of the hypotheses suggested. These preliminary efforts to apply the method of science to comparative political systems can still be considered only as illustrative since we can say so little about actual variations in national social structures. Considerably more research must be done specifying the boundaries of various societies along many dimensions before reliable comparative analysis of the sort attempted here can be carried out. Although the task obviously presents tremendous difficulties, it is only through such methods that we can move beyond the conventional semi-literary methods of giving illustrative examples to support plausible interpretations.

The data available are, however, of a sufficiently consistent character to support strongly the conclusion that a more systematic and up-to-date version of Aristotle's hypothesis concerning the relationship of political forms to social structure is valid. Unfortunately, as has been indicated above, this conclusion does not justify the optimistic liberal's hope that an increase in wealth, in the size of the middle class, in education, and other related factors will necessarily mean the spread of democracy or the stabilizing of democracy. As Max Weber, in discussing the chances for democracy in Russia in the early 20th century pointed out: "The spread of Western cultural and capitalist economy did not, *ipso facto*, guarantee that Russia would also acquire the liberties which had accompanied their emergence in European history. . . . European liberty had been born in unique, perhaps unrepeatable, circumstances at a time when the intellectual and material conditions for it were exceptionally propitious."[12]

These suggestions that the peculiar concatenation of factors which gave rise to western democracy in the nineteenth century may be unique are not meant to be unduly pessimistic. Political democracy exists and has existed in a variety of circumstances, even if it is most commonly sustained by a limited cluster of conditions. To understand more fully the various conditions under which it has existed may make possible the development of democracy elsewhere. Democracy is not achieved by acts of will alone; but men's wills, through action, can shape institutions and events in directions that reduce or increase the chance for the development and survival of democracy. To aid men's actions in furthering democracy was in some measure Tocqueville's purpose in studying the operation of American democracy, and it remains perhaps the most important substantive intellectual task which students of politics can still set before themselves.

[12] Richard Pipes, "Max Weber and Russia," *World Politics,* vol. 7 (1955), p. 383.

11. An Assessment of Democracy*

ROBERT A. DAHL

To one who believes in the essential worth of a democratic polity, how much opposition is desirable, and what kinds? What is the best balance between consensus and dissent? Even among democrats there is not much agreement on the answers to these questions.

It is easy to see why. These questions seem to demand nothing less than a complicated assessment of democracy itself. Or to put the matter more precisely, one can judge the desirability of different patterns of political opposition only by employing a number of different criteria that would be used if one were

*From "Reflections on Opposition in Western Democracies," *Government and Opposition,* vol. 1, no. 1 (November 1965), pp. 7–24. Reprinted by permission of the author and the journal. This study is an extract from *Political Oppositions in Western Democracies.* Copyright © 1966 by Yale University.

appraising the extent to which a political system as a whole achieves what are usually considered democratic goals or values.

Eight of these standards seem directly relevant in judging different patterns of opposition. In comparison with other possible arrangements, one might ask, to what extent does a particular pattern maximize:

1. Liberty of thought and expression, including opportunities for dissenting minorities to make their views known to other citizens and policy-makers?

2. Opportunities for citizens to participate in political life?

3. When political conflicts occur, control over the decisions of government by majorities (rather than minorities) of citizens, voters, and elected officials?

4. Rationality in political discussion and decision-making, in the sense of increasing understanding by citizens and leaders of the goals involved and the appropriate means?[1]

5. Consensus in political discussion and decision-making, in the sense that solutions are sought that will minimize the size, resentments, and coercion of defeated minorities, and will maximize the numbers of citizens who conclude that their goals have been adequately met by the solution adopted?

6. The peaceful management of conflicts and the minimization of political violence?

7. Resolution of urgent policy questions, in the sense that the government directs its attention to any question regarded as urgent and important by a substantial proportion of citizens or leaders, and adopts solutions satisfactory to the largest number of citizens?

8. Widespread confidence in and loyalty to a constitutional and democratic polity?

A number of other criteria might be advanced, but these are enough to give an idea of the magnitude of the problem of evaluation. What is most obvious and most important about these criteria is that, like most standards of performance for complex achievements, they conflict with one another; if a political system were to maximize one of these ends it would probably do so only at considerable cost to some of the others. Moreover, because different individuals disagree about the relative importance of different goals, they disagree as to what is the best solution in general, and even for a specific situation. How then can one prescribe an optimal balance among competing goals, when the goals are nonquantitative and imprecise, and when one man's optimum may be another man's prison? Nor are these the only sources of disagreement. The eight criteria conflict with one another; there is a certain tension among them; we cannot maximize one goal beyond some range without sacrificing another goal.

In spite of all these obstacles to finding an 'optimal solution', it is possible to clarify some of the costs and gains of different solutions, actual or proposed. Let me start by examining the tension created by wanting—as most good democrats do—freedom, dissent and consensus.

---

[1] Cf. Bagehot, who refers to 'one of the mental conditions of Parliamentary Government, by which I do not mean reasoning power, but rather the power of hearing the reasons of others, of comparing them quietly with one's own reasons, and then being guided by the result'. *The English Constitution*, p. 44. See also p. 280.

FREEDOM, DISSENT AND CONSENSUS

The first criterion listed above emphasizes opportunities for dissent; and it is no doubt their concern for this goal that explains, in the main, why liberals and radicals have usually been keenly sensitive to problems of political opposition. For to look at any political system from the point of view of an opposition inclines one to stress the virtues of dissent, of *opposing*. Yet the last criterion in our list emphasizes the virtues of stability; and the penultimate criterion, the importance of resolution and dispatch, avoiding deadlock, paralysis, impotence in government. Sensitivity to these criteria leads one to be concerned with the high costs of unlimited dissent and to stress the importance of consensus, particularly if governments willing to protect dissent are to survive.

There are, we all know, many varieties of freedom. One variety of freedom exists to the extent that every citizen has opportunities to engage in political activities without severe social and governmental constraints. In all political systems this freedom—let me call it Freedom in Political Action—is, like other freedoms, limited by government and society; yet it is the differences in these limits that distinguish libertarian from authoritarian systems. In libertarian systems the right to dissent from the views of government—to oppose the government—is a vital form of Freedom in Political Action. And political oppositions are a crucial expression of this Freedom.

Yet the very existence of dissent and political opposition is a sure sign that someone is constrained by government to do or to forbear from doing something that he would like to do and very likely feels he has a moral right, or even an obligation, to do. To feel politically free because one obeys laws one believes in, to obey a government one approves of, to obey governmental policies one wants or agrees with—here is a second variety of freedom. Since this variety, like the other, bears no accepted name, let me call it Freedom in Political Obligations.

Now if the existence of political opposition is evidence of Freedom in Political Action, it is also a symbol of the Unfreedom[2] in Political Obligations of those opposed to the government. I expect that some readers will now move a well-known objection. Even citizens who are opposed to the laws enforced by their government may nonetheless yield their implicit consent, provided these laws are adopted by procedures they regard as legitimate; in this sense, their Freedom in Political Obligations is not diminished by their need to obey specific laws to which they object. Let me recognize the force of this familiar argument and put it to one side as irrelevant here. I do so in order to distinguish (1) a polity in which a large and permanent minority accepts the constitutional procedures and arrangements, yet detests the policies of government, which seems to it tyrannical in what it does if not in the way it acts; from (2) a polity in which agreement is so extensive that minorities are microscopic and evanescent, and no one ever feels much injured by the laws he is obliged to obey. In the

---

[2] The notion of 'unfreedom' is defined in Felix E. Oppenheim, *Dimensions of Freedom* (New York, 1961), chap. 4, 'Unfreedom'.

first case, members of the outvoted minority might accept the obligation to obey the laws because these were adopted according to legitimate constitutional processes, and yet feel constrained to obey laws they hold wrong. In the second case, they would feel no such constraint.

If you will allow me this distinction, it follows, I think, that in a democratic system where Freedom of Political Action is widely enjoyed, the less the dissent, the greater the Freedom in Political Obligations. In fact the only system in which every citizen would be completely free in his Political Obligations would be one in which political consensus was perfect; for no citizen would then feel constrained by government to do something he believed he should not do. The more extreme the dissent permitted, the greater the range of Freedom in Political Action; yet the more numerous the extreme dissenters, the greater the number who are (at least temporarily and perhaps indefinitely) Unfree in their Political Obligations.

Let me try to make these abstractions more concrete by comparing a high-consensus system like Sweden with a low-consensus system like Italy. In a high-consensus system most citizens are only moderately opposed, if at all, to the character and conduct of government; by comparison, in a low-consensus system a great many more people are strongly opposed to the conduct and even the form of government. The proportion of citizens who feel themselves coerced or constrained by government, and thus Unfree in Political Obligations is, naturally, much larger in the low-consensus systems than in the high-consensus ones.

Yet an extreme dissenter may enjoy more freedom to express his dissent in a low-consensus system like Italy than in a system with considerably more consensus like the United States. For (aside from any other reasons) the very magnitude of extreme dissent in Italy and France limits the extent to which dissent is coerced by social and governmental actions; in the United States, however, where extreme dissent is so small that it can be coerced at less cost, social and governmental constraints are rather powerful. Thus in the United States opportunities for discussing one's views with others, attending meetings, reading newspapers sympathetic to one's cause, joining in a like-minded party, and voting for like-minded candidates are extensive for most citizens—but not, often, for the extreme dissenter.

Thus a low-consensus country like Italy may actually provide more Freedom in Political Action (to Communists, Monarchists and Fascists, for example) than a country like the United States where there is considerably higher consensus. Is low consensus a better guarantee of political freedom, then, than high consensus? Hardly, for a low-consensus system greatly increases the amount of Unfreedom in Political Obligations among its citizens. What is more, widespread Unfreedom in Political Obligations is inescapable as long as consensus remains low; for even if the Outs were to displace the Ins, their positions would only be reversed. The Freedom in Political Obligations of the one-time Outs would now be greater; but so would the Unfreedom in Political Obligations of the one-time Ins. Then, too, a low-consensus system is much more likely to impose other costs such as deadlock, political violence, constitutional instability and destruction of democracy itself.

If, then, the most desirable long-run solution for a low-consensus country would be to increase consensus, surely the most desirable long-run solution for a high consensus country would not be deliberately to foster extreme dissent! An obvious alternative solution would be to reduce the legal obstacles that limit the Freedom of Political Action among dissenters until they are legally on a par with all other citizens. This is, in fact, the solution adopted in a number of high-consensus countries. In this respect, the United States is a somewhat deviant case: most other stable democracies have not imposed as severe a set of legal and social obstacles to political dissent as exist in the United States.

RATIONALITY, DISSENT AND CONSENSUS

If freedom of dissent is thought (by most libertarians and democrats) to be a desirable freedom in itself, advocates of libertarian democracy have usually contended, as John Stuart Mill did, that an opportunity for the expression of dissenting opinions is also a necessary (though definitely not a sufficient) condition for 'rational' political action. The citizens of any country, in this view, need dissenters and oppositions in order to act wisely, to explore alternatives, to understand the advantages and disadvantages of different alternatives, to know what they want and how to go about getting it. Yet there is a certain conflict, one not always recognized, between the conditions required for a relatively rational consideration of alternatives, and the existence of extensive dissent or extensive consensus.

Where dissent is slight, the alternatives presented by political leaders for consideration among themselves and by the voters are likely to represent relatively small marginal changes. For in a society where nearly everyone is already rather satisfied with the conduct of government, alternatives profoundly opposed to existing government policy are not likely to be generated, proposed, or considered. Changes are likely to come about by paying attention to a relatively small number of marginally different alternatives to existing policies, examining a limited set of possible consequences, comparing the results of whatever changes are made, and making whatever further modifications are suggested by subsequent experience: in short, by incremental action.

Although incrementalism evidently seems to a great many people a less rational process than comprehensive and deductive approaches, in fact it offers great advantages as a process for relatively rational change.[3] The characteristics and effects of existing policies and institutions are more easily, more accurately, and more confidently known than for hypothetical policies and institutions. The effects of small changes are usually much easier to predict than the effects of

[3] Cf. the discussion in R. A. Dahl and C. E. Lindblom, *Politics, Economics, and Welfare* (New York 1953), pp. 82 ff., and the much more highly developed theory in C. E. Lindblom and D. Braybrooke, *A Strategy of Decision* (Glencoe, Ill., 1963), chap. 5, 'The Strategy of Disjointed Incrementalism', and chap. 6, 'Why Analysts Use The Strategy'.

large changes. Current processes generate information about effects, and since this information can be fed back to policy-makers, changes can be reversed, accelerated, or altered. In practice, moreover, peaceful change is usually highly incremental. Partly for this reason, no doubt, incremental change is the characteristic method of democracies: liquidation of the Kulaks and the Great Leap Forward would not have been carried out by parliamentary governments.

Yet if high-consensus societies can profit from the advantages of incremental change, they run an opposite danger. Where there is little dissent, both political leaders and citizens escape the compulsion to weigh the relative advantages offered by a comprehensive, large-scale change, even when a large-scale change might prove less costly in the long-run than either the *status quo* or a series of incremental changes. The history of politics is writ large with the results of costly timidities that have produced too little, too late.

Reflecting that incremental responses have frequently failed to match the magnitude of a challenge, one is tempted to conclude that sharp political conflict, clashing ideologies, and even low consensus are needed for a rational examination of alternatives. Yet the historical record seems to offer little support for this view. For intense conflicts create their own irrationalities, particularly when conflict is fortified by ideology. It is a reasonable hypothesis that the greater the discrepancy between the goals of the parties to a conflict, the more problem-solving and persuasion are likely to give way to bargaining and coercion.[4] The true believer does not judiciously appraise the arguments of the infidel. Has the clash of ideologies in France and Italy provided a more 'rational' examination of alternatives than the low-tension conflicts and unideological analyses among Britons and Swedes?

In sum, high-consensus polities are able to give relatively rational consideration to small changes but they are prone to ignore the possible advantages of radical changes in the *status quo*. Low-consensus polities may find it difficult to profit from the advantages of incremental changes; yet posing radically conflicting alternatives to citizens and leaders is accompanied by the irrationalities of ideological controversy.

Is it possible to have the best of both worlds? A society where dissent is low enough to encourage a relatively calm and objective appraisal of alternatives, and yet sufficient to make sure that radical alternatives will not be ignored or suppressed? Among the Western countries, if Italy lies at the one extreme, the United States is at the other. Possibly some of the north-European democracies come closer to the balance we seek. Yet if their high-consensus endures and increases, will not they, too, suffer the disadvantages of weak dissent?

DISPERSION, CONCENTRATION AND MAJORITY RULE

Does the two-party system offer a solution? Probably no other cure is so often proposed for the ailments of a sick polity. Does it not solve the problem

---

[4] James G. March and Herbert A. Simon, *Organizations* (New York, 1958), pp. 129 ff.

of how to balance a large measure of consensus with a satisfactory amount of rational dissent? For cannot one party embody the values of stability and consensus, and the other the values of change and dissent?

The only country where a two-party system of this kind has ever endured in a relatively clear form is Britain, which does, I believe, exhibit many of the virtues claimed for the two-party system. Should it be more widely copied?

Unfortunately, the two-party system presents two imposing difficulties as a general solution. It is evidently not viable in many countries. And even if it were, it would not in all circumstances produce the results found in Britain.

The very rarity of the two-party system argues that the existence of such a system requires an unusual combination of circumstances. The absence of one or more of these circumstances greatly reduces the likelihood that a two-party system will exist, or, if it does exist, that it will have the results expected of it.

The conditions under which a two-party system would provide an optimal solution for meeting the eight goals listed earlier probably include these:

1. The parliament is sovereign in law and in fact.

2. Within parliament, the principle of majority rule is applied to decisions.

3. Among citizens, and markedly among political activists, there exists a high degree of consensus on the desirability and legitimacy of the first two conditions; on the other characteristics of the constitutional system; on the rights, liberties and duties of individuals and groups; and on a great many social and economic goals, institutions and arrangements.

4. Of all questions about which there are conflicting views, and for which governmental action is regarded by some people as desirable, most citizens divide into only two great clusters of opinion. These opinions, though stable for long periods, are not rigidly fixed but change with time, as does the size of the two opinion-clusters.

5. There are two political parties, and neither of these parties is, or expects to be, indefinitely out of office.

In these circumstances, two unified parties, each having a programme and policies directed towards one of the two great clusters of opinion and competing actively for office, meet a great many of the criteria listed earlier. As long as most conflicting opinions fall into one of the two great clusters, the two-party system would provide an outlet for expressing views, including criticizing the government (Criterion 1), and opportunities for citizens to participate in political life (Criterion 2). Any fair system for apportioning parliamentary seats would ensure that the government would represent the larger opinion-cluster rather than the smaller (Criterion 3). The existence of two divergent sets of public attitudes bounded by extensive consensus would facilitate rationality in political discussion and decision-making (Criterion 4), by ensuring that alternatives would be posed, providing a reasonably clear choice to voters, and enabling a rather high degree of coherence of policies and programmes. Rationality would also be enhanced because an opposition's past experience in office and its expectation of future responsibility as the governing party would encourage its members to avoid demagogic and irresponsible appeals for unworkable and unrealistic solutions. The existence of widespread consensus and the experience and expectation of governing would help to minimize the resentments of the opposition and the need for coercion (Criterion 5) and also to ensure that conflicts would be peacefully resolved (Criterion 6). Policy questions uppermost in the minds of any large group of people would almost certainly be brought forward by one of the two parties; and in due time each party would have an oppostunity to enact its own solution (Criterion 7). Finally, all these conditions taken together would surely go very far toward creating widespread loyalty to democracy and constitutional government (Criterion 8).

It is easy to see why the two-party model, especially in the idealized form in which it is often described, has charmed so many political observers. Yet the conditions I have just specified are an unusual combination; they have not always existed even in Britain.

In the first place, if a society is polarized into highly antagonistic camps, then the two-party system might actually increase the intensity of conflicts by wiping out the mediating centre.

Secondly, opinions may fall into more than two clusters, as they generally do in Belgium, Holland, Italy and the United States. In these circumstances, there would have to be more than two parties; or, as in the United States, the two parties would not be highly unified. Moreover, if a system of disciplined parties existed, it could produce flagrant contradictions with several of our criteria. Specifically, the applications of the principle of majority rule and parliamentary sovereignty could lead to minority government, negate majority rule, and thus violate Criterion 3. For if a faction in one party, even if it were a majority faction, could use the instruments of party discipline to impose its policies on that party, and if that party had a majority in parliament, then the policies adopted by the government and agreed to by the parliamentary majority might well be policies preferred only by a minority and opposed by a majority of the whole country. When there are more than two large clusters of opinions it would be necessary, in order to satisfy our criterion, for different majority coalitions to form on different issues. Thus a multiparty system or two heterogeneous parties without strong discipline would be preferable.

Thirdly, the government and the opposition parties might not alternate in office. In this case, an opposition might find demagogic and unrealistic appeals increasingly attractive. Even if the problem of a permanent opposition is not at all peculiar to a two-party system, there is nothing inherent in the dynamics of a two-party system that guarantees an alternation between the two parties.

A system with two disciplined and strictly competitive parties, one controlling the government and the other providing a concentrated focus for opposition, is not always, therefore, a desirable solution. The circumstances under which it is the optimal solution may be, in fact, rather uncommon. The typical solution of democracies is not concentration but dispersion, not strict competition but bargaining and coalescent strategies. Given the conditions of political life in most countries, quite possibly this solution is preferable; for it is often possible where the other solution is not, and it may come somewhat closer to satisfying our various criteria.

MAJORITY RULE, MINORITIES AND ORGANIZED PLURALISM

Every solution to the problems of opposition that focuses upon party systems runs the danger of neglecting a palpable fact of political life: many important decisions are not made in parliament. To the extent that an opposition concentrates on elections and parliamentary action, it may be powerful in unimportant encounters and feeble or even absent when key decisions are made.

As the extent of governmental intervention and control in social and economic affairs has expanded, the work of parliaments has also multiplied. But even with the enormously increased work load of parliaments and the much greater weight and range of the effects that laws passed by parliament now have on social and economic behaviour, the *relative* importance of parliaments in making important decisions has not increased in the same proportion; the 'decline of parliaments' has become a familiar topic and a source of concern.

No single curve could summarize the historical changes in the power of various parliaments. But in a number of countries two kinds of developments have helped to increase the *relative* importance of other sites. One is a pronounced growth in many Western democracies in the power of a plebiscitary executive who acquires great political resources by winning a national election. Although this development is clearest in the United States and the Fifth French Republic, the rise of highly disciplined parties has led by a different route to similar results in Britain, Norway, Sweden, Austria, and a number of other democracies. In France and the United States, the constitution, laws, and political practices grant extensive discretionary power and authority to an elected chief executive; in the other countries, if a party or coalition wins a majority of seats in parliament, party discipline ensures that it will form a government whose policies cannot, for all practical purposes, be defeated by opponents in parliament. Although the development is highly uneven and the pattern is markedly different from one country to another, the importance of the legislature as a site for encounters between opposition and government is reduced to the extent that a plebiscitary executive (whether president or cabinet) has acquired the power to make key decisions without much restraint by parliament.

The other development that creates a powerful rival for parliament is the fact that the evolution of national bargaining among employers, trade unions and other interests has led to a process for making decisions of great economic and social importance over which parliaments and sometimes even executives exercise scant control.

What these two developments have in common is the creation of highly strategic sites outside parliament—rivals to parliamentary power. Where they differ is in the importance of national elections. For if the rise of a plebiscitary executive has reduced the relative influence of parliament, that development has, if anything, made elections even more crucial. Yet because the concrete alternatives open to voters are few and simple in comparison with the great range of problems confronting a modern state, an election furnishes a vague mandate at best; and at worst it simply allows winners and losers to provide their own interpretations of the election returns.

Bargaining with the executive, bargaining among private and public bureaucracies, negotiations among the great national associations, all these provide ways of supplementing, interpreting, offsetting and even negating the election returns. This is exactly the source of both the advantages and the dangers of organized pluralism and national bargaining.

Organized pluralism meets many of the criteria for opposition in a democracy that I proposed at the beginning of this study. For example, because it often enables key groups to arrive at decisions they find more acceptable than decisions imposed by legislature or executive order, bargaining is an instrument for gaining consensus and enlarging the area of Freedom in Political Obligations. It provides additional sites for effective expression of views, dissent, criticism. Often it ensures that the specialized knowledge of the groups most deeply involved in some activity will be brought to bear on a solution. Yet if it has many advantages—and it is in any case inevitable in every modern libertarian industrial society—organized pluralism creates two problems that have not yet been solved anywhere. For one thing, since all resources except the vote are unequally distributed, some minorities (one thinks of the uneducated poor in the United States) may not have much in the way of political resources to bargain with: they have the ballot—and little else. In addition, to the extent that parliament is excluded from the process and elections provide only a vague and rather uncertain control over national leaders, there is no political institution in which majorities weigh heavily that can control the great bargained decisions by means of public review, appraisal, opposition, amendment, or veto.

Perhaps organized pluralism would weaken democracy in a small city-state, as Rousseau and his admirers would argue, for it encourages a citizen to take only a fragmentary view of his interests. And faction has always been the mortal disease of the city-state. Yet in the modern nation-state, it is difficult to imagine an alternative to organized pluralism that would not leave the plebiscitary executive and the official bureaucracies without effective oppositions, criticism and control.

What is not yet perfectly clear, however, is how organized pluralism and national bargaining are to be reconciled with systems in which political equality and majority rule are major principles of legitimacy.

OPPOSITIONS IN WESTERN DEMOCRACIES: THE FUTURE

There is a tension, then, among our goals, a tension that seems to be inescapable. The demands imposed by the values of democracy are extraordinarily severe.

To one who accepts these values, one perennial problem of opposition is that there is either too much or too little. The revolutionary parts of the world have a surplus of poverty and a deficit of order. The authoritarian countries have a surplus of order and a deficit of political freedom. Some of the Western democracies are achieving a mounting surplus of riches and consensus.

To be concerned over the decline of structural oppositions in most Western democracies may very well be an anachronism, a throwback to 19th-century styles of thought, on a par with a nonrational faith in the virtues of a balanced budget or the conviction that a seven-day working week is indispensable if the working classes are not to become dissolute from having too much spare time on their hands. Should we not begin instead to adjust our minds to the notion that in the future—or at least in that short-run future into which it is not wholly senseless to extrapolate present trends—a great many Western democracies will have rather high levels of agreement and not much structural opposition?

That a large number of democracies have won the battle for the allegiance of their citizens among all social strata is, surely, a satisfying victory to anyone who believes in the values of a democratic polity. Yet it is difficult to disregard the sense of disquiet that follows hard upon one's awareness that severe criticism of social and economic structures has all but disappeared from the political life of many Western democracies—or else has become a monopoly of political forces like the Communists and the Radical Right whose allegiance to democratic values is, to say the least, doubtful. If the growth of extreme dissent can endanger a democratic system, universal but quite possibly superficial and irrational 'consensus' may also be undesirable, for reasons I have just been exploring.

But is the trend evident in so many Western democracies over the past several decade toward greater consensus likely to continue? Might it level off, or even be reversed?

No way of conjecturing about the future, as Bertrand de Jouvenel has remarked, is more compelling than the temptation to project recent trends, 'to suppose that tomorrow is going to differ from today in the same way that today differs from yesterday.'[5] And as M. de Jouvenel also reminds us, it is the extrapolation of recent trends that has so often led men who understood their own time well to miss completely the large changes and abrupt reversals that transform the future into something radically different from the past. Suppose, then, that we make two assumptions about the future: that there will be no holocaust, an assumption without which it would be futile to speculate about the future of politics; and that Western societies will continue to develop greater affluence, higher consumption, reduction of poverty, wider educational opportunities and steadily increasing technical and technological resources. Under these conditions, what can we conjecture about the future of oppositions in Western democracies?

To begin with, even the growth of affluence does not automatically wipe out conflicts over the distribution of the national income and opportunities of all kinds. There is no reason to assume a decline in the familiar conflicts among

[5] *L'Art de la Conjecture* (Monaco, 1964), p. 82.

different interest groups, each striving to ensure that its members gain a satisfactory share. Indeed, since a just or satisfactory share probably cannot be defined so as to command general assent, and since any particular allotment reveals itself more and more clearly nowadays to be a product of political decisions and less and less an act of God, nature, or the inexorable operation of economic laws, conflicts over the distribution of income might, if anything, become more numerous even if less intense.

International policies will also remain, surely, subjects of conflict. Since there is small chance that international politics will diminish in importance and salience in the next half century, and since judgments of alternative policies and proposals will necessarily rest on highly controversial assessments of very great risks, gains and costs, a variety of foreign policies, military affairs, treaties, regional and international organizations and alliances all promise a steady flow of internal conflict.

In many cases, conflicts over international politics and the distribution of national income and opportunities may not generate anything more than the kinds of policy oppositions with which we are already familiar in Western democracies. To this extent the future looks rather like the immediate past. Yet this may not be the whole picture. For these two kinds of conflicts need not necessarily entail only narrow group interests or technical matters. The more the distribution of incomes and other opportunities is thought to be subject to determination by government, the more relevant may become the ancient and evidently inextinguishable controversies over the issue of equality versus differential awards. And conflicts over international affairs will in some cases involve nothing less than alternative views of how the nation, the civilization, even the species itself are most likely to survive or perish.

Yet neither of these kinds of issues inevitably entails structural oppositions. Are there possible sources of alienation in Western democracies that might foster new structural oppositions? Since alienation has lately become a fashionable topic, let me hasten to add that I do not mean to imply anything about social or psychological alienation, whatever these may be. I speak only of political alienation. A citizen is alienated from his political system to the extent that he has unfavourable feelings, evaluations and attitudes toward it. I assume that a citizen might be alienated from the political system in which he lives without necessarily being neurotic, rootless, excessively anxious over his social standing, or otherwise much different in personality and social characteristics from his fellow citizens. In short, I wish to leave completely open the murky empirical question of how political alienation may be related, if at all, to strictly social and psychological factors.

Among the possible sources of alienation in Western democracies that may generate new forms of structural opposition is the new democratic Leviathan itself. By the democratic Leviathan I mean the kind of political system which is a product of long evolution and hard struggle, welfare-oriented, centralized, bureaucratic, tamed and controlled by competition among highly organized élites, and, in the perspectives of the ordinary citizen, somewhat remote, distant and impersonal even in small countries like Norway and Sweden. The politics of this new democratic Leviathan are above all the politics of compromise, adjustment, negotiation, bargaining; a politics carried on among professional and quasi-professional leaders who constitute only a small part of the total citizen body; a politics that reflects a commitment to the virtues of pragmatism, moderation and incremental change; a politics that is un-ideological and even anti-ideological.

The traditional opposition to the new democratic Leviathan has come from critics on the Right. In most European countries this traditional opposition has been greatly enfeebled. In the United States a Radical Right has become alienated from the existing political system, for the principal leaders in the American system—whether in the Administration's coalition or nominally in opposition—accept policies, express views and engage in conduct that the Right passionately rejects as evil; being a minority and unable to win national elections (and not many state or local elections) the Right has steadily suffered the humiliation of political impotence and rejection.

Is it likely that the wheel of history may make a full turn, that opposition to the democratic Leviathan may arise from a new quarter? There are already faint signs, not only in the United States but in high-consensus European systems like Sweden, Norway and Britain, that many young people, intellectuals, and academics reject the democratic Leviathan—not because it is democratic but because, in their view, it is not democratic enough: this new Leviathan is too remote and bureaucratized, too addicted to bargaining and compromise, too much an instrument of political élites and technicians with whom they feel slight identification. Political isolation, alienation and rebellion among youth, intellectuals and academics are not, of course, new. Yet in the past half century the Left has, on the whole, sought to channel these feelings into support for policies and programmes that have encouraged, not retarded, the development of the new democratic Leviathan. Is it not possible, however, that political alienation will increase, and that a new Left—if one can stretch traditional terms to cover the case—might channel these feelings into radical efforts (the shape of which we cannot foresee) to reconstruct the Leviathan to a more nearly human scale?

None of the three possible sources of future oppositions that I have been describing can be reduced, I imagine, to strictly technical questions. Although most issues involving the distribution of incomes and opportunities, international politics and the democratic Leviathan have strictly technical aspects, few of them can be settled by strictly technical answers. The position one takes must depend in part on non-technical factors—on values more implicit than explicit, psychological orientations and predispositions, identifications, feelings of hate, hostility, fear, jealousy, pride, self-confidence, respect, solidarity. If factors of this kind are to play a part, then there is good reason for expecting that political conflict will encourage the birth of new ideologies. For political élites and involved citizens alike will sense a need for broad, integrated views of the world to provide guidance, validity and authority for their judgments on specific issues. And it will be surprising if these views of the world do not differ considerably in their perspectives, goals, evaluations, and assumptions about the nature of man and society.

Yet should these conflicting issues and ideologies develop it seems unlikely that they will be strongly associated, at least in the Western democracies with the familiar social and economic characteristics that have done such yeoman service in social theory in the recent past. For differences in political demands will probably become in large measure detached from general socio-economic factors. At one end of the scale, new oppositions may reflect no more than conflicts among shifting coalitions of interest groups. At the other extreme, conflicting demands are likely to be attached to relatively durable orientations, perspectives, 'mentalities', political philosophies, or ideologies that are related only casually to the kinds of social forces that have played such an important part in the political life of Western democracies in the past century.

In short, differences in basic political ideas and evaluations are likely to become more and more important in explaining differences in political behaviour and therefore in patterns of opposition. Yet these crucial differences in political ideas and evaluations will probably be less and less traceable to differences in social and economic characteristics. In this sense, political ideologies, far from waning, will be ascendant.

To be sure, the traditional ideologies that have played so great a role in Western politics in the past centuries show every sign of being well on the way to ultimate extinction. But democracies have not eliminated all causes of political conflict; and if we agree with James Madison that 'the latent causes of faction are sown in the nature of man', then democracies will not and cannot eliminate all causes of political conflict. If democracies cannot eliminate all the causes of conflict, is it not reasonable to expect that with the passage of time the clash of governments and oppositions, indeed of one opposition with another, will generate—and will be generated by—new political perspectives that we cannot now accurately foresee?

chapter V

MODERN DICTATORSHIP

The emphasis on procedure in parliamentary democracies is rejected by Fascists and Communists alike as irrelevant. Legitimacy for the antidemocratic critics derives from some other source—the nation or class or race. It can never be the product of argument and opinions of groups and individuals. Communist theorists have always distinguished between "bourgeois parliamentarism" and "Soviet democracy." Parliamentarism, Marx contended, means that the people have only the right to decide which members of the ruling class will have the privilege of exploiting them for the next few years. Parliamentary "prattle" is designed mainly to delude the masses into believing that they have some political importance, whereas in reality power is firmly in the hands of capitalists, operating through the bureaucracy. In Communist regimes, legitimacy comes mainly through manipulation and control but ultimately, if the government is to survive, from achievement and performance.

Fascism secures the obedience of the people largely by exploiting nationalist sentiment. Adolf Hitler strove to liberate Germany from the restrictions imposed by the Treaty of Versailles, mobilize popular support in the name of the uniqueness of the German race and destiny, and then to bring about the unification of Europe by conquest. It is apparent that the great majority of the German people considered these aims proper, and that the Nazi Party and State were thereby "legitimized."

The student is urged to apply the same kind of analysis to legitimacy in modern dictatorships that he previously employed with reference to modern democracies. First, what are the basic values through which these regimes seek legitimacy? Franz Neumann, for example, distinguishes among simple, Caesaristic, and totalitarian systems. To what extent are these values accepted by the major groups in the population? In the absence of reliable indicators of legitimacy, such as freely contested elections and public opinion surveys, the degree of consensus must be appraised through broad historical analysis, with particular attention to crises of leadership and succession. Some authoritarian regimes have been unstable, while others have demonstrated a remarkable ability to mobilize popular support. Most important, are there any social or economic correlates of consensus under authoritarian regimes? Ultimately the analysis must be extended to include the whole range of factors making for revolution and political change (dealt with in Part Five, below).

On modern dictatorship the student may consult: C. J. Friedrich, ed., *Totalitarianism* (1954); C. J. Friedrich and Z. Brzezinski, *Totalitarian Dictatorship and Autocracy* (1956); Hannah Arendt, *The Origins of Totalitarianism* (1958); Franz L. Neumann, *Behemoth* (1944); and Merle Fainsod, *How Russia Is Ruled* (1963).

12. Notes on the Theory of Dictatorship*

FRANZ L. NEUMANN

DEFINITION OF DICTATORSHIP

Strange though it may seem, we do not possess any systematic study of dictatorship. The historical information is abundant, and there are many analyses of individual dictators in various countries. But there is no analysis that seeks to generalize not only from the political experience of the twentieth century, but from the political systems of the more distant past. The present paper attempts to outline the theoretical problems encountered in the analysis of dictatorship and to indicate whatever answers now can be supplied.

By dictatorship we understand the rule of a person or a group of persons who arrogate to themselves and monopolize power in the state, exercising it without restraint.

The first question raised by this definition is whether the Roman dictatorship and the absolute monarchy should be included in its scope.

It seems more appropriate to classify the Roman dictatorship (prior to Sulla) not as a dictatorship properly speaking, but as a form of Crisis Government. This may seem arbitrary, for the very word "dictator" derives from Roman constitutional law. Nevertheless, the Roman dictatorship was a magistracy, clearly defined in authorization, scope and duration, and it ought not to be confused with a political system in which power is arrogated by an individual or a group, and which does not circumscribe either the scope or the duration of dictatorial power. The Roman dictator was appointed by one of the consuls for a period

*Reprinted with permission of the publisher from *The Democratic and Authoritarian State* (Glencoe, Ill.: Free Press, 1957). Copyright 1957 by The Free Press, a corporation.

not to exceed six months, to defend the country against an external enemy or to cope with internal dissension. He was duty-bound to appoint at once a Master of the Horse for the command of the cavalry; he had no authority to change the constitution, to declare war, to intervene in civil law suits, or to impose new fiscal obligations upon Roman citizens. Within these limits, the sovereign power of the Roman people was concentrated in his hands. The consuls became his subordinates; the tribunician power of intercession did not apply against his acts; nor could a citizen condemned in a criminal trial invoke the normal right of appeal (*provocatio*) against him.

The Romans resorted to dictatorship because the collegiate nature of the magistracy, including the consulate, and the one-year restriction on its term, made the conduct of war extremely difficult. But the dictatorship itself was to prove unsuitable for wars of long duration. By the end of the fourth century it was already in decline, reappearing in irregular forms during the Punic Wars and disappearing at the end of the Second Punic War (201 B.C.). From then on, the Roman dictatorship (e.g., Sulla's and Caesar's) changes its character radically.

The second problem that our definition raises is the relation between monarchy and dictatorship. The title of the absolute ruler—whether he is designated King, Emperor, Leader or Duce—is not decisive here. This was already recognized by Aristotle, who held the rule of kings among non-civilized (non-Hellenic) peoples to be "similar to that of tyranny" and who defined his fifth type of kingship, the case "where a single power is sovereign on every issue, with the same sort of power that a tribe or a polis exercises over its public concerns," as a *Pambasileia,* an all-kingship or super-kingship.

Actually, from the standpoint of the exercise of power the absolute monarch is a dictator, but from the standpoint of the legitimacy of power, he is not. We may speak of legitimate monarchical rule whenever accession to power is constitutionally regulated by heredity or by election and monarchical rule is generally accepted as the normal form of government. These criteria are rather vague—but so is the actual situation. In the history of political and constitutional thought, the ruler who comes to power through a *coup d'état* (*absque titulo*) is held to be an usurping tyrant, but he may rid himself of this stigma if he succeeds in formally establishing his rule and that of his line, which then becomes "legitimate." On the other hand it was also generally held that a monarch who acceded to the throne legitimately could degenerate into a tyrant through his acts (*quoad exercitio*). Thus, while one may distinguish in principle between monarchy and dictatorship, one must realize that the principle suffers many exceptions and that, consequently, certain forms of the absolute monarchy must also be treated as forms of dictatorship.

Our definition, furthermore, envisages dictatorship only in the state, and in no other social organization. There may be situations in which absolute power of a party boss or of the pater familias may help us understand the mechanisms leading to a dictatorship or serving to maintain its power. But there is as yet no convincing evidence that the dictatorial structure of social organizations necessarily leads to or facilitates political dictatorship. An example is the ambiguity of the social and psychological role of the so-called "authoritarian family."[1] The authoritarian (quasi-dictatorial) family may lead, as some maintain, to a more ready acceptance of political dictatorship,[2] but dictatorship may also be promoted (and more frequently, perhaps) by the decay of traditional authority, by the very undermining of the authority of the father. The relation between political and social forms of authoritarianism must, therefore, be taken as a special problem, and not as an automatic correlation.

Moreover, we deliberately do not distinguish among a dictator, a tyrant, and a despot. Tyranny and despotism have no precise meaning. One usually associates despotism with oriental dictatorships, whereas tyranny is often used to designate any system of government that either in its origin or in its practice is tainted by unconstitutional practices or characterized by lack of restraints. Both words are emotionally charged and exhibit in varying degrees rejection and resentment of these systems of government.

Rejection of the terms "tyranny" and "despotism" does not mean, however, that within the general definition of dictatorship there are no subtypes. A number of distinctions are significant.

The first pertains to the scope of the political power monopolized by the dictator. The dictator may exercise his power through absolute control of the traditional means of coercion only, i.e., the army, police, bureaucracy and judiciary. We may call this type a *simple dictatorship.*

In some situations, the dictator may feel compelled to build up popular support, to secure a mass base, either for his rise to power or for the exercise of it, or for both. We may call this type a *caesaristic dictatorship,* which, as the name indicates, is always personal in form.

Even this combination of monopolized coercion and popular backing may be insufficient as a guarantee of power. It may be necessary to control education, the means of communication and economic institutions and thus to gear the whole of society and the private life of the citizen to the system of political domination. The term for this type is totalitarian dictatorship. It may be either collective or personal, that is, it may or may not have a caesaristic element.

It need hardly be mentioned that these classifications are ideal types which will only approximate historical realities. They will help us, however, to understand the structure of the various cases of dictatorship.

CAESARISTIC DICTATORSHIP

The simple dictatorship—whether it be military or bureaucratic, the rule of a junta, a caudillo, or even an absolute monarch—is exercised primarily through the control of what one may call the classical instruments of rule: army, police, bureaucracy, judiciary. This limitation is due less to self-imposed restraints than to the absence of any need for more extensive controls. Simple dictatorship

---

[1] Which, however, need not necessarily be a dictatorial family, because the power of the *pater familias* may well be founded in reason: "rational authority."

[2] T. W. Adorno *et al., The Authoritarian Personality* (New York, 1950).

usually occurs in countries where the masses of the people lack political awareness, where politics is the affair of small cliques who compete for favors and
hope to gain prestige and wealth by association with the dictator. The mass of
the people pay taxes and may have to serve in the army, but otherwise have little
to do with political life. The only social controls which may be needed are
bribery and corruption of a few influential individuals in order to tie them
closely to the system.

In the *caesaristic dictatorship* a new element enters: the need for popular
support. The term "caesarism" was apparently coined by Romieu in his little
book *L'Ere des Césars* (1950) and its climate most adequately described by
Guizot, Louis Philippe's Prime Minister after the revolution of 1830.

"Chaos," says Guizot, "is now hiding under one word—democracy. This is
now the ultimate and universal word all seek to appropriate as a talisman. The
Monarchists say: Our Monarchy is a Democratic Monarchy; it differs essentially
from the ancient monarchy and is adapted to modern conditions of society. The
Republicans say: The Republic is Democracy governing itself. This is the only
form of government in harmony with democratic society, its principles, its
sentiments, and its interests.

"Socialists, Communists, Montagnards wish that the Republic should be pure
and absolute democracy. This is for them the condition of its legitimacy.

"Such is the power of the word democracy that no government or party
dares to exist or believes it can exist without inscribing that word upon its
banner." [3]

Caesarism becomes a necessity when the masses tend to become politically
articulate. . . . Much . . . is to be learned from Julius Caesar whose name came to
designate this type of dictatorship.

The gradual disintegration of the Roman constitution between the Second
Punic War and the murder of Caesar is familiar in its major outlines and need not
be elaborated in detail. Personal dictatorship was foreshadowed as early as the
close of the Second Punic War by the political pre-eminence of Scipio Africanus.
And the first clear-cut rejection of the Roman constitution was Sulla's dictatorship about a century later, for although it traded on the name of the classical
emergency magistrate, it was a dictatorship for life and its purpose was to change
the constitution by undoing such semi-democratic reforms as the new powers of
the tribunate and by restoring the sway of the senatorial oligarchy (*optimates*).
But Sulla's system could not achieve this restoration. Less than ten years after
his departure from the political scene, his system collapsed and the Republic
was in full decline. "Non mos, non ius" said Tacitus, describing the collapse of
morality and law. "You see that there is no Republic, no Senate, no dignity in
any of us"—thus wrote Cicero in a letter to his brother Quintus.

Julius Caesar's rise to power is due to a number of factors: the disintegration
of the constitution; his personal control of a dedicated army; the support of the
so-called party of the *populares;* the rise of the equestrian order to economic

---

[3] Guizot, *La Démocratie en France* (Leipzig, 1849), p. 2.

power; the discontents of the non-Roman Italian population; and the expansion of the Empire. His position, by the time of his death, could not conceivably be reconciled with the constitutional structure of the Republic. He was an absolute monarch in fact. But it is important to note that, much as Caesar would have liked it, he could not, in view of public opinion, take on the title of King. Brutus' deed shows the strength of republican feelings in Rome which are important for the understanding of Augustus' constitutional arrangements.

Modern historians do not tire of arguing that there really was no "democratic" party or movement in Rome, that the populares were in reality a city mob manipulated and bribed by aristocratic cliques held together by the institution of *amicitia* (friendship) and organized into *factiones* or *partes*. This is undoubtedly true. Yet it would be dangerous to construe Roman politics simply as a fight of the "ins" against the "outs" and thus to overlook the political impact of major social problems: the equestrian order's rise to economic power—without corresponding political recognition; the control of political power by a landed oligarchy that no longer monopolized economic power; the deterioration of the position of the small peasants (the Gracchi had already attempted to create an absolute, caesaristic monarchy with their support); the existence of a city plebs—legally defined as those without income or occupation but, through its assemblies and tribunes, exceedingly powerful politically; and finally, the problems of an ever growing empire—the need for defense and communications, and the struggles for participation in the spoils. Seen against this background, caesarism was more than the attempt of a powerful person to make himself supreme; it was in fact the means for reorganizing Rome, Italy, and the Empire. And even if we do not accept Mommsen's image of Caesar as the genius who from the very beginning had set out to do precisely this, the fact remains that these problems brought him into power and that he coped with them, often quite successfully.

Augustus' triumph serves to underline the fact that these social and economic changes had made monarchy inevitable. As Dion Cassius put it: "at this time [after the defeat of Antonius at Actium in 31] the government assumed a better and more salutary form, for it was quite impossible for the Romans to save themselves with the Republican constitution."[4] But what kind of monarchy? The resurrection of the old Roman kingship (the *Rex*) proved impossible. Caesar's death was a warning not to attempt it. The Hellenistic (oriental) monarchy with the deification of the monarch, the proskynesis, and the complete identification of monarch and state was not only an alien tradition, but was associated with Antonius and Celopatra and ruled out by their defeat. Dictatorship for life, voted by the people, had become almost equally disreputable. Augustus, with his unusual political shrewdness, realized that his personal power must be made to fit the constitution. Prior to 27 B.C., all positions he held—admission to the Senate at the age of 19, consular rank, etc.—were irregular but, so he says, "All Italy took the oath to me spontaneously and demanded me as

[4] For details see Leon Homo, *Roman Political Institutions from City to State* (New York, 1947), p. 202.

leader in the war in which I won the battle of Actium. . . ." After 27 B.C., in what Homo calls the organic period, Augustus' Principate was established in what he alleged to be a completely constitutional form. "The Dictatorship was conferred upon me, in my absence and in my presence, by the People and Senate . . . and I did not accept it (22 B.C.). The Consulship for the year and for life was given me at the same date, and I did not accept it . . . I accepted no function contrary to the usages of our fathers. . . . When the people offered me the position of Pontifex Maximus (which my father had held) . . . I refused it." And he continues: ". . . When I had put an end to the civil wars . . . , I transferred the government of the State from my hands to those of the Senate and the Roman people. In return for this service, I was given the title of Augustus. . . . Since that time I have been above all in authority [*auctoritate*] but have had no more power [*potestas*] than those who have been my colleagues in magistracies."

This touching modesty came cheap enough, for Augustus had already proscribed the bulk of his opponents and now, invoking his *auctoritas*, he saw to it that his own men occupied all the positions of influence and power. The patronage system was thus refined and skillfully employed. The Senate was purged, mainly to eliminate adherents of the late Antonius; wealthy plebeians friendly to Augustus rose easily into the equestrian order, and equestrian bankers and traders were elevated to the rank of *optimates*. Moreover, propaganda and the suppression of oppositional and critical literature were used to consolidate support, and in his later years Augustus assumed the religious dignity of the Pontifex Maximus in order to further his prestige. But the political victory was consolidated, above all, by changes in the social hierarchy: the doom of the *nobiles* and the rise of *homines novi* in society and politics.

After 27 B.C. Augustus depended for his constitutional powers primarily on two positions: the *imperium proconsulare maius* and the *potestas tribunicia*—both of which he held for life. The former gave him command of the armies in Rome and in the provinces; the latter—granted to him with extended powers—sacrosanctity, the right of intercession, and above all, the democratic legitimation.

This last point is especially important, because the *potestas tribunicia* is the source of the *lex regia* which, in the formula attributed to Ulpian, was the principle that "the will of the *Princeps* has the force of law for, in virtue of the *lex regia* . . . the people . . . transfers to him all its *imperium* and all its *potestas*." And again in the Code of Justinian: "In virtue of the ancient law which was called *lex regia*, all the right and all the *potestas* of the Roman people have been transferred to the Imperial *potestas*." We now know that some such formula was actually enacted, although of course popular sovereignty after Claudius became a mere fiction. And the Roman people (*populus Romanus*) remained sovereign in law and the source of all political authority, even though the later emperors, influenced by Hellenistic conceptions, added a divine legitimation to the pseudo-democratic *lex regia* . . . .

TOTALITARIAN DICTATORSHIP

Totalitarian dictatorship, to which our attention now will be directed, ought not to be confused with caesarism. Up to the nineteenth century at least, caesaristic dictatorship does not necessarily lead to a totalitarian system, nor is the totalitarian state necessarily the result of a genuine caesaristic movement. Totalitarianism is thus a separate problem. For the purpose of a brief discussion the modern totalitarian dictatorship may be reduced to five essential factors.

The first of these is the transition from a state based upon the rule of law (the German *Rechtsstaat*) to a police state. The rule of law is a presumption in favor of the right of the citizen and against the coercive power of the state. In the totalitarian state this presumption is reversed. Details need not concern us here, since the power of executive agencies in totalitarian states to interfere at discretion with life, liberty and property may be taken as the best-known feature of this kind of dictatorship.

The second factor is the transition from the diffusion of power in liberal states to the concentration of power in the totalitarian regime. This concentration may vary in degree as well as form. But there is no role in any totalitarian state for the various liberal devices of diffusing power, such as separation of powers, federalism, a functioning multiparty system, bicameralism, etc.

These first two elements, however, are to be found in the absolute monarchy as well as in the totalitarian dictatorship. What distinguishes totalitarianism politically is the third element, namely, the existence of a monopolistic state party. Such a party is required because the traditional instruments of coercion do not suffice to control an industrial society, and all the less so since bureaucracies and armies may not always be reliable. The monopolistic party is a flexible instrument which provides the force to control the state machine and society and to perform the gigantic task of cementing the authoritarian elements within society together.

Moreover, the monopolistic party involves a socio-psychological aspect pertaining to what is commonly called a "mass" society. Since modern totalitarian dictatorships arise, almost without exception, within and against democracies (weak though the democratic structures may have been), the totalitarian clique has to assume the shape of a democratic movement and to retain this façade even after it has come to power. In other words, it is forced to practice the ritual of democracy even though the substance is totally denied.

The role of the monopolistic party involves the fourth element of the totalitarian dictatorship: the transition from pluralist to totalitarian social controls. Society ceases to be distinguished from the state; it is totally permeated by political power. The control of society, now as important as the control of the state, is achieved by the following techniques:

1. The leadership principle—to enforce guidance from the top and responsibility to the top.

2. The "synchronization" of all social organizations—not only to control them, but to make them serviceable to the state.

3. The creation of graded elites—so as to enable the rulers to control the masses from within and to disguise manipulation from without, i.e., to supplement bureaucracies in the narrow meaning of the term with private leadership groups within the various strata of the population.

4. The atomization and isolation of the individual, which involves negatively the destruction or at least weakening of social units based on biology (family), tradition, religion, or co-operation in work or leisure; and positively the imposition of huge and undifferentiated mass organizations which leave the individual isolated and more easily manipulable.

5. The transformation of culture into propaganda—of cultural values into saleable commodities.

The final factor in totalitarianism is the reliance upon terror, i.e., the use of noncalculable violence as a permanent threat against the individual. Care must be taken, however, not to define a totalitarian dictatorship simply as the rule of violence. Without it, it is true, such regimes could not survive. But they could not endure for any length of time without considerable identification by the oppressed people with its rulers.

These, in brief outline, are the features of the most repressive of political systems. What distinguishes it from absolutism is not primarily the caesaristic element, for this was also characteristic of the absolute monarchy in certain periods of its history, but rather the destruction of the line between state and society and the total politicization of society by the device of the monopolistic party. This is not merely a question of more or less political power. The difference is one of quality, not quantity. Where, as in the absolute monarchy, power is primarily exercised through the traditional bureaucratic instruments of coercion, its operation is governed by abstract, calculable rules, although their execution often may be arbitrary. Absolutism, therefore, already contains the major institutional principles of modern liberalism. Totalitarian dictatorship, on the other hand, is the absolute negation of these principles because the main repressive agencies are not courts and administrative bodies, but the secret police and the party.

A fully developed totalitarian dictatorship is the form an industrial society may adopt if it should become necessary to maximize its repressive elements and eliminate its liberal ones. But totalitarian dictatorship is not the child of modern industrialism alone. Sparta . . . may be briefly discussed as an illuminating earlier experiment.

Those who call Sparta a democracy perniciously forget that the Perioici and, more importantly, the Helots (state serfs) were decisive for its institutions. The case is perhaps otherwise with Athens, where, as Westermann and Jones[5] have shown, slavery was relatively insignificant. But the ratio of Spartans to Helots

---

[5] W. L. Westermann, "Athenaeum and the Slaves of Athens," in *Athenian Studies presented to W. S. Ferguson* (London, 1940); A. H. M. Jones, "The Economic Basis of Athenian Democracy," in *Past and Present,* no. 1 (February 1952), pp. 13–31.

was about 1:20, and the perpetual danger from the Helots required a system of total repression. Plutarch saw the problem when he described the horrors of the infamous Crypteia, the missions of young Spartans armed with daggers, which the Ephors sent out secretly "from time to time" to terrorize and assassinate Helots. Thucydides also refers to the appalling slaughter of 2,000 Helots in 424 B.C. Service in this dreadful secret police was part of the training of the Spartan youth, for terror, rather than criminal sanction, constituted the backbone of the Spartan system.

The cohesion of the ruling stratum was achieved by the total control of society and of private life through such well-known institutions as the transfer of the children at the age of six to barracks, and the rigid system of state education emphasizing cunning and violence. It is most illuminating to compare Plutarch's description of the Spartans' "liberal" education with Himmler's recipe for the education of Russians under German occupation. Plutarch says, "They learned to read and write for purely practical reasons, but all other forms of education they barred from the country, books and treatises being included in this as much as men." And Himmler: "All they may learn is to count till 12 and to write their names. Beyond this, education is dangerous and not to be countenanced."

We must remember that this totalitarian dictatorship was without a caesaristic element. None was needed due to the completely static character of Sparta's economy and society. Wealth had only two sources: agriculture and robbery (through war). Corruption was enough to make the system function so long as its static character (the pattern of land-holding) was maintained. It was the gradual concentration of wealth in the hands of a few which produced Clemenes' unsuccessful effort to revitalize Sparta through a caesaristic dictatorship. In the end, the Spartan government degenerated into the personal rule of Nabis, who, with the cruelty of an oriental despot, seems to have restored the agrarian system and much of the discipline. . . .

DEMOCRACY AND DICTATORSHIP

If we review the various types of dictatorships outlined above, we are forced to conclude that the usual confrontation of liberal democracy vs. dictatorship as an antithesis of good and evil, cannot be maintained from a historical point of view. Moralizing about political systems makes it difficult to understand their functions. The relationship between democracy and dictatorship is not as simple as is sometimes stated.

1. Dictatorships may be an implementation of democracy. But this refers to emergency dictatorships with functions similar to the classical Roman type, which we prefer to classify as a kind of magistracy.

2. Dictatorships may be the preparation for democracy. We may then speak of an educational dictatorship.

3. Dictatorships may be the very negation of democracy and thus be a totally regressive system.

Pisistratus' rule is probably a classical example of an educational dictatorship. As Werner Jaeger puts it: "The masses were still politically inexperienced, so that democracy was far away: it could not come until the aristocracy had been brought low by the Pisistratic tyrants." We may add that the great function of the Pisistratidae was the creation of an Athenian national (or collective) spirit. This was done by facilitating the emergence of a "middle class," which Aristotle believed to be the social prerequisite of democracy. Hence, without the work of Pisistratus the regimes of Cleisthenes and Pericles would hardly be conceivable.

It is well to remember that the Marxist-Leninist conception of a dictatorship of the proletariat was democratic precisely in this sense of a preparatory dictatorship. The concentration of power in the hands of the proletariat was to be used to abolish class rule altogether and to herald a new epoch of freedom in a classless society. That it was not this expectation but the very opposite which materialized cannot be discussed in detail here. However, we may cite the basic reasons why, under modern conditions, every dictatorship tends to be a totalitarian dictatorship and to involve the negation of democracy.

The democratic ideology has become so universal that Guizot's statement seems even truer today than it did in 1848. All modern dictatorships arose from democratic conditions. This is true of Italy, Germany, Spain, Argentina, and perhaps even of the U.S.S.R., although to a lesser degree.

The dictator is therefore compelled to seek mass support and, having obtained it, to practice the ritual of democracy even if its substance is withheld. As Engels already saw, a *coup d'état* seems hopeless against a modern army; the dictator can come to power only with the help or toleration of the army, but to sustain his power, he depends on a mass base.

There is, however, an important distinction between the Fascist-Nazi type and the Bolshevik. In the former, the dictator could rely upon substantial sectors of the traditional ruling groups (industry, finance, agrarians, army, bureaucracy, judiciary) which were committed to a minimum of formal legality since overt rebellion would have jeopardized their own status and security. Consequently, the dictatorship in its rise to power had to play the democratic game (compare Hitler's strategy before his Beer Hall Putsch of 1923 and afterwards). And once it had attained this goal, the requirements of competition with the outside world and the need to secure the active or passive co-operation of industrial labor, led the Nazi-Fascist type of dictatorship to present itself as a higher and nobler form of democracy.

For the Bolsheviks the need for mass support is of a different nature. The original theory of the dictatorship of the proletariat as the dictatorship of the majority over a minority was compatible at least with one version of democracy. But the Russian proletariat was a small minority in 1917, and with the Bolshevik rejection of Trotsky's theory of a permanent revolution, the democratic mass base had to be secured from among the peasants. When this was not voluntarily forthcoming the Bolshevik regime evolved into a full-blown totalitarian dictatorship.

But even in agrarian, colonial, and semi-colonial countries, where democracy did not exist or was inadequately practiced, modern dictatorship tends to become totalitarian. Today every nation experiences democracy vicariously. Due to the world-wide scope of communications, even the most backward peoples have become aware of democracy and want it, awakening mass consciousness usually taking the form of a demand for national emancipation. Consequently, here too a dictator must attempt to be a Caesar by acting out the democratic ritual even if he is compelled to go on towards a totalitarian regime.

THE SOCIAL FUNCTION OF DICTATORSHIP

Neither the attraction of a democratic ideology nor the scope of the dictatorship can fully explain the phenomena of caesarism and totalitarianism. An understanding of the social function of dictatorship would require a comprehensive analysis based upon the following elements:

a) The economic system;
b) The class relationship;
c) The personality structure.

In each historical situation these factors—economic, social, and psychological—must be treated as a unity, not as isolated, independent causes. An index of changes in these elements will frequently—I would even say invariably—be found in the intellectual and artistic trends of a given period, i.e., in philosophy, literature, and the arts. I should like to indicate certain principles that may help in the search for the causes and functions of the various types of dictatorships.

In terms of *class relationships,* the function of dictatorship may be related to three basic and recurring situations:

1. Disenfranchised and insurgent social classes demand recognition of their interests which the political power-holders refuse to grant. There are two alternatives, depending upon the political maturity of the ascending classes:

If they are politically mature—as the bourgeoisie in England in the seventeenth or in France in the eighteenth century—caesarism will be merely a transitory phenomenon (Cromwell and Robespierre). The new classes, in power and commanding a majority, will for various reasons demand a liberal political system.

But if they are not mature, or too weak, the caesaristic movement will become a dictatorship as in the case of Pisistratus, Cola di Rienzo, or Lenin.

2. The second case is the attempt of a social class threatened with decline and striving to preserve its status and power. Dictatorship may then arise as an attempt to preserve the *status quo.* The most striking examples are Sparta, to a lesser extent the half-hearted efforts of Napoleon I, and probably the regimes of Franco and Perón.

3. The third possibility is the attempt of what one might call doomed classes to change radically the socio-economic situation, to reverse it, and to install a political system that would restore them to their old preeminence. This is the kernel of the German and Italian Fascist movements.

These class relationships must be studied in the light of changing economic systems. Totalitarianism, although not a new phenomenon, is determined in its modern form by the features of an industrial society. Modern industrialism is politically ambivalent because it contains and intensifies two diametrically opposed trends in modern society: the trend toward freedom and the trend toward repression. Sociologists usually define this as the problem of "moral lag," holding that the growing potentialities of modern technology outstrip the progress of "morality." This may or may not be true, but it is not, in my opinion, the decisive factor.

It is easy to say that technology is neutral politically and socially, so that any desired result can be attained depending upon the persons who use it and upon their aims. Technological optimists (like Georges Sorel and Thorstein Veblen) hold that only the full development of technological resources and their efficient utilization (e.g., exclusion of "conspicuous consumption"), can bring mankind to its highest perfection. We do not challenge this statement, but should like to explore some of its implications.

Large-scale technology on the one hand may imply the total dependence of the industrial population upon a complex, integrated mechanism, which can be operated only in a highly organized, stratified, and hierarchic system. This system must instill the virtues of discipline, obedience and subordination—no matter who owns the means of production. Thus, modern industrialism preaches the very virtues which every authoritarian political system seeks to cultivate. These virtues are repressive because they are opposed to man's self-determination.

On the other hand, the very opposite virtues may also be strengthened by technology: self-reliance, awareness of one's power and, most particularly, the feeling of solidarity—that is, a spirit of co-operation as opposed to authoritarianism.

THE PSYCHOLOGICAL PROCESSES OF DICTATORSHIP

These two antagonistic trends of industrialism are, in my opinion, essential for the understanding of modern dictatorship. The authoritarian element facilitates the rise of a dictatorship. But the co-operative aspect forces the dictatorship to find some way of replacing solidarity based on a rational interest (such as class interest) with some other identification that does not undermine but rather strengthens the dictatorship. Mussolini tried corporatism; Hitler, the doctrine of folk-community; Stalin, that of the classless socialist state. But in varying degrees all these identifications were a fake. That they nonetheless "succeeded" leads us to our final problem: the psychological processes connected with dictatorship. The basic problem is anxiety and fear and their function in political life.

Freud has defined anxiety as an "increase in tensions arising from non-gratification of [the individual's] need."[6] Anxiety is thus always present—at least

6 *The Problem of Anxiety,* trans. by H. A. Bunker (New York, 1936), p. 76.

potentially—as a situation or a state of indefiniteness. Fear, in turn, is the recognition of a specific danger.

Therefore, external dangers, arising in specific situations and from specific objects, are experienced in the light of internal anxiety, which then becomes externalized and activated.

But this externalization of anxiety through fear is by no means always dangerous to the personality. One may distinguish three functions of fear:

Fear as a warning;

Fear as protection; and

Fear as destruction.

Thus, an external danger may well have a kind of monitoring function: it may warn the individual that something terrible may happen to him. And the reaction to the threat may then perform a protective or even cathartic function. It may not only remove the concrete danger, but allay the anxiety as well and thus make the individual more free. On the other hand, fear may activate anxiety (particularly neurotic anxiety) to the point of making it destructive. (Indeed there are psychoanalysts who derive anxiety from destructive impulses.) Hence, in some individuals, fear becoming operative or latent anxiety may either paralyze the personality and make it incapable of defense (depressive anxiety) or heighten its aggressive instincts (persecutory anxiety).

This bare (and rather thin) analysis of certain terms of individual psychology may now be put to use in understanding the rise of totalitarian movements and the operation of the totalitarian state.

As an illustration let me again take the Spartan state. Plutarch says, ". . . [T]he Spartans dealt with them [the Helots] very hardly: for it was a common thing to force them to drink to excess, and to lead them in that condition into their public halls, that the children might see what a sight a drunken man is; they made them to dance low dances, and sing ridiculous songs . . ." Then they assassinated them. There is little difference between the Spartan aristocracy's behavior toward the Helots and the Nazis' treatment of the Jews. The ancients were well aware of the fact that the passive element in the Spartan character was fear, that this fear was systematically cultivated and that the Spartans' famous courage in battle was nothing but fear of being stigmatized if they failed in their military duty. The actual or feigned fear of the Helots is the integrating principle of the Spartan ruling class, their anxieties being activated into aggressiveness and destruction. The totally repressive character of Sparta (as compared to Athens) rests precisely in this fact.

In totalitarian movements (as contrasted with totalitarian states), there appears a similar element. A distinction should be made between the Nazi-Fascist movement and Lenin's party prior to 1917. The Bolshevik party at that time was not a totalitarian movement, nor may Lenin (in contrast to post-1928 Stalin) be considered a totalitarian leader. The Bolshevik party then did not manipulate fear; this is a later development which began with the defeat of the revolutionary movements in Western Europe.

In contrast, the Nazi-Fascist movement activated the anxieties of the middle classes and turned them into channels of destruction which were made legitimate by means of the masses' identification with a leader, the hero. The nature of such identification has already been discussed by Freud.[7] This phenomenon appears in all caesaristic and totalitarian movements, in various degrees, of course, and with varying historical functions. . . .

[7] Sigmund Freud, *Group Psychology and the Analysis of the Ego*, trans. S. J. Strachey (New York, 1949).

13. A Comparative Politics of Movement-Regimes*

ROBERT C. TUCKER

Those who specialize in the study of Soviet government and politics are beginning to feel and acknowledge the need for a more effective theoretical apparatus. The post-war years of expanded research in this field have been fruitful in empirical studies of Soviet political history and institutions, but the theoretical development has not kept pace; and now the lag is beginning to inhibit the further fruitful progress of empirical research itself. Instead of a gradually developing body of theory, we still have a melange of "ten theories in search of reality," as Daniel Bell has summed it up in the title of a recent article.[1]

The purpose of the present paper is not to propound an eleventh theory. It is only an exploratory effort, a consideration of a somewhat different approach to the problem than has been customary in the field of Soviet studies. In presenting it, I shall try to shed the blinkers of a Russian specialist and take a look at the whole political galaxy in which Russia is only the biggest star and probably no longer the brightest one.

I

The best way out of the theoretical difficulty may lie in making the study of Soviet government and politics more comparative than it has generally been so far, thus bringing it into much closer working relations with political science as a whole and particularly with the slowly growing body of theory in comparative

*From "Towards a Comparative Politics of Movement-Regimes," *American Political Science Review*, vol. LV, no. 2 (June 1961), pp. 281–89. Article and footnotes abridged by the editors. Reprinted by permission of the American Political Science Association and the author.

[1] "Ten Theories in Search of Reality: The Prediction of Soviet Behavior in the Social Sciences," *World Politics* (April 1958). The article is reprinted in A. Dallin, ed., *Soviet Conduct in World Affairs*.

politics. As this statement implies, our work on Soviet government and politics has been characterized by a certain theoretical isolationism. The underlying assumption of a great deal of it is that Soviet politics constitutes a unique subject matter, a political world apart that can only be understood in terms of its own queer if not inimitable laws or motivations. Among the ten approaches surveyed by Bell we encounter, for example, "diaperology," or the view that Soviet politics is what it is largely because the leading participants may have been swaddled in babyhood. . . .

It would not be accurate, however, to say that no one has studied the Soviet political system in a comparative political way. Indeed, much of the work done on this subject in the past fifteen years or so has been built around a kind of comparative concept—"totalitarianism." This term, it may be noted, was not originated by political scientists, but by totalitarians. It appears to have been put into currency by Mussolini or members of his circle.[2] Beginning in the late 1930s, however, Western students of dictatorship began to make use of it. The phenomenon of the totalitarian or all-embracing state was conceived as a distinctively new, twentieth-century development in the theory and practice of despotism. The Soviet Russian state, as reshaped under Stalin in the 1930s, was coupled with the nazi-fascist type of system under the general heading of "totalitarianism." They represented respectively the totalitarianism of the "left" and the totalitarianism of the "right"—two different species of one and the same new political genus. Though the political symbolisms differed, in all essentials the two types of system were identical. They shared the *Fuehrerprinzip*, the mass party brooking no opposition and extending its tentacles into all other organizations, the aggressive ideology and dynamism of external expansion, the use of the mass communications media to keep the controlled population always keyed up, the development of terror by concentration camp into a system of power, the penetration of the total state into every pore of the "atomized" society, and so on.[3]

There was an obvious basis for this trend of thought. The fact is that Stalinism was essentially identical with Hitlerism and the other expressions of fascism. Unfortunately, however, the concept of the twin totalitarianisms of the left and the right did not clearly fix and delimit this fact. The theory of totalitarianism has tended to equate not Stalinism and fascism but communism and fascism, and this is a mistake. The two phenomena have a great deal in common,

[2] Mussolini wrote the following in his article on the doctrine of fascism in the *Enciclopedia Italiana* in 1932: "The Fascist conception of the State is all-embracing; outside of it no human or spiritual values may exist, much less have any value. Thus understood, Fascism is totalitarian and the Fascist State, as a synthesis and a unit which includes all values, interprets, develops and lends additional power to the whole life of a people."

[3] The outstanding and most influential book written from this point of view is Hannah Arendt's *The Origins of Totalitarianism* (1951). A notable attempt to develop the approach systematically has been made by Carl J. Friedrich and Zbigniew K. Brzezinski in *Totalitarian Dictatorship and Autocracy* (1956). Another effective proponent of the view is Bertram D. Wolfe, who calls totalitarianism "a total-power system" under which the state "strives to be *co-extensive* with society." "The Durability of Soviet Despotism," *Commentary*, August 1957, reprinted in Dallin, *op. cit.*

but they also differ significantly. The difference is visible and traceable within the political history of the Soviet Union itself. That is, communism differs from fascism as Leninism (or Bolshevism) differs from Stalinism. And a clear recognition of this is an essential prerequisite for the advancement of theory in comparative politics as it affects Russia and numerous other countries.

It must be said, too, that the theorists of totalitarianism are conscious of this difference. They show it by suggesting in various ways that Soviet totalitarianism is preeminently a phenomenon of the Stalin era. According to Wolfe, "the Soviet government had been established for more than a decade before Stalin, late in the twenties and into the early thirties, began to impose totalitarian controls upon it." Arendt writes in the same general vein that "To change Lenin's revolutionary dictatorship into full totalitarian rules, Stalin had first to create artificially that atomized society which had been prepared for the Nazis in Germany by historical circumstances." Friedrich and Brzezinski observe, for their part, that the emergence of totalitarian government in the Soviet Union "is marked by Stalin's liquidation of his erstwhile colleagues in the USSR's leadership and more particularly by his epochal struggle with Trotsky."

The implication of these statements is that something in the nature of a change of political configuration, a transformation of regime, occurred in Soviet Russia between Lenin's time and Stalin's, and this is quite true. Lenin's system— a "revolutionary dictatorship"—was revolutionized by Stalin in a process that involved, among other things, the repression of Lenin's Bolshevik Party, and was supplanted by a Stalinist totalitarian autocracy. This process of transformation is accurately describable as a political revolution, although Stalin, for psychological and political reasons of his own, never admitted that fact. He never permitted his own new political order to be officially described as "Stalinism," and maintained to the end the myth of complete continuity between the regime created in the October Revolution and the new regime created in and through his own political revolution from above.

The theorists of totalitarianism, as has been indicated, recognize that a virtual change of regime occurred, but their theory does not. In effect, it says that the communist political system, established by Lenin and the Bolshevik Party, *is what it became* after Stalin revolutionized it and transformed it into a Stalinist political system. This is a questionable procedure from an analytical point of view. That Lenin's revolutionary dictatorship of the Bolshevik Party paved the way for Stalinism, and that the later system had much in common with the one it supplanted, is true. But if, on this account, we ignore the significant differences between them and view Stalinism as the effective reality of communism, we deprive ourselves of the theoretical basis for a comparative politics of the Soviet Union over time as well as a comparative politics of communism and fascism as two significantly different species of one genus.

A good comparative concept should perform a dual discriminating function: it should direct attention to the ways in which similar phenomena differ, and simultaneously to the ways in which differing phenomena resemble each other. I have suggested that the concept of totalitarianism is deficient in the former respect since it fails to direct attention to significant differences between the closely resembling political phenomena of communism and fascism. I must now extend the argument by suggesting that it also fails to direct attention to significant resemblances between *both* these phenomena and a further class of phenomena belonging to the same genus: single-party systems of the nationalist species.[4]

This century has seen the rise of a large and still growing number of revolutionary nationalist regimes under single-party auspices. Turkey under Kemal-Ataturk, Nationalist China under Sun Yat-sen and Chiang Kai-shek, Tunisia under Bourguiba, Egypt under Nasser and Ghana under Nkrumah are some among the many examples that might be cited. If we disregard all considerations of international relations and look at these regimes simply as regimes, we see a political phenomenon that calls for comparison with communist and fascist regimes. We see the need for a comparative-political framework within which communist, fascist and nationalist single-party regimes may be analyzed in terms of their significant similarities as well as their significant differences, or as three species of a single political genus.

The definition of the political genus presents obvious difficulties. Ideally this definition should fix upon (1) that which is common to all phenomena of the class and specific to no one of the three postulated sub-classes, and (2) that which differentiates this whole class of phenomena from others that may be more or less closely related to it. As a rough attempt I would propose the following formula: *the revolutionary mass-movement regime under single-party auspices.* For brevity I shall refer to it as the "movement-regime."

In advocating this category as a tool of comparative analysis, it is not my object to suggest that the notion of totalitarianism is useless or ought to be discarded from political science. The frequency with which we employ it in political discourse strongly indicates that it answers to a genuine need of intellectual communication. My thesis is simply that the concept of totalitarianism has not adequately stimulated the progress of research in the comparative study of the novel forms of authoritarianism that have arisen in profusion in this century, and that it will have its scientific uses *within* a comparative politics of movement-regimes. Otherwise expressing it, the totalitarian dictatorship as such is not the novel political phenomenon of the present century, but at most one of the forms that this phenomenon takes. The distinctively new type of political formation that needs to be studied as a general form and in its specific varieties is the revolutionary mass-movement regime under single-party auspices.

II

The first element of the formula—"revolutionary"—establishes that we are dealing with regimes born in revolutionary struggle and that once in being they

[4] It must be said to the credit of Arendt that she stresses the relationship between the nineteenth-century "pan-movements" of nationalism and the totalitarian movements of the present century. Unfortunately, however, she considers the nationalist movements as simply historical forerunners of totalitarianism, and non-European nationalisms are more or less left out of the picture.

strive to maintain revolutionary momentum. The movement to displace the pre-existing system of order then becomes a revolutionary movement for national renovation, or a movement to carry the revolution beyond the national borders, or both. In the case of the nationalist movement-regimes, especially in more recent times, the original revolutionary struggle is typically directed against a foreign colonial regime or regime of foreign dependency. With communist and fascist regimes, the typical—though not necessary or invariable—pattern is one of revolutionary struggle against an indigenous order that is treated *as though* it were foreign. So Lenin in 1902 conceived the Russian revolutionary movement as a nation-wide resistance movement against an essentially alien Tsarist monarchy and its supporters, and for Hitler the Weimar Republic was an un-German phenomenon. Stalin's was a marginal case in which the revolution against the pre-existing (Bolshevik) system of order was conducted from above. It is notable, however, that the purged old Bolshevik leadership was condemned as a treasonable, anti-national element.

The reader may have wondered why "ideology" was not included as an independent element of the formula. It might have been, but for simplicity's sake it seems preferable to consider this extremely important factor under the "revolutionary" heading. The ideology is, in its core, a philosophy of the revolution and program of the revolutionary struggle. As such it not only provides political orientation but serves as a powerful organizing instrument in the hands of the leadership. As Lenin said, "Without a revolutionary theory there can be no revolutionary movement."[5] Every movement-regime is associated with an ideology. As will be suggested later in this paper, comparative analysis of the ideologies may be useful in differentiating communist, fascist and nationalist forms of the movement-regime.

Revolutionary regimes are not at all new in history, but the revolutionary *mass-movement* regime is a relatively novel phenomenon. The idea is traceable at least as far back as Mazzini, and earlier intimations of it are to be found in eighteenth-century France.[6] Thus, Mazzini's contemplated revolution of national liberation and unification of Italy was to bring into being a third and greater Rome, "the Rome of the People," which in turn would provide leadership for all of Europe in creating a Europe of the people. The revolution was to be accomplished, moreover, with the active participation of masses of the people under the guidance and energetic leadership of an elite organization, Young Italy.

The history of politics in the twentieth century could be written in terms of the realization of the dreams of the nineteenth—and the discrepancy between dream and reality. The contemporary world contains a multitude of regimes, born in revolution, that rest upon and represent—or claim to—mass movements of a national or trans-national scope. In the typical case the mass movement is organized during the revolutionary struggle for power and as a means of waging

[5] *What Is To Be Done?*, in *Selected Works* (Moscow, 1946), vol. I, p. 165.
[6] J. A. Talmond discusses the eighteenth-century background in his *Origins of Totalitarian Democracy* (1952).

this struggle. Once the regime is in being, the mass movement is enlarged and given new tasks of various kinds in the continuing revolution of national renewal. In some instances (present-day Egypt, for example) the development of the mass movement occurs after the conquest of power. In some instances too, it remains largely a political artifact or pretence of a mass movement. Some of the Soviet satellite regimes might be cases in point.

The third common element is the militant centralized revolutionary party, or "vanguard" party as we may call it, which takes power in the name of the movement and the nation and then assumes the new function of governing the country single-handedly. Mazzini's phrase "party of action" foreshadowed the nature of this new type of party. Its character is largely determined by the circumstances of its origin. Since it arises outside of, and in opposition to, an existing system of law and order, electioneering is not its *métier*. Though it may take part in a given election for tactical purposes, it exists to overthrow a political order rather than to come to power within it. In the typical case it develops as a disciplined elite connected with a mass following through party "cells" in the enemy-order, and usually has a single dominating personality as its top leader and organizer. It is in essence a political warfare organization, and as such tends toward conspiratorial habits and a quasi-military, authoritarian concept of its internal organization and relation to the mass following. Since its revolutionary ends transcend the destruction of the old order, the latter event is simply a new beginning. The party becomes the staff headquarters of the new revolutionary movement-regime, the territorial committees and cells become units of rule, and the single-party state is born.

The concept of the revolutionary vanguard party, with its "cellular structure" penetrating the pores of the old society, was rather well developed already in the nineteenth century, particularly among the Russian Populists. But it found its most influential exponent early in the twentieth century in Lenin. Unlike Marx, who tended to think that history itself would make the revolution, Lenin based all his thinking on the premise that revolutions have to be organized. His theory and practice of revolutionary "party construction" not only shaped the organization of communist movements everywhere; it also radiated far and wide into nationalist and fascist movements. A well known instance of this diffusion occurred in the early 1920's, when Sun Yat-sen decided to remodel the Chinese national revolutionary party (Kuomintang) in accordance with the Leninist concept, and the Russian Bolshevik Mikhail Borodin was sent to supervise the overhauling. A little later Chiang Kai-shek gave the Russians a lesson in what might be called "anti-Communist communism" by turning the assimilated Bolshevik-type organizational forms against the Chinese Bolsheviks and their Muscovite mentors. The lesson was not lost on Stalin, who in the 1930s made use of Bolshevik organizational forms in destroying the *Russian* Bolsheviks, save for those whom he permitted to survive as Stalinists.

An instructive present-day example of a nationalist movement-regime with a ruling party shaped in the Leninist image may be found in Tunisia. President Bourguiba's Liberal Constitutional (Neo-Destour) party "has covered the whole country with a network of a thousand cells" which "replace the 'infrastructure' of the modern state." "The party members who are organized in cells form the party Congress, which elects an executive, the Political Bureau. The Political Bureau is the main instrument of government. . . . The Political Bureau exercises tight control over the party machine, in which it has established a kind of 'democratic centralism.' . . . The Liberal Constitutional party has established a large network of organizations which embrace practically the whole population."[7] The exquisite irony of the situation is that the Communist Party of Tunisia is the sole opponent of President Bourguiba's regime.

One further generalization may be offered regarding the movement-regimes as a class. Since the militant centralized revolutionary party becomes the new foundation of political authority, and its cellular structure the "infrastructure" of the new state, the movement-regime takes on the authoritarian character of the founding organization. In certain instances (about which more later) it subsequently grows much more authoritarian, and the adjective "totalitarian" may become applicable. However, the leadership of the authoritarian movement-regime insists that it is also democratic in a "new way" (*i.e.*, not the liberal Western way). This mode of thought, in which the dichotomy of "dictatorship—democracy" is rejected, is an outgrowth of the original concept of the revolutionary struggle as a mass movement for national or supra-national objectives under guidance of a disciplined political elite organization. The result is one or another version of the doctrine of "guided democracy," of which, again, Lenin was the preeminent exponent.

The notion should not be dismissed as simple hypocrisy, although it may be that in any given instance. If "democracy" here loses the connotation of effective popular control over the regime (which is, by self-definition, the group that knows best what is in the interests of the people), it simultaneously acquires the connotation of mass popular participation in the continuing revolution of national renewal. In practice this means the enlisting of masses of people in the activities of trade unions, youth, professional and other organizations that are formally non-party in character but are operated under party guidance and supervision via directorates from top to bottom in which disciplined party members predominate (the so-called "transmission belts" of Leninist theory). A large proportion of the population is thus drawn into the whirlpool of guided public life, and many may derive an experience of political participation that was denied them under the old regime. In Russia the foremost non-party organs of controlled participation are the soviets or local councils, which arose before the October Revolution and independently of communism but were later reshaped into components of the Bolshevik movement-regime. Today they form a pyramidal network of thousands of party-guided bodies at village, town, district and province level, with deliberative and administrative functions in which several millions of deputies and sub-committee members take part. Very many of these people have no direct Communist party affiliation.

---

[7] Hans E. Tutsch, "Bourguiba's Tunisia—I," *The New Leader*, February 29, 1960, p. 7.

This brings us again to the principle of transferability of organizational forms among movement-regimes of different types. Recently, for example, a pyramidal system of "councils," quite comparable in concept if not in all details to the one just described, has been introduced under the auspices of President Nasser's National Union regime in Egypt, and President Mohammed Ayub Khan's new regime in Pakistan is now introducing a similar setup there under the heading of "basic democracy." A close associate of President Nasser's has explained to a Western journalist that the purpose of the Egyptian councils is to enlist mass participation at the village level in the revolution of national renewal: "The real revolution must come in the villages. . . . Every village has elected a council, replacing the old appointed Mayor. The council constitutes itself a cooperative and works with the Government's agricultural experts." The journalist reports that Nasser aides are not insulted if this system is described as "guided democracy," and he quotes the close associate further as saying: "We have a concept of democracy, it differs from yours. . . . We need something more dynamic, more realistic. . . . If we use your system the Communists will succeed, because they can speak to the masses." Thus, there can be anti-Soviet sovietism in the field of "guided democracy," as well as the previously mentioned phenomenon of anti-Communist communism in the field of party organization.

A final observation about the movement-regime is that it has no restricted habitat in the world. A comparative politics of movement-regimes is not a regional affair, and defies the classifications of political systems according to geographic zone. There is a rough correlation between antecedent colonialism and the rise of nationalist movement-regimes or alternatively of communist movement-regimes that ride to power on a wave of nationalist revolution. There is a related and still rougher correlation between the movement-regime and the conditions of economic and cultural backwardness, feudalism, stagnation, etc., that lend a special cogency to the revolutionary call for renovation of the nation. All this might suggest the thought that the specific habitat of the movement-regime is the "East" or, more broadly, the "under-developed areas." Yet such regimes, in one form or another, have appeared not only in Russia, Asia, the Middle East, Africa, Latin America and Eastern Europe, but also in parts of Western Europe (Germany, Italy, Spain, Portugal); and Hitler's Germany was hardly an under-developed area. Moreover, movements bearing within themselves the germs of potential movement-regimes have arisen in many other countries, including Great Britain and the United States. The movement-regime is a political phenomenon to which no nation and no part of the world is completely immune.

III

The differentiation of the species of movement-regime presents a much more difficult and complex problem than the definition of the genus. There are many avenues of approach to it, variously emphasizing social, economic, historical, religious and psychological factors, etc. The most that can be attempted here is to present a few notes on the problem.

First, it must be said that we are dealing with classes of phenomena that may be distinguishable but are not fully distinct. Thus, elements of nationalism are to be found in both communist and fascist movement-regimes, and any formulae for the latter that excluded this fact would be useless. It therefore appears inadvisable to segregate the species under conceptually pure "ideal types." Allowance must be made for complexity of character and even for the possibility of genuine hybrids. In short, nationalist, fascist and communist movement-regimes are best differentiated according to their characteristic *prevailing tendencies.*

What has been said above about the transferability of organizational forms among movement-regimes of different types argues against any attempt to differentiate the types primarily in organizational terms. A more promising basis of differentiation, it seems to me, lies in the motivation of revolutionary politics, or what is often called the "revolutionary dynamism." All the movement-regimes originally have a revolutionary dynamism. They come into being by the revolutionary displacement of a pre-existing order, and seek to maintain revolutionary momentum after they come to power. They may, of course, fail to do so. They may lose revolutionary momentum eventually. When this happens they become what I shall call "extinct" movement-regimes. Like a star that has ceased to give off light, an extinct movement-regime may go on existing for a long while without a revolutionary *raison d'être.* We may say of such a regime what Herzen in 1853 said of the contemporary Russian monarchy, that it "exercises power in order to exercise power."

The revolutionary dynamism of the nationalist movement-regime is relatively restricted in scope and easy to define. Here the goal of the revolutionary movement is, first, national independence, the creation of a sovereign nation-state. Second, the revolutionary movement is aimed at the modernization of the newly independent state, and this typically involves many elements of an internal social revolution. Old class relations in society, old patterns of land tenure, old customs, old traditions of thought and generally old ways of conducting the business of life are assailed in an internal revolution of national renewal. However, purely nationalist revolutionary movement-regimes show a definite tendency to spend their revolutionary force rather early. In some cases this happens soon after the achievement of the original revolutionary goals and prior to the completion of the revolutionizing of the old society. In other words, the nationalist movement-regime is peculiarly the prey of the phenomenon of "extinction."

In the best of cases, of which the Kemalist movement in Turkey might be an example, the revolution of national renewal is carried through far enough under the auspices of the movement-regime to make possible an orderly further development in a new and more democratic direction. More typical, however, may be the case of the Chinese Kuomintang, where the early subsiding of revolutionary dynamism paved the way for the displacement of the nationalist movement-regime by a communist movement-regime that came to power under the slogan of carrying through the "betrayed" revolution of national renewal. In general, communist movement-regimes, where not installed by direct action of a foreign power (as in most of Eastern Europe, North Korea, etc., after World War II), tend to arise as the penalty for either the absence of an effective national revolutionary movement where conditions call for it, or the inability of nationalist movement-regimes, once in being, to maintain their initial revolutionary momentum.

The relatively low revolutionary dynamism of the nationalist movement-regime is correlated with a relatively restricted revolutionary "constituency." The ideology of the national revolution is itself national. The sovereign independence and renovation of the nation are the objectives. Once installed in power, the nationalist movement-regime may develop an active foreign policy within what is likely to be a neutralist orientation in world affairs. But this will not be a policy of active export of the revolution to other lands. Such revolutionary expansionism is, on the other hand, a distinctive characteristic of *both* communist and fascist movement-regimes. Here the sphere of outlet for revolutionary energy is not confined to the national homeland. The politics of revolution embrace not only the revolutionary capture of power and subsequent internal revolution, but also, in varying manner and degree, the turning of the revolutionary dynamism out upon the world. Thus when a new movement-regime embarks upon a course of active export of the revolution to other countries, this may be taken as a fairly strong indication that it belongs not to the nationalist species but to one of the other two. The Castro regime in Cuba would be a case in point.

Communism and fascism are often contrasted on the ground that the one has an international "class appeal" while the other has a "national appeal" and is nationalist in essence. There is something in this idea, but it is also quite misleading. The dichotomy of communist internationalism *versus* fascist nationalism overlooks the fact that national and international elements commingle in both phenomena. On the one hand, the communist movement-regime is committed to a form of the national revolution as well as to the goal of world communism. It appropriates not only the appeals of the revolution of national renewal but also the task of carrying it through (in its own special way) when the movement comes to power.

On the other hand, the fascist revolutionary dynamism shares with the communist a supra-national scope. Both give ideological expression to this by proclaiming a supra-national revolutionary constituency and also an international *enemy* of the revolution. In the classic Bolshevik conception, the revolutionary constituency begins with the working classes of the revolutionary homeland and embraces the working classes of all countries, and the international bourgeoisie (or "international imperialism") is the enemy. Fascist regimes differ in their ideologies, but those regularly show a dualism that is comparable in kind if less comprehensive in scope. They take the *nation* as the nucleus of a large whole, a supra-national revolutionary constituency or sphere of revolution. Thus, for Hitler the German *Volk* was the nucleus of the "Nordic race," and international Jewry or international imperialism was the enemy of the national-socialist revolution. For Mussolini "Romanism" was the key word, and the larger sphere of revolution was reflected in the slogan: "Italy today, tomorrow the Roman Empire!" Examples could be multiplied. The dual symbolism of President Nasser's movement-regime, which views Egypt or the U.A.R. as the nucleus of a vast "Arab nation" embracing all the separate Arabic nations and Arabs wherever they are, belongs to the pattern in question. Taken in conjunction with Nasserist activity in the export of the revolution to neighboring countries, this suggests that it would be a mistake to construe Nasserism as nationalist in essence although it does display various features of a nationalist revolutionary movement.

In certain instances, typically occurring in smaller countries, we see the phenomenon of "national communism" or, alternatively, "national fascism" (of which present-day Francoist Spain might be a good example). This development may be, and in the latter case no doubt is, indicative of a general loss of revolutionary momentum and the tendency to grow "extinct." On the other hand, it may, as in the case of Titoist Yugoslavia, be accompanied by something in the nature of an internal political "reformation" in which the movement develops with new vigor but in different directions.

One further consideration should be noted in connection with the fascist form of movement-regime. Although its sphere of revolution is not confined to the national homeland, it does typically indulge in strident national self-glorification. It proclaims its nation to be supreme in all the recognized national virtues, and declares that the good of the nation is the highest goal of the regime. This has led some scholars to see in fascism "an inflammation of nationalism."[8] It seems, however, that this inflamed nationalism is essentially a pseudo-nationalism, and that fascists must be distinguished from authentic nationalists as being, at best, the pharisees of nationalism. Thus, when Hitler saw that all was lost, he desired the destruction of the German nation as punishment for its unworthiness. Germany had not been worthy of its *Fuehrer.* Obviously, the supreme value was not the German nation but the Hitlerite self, and the official glorification of the nation had been a cover and vehicle of the leader's self-glorification.

I take this to be indicative of a critically important general fact about the fascist type of movement-regime, viz., that here the psychology or more accurately the psychopathology of the leader becomes the driving force of the political mechanism. The regime is shaped into a highly complicated instrumentality for acting out the needs of the paranoid leader-personality, whose psychodynamics are politicalized, *i.e.*, expressed in political action. Thus, the Nazi regime started the second World War in 1939 at a time when it was militarily not yet prepared and to the chagrin of many of its highest officials, military and civilian. It was propelled into this action not by a cold calculation of relative forces and risks, but by the compulsive need of Hitler for revenge against his enemies. When his advisers warned him against it on the ground of the enemies' strength, he replied: "Then I will build U-boats! U-boats! U-boats! . . . I will build airplanes! airplanes! airplanes! *and I will exterminate my enemies.*"

[8] Hans Kohn, *Nationalism: Its Meaning and History* (1955), p. 79.

Comparable in character (though not in consequence) was the statement reportedly made by Stalin on the eve of his public assault on Tito in 1948: "I will shake my little finger—and there will be no more Tito. He will fall."

In order to shape the regime into a means of expression of his personal needs, the leader must reduce the ruling party to the role of an important cog in the apparatus of the state. It was pointed out earlier that movement-regimes tend to be headed by a dominating individual personality. This, however, does not imply that they are absolute autocracies. In fact, the broad tendency is oligarchical rule by the top leadership of the ruling party under the overall direction of the dominant personality. The fascist movement-regimes deviate from this pattern and show a pronounced tendency to absolute autocracy, which involves the subordination of the party to the state as embodied in the leader. He emancipates himself from the control of the party oligarchy, and relies heavily upon the secret police and permanent pervasive terror through this organization to ensure unquestioning compliance with his least wishes on the part of everyone from the lowliest man in the street to the highest dignitaries of the regime. Consequently, fascist regimes tend to become highly *statist* in orientation, and the state as personified in the leader displaces the party as the supreme symbol and object of official adoration. For these reasons the most accurate general term for the various fascist movement-regimes would be "fuehrerism," and the most accurate title in each individual instance would be the one formed from the leader's name (*e.g.*, "Hitlerism" rather than "Nazism").

It was said above that movement-regimes may undergo "extinction" when the revolutionary dynamism subsides. Another possible process is "metamorphosis" as a result of the *alternation* of the dynamism. A movement-regime of one species turns into one of another species as a consequence of a qualitative change in the motivation of revolutionary politics. Such a change is determined in its turn by a change or changes in the leadership situation within the regime. For various reasons it may not be possible for the leadership of the metamorphosed movement-regime to admit (even to itself) that the metamorphosis has occurred. The evidence of it must therefore be sought not in the regime's official self-definition but rather in changes in the observable complex of ideological and behavioral patterns.

In conclusion I suggest that the political history of Soviet Russia probably offers the best laboratory for the study of the phenomenon of metamorphosis of movement-regimes. From the standpoint of a comparative politics of movement-regimes, this history is one of different *movements* and of different Soviet *regimes* within a framework of continuity of certain (transferable) organizational forms and official nomenclature. The rise of Stalinism between 1928 and 1938 involved a process of change far more deep and pervasive than is generally realized. It was the metamorphosis of the original communist or Bolshevik movement-regime into a new movement-regime of the fuehrerist type. As indicated at the outset of this paper, the metamorphosis was not accompanied by any change in the regime's official self-definition (although it is significant that Stalin in 1952 banned the word "Bolshevik" from the name of the party and from all Soviet official usage). It was, however, reflected in a whole system of changes in the political process, the ideological pattern, the organization of supreme power, and official patterns of behavior. Partly because of the inadequacy of our theoretical apparatus, and partly too because of the unduly large influence of the Soviet regime's self-image upon our conceptions, Western thinking has not, on the whole, assessed the full significance of the change from the Bolshevik to the Stalinist political system. A basic continuity of the Bolshevik movement-regime has been postulated, as is implicit, for example, in the following statement by Bertram Wolfe: "When Stalin died in 1953, Bolshevism was fifty years old."[9]

Very real and important issues affecting the understanding and interpretation of the political changes in Russia since Stalin's death are involved in what may seem to be a problem of merely historical interest. On the postulate of continuity of the Bolshevik movement-regime from 1917 to 1953, "significant change" will logically mean change *away* from Bolshevism or communism. This assumption results in a tendency to deprecate the significance of the post-Stalinist changes in Soviet political processes and policies. If, on the other hand, we operate on the premise that Stalin's political revolution from above transformed the original Bolshevik movement-regime into a new one that was fuehrerist in its inner dynamism and political tendency, we shall reason that when Stalin died in 1953 Bolshevism had been moribund in Russia for fifteen years, and that the main issue was whether it would revive and if so to what extent. This opens the way to a recognition that a whole complex of quite significant political changes have occurred in post-Stalinist Russia within the broad framework of a conscious movement under the aegis of Khrushchev to reconstitute the political system of Bolshevism.

[9] Dallin, *op. cit.,* p. 268.

part THREE
Political Dynamics

The pursuit of power—the capacity to command the actions of others—by individuals and groups is a universal phenomenon. Individuals and groups are organized through specialized associations representing their interests; they also promulgate or associate themselves with ideological orientations. By *political dynamics* we mean the interplay of social groups, organized interests, and ideologies, generally taking place through political parties and institutions in order to shape public policy.

THE GROUP UNIVERSE

The process whereby groups compete for positions and advantage takes place in all political systems, and hence can be studied functionally and comparatively. In some political systems, groups press their demands and claims mainly through "interest" or "pressure" groups; in others, through the parties or administration. Comparative analysis can be conducted by studying the diverse patterns of interest articulation. Interest groups can be considered in terms of their size, membership, leadership, organization, relations with political parties, and means used to mobilize public opinion, gain access to the state, and influence decisions. Group analysis has the merit of bringing the student directly into the heart of the political process—social conflict and its resolution. By studying the "interest group universe" in a given political system, we gain a good insight into the distribution of power in that society and the manner in which interests are organized and expressed.

One of the striking features of industrialized societies is the development and proliferation of specialized groups. In a modern society they represent every conceivable social, economic, religious, and professional interest. The largest and most powerful groups, speaking on behalf of the major social classes, are the business, labor, and agricultural organizations. Every modern political system must provide these associations or interest groups with the opportunity to gain access to the policy makers and make known their proposals or demands.

183

Reconciliation of the demands of interest groups and, broadly speaking, of social forces, is perhaps the most serious single challenge confronting any political system. We are not referring here to the demands, say, of trade unions and management for a minimum wage fixed at a particular level, though this kind of conflict is quite intense. We refer rather to the attitude of social groups toward the political process itself, the acceptance of the "rules of the game" by all the players. For example, there is a complex network of specialized associations in both Great Britain and France. In both countries we find powerful trade unions, business groups, churches, and associations of farmers, veterans, teachers, and so on. Some French groups are more powerful than their opposite numbers in Britain (for example, farmers, small merchants, lay Catholics) and vice versa (British trade unions and business groups are more highly organized than their counterparts in France). Yet the basic attitudes of the groups are significantly different. In spite of their political rivalry, expressed through support of the Labor and Conservative Parties, the trade unions and management groups in Great Britain accept a commitment to parliamentary institutions. With a few exceptions (such as the Irish nationalists), they are willing to work within the existing system in order to realize their goals, and do not turn against it when they lose. The habits of compromise are solidly established in British society. The actors abide by fundamental rules which are embodied in the constitutional system.

In France, however, the same economic or social interests are *not* in agreement upon the values of the state or on political procedures to be used in the resolution of group conflicts. The labor and business groups are fundamentally hostile to each other, and constantly strive to change the rules of the game or the system itself so as to secure a more advantageous position. The most powerful trade union in France, the General Confederation of Labor, is Communist controlled and Communist oriented. That is, the industrial proletariat in France largely expresses its demands through a union and a party which reject the system. Important elements of the business community, on the other hand, not only distrust the workers, but wish to introduce a "strong" state to deal with them. The parliamentary system is held in low repute by other important interests as well. Political debates and meetings are marked by verbal and physical violence. In practice the disaffected groups are generally unable to overthrow the system, and accept it provisionally. Compromise is difficult to achieve and breaks down altogether during political crises. There is a distinct tendency to change the rules of the game (usually by promulgating a new constitution) whenever the balance shifts and one constellation of groups or forces gains the upper hand. Thus, one of the most important questions to pose about a political system is the attitude of the principal organized groups toward each other and toward the system itself.

POLITICAL PARTIES

Max Weber's definition of party is useful for placing the subject in broad social and historical perspective. "The term political party," he suggested, "will be employed to designate an associative type of social relationship, membership in which rests on formally free recruitment. The end to which its activity is devoted is to secure power within a corporate group for its leaders in order to attain ideal or material advantages for its active members. These advantages may consist in the realization of certain objective policies or the attainment of personal advantages or both." As Weber uses the term, a "party" can exist in any corporate group—unions, fraternal orders, churches, university faculties, and corporations. It can be oriented toward personal interest or toward broad policy. When the rules of the corporate group provide for campaigns and elections, the parties coalesce around interests. Political victory in party terms means that its adherents, in assuming direction of the state, can realize party proposals. Political parties thus tend to be complex social institutions holding together those who have a common program and those who strive for power and personal advantage.[1] In a sense they are specialized associations *within* specialized associations and become more complex, organized, and bureaucratic as a society approaches the "modern" type.

It is therefore understandable that political parties were not studied systematically until the modern period, when they were fully developed. John Stuart Mill's treatise *On Representative Government,* written in 1861, contained an extensive plea for proportional representation but no analysis of parties. Insofar as parties were brought under scrutiny, they were generally denounced as expressions of factionalism. In a classic criticism of political parties, James Bryce expressed his fear that insofar as parties are permitted to run the government a community falls below the level of ideal democracy. "In the ideal democracy every citizen is intelligent, patriotic, disinterested. His sole wish is to discover the right side in each contested issue, and to fix upon the best man among competing candidates. His common sense, aided by a knowledge of the constitution of his country, enables him to judge easily between the arguments submitted to him while his own zeal is sufficient to carry him to the polling booth. . . ." But, Bryce continues, the electorate is *not* informed or interested. Hence, politicians discover the advantages of organization. "Organization and discipline mean the command of the leaders, the subordination and obedience of the rank and file; and they mean also the growth of a party spirit which is in itself irrational, impelling men to vote from considerations which have little to do with a love of truth or a sense of justice."[2]

Most students of political parties at the turn of the century, like Bryce, were concerned with the shortcomings and deficiencies of the political parties: with bossism, corruption, and the inability of the parties to put forward coherent programs and implement them once in power. M. I. Ostrogorski's classic treatise on *Democracy and the Organization of Political Parties* emphasized especially the sordid side of politics—above all, the politicians' craving for spoils. The thesis argued by Bryce and Ostrogorski concerning American parties was strengthened

[1] See Max Weber, *The Theory of Social and Economic Organization* (Oxford University Press, 1947), pp. 407–12.

[2] From James Bryce's preface to M. Ostrogorski, *Democracy and the Organization of Political Parties* (New York, 1902).

by Robert Michels' study of the German Social Democratic party. From the viewpoint of comparative analysis Michels' work marked an advance, since his "iron law of oligarchy" could be construed as a general theory in the light of which all political parties may be examined. Bryce, Ostrogorski, and Michels, taken together, offered a full-fledged theory of parties and their role in democracies. They fully documented the growth of mass political parties with complex structures in the United States, Britain, and Germany. They assumed that democracy somehow involves meaningful participation by the masses in the making of important decisions. They agreed that parties were controlled by a handful of politicians and leaders. Democracy therefore becomes less and less feasible as parties become more and more complex.

Theory regarding the role of parties in a democracy has undergone sweeping change since then. The widespread view of parties as destructive of democracy has given way to an almost equally widespread view that parties are indispensable to the operation of democratic institutions. American political scientists were especially affected by the New Deal, which seemed to demonstrate the potential utility of political parties in mobilizing public support for a program of social reform. Also, the hostile reaction to the Nazi regime included searching appraisal of the one-party system. In defense of Western democracy against the challenge of fascism and communism, it was discerned that democracy was bound up somehow with the existence of at least two parties. The previously despised parties were elevated to positions of great prestige by political philosophers and researchers.

Stress was laid upon the role of parties in the democratic process by such writers as A. D. Lindsay, R. M. MacIver, C. J. Friedrich, Joseph Schumpeter, and Walter Lippmann, to name but a few.[3] They argued that a distinct element of democracy, as contrasted with fascism and communism, was the existence of an opposition. But it is not sufficient to grant an abstract right of opposition to individuals. To be effective, opposition must be enabled to organize, that is, form a party. In the absence of parties, there would be no check upon the egoistic impulses of the rulers. Also, the masses can participate effectively in government only through the agency of parties. Thus, parties organize the "chaotic public will," educate the private citizens to public responsibility, connect government with public opinion, and select the political leadership. In answer to Michels' criticism of oligarchy, it has been argued that even oligarchical parties may serve democratic purposes—provided that there is free competition among the parties.[4] Thus, Gwendolyn Carter concludes her survey of parties in the Commonwealth: "Political parties . . . are not only an aid to democracy but an essential element in making it possible." Similarly, E. E. Schattschneider on the American parties: "The major parties have become the crucial and competing

[3] See A. D. Lindsay, *The Modern Democratic State* (New York, 1947); R. M. MacIver, *The Web of Government* (New York, 1947); Carl J. Friedrich, *Constitutional Government and Democracy* (Boston, 1946); Joseph Schumpeter, *Capitalism, Socialism and Democracy* (New York, 1947); and Walter Lippmann, *Public Opinion* (New York, 1945).

[4] See the argument in R. T. McKenzie, *British Political Parties* (London, 1955).

channels of policy formulation in our national democracy." And Maurice Duverger contends that in all advanced societies, "liberty and the party system coincide.[5] The contrast with Bryce, Ostrogorski, and Michels is complete!

However, the pervasive crisis of parliamentary democracy since World War II has been reflected in a revival of criticism of political parties. This is especially the case in countries where large social groups have not been fully integrated into the political system, as evidenced by massive support for antiparliamentary parties. In France, for example, there is now an extensive literature critical of the role played by parties in the democratic process.

In developing nations, competitive political parties generally have fallen into disrepute. In many countries, as in Burma, Turkey, South Korea, Pakistan, Egypt, Ghana, and Nigeria, the army seized power professedly in order to defend the national interest against the corrupt parties. In India, disciples of Mahatma Gandhi urge the conversion of Congress into a national movement and the creation of a "party-less democracy." Ben Bella declared after coming to power that the "Front" ruling Algeria must never degenerate into a mere party. But it would be misleading to consider all criticism of parties as manifestations of a dictatorial impulse. Most students of developing nations recognize that in fact there are genuine difficulties in transferring democratic institutions from Europe and North America to the rest of the world. Democracy does not appear appropriate in societies where the overwhelming majority of the people is illiterate and therefore not in a position to judge intelligently between candidates and programs. Different kinds of questions about both parties and democracy are raised: how the elite is recruited, what role is played by the party in mobilizing the masses and breaking up the traditional society, what kind of values are held by the educated elite, and so on. The trend in interpreting the democratic nature of parties in developing nations is to assess their role in the transition from traditional to more modern forms of social organization. Mass participation in politics is one of the social conditions of democratic government. In some cases the party asserts a monopoly of power in order to create a modern society with the support, even if without the understanding, of the peasantry. In other cases, the party seeks to preserve the power of a traditional group. Dominant parties may seek to crush opposition, or may tolerate criticism and respect an independent judiciary. Theory concerning the role of parties in a democracy is thus being modified in the light of the experience of the developing nations.

GROUPS AND PARTIES

The political party is the most important single link between groups, the people, and the government in a democracy. Through the party, leadership is able to reach out into the masses for support and new sources of strength, while

---

[5] See contributions by Gwendolyn Carter and E. E. Schattschneider in Sigmund Neumann, ed., *Modern Political Parties* (Chicago, 1956), pp. 103 and 215; and M. Duverger, *Les partis politiques* (Paris, 1954), p. 465.

the masses in turn are able to focus criticism and make demands upon it. The party, if backed by a majority of the electorate, coordinates the multifarious functions of the government in order to achieve coherently stated aims. A minority party gives like-minded individuals and groups an opportunity to rally their forces, develop a program, and prepare for the day when power might be wielded or at least shared.

But the mass party also characterizes modern dictatorships. In the Soviet Union the Communist Party attempts to coordinate the activities of all major interests in the nation; while in Great Britain the majority party recognizes the right of other parties to seek the support of the electorate. Yet in both countries the party remains the most important instrument used by social groups in their quest for power. In a dictatorship the overriding task of the party is to mobilize the masses. This is the dominant trend also in developing nations, where a small, educated elite is determined to bring about modernization. Even in parliamentary democracies parties must be able to generate widespread popular support for the policies of the executive, or else the regime is in serious trouble. Totalitarian parties in particular secure the adherence of masses of people by offering them an opportunity to gratify social impulses, but democratic parties likewise engage in some of the same activities. Most studies of totalitarian parties have emphasized the role of the party as an instrument of the leadership, while most studies of democratic parties stress the role of the party in limiting leadership and permitting popular participation in the decision-making process. Yet, all parties may be viewed and compared in both ways.

Thus, groups organize, present their claims to the parties, and are in turn courted by party leaders. Decision makers are themselves members of parties and are dependent upon the support of groups for maintenance in office. The delicate process of compromising pressures must take place somewhere within the political system: Is it within the single party, or the major party of a two-party system, or a parliamentary assembly? Does the nature of the relationship between leaders and followers in British, American, French, and Russian parties reveal differences or similarities? If we compare parties as regards function, we may discover that social conflict is expressed and resolved in different ways in these countries. Comparative study of party structure may reveal the existence of common organizational trends in all party systems.

CLASSIFICATION OF PARTY SYSTEMS

Classification is a first step in comparison since it enables the observer to select for analysis the like elements of various political systems. One such classification is based on the means employed in appealing to the electorate and organizing opinion. Some commentators distinguish between parties of interest and parties of principle, or parties of personalities and parties of program, "broker" parties and "missionary" parties. American parties would thus be considered examples of interest appeal and personalities, while British and continental parties would be programmatic. Yet this classification does not fully explain modern trends. American parties reflect ideological orientations, and continental parties represent interests and may be led by forceful personalities. As Sigmund Neumann has persuasively argued:

> The reality of modern politics represents a much more complex picture than is suggested by the simple array of insiders and outsiders, of parties of patronage and parties of principles, of expediency, interests and Weltanschauung, of personages and programs. Such precise but utterly imaginary partitions fail to reveal the inner dynamics and tensions of a functioning democracy. In fact, it is the inexhaustible mixture of all these elements that comprises the life of modern political parties—and perhaps escapes any rigid classification.[6]

A more useful scheme of classification is in terms of degree of centralization and discipline. Robert Michels, in his classic study of *Political Parties,* argued that the dominance of the leadership characterizes *all* mass parties, including those whose ideology is militantly democratic. Michels raised a significant problem of democratic theory. Democracy obviously involves some kind of control over the rulers by the people. Every democracy is run by political parties. But who runs the parties? To what extent can the leaders be controlled by those who hold subordinate positions in the organization?

Democratic parties vary greatly as regards the relative power of local units, members, national agencies, and leaders. American parties, for instance, are federations of state political organizations. There is no formal chain of command. National leadership results from coalitions among local party leaders, not from the directives of a powerful center. British parties, on the other hand, are national organizations with local branches. In both the Conservative and Labor parties decision making is vested in the leaders. Parties in parliamentary democracies run the gamut from the British model to the American. The two large parties of the Federal Republic of Germany are structurally similar to the British parties. Leadership in both the Social Democratic party and the Christian Democratic Union is concentrated at the national level and personalized. On the other hand, conservative and moderate parties in multiparty systems have relatively few active members, and are run almost exclusively by parliamentarians.

In authoritarian systems the parties are always highly centralized and serve as admirable instruments of coordination and control. In all Communist parties relations between local units and national bodies are proclaimed to be "democratic"—that is, each local unit elects delegates to the next highest organization, and all delegates are urged to "discuss" party policy. The impression is carefully cultivated that "democratic centralism" enables the party to act as a unity, on the basis of widespread debate within the party ranks. In practice, however, "democratic centralism" vests plenary control of the party in the leadership and confines the role of militants to the execution of policy.

The degree of centralization and discipline within parties largely determines the "style" of the political process, that is, the level of the political system at

6 Sigmund Neumann, ed., *Modern Political Parties* (Chicago, 1956), p. 401.

which compromises are made, the degree of cohesion of parliamentary groups, and the nature of electoral appeals. Yet in all parties there is a sharp distinction between the leadership and the followers, and the latter are rarely in a position to shape or control policy.

Perhaps the most popular classification of party systems is in terms of the number of parties in the field. In his influential book, *Political Parties,* Maurice Duverger points out that the one-party, two-party, and multiparty systems tend to correspond to the major types of contemporary regimes. Thus, dictatorships are characterized by the single party, and democracies by either a two, or multi-party system. The two-party system is frequently held up as a model form, permitting the majority to govern and the minority to criticize. Multiparty systems are usually considered less stable, but offer the voter a greater choice of alternatives. However, this classification has come under attack. Some observers have suggested that one-party systems may serve as transitional forms, making possible the creation of a more democratic regime at a later time. Mexico is frequently cited as an instance where one-party rule is compatible with democracy because debate can take place within the dominant party.

The customary distinction between two and multiparty systems has also been questioned, particularly with regard to France and Scandinavia. French political scientists have called attention to the agreements (electoral alliances and cabinet coalitions) between parties of the same political family, which provide a measure of coherence. Thus, François Goguel speaks of the "party of order" and the "party of movement" in interpreting the conflict among the various parties of the Third Republic, in his *La Politique des partis sous la IIIe République* (1946). In run-off elections under the Third and Fifth Republics the French voter has frequently been presented with a choice between only two or three serious candidates. Similarly, students of Scandinavia have pointed out that these multi-party systems are capable of sustaining dynamic and stable governments. The parties form coalitions in the same way that wings of a major party in Britain or the United States come to agreement on a common policy or leader. It may be more fruitful to view party systems in terms of the nature of the national consensus, that is, whether or not the major parties (within either a two- or multi-party system) and in turn the major social groups on which they are based, share the same attitudes toward basic values and goals and the means by which they are to be attained.

In recent years party systems have been reappraised in the context of the general process of modernization. As a traditional society breaks up and takes on the characteristics of "modernity," it goes through a series of political crises. The first is a crisis of *legitimacy.* Values sanctioning rule by a traditional monarchy or aristocracy are called into question, and are eventually replaced by values such as parliamentary democracy or nationalism that are more consonant with mass participation in the political system. This goes hand-in-hand with a crisis of *participation.* New social groups, in particular an industrial middle class and a working class, make their appearance and demand entry into the political system. In mature industrial societies there is a continuing crisis of *conflict-*

management. The political system is confronted by the need to facilitate economic growth, reconcile the claims of powerful social groups for a greater share of wealth and power, and ensure the continued adherence of these groups to the system itself.

Political parties, it may be argued, have gone through stages of development that correspond to the successive crises of legitimacy, participation, and conflict-management. Parties throughout Europe in the early part of the 19th century were primarily concerned with new principles of legitimacy and the representation of fairly narrow interests. With the extension of the suffrage in the course of the 19th century the parties created mass organizations outside of parliament. Mass parties, like the German Social Democrat, British Liberal, and, later, Labor parties sought to defend the interests of the new middle and working classes, and to mobilize popular support for their policies. At this stage the parties tended to reflect sharp ideological orientations. The "parties of participation" had to make adjustments in order to cope with the demands of late industrialization, when problems became more complex and less susceptible to ideological solutions. They became more concerned with the management of conflict and tensions when in power, and more pragmatic in their appeals to the electorate.

One of the most noticeable trends affecting parties at present is the development of plebiscitary government. Its main trait is the bypassing or the diminution of the powers of all representative bodies in favor of personalized leadership stemming from direct popular support in periodic elections. In France under the Gaullist constitution, the President, as the political leader and head of the executive, now derives his powers from direct election. This is also the case for the American president and the British cabinet under the leadership of the prime minister, who is head of the majority party. The political parties select and nominate a leader who then appeals directly to the public. Although the parties may set broad policy guidelines, the personal appeal of the leader and his ability to secure widespread support may, in the last analysis, be the decisive factor for victory or defeat at the polls.

In France, plebiscitary government has an old and venerable lineage that goes back to Bonapartism. In all countries it is a reflection of profound social changes that have led to an increasingly homogeneous body politic. Under these altered circumstances the parties can no longer sell their ideological or policy programs. Large national formations vie for support on the basis of broadly similar appeals to consumer interests. As a result, identification with party becomes weaker, or, to put it another way, the personality of a leader becomes more important. Correspondingly, the ratio of party members to voters, for the whole community and for each party, goes down, while there are growing numbers of independents or "floaters."

In totalitarian systems the ruling party excludes competition and uses the election as a well-controlled plebiscitary instrument. The leader in a communist system is likely to emerge only after he has proven himself within the party, which remains a powerful recruitment and screening agency. In presidential democracies nonparty men may, without any prior screening or testing, avail themselves of the plebiscitary character of the election. Even in Britain and other parliamentary democracies the struggle for leadership of the party, and certainly the general election itself, is greatly influenced by the personal qualities of the contending leaders. The logic of plebiscitary government applies to both Western democracies and totalitarian systems. The intermediary organs—including the parties and representative assemblies—are weakened, and power is concentrated in the political executive. A continuing problem in all modern political systems is to create institutions that might counterbalance the tremendous political and decision-making powers of plebiscitary leaders.

POLITICAL IDEOLOGIES

The term "ideology" was first popularized by Napoleon when he used it in a derogatory fashion to refer to intellectuals opposing his policies. It was taken up by Marx and Engels, who distinguished between the material basis of society and the "superstructure" (including ideology, religion, legal systems, etc.) which rests upon it. Law, politics, morality, and religion in the Marxist view reflect the interests of the class in power.

At the other extreme from the Marxist theory of ideology is the view that ideas command interests. Even an observer as sympathetic to Marxism as Karl Mannheim suggested the existence of a "utopian" mentality, which does not derive from the life situation of the individual concerned. "A state of mind is utopian when it is incongruous with the state of reality within which it occurs." Thus, a businessman could develop ideas that transcend the reality of his economic or class interests. The modification is important. It admits the possibility that ideas might not emerge directly out of interests. Max Weber has argued cogently that some key belief systems—Protestantism, for example—may permit transformation of an existing reality. In encouraging thrift and hard work, Protestant ideology undermined feudal society and paved the way for the emergence of capitalist production.[7]

The controversy between the theorists of "ideology" and "utopia" has perhaps obscured a central feature of the political process: that generally ideologies are related to economic and social groups. In all political systems there is an understandable tendency for individuals and groups to define and defend their interests in universal or idealistic terms. Every group attempts to rationalize its position or program, even if only for tactical reasons. In a general way, all major social groups try to identify themselves with the nation as a whole. Thus, what's good for business (or even a single firm, like General Motors) is good for the country; the workers are the sole creators of value; and a sturdy peasantry is the backbone of the nation. These transparent rationalizations are usually recognized as such by politicians and the public alike.

More important, each of the major social classes in a modern society also

[7] See Karl Mannheim, *Ideology and Utopia* (New York, 1949), and Max Weber, *Protestant Ethic and the Spirit of Capitalism.*

tends to associate itself with a particular interpretation of politics. This is not to say that all workers or businessmen or farmers think and vote alike, but merely that certain voting and ideological trends may usually be discerned. The clash of social forces is generally paralleled by a somewhat more complex clash of political ideologies. Socialism, conservatism, liberalism, and communism are all connected in some fashion with social classes, but these ideologies are not necessarily rationalizations of class interests. There are also ways of looking at the world in terms of key analytic concepts, *attempts to change reality* and not merely to justify it.

In industrialized nations, for example, the middle classes tend to support conservative parties and ideologies, while the working class usually supports socialist or communist parties and ideologies. The complex relationship between groups, parties, and ideologies is one of the most important subjects of comparative analysis. As regards the ideologies themselves, all three trends mentioned above—conservatism, socialism, and communism—are undergoing internal crises and transformation. Throughout the Western world there is considerable controversy within the *conservative* movement over the merits of laissez-faire and state action. Those in the tradition of Tory Democracy have accepted the general philosophy of John Maynard Keynes, according to which the State creates suitable conditions for economic expansion by means of fiscal and credit controls. Some continental conservatives also hope to transcend the class struggle by "integrating" the workers in the economic and social structure. Thus the Christian Democrats in Germany advocate "co-management" of industry by owners and workers, and the Gaullists in France have proposed a scheme of labor-management associations. Important elements within the conservative movement, however, reject both Keynesian economics and codetermination in favor of free enterprise and competitive capitalism. The necessity of winning electoral majorities has tended to isolate the advocates of laissez-faire and has given an advantage to those who wish to make use of the State in stimulating and directing the economy. Successful conservative parties have thus found it increasingly necessary to compromise the beliefs of their most militant supporters.

Similarly, all *socialist* movements are going through a period of ideological reassessment and adjustment. Throughout the 19th century socialist parties were split by the conflict between revolutionaries and moderates. The former argued that the interests of the workers can be realized only by eliminating the capitalist system. The moderates disagreed with the Marxist emphasis on revolution, and urged participation by the workers in the institutions of the democratic state. These controversies have continued and have seriously reduced the effectiveness of socialist parties. The French Socialist party, for example, retains many revolutionary symbols, yet cooperates with other democratic parties in both elections and parliament. As a consequence, it has frightened away both middle-class supporters (because of its platform) and working-class militants (because of alliances with bourgeois parties).

The dilemmas of contemporary socialism are especially evident in Great

Britain—the only major nation in which a social democratic party has gained power. A bitter debate within the party has been taking place over program and tactics. The moderates fear that the middle class is being alienated by undue emphasis on nationalization of industry. They urge the party to concentrate on central planning (rather than public ownership) of the economy, along with elimination of class and social inequalities. The Left-wing leaders contend that nationalization should be accelerated, and that the workers should be given direct powers of management and control in the publicly owned industries. The vitality of the socialist movement would be restored, they claim, and electoral victory assured.

Communist ideology has also been modified significantly in the past century. It has been found necessary to reinterpret key doctrines in order to explain developments within both capitalist and communist systems. Even orthodox Marxists have admitted that the development of capitalism does not inexorably bring about poverty and degradation, and with it a sharpened class consciousness. Such highly industrialized nations as the United States and Great Britain do not have proletarian revolutionary movements. It is in the economically retarded nations that the "communist" revolution has triumphed. Lenin tried to explain the shortcomings in Marx's analysis by postulating a further stage in the development of capitalism: imperialism. As a result of imperialist adventures, he contended, capitalists are able to secure "super-profits" enabling them to buy up or "bribe" certain labor leaders and even some segments of the working class. The trade unions become concerned above all with extracting concessions from the capitalists rather than overthrowing the whole capitalist system. Yet Lenin did not expect capitalism to collapse because of the contradictions described by Marx. It becomes necessary, then, to create a revolutionary party that will do the job originally assigned to the revolutionary proletariat.

Marxist "revisionists" argue that Lenin failed to appreciate an important political development in the West. Modern democracies, they point out, accept responsibility for sparing the masses the kind of suffering Marx believed would explode in revolution. The involvement of the democratic state with the economy, usually over the determined opposition of capitalist interests, has had the consequence of improving conditions of labor and stimulating production in whose profits workers share. The "class struggle" in a modern democracy, they contend, is not a straight fight between only two classes, but a rivalry of multifarious groups and interests for a greater share of political and economic power.

The comparative study of ideology involves the identification of specific ideologies in various countries, and tracing them to dominant social groups. What is the nature of conservative, or communist, or socialist ideology in different nations? The student should attempt to compare these ideologies in terms of content (for example, conservatism in Britain and the United States, or communism in Europe and Asia), and relationship to groups. Communism in an advanced country like France may receive major support from the industrial workers; in an underdeveloped country, where there is no proletariat, it may be primarily an intellectual or agrarian movement. Attention might be focused on particular groups, like the working class in the United States and continental Europe, and comparison made between their ideologies. The nature and intensity of ideological conflict should also be studied comparatively, since this is a fairly reliable indicator of stability or instability, consensus or lack of consensus, in a political system. Generalizations concerning groups and ideologies will reveal both differences and similarities, which can be explained only in terms of "conditioning factors," such as development of habits of compromise, dynamism of political leadership, effectiveness of political parties, viability of the economy, and so on. Certain social groups are of particular importance during periods of rapid political change, for example, the intellectuals. In short, virtually every significant part of the political system can be explored by using the relationship between groups and ideologies as an interpretive tool.

chapter VI
GROUP THEORY

The early literature on groups shared many of the characteristics of studies of political parties. Groups, like parties, were either ignored, treated casually, or considered a dread disease. The first major theoretical discussion of groups was A. F. Bentley's *Process of Government* (1908). It was a serious attempt to view groups analytically, without condemnation and exhortation as a primary goal. But his book had little immediate influence. It was not until the 1920's that monographs began to appear on groups, and most were case studies of individual groups or of conflict situations involving group pressures. Mention may be made of Peter Odegard's book on *The Anti-Saloon League* (1928), E. P. Herring's *Group Representation before Congress* (1929), E. E. Schattschneider's *Politics, Pressures and the Tariff* (1935), the work of Belle Zeller and Dayton McKean on the state legislatures of New York and New Jersey (1938), Oliver Garceau's *Political Life of the American Medical Association* (1941), Avery Leiserson's *Administrative Regulation* (1942), and Stephen K. Bailey's *Congress Makes a Law* (1946). Although some of these writers were concerned with the theoretical implications of group analysis, most were drawn to the study of groups because it was "reality." Group study reflected disenchantment with the formal and juridical study of political institutions.

The most important single analytic work since Bentley is David Truman's *The Governmental Process* (1951). While most early writers sought to expose and condemn groups, Truman perceived them as vital parts of the political system. "Without some working conception of the political role of interest groups, their function, and the ways in which their powers are exercised," he wrote, "we shall not be able adequately to understand the nature of the political process."

Up to the time of the publication of *The Governmental Process* most monographs were by Americans and on American groups. Indeed, there was long an impression that lobbies and pressure groups were peculiarly American phenomena. In the early 1950's interest groups were discovered by European political scientists. The outpouring of literature on European interest groups has

196

been torrential, as evidenced by: Jean Meynaud, *Les Groupes de Pression en France* (1958) and *Nouvelles études sur les Groupes de Pression en France* (1962); Samuel E. Finer, *The Anonymous Empire* (1958); Allen Potter, *Organized Groups in British Politics* (1961); Henry Ehrmann, ed., *Interest Groups on Four Continents* (1958); and J. LaPalombara, *Interest Groups in Italian Politics* (1964). Thirty years ago the literature on interest groups was so sparse that comparison of American and European groups was virtually impossible. Today, the literature on interest groups both in and outside the United States is so vast that comparison is unavoidable. The expansion of our substantive knowledge of interest groups is by itself of considerable theoretical importance, since it is now more feasible to check hypotheses concerning political behavior.

A number of significant attempts have been made to apply group theory to comparative study. Professor Almond's "Research Note: A Comparative Study of Interest Groups and the Political Process," reprinted below, is perhaps the most stimulating of these analytic efforts. The reader is also referred to the suggestive article by Joseph LaPalombara, "The Utility and Limitations of Interest Group Theory in Non-American Field Situations," *Journal of Politics,* February 1960; and also H. Eckstein, *Pressure Group Politics* (1960).

Study of groups is a means, perhaps the best single means, of approaching and understanding any political system. Groups constitute the raw material, the "stuff" of politics. Description of groups, their internal organization, access to decision makers and the way in which they exert influence is extremely important in the comparative analysis of political systems. But the student should also remember that groups cannot be understood in a vacuum. They must be related to the social structure, culture, and political institutions of a nation. The universe of comparative analysis should consist of as large a number of relevant factors as is possible—not only parties and interest groups, but social groups, ideologies, values, and policy decisions. In the final analysis, a theory of groups must be part of a larger theory of the political system.

14. Interest Groups and the Political Process*

GABRIEL A. ALMOND

THE GENERAL OBJECTIVES

Comparative analyses of political institutions have thus far been confined to formal governmental institutions, and to political party and electoral systems. Dissatisfaction with these formal comparisons is widespread in view of the generally appreciated fact that formally similar governmental and party systems often function in radically different ways. And the search for explanation of the formally similar but differently functioning political systems has turned to vague residual categories such as "social structure," "national character," "consensus" or its absence, and "public opinion." . . .

We turn to the comparative study of interest groups not with the hope that these rather than parties or governmental institutions will yield *the principles* of discrimination between types of political systems, but rather with the expectation that the systematic examination of interest groups in their complex interrelations with public opinion, political parties and formal governmental institutions will enable us to differentiate more accurately between political systems as *wholes.* In other words, the growing concern among scholars with interest groups and public opinion is the consequence of a search for a more complete and systematic conception of the political process as a whole, rather than a search for an approach which is an *alternative* to the present emphasis on formal governmental institutions. . . .

The kinds of interest groups which are present in a society, the specificity or diffuseness of their demands, their conceptions of the political arena and of the "rules of the game," the ethos which they bring with them into the political process—these are the "raw materials" of politics—the unaggregated demands—which some set of mechanisms must transform into political personnel and public policy.

These general observations about interest groups not only suggest their importance as a subject of study, but set certain specifications in research design if the maximum value of a comparative study is to be attained. A good research job on interest groups in a particular country, which may make possible meaningful comparisons with other countries, must examine the interest group system in its relations with the social structure and culture on the one hand and the other parts of the political structure on the other. In identifying the interest

*From "Research Note: A Comparative Study of Interest Groups and the Political Process," *American Political Science Review,* vol. LII, no. 1 (March 1958). By permission. [This article is a summary of the work of the Committee on Comparative Politics of the Social Science Research Council.]

group system in any particular country this broad functional approach will prevent us from identifying interest groups with any particular kind of structure. The function of articulating and transmitting group interests may be performed in one system typically by the well organized and bureaucratized "pressure groups" familiar in the West, or it may be performed in another system typically through an informal and intermittent process of communication between and among class and status groups such as large landholders or businessmen, and cliques of bureaucrats and/or army officers. If it is possible to state the theme of the comparative study in the form of a single question it might be: What form does the articulation of political interests take in various societies, and how are these interests transmitted to other parts of the political and governmental structure, and translated into choices of political personnel and public policy?...

INTEREST GROUPS AND PUBLIC OPINION

One of the central problems in interest group theory is the relation between manifest and latent interests. To what extent can organized, overt interests be taken as reflecting the interest tendencies of the general population? The phenomena of the mob in non-Western countries, of riots in totalitarian countries, of "Caesarism," "Poujadism," and "incivisme," in the European area suggest that popular attitudes and tendencies are a separable factor in the political process, the properties of which cannot be inferred from the existing organized tendencies and from electoral behavior. Any characterization of a political system would be incomplete if it was confined solely to a description of current organizational patterns and processes. Latent interests may not only result in future changes in organization and process, it establishes an atmosphere which affects the contemporary operations of the political process. . . . The ways in which interest groups conceive of their audiences, and the ways in which they represent their interests to the public should throw light on the functioning of the political system as a whole. For example, French business associations are different from the American in that they do not engage openly and on large scale in public "informational" activities. This may reflect a general condition of fragmentation in political communication in France, a condition of distrust and alienation among interests. . . .

INTEREST GROUPS AND POLITICAL PARTIES

In the Anglo-American type of political system the functions of political parties and interest groups are sharply differentiated. Interest groups articulate political demands in the society, seek support for these demands among other groups by advocacy and bargaining, and attempt to transform these demands into authoritative public policy by influencing the choice of political personnel, and the various processes of public policy-making and enforcement. Political parties tend to be free of ideological rigidity, and are aggregative, *i.e.,* seek to form the largest possible interest group coalitions by offering acceptable choices of political personnel and public policy. Both the interest group systems and the party systems are differentiated, bureaucratized, and autonomous. Each unit in the party and interest group systems comes into the "market," so to speak, with an adjustive bargaining ethos. Furthermore, the party system stands between the interest group system and the authoritative policy-making agencies and screens them from the particularistic and disintegrative impact of special interests. The party system aggregates interests and transforms them into a relatively small number of alternative general policies. Thus this set of relationships between the party system and the interest group system enables choice among general policies to take place in the legislature, and assures that the bureaucracy will tend to function as a neutral instrument of the political agencies.

We might take as our second type a model summarizing the properties of the political systems which are to be found in Asia, the Middle East and Latin America in which neither parties nor interest groups are fully differentiated. Associational interest groups such as trade unions and business associations may exist in the urban Westernized parts of the society, but in the village and the countryside interest organization takes the form of lineage, caste, status, class and religious groups, which transmit political demands to the other parts of the political structure by means of informal communication. In one version of this class of systems parties tend to be *ad hoc* coalitions without permanent bureaucracies, and without grass roots organization. They exist primarily in election periods and in effect cease to exist in the intervals between. Given such weak and non-aggregative party systems the capacity of the legislatures to formulate alternative policy choices may be seriously impaired, as is their capacity to control the bureaucracies. In many of these political systems the significant political groups are neither the parties, nor the associational interest groups, but elements or cliques within the bureaucracy, and the army; and cliques, informal groupings and powerful families formed within such nonassociational interests as religious communities, the large landowners, the business community, and the like. The political process consists of the informal communication and flow of influence between these informally organized interests, and groups within the bureaucracy and the army.

The instabilities of this type of political system arise out of the fact that the agencies for the articulation, communication, and aggregation of interests are incomplete and unrepresentative, as well as out of the fact that the demands transmitted into the political system from interest groups are vague, diffuse, and of radically unlike content and intensity. Latent interests, lacking overt and organized channels of expression may suddenly break into the political arena. The information available to influential groups and individuals about the expectations and attitudes of the various interests in the society cannot be complete or accurate. Hence, calculation is impossible, and the flow of political interaction involves under-reaction and over-reaction, violence and apathy, alternations of periods of political latency, with sudden and violent shifts in power.

Given the basic instability of this general class of political systems, authoritarian stabilizations are a frequent event. Indeed, in many of them the developmental pattern is one of a shift from an unstable pluralism to authoritarianism, and then back again, or a shift from the authoritarianism of one clique to that of another. Authoritarianism may be based on control of the army either by a clique of army officers, or a clique of bureaucrats controlling the army, or by a coalition of both. Still another pattern is one in which the desire on the part of a controlling group to secure its own power and destroy opposition, or to mobilize the society for industrialization and national expansion, leads to the formation of an authoritarian party which actually penetrates the countryside. In some cases, as in Turkey and in India, the objectives of the ruling groups and of the dominant party are tutelary. That is, the function of the party is not only control and mobilization, but also political acculturation, the preparation of the ground for the emergence of a Western-type associational system and of a Western-type party system with a coherent, responsible, and loyal opposition.

Thus, it should be quite clear that there are many kinds of non-Western political systems. They all appear to have in common (1) a fragmented political culture as a consequence of Westernization, in many cases added on to an indigenous cultural heterogeneity, (2) poor political communications and a high degree of interest latency which renders political calculation difficult if not impossible, and (3) a party system which is incapable of aggregating and synthesizing interest demands into a small number of political alternatives either of personnel or of public policy. On a scale of political differentiation one would have to say that certain kinds of structures such as associational interest groups, the mass media of communication, and the kind of party system common in the West and essential for the functioning of a modern mass-suffrage parliamentary system, are present at best in only a limited degree. On a scale of functional specialization one would have to say that in the absence of fully developed associational groups, party systems, and modern media of communication, the functions of interest articulation, aggregation, communication and transmission are largely performed by bureaucratic or army cliques, traditional structures such as lineage or status groupings, and by mobs, street demonstrations and the like, which serve as one of the agencies by means of which latent interests are articulated and transmitted.

A third type of political system is exemplified by France and Italy and by the Germany of the Weimar Republic. Contemporary Germany appears to be moving in the direction of an autonomous interest group system and an aggregative two-party system; toward the Anglo-American model, in other words. In the French and Italian political systems parties and interest groups are organized and bureaucratized, but they are not autonomous systems. They interpenetrate one another and consequently fail to realize the two-stage pattern of the political process characteristic of the English and American systems. There are some parties which more or less control interest groups (e.g., the Communist party and the Communist-dominated trade unions, and to a lesser extent the Socialist parties and the Socialist trade unions). There are some interest groups which more or less control other interest groups and parties (e.g., the Church, the

Catholic trade unions, and the Catholic parties, business interest groups, and the center and right wing parties, and the like).

When parties control interest groups they inhibit the capacity of interest groups to formulate pragmatic specific demands; they impart a political-ideological content to interest group activity. When interest groups control parties they inhibit the capacity of the party to combine specific interests into programs with wider appeal. What reaches the legislative process from the interest groups and through the political parties thus are the "raw," unaggregated demands of specific interests, or the diffuse, uncompromising, or revolutionary tendencies of the Church and the movements of the extreme right or left. Since no interest group is large enough to have a majority, and the party system cannot aggregate different interests into a stable majority and a coherent opposition, the electoral and legislative processes fail to provide alternative, effective choices. The result is a legislature penetrated by relatively narrow interests and uncompromising ideological tendencies, a legislature which can be used as an arena for propaganda, or for the protection of special interests, by veto or otherwise, but not for the effective and timely formulation and support of large policy decisions. And without a strong legislature, special interests and ideological tendencies penetrate the bureaucracy, and undermine its neutral, instrumental character.

A fourth type of political system is exemplified by the Scandinavian and Low Countries. These systems appear to differ from the French and Italian in two respects. First, the party systems tend to be aggregative (e.g., the Scandinavian Socialist parties, the Belgian Socialist and Catholic parties). Second, the relations between parties and interests appear to be more consensual, which makes stable majority and opposition coalitions possible. Thus, though the party systems fail to aggregate interests as thoroughly as in the British case, the public policy-making function of the legislature is not undermined to the same extent as in the French and Italian cases. What appears to happen in the Scandinavian and the Low Countries is that the function of interest aggregation and general policy formulation occurs at both the party and parliamentary levels. The parties are partly aggregative of interests, but "majority-minority" aggregation takes place finally in the coalition-making process in the legislature. This coalition-making process may be organized by parties in the formation of cabinets and the enactment of legislation or it may take the form of interest coalitions organized around issues of public policy. The capacity for stable majority-minority party coalitions and for relatively flexible issue-oriented interest coalitions is dependent upon the existence of a basic political consensus which affects both parties and interest groups. These appear to be the properties of the so-called "working multi-party systems." . . .

The relation between political parties and interest groups could be viewed as a continuum with substantial autonomy at one limit and sub- and super-ordination at the other. The relationship patterns which exist in historical political systems always involve two-way flows of influence, which differ from one another in the dominant direction of the flow and the different patterns which are occasioned by different kinds of issues. Thus the extreme case of the Communist Party—Communist trade union dominance still involves a flow of information and influence from trade union to party, but the dominant direction of the flow is from party to trade union. In the case of the church and Catholic parties the flow of influence varies from country to country, and even among regions within countries. In addition, in certain areas of policy Catholic parties may be relatively free of church influence, or may even influence the church to take a position consistent with or supportive of that of the party. In Germany, for example, the fact that the CDU has both Protestant and Catholic support seriously limits the power of the Catholic church to intervene in party policy-making. In other legislative fields, the freedom of Catholic parties may be sharply circumscribed by a rigid church position, as in the field of educational subsidies and the like. In other policy areas, *e.g.,* social-economic, there may be more give and take in the relations between church and Catholic party.

These considerations suggested that analysis of the flow of influence between parties and interest groups would require not only an examination of the interconnections through financing, interlocking memberships and directorates, sharing of ideological beliefs and the like, but would also require a judicious use of case study methods to discover the way in which different kinds of legislative issues affected the flow and pattern of influences between interest groups and parties. . . .

INTEREST GROUPS AND THE LEGISLATIVE PROCESS

Interest groups tend to seek out the important points of access in the legislative process; the points where legislative policy is initiated, and where revision, vetoing, and favorable action are possible. Hence, the constitutional separation and distribution of powers, legislative organization and procedure, the characteristics of the electoral system and the parliamentary party organization, set the problem of interest group access in the legislative process. Thus, the American system of federalism, and separation of powers, creates a different interest group "target structure" than does the British parliamentary-cabinet system. The American federal system produces a party structure with its center of gravity at the state level. This kind of decentralized party organization limits the possibilities of congressional party discipline and hence opens the legislative process to interest group penetration. The susceptibility of the legislature to interest group penetration is enhanced by the American single-member district electoral system which frequently exposes the legislator to the effective pressure of interests which may be especially concentrated in his constituency. In addition, the American separation of powers system grants a powerful and independent role in legislation to both the House and Senate. And since relatively large collegial bodies are, other things being equal, less able to aggregate interests and protect themselves against interest penetration than Cabinet-dominated parliaments, this aspect of American constitutional structure contributes significantly to interest group action in the legislative process. If we consider this constitutional and statutory structure on the one hand, and the economic, regional, ethnic, and religious composition of the American population on the other, it is hardly surprising that the penetration of the legislative process by interest groups in the United States is greater than in the United Kingdom. There, a unitary constitution, and a Cabinet-dominated parliament make possible a disciplined parliamentary party system which protects the legislative process from effective interest group penetration. The main targets of interest groups are the upper levels of the parliamentary and extra-parliamentary party structure where power is concentrated, and the bureaucracy. And because of the cohesion of the party system and the concentration of legislative power in the Cabinet, the impact of any single interest group—with the exception of the trade unions—is quite limited.

France presents yet another problem of interest group access. In the United States aggregation and synthesis of interests is performed by the party system and a powerful presidency responsible to a national constituency. France has neither a powerful executive nor an aggregative party system. A culturally and politically fragmented society choosing its legislators by means of proportional representation produces a legislature capable of producing only weak and unstable coalitions. The standing committees of the *Assemblée* are in many cases colonized by powerful interests. The net effect of this situation is a legislative process which can only rarely enact significant "national-interest" legislation, but which regularly and characteristically protects and subsidizes special interests. Still a fourth type of legislative interest group pattern is to be found in the Scandinavian countries where a stronger executive and a more aggregative party system limits the impact of interest groups in the legislative process.

These characteristics of constitutional, legislative, and party structures affect not only the tactics of interest groups, but the very goals and objectives which they can reasonably attain. A disciplined party system and a powerful executive forces interest groups to direct their energies to the upper levels of the executive and the bureaucracy where only moderate claims, well supported with technical information, become possible. A non-aggregative and undisciplined party system as in France opens up the legislative process to covert interest group domination of legislative committees and agencies, or to propagandistic interest group maneuvers of which "Poujadism" is only an extreme instance.

These hypotheses about patterns of interest-group-legislative relations in the European area suggest the importance of a careful analysis of the functioning of the constitutional, legislative, electoral, and party systems as they relate to interest group access. In other words, the aim of research in interest-group-legislative relations will be to determine the extent to which the parliamentary parties, or extra-parliamentary legislative institutions such as the American Presidency, are able to maintain independence of interest groups and relative freedom to legislate or influence legislation (a) by combining several interest groups in their support, and (b) by establishing and maintaining the discipline of the parliamentary system as a means of withstanding interest group pressures....

COMPARISON OF WESTERN AND NON-WESTERN INTEREST GROUPS

. . . Every independent society makes political choices, *i.e.,* broad policy decisions which are backed up by severe sanctions. In making and enforcing these political decisions all societies have some way of articulating and communicating political demands, aggregating these demands, translating them into choices of political personnel and public policy, executing these decisions in specific cases, and testing the appropriateness of these specific actions. In studying interest groups comparatively the participants in the study are primarily concerned with the structures, institutions and processes by means of which these functions are accomplished. Research conclusions as to which structures and processes perform which functions in different societies, and how they perform them, will provide the basic materials for comparative analysis.

Not only are these functions performed in all independent political systems—Western and non-Western—but the structures and processes which perform them in both areas overlap to a considerable extent. The West is more like the non-West than we sometimes think. Even in the most differentiated and specialized political systems in the West, such interest groups as families, status groups, and religious communities affect the political process. And in most of the non-Western countries—however "underdeveloped"—the beginnings of functionally specialized political parties, and associational interest groups such as trade unions and trade associations, may be found. Even in the field of political communication the highly elaborated mass communication systems of Western societies should not obscure the fact that informal and face-to-face communication is still a political factor of enormous importance.

In still another respect Western and non-Western systems are alike. While it is true in general that Western political structures are more specialized than the non-Western, there is much "multi-functionalism" in the West. Thus in a country such as France political parties and interest groups are not sharply differentiated from one another. And in all countries the structural specialization of policy-making and administration is by no means complete, nor can it ever be complete. If it is peculiar to non-Western countries that bureaucracies are penetrated by interest groups and ideological tendencies, this situation differs only in degree from the Western pattern where rationality, responsibility, and neutrality are only partially realized at best.

15. Groups and Group Theory*

ROY C. MACRIDIS

Without attempting to enter into a detailed discussion it would seem to me that group analysis is (epistemological labels may be used without implying any guilt by association) a crude form of determinism. Interest is the primary propelling force and every action is based upon sharing of interest. Power configuration is basically the configuration of competing and struggling interests organized into groups. Ideology, values, the state, the formal organization of political decision-making, and the content of decisions are determined by the parallelogram of group forces. Perhaps this may be an oversimplification, but I do not think that it does violence to the scheme of group analysis. It is interesting, for instance, that not only concern with the state recedes into the background in the writings of all proponents of the group theory, but also the role of ideology, of extra-economic and non-rational motivational patterns, and of the political system as an independent factor influencing group behavior.

But while Marx with his class theory and its deterministic underpinnings provided a broad theory of history and development through which man would ultimately be able to shed interest in order to attain freedom—that is, while Marxist determinism led progressively to higher stages of consciousness and perception of the environment, group theorists anchor man's life into the perennial group conflict which by their very nature groups can never transcend. Not only our lives remain intolerably and unredeemably "nasty and brutish," but our theoretical universe in terms of which we can explain behavior becomes unduly restricted. Interest is the propelling force and man is forever destined to live in an environment that mirrors interest. It may be argued that group theory is "realistic" and, furthermore, that the "group" is a far more useful concept analytically than "class." I doubt it very much—first, because group analysis as I have noted has normative implications and second and more important, because the concepts of "interest" and "group" are fuzzy analytically, perhaps just as much as that of the "class."

But the above criticisms involve philosophic questions that are highly controversial. What is more important for our discussion is that group theory puts exaggerated demands upon empirical research and data collection. If an understanding of a political system at a given moment depends upon the study of the total configuration of interests the task of the political scientist becomes stupendous. We have to study every and all interest groups, index them and measure carefully and constantly the increments of power and influence they generate before we can make any statements about the most meaningful aspects of politics—the resolution of conflict and policy-making, including foreign

*From "Interest Groups in Comparative Analysis," *The Journal of Politics,* vol. 23, no. 1 (February 1961). By permission.

policy. We would have to elaborate precise units of power in order to assess and reassess continuously group power. But such a measurement would involve so many variables that meaningful measurement and quantification would become hopeless. . . . Where then do we start and even more important where do we stop indexing and measuring group power and interaction: business interests, economic interests, labor interests, religious interests, local interests, bureaucratic interests, organized interests, to say nothing of potential groups that hide in their bosom potential interests that are ready to blossom forth? How many of them do we study and exactly for what purpose? The index of power at any given moment would be inaccurate unless we measure the potential counter-power that can be generated by the potential groups. How can we tell exactly under what conditions groups will compromise? What can we learn about the perception that groups have of other groups or the total group configuration? How can we measure the adherence of groups to the "rules of the game" that in all political systems curb, limit and often shape group action? What I am saying, of course, is that group analysis may prove to be both self-defeating and misleading. We cannot know the power configuration in a society unless we have studied all groups as they interact, and when we do so we still do not know why groups interact in one manner rather than another.

Finally, group analysis seems to beg rather than answer the very question it purports to ask—to give us an explanatory frame of reference in terms of which we can account for differences and uniformities in political behavior and action. This is the central problem of comparative analysis. Group theory assumes the existence of organized groups or interests that can be defined in objective terms; labor, business, and agriculture are some of the more obvious and frequently studied ones. It is further assumed that their members have a common perception of the interest involved which accounts for the very formation of the group and its organization and articulation. So far so good. Descriptive and comparative study immediately presents us with extreme variations in the organization, cohesiveness, membership strength, forms of action and patterns of interaction among these groups. It reveals some striking differences in the manner in which interest groups in various political systems relate to the political parties and the political processes.

To attempt to explain such differences in terms of a group theory is impossible. Why are, for instance, agricultural groups so well organized under the National Farmers Union in England, to which more than 90 per cent of the farmers belong, but dispersed and relatively unorganized in the United States and France? Why are more than 85 per cent of all manufacturing concerns in England represented in their national association while not more than 6 per cent are so represented in the United States? Why do more than 50 per cent of the British workers belong to trade unions which are almost all represented in their peak organization, the TUC, while in France membership remains low and articulation of labor interest dispersed in at least four Trade Union organizations? Why is it that in England interest groups avoid large publicity campaigns and center their attention on the Party and the Cabinet, while in the United

States interest groups perform important publicity and propaganda functions through the media of communications and center their efforts on the electorate and the legislature, primarily, while French interest groups shy publicity and center their activities upon the legislature and the administration?

A number of answers can be given to these questions in the form of propositions to be carefully investigated, but I submit none of them are researchable in terms of group analysis. The answers are often given (without adequate evidence, to be sure) in terms of other categories: the American political system *with multiple foci* of decision-making, for instance, makes the legislature and more particularly individual legislators more susceptible to pressure either directly or indirectly; *the diffusion of power* in the political party in the United States makes any effort to control or influence the Party unrewarding for pressure groups; the same applies for France, where it is often pointed out that "interest" and "interest groups" are divided and sub-divided and lose their "objective" or "real" interest *because of political reasons.* The workers, the farmers, the teachers have no spokesmen and no cohesive and disciplined interest articulation because they are divided into a number of "political" or "ideological" families. As for group interaction, again the differences are striking: in some cases, groups interact within a given political party and compromise their differences; in other cases, compromise is made outside of the political parties, or is not made at all, leading to immobility; elsewhere compromise is made impossible by virtue of the fact that interests are "colonized" by ideological parties so that interest groups mirror the ideological divisions of the society instead of causing them.

In all cases the reasons advanced for a given pattern of group organization, action and interaction derive from categories other than group analysis would suggest: the formal organization of power; the cohesiveness or dispersal of political power; the two-party or multi-party configuration; the "climate of public opinion"; the intensity of consensus or lack of same in given political systems. . . .

Let me further illustrate the shortcomings of group analysis as an explanatory theory by borrowing from the conclusions of authors interested in comparative study or who did field work in foreign political systems. Professor Ehrmann writes in his introduction to *Interest Groups on Four Continents:* "The political system, as well as the social structure, will often decide whether claims raised in the name of special interests will be successful or not; it may determine the 'style' used by pressure groups when raising their demands."[1] Professor Lavau, after indicating in detail the fragmentation of many French interests because of ideological reasons, points out that "This hostile ideological and moral climate surrounding pressure groups in France reacts in turn upon their behavior. . . ." He indicates that some pressure groups if *not politicized* play an aggregative and integrative role that the French political parties do not play. This is, for instance, the case with some peak organizations that include a variety of

---

[1] Henry Ehrmann, *Interest Groups on Four Continents* (1959), p. 1.

professional groups. "Since it is [their] function to arbitrate or mediate possible conflicts between different member organizations, this role confers upon [them], in the eyes of the administration and the politicians, a considerable dignity."[2] In fact one of the most pervasive efforts of the French interest groups is to liberate themselves from a divided political culture and be able to organize their membership on the basis of interest alone. That they fail more often than they succeed is an indication of the importance, and what is more, the independence, of political and ideological factors. Professor Sam Finer accepts Beer's emphasis upon the British "consensus" and the general agreement of the British leadership on a number of policy issues as a factor that shapes and structures group action. He adds that such beliefs are brought together in English political life by the myth of "public interest" which provides a yardstick in terms of which interest claims are judged. The image of the national interest acts as a cohesive force. Professor Beer in an excellent analysis points to the parallel development in Great Britain of well organized and integrated political parties with well organized national interest groups.[3] For the purpose of our discussion this parallelism between interest organization and party organization is striking and one cannot avoid the impression that British interests gradually evolved a pattern of organization and cohesiveness *that corresponds* to and *parallels* the highly centralized and cohesive political system; that perhaps their "style" of action was conditioned by the cohesiveness of the political culture and the organization of political parties very much as the dispersion of the French interest groups may well have been shaped by the diversity of the French political culture and multi-partism. Joseph LaPalombara,[4] points out bluntly that many interest groups in Italy (and the same applies to France) operate within the political sub-cultures of the system (communist, catholic, socialist, etc.) resulting in an enormous proliferation (and the same applies to France) of pressure groups. Writing for the Swedish pressure groups Gunnar Heckscher points out that ". . . there is hardly any point at which this term (politics of compromise) seems more definitely warranted than with regard to interest organizations: an equilibrium is maintained chiefly through the willingness of each of them to make concessions in order to achieve important results. . . ." But why? Because "the pluralistic character of the Swedish society is openly accepted on all sides."[5] Back we come to the general values of the community in terms of which the role of pressure groups and pressure group action and interaction can be explained. Jean Meynaud, in his comprehensive study of French pressure groups in France[6] comes very close to a very important theoretical insight, when he points out that the fragmentation of parties like the frag-

[2] *Ibid.,* pp. 61 and 78.

[3] Samuel Beer, "Group Representation in Britain and the United States," *The Annals* (September 1958).

[4] "The Utility and Limitations of Interest Group Theory in Non-American Field Situations," *Journal of Politics* (February 1960).

[5] "Interest Groups in Sweden," in Ehrmann, *op. cit.,* p. 170.

[6] Jean Meynaud, *Les Groupes de Pression en France* (1959), particularly chaps. i and v.

mentation of the groups has its origin in the divisions in the public mind. Political ideologies and religious considerations destroy the unity that would result from objective professional and interest considerations. A number of organizations mushroom *within the same* professional sector because of ideological reasons. One might hypothesize indeed that this parallelism between the political system and the interest configuration is true everywhere. *Whenever the political governmental organization is cohesive and power is concentrated in certain well established centers the pressure groups become well organized with a similar concentration of power and vice versa.*

Despite the reputed advantage of concreteness, groups appear to be as elusive as some of the much criticized terms used in the past—such as the state, consensus, social structure, national character, or class; implicitly accepting the power theory, group analysts tend to embrace a theory of group determinism in which interest groups appear to be the most significant actors within a system with the individual, on the one hand, and the state on the other, receding in the background; from the standpoint of research in a political system group analysis compels the student, if he is to gain a solid view of a system, to study all groups and all patterns of group interaction—no clear-cut discrimination of what is relevant and what is not being offered. Indeed, when David Truman brings the potential groups into the picture any discriminating feature that group analysis might offer goes to the winds; finally, and what is very revealing, researchers who start with a group orientation finish by admitting the inadequacy of their approach—they tell us that in order to understand how groups behave and how they interact, we must study the political system, the overall behavior patterns, the values and beliefs held by the actors, the formal organization of authority, the degree of legitimacy, etc., etc. Without realizing it, they reverse their theoretical position. They start with the groups only to admit the primacy of the political phenomenon and suggest that in order to explain group behavior we must start with what group behavior purported to explain—the political system!

*   *   *

The road to theory in comparative politics is a long one. Group theory claims that it is more "comprehensive" and "operational" in that it directs the student to the study of concrete and observable entities—the groups—and leads him immediately to the promised heaven of data-accumulation and explanation. When the real test of the utility of the theory comes, however—field work— groups prove to be just as stubborn in yielding their secrets as other structures and units of a system. Their pulsating reality often proves to be nothing but a ghost that haunts the field worker from one interest group office and organization to another, from one interest group publication to another. In some cases, especially in the underdeveloped systems where interest articulation is weak, the office may be vacant. Even where interest articulation and interest groups pulsate with life and vigor the student soon discovers that the "interest universe" overlaps with the political universe; that it is indeed enmeshed with the political universe in which tradition, values, habits, styles and patterns of leadership and the governmental organization must be carefully studied before we begin to understand the system as a whole. The dichotomy between "interest" and "government" appears increasingly tenuous and the student has often to study the latter in order to understand better not only the manifestations and actions but also the motivation and organization of the former. He is soon forced to the conclusion that "interest" like any other activity in a system is conditioned by secular forces that have shaped the political culture of the community and that the best way to a theory of comparative politics is at this stage a comprehensive comparative look at the main features of a political system—political culture, social configuration, leadership and governmental institutions. It is only such an approach, which requires a good understanding of the historical dimension of any and all political systems, that may help us differentiate between political systems and isolate those factors that may account for the diversities and similarities we observe.

chapter VII

PARTY SYSTEMS

Reproduced below is an extract from one of the first classic analyses of political parties, by Robert Michels. His thesis concerning the inability of masses to control their leaders has become especially timely in view of current demands for mass participation in the decision-making process.

The position of members within parties is analogous then to that of the people within the democratic state. In neither case can the masses directly control the organization that acts in their name. All large groups, including political parties, are run by a band of interested persons united by a common set of beliefs or desire for power or both. Political parties are especially susceptible to oligarchical tendencies. While various techniques have been devised to mitigate these tendencies, mass parties remain under the control of a relatively few key individuals.

Among many works on this problem are: Gaetano Mosca, *The Ruling Class* (1939); Walter Lippmann, *The Phantom Public* (1925); James Burnham, *The Managerial Revolution* (1941); Carl J. Friedrich, "Oligarchy," *Encyclopedia of the Social Sciences;* C. Wright Mills, *The Power Elite* (1957); and T. B. Bottomore, *Elites and Society* (1964). The critics of Michels generally agree that all parties tend to be oligarchic, but argue that even oligarchy can serve democratic purposes. Democracy is distinguished not by the size of the ruling body, but by the right of other interested persons to dispute the actions of the government and to replace the leadership without recourse to violence. The most effective check on party autocracy would thus be the existence of a well-organized opposition enjoying guaranteed freedom to expose mistakes, indiscretions, or abuses on the part of party leaders. But does it work out this way in practice? The student should compare the organization of power within several different parties, ascertain the extent to which the leadership is responsible to the members, and appraise the party organization as it functions within the total political system.

We have also called attention to the changing functions of parties within political systems, generally reflecting the stages of modernization. Parties are clearly the most important channels between government and the public during the "crisis of participation," when groups previously excluded from power enter politics and seek to influence the state. But it appears that the role of parties may well decline when the major problem confronting a society is the management of a complex technology. Otto Kirchheimer and Anthony King present below new appraisals of the functions of political parties.

Important recent books on parties include: Maurice Duverger, *Political Parties* (1951); Avery Leiserson, *Parties and Politics* (1958); Leon D. Epstein, *Political Parties in Western Democracies* (1967); Roy C. Macridis, ed., *Political Parties* (1967); S. P. Huntington and C. H. Moore, eds., *Authoritarian Politics in Modern Society: The Dynamics of Established One-Party Systems* (1970), R. Alford, *Party and Society* (1964); and S. M. Lipset and S. Rokkan, eds., *Party Systems and Voter Alignments* (1967). A developmental approach to parties is presented in two stimulating recent books: Samuel H. Beer, *British Politics in the Collectivist Age* (1965); and Joseph LaPalombara and Myron Weiner, eds., *Political Parties and Political Development* (1966)—which also contains a useful bibliography.

16. The Iron Law of Oligarchy*

ROBERT MICHELS

DEMOCRACY AND ARISTOCRACY

In modern party life aristocracy gladly presents itself in democratic guise, whilst the substance of democracy is permeated with aristocratic elements. On the one side we have aristocracy in a democratic form, and on the other democracy with an aristocratic content.

The democratic external form which characterizes the life of political parties may readily veil from superficial observers the tendency towards aristocracy, or rather towards oligarchy, which is inherent in all party organization. If we wish to obtain light upon this tendency, the best field of observation is offered by the intimate structure of the democratic parties, and among these, of the socialist and revolutionary labour party. In the conservative parties, except during elections, the tendency to oligarchy manifests itself with that spontaneous vigour and clearness which corresponds with the essentially oligarchical character of these parties. But the parties which are subversive in their aims exhibit the like phenomena no less markedly. The study of the oligarchical

*From *Political Parties* (New York, Dover Publications, Inc.).

manifestations in party life is most valuable and most decisive in its results when undertaken in relation to the revolutionary parties, for the reason that these parties, in respect of origin and of programme, represent the negation of any such tendency, and have actually come into existence out of opposition thereto. Thus the appearance of oligarchical phenomena in the very bosom of the revolutionary parties is a conclusive proof of the existence of immanent oligarchical tendencies in every kind of human organization which strives for the attainment of definite ends. . . .

THE NEED FOR ORGANIZATION

Democracy is inconceivable without organization. A few words will suffice to demonstrate this proposition.

A class which unfurls in face of society the banner of certain definite claims, and which aspires to be the realization of a complex of ideal aims deriving from the economic functions which that class fulfils, needs an organization. Be the claims economic or be they political, organization appears the only means for the creation of a collective will. Organization, based as it is upon the principle of least effort, that is to say, upon the greatest possible economy of energy, is the weapon of the weak in their struggle with the strong.

The chances of success in any struggle will depend upon the degree to which this struggle is carried out upon a basis of solidarity between individuals whose interests are identical. In objecting, therefore, to the theories of the individualist anarchists that nothing could please the employers better than the dispersion and disaggregation of the forces of the workers, the socialists, the most fanatical of all the partisans of the idea of organization, enunciate an argument which harmonizes well with the results of scientific study of the nature of parties.

We live in a time in which the idea of cooperation has become so firmly established that even millionaires perceive the necessity of common action. It is easy to understand, then, that organization has become a vital principle in the working class, for in default of it their success is *a priori* impossible. The refusal of the worker to participate in the collective life of his class cannot fail to entail disastrous consequences. In respect of culture and of economic, physical, and physiological conditions, the proletarian is the weakest element of our society. In fact, the isolated member of the working classes is defenceless in the hands of those who are economically stronger. It is only by combination to form a structural aggregate that the proletarians can acquire the faculty of political resistance and attain to a social dignity. The importance and the influence of the working class are directly proportional to its numerical strength. But for the representation of that numerical strength organization and coordination are indispensable. The principle of organization is an absolutely essential condition for the political struggle of the masses.

Yet this politically necessary principle of organization, while it overcomes that disorganization of forces which would be favourable to the adversary, brings other dangers in its train. We escape Scylla only to dash ourselves on

Charybdis. Organization is, in fact, the source from which the conservative currents flow over the plain of democracy, occasioning there disastrous floods and rendering the plain unrecognizable. . . .

Is it impossible for a democratic party to practise a democratic policy, for a revolutionary party to pursue a revolutionary policy? Must we say that not *socialism* alone, but even a socialistic *policy,* is utopian?

Within certain narrow limits, the democratic party, even when subjected to oligarchical control, can doubtless act upon the state in the democratic sense. The old political caste of society, and above all the "state" itself, are forced to undertake the revaluation of a considerable number of values—a revaluation both ideal and practical. The importance attributed to the masses increases, even when the leaders are demagogues. The legislature and the executive become accustomed to yield, not only to claims proceeding from above, but also to those proceeding from below. This may give rise, in practice, to great inconveniences, such as we recognize in the recent history of all the states under a parliamentary regime; in theory, however, this new order of things signifies an incalculable progress in respect of public rights, which thus come to conform better with the principles of social justice. This evolution will, however, be arrested from the moment when the governing classes succeed in attracting within the governmental orbit their enemies of the extreme left, in order to convert them into collaborators. Political organization leads to power. But power is always conservative. In any case, the influence exercised upon the governmental machine by an energetic opposition party is necessarily slow, is subject to frequent interruptions, and is always restricted by the nature of oligarchy. . . .

As the organization increases in size, the struggle for great principles becomes impossible. It may be noticed that in the democratic parties of to-day the great conflicts of view are fought out to an ever-diminishing extent in the field of ideas and with the weapons of pure theory, that they therefore degenerate more and more into personal struggles and invectives, to be settled finally upon considerations of a purely superficial character. The efforts made to cover internal dissensions with a pious veil are the inevitable outcome of organization based upon bureaucratic principles, for, since the chief aim of such an organization is to enrol the greatest possible number of members, every struggle on behalf of ideas within the limits of the organization is necessarily regarded as an obstacle to the realization of its ends, an obstacle, therefore, which must be avoided in every possible way. This tendency is reinforced by the parliamentary character of the political party. "Party organization" signifies the aspiration for the greatest number of members. "Parliamentarism" signifies the aspiration for the greatest number of votes. The principal fields of party activity are electoral agitation and direct agitation to secure new members. What, in fact, is the modern political party? It is the methodical organization of the electoral masses. The socialist party, as a political aggregate endeavouring simultaneously to recruit members and to recruit votes, finds here its vital interests, for every decline in membership and every loss in voting strength diminishes its political prestige. Consequently great respect must be paid, not only to new members, but also to possible adherents, to those who in Germany are termed *mitläufer,* in Italy *simpatizzanti,* in Holland *geestverwanten,* and in England *sympathizers.* To avoid alarming these individuals, who are still outside the ideal worlds of socialism or democracy, the pursuit of a policy based on strict principle is shunned, while the consideration is ignored whether the numerical increase of the organization thus effected is not likely to be gained at the expense of its quality. . . .

THE IRON LAW OF OLIGARCHY

The party, regarded as an entity, as a piece of mechanism, is not necessarily identifiable with the totality of its members, and still less so with the class to which these belong. The party is created as a means to secure an end. Having, however, become an end in itself, endowed with aims and interests of its own, it undergoes detachment, from the teleological point of view, from the class which it represents. In a party, it is far from obvious that the interests of the masses which have combined to form the party will coincide with the interests of the bureaucracy in which the party becomes personified. The interests of the body of employees are always conservative, and in a given situation these interests may dictate a defensive and even a reactionary policy when the interests of the working class demand a bold and aggressive policy; in other cases, although these are very rare, the roles may be reversed. By a universally applicable social law, every organ of the collectivity, brought into existence through the need for the division of labour, creates for itself, as soon as it becomes consolidated, interests peculiar to itself. The existence of these special interests involves a necessary conflict with the interests of the collectivity. Nay, more, social strata fulfilling peculiar functions tend to become isolated, to produce organs fitted for the defence of their own peculiar interests. In the long run they tend to undergo transformation into distinct classes.

The sociological phenomena whose general characteristics have been discussed in this chapter and in preceding ones offer numerous vulnerable points to the scientific opponents of democracy. These phenomena would seem to prove beyond dispute that society cannot exist without a "dominant" or "political" class, and that the ruling class, whilst its elements are subject to a frequent partial renewal, nevertheless constitutes the only factor of sufficiently durable efficacy in the history of human development. According to this view, the government, or, if the phrase be preferred, the state, cannot be anything other than the organization of a minority. It is the aim of this minority to impose upon the rest of society a "legal order," which is the outcome of the exigencies of dominion and of the exploitation of the mass of helots effected by the ruling minority, and can never be truly representative of the majority. The majority is thus permanently incapable of self-government. Even when the discontent of the masses culminates in a successful attempt to deprive the bourgeoisie of power, this is after all, so Mosca contends, effected only in appearance; always and necessarily there springs from the masses a new organized minority which raises itself to the rank of a governing class. Thus the majority of human beings, in a condition of eternal tutelage, are predestined by tragic necessity to submit to the dominion of a small minority, and must be content to constitute the pedestal of an oligarchy. . . .

Thus the social revolution would not effect any real modification of the internal structure of the mass. The socialists might conquer, but not socialism, which would perish in the moment of its adherents' triumph. We are tempted to speak of this process as a tragicomedy in which the masses are content to devote all their energies to effecting a change of masters. All that is left for the workers is the honour "de participer au recrutement gouvernemental."[1] The result seems a poor one, especially if we take into account the psychological fact that even the purest of idealists who attains to power for a few years is unable to escape the corruption which the exercise of power carries in its train. In France, in work-class circles, the phrase is current, *homme élu, homme foutu.*[2] The social revolution, like the political revolution, is equivalent to an operation by which, as the Italian proverb expresses it: "Si cambia il maestro di cappella, ma la musica è sempre quella."[3] . . .

History seems to teach us that no popular movement, however energetic and vigorous, is capable of producing profound and permanent changes in the social organism of the civilized world. The preponderant elements of the movement, the men who lead and nourish it, end by undergoing a gradual detachment from the masses, and are attracted within the orbit of the "political class." They perhaps contribute to this class a certain number of "new ideas," but they also endow it with more creative energy and enhanced practical intelligence, thus providing for the ruling class an ever-renewed youth. The "political class" (continuing to employ Mosca's convenient phrase) has unquestionably an extreme fine sense of its possibilities and its means of defence. It displays a remarkable force of attraction and a vigorous capacity for absorption which rarely fail to exercise an influence even upon the most embittered and uncompromising of its adversaries. From the historical point of view, the antiromanticists are perfectly right when they sum up their scepticism in such caustic phraseology as this: "Qu'est ce qu'une révolution? Des gens qui se tirent des coups de fusil dans une rue: cela casse beaucoup de carreaux; il n'y a guère que les vitriers qui y trouvent du profit. Le vent emporte la fumée. . . ."[4] Or we may say, as the song runs in *Madame Angot:* "Ce n'est pas la peine de changer de gouvernement!" In France, the classic land of social theories and experiments, such pessimism has struck the deepest roots.

FINAL CONSIDERATIONS

We are led to conclude that the principal cause of oligarchy in the democratic parties is to be found in the technical indispensability of leadership.

The process which has begun in consequence of the differentiation of

[1] ["The honor of being recruited in the government."]

[2] ["A man elected is a man lost."]

[3] ["There is a new conductor but the music is the same."]

[4] ["What is a revolution? People who fire on each other in the street; that breaks a lot of windows; only the window makers profit. The wind carries away the smoke."]

functions in the party is completed by a complex of qualities which the leaders acquire through their detachment from the mass. At the outset, leaders arise *spontaneously;* their functions are *accessory* and *gratuitous.* Soon, however, they become *professional* leaders, and in this second stage of development they are *stable* and *irremovable.*

It follows that the explanation of the oligarchical phenomenon which thus results is partly *psychological;* oligarchy derives, that is to say, from the psychical transformations which the leading personalities in the parties undergo in the course of their lives. But also, and still more, oligarchy depends upon what we may term the *psychology of organization itself,* that is to say, upon the tactical and technical necessities which result from the consolidation of every disciplined political aggregate. Reduced to its most concise expression, the fundamental sociological law of political parties (the term "political" being here used in its most comprehensive significance) may be formulated in the following terms: "It is organization which gives birth to the dominion of the elected over the electors, of the mandataries over the mandators, of the delegates over the delegators. Who says organization, says oligarchy."

Every party organization represents an oligarchical power grounded upon a democratic basis. We find everywhere electors and elected. Also we find everywhere that the power of the elected leaders over the electing masses is almost unlimited. The oligarchical structure of the building soffucates the basic democratic principle. That which *is* oppresses *that which ought to be.* For the masses, this essential difference between the reality and the ideal remains a mystery. Socialists often cherish a sincere belief that a new *élite* of politicians will keep faith better than did the old. The notion of the representation of popular interests, a notion to which the great majority of democrats, and in especial the working-class masses of the German-speaking lands, cleave with so much tenacity and confidence, is an illusion engendered by a false illumination, is an effect of mirage. In one of the most delightful pages of his analysis of Modern Don Quixotism, Alphonse Daudet shows us how the "brav' commandant" Bravida, who has never quitted Tarascon, gradually comes to persuade himself, influenced by the burning southern sun, that he has been to Shanghai and has had all kinds of heroic adventures.[5] Similarly the modern proletariat, enduringly influenced by glib-tongued persons intellectually superior to the mass, ends by believing that by flocking to the poll and entrusting its social and economic cause to a delegate, its direct participation in power will be assured.

The formation of oligarchies within the various forms of democracy is the outcome of organic necessity, and consequently affects every organization, be it socialist or even anarchist. . . . In every form of social life relationships of dominion and of dependence are created by Nature herself. The supremacy of the leaders in the democratic and revolutionary parties has to be taken into account in every historic situation present and to come, even though only a few and exceptional minds will be fully conscious of its existence. The mass will never

---

[5] Alphonse Daudet, *Tartarin de Tarascon,* Marpon et Flammarion (Paris, 1887), p. 40.

rule except *in abstracto.* Consequently the question we have to discuss is not whether ideal democracy is realizable, but rather to what point and in what degree democracy is desirable, possible, and realizable at a given moment. . . .

The objective immaturity of the mass is not a mere transitory phenomenon which will disappear with the progress of democratization *au lendemain du socialisme.* On the contrary, it derives from the very nature of the mass as mass, for this, even when organized, suffers from an incurable incompetence for the solution of the diverse problems which present themselves for solution—because the mass *per se* is amorphous, and therefore needs division of labour, specialization, and guidance. "L'espèce humaine veut être gouvernée; elle le sera. J'ai honte de mon espèce," wrote Proudhon from his prison in 1850.[6] Man as individual is by nature predestined to be guided, and to be guided all the more in proportion as the functions of life undergo division and subdivision. To an enormously greater degree is guidance necessary for the social group. . . .

The writer does not wish to deny that every revolutionary working-class movement, and every movement sincerely inspired by the democratic spirit, may have a certain value as contributing to the enfeeblement of oligarchic tendencies. The peasant in the fable, when on his deathbed, tells his sons that a treasure is buried in the field. After the old man's death the sons dig everywhere in order to discover the treasure. They do not find it. But their indefatigable labour improves the soil and secures for them a comparative well-being. The treasure in the fable may well symbolize democracy. Democracy is a treasure which no one will ever discover by deliberate search. But in continuing our search, in labouring indefatigably to discover the undiscoverable, we shall perform a work which will have fertile results in the democratic sense. We have seen, indeed, that within the bosom of the democratic working-class party are born the very tendencies to counteract which that party came into existence. Thanks to the diversity and to the unequal worth of the elements of the party, these tendencies often give rise to manifestations which border on tyranny. We have seen that the replacement of the traditional legitimism of the powers-that-be by the brutal plebiscitary rule of Bonapartist parvenus does not furnish these tendencies with any moral or aesthetic superiority. Historical evolution mocks all the prophylactic measures that have been adopted for the prevention of oligarchy. If laws are passed to control the dominion of the leaders, it is the laws which gradually weaken, and not the leaders. . . .

In view of the perennial incompetence of the masses, we have to recognize the existence of two regulative principles:—

1. The *ideological* tendency of democracy towards criticism and control;

2. The *effective* counter-tendency of democracy towards the creation of parties ever more complex and ever more differentiated—parties, that is to say, which are increasingly based upon the competence of the few.

To the idealist, the analysis of the forms of contemporary democracy cannot fail to be a source of bitter deceptions and profound discouragement. Those

6 ["The human species wants to be governed; it will be. I am ashamed of my species."]

alone, perhaps, are in a position to pass a fair judgment upon democracy who, without lapsing into dilettantist sentimentalism, recognize that all scientific and human ideals have relative values. If we wish to estimate the value of democracy, we must do so in comparison with its converse, pure aristocracy. The defects inherent in democracy are obvious. It is none the less true that as a form of social life we must choose democracy as the least of evils. The ideal government would doubtless be that of an aristocracy of persons at once morally good and technically efficient. But where shall we discover such an aristocracy? We may find it sometimes, though very rarely, as the outcome of deliberate selection; but we shall never find it where the hereditary principle remains in operation. Thus monarchy in its pristine purity must be considered as imperfection incarnate, as the most incurable of ills; from the moral point of view it is inferior even to the most revolting of demagogic dictatorships, for the corrupt organism of the latter at least contains a healthy principle upon whose working we may continue to base hopes of social resanation. It may be said, therefore, that the more humanity comes to recognize the advantages which democracy, however imperfect, presents over aristocracy, even at its best, the less likely is it that a recognition of the defects of democracy will provoke a return to aristocracy. Apart from certain formal differences and from the qualities which can be acquired only by good education and inheritance (qualities in which aristocracy will always have the advantage over democracy—qualities which democracy either neglects altogether, or, attempting to imitate them, falsifies them to the point of caricature), the defects of democracy will be found to inhere in its inability to get rid of its aristocratic scoriae. On the other hand, nothing but a serene and frank examination of the oligarchical dangers of democracy will enable us to minimize these dangers, even though they can never be entirely avoided.

The democratic currents of history resemble successive waves. They break ever on the same shoal. They are ever renewed. This enduring spectacle is simultaneously encouraging and depressing. When democracies have gained a certain stage of development, they undergo a gradual transformation, adopting the aristocratic spirit, and in many cases also the aristocratic forms, against which at the outset they struggled so fiercely. Now new accusers arise to denounce the traitors; after an era of glorious combats and of inglorious power, they end by fusing with the old dominant class; whereupon once more they are in their turn attacked by fresh opponents who appeal to the name of democracy. It is probable that this cruel game will continue without end.

17. The Transformation of the Western European Party Systems*

OTTO KIRCHHEIMER

[Editors' Note. *Mention is made in this excerpt of parties of "individual representation" and "mass integration." Professor Kirchheimer explains earlier that parties of individual representation, such as the bourgeois parties of the Third French Republic, are based on "the local parish pump and the operation of the parliamentary factions." These parties are unable to function as transmission belts between the population and the government. By political integration he means "the capacity of a political system to make groups and their members previously outside the official fold full-fledged participants in the political process." A mass integration party is one that helps perform this function.*]

THE POSTWAR CATCH-ALL PARTY

Following the Second World War, the old-style bourgeois party of individual representation became the exception. While some of the species continue to survive, they do not determine the nature of the party system any longer. By the same token, the mass integration party, product of an age with harder class lines and more sharply protruding denominational structures, is transforming itself into a catch-all "people's" party. Abandoning attempts at the intellectual and moral *encadrement* of the masses, it is turning more fully to the electoral scene, trying to exchange effectiveness in depth for a wider audience and more immediate electoral success. The narrower political task and the immediate electoral goal differ sharply from the former all-embracing concerns; today the latter are seen as counter-productive since they deter segments of a potential nationwide clientele.

For the class-mass parties we may roughly distinguish three stages in this process of transformation. There is first the period of gathering strength lasting to the beginning of the First World War; then comes their first governmental experience in the 1920's and 1930's (MacDonald, Weimar Republic, *Front Populaire*), unsatisfactory if measured both against the expectations of the class-mass party followers or leaders and suggesting the need for a broader basis of consensus in the political system. This period is followed by the present more or

*From Joseph LaPalombara and Myron Weiner, eds., *Political Parties and Political Development*. Copyright © 1966 by Princeton University Press: Princeton Paperback, 1968, pp. 184–200. Reprinted by permission of Princeton University Press. Article and footnotes abridged by the editors.

less advanced stages in the catch-all grouping, with some of the parties still trying to hold their special working-class clientele and at the same time embracing a variety of other clienteles.

Can we find some rules according to which this transformation is taking place, singling out factors which advance or delay or arrest it? We might think of the current rate of economic development as the most important determinant; but if it were so important, France would certainly be ahead of Great Britain and, for that matter, also of the United States, still the classical example of an all-pervasive catch-all party system. What about the impact of the continuity or discontinuity of the political system? If this were so important, Germany and Great Britain would appear at opposite ends of the spectrum rather than showing a similar speed of transformation. We must then be satisfied to make some comments on the general trend and to note special limiting factors.

In some instances the catch-all performance meets definite limits in the traditional framework of society. The all-pervasive denominational background of the Italian *Democrazia Cristiana* means from the outset that the party cannot successfully appeal to the anticlerical elements of the population. Otherwise nothing prevents the party from phrasing its appeals so as to maximize its chances of catching more of those numerous elements which are not disturbed by the party's clerical ties. The solidary element of its doctrinal core has long been successfully employed to attract a socially diversified clientele.

Or take the case of two other major European parties, the German SPD (Social Democratic party) and the British Labour party. It is unlikely that either of them is able to make any concession to the specific desires of real estate interests or independent operators of agricultural properties while at the same time maintaining credibility with the masses of the urban population. Fortunately, however, there is enough community of interest between wage-and-salary earning urban or suburban white- and blue-collar workers and civil servants to designate them all as strategic objects of simultaneous appeals. Thus tradition and the pattern of social and professional stratification may set limits and offer potential audiences to the party's appeal.

If the party cannot hope to catch all categories of voters, it may have a reasonable expectation of catching more voters in all those categories whose interests do not adamantly conflict. Minor differences between group claims, such as between white-collar and manual labor groups, might be smoothed over by vigorous emphasis on programs which benefit both sections alike, for example, some cushioning against the shocks of automation.

Even more important is the heavy concentration on issues which are scarcely liable to meet resistance in the community. National societal goals transcending group interests offer the best sales prospect for a party intent on establishing or enlarging an appeal previously limited to specific sections of the population. The party which propagates most aggressively, for example, enlarged educational facilities may hear faint rumblings over the excessive cost or the danger to the quality of education from elites previously enjoying educational privileges. Yet the party's stock with any other family may be influenced only by how much more quickly and aggressively it took up the new national priority than its major competitor and how well its propaganda linked the individual family's future with the enlarged educational structures. To that extent its potential clientele is almost limitless. The catch-all of a given category performance turns virtually into an unlimited catch-all performance.

The last remark already transcends the group-interest confines. On the one hand, in such developed societies as I am dealing with, thanks to general levels of economic well-being and security and to existing welfare schemes universalized by the state or enshrined in collective bargaining, many individuals no longer need such protection as they once sought from the state. On the other hand, many have become aware of the number and complexity of the general factors on which their future well-being depends. This change of priorities and pre-occupation may lead them to examine political offerings less under the aspect of their own particular claims than under that of the political leader's ability to meet general future contingencies. Among the major present-day parties, it is the French UNR . . . [Union for the New Republic] a late-comer, that speculates most clearly on the possibility of its channeling such less specialized needs to which its patron saint De Gaulle constantly appeals into its own version of the catch-all party. Its assumed asset would rest in a doctrine of national purpose and unity vague and flexible enough to allow the most variegated interpretation and yet—at least as long as the General continues to function—attractive enough to serve as a convenient rallying point for many groups and isolated individuals.

While the UNR thus manipulates ideology for maximum general appeal, we have noted that ideology in the case of the *Democrazia Cristiana* is a slightly limiting factor. The UNR ideology in principle excludes no one. The Christian Democratic ideology by definition excludes the nonbeliever, or at least the seriously nonbelieving voter. It pays for the ties of religious solidarity and the advantages of supporting organizations by repelling some millions of voters. The catch-all parties in Europe appear at a time of de-ideologization which has substantially contributed to their rise and spread. De-ideologization in the political field involves the transfer of ideology from partnership in a clearly visible political goal structure into one of many sufficient but by no means necessary motivational forces operative in the voters' choice. The German and Austrian Social Democratic parties in the last two decades most clearly exhibit the politics of de-ideologization. The example of the German Christian Democratic Union (CDU) is less clear only because there was less to de-ideologize. In the CDU, ideology was from the outset only a general background atmosphere, both all-embracing and conveniently vague enough to allow recruiting among Catholic and Protestant denominations.

As a rule, only major parties can become successful catch-all parties. Neither a small, strictly regional party such as the South Tyrolian Peoples' party nor a party built around the espousal of harsh and limited ideological claims, like the Dutch Calvinists; or transitory group claims, such as the German Refugees; or a specific professional category's claims, such as the Swedish Agrarians; or a limited-action program, such as the Danish single-tax Justice party can aspire to a catch-all performance. Its raison d'être is the defense of a specific clientele or the lobbying for a limited reform clearly delineated to allow for a restricted appeal, perhaps intense, but excluding a wider impact or—once the original job is terminated—excluding a life-saving transformation.

Nor is the catch-all performance in vogue or even sought among the majority of the larger parties in small democracies. Securely entrenched, often enjoying majority status for decades—as the Norwegian and Swedish Social Democratic parties—and accustomed to a large amount of interparty cooperation,[1] such parties have no incentive to change their form of recruitment or their appeal to well-defined social groups. With fewer factors intervening and therefore more clearly foreseeable results of political actions and decisions, it seems easier to stabilize political relations on the basis of strictly circumscribed competition (Switzerland, for instance) than to change over to the more aleatory form of catch-all competition.

Conversion to catch-all parties constitutes a competitive phenomenon. A party is apt to accommodate to its competitor's successful style because of hope of benefits or fear of losses on election day. Conversely, the more a party convinces itself that a competitor's favorable results were due only to some non-repetitive circumstances, and that the competitor's capacity of overcoming internal dissension is a temporary phenomenon, the smaller the overall conversion chance and the greater the inclination to hold fast to a loyal—though limited—clientele.

To evaluate the impact of these changes I have found it useful to list the functions which European parties exercised during earlier decades (late in the nineteenth and early in the twentieth centuries) and to compare them with the present situation. Parties have functioned as channels for integrating individuals and groups into the existing political order, or as instruments for modifying or altogether replacing that order (integration-disintegration). Parties have attempted to determine political-action preferences and influence other participants in the political process into accepting them. Parties have nominated public officeholders and presented them to the public at large for confirmation.

The so-called "expressive function" of the party, if not belonging to a category by itself, nevertheless warrants a special word. Its high tide belongs to the era of the nineteenth-century constitutionalism when a more clear-cut separation existed between opinion formation-and-expression and the business of government. At that time the internally created parliamentary parties expressed opinions and criticism widely shared among the educated minority of the population. They pressed these opinions on their governments. But as the governments largely rested on an independent social and constitutional basis, they could if necessary hold out against the promptings of parliamentary

---

[1] . . . For both weighty historical and contemporary reasons the Austrian Social-Democratic party forms a partial exception to the rule of less clear-cut transformation tendencies among major class-mass parties in smaller countries. It is becoming an eager and rather successful member of the catch-all club. For the most adequate treatment see K. L. Shell, *The Transformation of Austrian Socialism* (New York, 1962).

factions and clubs. Full democratization merged the opinion-expressing and the governmental business in the same political parties and put them in the seat either of government or an alternative government. But it has left the expressive function of the party in a more ambiguous state. For electoral reasons, the democratic catch-all party, intent on spreading as wide as possible a net over a potential clientele, must continue to express widely felt popular concerns. Yet, bent on continuing in power or moving into governmental power, it performs this expressive function subject to manifold restrictions and changing tactical considerations. The party would atrophy if it were no longer able to function as a relay between the population and governmental structure, taking up grievances, ideas, and problems developed in a more searching and systematic fashion else-where in the body politic. Yet the caution it must give its present or prospective governmental role requires modulation and restraint. The very nature of today's catch-all party forbids an option between these two performances. It requires a constant shift between the party's critical role and its role as establishment support, a shift hard to perform but still harder to avoid.

In order to leave a maximum imprint on the polity a party has to exercise all of the first three functions. Without the ability to integrate people into the community the party could not compel other powerholders to listen to its clarions. The party influences other power centers to the extent that people are willing to follow its leadership. Conversely, people are willing to listen to the party because the party is the carrier of messages—here called action prefer-ences—that are at least partially in accord with the images, desires, hopes, and fears of the electorate. Nominations for public office serve to tie together all these purposes; they may further the realization of action preferences if they elicit positive response from voters or from other powerholders. The nomina-tions concretize the party's image with the public at large, on whose confidence the party's effective functioning depends.

Now we can discuss the presence or absence of these three functions in Western society today. Under present conditions of spreading secular and mass consumer-goods orientation, with shifting and less obtrusive class lines, the former class-mass parties and denominational mass parties are both under pressure to become catch-all peoples' parties. The same applies to those few remnants of former bourgeois parties of individual representation which aspire to a secure future as political organizations independent of the vagaries of electoral laws and the tactical moves of their mass-party competitors.[2] This change involves: (a) Drastic reduction of the party's ideological baggage. In France's SFIO, for example, ideological remnants serve at best as scant cover for what has become known as *"Molletisme,"* the absolute reign of short-term tactical considerations. (b) Further strengthening of top leadership groups,

[2] Liberal parties without sharply profiled program or clientele may, however, make such conversion attempts. Val Lorwin draws my attention to the excellent example of a former bourgeois party, the Belgian Liberal party, which became in 1961 the "Party of Liberty and Progress," deemphasizing anticlericalism and appealing to the right wing of the Social Christian party, worried about this party's governmental alliance with the Socialists.

whose actions and omissions are now judged from the viewpoint of their contribution to the efficiency of the entire social system rather than identification
with the goals of their particular organization. (c) Downgrading of the role of
the individual party member, a role considered a historical relic which may
obscure the newly built-up catch-all party image. (d) De-emphasis of the *classe
gardée,* specific social-class or denominational clientele, in favor of recruiting
voters among the population at large. (e) Securing access to a variety of interest
groups. The financial reasons are obvious, but they are not the most important
where official financing is available, as in Germany, or where access to the most
important media of communication is fairly open, as in England and Germany.
The chief reason is to secure electoral support via interest-group intercession.

From this fairly universal development the sometimes considerable remnants
of two old class-mass parties, the French and the Italian Communist parties, are
excluding themselves. These parties are in part ossified, in part solidified by a
combination of official rejection and legitimate sectional grievances. In this
situation the ceremonial invocation of the rapidly fading background of a remote
and inapplicable revolutionary experience has not yet been completely abandoned as a part of political strategy. What is the position of such opposition
parties of the older class-mass type, which still jealously try to hold an exclusive
loyalty of their members, while not admitted nor fully ready to share in the
hostile state power? Such parties face the same difficulties in recruiting and
holding intensity of membership interest as other political organizations. Yet, in
contrast to their competitors working within the confines of the existing
political order, they cannot make a virtue out of necessity and adapt themselves
fully to the new style of catch-all peoples' party.[3] This conservatism does not
cost them the confidence of their regular corps of voters. On the other hand, the
continued renewal of confidence on election day does not involve an intimate
enough bond to utilize as a basis for major political operations.

The attitudes of regular voters—in contrast to those of members and activists—
attest to the extent of incongruency between full-fledged participation in the
social processes of a consumer-goods oriented society and the old political style
which rested on the primordial need for sweeping political change. The latter
option has gone out of fashion in Western countries and has been carefully
eliminated from the expectations, calculations, and symbols of the catch-all
mass party. The incongruency may rest on the total absence of any connection
between general social-cultural behavior and political style. In this sense electoral
choice may rest on family tradition or empathy with the political underdog
without thereby becoming part of a coherent personality structure. Or the
choice may be made in the expectation that it will have no influence on the
course of political development; it is then an act of either adjusting to or, as

---

[3] However, even in France—not to speak of Italy—Communist policies are under pressure
to accommodate to the new style. For a concrete recent example see W. G. Andrews,
"Evreux 1962: Referendum and Elections in a Norman Constituency," in *Political Studies,*
vol. 11 (October 1963), pp. 308–326. Most recently, Maurice Duverger, "L'Eternel Marais,
Essai sur le Centrisme Français," in *Revue Française de Science Politique,* vol. 14 (February
1964), pp. 33 and 49.

the case may be, signing out of the existing political system rather than a manifestation of signing up somewhere else.

THE CATCH-ALL PARTY, THE INTEREST GROUP, AND THE VOTER: LIMITED INTEGRATION

The integration potential of the catch-all mass party rests on a combination of factors whose visible end result is attraction of the maximum number of voters on election day. For that result the catch-all party must have entered into millions of minds as a familiar object fulfilling in politics a role analogous to that of a major brand in the marketing of a universally needed and highly standardized article of mass consumption. Whatever the particularities of the line to which a party leader owes his intraparty success, he must, once he is selected for leadership, rapidly suit his behavior to standard requirements. There is need for enough brand differentiation to make the article plainly recognizable, but the degree of differentiation must never be so great as to make the potential customer fear he will be out on a limb.

Like the brand whose name has become a household word, the catch-all mass party that has presided over the fortunes of a country for some time, and whose leaders the voter has therefore come to know on his television set and in his newspaper columns, enjoys a great advantage. But only up to a certain point. Through circumstances possibly outside the control of the party or even of the opposition—a scandal in the ranks of government, an economic slump—office-holding may suddenly turn into a negative symbol encouraging the voter to switch to another party as a consumer switches to a competitive brand.

The rules deciding the outcome of catch-all mass party competition are extremely complex and extremely aleatory. When a party has or seeks an almost nationwide potential constituency, its majority composed of individuals whose relation to politics is both tangential and discontinuous, the factors which may decide the eventual electoral outcome are almost infinite in number and often quite unrelated to the party's performance. The style and looks of the leader, the impact of a recent event entirely dictated from without, vacation schedules, the weather as it affects crops—factors such as these all enter into the results.

The very catch-all character of the party makes membership loyalty far more difficult to expect and at best never sufficient to swing results. The outcome of a television contest is dubious, or the contest itself may constitute too fleeting an exposure to make an impression that will last into the election. Thus the catch-all mass party too is driven back to look out for a more permanent clientele. Only the interest group, whether ideological or economic in nature or a combination of the two, can provide mass reservoirs of readily accessible voters. It has a more constant line of communication and higher acceptance for its messages than the catch-all party, which is removed from direct contact with the public except for the comparatively small number intensively concerned about the brand of politics a party has to offer these days—or about their own careers in or through the party.

All the same, the climate of relations between catch-all party and interest groups has definitely changed since the heyday of the class-mass or denominational integration party. Both party and interest group have gained a greater independence from each other. Whether they are still joined in the same organization (like British Labour and the TUC [Trades Union Congress]) or formally enjoy complete independence from each other (like the German SPD and the DGB [Workers' Federation]), what matters most is the change of roles.[4] Instead of a joint strategy toward a common goal there appears an appreciation of limited if still mutually helpful services to be rendered.

The party bent on attracting a maximum of voters must modulate its interest-group relations in such a way so as not to discourage potential voters who identify themselves with other interests. The interest group, in its turn, must never put all its eggs in one basket. That might offend the sensibilities of some members with different political connections. More important, the interest group would not want to stifle feelings of hope in another catch-all party that some moves in its direction might bring electoral rewards. Both party and interest group modulate their behavior, acting as if the possible contingency has already arrived, namely that the party has captured the government—or an important share in it—and has moved from the position of friend or counsellor to that of umpire or arbitrator. Suddenly entrusted with the confidence of the community as a whole, the government-party arbitrator does best when able to redefine the whole problem and discover solutions which would work, at least in the long run, in the favor of all interest claimants concerned.

Here there emerges a crucial question: What then is the proper role of the catch-all party in the arbitration of interest conflicts? Does not every government try to achieve the best tactical position for exercising an effective arbitration between contending group claims? Is the catch-all party even needed in this connection? Or—from the interest viewpoint—can a society dispense with parties' services, as France now does?

A party is more than a collector of interest-group claims. It functions at the same time as advocate, protector, or at least as addressee of the demands of all those who are not able to make their voices felt as effectively as those represented by well organized interest groups: those who do not yet have positions in the process of production or those who no longer hold such positions, the too young and the too old, and those whose family status aligns them with consumer rather than producer interests.

Can we explain this phenomenon simply as another facet of the party's aggregative function? But functionalist phraseology restates rather than explains. The unorganized and often unorganizable make their appearance only on election day or in suddenly sprouting pre-election committees and party activities arranged for their benefit. Will the party be able and willing to take their interests into its own hands? Will it be able, playing on their availability in

---

[4] See the conclusions of Martin Harrison, *Trade Unions and the Labour Party Since 1945* (London, 1960).

electoral terms, not only to check the more extreme demands of organized groups but also to transcend the present level of intergroup relations and by political reforms redefining the whole political situation? No easy formula will tell us what leader's skill, what amount of pressure from objective situations has to intervene to produce such a change in the political configuration.

In this job of transcending group interests and creating general confidence the catch-all party enjoys advantages, but by the same token it suffers from an infirmity. Steering clear of sectarianism enhances its recruiting chances in electoral terms but inevitably limits the intensity of commitment it may expect. The party's transformation from an organization combining the defense of social position, the quality of spiritual shelter, and the vision of things to come into that of a vehicle for short-range and interstitial political choice exposes the party to the hazards of all purveyors of nondurable consumer goods: competition with a more attractively packaged brand of a nearly identical merchandise.

LIMITED PARTICIPATION IN ACTION PREFERENCE

This brings us to the determination of action preferences and their chances of realization. In Anthony Downs's well-known model action preference simply results from the party's interest in the proximate goal, the winning of the next election. In consequence the party will arrange its policies in such a way that the benefits accruing to the individual members of the community are greater than the losses resulting from its policy.[5] Downs's illustrations are frequently, though not exclusively, taken from fields such as taxation where the cash equation of political action is feasible. Yet Downs himself has occasionally noted that psychological satisfactions or dissatisfactions, fears or hopes, are elements in voters' decisions as frequently as calculations of immediate short-term benefits or deprivations. Were it different, the long-lasting loyalty of huge blocks of voters to class-mass integration parties in the absence of any immediate benefits from such affiliation could scarcely be explained. But can it be said that such short-term calculations correspond much more closely to the attitudes connected with the present-day catch-all mass party with its widely ranging clientele? Can the short-term benefit approach, for example, be utilized in military or foreign-policy issues?

In some countries in the last decade it has become the rule for catch-all parties out of office simply to lay the most recent shortcomings or apparent deterioration of the country's military or international position at the doorstep of the incumbent government, especially during election campaigns: thus in the United States the Republican party in 1952 with regard to the long-lasting indecisive Korean War, or in Germany more recently the Social Democrats with regard to Adenauer's apparent passivity in the face of the Berlin Wall. In other instances, however, the opposition plays down foreign or military issues or treats

[5] "It always organizes its action so as to focus on a single quantity: its vote margin over the opposition is the test at the end of the current election period." In A. Downs, *An Economic Theory of Democracy* (1957), p. 174.

them in generalities vague enough to evoke the image of itself as a competitor who will be able to handle them as well as the incumbent government.

To the extent that the party system still includes "unreformed" or—as in the case of the Italian Socialist party—only "half-reformed" class-mass integration parties, foreign or military issues enter election campaigns as policy differences. Yet even here the major interest has shifted away from areas where the electorate could exercise only an illusory choice. The electorate senses that in the concrete situation, based in considerable part on geography and history, the international bloc affiliation of the country rather than any policy preference will form the basis of decision. It senses too that such decisions rest only partially, or at times nominally, with the political leadership. Even if the impact of the political leader on the decision may have been decisive, more often than not election timetables in democracies are such that the decision, once carried out, is no longer contested or even relevant to voter choices. As likely as not, new events crowd it out of the focus of voters' attention. Few voters still thought of Mendès-France's 1954 "abandonment" of Indo-China when Edgar Faure suddenly dissolved the Assembly in December 1955. While a party may benefit from its adversary's unpopular decisions, such benefits are more often an accidental by-product than the outcome of a government-opposition duel with clearly distributed roles and decisions.

A party may put up reasonably coherent, even if vague, foreign or military policies for election purposes. It may criticize the inept handling of such problems by the government of the day, and more and more intensively as it gets closer to election day. But in neither case is there a guarantee of the party's ability to act as a coherent body in parliament when specific action preferences are to be determined. Illustrative of this dilemma are the history of EDC in the French Parliament and the more recent battles within the British parties in regard to entrance into the Common Market (although the latter case remains inconclusive because of De Gaulle's settling the issue in his own way, for the time being). Fortuitous election timetables and the hopes, fears, and expectations of the public do not intermesh sufficiently with the parliamentary representatives' disjointed action on concrete issues before them to add up to the elaboration of clear-cut party action preference.

The catch-all party contributes general programs in the elaboration of domestic action preferences. These programs may be of a prognostic variety, informing the public about likely specific developments and general trends. Yet prognostics and desirability blur into each other in this type of futurology, in which rosy glasses offer previews of happy days for all and sundry among the party's prospective customers. These programs may lead to or be joined with action proposals in various stages of concretization. Concrete proposals, however, always risk implying promises which may be too specific. Concretizations must remain general enough so that they cannot be turned from electoral weapons to engines of assault against the party which first mounted them.

This indeterminacy allows the catch-all party to function as a meeting ground for the elaboration of concrete action for a multiplicity of interest groups. All the party may require from those who obtain its services is that they make a maximal attempt to arrive at compromises within the framework of the party and that they avoid coalescing with forces hostile to the party. The compromises thus elaborated must be acceptable to major interest groups even if these groups, for historical or traditional reasons, happen not to be represented in the governing party. Marginal differences may be submitted to the voter at elections or, as older class-mass parties do on occasion, via referenda (Switzerland and Sweden). But expected policy mutations are in the nature of increments rather than major changes in intergroup relations.

It is here that the difference between the catch-all and the older form of integration party becomes most clearly visible. The catch-all party will do its utmost to establish consensus to avoid party realignment. The integration party may count on majority political mechanisms to implement its programs only to find that hostile interests frustrate the majority decision by the economic and social mechanisms at their disposal. They may call strikes (by labor or farmers or storekeepers or investors), they may withdraw capital to safe haven outside the country, they may undermine that often hypocritically invoked but real factor known as the "confidence of the business community."

INTEGRATION THROUGH PARTICIPATION IN LEADERSHIP SELECTION—THE FUTURE OF THE POLITICAL PARTY

What then remains the real share of the catch-all party in the elaboration of action preferences? Its foremost contribution lies in the mobilization of the voters for whatever concrete action preferences leaders are able to establish rather than *a priori* selections of their own. It is for this reason that the catch-all party prefers to visualize action in the light of the contingencies, threats, and promises of concrete historical situations rather than of general social goals. It is the hoped-for or already established role in the dynamics of action, in which the voters' vicarious participation is invited, that is most in evidence. Therefore the attention of both party and public at large focuses most clearly on problems of leadership selection.

Nomination means the prospect of political office. Political office involves a chance to make an impact via official action. The competition between those striving to influence official action puts into evidence the political advantage of those in a position to act before their political adversaries can do so. The privilege of first action is all the more precious in a new and non-repetitive situation where the political actor can avoid getting enmeshed in directives deriving from party action preferences. Much as the actor welcomes party support on the basis of revered (but elastic) principles, he shuns specific direction and supervision. In this respect the catch-all party furnishes an ideal background for political action. Where obtaining office becomes an almost exclusive preoccupation of a party, issues of personnel are reduced to search for the simplest effective means to put up winning combinations. The search is especially effective wherever the party becomes a channel by which representatives of hitherto excluded or neglected minorities may join in the existing political elite.

The nomination of candidates for popular legitimation as officeholders thus emerges as the most important function of the present-day catch-all party. Concentration on the selection of candidates for office is in line with an increasing role differentiation in industrial society. Once certain levels of education and material welfare are reached, both intellectual and material needs are taken care of by specialized purveyors of communications and economic products. Likewise the party, which in less advanced societies or in those intent on rapid change directly interferes with the performance of societal jobs, remains in Western industrial society twice removed—through government and bureaucracy—from the field of direct action. To this state of affairs correspond now prevailing popular images and expectations in regard to the reduced role of the party. Expectations previously set on the performance of a political organization are now flowing into different channels.

At the same time, the role of the political party as a factor in the continued integration of the individual into the national life now has to be visualized in a different light. Compared to his connection with interest organizations and voluntary associations of a non-political nature and to his frequent encounters with the state bureaucracy, the citizen's relations with the political party are becoming more intermittent and of more limited scope.

To the older party of integration the citizen, if he so desired, could be closer. Then it was a less differentiated organization, part channel of protest, part source of protection, part purveyor of visions of the future. Now, in its linear descendant in a transfigured world, the catch-all party, the citizen finds a relatively remote, at times quasi-official and alien structure. Democratic society assumes that the citizen is finally an integral and conscious participant in the affairs of both the polity and the economy; it further assumes that as such he will work through the party as one of the many interrelated structures by which he achieves a rational participation in his surrounding world.

Should he ever live up to these assumptions, the individual and society may indeed find the catch-all party—non-utopian, non-oppressive, and ever so flexible—an ingenious and useful political instrument.

What about the attitude toward the modern catch-all party of functional powerholders in army, bureaucracy, industry, and labor? Released from their previous unnecessary fears as to the ideological propensities and future intentions of the class-mass party, functional powerholders have come to recognize the catch-all party's role as consensus purveyor. In exchange for its ability to provide a clear-cut basis of legitimacy, functional powerholders are, up to a point, willing to recognize the political leadership claims of the party. They expect it to exercise certain arbitration functions in intergroup relations and to initiate limited political innovations. The less clear-cut electoral basis of the party's leadership claim and the closer the next election date, the smaller the credit which functional powerholders will extend to unsolicited and non-routine activities of the political powerholders impinging on their own positions. This lack of credit then sets the stage for conflicts between functional and political leadership groups. How does the catch-all party in governmental positions treat such conflicts? Will it be satisfied to exercise pressure via the mass media, or will it try to re-create a militant mass basis beyond the evanescent electoral and publicity levels? But the very structure of the catch-all party, the looseness of its clientele, may from the outset exclude such more far-reaching action. To that extent the political party's role in Western industrial society today is more limited than would appear from its position of formal preeminence. Via its governmental role it functions as coordinator of and arbitrator between functional power groups. Via its electoral role it produces that limited amount of popular participation and integration required from the popular masses for the functioning of official political institutions.

Will this limited participation which the catch-all party offers the population at large, this call to rational and dispassionate participation in the political process via officially sanctioned channels, work?

The instrument, the catch-all party, cannot be much more rational than its nominal master, the individual voter. No longer subject to the discipline of the party of integration—or, as in the United States, never subject to this discipline—the voters may, by their shifting moods and their apathy, transform the sensitive instrument of the catch-all party into something too blunt to serve as a link with the functional powerholders of society. Then we may yet come to regret the passing—even if it was inevitable—of the class-mass party and the denominational party, as we already regret the passing of other features in yesterday's stage of Western civilization.

18. Political Parties: Some Sceptical Reflections*

ANTHONY KING

A glance at the bookshelves of most political scientists or at the index of almost any professional journal would satisfy most of us that one of the major concerns of political science is the political party. Parties, having once been neglected by scholars, are now the subject almost of a sub-discipline within the profession. To take one simple measure, parties have featured more prominently in the pages of the *American Political Science Review* over the past decade than any other single process or institution. Moreover, the claims made on behalf of

*From "Political Parties in Western Democracies: Some Sceptical Reflections," *Polity*, vol. II, no. 2 (Winter 1969), pp. 111–41. Article and footnotes abridged by the editors. Reprinted by permission of the author and the journal.

the political party are often extreme. It is said not merely that parties, like executives and legislatures and electoral systems, are essential prerequisites of modern democracy but that parties perform an extraordinarily wide range of political functions, sometimes to the virtual exclusion of other political structures. The party, like some vast commercial enterprise, is seen as operating in a wide variety of political markets and as wielding something approaching monopoly power in a considerable number of them. . . .

. . . Do parties play as large a role in Western democracies as is usually assumed? How crucial are parties to the performance of certain important political functions?

PARTIES IN ACTION AND PARTY FUNCTIONS

Two ways of dealing with these questions suggest themselves, one highly impressionistic but perhaps suggestive, the other more systematic. The first is to select a number of important episodes in the recent history of Western democracies and to ask what role political parties played in them. If parties are as important as political scientists are inclined to suppose, then they ought, either as groups or as sets of patterned actions, to have featured prominently in the cases chosen—and in most of the other cases that might have been chosen. Three examples come to mind, one chosen from each of three major Western countries: the Negro revolution in the United States; the efforts of two British governments to gain entry to the European Economic Community; and the upheaval in France in the summer of 1968. Each of these developments was at least potentially critical for the country concerned. Two of the three—the Negro revolution and the May riots in France—directly involved large numbers of people. All three raised questions, central to the putative functions of political parties, concerning the relationship in a democracy between governors and governed. The main facts concerning the three are reasonably well known, and there is no need to go into detail here.

What seems fairly obvious is that neither the political parties of the three countries nor (except very indirectly) their party systems played a central role in any of these developments. Historical accounts of them could be produced, and indeed have been, in which political parties figure hardly at all. Moreover, few political scientists analyzing these events as case studies in the workings of particular political systems would single out parties as having been critical actors. If parties were made the focus of scholarly attention, it would probably be with a view to showing that the parties and party systems of all three countries had in one way or another failed to perform the functions that are conventionally attributed to them. Any amount of evidence can be drawn on to reinforce these points. Many of the leading figures in all three episodes—Martin Luther King, Sir Eric Roll, Daniel Cohn-Bendit, not least General de Gaulle himself—were recruited outside the party system. To the extent that political integration and mobilization took place, they occurred in structures largely set apart from the parties: civil rights organizations in America, the Campaign for Europe and other less formal groupings in Britain, trade unions and student organizations in France. In no case did a political party, as a party, formulate policy in any strict sense; nor, except briefly in Britain (1963–65), did the political parties structure the choices available to either the mass publics or the governments concerned. The aggregation of interests proceeded to a greater or less degree in all three countries, but political parties were seldom the chief agencies involved.

But, it may be objected, to proceed in this way, episode by episode, is to miss a large part of the point. Individual parties may or may not be critical actors in particular situations; but parties and party systems play a large part in creating and maintaining the political culture and political structures which characterize political systems as a whole and in the context of which particular situations develop. To take the British case, the Conservative and Labour Parties as such may not have had much to do with the efforts to enter Europe; but the British party system produced the governments which took the decisions, recruited the chief political decision-makers, and (at least in 1964) created the circumstances in which the electorate could choose between a party committed to entering Europe and one not so committed. In other words, even though parties and party systems may in large part be the products of their political environment, nonetheless they perform, it is claimed, certain critical functions in all Western democratic systems.

This line of reasoning has to be treated with respect, and it brings us to the second, more systematic way of assessing the importance of parties. This is to analyze in turn each of the alleged functions of party. . . .

What, then, are the alleged functions of party, and what can be said about them? It probably does relatively little violence to the complexity of the subject to discuss six, and only six, of the most general functions: (1) the structuring of the vote; (2) the integration and mobilization of the mass public; (3) the recruitment of political leaders; (4) the organization of government; (5) the formation of public policy; and (6) the aggregation of interests. Other functions will be touched on in passing, but these seem to be the main ones referred to in the literature.

STRUCTURING THE VOTE

"Structuring the vote," in Epstein's words, "is the minimum function of a political party in a modern democracy."[1] A group or organization that did not attempt to structure the vote in its own favor would not normally be called a party; a group that did would generally be regarded as a party even if, like the typical French rally, it tried to claim it was not one. Efforts to structure the vote can range from the simple allocation of party labels to candidates to the conduct of large-scale educational and propaganda campaigns. Indeed, vote-structuring is often bound up with the educational, persuasive, and representational functions to which many writers refer. Whether in a particular political

[1] Leon D. Epstein, *Political Parties in Western Democracies* (New York: Praeger, 1968), p. 77.

system the parties are in fact performing a vote-structuring function depends ultimately on whether the voters respond (at a single election or over a longer period) to the labels the parties present. On the one hand, parties might make heroic efforts, yet find that the voters responded much more to considerations of class or race or personality. On the other hand, the parties might (say, in a particular election) make few efforts to appeal to voters, yet discover when the behavior of voters was analyzed that party had been the main structuring factor. In the latter case one would probably want to say, not simply that party had structured the vote, but rather that the vote had been structured along party lines as a consequence of past or present party activity, or as a consequence of the past or present workings of the party system.

The political scientist is thus presented with two broad questions: What entities seek to structure the vote? What entities, as the result of their activities or even of their mere existence, have the effect of structuring the vote? And of course political scientists are right in asserting that the best single answer to both questions is "political parties." Formally-organized political parties in all Western democracies attempt to structure the vote more assiduously, more continuously, and more single-mindedly than any other kind of agency. As regards how the vote is actually structured, it is clear from an abundance of studies that in most countries at most times the major electoral alignments are in large part party alignments.[2] The scholar who wishes to study vote-structuring will inevitably find himself studying parties—although not only parties, since parties in all Western systems share this function with a wide variety of other agencies: candidates, who may not wish (especially in the United States) to associate themselves too closely with the party label, elements in the media of communications, interest groups and broader social movements, and other kinds of citizen groups. And in exceptional circumstances vote structuring may take place without parties at all, as in the numerous American jurisdictions with nonpartisan elections.

But there is another point to which attention ought to be drawn. The term "structuring" and others like it—Bryce referred to parties' "bring[ing] order out of chaos"[3]—may be used in rather different senses. They may refer simply to parties' efforts to persuade voters to respond to particular party labels, and to voters' responses to those labels. Or they may refer to parties' efforts to persuade citizens to adopt particular opinions, and to the consequences of party activity and the configuration of the party system for the structure of political opinion in a community. Epstein is clearly using the term in its minimal sense when he writes:

All that is meant by the awkward word "structuring" is the imposition of

---

[2] Although true, this point may on occasion be fairly jejune. If, for example, the party division within a particular country is in some way a consequence of a pre-existing class division, it will not be adding very much to say that the resulting alignment is a "party" alignment. . . .

[3] Sigmund Neumann, ed., *Modern Political Parties: Approaches to Comparative Politics* (Chicago: University of Chicago Press, 1956), p. 396.

an order or pattern enabling voters to choose candidates according to their labels. . . . The structure may be little more than that provided by the label itself and the voters' acquaintance with it. . . .[4]

But Neumann, although using similar terminology, evidently had something more elaborate in mind when he said of parties:

They are brokers of ideas, constantly clarifying, systematizing, and expounding the party's doctrine. . . . They maximize the voters' education in the competitive scheme of at least a two-party system and sharpen his free choice.[5]

Vote-structuring, in short, is related to opinion-structuring.

To some extent the point is obvious. Political scientists have long been aware, for instance, that political parties are programmatic in widely varying degrees, the communist and social democratic parties of Western Europe contrasting with the mainly nondoctrinal parties of the United States and Canada. They have long been aware, too, that even doctrinal parties often fail to communicate their doctrines to the mass of voters or even to their own supporters. But there is another more profound point at issue. Irrespective of whether the parties in a system seek to structure opinion in any elaborate way, there may come to exist, for one reason or another, a radical discontinuity between the structure of alternatives presented to the electorate by the parties and the attitudes and demands of the electorate or of important sections of it. There may, in other words, cease to be a high degree of "fit" between the pattern of party opinion and the pattern of mass opinion.

That this is not a remote possiblity is suggested by the recent history of a number of Western countries. The last half-decade has witnessed the increasing violence of the Negro revolution in the United States and the mounting evidence of Negro alienation from conventional political life, the rapid growth in Britain of Scottish and Welsh nationalist movements intent on breaking up the United Kingdom, the momentary descent of France into chaos in 1968, the student unrest in West Germany following on the creation of the grand coalition, and the growth of French Canadian separatism. The list could be extended further.

It is not yet possible to explain these phenomena fully. In particular, it is not clear to what extent the explanation for them lies in the "malfunctioning" (however that term is used) of the party system in the countries in question; indeed it may be that the nature and workings of the various party systems have been such as to reduce levels of conflict that might have been even higher under other circumstances. Even so, the altered temper of a good deal of Western politics in the late 1960s raises serious questions: To what extent are parties performing an opinion-structuring function? Is it necessary that this function be performed? If so, is it necessary that it be performed by parties? If not by parties, then by what other agencies? If by other agencies, then what are the

[4] Epstein, *op. cit.,* p. 77.
[5] Neumann, *op. cit.,* p. 396.

consequences for parties and party systems and for the other functions of party? Whatever the answers to such questions, it is evident that when political scientists speak of the representational or linkage or communication functions of parties they are speaking of functions that parties may perform completely, incompletely, or not at all. And the extent to which they are performing such functions is to be determined by empirical inquiry, not by fiat.

At this point discussion has shifted from the structuring of the vote to another alleged function of party: the integration and mobilization of the political community.

INTEGRATION AND MOBILIZATION

This function, like most of the others, has been described in a variety of ways. LaPalombara and Weiner note that somehow "the party must articulate to its followers the concept and meaning of the broader community. . . ."[6] Kirchheimer similarly observes that parties have functioned "as channels for integrating individuals and groups into the existing political order. . . ."[7] Neumann went rather further and maintained that parties transformed the private citizen himself:

> They make him a *zoon politikon;* they integrate him into the group. Every party has to present to the individual voter and to his powerful special-interest groups a picture of the community as an entity.[8]

Such ideas are clearly part of what is normally understood by the concept of political socialization. However the ideas are phrased, those who use them are referring to the processes whereby individuals acquire psychological and social attachments to political parties and, through them, to the wider political order. (It goes without saying that some parties seek to do the reverse, to engender hostility to the established order; but in a discussion as brief as this such parties will have to be ignored even though they raise serious conceptual problems in connection with almost any kind of functional analysis.)

The problems that confront the political scientist are to ascertain whether political integration and mobilization are taking place at all and, if so, to what extent and with respect to whom; and also, if integration is taking place, to discover which agencies or processes are responsible for it. In this connection it is worth noting that students of politics, especially students of Western politics, have tended to assume, sometimes in a rather Panglossian way, that a satisfactory degree of integration is in fact taking place. They have assumed, in other words, that the mass publics of Western democracies (at any rate the assertive elements in them) accept the existing political order or at least accept the existing rules

---

6 Joseph LaPalombara and Myron Weiner, eds., *Political Parties and Political Development* (Princeton, N.J.: Princeton University Press, 1966), p. 3.

7 Otto Kirchheimer, "The Transformation of the Western European Party Systems" in LaPalombara and Weiner, *op. cit.,* pp. 188–89.

8 Neumann, *op. cit.,* p. 397.

for changing it. Events in the past two decades in the United States, France, Canada and elsewhere should give one pause before this assumption is made too readily—quite apart from the political turmoil that has characterized the history of many European countries since at least the beginning of this century.

But insofar as integration is taking place, is it taking place as a consequence of the presence and activities of parties? A full answer to this question would have to be very complex, since parties could in principle perform an integrative function in various ways. Individuals and groups in mass publics could be integrated into the political system by party because they developed favorable attitudes toward parties and party systems as such; or because they came to have favorable attitudes toward particular parties (which were not themselves hostile to the system); or because, in addition to developing favorable attitudes, they came into personal contact with parties either as citizens whose votes were being solicited or as party members or activists.

Comparatively little empirical work has been done on any of these processes; some of them, indeed, would be extraordinarily hard to study, certainly within the confines of any one country. But what few findings are available cast doubt on the centrality of party's role. Dennis investigated support for the American Party system amongst a section of the American public and found "mixed and not highly supportive feelings about the institution of party." He concluded:

> In our system, as no doubt in many others—where leaders from Mobutu to de Gaulle have been calling for an end to partisan politics—anti-party norms and images are present as a living part of the political culture.[9]

Parties can hardly be said to be performing a positive integrative function if there exists widespread antipathy or even indifference toward them; rather the reverse. As Dennis points out, lack of enthusiasm for parties could at a time of great environmental stress deprive a political system of an important potential source of support.

Equally problematical is the strength of the psychological bond connecting citizens to individual parties and thence to political systems as a whole. Most American research testifies to the widespread incidence and strength of partisan identifications in the United States, and it seems reasonable to suppose that in America favorable dispositions toward a particular party as one main element in the citizen's political universe are associated with, and even reinforce, favorable views of much else in his universe. Certainly the stronger the individual's sense of attachment to one of the parties, the greater his psychological involvement in politics generally, although the nature of the causal nexus here is far from clear.[10] Moreover, when the pattern of party identification is fairly stable, as it is in the United States, an important stabilizing factor is thereby introduced into the political system as a whole.

It seems, however, that what is true for America—and probably most of the

[9] Jack Dennis, "Support for the Party System by the Mass Public," *American Political Science Review*, LX (September 1966), pp. 613 and 615.

[10] Angus Campbell *et al., The American Voter* (New York: Wiley, 1960), p. 143.

other Anglo-Saxon democracies—is not true for some of the continental countries in Europe, notably France. Kirchheimer noted that, "In the single-load job
of integrating the *couches populaires* into the French polity the performance of
the political party remained unimpressive."[11] He was referring to the Third
Republic, but recent French history suggests that French parties and the French
party system have not performed an integrative function any more effectively
since the war than before. This conclusion is buttressed by the well-known
finding of Converse and Dupeux that the incidence of party identification is
much lower in France than in the United States.[12] If parties are playing a part
in integrating successfully the political communities of West Germany and Italy,
it would seem that they have been doing so only fairly recently, given the
frequent changes of both regime and party system in both those countries.

Political integration may take a purely psychological form; it may in addition
involve the mobilization of men and women into active political work. Political
activists may, as a by-product of their activities, more fully integrate their less
active fellows into the political system; persons not active in politics may become more completely members of the political community as the result of
having their votes solicited on the doorstep or of attending a party picnic or
bazaar. At the same time, the political activists may themselves become more
fully integrated into the system as a consequence of their efforts.

Leaving aside the question of how important political mobilization is for the
achievement of political integration (assuming that the two are not defined as
the same thing), we can question the effectiveness of the activities of those active
in political parties as distinct from other agencies. We can also ask how important parties are generally in promoting political activity.

There exist several studies dealing with the impact of party activity on the
mass public. Their findings are broadly similar, and it is probably fair to take
Eldersveld's study of Wayne County as representative (although how far the
data gathered in one American city are useful for comparative purposes is of
course open to question). Exposure to party activity, Eldersveld found in
Detroit, did have an impact on individuals' political dispositions. For example,
an analysis of the relationship between exposure to party activity and indices of
political optimism and pessimism led Eldersveld to conclude: "Party contact
appears . . . to fortify and accentuate public confidence by making the citizen
feel that he has some importance in our complex political system."[13] Yet at
the same time, even though the Wayne County study was conducted in a
densely-populated urban area with a highly-articulated party system, fully 44 per
cent of the sample had not been exposed to party activity at all. The writer notes
that as a result "party impact is severely restricted."[14] Moreover, when Elders-

[11] Kirchheimer in LaPalombara and Weiner, *op. cit.,* p. 180.

[12] Philip E. Converse and Georges Dupeux, "Politicization of the Electorate in France
and the United States" reprinted in Angus Campbell *et al., Elections and the Political Order*
(New York: Wiley, 1966), pp. 269–91.

[13] Samuel J. Eldersveld, *Political Parties: A Behavioral Analysis* (Chicago: Rand McNally,
1964), p. 500.

[14] *Ibid.,* pp. 442 and 526.

vled tried to assess the relative roles of television and party in fostering support for the political system, television seemed at least as powerful an agency as party. And there are many other agencies at work: family, friends, work associates, formal associations, the press, contact with government officials. Some of these agencies mediate the influence of party, but others do not, at least not in any direct way.

It remains to consider, not the impact of political activity, but the activists themselves, whether their participation takes place via party or through other channels. Active political participation often leads to consensus and integration. The acts of participation—voting, soliciting votes, collecting campaign contributions, speaking at meetings, leading delegations, and so on—may themselves contribute to the functioning of political systems; and active participants in politics usually have, if anything, a more favorable attitude toward existing political procedures than do mass publics. One may recall the famous dictum that two deputies, one of whom is a revolutionary, have more in common than two revolutionaries, one of whom is a deputy. But of course participation may on occasion be linked to profound disagreements and may lead to dissensus and even disintegration.

Whatever its impact on integration, to what extent in modern democracies does political activity take the form of party activity? Although hard data are not easy to come by, the incidence of specifically partisan activity has almost certainly declined in most Western countries, perhaps partly as a result of the growing professionalization of party politics. Other kinds of politically-engaged groupings, however, appear to flourish. In the United States in recent years an increasing proportion of political activity has been channelled through civil rights and student organizations, citizens' political clubs, protest movements, (of right as well as left), and the followings of individual candidates for office. All seek to influence party structures; but many combine outside the existing party system, some against it. As Sorauf has noted:

> . . . men and women continue to participate in the political process and perform the traditional political services. But they no longer work exclusively or largely within the political party. . . . the political party in the United States finds it progressively harder to monopolize its traditional political activities.[15]

And of course a significant proportion of current political activity in America (as elsewhere) is not "traditional" in any usual sense.

In most European countries political parties still play a more dominant role. A larger proportion of political participation has long been organized via the party, and the more militant parties continue to perform an expressive function not undertaken by the parties of the United States. Even so, there have been manifestations of anti-party activism in France, Germany, the Netherlands and Denmark, and Britain is frequently reported, possibly accurately, to be going through a phase of disillusionment with traditional party politics. More to the

[15] Frank J. Sorauf, *Political Parties in the American System* (Boston: Little, Brown, 1964), p. 55; cf. p. 56.

point, Epstein has thoroughly documented the secular decline in the mass-membership basis of many of Europe's major parties. In France, to take the extreme case, the membership of the Communist Party declined from more than 900,000 just after the war to about 500,000 in the late 1950's; the Socialists' membership fell from a peak of 354,000 to about 50,000, the MRP's from 400,000 to roughly 40,000.[16] In Europe as in America, party is likely to remain one important factor in political integration and mobilization: in Europe as in America it has never been the only one and it seems possible that its importance is declining.

So far we have considered two functions having to do with mass politics. The next has to do with political leadership and with the relationship between political leaders and led.

LEADERSHIP RECRUITMENT

The recruitment function can be dealt with somewhat more straightforwardly, partly because the concept of recruitment is itself tolerably precise, and partly because the role of party in recruitment is relatively—though only relatively—easy to delimit. All those who have catalogued party functions refer to leadership recruitment. It is seldom defined in detail as a function, but presumably it has to do with the processes by which men and women are selected out of the broader society to fill political positions or to play more or less full-time political roles. A full discussion of recruitment would have to deal with, among other things, the motives which lead individuals to seek or accept political roles or inhibit them from doing so; the "catchment pools" from which the political classes are drawn, whether social strata, parties or other groupings; the criteria by which they are selected; and the characteristics and aims of those selecting them.

That recruitment does take place in Western democracies—that the recruitment function is being performed—is beyond question. Whether it is performed well or badly in particular systems is not immediately relevant; what we are interested in is how important a part political parties play in the recruitment process. Certainly the claims made on behalf of party in this connection are sometimes extreme. Seligman, while not sharing this view fully himself, notes that, "for some, the functions of nominating and electing candidates for political elective office are attributed exclusively to political parties."[17] He observes at another point that "in selection of leadership, political parties play a special and sometimes exclusive function."[18]

There is one sense in which the central role of parties cannot be doubted. Insofar as political leaders are popularly elected, and insofar as parties play a

16 Epstein, *op. cit.,* pp. 253-54; see generally pp. 164–65, 251–55.

17 Lester G. Seligman, "Political Parties and the Recruitment of Political Leadership" in Lewis J. Edinger, ed., *Political Leadership in Industrialized Societies* (New York: Wiley, 1967), p. 295.

18 *Ibid.,* p. 315.

large part in elections, parties are undoubtedly deeply implicated in the performance of the recruitment function. To assess the overall role of parties,
however, requires asking, among other things, the extent to which political
leaders are in fact popularly elected. Much depends on how broadly or narrowly
the notion of political position or role is defined. It is often defined—by
Seligman in his work and Schlesinger in his—in such a way that parties are bound
to loom large.[19] Schlesinger, for example, confines himself (perfectly appropriately, given his interests) to senators and governors, and notes that others have
analyzed the backgrounds and careers of presidents, cabinet members, Supreme
Court justices, congressmen, and state legislators.[20] Epstein (again appropriately,
given his concerns) deals exclusively with the selection of candidates for elective
office.[21]

Yet to narrow the definition of political position in this way is to introduce
distortion, since by any of the usual criteria the chief political decision-makers
in developed political systems include not only elective office-holders but also
appointed executive officials, senior civil servants, military officers, judges appointed rather than elected, and the leading figures in interest groups and social
movements. Occupants of some of these positions may be appointed by elected
officials who have themselves been recruited via the party system, but the role
that party plays is no more than indirect. It may be that Europeans are more
sensitive than Americans to this fact, given Europe's long history of a strong,
nonpartisan civil service and the relatively recent appearance in some countries
of party government. Daalder has suggested that:

> Perhaps the best measure to distinguish the relative hold of party elites on a
> political system as against that of other elites is to ask how far positions of
> political influence can be obtained through, as compared to outside, party
> channels.[22]

By this measure, Daalder implies, European countries would vary considerably.
And even in the United States it would seem that the hold of party on political
recruitment is weaker than some writers suggest. American cabinet officers, not
to mention senior career bureaucrats, military officers and interest group leaders,
are often selected irrespective of party affiliation and by procedures which have
little or nothing to do with party.

Even in connection with recruitment to elective offices, the role of party is
at least problematical. Seligman and Sorauf have testified to the importance of

[19] Seligman, on p. 307 of "Political Parties," writes: "The full leadership recruitment
tasks of parties include the following: (1) the nomination of candidates for public
office . . . ; (2) the selection of officials for executive positions; and (3) the selection of
party organization officials. Throughout this chapter, we shall refer only to the selection
of parliamentary candidates." See Joseph A. Schlesinger, *Ambition and Politics: Political
Careers in the United States* (Chicago: Rand McNally, 1966).

[20] Schlesinger, *op. cit.*, p. 12.

[21] Epstein, *op. cit.*, pp. 167 and 201.

[22] Hans Daalder, "Parties, Elites and Political Developments in Western Europe" in
LaPalombara and Weiner, *op. cit.*, p. 75.

"self-recruitment" in leading individuals to seek candidatures in the United States, and there is reason to believe that in all countries the motives that lead men to seek elective office may arise independently of party.[23] In most jurisdictions in the United States it is hard for candidates to be elected who do not bear a party label; they are thus recruited by party in the sense that the law provides mechanisms for attaching labels to candidates and voters respond almost exclusively to label-bearing candidates. In this sense the successful candidates are recruited to political office via the party system. At the same time, however, the role of party, conceived of as group or organization, may be quite limited. The institution of the direct primary makes it possible for men to seek nominations (especially at state and substate level) who have little or no connection with organized party; the primary electorate in turn is likely to consist of voters few of whom are party "members" in any more than a psychological sense (and perhaps not even in that); primary electors may consciously cast their ballots for candidates they believe to be independent of organized party. "The fact is," in the words of Epstein, "that there are large areas of American politics in which candidate selection is not controlled by any regular party process."[24] Parties, indeed, monopolize the candidate-selection aspect of recruitment more successfully in Europe than in America.

Thus, although parties are everywhere deeply implicated in the leadership recruitment process, the importance of the role they play varies and it may on occasion be little more than tautologous to say that parties perform the recruitment function. The same point can be made in connection with the next alleged function of party, which has to do with one of the roles of party in government.

ORGANIZATION OF GOVERNMENT

In dealing with recruitment, we touched on what might be called the "reach" of political parties; i.e., the range of decision-making positions—legislative, executive, judicial, etc.—which are filled by men chosen by or from the parties or somehow via the party system. The reach of party may extend into the judiciary and the upper echelons of the administration as in the United States, or it may be restricted to legislature and cabinet as in Britain. When we come to deal with the organization function, we are concerned with the "grasp" of parties: how far they are able as organized entities to extend their authority over the various elements of government, or alternatively how far the conduct of government bears the imprint of the presence of parties, their nature and their activities. It is apparent that parties in one system may recruit for a wide range of decision-making offices yet have little subsequent impact on the decision-makers. Equally, in another system the parties may recruit to few

[23] See, e.g., Lester G. Seligman, "Political Recruitment and Party Structure: A Case Study," *American Political Science Review*, LV (March 1961), pp. 77–86; and Frank J. Sorauf, *Party and Representation* (New York: Atherton, 1963), pp. 107–20.

[24] Epstein, *op. cit.*, p. 205; cf. Sorauf, *Parties in the American System*, pp. 113–15.

offices but have an impact on many. The Anglo-American contrast comes to mind once again.

The organization function is referred to in almost all writings on parties but, like the recruitment function, is seldom defined precisely. In some contexts words like "control" and "integration" are as appropriate as "organization." What is meant is the arrangements under which, or the processes whereby, persons in government or the various elements of government come to act in concert. Unlike the recruitment function, the organization function is one that need be performed not at all, or at least only to a limited degree. Men in government and the various elements of government may not act in concert; on the contrary, governments are at least as likely to be at the mercy of centrifugal as centripetal forces, with colleague divided from colleague, department from department, judiciary from executive, executive from legislature.

To the extent that organization in this sense takes place, it may be achieved constitutionally, extra-constitutionally, formally or informally. There is likely to be not one organizing agency but many: administrators and their allies in the legislature, friendship networks, groups that come together *ad hoc* on the basis of shared interests. But such agencies are unlikely to have the effect of organizing more than fragments of government. If more general integration is to occur, it will almost certainly have to be as the result of the presence and activities of more highly articulated, probably more formal structures. Governments have from time to time been organized by military juntas, religious sects, powerful industrial combines, and even (if certain nineteenth-century writers are to be believed) by the Freemasons. But in modern democracies it seems fairly clear that the only entity through which governments can be organized—if they can be organized at all—is the political party.

How far is party an organizing agency in governments in the West? The question is not a simple one, partly because this is clearly a point at which it is essential to make overt the distinction between party conceived of as a cluster of individual human beings and party conceived of as a patterned set of actions or behaviors. If party is thought of as a group of human beings, then the question "Did party have influence?" will usually refer to a party or coalition of parties and will be resolvable into questions of the form, "Did the party leader, or the legislative party, or the party activists, have influence?" Similarly, questions about party policy resolve themselves into questions about the authoritative procedures for making policy within the party (if any) and about the decisions taken by particular individuals or groups in the context of those procedures. If, however, party is conceived of not as an actor or actors but as a set of patterned activities, then the question "Did party have influence?" resolves into a number of questions, possibly quite a large number, about men's recruitment and socialization into parties, their psychological ties to them, their associations within them, their ambitions, the place of party in their attitude structures, and so on. Conceived of in this way, party may have influence without any party leader or group attempting to wield influence and possibly without any individual's being aware that his attitudes or behavior are in fact party-influenced. Greenstein and Jackson have shown that the answers to the question "Did party have influence?" may be very different indeed depending on which concept of party is being used.[25] The disadvantage of the group concept, as we have already remarked, is that it may be unnecessarily restrictive. The disadvantage of the patterned-behaviors concept is that it may be extremely difficult to use operationally: it may be very hard to separate "party" influence from other kinds of influence.

Whichever concept is used, it remains to be determined empirically how firm the grasp of party is in a particular government and into how many elements of government it extends. This is a point on which a certain amount of evidence exists, at least as regards the United States, because of course the whole question of party-in-government got caught up some twenty years ago in the (by now rather tiresome) debate over whether or not the American parties should become more "responsible." The proponents of the idea of responsible party government agreed on using a group concept of party—as they were bound to do given their reformist aims—and both they and their critics agreed that party grasp of government in the United States was in fact quite limited. Grodzins went so far as to describe American parties as "anti-parties," since they dispersed segments of power instead of gathering them together and wielding them as one.[26] Looking abroad, both sides in the debate also agreed on the existence of a sharp contrast between the United States and most countries in Europe. In America political parties, for good or ill, did not govern; in Europe, for good or ill, they did. The matter is too complex to be gone into in detail here, but this contrast almost certainly was—and is—overdrawn. Britain provided the model to which most advocates of responsible party government looked, yet in a recent paper Rose concludes that Britain has "a political system in which administrative government is much more nearly the case than party government."[27] Daalder has similarly noted that:

Partly as a consequence of historical factors European parties have differed greatly in the extent to which they have permeated and enveloped other political elites. In some countries the role of parties has become all-pervasive; in others the parties have penetrated far less successfully to the mainsprings of political power.[28]

Certainly party cohesion is greater in the parliaments of Europe than in American legislatures, but of course it does not follow from this that European parties

[25] Fred I. Greenstein and Elton F. Jackson, "A Second Look at the Validity of Roll-Call Analysis," *Midwest Journal of Political Science*, VII (May 1963), pp. 160–64.

[26] Morton Grodzins, "Party and Government in the United States" in Robert A. Goldwin, ed., *Political Parties, U.S.A.* (Chicago: Rand McNally, 1964), pp. 132–33.

[27] Richard Rose, "Party Government vs. Administrative Government: A Theoretical and Empirical Critique," paper delivered to the Political Studies Association of the United Kingdom, York, April 1969, p. 13.

[28] Daalder in LaPalombara and Weiner, *op. cit.*, p. 58; this essay as a whole is full of interest.

have also been able to extend their grasp over the executive and administration and, for example, publicly-owned industries.

Moreover, a party's or coalition's grasp of government, even if it were firm and extensive, and even if it achieved concerted action, might not serve ends which were distinctively its own. The policies of the authoritative decision-makers, although acquiesced in or even enforced by the party or coalition, might not have emanated from party sources and indeed might run counter to the declared aims of the party or parties in government. . . .

POLICY FORMATION

. . . The policy-making role of party can be discussed from two different points of view: in terms of the relationship between party and electorate (Schattschneider and the party reformers, for instance, wanted parties to formulate policy so that they could perform their representational function more effectively); and in terms of the relationship between party and government. Parties in government may implement party policy for electoral reasons; they may implement it for all sorts of other reasons ranging from conscientious ideological belief to pressure from (say) the party militants; or they may not implement it at all. The electoral aspect of the policy function has been discussed fully elsewhere, notably by Epstein.[29] It is worth saying a word here about the governmental aspect.

The question is: How far in Western democracies are parties as associations or organizations influential in the making of public policy? Of course, if a particular government is organized by party, there is a wholly trivial sense in which it can always be said that the government's policies are *ipso facto* party policies.[30] But there are probably only three strict ways in which political parties can influence public policy apart from the role they play in the selection of political leaders: by influencing the content of political thought and discussion; by adopting specific policies or programs which the party's leaders, once elected, feel constrained (for whatever reason) to implement; or by successfully bringing pressure to bear on government, as when a governing party's followers in the legislature or in the country use the processes of the party to force the government to adopt particular policies.

Simply to list these three possibilities is to be reminded that organized parties in the United States do not play a central role in forming public policy and probably never have. American parties are not major forums for policy discussion; party platforms in the United States are more significant as indices of the strength of party factions than as statements of what future administrations are likely to do; American party organizations seldom wield much influence in

---

[29] See Epstein, *op. cit.,* chap. X.

[30] Labour prime ministers in Britain are sometimes sophistical in this way, when they reply to the criticism that they are deviating from party policy by claiming that whatever is the policy of a Labour government is automatically also the policy of the Labour Party. See the pertinent remarks of Scarrow, "The Function of Political Parties," *Journal of Politics,* 29 (November 1967), pp. 783–85.

government, certainly not at the federal level and in most of the larger states. So much is generally agreed. What is less widely recognized is that the policy role of party is also sharply restricted outside the United States. With the general decline of parties as bearers of ideology has gone a reduction in the role that parties play as vehicles for policy innovation, and also in the importance that even socialist parties attach to detailed programs and platforms. To take a simple example, the British Labour party manifesto of 1945 consisted of a detailed catalog of pledges which both electors and party members could regard as authoritative; the same party's manifesto in 1966 had about the same uncertain status as an American presidential platform. The same tendencies have been manifested widely in Europe and the white Commonwealth, although perhaps rather less in Italy than elsewhere. Epstein has concluded:

> The plain fact of the matter is that a cohesive party, assuming an organizational responsibility for governing in the style of a British parliamentary party, is only somewhat more of a policy-maker than a loose American party. It may enact policies as a party in a way that an American party cannot regularly manage, but the policies may be the product of particularized interest groups rather than of any programmatic commitments backed by majority support.[31]

The policies may, as Epstein says, be the product of interest groups. They may also be the product of individual politicians, civil servants, departments and interdepartmental committees, academics, television and the newspapers. They may also, as often as not, be the product largely of force of circumstances.

Nor have party organizations outside the United States been particularly successful in imposing their will when their own leaders have either formed the government or participated in a governing coalition. The past decade or so in Europe provides several examples of new governments, mainly radical ones, pursuing much the same policies as the governments they replaced, and of existing governments executing abrupt policy shifts without prior warrant from the party organizations of their supporters and sometimes in the face of strong party opposition. To refer to Britain again, the Labour administration elected in 1964 has applied to join the Common Market despite the Labour Party's hostility to joining, expressed both before and after the 1964 and 1966 elections; and the government persisted in supporting United States policy in Vietnam despite the passage at successive Labour Party conferences of resolutions calling on the Labour government to dissociate itself from America. Similarly, when the socialist parties of Germany and Italy joined coalition governments in those countries, the policy changes that followed were at the margin only. The role of party in policy-making in France has been negligible at least since 1958. Organized party generally remains one of the forces with which Western governments must contend in the formation of public policy; but it has never been the only one, and there is reason to suppose that in many countries in the late 1960's it is not even a major one.

<hr>

[31] Epstein, *op. cit.*, p. 282; see in general pp. 272-88.

It may be contended, however, that although the policy role of parties is circumscribed they nevertheless perform a related, perhaps more important function, one that may indeed subsume the policy-making function: the function of interest aggregation. This is the sixth and last of the functions in our catalog.

INTEREST AGGREGATION

The aggregation of interests is the newest functional concept to be associated with party (at least the phrase is new), and it deserves separate treatment even though it overlaps all of the functions discussed already. As it happens, however, the concept is not an easy one to work with. Etymologically the verb "to aggregate" means simply to gather together, to unite; the noun "aggregation" has two distinct meanings, referring either to the act of aggregating, or to the whole or mass formed as the result of acts of aggregation. In political analysis, by contrast, the concept has not been defined precisely. Almond in one of the original formulations wrote:

> Every political system has some way of aggregating the interests, claims, and demands which have been articulated by the interest groups of the polity. Aggregation may be accomplished by means of the formulation of general policies in which interests are combined, accommodated, or otherwise taken account of, or by means of the recruitment of political personnel, more or less committed to a particular pattern of policy.[32]

Almond and Powell say simply that, "The function of converting demands into general policy alternatives is called interest aggregation."[33] . . .

In a diffuse way interest aggregation of one sort or another undoubtedly takes place in all political systems just as it takes place in all societies, associations, interest groups, trade unions, bowling clubs, and families. It is a matter of contingent fact whether interest aggregation in the sense of accommodation takes place in any given system in such a way as to contribute to the system's capacity to maintain and adapt itself. Almond and Powell suggest that the "political party may be considered the specialized aggregation structure of modern societies," yet they also note that "party may or may not be a major interest aggregator in a given system."[34] Given that interest aggregation occurs everywhere to some extent, whether or not successfully in the system-maintenance sense, the question arises: Are parties in fact the major interest aggregators in the West?

The answer, irrespective of whether aggregation is used in its accommodation-of-interests sense or in its general-policy-alternatives sense, would seem to be "no"—that the interest aggregation function, like most of the others discussed here, is performed by a variety of structures of which the political party is only

[32] Gabriel A. Almond and James S. Coleman, eds., *The Politics of the Developing Areas* (Princeton, N.J.: Princeton University Press, 1960), p. 39.

[33] Gabriel A. Almond and G. Bingham Powell, Jr., *Comparative Politics: A Developmental Approach* (Boston: Little Brown, 1966), p. 98; cf. p. 29.

[34] Almond and Powell, *op. cit.,* p. 102.

one and not necessarily the most important. As regards the reaching of accommodations and compromises, the workings of party systems in some countries
do appear to contribute to the creation of a political climate conducive to
accommodation and compromise (although of course it is usually hard to say
whether a particular kind of party system engenders a particular kind of political
culture, or vice versa). But the role of the parties themselves is often rather
peripheral. One can think of trade union demands in France, which are increasingly dealt with at the centre by face-to-face confrontations between unions and
government; or of the claims of the North and the Mezzogiorno in Italy, which
are accommodated, if at all, by the civil service, semi-autonomous public bodies,
and loose alliances of individual politicians, hardly at all by the parties; or of the
claims of different sections of the farming community in the United States,
which are typically adjusted by the Department of Agriculture and by Congress
and its committees; or of the competing demands of rival linguistic and religious
groups in Belgium and the Netherlands, which tend to be compromised, if at all,
as much in the national legislatures and bureaucracies as by political parties; or
of the competing claims of European co-operation and an independent aircraft
industry in Britain, which have hardly ever been discussed, much less compromised, in any party arena.

As regards the conversion of demands into broad policy alternatives, here too
the role of organized parties is often not central. Instead alternatives are typically formulated by individual political leaders, as when de Gaulle offered the
French people the choice between regional devolution and continuing centralization; by cabinets, as with the British government's 1969 proposals for the
reform of trade union law; by civil servants, as witness the determining part
played by the Department of Health, Education and Welfare in structuring the
medicare debate in the United States; by individual politicians, publicists and
intellectuals, as in the American debate over Vietnam. The most that parties
seem generally able to do is to present electorates with highly generalized platforms and with alternative candidates committed to very general policy stand-
points. Probably on major issues, given their desire to mobilize the maximum
number of votes, most parties in the West could do little else. But they thereby
leave the function of interest aggregation largely to others.

CONCLUSIONS

This brings us to the end of our discussion of the six major functions which,
it is claimed, political parties perform in Western systems. . . . Throughout the
subsequent discussion a good deal of attention was paid to the importance,
whether in analyzing parties or party functions or both, of conceptual clarity.
The discussion has been brief, and almost every point that has been made is open
to some sort of qualification and elaboration. Nevertheless, on the basis of the
discussion it would seem that we are entitled, at the very least, to a certain
scepticism concerning the standard catalog of party functions, and also con-

cerning the great importance attached to parties in large segments of the political science literature. What conclusions should we draw?

There is one conclusion that we should not draw: namely, that parties are unimportant and therefore undeserving of study. It has been suggested that political parties are, after all, "organizations whose purpose it is to affect a process which would continue with or without them."[35] This is undoubtedly true as stated, and indeed there exist in most countries small jurisdictions in which parties are scarcely active and have hardly any impact. But the experience of all Western societies suggests that, where there is any degree of freedom and where power is both worth having and hard to get, men and women will combine to form political parties. The parties they form are certain to play a large part in almost every process of democratic politics, the electoral, the legislative, the administrative, even the judicial. If the study of political parties did not exist, it would clearly have to be invented.

The conclusions suggested by the argument of this paper have to do, not at all with abandoning the study of parties, but rather with the way in which parties should be studied. In the first place, if the role played by party in the performance of this or that political function is to be assessed, it is crucial that the function in question be defined precisely and in detail. Too many discussions of party function are bogged down by conceptual muddle, although the authors of them often seem unaware of it (indeed this paper may well not have escaped entirely). In the second place, if a party function is to be studied, the focus should almost certainly be on the function and not on the party, since otherwise the importance attached to party is likely to be exaggerated simply as the result of the approach employed. It may be that in future the most significant findings about political parties will emerge from studies that, in conception at least, have not focused on party at all. In the third place, . . . what is needed above all else are attempts to specify the conditions under which political parties and other political structures will or will not perform the various political functions. Many of the statements in this paper may well be shown to be false by future research. Even if they all turn out to be true, they will not constitute in themselves the kind of comparative empirical theory required.

Once the theory exists—and constructing it, although a difficult task, ought not to be an impossible one—what will be its general import? My hunch is that it will show, in the words of Kirchheimer, that "the political party's role in Western industrial society today is more limited than would appear from its position of formal preeminence."[36] But that is only a hunch, and hunches are no substitute for disciplined inquiry.

[35] Joseph A. Schlesinger, "Political Party Organization" in James G. March, ed., *Handbook of Organizations* (Chicago: Rand McNally, 1965), p. 774.

[36] Kirchheimer in LaPalombara and Weiner, *op. cit.,* p. 200.

chapter VIII
SOCIAL AND IDEOLOGICAL TRENDS

Many political observers have discerned a trend towards "depoliticization" or the "end of ideology" in modern democracies. The conflict between capitalism and socialism, they argue, is being muted. All modern states are involved in regulating or stimulating the economy. Capitalism or private enterprise is evolving toward the welfare state and the planned economy. Democratic socialist parties are moving away from nationalization as a policy, in favor of the welfare state and the planned economy. Thus the differences between conservatives or liberals and socialists are becoming a matter of political tactics in dealing with concrete problems rather than of clashing ideologies.

The decline in the intensity of ideological controversy may be caused by a transformation of social structure which seems to take place in industrial societies at a certain stage of their development. Members of the working and middle classes increasingly share a common way of life and experience the same kind of social discipline. Politics becomes a matter of allocating the national revenue; and while this issue may be important and dramatic, it does not involve the fate of the political institutions themselves.

However, one striking development in all industrial societies today has been the sudden outburst of ideological controversy and student unrest. The observer may be disposed to welcome this trend as the ushering in of a higher form of consciousness, or to view with alarm the disintegration of liberal values. Whatever one's political orientation, the resurrection of ideology will be a high-priority item on the agenda of political science for a long time to come.

In the readings below we present a discussion of the decline of ideology with reference especially to the working class by Val Lorwin and Joseph LaPalombara, and one case study of student unrest—the French revolt of May 1968. The theme of alienation of the intellectuals is further developed in Part Five, below. The reader is referred to: Daniel Bell, *The End of Ideology* (1960), and S. M. Lipset, *Political Man* (1960) and "The Changing Class Structure and Contemporary European Politics," *Daedalus* (Winter 1963). For a sympathetic view of the

252

revival of ideology among intellectuals, see Herbert Marcuse, *One-Dimensional Man* (1964) and Charles Reich, *The Greening of America* (1970). For a more critical appraisal: Raymond Aron, *The Elusive Revolution* (1969), and Zbigniew Brzezinski, *Between Two Ages: America's Role in the Technetronic Era* (1970). On student unrest, see notably S. M. Lipset, ed., *Student Politics* (1967).

19. Working Class Politics in Western Europe*

VAL R. LORWIN

How far has economic development conditioned working-class politics in Western Europe in the last century and a half? Are there stages of economic development in which protest is always sharp and others in which it is dull? To what extent are the differences in protest among the nations due to differences in economic growth, to what extent to different patterns of general historical development caused by other factors? What types of studies may promote our understanding of these questions? These are questions I propose to raise or to discuss here. . . .

Working-class protest, like economic development, has been a matter of some agitated public concern since the Second World War. But people have been proclaiming it a chief problem of modern times since Carlyle wrote of the "bitter discontent gone fierce and mad, the wrong conditions therefore or the wrong disposition of the Working Classes of England"[1] and Harriet Martineau warned that "this great question of the rights of labor . . . cannot be neglected under a lighter penalty than ruin to all."[2] . . .

Political protest can be measured in some of its more orderly forms: party membership, election results, and—for the most recent years, in many nations—whatever it is people tell to those who take public opinion polls. For periods before the working class attained full suffrage, however, the test of votes is only partially applicable, and complete and equal manhood suffrage was not attained until the First World War in most of the advanced European nations. We do not know how workers voted, moreover, or who voted for the parties claiming to represent the working class, except in some one-industry areas like the miners'

---

*From "Working Class Politics and Economic Development in Western Europe," *American Historical Review,* vol. LXIII, no. 2 (January 1958), pp. 338–51. By permission.

[1] Thomas Carlyle, "Chartism," *Critical and Miscellaneous Essays,* in *Works,* 30 vols. (New York, 1900), vol. XXIX, p. 119.

[2] *A History of the Peace: Being a History of England from 1816 to 1854,* 4 vols. (Boston, 1866), vol. IV, p. 622.

constituencies. Nor have all Socialist votes or all Communist votes been of equal intensity as protests. Some votes have implied rejection of the social order; others, merely hopes of immediate economic self-interest; still others, vague and diffuse frustrations.

On the eve of the Industrial Revolution, Henry Fielding remarked: "The sufferings of the poor are less observed than their misdeeds. . . . They starve, and freeze, and rot among themselves, but they beg, and steal, and rob among their betters."[3] Soon the laboring poor were able to do more, when they were thrown out of work or their wages were cut, than "beg and steal and rob among their betters." Modern economic development created a new sort of political protest by generating the industrial, essentially urban, wage-earning groups in such numbers and force that they were, for all their medieval and early modern predecessors, in most ways a new class—as yet only "camped in society . . . not established there."[4] This was, said the ex-worker Denis Poulot, "the terrible sphinx which is called the people . . . this great mass of workers which does not know what it is, except that it suffers."[5] Huddled in the wretched new factory towns or in the slums of renowned old cities, oppressed by long hours of work, arbitrary shop rules, and monotony, sorely tried by recurrent unemployment, unlettered, this mass inspired more fear than solicitude. Lord Liverpool, congratulated by Chateaubriand on the solidity of British institutions, pointed to the capital outside his windows and replied: "What can be stable with these enormous cities? One insurrection in London and all is lost."[6]

Hunger will turn political. In the hard year of 1819 the banners of the crowd at Peterloo, before the Yeomen rode them down, typified the mixture of the economic and the political: "A Fair Day's Wage for a Fair Day's Work," "No Corn Laws," and "Equal Representation or Death."[7]

It was not hunger alone. "The poor have hearts as well as stomachs," said Cooke Taylor but deemed it a fact not known to many who passed for wise men.[8] Carlyle knew it: "It is not what a man outwardly has or wants that constitutes the happiness or misery of him. Nakedness, hunger, distress of all kinds, death itself have been cheerfully suffered, when the heart was right. It is the feeling of injustice that is insupportable to all men. . . . No man can bear it or ought to bear it."[9]

Michel Chevalier looked at manufacturing and said: "Fixed points are totally lacking. There is no bond between superior and inferior, no rapprochement

[3] *A Proposal for Making an Effectual Provision for the Poor, 1753,* in *Works,* 16 vols. (New York, 1902), vol. XIII, p. 141.

[4] Michel Chevalier, *De l'industrie manufacturière en France* (Paris, 1841), p. 37.

[5] *Le Sublime,* 3d ed. (Paris, 1887; first pub. in 1870), p. 27.

[6] Chateaubriand, *Mémoires d'outre-tombe* (Brussels, 1849), vol. IV, p. 210.

[7] F. A. Bruton, ed., *Three Accounts of Peterloo by Eyewitnesses* (Manchester, 1921); William Page, ed., *Commerce and Industry,* 2 vols. (London, 1919), vol. II, p. 47.

[8] *Notes of a Tour in the Manufacturing Districts of Lancashire . . .* (London, 1842), p. 157.

[9] "Chartism," pp. 144–45.

between equals. . . . Nothing holds, nothing lasts." [10] Slowly, "fixed points" were established; the working classes gained in education, self-discipline, and political experience. In the course of industrialization in every Western country, despite crises and wars, workers' levels of living improved vastly. Did this resolve working-class protest?

Continuing economic development would resolve the very protest it brought into being, Marx argued, but only by the inevitable substitution of a new order for the capitalist society, which would prove incapable of continuing the triumphant progress of economic growth. Until the coming of the new order, declared the *Communist Manifesto,* "the development of class antagonism keeps even pace with the development of industry," and in *Capital* Marx affirmed that "there is a steady intensification of the wrath of the working class." (I use a few of Marx's significant statements as beginning points for discussion, not attempting an analysis of Marx or Marxism.)

These predictions have been contradicted by the experience (thus far) of all the Western nations except France and Italy—nor do France and Italy actually support the prophecy. Here is one of the ironies of the history of Marxist prediction. Only in the two countries where, among all the great industrial nations of the free world, capitalism has shown the least sustained dynamism has the "wrath of the working class" permitted the Communist party to take and hold a preponderant position among workers. [11] These two countries require a closer look.

In France and Italy, economic growth alone could not resolve the noneconomic problems created by wars, religious tensions, social distance, and the relations between the individual and the state. We cannot go into the noneconomic factors here. But the sense of injustice in these countries also grew, in part, out of the qualities of economic growth: the character of entrepreneurship, the distribution of income, and—even more—the nature of employer authority. The bourgeoisie of France and of Italy were insistent in their demands for protection against labor as well as protection against competition. Niggardly and tardy in concessions to their workers, they flaunted inequalities by their style of living. Their class consciousness helped shape the class consciousness of workers.

Workers, moreover, doubted the ability of their superiors to fulfill their economic functions as an entrepreneurial class. The slowness of economic growth evoked protest, particularly in France. Before the First World War, labor leaders shared with many orthodox economists and publicists the impression that their country was stagnating, although it was progressing in the two decades before the war. The gloomy view arose in part from comparisons with the industrial growth of the United States and with the industrial and military

[10] *Op. cit.,* p. 38.

[11] Nor, clearly, has the experience in the Soviet orbit borne out the Marxian prophecy any better, since revolution won only in countries in early stages of industrial capitalism and had to be imposed from without on more advanced countries.

growth of Germany. That view also reflected the state of labor organization, greater in the stagnant old industries such as building and in the thousands of small workshops of Paris than in the newer industries such as the booming steel mills of Lorraine. Later, in the interwar period, the labor movement was strong in the civil administration and public service industries rather than in the new and technically progressive branches of private industry—chemicals, synthetic fibers, automobiles.

French employers groaned constantly about their high costs, especially of labor, and their inability to compete with foreign producers. Labor leaders argued, however, that the employers' difficulties really came from their sterility; "their very slow progress, from their timidity; their uncertainty, from their lack of initiative. We ask the French employers to resemble the American employer class. . . . We want a busy, active, humming country, a veritable beehive always awake. In that way our own force will be increased."[12] But the unions' own force remained weak. Their weakness, along with pessimism about the country's economic growth, gave to French labor that curious combination of low immediate hopes and utopian dreams which has characterized it during most of this century.

Management's own leaders praised smallness of scale and slowness to mechanize. In 1930 the president of the General Confederation of French Manufacturers congratulated his members on "the spirit of prudence in the management of firms, which is the surest guarantee against the dangers of a fearful crisis," and on "the French mentality of counting on regular and steady dividends, rather than on the saw-toothed variation of dividends fashionable in some great industrial nations." The year of this speech marked the beginning of fifteen years of economic decline and stagnation in France.

The dramatic inequalities between the poorer, agricultural areas and the industrialized regions of both Italy and France created further tensions in each nation. Finally, the bourgeoisie showed a fear of the people and a political bankruptcy at history's critical hours. Workers in Italy and France tended to merge judgments of the political and the economic performance of the powers that were. Their doubts as to the competence and courage of the bourgeoisie deepened their feelings of both the injustice and the fragility of the social and political order. Here let us leave France and Italy to return to the general question.

Some would turn the Marxian assertion upside down and argue that there is a "hump of radicalism" early in a nation's industrial development and that once the economy, by a big "initial push," surmounts its early difficulties, protest inevitably falls off. The history of a number of countries gives support to this analysis. But, despite Marx and many anti-Marxists, in the history of social relationships the several factors never long "keep even pace" with each other. In England the working class has not seriously threatened the political order since Chartist times, to be sure; but the syndicalists of the immediate pre-1914 period

---

[12] Victor Griffuelhes, "L'Infériorité des capitalistes français," *Mouvement socialiste*, no. 226 (December 1910), pp. 329–32.

and the Socialists of the post-1918 period were far more critical of the social and economic order than the New Model unionists and the "Lib-Labs" of the 1850's, 1860's, and 1870's. France and Italy show a series of humps of radicalism.

Economic development has attenuated early protest by changes in the structure of the working classes. "Within the ranks of the proletariat," announced the *Communist Manifesto,* "the various interests and conditions of life are more and more equalized, in proportion as machinery obliterates all distinction of labor, and nearly everywhere reduces wages to the same low level. . . . The modern laborer, instead of rising with the progress of industry, sinks deeper and deeper below the conditions of existence of his own class." Marx was observing a period of development in which the machine was breaking down old skills, especially in the textile trades. The historian was being unhistorical in assuming that the trend must continue.

By the turn of the century it was already clear to a good observer like Eduard Bernstein (who was aided by residence in England) that economic growth and social reforms were blurring the sharpness of class among wage and salaried workers.[13] This is the now familiar phenomenon of the rise of the "new middle class." (Let us accent the word "new," for we use the old, imprecise words "middle class" for lack of a more descriptive phrase.) George Orwell spoke of the "upward and downward extension of the middle class" and of the growing importance of the people of "indeterminate social class."[14] This is the result of the swelling of the so-called tertiary sector of the economy—of public administration, commerce, services, and, with the industrial sector itself, the expansion of professional, technical, and administrative jobs. Even among those in traditional forms of wage employment, middle-class attitudes have flourished, made possible not only by higher real wages and greater leisure but also by enhanced security, housing in socially mixed communities, longer schooling, and an increasingly classless culture wafted on mass communications.

The people of the new middle class have most often sought individual rather than collective solutions. Their political preferences have been divided—although unevenly—among almost all the parties. On the Continent in crisis times, fearful of being dragged down to proletarian status, many have hearkened to authoritarian voices. The new middle class called into question many of the traditional appeals of working-class politics. The parties of labor were obliged to appeal to other classes and to more complex attitudes than, rightly or wrongly, they formerly took for granted among workers.

Another change which came with economic growth was the differentiation between the economic and the political organizations of the working classes. Early forms of action had confused the economic and political. Then there generally came a separation between unions and political parties and, albeit with

---

[13] *Evolutionary Socialism: A Criticism and Affirmation,* trans. by E. C. Harvey (London, 1909), esp. pp. 103–106, 206, 207, and 219. See also Peter Gay, *The Dilemma of Democratic Socialism: Eduard Bernstein's Challenge to Marx* (New York, 1952).

[14] *The Lion and the Unicorn* (London, 1941), pp. 53–54.

interlocking directorates and memberships, a cooperative division of function. France, Italy, and Spain, however, did not achieve this division of labor; while England was developing "Sidney Webbicalism,"[15] they developed syndicalism. This was the confounding of politics and economics in the name of "a-political" action. Anarcho-syndicalism, with its refusal to recognize the reality of politics and its disdain for parliamentary democracy, had fateful consequences. It prevented an effective working relationship of the unions with the socialist parties, to the great mischief of both, and helped leave workers poorly prepared later to distinguish between democratic political protest and communist politics.

Politics could not be denied, however much some workers' leaders might plead the sufficiency of economic action. No movement came to be more dependent on political action for economic gains than the "a-political" French unions. Even the robust British workers' consumer cooperatives, founded on the Rochdale principle of political neutrality, formed a Cooperative party (which became a small tail to the Labour party kite). When British labor attempted in the 1926 general strike to solve by industrial action a problem too big for industrial action alone, the result was catastrophe. Even there, moreover, the Trades Union Congress used its economic power in only a halfhearted way for fear of damaging the nation's political foundations.

The once lively anarchist and syndicalist movements practically disappeared under the hammer of economic development. The libertarian movements could not survive in the climate of assembly line production, modern industrial organization, or the modern welfare state. It was the communists, opposed though they were to the deepest libertarian impulses, who by their militant rejection of bourgeois society claimed most of the anarchists' and syndicalists' following. To the completely power-centered movement fell the heritage of those who had refused to come to any terms with political power.

Among the socialists, the bearded prophets gave way to the smooth-chinned organizers, parliamentarians, and planners. Socialist militancy was a victim of socialist success, itself made possible by economic growth. Economic growth produced a margin of well-being and facilitated the compromises and generosity which reconciled groups to each other in most of the liberal democracies.

Along with socialist militancy, socialist certitudes faded. The motto of "Socialism in our time" was amended, at least *sotto voce,* to "Socialism . . . but not in our time." Socialism became less than ever a doctrine and more a political temper. Despite an addiction to worn-out slogans, it was mellowed and strengthened, particularly after the First World War, by its identification with the non-economic values of national life against threats from extreme left and extreme right.

Where it was most doctrinal, socialism was least effective—and often least true to its own doctrine. It proved most effective where it was most pragmatic, in the lands where the habits of civic responsibility and political compromise were strong; these were all (except Switzerland) constitutional monarchies. In France

---

[15] The term is *Punch's,* quoted by G. D. H. Cole, *The World of Labour,* 4th ed. (London, 1920), p. 3. In Italy syndicalism was important but not the dominant current.

and in Italy, however, the Communist party rushed into the gap between socialist reasonableness and workers' old resentments, between socialist uncertainties and workers' pent-up hopes. Spain and Portugal were limiting cases; their hours of democracy were of the briefest, in part because of long economic stagnation.

"Modern industrial labor, modern subjugation to capital, the same in England as in France, in America as in Germany, has stripped [the proletarian] of every trace of national character. . . . National differences, and antagonisms between people, are daily more and more vanishing," said the *Communist Manifesto*. Instead, the working-class movements have all followed different national patterns. For many years it could be said that the only thing the socialists had nationalized was socialism.

Britain developed a labor movement of class solidarity and class organization without class hatred; France and Italy, class hatred but ineffectual class organization. Scandinavia developed on the British pattern, overcoming class conflict and moving on to an even higher degree of class restraint and responsibility than Britain's. The Belgian, Dutch, and Swiss working classes have shown a remarkable degree of responsibility, although their highly developed class organizations have followed the religious and political cleavages in each nation. The Communist Internationals have exercised central controls, but over parties which have differed not only from continent to continent but also from nation to contiguous Western European nation.

"A number of things govern men," said Montesquieu, "climate, religion, laws, maxims of government, the examples of things past, customs, manners; from all this there is formed a general spirit."[16] Economic development was only one of the factors that influenced social structures, cultural patterns, political habits and institutions, and what for short we call national character.

National character is often a bundle of contradictions, however, and it changes in time. The form and temper of working-class action also change. In Norway, for example, the tremendous onrush of industrialization early in this century evoked a radical protest which gave the union movement a syndicalist turn and took the Labor party into the Communist International. But the party soon broke with the Comintern, and party and unions developed into one of the most solid—yet independent and imaginative—labor movements in the world.

In Belgium, about 1891, social conflict seemed so irreconcilable that Paul Vinogradoff thought revolution must break out in this "overcrowded country, where the extremes of socialist and Catholic opinion were at that time most in evidence,"[17] and that such a revolution would touch off a general European war. But before the First World War, Belgian workers had somehow assimilated their conflicts in a structure of compromise and appeared as among the most moderate in Europe.

---

[16] The year 1956 reminded us again, in hope and tragedy, of the "general spirit" of peoples. Upsurge against Soviet rule came, where if anywhere among the satellites one might have expected it, from the "brave" and "romantic" Poles and Hungarians.

[17] H. A. L. Fisher, "Memoir," in *The Collected Papers of Paul Vinogradoff*, 2 vols. (Oxford, 1928), vol. I, p. 19.

The study of differences and similarities between the nations, as well as change within the nations, sheds light on our problems. One may, for example, compare France and Belgium, separated by a rather artificial frontier but by many historical differences. The reconciliation of the Belgian working class to the political and social order, divided though the workers are by language and religion and the Flemish-Walloon question, makes a vivid contrast with the experience of France. The differences did not arise from the material fruits of economic growth, for both long were rather low-wage countries, and Belgian wages were the lower. In some ways the two countries had similar economic development. But Belgium's industrialization began earlier; it was more dependent on international commerce, both for markets and for its transit trade; it had a faster growing population; and it became much more urbanized than France. The small new nation, "the cockpit of Europe," could not permit itself social and political conflict to the breaking point. Perhaps France could not either, but it was harder for the bigger nation to realize it.

Comparisons of different groups within nations and among nations are of the essence too. Some occupations seem prone to long phases of radicalism. Dangerous trades, unsteady employment, and isolation from the larger community are some of the factors which make for radicalism among dockers, seamen, lumbermen, and miners in many—though not all—countries. Yet radicalism has had successes among the more stable occupations too.

It is not generally those who are in the greatest economic distress who are the leaders in protest. First, one may recognize the element of chance in the occupational selection of leaders of protest (as in all selections of leadership). It is happenstance that the lifelong leader of the French unions, Léon Jouhaux, came out of a match factory and that the great leader of Danish Social Democracy, Thorvald Stauning, came out of the cigar maker's trade. Beyond the chance elements, however, there is a process of selection for leadership of protest from strength rather than misery, by the capacity of the group rather than its economic distress. First those in the skilled artisan trades (notably the printers and building craftsmen), then the metal workers, miners, and railroad men have been in the vanguard in many lands. In relation to economic development, some of the leaders have come from the groups of skilled operatives menaced by technological change, others from skilled or semi-skilled workers in positions of continuing opportunity or in stable, strategic locations in the industrial process. . . .

Apparently similar economic trends may give rise to, or at least be accompanied by, different consequences of protest. British miners' protest mounted bitterly as the coal industry sank into the doldrums of the 1920's. On the other hand, the porcelain workers of Limoges, vigorous socialists at the turn of the century, became torpid as their industry declined into torpor.

If only in passing and by inference, I hope to have recalled some examples of the particular subjects which invite the historian and some of the values of comparative studies. We need to study many more individuals, in biographies, and many more occupations and industries, in their settings of period and place, as, with fond intensity and imaginative erudition, George Duveau has studied the workers of the Second Empire,[18] before we can safely generalize. But men will, as men should, generalize long before they can safely generalize.

Here I have thought that modest ground-clearing considerations would be most useful. To assume my share of responsibility, however, I offer a few working hypotheses. For some of them, the nature of the evidence has been hinted at in the preceding pages; for others, not even that. They are not meant to be "laws" or "universal" but to sum up a few aspects of the experience of the past 150 years in one area of the world, an area full of intriguing differences yet with enough homogeneity in culture and industrial development to make generalization valid and comparison significant.

Economic development is process, environment, and goal; it provides a framework, and sets problems, for man's capacities for political and social action.

Rapid growth in the early stages of industrialization generates protest by reason of the bewildering dislocations and (for many) the sacrifices out of current consumption which it imposes. Continued economic growth permits the satisfaction of much of this protest. But some attitudes of protest persist well beyond the economic conditions which aroused them.

Sluggish economic growth may generate the deepest and longest lasting protest by reason of the society's inability to provide well-being and social justice to match social aspirations and by reason of the economic elite's failure to inspire confidence. Slow growth of cities and slow recruitment of the industrial work force facilitate the carry-over of traditions of protest from generation to generation.

The gradual delineation of the separate (but overlapping) spheres and organizations of political and industrial protest makes for reconciliation and absorption of protest in each sphere.

The labor movements most dependent on the state may show the greatest hostility to the state. The working classes best integrated with their national communities are those which have built labor movements that are more or less autonomous centers of power.

The successive phases of a nation's economic development are not inevitably reflected in corresponding attitudes and behavior of labor protest. Moreover, different phases of development exist side by side in the same regions and industries. Different forms of working-class politics also exist side by side.

[18] *La Vie ouvrière en France sous le Second Empire* (Paris, 1946) and *La Pensée ouvrière sur l'éducation pendant la Seconde République et le Second Empire* (Paris, 1948).

National differences shape the response of workers and labor movements to economic change. These differences are only in part due to the differences in patterns of economic development. In large part they are due to noneconomic factors—politics and religion, cultural patterns and class structure—and to historical accident and personalities. ("Everything is dependent on everything," however, and most of the noneconomic factors are themselves conditioned by economic change.)

These are a few of the problems on which we need further descriptive findings and further comparative analysis. Comparative studies may remind those of us who wear monographic spectacles to look up to the horizon from time to time and may remind those who strain at the horizon to put on the spectacles occasionally for closer observation.

It is to the more modest forms of comparative historical work that I refer, not to the abused "grand manner" of universal history. Yet even modest comparative studies will help put our problems in their broader settings of the history of man's relation to his work and his fellows, of the history of social organization and political striving, of the endless searches for justice, order, and freedom.

20. Decline of Ideology: A Dissent and an Interpretation*

JOSEPH LAPALOMBARA

INTRODUCTION

With increasing frequency and self-assurance, the scientific objectivity of American social science is proclaimed by some of its prominent practitioners. Various explanations are offered for the onset of social science's Golden Age, but central to most of them is the claim that modern social science has managed to resolve Mannheim's Paradox,[1] namely, that in the pursuit of the truth the social scientist himself is handicapped by the narrow focus and distortions implicit in ideological thought. Presumably, the social scientist can now probe any aspect of human organization and behavior as dispassionately as physical

*From *The American Political Science Review*, vol. LX, no. 1 (March 1966), pp. 5–16. Reprinted by permission of the American Political Science Association and the author. Article and footnotes abridged by the editors.

[1] This term is used by Clifford Geertz in "Ideology as a Cultural System," in D. E. Apter, ed., *Ideology and Discontent* (London, 1964), pp. 48 ff.

scientists observe the structure of the atom or chemical reactions. For this reason, it is claimed by some that the ideologically liberated social scientists—at least in the United States—can expect to be co-opted into the Scientific Culture, or that segment of society that is presumably aloof from and disdainful toward the moralistic speculations and the tender-heartedness of the literary intellectuals.

The behavioral "revolution" in political science may have run its course, but it has left in its wake both obscurantist criticisms of empiricism, on the one hand, and, on the other hand, an unquestioning belief in "science." Quite often the latter belief is not merely anti-historical and anti-philosophical but also uncritical about the extent to which empirical observations can be colored by the very orientation to values that one seeks to control in rigorous empirical research. . . .

One interesting extrapolation from these assumptions about social science objectivity, and of the essential incompatibility of social science and normative orientations, is found in the so-called "decline of ideology" literature. Presumably, social-scientific generalizations have been made about the waning of ideology. The irony attaching to arguments in and against these "findings" is that they have themselves taken on many of the undeniable earmarks of *ideological* conflict. Thus, I wish to acknowledge that my own effort in this paper may be in part—and quite properly—identified as ideological. Indeed, the underlying theme of my argument here is that we have not, in fact, resolved the Mannheim Paradox and that perhaps the future of social science will be better served if we acknowledge this fact and face up to its intellectual and theoretical implications.

More particularly, however, I wish to deal in this paper with these topics: 1) what it is that is meant when social scientists write about the "decline of ideology"; 2) an examination of some empirical evidence from the West that strongly challenges some of the "findings" of these writers; and 3) a somewhat tentative ideological-social scientific interpretation of what these writings may represent in contemporary American society.

THE MEANING OF IDEOLOGY

It is abundantly clear that those who write about ideology's decline, with few exceptions,[2] intend a pejorative denotation and connotation of the term. Taking their lead from Mannheim, these writers contend that ideological thought means at least that such ideas are "distorted," in the sense that they lack "congruence"

---

[2] One exception would be Otto Kirchheimer, who was greatly concerned about the possible consequence of, say, the emergence of the "catch-all" political party in a country like the West German Republic. See his "The Transformation of the European Party System," in Joseph LaPalombara and Myron Weiner, eds., *Political Parties and Political Development* (Princeton, 1966). Cf. his "The Waning of Opposition in Parliamentary Regimes," *Social Research* 24 (1957), pp. 127–156. I am uncertain as to whether what Kirchheimer describes is a decline of ideology, but it is noteworthy that he was one of those who didn't think that what he saw was "good" for Western societies.

with reality. Beyond this, however, they seem to support the Mannheim view that the lack of congruence may be either emotionally determined, and therefore the result of subconscious forces, or "conscious deception, where ideology is to be interpreted as a purposeful lie."[3]

It can be argued, of course, that one is free to define ideology as it happens to suit one's mood or purpose, and we have a vast literature demonstrating the considerable range of meaning that can be assigned to the concept. But if one elects a definition that is based too heavily on the notion of wilful or unintended deception or distortion, much of what social scientists generally identify as ideological would simply have to be ignored, or called something else. Moreover, if the central purpose of the analysis is to demonstrate something as significant as ideology's decline, it seems to me to be the essence of intellectual legerdemain, or downright slovenliness, to leave the definition of ideology vague, or to confuse the demonstrable decline of something one finds objectionable with presumably empirical generalizations about the gradual disappearance of something which is much broader in meaning.

My usage of ideology is quite close to the definition suggested by L. H. Garstin, in that it involves a philosophy of history, a view of man's present place in it, some estimate of probable lines of future development, and a set of prescriptions regarding how to hasten, retard, and/or modify that developmental direction.[4] While the concept, ideology, is certainly one of the most elusive in our vocabulary, we can say about it that, beyond the above, it tends to specify a set of values that are more or less coherent and that it seeks to link given patterns of action to the achievement or maintenance of a future, or existing, state of affairs. What makes such formulations of particular interest to political scientists is that ideologies frequently insist that in order to achieve or maintain desired ends, deemed to be morally superior and therefore desirable for the entire collectivity, public authority is expected to intervene.

It is in this broad sense, then, that I am using the concept in this paper. This being the case, several caveats are in order. For example, an ideology may or may not be dogmatic; a relative lack of dogmatism does not necessarily make a given set of cognitions, preferences, expectations and prescriptions any the less ideological. An ideology may or may not be utopian. I assume that conservative movements of the last century or two, as well as the so-called Radical Right in the United States at present have strong ideological dimensions, notwithstanding their vociferous denials of utopias. Similarly, Catholicism is no less ideological in many of its political dimensions by reason of its rejection of the Enlightenment's assumptions concerning man's perfectibility. An ideology may or may not be attuned to the claimed rationality of modern science; the place of scientific

---

[3] Karl Mannheim, *Ideology and Utopia* (London, 1936), pp. 175–176. Mannheim's second chapter in this volume, pp. 49–96, from which the volume's title is derived, is of course the classic statement of the origins of the term "ideology," its particular and general formulations, its relationship to Marxism and its catalytic impact on the sociology of knowledge.

[4] L. H. Garstin, *Each Age Is a Dream: A Study in Ideologies* (New York, 1954), p. 3.

thought in ideological formulations is an empirical question that should not be begged by the assumption that science and ideology are incompatible. Technocrats and others who enshrine the Managerial Society certainly engage in the most fundamental kind of ideological reasoning. Ideology may or may not emphasize rhetoric or flamboyant verbal formulations. The language of ideology is also an empirical question; it will surely be strongly influenced by the sociohistorical context in which it evolves, and a decline or, better, change in rhetoric should not be confused with a decline in ideology itself. Finally, an ideology may or may not be believed by those who articulate it. Whether an ideology is cynically used as a weapon or instrument of control; whether it emanates from subconscious needs or drives or is rationally formulated and incorporated into one's belief system; indeed, whether it is narrowly or widely, publicly or privately shared with third persons are also legitimate and fascinating questions that require careful investigation rather than a priori answers.

It seems to me that the "decline of ideology" writers[5] commit one or more of all of the errors implied above. For example, ideology is said to apply to passionately articulated prescriptions, evidently not to those which manifest calm rationality. As Daniel Bell puts it, "ideology is the conversion of ideas into social levers. . . . What gives ideology its force is its passion."[6] Lipset, in his personal postscript on ideology's passing, tells us that "Democracy in the Western world has been undergoing some important changes as serious intellectual conflicts among groups representing different values have declined sharply."[7] In the case of Aron, his passionate and intemperate attacks on the ideas of certain French intellectuals are so extreme as to represent not so much social science analysis as they do a fascinating example of the rhetorical aspect of ideological exchange.[8]

It seems equally apparent that what these writers mean by ideology is not any given set of values, beliefs, preferences, expectations and prescriptions regarding society but that *particular* set that we may variously associate with Orthodox Marxism, "Scientific Socialism," Bolshevism, Maoism, or in any case with strongly held and dogmatically articulated ideas regarding class conflict and revolution. Thus, "the exhaustion of political ideas in the West" refers to that particular case involving the disillusionment experienced by Marxist intellectuals when it became apparent that many of Marx's predictions were simply not borne

[5] I refer here primarily to the following: Raymond Aron, "Fin de l'age ideologique?" in T. W. Adorno and W. Dirks, eds., *Sociologica* (Frankfurt, 1955), pp. 219–233; R. Aron, *The Opium of the Intellectuals* (New York, 1962); Talcott Parsons, "An Approach to the Sociology of Knowledge," *Transactions of the Fourth World Congress of Sociology* (Milan and Stresa, 1959), pp. 25–49; Edward Shils, "The End of Ideology?" *Encounter* 5 (November 1955), pp. 52–58; S. M. Lipset, *Political Man* (Garden City, 1960), pp. 403–417; Daniel Bell, *The End of Ideology* (Glencoe, Ill., 1960), esp. pp. 369–375; and S. M. Lipset, "The Changing Class Structure and Contemporary European Politics," *Daedalus* 93 (Winter 1964), pp. 271–303.

[6] Bell, *op. cit.,* pp. 370 and 371.

[7] Lipset, *Political Man,* p. 403.

[8] Aron, *The Opium of the Intellectuals.*

out, and when the outrages of the Stalinist regime were publicly revealed. We need not document the evidence for the widespread disillusionment, or for the agonizing ideological reappraisals to which it has led. But, as I shall briefly document below, to limit the meaning of ideology to absolute utopias, to concentrate one's analytical attention upon what some Marxian socialists may be up to, and to equate certain changes in rhetoric with ideological decline is to narrow the meaning of the central concept to the point where it has very limited utility for the social scientist.

The writers I have in mind also seem to see ideology as a dependent phenomenon, whose rise and fall is conditioned by a number of ecological factors, most of them economic. This curious determinism suggests that if there are marked differences in poverty and wealth—or in life styles—ideology emerges; if these differences are reduced, ideology (i.e., class-conflict ideology) declines. Thus, Lipset tells us that "Ideological passion may no longer be necessary to sustain the class struggle within stable and affluent democracies." At another place he says, "As differences in style of life are reduced, so are the tensions of stratification. And increased education enhances the propensity of different groups to 'tolerate' each other, to accept the complex idea that truth and error are not necessarily on one side." [9]

These writers are far too sophisticated to suggest that there is a simple correlation between increases in economic productivity or distribution and decline of ideology. They recognize, for example, that religious and other cleavages may cut against tendencies toward ideological quiescence. Nevertheless, I came away from this literature with the uncomfortable impression that these writers claim that moral imperatives, differences of opinion regarding the "good life," and opposing formulations regarding public policy must necessarily give way before the avalanche of popular education, the mass media and greater and greater numbers of washing machines, automobiles and television sets. How else judge the assertion—as clearly debatable as it is subjective and ideological—that ideology is in decline because "the fundamental problems of the Industrial Revolution have been solved." [10]

There are certainly thousands of European intellectuals, as well as tens of millions of other Europeans, who would react to the last quoted statement sardonically, or in sheer disbelief.

Since the generalizations about ideology's alleged decline apply to the West, and therefore to Europe as well as the North American continent, it may be instructive to look at one of these countries, Italy, to see exactly how accurate these generalizations are. It should be noted that the time span I will consider are the years since World War II; my point will be that since generalizations for such a short period are so manifestly inaccurate, it is useless to lend any kind of serious attention to prognostications about where we will be a century or two from now. Keynes, I believe, authored the most appropriate aphorism about the "long run."

9 Lipset, *Political Man,* p. 407, and Lipset, "The Changing Class Structure . . . ," p. 272.
10 Lipset, *Political Man,* p. 406.

IDEOLOGY IN ITALY

The points I wish to stress about Italy can be briefly stated, although their detailed documentation would require more space than is available here. First, notwithstanding the existence within the Italian Communist party of both a "crisis of intellectuals" and a "crisis of ideology," there has recently occurred within that party a new ferment of ideas which in a certain sense has actually enriched rather than diminished attention to ideology. Second, if one bothers to look away from the Communist party (P.C.I.) and toward Christian Democracy (D.C.), it is possible to conclude that ideology in the latter is actually on the upswing. Third, and following from these two observations, the so-called decline-of-ideology theory is simply not valid for the Italian case.

The Italian Communist Party. The most frequent—and most wishful—interpretation of P.C.I. is that it is moving in a reformist direction that will eventuate in its accepting the existing system and limiting its demands to social, political and economic manipulations designed to effect needed, but not revolutionary, reforms from time to time. This view of the party is superficial in the sense that "reformism" dates back to 1944 when Palmiro Togliatti returned from Moscow articulating a moderate line which was as unnerving as it was unexpected. This line was carefully followed in the Constituent Assembly, which drafted the Italian Constitution, and in this broad sense, the party has been "reformist" throughout the postwar years.

What has changed in recent years is neither the party's will to power nor its commitment to a basically socialist ideology. Rather, I would say that the changes include: 1) the party's use of extreme rhetoric; 2) its now openly expressed polycentrist view regarding the nature of the international socialist or communist movement; and 3) the party's notions regarding how the class struggle should be conducted in contemporary Italy. The debates and agonizing reappraisals that the party has experienced in recent years must be construed not as a sign of ideological decay but, rather, as a sign of ideological vigor which is largely responsible for the party's steady and increasing attraction at the polls.

The list of P.C.I. errors in prognosticating about Italian society is long and impressive; it led observers at Bologna not long ago to comment on what a "grotesque assumption" was the party's belief that only it possessed a scientifically infallible method for analyzing reality. The errors included such things as predictions about the comparative rate of economic growth in Communist and free countries, expectations regarding the European Common Market, impending economic crises in capitalistic countries, etc. One observer of this pattern of inaccurate prognosticating notes that it was not until the middle of 1961 that the "Communists awoke from their dogmatic dream and almost in a flash learned that their judgments did not correspond to reality."[11]

The truth is that the alarm had sounded for P.C.I. several years before, and precisely at the VII Party Congress of 1956. It was here that the party's activities

[11] G. Tamburrano, "Lo Sviluppo del capitalismo e la crisi teorica dei communisti italiani," *Tempi Moderni,* 5 (July-September 1962), p. 22.

in the underdeveloped South first received a public airing. The critics of the party's *"Movimento di Rinascita"* in southern Italy openly noted that the movement was in crisis and that the crisis grew out of the party's failure to adapt ideology and consequently policy to the concrete conditions of Southern Italy. Members of the party itself scored it for its "sterile and negative" approach to national problems, for its rigid and doctrinaire adherence to fixed schemes, for its permitting the movement to lose whatever dynamism it may have had in earlier years.

Both Togliatti and Giorgio Amendola (the latter considered the leader of the P.C.I.'s "reformist" wing) urged that the party must be flexible and overcome the inertia of pat formulations. They admitted that both the party and its trade union wing seemed to be unprepared to confront the great changes in local conditions that had occurred in the years since 1945. It is possible that, within the party's secret confines, this kind of self-appraisal had begun before 1956, but in those earlier days one would not have expected Togliatti to say publicly that the party was not keeping up with basic social and economic transformations in Italy or that it was necessary for that organization to engage in the kind of total re-examination that will finally sweep away "ancient and recent moldiness that impede the action of P.C.I."

To be sure, removing ideological mold is not easy for Communists, who tend to be ultra-intellectual in a society where intellectual elegance is highly prized. One can therefore note in the party's literature the care—and the web-like logic—with which recent changes are reconciled with Marx and Lenin, and particularly with the writings of Antonio Gramsci, the intellectual fountainhead of Italian Communism, and a formidable dialectician whose work is too little known in the English-speaking world.[12] Nevertheless, the party's public posture has changed radically. The most recent and important indication of this change is the party's decision to seek alliances with elements of the middle class—peasants, small landowners, artisans, small and medium industrialists and even with entrepreneurs who are not involved with industrial monopolies.[13] The importance of this change should be strongly emphasized; the P.C.I. has managed in one stroke to shift largely to monopoly capitalism all of the attacks that had previously been leveled against an allegedly retrograde, decadent bourgeoisie. The party's open strategy is to attract to its ranks the mushrooming members of the middle and tertiary strata that large-scale industrial development tends to proliferate. The fire of opposition is no longer directed against proprietors in general but against the monopolists who allegedly exploit all others in society, who are oppressive, and who increase the degree of imbalance or disequilibrium in the social system.

This, then, is not the party of the Stalin Era. Not many who followed the antics of P.C.I. up to the Hungarian Rebellion would have predicted changes in orientation such as the ones so briefly summarized. The fascinating question to

---

[12] Palmiro Togliatti, *Il Partito Communista Italiano* (Rome, 1961), p. 55; Antonio Gramsci, "Alcuni temi della questione meridionale," in *Antologia degli scritti* (Rome, 1963), pp. 51 and 69.

[13] Tamburrano, *op. cit.,* p. 23.

pose here, however, is whether what has happened represents a *decline* in P.C.I. ideology, or something else. If by decline is meant the abandonment of some of the rhetoric, the verbal symbols, the predictions and expectations voiced until the late fifties, there seems little doubt about the validity of such a judgment, although the more appropriate word would be *change*. However, if by decline is meant that P.C.I. is becoming bourgeois or "social-democratized," or that it is abandoning any commitment to ideological formulations, I believe one should hesitate before leaping to such a conclusion. As Palmiro Togliatti significantly put it, "There is no experience regarding the way in which the battle for socialism can or must be waged in a regime of advanced monopolistic state capitalism. . . . There do not even exist explicit prescriptions in the classics of our doctrine."[14]

Communist leaders who spearhead this reappraisal are not calling for ideological retreat but, rather, for a concerted search for new ideological underpinnings for party policies and actions. In noting that Marxism offers, at best, vague guides to party behavior in modern Italian society, these leaders seem to me to be a long way from abandoning such key concepts as class dialectical conflict, the exploitative nature of monopoly capitalism, and the fundamental need for effecting structural—not mild, reformist—changes in the social system. They, and the millions of Italians who support them at the polls, are far from concluding, if this is the acid test for the inclination toward ideological decline, that the problems created by the Industrial Revolution have been largely solved.

The effort to attune the party's ideology to present Italian realities is a complementary side of the vigorous campaign for polycentrism which the party has been conducting within the international communist movement. Beginning in 1956, P.C.I. frankly asserted that the Soviet model could no longer be a specific guide to Communist parties in every country and that it would be necessary to find a "national path to socialism." Togliatti made this point forcefully in the last book he published before his death.[15] In November, 1961, the P.C.I. Secretariat formulated a resolution which said in part that "There do not exist and there cannot exist either a guiding party or state or one or more instances of centralized direction of the international Communist movement. Under existing conditions there must be and there must increasingly be a greater articulation of the movement in a context of full independence of individual parties."

These are brave words, and it is still much too early to conclude with any confidence what the result of the P.C.I.'s campaign will be. What is important is the apparent P.C.I. conviction that it can come up with a new strategy—a new formula for achieving power—for Communist parties operating in Western European and other countries of advanced capitalism. It is important to bear in mind that, in doing this, the party purports to be able to provide an up-dated ideologi-

[14] *Ibid.*, p. 69. See the important statement by Bruno Tentin, one of the most important of the party's young leaders, intellectuals and ideological architects, "Tendenze attuali del capitalismo italiano," in *Tendenze del capitalismo italiano: Atti del convegno economico dell'Istituto Gramsci* (Rome, 1962), p. 43 ff.

[15] Togliatti, *op. cit.*, p. 131.

cal rationale for action. Some of the "moldiness" of "Scientific Socialism" has certainly been scraped away. What remains, coupled with some of the newer ideas currently in ferment, amounts to much more ideology than one might detect from the simple notation that the language of the late forties and early fifties is no longer in vogue.

Italian Christian Democracy.   The genius of Alcide DeGasperi is that for a decade following the birth of the Italian Republic he was able to hold together within the Christian Democratic party (D.C.) strongly opposed ideological factions that managed to play down ideology in the interest of holding on to power. This was no mean achievement. Although the popular image of the D.C. is that of an opportunistic, anti-ideological "brokerage" party, the truth is that, from the outset, strong factions that would have emphasized ideology, even at the risk of splitting the party, had to be suppressed or defeated. DeGasperi's hegemonic control of the organization was secured only after he had managed to beat down early competition for leadership emanating from such ideologues as Giuseppe Dossetti, Amintore Fanfani and Giovanni Gronchi. One might well conclude that, in an age of alleged ideological decline and after a decade of enjoying the many fruits of political power, ideology would have become a much less salient issue within the D.C.

Exactly the opposite tendency is apparent, however. Since the death of De-Gasperi, and the advent of Fanfani as a major party leader in 1954, the ideological debate has not only intensified but has also broken into public view, revealing a party organization under deep internal stress. I believe that the facts will clearly demonstrate that since that date the role of ideology within the D.C. has actually increased rather than diminished, and a few central occurrences will serve to bear out this conclusion.

In September, 1961, the D.C. held at San Pellegrino the first of three annual "ideological" conventions. They represented a long and successful effort on the part of those in the party who had fought for making the party ideologically coherent, something more than the "brokerage" party the D.C. had been under DeGasperi's leadership. Looming over these proceedings were two of the party's perennial dilemmas: First, to what extent should the D.C., a party drawing much of its strength from the political right, articulate a left-wing ideology as a guide to policy? Second, how much ideological freedom could the party express *vis-à-vis* a Catholic Church to which it must necessarily remain closely tied? Those who favored stronger articulation of a coherent left-wing ideology were strongly spurred by an undeniable gradual movement to the left by the Italian electorate, by the increasing willingness of the Italian Socialist party to consider active coalition with the D.C., and certainly not least by the kinds of ideological changes in the Vatican triggered by the innovating papacy of John XXIII.

Speakers at the conferences reviewed the party's ideological history, noting that at war's end it appeared that the party would lead the country left and that, in those years, DeGasperi himself stated that the old order based on the domination of rural landowners and urban industrialists would not remain intact. But it was lamented that whenever the D.C. confronted issues concerning which the party's ideology seemingly required socialist solutions, ideology was arrested in favor of not pushing to the breaking point the ideological centrifugal tendencies within the organization. As Franco Malfatti, one of the followers of Giuseppe Dossetti and Amintore Fanfani, points out, the revolutionary tone of early D.C. pronouncements was gradually transformed into the muted notes of a purely formalistic democracy and of a great concentration of governmental power at Rome.[16]

As the D.C. moved self-consciously toward the "Opening to the Left" which would bring the Socialists into the government, the party's ideologues would no longer accept the DeGasperi formula whereby all concern about or dedication to ideology was to be obscured in favor of the overriding value of party unity. At San Pellegrino, Malfatti put the new posture of the ideologues pointedly. "The problem of [party] unity," he said, "is a great one of fundamental importance but it is also a problem that runs the risk of losing all its value if used as a sedative, or as the Hymn of Garibaldi, every time there is conflict between clerical and anti-clerical elements."[17] If the party wished to be free of all internal ideological conflict, nothing would remain of it except an agreement "to hold power for power's sake."[18]

According to Achille Ardigo, a sociologist and long-time member of the party's national executive committee, the major milestones in the D.C.'s ideological evolution are the following: First, the development of the concept of the political autonomy of Catholics, unconstrained by specific direction of clerical forces. Second, the growth of the idea of the autonomous function of intermediate groups (such as family, community and social class) against the excesses of the centralizing, modern liberal state. Third, the defense and consolidation of liberty, in a government of laws, through an alliance of the democratic forces of the nation against political and ideological extremes. Fourth, the materialization of the ideology of the "new party" led by Amintore Fanfani. Finally, the emergence of a new concept of the state as an artifice of harmonious and planned development—the idea of the state as an instrument of dynamic intervention in the economic sphere and of the modification of the rights of property in favor of the well-being of the collectivity. It is the evolution of this last, self-consciously ideological stage that permitted the party's recent shift to the left and the acceptance of coalition with the Socialists.[19]

One can identify many reasons for this shift to the left, including Italian

[16] Franco M. Malfatti, "La Democrazia Cristiana nelle sue affermazioni programmatiche dalla sua ricostruzione ad oggi," in *Il Convegno di San Pellegrino: Atti del I Convegno di Studi della D. C.* (Rome, 1962), pp. 325–341. For examples of the early, postwar ideological statements of the party, see, for example, Alcide DeGasperi, "Le Lineo programmatiche della D.C.," in *I Congressi Nazionali della Democrazia Cristiana* (Rome, 1959), p. 23; Gianni Baget Bozzo, "Il Dilemma della D.C. e del suo prossimo Congresso," *Cronache Sociali,* vol. 3 (April 30, 1949), p. 17; and Achille Ardigo, "Classi sociali e sintesi politica," in *Il Convegno di San Pellegrino . . . , op. cit.,* pp. 135 ff.

[17] Franco M. Malfatti, "L'Unità della D.C. e il problema delle tendenze," *Cronache Sociali,* 3 (February 15, 1949), p. 15.

[18] Ardigo, *op. cit.,* p. 145.

[19] *Ibid.,* pp. 155–165.

voting patterns that have clearly led the D.C. in this direction. To the many social and economic pressures leading to the emergence of a Catholic Socialism, one would have to add the liberating impact of John XXIII's revolutionary encyclical, *Mater et Magistra*. In the light of this radical departure from the conservative, often reactionary, political utterances of Pius XII, it is easy to understand why the D.C. left should be spurred to a more purposeful and ideologically rationalized attack on Italian society's ills.

It is important to recognize that the San Pellegrino meetings mean not that the D.C. has moved left on a purely opportunistic basis, but, rather, on the basis of a "rediscovery" of the ideological formulations laid down by Dossetti and others in the late forties. To be sure the current ideology is not socialism and, indeed, leaders like Aldo Moro have been careful to distinguish D.C. ideology from socialism and communism. Nevertheless, the D.C. is today a dramatically less catch-all party than it was under DeGasperi. It now has a somewhat official and publicly articulated ideology. If ideology is in fact in significant decline elsewhere in Europe, Italy will certainly have to be excepted from such easy generalizations. In the P.C.I., ideology has changed and appears to be vigorously reasserting itself; in the D.C. the era of suppressed ideology has passed, and ideological debate and commitment are clearly resurgent.

*   *   *

. . . A few concluding remarks about the extent to which phenomena associated with the alleged decline of ideology reflect in great measure certain kinds of adaptations to the crisis confronting Western intellectuals. The Italian case will serve as one concrete illustration of this, although similar patterns can also be explicated for other Western countries.

At the end of World War II, Italian intellectuals—like their counterparts elsewhere in Western Europe—felt deeply involved in a concerted and apparently promising effort to transform Italian society. This was a period in which "The sacred texts were dusted off and the people were enlightened in order to create the maximum degree of consensus and to realize the maximum degree of support and conversions."[20] But romantic notions of socialist revolution—widely fostered by intellectuals—were of very short duration. Failure of Italian society to move directly toward socialism caught many intellectuals flat-footed. They remained tied to a permanent anti-Fascism which led them to ritualistic rhetorical statements about Italian society's ills and the paths to salvation. For almost fifteen years, these intellectuals repeated with startling monotony themes and prescriptions which were simply out of joint as far as the changing conditions of Italian society were concerned. In this sense, certainly, Aron and others are right in scoring the stultifying consequences of doctrinaire ideological formulations.

These were years of demoralization for intellectuals who expected revolutionary change and were treated instead to a great deal of temporizing under DeGasperi; but the intellectuals were also blinded to certain social and economic changes that made the traditional rhetoric of Marxism alien to growing numbers

[20] Antonio Carbonaro and Luciano Gallino, "Sociologia e ideologie ufficiali," *Tempi Moderni,* 4 (January-March 1961), p. 31.

of Italians. The irony in all of this is that the intellectuals were the last to appreciate the néed for new rhetoric and, indeed, for new ideological formulations. They had been preceded by political leaders not only in the Communist party, but in the ranks of Christian Democracy as well. The politicians evidently quickly understood that no large-scale intervention of the public sector in any kind of development was likely to proceed for long without some kind of *ideological* justification.

To some extent, the isolation of intellectuals from social realities was encouraged by the P.C.I. In keeping the party's intellectuals organizationally separated from mass members, the P.C.I. was able to capitalize on a tendency which is deeply rooted in Italian culture. As Guiducci points out, Italian intellectuals were strongly influenced by the Crocian idea that they were a caste apart, superior to and removed from the masses, and thus failed to maintain an open and realistic contact with the broader population. Even in a context of deep ideological commitment, they managed to adhere to "a position which is traditional with the Italian man of culture, estranged as he is from reality, tied as he is to a culture which is literary and humanistic in the narrowest sense of the words."[21]

The striking thing about Italy in recent years is that the country's intellectuals (largely of the left, but also of the right) seem to be emerging from the kind of isolation Guiducci mentions. Their confrontation of the realities of Italian society has not led, however, to a decline of ideology. Rather, I would suggest that what has happened involves in part ideological clarification and in part the framing of new ideologies to which striking numbers of Italians and European intellectuals now adhere. These new ideologies in a profound sense involve substituting new myths for old. The new myths, which form the core of the ideological structure of many intellectuals, are those of the welfare state and of economic planning. As Henri Jarme rightly puts it, "The myth of planning is only the socialist variant of the myth of progress."[22] But such myths, if Italy is any test, attract more than segments of former orthodox Marxists; they are woven as well into the kind of new ideology that Christian Democrats create.

To be sure, the emergence of new myths creates new symbols and vocabulary. This sort of change should not be construed, however, as an end of ideology. As Giovanni Sartori notes, "Granted that in an affluent society the intensity of ideology will decrease, a lessening of its intensity should not be confused with a withering away of ideology itself. . . . The temperature of ideology may cool down but this fact does not imply that a society will lose the habit of perceiving political problems in an unrealistic or doctrinaire fashion; and it implies even less that a party system will turn to a pragmatic approach."[23]

Two points are relevant here. First, it is obvious that many Italian intellec-

[21] Roberto Guiducci, *Socialismo e verità* (Turin, 1956), pp. 23 ff. Cf. Gaetano Arfè, "La Responsibilità degli intellettuali," *Tempi Moderni,* 4 (January-March 1961), pp. 31–32; Paolo Prandstraller, *Intellettuali e democrazia* (Rome, 1963).

[22] Henri Jarme, "Le Mythe politique du socialisme democratique," *Cahiers Internationaux de Sociologie,* 33 (July-December 1962), p. 29.

[23] Giovanni Sartori, "European Political Parties: The Case of Polarized Pluralism," in LaPalombara and Weiner, *op. cit.*

tuals seem to have rediscovered a valid—or at least personally satisfying—function in society, namely, providing an ideological rationale, as well as rational alternatives, for economic planning activity. Second, in achieving this redefinition of role, the intellectual seems to have reaffirmed his responsibility for creating the ideological system within which contemporary activity is justified. Needless to say, some of these intellectuals will phrase ideology in the language of science and rationality, whether they are in favor of radical change or of the preservation of the status quo. There is certainly little evidence in Italy, in any event, that, say, a commitment to social science miraculously resolves the nagging problem of Mannheim's Paradox, nor, indeed, that it should.

When we turn to the decline-of-ideology writers, it is possible to detect that they, too, are in search of a definable role in contemporary American society. Whether that role involves the use of social science to criticize America's failings or to extol its consensual or managerial character is a fascinating empirical question. But surely the exploration of this problem would require of a mature social science a certain amount of caution and humility regarding the danger of translating highly selective data gathering or personal predilections or ambitions into sweeping historical projections and "scientific" generalizations. Clifford Geertz, I believe, has put this most succinctly: "We may wait as long for the 'end of ideology' as the positivists have waited for the end of religion."[24]

24 Geertz, *op. cit.*, p. 51.

21. The French Student Revolt*

BERNARD E. BROWN

Nous ne sommes pas en face de besoin de réformes, mais en face d'une des crises les plus profondes que la civilisation ait connue. . . . Cette répétition générale d'un drame suspendu montrait, chez les grévistes comme chez ceux qui les regardaient passer, la conscience de la fin d'un monde. . . . Notre société n'est pas encore adaptée à la civilisation des machines.—André Malraux, Le Monde, June 22, 1968.

The student uprising and general strike of May 1968 mark a turning point in the evolution of postwar France. All universities and many high schools in France were occupied by students, ten million workers were on strike, and bloody battles raged on the streets of Paris. The proud Gaullist regime seemed no longer to exercise authority. Though fighting desperately to retain power,

*From Bernard E. Brown, *The French Revolt: May 1968* (New York: McCaleb-Seiler, © 1970). Abridged by the editors. Reprinted by permission of General Learning Corporation. *Note:* Abbreviations are explained on p. 290.

Prime Minister Pompidou admitted publicly that "nothing can ever be quite the same as before." The regime counterattacked, but in spite of the Gaullist triumph at the polls in June nothing was quite the same. The fragility of the Fifth Republic had been revealed. A year later De Gaulle was repudiated in a referendum, and the "solitary exercise of power" came to an end.

The May Revolt is important to students of French politics; but its significance transcends the immediate context. It has been an article of faith among social scientists that revolutionary uprisings are characteristic of societies in the early stages of modernization. It has been fashionable to speak of a "decline of ideology"—or rather, a decline in the intensity of ideological conflict—in the West. But in 1968 a revolt of major proportions took place in an advanced industrial society with a parliamentary democracy and free elections. All current theories concerning the integration of social classes during the process of modernization need re-examining in the light of this dramatic, near cataclysmic event. We must even return to the question posed by General de Gaulle's minister of culture, André Malraux, whether this signals "the end of a world."

. . . .

THE REVOLUTIONARIES

The "detonator" of the May Revolt was fashioned by student militants. But these militants—and this point is crucial for an understanding of the course of events—were fragmented politically, were working at cross purposes, and were striving to attain wholly contradictory goals. For a brief moment they were united in their desire to bring down the bourgeois university, but even on this relatively minor aspect of their far-reaching programs they disagreed on tactics. The various student revolutionary organizations and movements reflected two wholly opposed outlooks. One set of organizations wished to create a corps of professional revolutionaries (in the tradition of Lenin, Trotsky, Mao) who would overturn the regime, establish total control of the society, and then drive on to more complete industrialization. On the other hand, a loose, diffuse "movement" of anarchists and assorted surrealists distrusted all organizations, denounced Lenin and Trotsky, expressed reservations even about Mao, Ho Chi Minh and Castro, and in effect sought to destroy the whole infrastructure of the modern economy. Their goal was not industrialization but a state of complete, untrammeled individual creativity. Neither group could possibly exist in a society created by the other; but the future struggle for power was subordinated to the immediate task of liberating students from the oppression of their bourgeois environment.

. . . .

THE SEIZURE OF POWER: TACTICS AND GOALS

There was no single theory of the seizure of power before the events of May. The minuscule revolutionary groups in France acted out the historic debate of the whole European social-democratic movement: organization versus spontaneity, Bolsheviks versus Mensheviks, Rosa Luxemburg versus Lenin, the Workers Opposition versus Trotsky. To this was added the debate among modern Communists over guerrilla war versus peaceful coexistence. Yet the debate seemed unreal. France was a highly industrialized society, its proletariat was largely integrated into the social system, the peasantry was hardly a revolutionary force. More important, the revolutionary groups did not have more than four or five thousand members altogether, and were opposed by the organized forces of the society, including notably the major trade unions and the Communist Party. Before May, the revolutionary groups (or at least the more realistic leaders) did not expect to seize power; they hoped at most to create a "pre-revolutionary" climate of opinion.

It was only after the explosion of May 3, and above all the general strike of May 14, that anything approaching a coherent theory of the seizure of power emerged. That is, the theory of the seizure of power came after the creation of a revolutionary situation. First, errors were admitted on all sides. The FER and M.L.s agreed that they had underestimated the potential of student revolt, and the anarchists were impressed with the penetration of the working class by the Maoists and Trotskyites. It was evident that each particular revolutionary group had made a contribution, in some cases unwittingly, and that as a result of a chain reaction in which all groups participated the "impossible" revolution was at hand. There was now a striking unity of views among the revolutionary leaders regarding the tactics to be used in creating a revolutionary situation. The key elements were: (a) "contestation," i.e., permanent, unrelenting criticism of the existing order; (b) exposure of the violent nature of bourgeois society through provocation; (c) extension of the revolt to the working class; (d) conversion of campuses and factories into revolutionary bastions; and (e) creation of a "dual power."

"Contestation," largely the contribution of the anarchists, means challenge of all existing values, institutions, and authority, from the immediate (for example, professors, university officials, policemen) to the global (De Gaulle, capitalism, reformist communism, bureaucracy, modern society). One method may be disrupting lectures and holding professors up to ridicule. At Nanterre, for example, a highly successful technique was simply to occupy a lecture hall and refuse to permit classes to be held there. On one such occasion the March 22 Movement appropriated a lecture hall assigned to the distinguished historian René Rémond and held a "debate" on Vietnam and other political topics. When Rémond opened the door, he was insulted and pushed out. Thus the anarchists expressed their contempt for the status of the professor, his pseudo-objective academic stance, and the irrelevance of university instruction to the concerns of revolutionaries.

The next key step is to expose the inherently repressive character of liberal and bourgeois-democratic institutions, even of that most liberal of all institutions, the university. As explained in one of the first pronouncements of the March 22 Movement, the revolutionaries are conscious of being a small minority.

The problem is how to arouse the political consciousness of the inert or apathetic masses. Our action, explained the revolutionaries, ". . . was a matter of making the latent authoritarianism come out (cf. the carloads of police ready to intervene) by showing the true face of the proposed 'dialogue.' As soon as certain problems are posed, the dialogue yields its place to the billy club." The sight of policemen beating students illuminates in a flash the repressive nature of the entire society. Then, through a spontaneous, instinctual movement of solidarity, the masses enter the fray. For example, on the critical day of May 3, most of the militant revolutionaries were in the custody of the police and were being evacuated peacefully from the courtyard of the Sorbonne. The silent mass that watched the proceedings suddenly intervened, and the spark of revolt was struck. The events of May 3 were a vindication of the anarchist theory of "spontaneity," as opposed to the Trotskyite and Maoist emphasis on the need for strict discipline.

Trotskyites, Maoists, and anarchists were in agreement that the revolution could take place ultimately only through the working class. The very first act of the students after the occupation of the Sorbonne on May 13 was to open the university to workers, who began to appear on the barricades along with the students. Above all, the FER and M.L.s were already implanted in a few factories and had a small following among young workers. The news of the occupation of Sud-Aviation was an electric shock, for it seemed to signal the transformation of a revolt into a revolution. . . .

How to exploit the wave of strikes? The strategy of the revolutionaries was clear: just as the students had occupied the Sorbonne, so must the workers occupy the factories. The bourgeois state must then face up to using violence to evacuate the students and workers. Thus, the orthodox Marxist view is borne out—the violence in revolution is not the workers', but rather the bourgeoisie's. And if the army and police were ordered to fire upon the students and workers, would they do so? No matter what happened, the bourgeois state would be disgraced. In fact, most occupied plants were turned into armed camps, topped by fluttering red flags.

The student revolutionaries urged the creation of workers councils in every factory to organize a return to production without the unwelcome aid of the capitalists. There would thus come into existence a "dual power": on the one hand, a functioning, self-sufficient economy run by the workers themselves, and on the other hand, a bourgeoisie deprived of its ownership of the means of production and utterly dependent on mercenaries. The victory of the proletariat and the overthrow of capitalism would be inevitable. Indeed, student leaders by the end of May believed that they had successfully adapted the theory of people's war to an advanced country. Industrial societies, they argued, cannot be overthrown by direct, frontal assault. Guerrilla war based on the peasantry was obviously impossible. But an *urban* guerrilla, made up of students and young workers, could provoke an industrial people's war (occupation of factories, self-defense, and workers control) that would topple the bourgeois regime.

. . . .

THE COMBUSTIBLE MATERIAL

The movement founded at Nanterre on March 22 by 142 students had as its purpose to destroy the bourgeois university and create "another Vietnam" in France. Consider the state of France on the afternoon of May 29, a scant two months later: over ten million workers were on strike; most factories were occupied by their workers and converted into armed camps; there was no mail, no public transport, no industrial production; all department stores were shut; all universities were occupied by students; the riots sweeping Paris in the preceding three weeks had resulted in injury to thousands of people and considerable damage to property; and there were signs of vacillation on the part of the police. The government itself seemed powerless, and the opposition leaders were beginning to talk about the formation of a provisional government as if the regime had already disappeared. In the midst of this social and political chaos, General de Gaulle flew out of beleaguered Paris and consulted with his generals commanding the French Expeditionary Force in Germany!

The detonator set off an explosion because the surrounding materials were combustible. The students had grievances in their schools and universities; the workers had grievances in their factories; and the middle classes had grievances in their offices. Elements of a revolutionary situation existed at each stage of the escalating violence. French social structures were simply not adapted to the needs of the time.

Nowhere has this been more evident than in the universities. Instruction is of the highest quality in the elite institutions of France, whose graduates are funneled directly into the top levels of the administrative and business hierarchies. These include the *Ecole Nationale d'Administration,* and its feeder institutions, the *Instituts d'Etudes Politiques,* the *Hautes Etudes Commerciales, Ecole Normale Supérieure,* and half a dozen technical institutes, including the famous *Polytechnique.* The Grandes Ecoles take care to screen their candidates, who must pass a stiff entrance exam. Once accepted, the students receive individual attention and the certainty of a good position after graduation.

The "faculties" of the twenty-three French universities present a sharp contrast. They are obliged to admit every student with a baccalaureate degree (in effect, the equivalent of a high school diploma). The number of students attending university has increased fivefold since World War II, with the greatest expansion under the Fifth Republic (123,000 in 1946; 202,000 in 1961; and 514,000 in 1968). In theory, students attend lecture courses throughout the year and pass exams at the end of their course of study. In practice, only a small fraction of the registered students ever attend lectures. Many cannot attend because they hold down jobs, frequently in other cities; others cannot successfully fight their way into an overcrowded lecture hall. Research papers are not required, and could not be prepared in any case; there are some 300 seats in the library of the Sorbonne, which is supposed to serve 30,000 students. Student associations make mimeographs of the lectures ("polycopiés") which are bought and memorized by the students. The attrition rate, under these circumstances, is harrowing; 50 per cent of all students drop out at the end of the first year and 70 per cent never receive a degree. Even when the student gets his degree, he may experience extraordinary difficulty in finding employment. There are no direct links between industry, business, and the state administration on the one hand, and the university faculties on the other.

The need to revamp the university system had been acknowledged by all political parties and all ministers of education for the preceding ten years. An impressive program of construction was launched in 1960, and seven wholly new campuses were created. But the structures of the new universities, as well as those of the old, remained unchanged. Hordes of students poured into the new campuses, and found themselves in the same crowded lecture halls, reading the same *polycopiés,* and taking the same highly stylized exams. A feeble attempt to introduce selection procedures, though rational in itself, simply added to the fears of the high school students. The human irritation and frustration created by this wasteful and irrational system was massive. Student associations became increasingly militant in demanding more buildings, more libraries, and more professors. It became customary for students to demonstrate in the autumn, during the opening of the university year, which produced inevitable clashes with police. The revolutionary groups were thus able to exploit genuine, long-standing grievances.

Student restiveness is widespread throughout Europe, but only in France has a student disruption sparked a working class strike. On the surface, the French workers seem to be no worse off than workers elsewhere in Western Europe. The French economy has performed well since the Liberation. Beginning in 1950, when industrial production finally reached its prewar level, economic growth averaged close to 10 per cent in most years. Reserves of gold and foreign currencies, practically zero in 1959, amounted to over 28 billion francs in 1968. By that year there were 12 million cars on the road, almost one for each family. The general strike of 1968 took place at a time not of depression and mass unemployment, but of relative prosperity.

This prosperity, however, was not evenly spread throughout the society. In the absence of a steep progressive income tax a disproportionate share of the wealth was in the hands of the upper middle class. The wage differentials were also much greater than in other advanced industrial societies. For example, in 1965 the average wage of a plant manager or engineer was about $750 a month, a middle-level manager earned about half that sum, a skilled worker made about $200 a month, and an unskilled laborer about $130 a month. One-third of all French workers earned less than $110 a month. The minimum salary was a derisory 40 cents an hour. The standard of living of the French worker has improved steadily in the past twenty years, but it remains low. Failure to redistribute income has been a major shortcoming of the French political system. Furthermore, competition from the other members of the Common Market forced adjustments in the French economy. By early 1968 unemployment amounted to half a million and particularly affected the young. Even more important, the French working class has a long tradition of class consciousness and political radicalism. Perhaps one-fourth of the workers have voted consistently for the Communist party in every election since the Liberation. This is a manifestation of a sense of alienation from the political system that was readily exploited by revolutionary groups in May.

One of the surprises of the May Revolt was the sudden expression of deeply felt grievances by large numbers of people in clerical, professional, and managerial categories. Low salaries accounted for some of this dissatisfaction, especially among shopgirls, teachers, and clerical workers. But the deepest protest was against French authority structures, which tend to vest responsibility and decision-making power in a relatively few people at the top of the pyramid. The organization of the university was a microcosm of all collective enterprise. A given discipline in a university was allotted one "chair," occupied by a full professor. The important policy decisions, including the appointment of assistants and associates, were his prerogative, along with the organization of courses, the assignment of topics, and the drafting of examinations. There was always a possibility of abuse of power by the professor, and a feeling of resentment and lack of dignity on the part of his subordinates. This relationship prevailed in hospitals and scientific laboratories as well as in liberal arts faculties. The "patron" ran everything in his little bailiwick. In the business world, too, authority was concentrated in the hands of the "patron," and his associates and subordinates suffered constant indignity. Once the explosion took place, those in inferior positions within bureaucratic structures gave vent to their resentment of the way their lives were organized. In the general revolutionary atmosphere of May, a whole society began to draw up its *Cahiers des doléances.*

THE FAILURE TO SEIZE POWER

Yet the revolt failed, and the Gaullists came back stronger than ever. We suggest the following reasons for the defeat of the revolution: (*a*) the strength of the tradition of parliamentary democracy; (*b*) widespread disillusion with the occupation of the universities; (*c*) the internal contradictions in the revolutionary coalition; (*d*) the hostility of the Communist party toward those who instigated the revolt; and above all, (*e*) the inability to adapt guerrilla war to an industrial society.

The revolutionaries were maneuvered into opposing the right of the electorate to determine its own fate. The Gaullists draped themselves in the mantle of the Republic, even renaming their party the *Union pour la Défense de la République* (UDR). Whatever may be said about the shortcomings of parliamentary democracy, ever since 1875 and except during the Vichy period the French have been in the habit of holding periodic elections in which all organized political forces could participate freely. The notion that opposition parties as well as individuals have the right to criticize those in power, and if possible vote them out of office, is strongly engrained. The student revolutionaries openly, proudly expressed their contempt for parliamentary democracy. In the best Marxist tradition they argued that revolutions are made not by counting votes, but rather by direct action in factories and in the streets. Alain Geismar's comments on parliamentary democracy were typical:

A parliamentary regime endowed with a majority and an opposition, let us even say a majority of the Left and a bourgeois opposition, cannot in my view impose . . . the necessary social transformation . . . , because from the moment the struggle envisages the liquidation of the bourgeois opposition, it cannot possibly take place within the framework of a parliamentary debate. . . . That, at a later time, diverse modes of expression can coexist does not in any way detract from the fact that during the months, the years of social transformation, when the class struggle is practically a fight for the survival of the bourgeois class, the dear parliamentary colleague is an element that has no place, and no meaning.

Relating how little interest the revolutionary students have in parliament Jacques Sauvageot even referred to that venerable institution as the "Chamber of Deputies"—a title it has not had since 1946. Particularly shocking was the vow to suppress the opposition and civil liberties. One student leader denounced Raymond Aron as an insidious bourgeois ideologist, and declared that he would not be permitted to teach at the Sorbonne. "Il est interdit d'interdire"—unless you happen to disagree!

The distrust of elections by revolutionary leaders was fully justified on purely pragmatic grounds. They had no electoral organization, no taste for electioneering, and would be easily outmaneuvered in an electoral campaign by the old hands. In the balloting on June 23 the only party in any way sympathetic to the revolution, the PSU, received 3.9 per cent of the vote—ludicrous in view of the actual power of the revolutionaries on the barricades. This almost total lack of electoral support was confirmed when Alain Krivine, leader of the JCR, ran for the presidency in June 1969. He received a bare 1 per cent of the vote, and PSU candidate Rocard 3.6 per cent.

In a sense, the success of the revolutionaries in taking over the Sorbonne and the Théâtre de France (Odéon) also led to their undoing. Things began to go sour when the lofty notions of the Commune were put into practice. On the day of the occupation of the Sorbonne all power was vested in a General Assembly, consisting of the mob that could make its way into the Grand Amphitheatre. To prevent "bureaucratization," a fifteen-member Occupation Committee was given executive power, but only for one day and one night. It was supposed to report to the General Assembly and be re-elected every night. The result was chaos. The Occupation Committee quickly became a permanent, irresponsible executive, while the General Assembly engaged in meandering, disorganized, and ineffective argument. The Trotskyites, JCR's, M.L.s and anarchists, however, were well organized, and they easily manipulated the mass debates and the election of the Occupation Committees. While the leadership ran things behind the scenes, the stage was taken up by such colorful characters as the "International Situationists," inheritors of the tradition of Dadaism and Surrealism. The sheer nihilism of the Situationists served to discredit the occupation of the Sorbonne and the Odéon.

A more serious matter was the infiltration of criminal elements—thugs, members of motorcycle gangs, and juvenile delinquents—who flocked to the occupied faculties and joyously helped the students battle with their common enemy, the police. At first the students welcomed "la pègre" on the grounds that they were the poor victims of capitalist society. But a group of thugs calling themselves the *Katangais* (a reference to the white mercenaries in Africa) took over a section of the Sorbonne by force. The students were shocked. Finally, the Occupation Committee marshaled its forces and after a violent battle expelled the "poor victims" of capitalist society. The Sorbonne and other occupied university faculties attracted bums, beatniks, hippies, and even dope addicts in increasing numbers, especially after the elimination of the barricades in the Latin Quarter. For example, by late June, when the police evacuated the Ecole des Beaux Arts they found that only 46 of the 103 persons on the premises were students. Many were just drifters, and 28 had criminal records.

The fervent activity within the occupied university buildings also produced mixed reactions on the part of the public. By far the most impressive work was accomplished by the art students, who turned out superb posters. Some serious proposals for reform were put forward by students in medicine, science, and political science. But by and large, the "liberation" courses conducted by student leaders were disappointing. The students went from one extreme to another. Before the May Revolt they listened docilely to the all-knowing professor, committing his lectures to paper and then to memory. Now they discussed current political topics—without information and without any critical apparatus. Typical of the contrast between promise and reality was the work of the revolutionary film students. *Le cinéma s'insurge* was the enticing title of a new documentary projected in June at the Faculty of Science. The camera picked up a middle-aged man as he wandered about the courtyard of the liberated Sorbonne. He happened to be a railroad worker (at least that was the part he played), and for a painful half hour he droned on about the evils of labor-saving devices recently introduced in the French railroad system. Presumably the message was that civilization had to serve man, and not vice versa. How this noble end could be achieved by retaining archaic work procedures in an industrial society was not explained.

The internal contradictions within the student movement came to the surface during the month-long occupation of universities. Trotskyites, Maoists, and anarchists could not agree on the future direction of their revolution—whether the factories would be run by workers alone or with the participation of managerial cadres, whether to drive forward to full industrialization based on atomic power and electronic calculators or to liberate man altogether from the tyranny of machines, whether to place a well-disciplined revolutionary party in power or govern through a network of local soviets, whether to permit all to express themselves or to wreak revolutionary vengeance upon the opposition.

There was also no agreement on the lessons to be learned from successful revolutions in the third world. The model that generated most enthusiasm was Castro's Cuba. Every occupied university building boasted its Che Guevara Hall, bedecked with portraits of the fallen hero. Ho Chi Minh's Vietnam and Mao's China were also held in high esteem generally, and to a lesser extent Yugoslavia and the kibbutzim in Israel. But what was the relevance of "participatory democracy," workers councils, decentralization, and the immediate sexual liberation of the individual to societies where power was highly centralized and sexual morality closely supervised and regulated? The professed goal seemed to have no relation to any existing reality. The anarchists were critical of everyone. As Cohn-Bendit put it: "I do not think that Castroism is really a model and believe that Cuba is heading toward a redivision of society into classes. . . . Alas, . . . in the Third World . . . socialism does not really exist." What, then, is socialism? The answer was evasive, vague, unsatisfactory. Said Alain Geismar:

> I am not a theoretician. For me socialism is defined negatively, by relation to a certain number of existing structures, by a refusal of all bureaucratization, of all central management, by giving power to producers on the very site of production. Let us say that it is essentially *autogestion,* even though this, too, is a vague word. . . . *Autogestion* and decentralization, the central power thus assuming a role of coordination and not of repression.

And how would the coordination be prevented from becoming repression? How could production take place without central direction? The revolutionaries voiced their confidence in the ability of the masses to devise the necessary structures, and then went on to other topics. The fantasy and unreality of this approach to problems of industrial organization and political relationships became increasingly manifest to the public.

Another major reason for the failure of the May Revolt was the refusal of the PCF to join forces with the student revolutionaries. From the outset the PCF was opposed to "adventurism" on the Left. After all, the anarchists and Trotsky-ites were engaged in vilification of the PCF. They claimed that the party bureaucracy within the Communist movement in France was playing the same exploitive role as the bureaucracy in the Soviet Union. The left extremists were deliberately trying to undermine the PCF apparatus. They demanded discussions at the "base" while condemning the leaders at the top, seeking constantly to drive a wedge between the leaders and the masses. The PCF leadership correctly viewed this threat as a matter of life and death for the party. It thrived on attacks from the right, but it could not survive if effectively outflanked on the left. There is no mystery, then, about the Communist reaction to the activists at Nanterre and the Sorbonne. These were the very elements that had been expelled from the UEC in the previous two years; these were the very people who heaped insults on the Communist and CGT leadership at every turn. After the mass protest parade of May 13, Cohn-Bendit exulted: "The Communist Party? Nothing gave me greater pleasure than to be at the head of a demonstration with all that Stalinist filth [*ces crapules Staliniennes*] bringing up the rear."

The PCF took pains to prevent the "adventurers" from contaminating their own student followers, and above all the workers.

A policy change took place after the first occupation of factories by workers on May 14. The party and the CGT did not precipitate the strikes, which were the initiative of militant local union officials, young workers, and Trotskyites. Not to be outflanked on the left, the CGT took charge. At this stage the PCF emphasized the material demands of the workers, and willingly entered into negotiations with the government in order to win concessions for its constituents. Communist leaders were careful to emphasize their concern for legality and continued to excoriate the "adventurers." The PCF had been confronted with a similar situation in 1947, when Trotskyites at the Renault plant provoked a strike against the wishes of the union leadership. The Communists then took over the strike, which led ultimately to their expulsion from the tripartite governing coalition.

When the Grenelle Accord was turned down by the striking workers at Renault, PCF policy changed again. Gingerly but methodically, the Communists now sought to make it impossible for the Gaullist regime to remain in power—not through an insurrection, but simply through the force of circumstances. The PCF troops began to make purely political demands—for De Gaulle's resignation, and for a *"gouvernement populaire."* Careful to avoid any move that might alarm the non-Communist public or the army, the PCF tried to draw recalcitrant Socialists into its orbit. If the Gaullist regime collapsed the PCF would be in an excellent position to return to power as part of a coalition, and if De Gaulle called for elections the PCF would be beyond reproach. The tactics were apt and shrewd—but did not work. In spite of the care taken by the Communists to avoid the appearance of illegality, De Gaulle centered his attacks during the election on the PCF, virtually disregarding the student revolutionaries, and successfully revived the specter of "totalitarian communism." Nevertheless the party survived the election, retained its organization and its bastions, and made a remarkable electoral comeback in the presidential contest of June 1969.

It is true that the PCF did not join forces with the Trotskyites and anarchists in May. Had it done so, and had the revolution succeeded, one can only speculate about the grim fate that would have awaited the leaders of the March 22 Movement at the hands of a Communist minister of the interior. But it would be too hasty to assert that the PCF is therefore no longer a revolutionary party. The PCF prides itself on not being a "party like the others," and its judgment in this respect is shared by the other parties. As late as December 1967, during discussions with Federation leaders concerning a common program, the sticking point was the insistence of the Communists that there would be no freedom for the "enemies of socialism" after the coalition of the Left was installed in power. In numerous public declarations Waldeck Rochet has stated as a matter of course that the bourgeoisie would be forcibly prevented from returning to power in a socialist state. That a PCF in power would suppress the opposition is assumed even by those elements in the left that favor collaboration with the Communists (provided they are kept away from the ministry of the interior).

Ever since 1962 the goal of the PCF has been to participate in a coalition government of the left, which it would gradually dominate through its more efficient organization and through the weight of popular pressure. The lesson of revolutionary uprisings in the modern era is that power is seized not against the state, but through the state. Whether the PCF would be willing ever again to abandon its share of power within a coalition government (as it did in 1947) is impossible to predict. But that the PCF has a vocation to power is not disproved by its refusal to support the May Revolt. The necessary condition for seizing power is to maintain the party apparatus, and the one overriding concern of the leadership is to preserve intact this instrument of the future revolution. When conditions are not favorable for an armed revolt, Waldeck Rochet has pointed out, an attempt at insurrection may lead to disaster "by affording a pretext for repression by reactionary forces." Perhaps the anarchists had forgotten about the French army but the PCF leadership had not. Waldeck Rochet cited the example of Indonesia in 1965, when an attempt was made by some leaders of the Indonesian Communist party, inspired by the ideas of Mao Tse Tung, to overthrow "reactionary generals" through a putsch. But they did not have the support of the masses.

Thus, the attempt failed, and we know the result: the reactionary forces, which went berserk, were able to massacre more than 300,000 Communists and decapitate a party which counted 2.5 million members without the popular masses of Indonesia being in any position to react effectively. This example—and there are others—demonstrates that the adventurism of the "left" which consists in advocating armed struggle "everywhere" and "any time" can cause the greatest harm to the revolutionary movement.

The lack of coordination between the Trotskyites, anarchists, and Communists was thus not "accidental." It was built into the structure of the situation, since the revolution desired by one partner would mean the doom of the others.

Probably the most important reason for the failure of the May Revolt was the misinterpretation by student revolutionaries of the nature of guerrilla war. Inspired by the heroic examples of Che Guevara and Ho Chi Minh, the student leaders raised high the banner of socialism, proclaimed their intention to destroy the existing social order, and plunged into battle with the mercenaries of capitalism. In so doing they mistook the end result of the Cuban and Asian revolutions for the revolutionary process itself. Mass support for an effective guerrilla war is secured through a reformist, moderate, and nationalist program. Only after the revolutionaries are in control of the state apparatus can the people be mobilized to "build socialism."

In Cuba, which was an inspiration for French student militants, the program of the revolutionaries during the period of armed struggle stressed the bourgeois notions of land ownership and liberalism. Che Guevara explained that the motor force of the revolution is not the working class, but the guerrilla. The guerrilla fighter, he continued, "interprets the desires of the great peasant mass to be owners of land. . . . Whatever the ideological aims that inspire the fight, the economic aim is determined by the aspiration toward ownership of land." Castro's program at the time was moderate, well within the established left reformist tradition. He called for restoration of the Constitution of 1940, guarantees of political freedom, and early elections. Once in power Castro quickly dismantled the old armed forces and replaced them with a popular militia. The state, its army and police were then used to bring about the real revolution. Similarly, in Asia the revolutionaries were careful to put themselves forward as reformers and nationalists. They appealed not only to workers and peasants, but also to the "urban petty bourgeoisie" and even to the capitalists.

Had the student leaders in France really adapted the tactics of Guevara, Mao, and Ho to their own situation, they would have tried to gain mass support for short-term and reformist objectives, toning down the revolutionary content of their program. Marx reserved his choicest epithets for those socialists who sought to raise the banner of revolution prematurely. These "German" or "true" socialists, these "fantastic" Utopians are all fundamentally reactionary, Marx observed, because they succeed only in frightening the bourgeoisie and bringing about a political alliance of the middle class and feudal elements in society against the proletariat. The leaders of the May Revolt did everything that Marx warned against, and brought about the very triumph of conservatism that Marx had predicted.

THE MAY REVOLT AS A CRISIS OF MODERNIZATION

During the debate in the National Assembly on May 14, Georges Pompidou reflected upon the profound meaning of the crisis. "Nothing would be more illusory than to believe that the events we have just lived through constitute a temporary flare-up." It is not simply a question of reforming the university, he continued, it is the whole problem of the place of youth in modern civilization, its obligations, and its morals. The social discipline of the past has disappeared; social relations among parents and children, teachers and pupils, have been weakened, and the advance of technology has eliminated the incentive to work. "Why is it surprising then if the need of man to believe in something, to have solidly anchored in himself some fundamental principles, is contradicted by the constant questioning of everything on which humanity has depended for centuries: the family is often dissolved or abandoned, the nation questioned, often denied. God is dead for some. The Church itself is debating the path to follow and is upsetting its traditions." Under these circumstances the students are at loose ends. Some are searching for solutions; others turn to negation, total refusal, and the desire to destroy. "Destroy what? What they have close at hand, and for the students that is the University. And then the society . . . society itself, modern society, materialistic and soulless." There followed a solemn conclusion:

> I see no other precedent in our history but that desperate period that was the fifteenth century, when the structures of the Middle Ages were collapsing

and when, even then, the students were revolting at the Sorbonne. At this stage, it is no longer, believe me, the government which is at stake, nor the institutions, nor even France. It is our civilization itself.[1]

Over a year later Pompidou (now President of the Republic) continued to express deep pessimism about the viability of modern society. In an interview reported by *Le Monde* on August 27, 1969 he spoke even of a possible "collective suicide." His disorientation is understandable. The May Revolt was no ordinary political crisis. The very fabric of the society was rent, and all social structures, all social discipline seemed to be collapsing. It may be suggested, however, that the May Revolt can better be understood as a crisis of modernization rather than of civilization.

All political systems are transformed by the development of science and technology. The economy shifts from agriculture to industry, social structures become more specialized and impersonal, the state becomes the most specialized and impersonal association of all, and the legitimating values of the state become more rational. But individual political systems are unique even though they all undergo a similar evolution. One fruitful way of studying the complex process of modernization is to view it as a series of crises or challenges, to which a number of different responses are possible. Some observers have distinguished among the crises of legitimacy, participation, and tension management. As European societies went through the experience of modernization they necessarily had to cope with each of these crises. Feudal societies could not survive the Enlightenment, and the concept of divine right gave way to more rational theories of political legitimacy. With industrialization new groups emerged (an energetic entrepreneurial class, a managerial and clerical class, and a massive working class); the existing political elites somehow had to deal with the demands of these new groups and integrate them into the political system. And as the European economy became more complex each national society had to devise a system of controls, enabling it to coordinate the activities of increasingly specialized associations.

Nothing is fated to work out in favor of modernization in any of these crises. Revolt against the monarchy may be crushed; reactionary forces may overthrow a republic and re-establish monarchy; new or greatly expanded social groups, in particular the working class, may not be effectively integrated into the political system; and a society may be unable to cope with the problems of coordination. But punishment for failure is severe. A country that falls behind is likely to come under the influence or even the rule of those who have been more successful in meeting these challenges. In France, the pressure in favor of modernization has been intense, since the preservation of French cultural and social integrity depended in the past on keeping up with the English and the Germans.

Nonetheless, at every stage of the process of modernization in France there has been strong opposition from some quarters—to the Republic, industriali-

[1] *Journal Officiel,* May 14, 1968, p. 1772.

zation, rationality, and science. The dividing line frequently runs right through the middle of otherwise coherent social groups. Thus some members of the capitalist and managerial class seek an accommodation with the workers, and others advocate repression; some workers seek greater benefits within an expanding economy, others wish to maintain outdated work practices or overthrow the system altogether; some intellectuals contribute to scientific advance and others glorify traditional society and values. The May Revolt likewise revealed fundamental contradictions within the revolutionary coalition. Some groups accepted modernization as a goal and wished to eliminate archaic barriers to facilitate mass participation in the modern society; some groups wished to continue the march toward ever elusive modernization by imposing totalitarian controls; and other groups were revolting against modern society and all its works in order to revert to an idyllic or imagined past.

The May Revolt reflected the ambiguity of all other conflict situations in France, involving a mix of reformism, revolution, and reversion to the past. It was similar, too, in the existence of an element of *anomie*—a term popularized by Durkheim in describing French society at the turn of the century. Durkheim assumed that the appetites and desires of men are infinite, and that every society must impose a discipline or "regulator" in order to survive. In traditional society the family and religion constitute the regulator. Every person knows his position within the family and within his church; his desires are limited by his own perception of social status. But when a traditional society breaks up, the family structure and the church are brought into question. New values and new social structures (the republic, science, the corporation, the university, and so on) arise, but frequently the individual in transition cannot accept them. He is caught between the traditional and modern forms, and may react by giving up completely (to apathy or even suicide). To Durkheim's analysis we add another possible reaction: lashing out in blind rage against the environment.

Throughout the process of modernization in France there has been a strong "anomic" reaction to social change. It has taken the form of violent opposition to all political authority and to urban industrial life. Anarchism has had a large following in France ever since the beginning of industrialization, and was quite widespread in the latter part of the nineteenth century. Hostility to industrial life has been especially vigorous in France among intellectuals, artists, and writers. The contrast has been sharply drawn between peaceful, bucolic nature on the one hand, and the dehumanizing discipline of factories and the chaos of cities on the other. Such literary movements as dada and surrealism have questioned science, rationality, and modern society, exulting instead in the gesture of the child, the unforeseen, unpredictable happening, and the immediate gratification of psychological and sexual desires. The anarchist, dadaist and surrealist traditions resurfaced in the May Revolt with astonishing force.

The May Revolt highlights in dramatic fashion the existence of a new dimension in the continuing crisis of participation. The problem of "entry into politics" in early industrialization involves mainly the capitalist and managerial classes, whose interests must be reconciled with those of a landholding aristocracy, and then the working class. In a later stage of industrialization the social force undergoing the greatest rate of expansion is the intellectual class—the scientists, researchers, librarians, communications specialists, engineers, administrators, economists, accountants, marketing specialists, technicians, and so on—who receive their training in scientific institutes and universities. Just as the assembly line provoked irritation and revolt on the part of the workers, so the organization of social activity on the basis of scientific and rational criteria creates a feeling of "dehumanization" in many intellectuals. Those who repudiate the old and fear or disdain to accept the new display the symptoms of anomie—resignation (retreat into political apathy or even a dream world of drugs) or rage (railing against all established authority).

In the scientific civilization what Durkheim called the "regulator" is more essential than ever. The intellectual must be imaginative, creative, and even enthusiastic if the collective scientific enterprise is to flourish. Doubts, hesitation, and withdrawal will block the system. But wherever freedom of criticism is permitted, opportunities for exploiting tensions are almost unlimited. The question may be raised whether parliamentary democracies like France can cope with the entry of the intellectuals as a massive social force into the political system. In a climate of freedom the intellectuals are even more likely to rebel than the old working class, and more likely to withdraw their cooperation from the establishment. It may well be that only total control of society by an authoritarian elite can eliminate that anarchy which is incompatible with the continued functioning and development of a scientific civilization. Raymond Aron has formulated the problem with his customary clarity.

I do not claim to prophesy; a civilization without religion, with a Church that questions itself and sometimes denies itself, deprived of the values of country and tradition, is perhaps entering into the ultimate phase that precedes death. A society founded on the voluntary cooperation of millions and millions of individuals in rationalized organizations risks being paralyzed by the violence of minorities and the disaffection of the many. Perhaps the events of May will appear tomorrow as revelatory of the fundamental precariousness of a liberal order in a scientific civilization. I do not state that those who admire the revolution of May are wrong. Perhaps the future will bear them out and the historians will see in what appears to me play acting [une comédie] the surging forth of subterranean and destructive forces.[2]

The May Revolt signals a revival of the ambiguous ideological conflict associated in the past with structural transformations of industrial societies. In all likelihood the parliamentary democracies that experienced great difficulty in securing the integration of the working class will continue to be unstable as they move into the "scientific civilization" and deal with the intellectual class. Even relatively consensual parliamentary democracies may have difficulty in adjusting to these new circumstances. Integration of the intellectuals into the political system may then take place forcibly, under other auspices. The political balance will shift, perhaps irrevocably, away from freedom and toward power.

[2] Raymond Aron, *La révolution introuvable* (Fayard, 1968), p. 134.

Note by the Editors: The following abbreviations were used throughout the above article.

CGT—*Confédération Générale du Travail* (Communist led trade union).

FER—*Fédération des Etudiants Révolutionnaires* (orthodox Trotskyite).

JCR—*Jeunesses Communistes Révolutionnaires* (Trotskyite student group founded in 1966).

March 22 Movement—Group created by about 150 students at Nanterre on March 22, 1968.

M.L.s—*Union des Jeunesses Communistes, Marxistes-Léninistes* (Maoist student group).

PCF—*Parti Communiste Français* (French Communist Party).

PSU—*Parti Socialiste Unifié* (Left wing socialist party).

UEC—*Union des Etudiants Communistes* (affiliate of the French Communist Party).

Among the personalities referred to in the text are:

Daniel Cohn-Bendit—a spokesman for the March 22 Movement, militant in anarchist groups.

Alain Geismar—secretary general of a university teachers organization, and subsequently active in a Maoist group.

Alain Krivine—leader of the JCR (Trotskyite).

Waldeck Rochet—secretary general of the French Communist Party.

Jacques Sauvageot—vice-president of the National Union of French Students, and a member of the PSU.

part FOUR

Political Institutions

Interests and interest groups are the raw material of politics. Through the political parties, or through other larger groupings, they press their claims upon the governmental structures and the decision-making organs of the political system. Policy is often the result of such claims. The farmers wish protection; the workers ask for wage increases; the military for special appropriations; the church for subsidies; the business community for lower taxes. To the uninitiated the striving for satisfaction by various interest groups, the multiplicity and the intensity of conflicts, the incompatibility of the interests involved, often make a political community seem something like a jungle where the survival of the fittest or the strongest appears to be the only rule.

Yet over and above interest and interest conflict there is a basic consensus on the fundamental rules of the game, that is, the acceptance of certain rules according to which conflict will be waged, interests articulated, and conflict resolved. All political systems are characterized by the existence of these rules—what A. D. Lindsay in his book *The Modern Democratic State* calls "operative ideals." That is, in every political society there is an organ which makes decisions according to certain procedures, and these decisions are accepted and obeyed. The state has authority and prestige, not only force.

CONSTITUTIONS

The general organization and structure of authority is in essence a "constitution." Whether written or unwritten a constitution expresses the "fundamental agreement" of the political society on how it will be governed. It usually defines the scope of governmental authority, the way in which decisions are made, and the manner in which decision makers are selected and held accountable. It both creates and limits power. The legacy of the Middle Ages was to define, what we call today, rights that limit arbitrary power and narrow the scope of the state's authority. With the beginning of the 19th century most political systems began

291

to establish responsibility of the governors to the governed through representative assemblies and periodic elections.

A system in which a constitution is widely accepted may be referred to as *consensual,* that is, the people in it agree on how they will resolve their differences. They do not "bicker about fundamentals." Political systems may well be classified, therefore, in terms of this criterion. In some systems the agreement on fundamentals is not widely shared or intensely felt—they have a *low degree of consensus or legitimacy.* In others, there is no such agreement—they are *highly divided or transitional systems.* In still others, the agreement is overtly manufactured through the control of the media of communication by a small group of political leaders—this is the case in authoritarian systems. But authoritarianism is not in itself evidence of low consensus, for in some cases leadership may bring about a high degree of unity and perhaps popular support.

The distinction between consensual and highly divided systems may be illustrated by the cases of Great Britain and France. In both countries the feudal scheme was disrupted, the traditional monarchy was severely restricted or overthrown, and parliamentary democracy was introduced. The British monarchy during the 17th century proved to be less adaptable than the French. The loss of its prerogatives was registered in the Declaration and Bill of Rights of 1689. That is, by the end of the 17th century parliamentary sovereignty was enunciated as the basic principle of the British Constitution. Political conflict did not disappear, and the monarch continued to exert great influence upon his ministers and the Parliament. With the extension of the suffrage in the 19th century, the political base of the House of Commons was transformed. Its legitimacy now derived from the people, whose will was expressed and shaped by mass political parties. While these new forces accepted the venerable principle of parliamentary sovereignty, they rejected the practice of parliamentary government. In theory the will of Parliament is unlimited, unfettered, and supreme. But under modern conditions Parliament consists of at least two well-organized and highly disciplined groups of members whose primary function is to support or criticize the ministry. The Cabinet controls deliberations of the House of Commons because its supporters constitute a majority in the chamber and therefore carry the day for the government so long as the majority remains solid. Juridically, Parliament can do anything; actually, Parliament enacts into law the program of the Cabinet.

The new interests and classes created by the Industrial Revolution thus found a ready-made instrument for the resolution of their conflicts. Slowly the system absorbed, or rather integrated, the new groups, notably the industrial middle class and the workers. But in so doing the political institutions were themselves greatly modified. The country was governed not by an independent and narrowly based House of Commons, but rather by disciplined parties, the Cabinet, and the civil service. The need for strong leadership and the increasing importance of the personality of the leader strengthened the position of the Prime Minister; on the other hand, the growing complexity of administration made it difficult for the Cabinet to function as a collective agency. The trend in the modern era has been toward the concentration of power in the Prime Minister, who dominates his Cabinet much as the Cabinet previously dominated Parliament. At times the system was subjected to great strain, particularly during bitter controversies over the workers' demands for a Charter (mid-19th century), and Home Rule for Ireland. Eventually the political institutions were used to work out satisfactory compromises. Government came to be looked upon as a problem-solving mechanism.

In France, and other countries of the continent, a radically different situation prevailed. Parliaments in these countries knew an uneasy and eventful life, becoming the source of unresolved opposition to the powers of the king or the nobility. The French representative assemblies were not allowed to meet for over a century and a half. When finally they met in 1789, they set aside the powers of the king and ushered in a period of turmoil. A democratic constitution was accepted only by a part of the population. The 19th century was a period of conflict and struggle in which sometimes democracy and sometimes monarchy or personal government (Bonapartism) triumphed. The working classes found it impossible to accommodate themselves with one or the other form and developed a utopian or revolutionary outlook. Thus by the end of the 19th century there was no widespread agreement in France about any constitution; sizable fractions of the population had not been integrated into the system; and people remained divided not only about interests and aspirations but also on how they should resolve their conflicts. The French found it difficult to "agree on how they were to disagree."

Throughout the 19th and 20th centuries, constitutional instability was also the rule in most other European countries where sharp incompatibilities and ideological divisions were very much in evidence. The threat of revolutionary uprising by the underprivileged groups that had never been fully integrated into the system was ever present. The Bolshevik Revolution of 1917 gave sharpness and meaning to their demands. The Nazi system in Germany and, to a lesser degree, the Fascist system in Italy, gave hope to the wealthier groups, to the military, some of the conservative elements of the Church, and to the many lower middle-class groups that a "strong" government, based on one-party rule, could provide stability and unity. Both the Bolshevik and Fascist movements imperiled democratic constitutionalism and provided their followers with an armed vision that undermined the tolerance and agreement on which democracy rests.

Constitutions are sometimes only empty forms, masking the real structure of power. In the Communist countries the disparity between written texts and reality is almost complete. In Latin America and the "new nations" solemn constitutional declarations and texts often conceal the real power which remains in the hands of a small group of leaders. Ceylon, Indonesia, the former British colonies in Africa and elsewhere, the new "Republics" of formerly French Africa and Madagascar, have written constitutions tailored after the British and French pattern, with some evidence of American influence. But in all these cases the "constitution" has not as yet gained acceptance, has no "legitimacy," and as a result remains precarious. Large segments of the population still live in their tribes. The masses are illiterate. Their living conditions afford them no possibility to think about politics intelligently or to organize and speak for themselves. They remain unintegrated in the political system. Yet the creation of a constitutional democracy will require the political integration of the masses. This in turn will be a gradual process based upon growing literacy, economic opportunities and well-being, the development of skills, the acquisition of property by a greater number of persons, and the free expression of interests and aspirations. Constitutional democracy faces, therefore, a severe challenge in the "new" states. There is a decided tendency on the part of the newly emancipated native leadership to follow the authoritarian model. They seem to prefer rapid activation and integration of the masses into a one-party system, along with rigorous discipline for the achievement of national objectives—particularly industrialization.

GOVERNMENTAL INSTITUTIONS

The decision-making functions of all political societies have been distinguished traditionally into three separate types: the executive, the legislative, and the judicial. However, this threefold division is not a realistic guide to the exercise of political power. In some systems the legislature assumed the totality of decision-making power, with the executive simply executing the will of the lawmakers and the judiciary applying and interpreting the law in case of litigation. In other instances, a precarious balance between the executive and the legislature was established, with the executive slowly assuming increased powers and independence of action. In other systems—notably those with a federal organization of power—the judiciary emerged as a genuinely independent organ with wide latitude to interpret the constitution and in so doing to limit the powers of the legislature and the executive.

The 19th century was the period of legislative supremacy in most of the Western constitutional democracies. Walter Bagehot, writing in the latter part of the century, pointed out that the Parliament nominated the members of the executive, passed laws, prepared and voted the budget, supervised the Cabinet and finally aired grievances and ventilated issues, thus helping to mold and shape public opinion. It was primarily a body of men who represented the upper and middle classes of the community, fundamentally in agreement about the policies to be pursued, unharried, embodying the complacency and stability of the Victorian period. They usually debated broad political problems—educational reform, extension of the franchise, the rights of associations and individuals, and international treaties. Controversy was resolved in compromise that could be spelled out in general parliamentary enactments. This was also the case in some other systems where parliamentary democracy developed—Sweden, Holland, Norway and Denmark. In the United States the pendulum swung between "presidential" government, especially in times of crisis, and "congressional" government.

On the continent representative assemblies were often regarded as the instruments of popular rule against the privileged groups. They claimed on behalf of the people the totality of political power, and relegated the executive to the role of an agent. This was notably the case of France, where the legislative assemblies reduced the Cabinet to a subservient role.

Outside of Western Europe, North America, and the British Dominions, representative government in the 19th century was virtually unknown. In the Balkans and Latin America, constitutions and parliamentary institutions were provided on paper, but the practice belied the constitutional forms. Most of these systems were oligarchies where political power, irrespective of the forms, was in the hands of the landowners, the military, or the church. Others were traditional societies, in which political rule was hereditary. They had not experienced the conflicts and modernization, associated with the French Revolution and industrialization, that led to progressive political emancipation of the masses in Europe. Their political systems were encrusted in tradition and immemorial custom.

With the beginning of the 20th century, an important change in the organization and functioning of democratic institutions can be discerned. The internal balance of power between the three organs—executive, legislative, and judicial—began to shift in favor of the executive. This trend reflects profound modifications in the social and political structures of modern societies.

Representative institutions operated well when the pressure upon them to make decisions was light. The free-market system provided an automatic mechanism of decision making. Matters of wages, hours of work, employment, social security, education, technological improvement, investment, and economic development were to remain outside of the province of the state. The increasing complexity of the industrial society called, however, for regulation of economic activity. The need for state intervention grew, and demanded special knowledge and skill. The legislature proved singularly unfit to perform these tasks. The legislature was cumbersome; its members had neither technical knowledge, nor expertise, nor time. Slowly the burden of decision making shifted to the political executive and the civil service.

Political reasons also accounted for this shift. Most significant were the extension of suffrage and the growth of large national parties. The two phenomena are historically associated. Elections became increasingly confrontations between two or more parties appealing to a mass electorate on specific issues or on a general program for action. Thus the legislature was bypassed, since victory at the polls meant that the leadership of the majority party would form a government to carry out its pledges. Wherever party discipline was strong, therefore, popular elections were equivalent to the selection of the "government," i.e., the executive.

Political and technical trends reinforced each other and during the interwar years the executive assumed more and more powers. Representative assemblies have lost virtually all of the functions attributed to them by Walter Bagehot in the 19th century. The vast majority of legislative projects emanate from the executive; the preparation of the budget has become an executive function in which the cabinet, in association with the top civil service or independent executive bodies, drafts the specifications involving public expenditures and revenue. Parliament has even virtually lost the power to nominate the cabinet. Finally, the very scope of lawmaking has changed. Special laws or regulations are needed which can best be made by those in touch with the problems of developed industrial societies—that is to say, by the executive departments and the civil service. Thus the legislature has fallen into the habit of drafting general laws in which regulatory powers are generously delegated to the executive. For all practical purposes such delegation is so broad as to invest the executive and civil service with virtual lawmaking powers.

Legislation has become a major task of the executive and of the various ministerial or interministerial committees. The legislature's function almost everywhere is to say "yes." When there is strict party discipline, the "yes" is given with a monotony reminiscent of the Supreme Soviet. When party support cannot be counted on, other devices to limit the legislature are introduced: its law-making functions are restricted; its power to amend government bills is qualified; the scrutinizing and deliberative functions of its legislative committees are limited; its power to debate issues leading to a vote are curtailed; its ability to censure the government is circumscribed; and the requisite majority to overthrow the cabinet is constitutionally defined to make it difficult for the opposition to coalesce. All these provisions are written into the Constitution of the Fifth Republic. The French National Assembly now deliberates under the shadow of a President whose power would be envied by his American counterpart. The President of the Fifth Republic may dissolve the Assembly and call for a new election; he may declare an emergency and rule by executive decree; and he may call for a referendum on virtually any question of policy, which, if approved, can set aside existing legislation or even existing constitutional provisions.

In West Germany the so-called "constructive" vote of no confidence makes it impossible for the Parliament to overthrow a Chancellor unless those who vote against the incumbent agree on his successor. This has not yet occurred; selection of the Chancellor—from Adenauer to Erhard, Kiesinger to Brandt—has taken place by prior party agreement and consultations rather than parliamentary deliberations and designation.

In modern political systems, then, leadership has shifted to the executive, with the legislature acting mainly as a forum for the airing of grievances. The executive has taken the initiative as regards general lawmaking, foreign and defense policy, and direction of the economy. Assumption of these responsibilities and the concentration of these functions in the executive branch have led to a proliferation of new agencies and bureaus. The political executive has become "bureaucratized." It initiates policy, coordinates policy decisions, and is responsible for their implementation and execution. Institutions have developed within the executive corresponding to these three phases of the policy-making process.

In both presidential and parliamentary systems, a small group of political leaders are in charge of overall policy initiation and formulation. They are the president, or the prime minister, and his immediate advisers. To assist the top leaders in the formulation of policy there are a number of "adjunct" administrative staff organizations. They draft policy papers on economic planning, foreign policy, defense, and the budget. In the United States, the Bureau of the Budget, the National Security Council, and the Council of Economic Advisers perform important deliberative and policy-initiation functions. In Britain and France, cabinet committees are responsible for similar activities. Thus deliberation is institutionalized at the executive level.

Policy proposals put forward by various executive agencies must then be coordinated. Suggestions and countersuggestions are thrashed out in the cabinet, or in small ministerial committees made up of top civil servants, the chiefs of staff, and the personal advisers to the president or prime minister. Reconciliation of conflicting proposals may require the ultimate intervention of the president or prime minister himself. The interdependence of military, economic, and foreign policy has called increasingly for such interdepartmental coordination.

Finally, it is necessary to execute decisions. This is the task of the vast majority of civil servants—to inspect, repair, perform, and check. They do what the employees of any large corporation do—they perform on the basis of orders and regulations decided by their superiors.

THE CIVIL SERVICE

It is one of the characteristics of industrialized societies, irrespective of their form of government, to develop a civil service recruited on the basis of specific technical requirements. "Bureaucratic administration means fundamentally the exercise of control on the basis of knowledge," observed Max Weber. It is above all a rational organization characterized by: (a) a clearly defined sphere of competence subject to impersonal rules: (b) a hierarchy which determines in an orderly fashion relations of superiors and subordinates; (c) a regular system of appointments and promotions on the basis of free contract; (d) recruitment on the basis of skills, knowledge, or technical training; and (e) fixed salaries.

The Prussian civil service was an early example of a professional service with clear-cut demarcation of spheres of competence, rigid rules of recruitment, and allocation of posts on the basis of skills. It reflected the high degree of military organization and centralization of that country. After the unification of Germany the same standards were made applicable to the whole German bureaucracy.

In Great Britain professionalization was introduced officially in 1853 by the Northcote-Trevelyan Report on the "Organization of the Permanent Civil Service," which opened the civil service to talent through competitive examinations. Until then civil service appointments were made on political considerations and were, by and large, restricted to the nobility. The civil service was divided into three "classes," each corresponding to a distinct function: 1) the Administrative Class, which is the highest policy-making group within the departments; 2) the Executive Class, whose main task is the execution of policies; and

3) the Clerical or Manipulative Class, whose work is primarily clerical and manual.

The educational requirements for entrance into the Administrative Class were unique. Until the end of the 19th century, applicants were supposed to have a thorough training in the humanities—Greek, Latin, philosophy, and mathematics. The advantage was thus given to the well-educated university man, as the term was interpreted during the Victorian age, rather than the specialist. Since this kind of education was provided only in the exclusive and expensive "public schools" (which despite their name were privately endowed) civil service applicants came either from the nobility or the wealthy middle classes. It was only after World War I that it became possible to offer specialized subjects in satisfying the entrance requirements. Expansion of scholarships and the growth of provincial universities also gave an opportunity to the lower middle classes, and even the working class, to receive the kind of education that prepared them for the examinations and admission. Nonetheless, the bias in the British recruitment system is still in favor of the "humanist" rather than the "specialist," the upper middle classes rather than the lower.

In France it was only after the Liberation in 1944 that drastic reforms—inspired in large measure by the organization of the civil service in Britain—were made. First, a general entrance examination has been established for all candidates. Previously each department did its own recruiting. The examination stresses law, political science, economics, and social sciences in general. Secondly, the civil service was broadly divided into two classes: (a) civil administrators (approximating the British administrative class) and (b) "secretaries of administration" (corresponding to the executive class). Thirdly, the *Ecole Nationale d'Administration* has been founded to serve as the training school for all prospective civil administrators. Students are considered public officials from the moment they enter, receive a stipend, and after successful completion of their studies and the passing of the final examinations, are assigned to an executive department. Throughout their training, which is jointly offered by civil servants and academicians, an effort is made to depart from the formalistic and legalistic approach so typical of the past and to create a self-reliant and imaginative civil servant.

The American civil service has also been "professionalized," beginning with the Pendleton Act of 1883. Recruitment is by competitive examinations, but the emphasis tends to be on specialized knowledge rather than a broad, liberal education. There is no clear-cut division between an administrative and executive class, in terms of rigidly separate educational requirements and examinations, though of course those who occupy the highest "general classes" within the hierarchy in effect perform the policy-making function. The American civil service thus is not as homogeneous as its European counterparts. American top-level administrators are graduates of universities all over the nation and are drawn from a wider range of social classes. There is also considerable movement of individuals between the civil service and private life (business, universities, and law practice, for example)—which is rare in Europe. The undoubted advantage of the European system is to create a corps of administrators who have demonstrated brilliance in academic studies during their youth, and who have shared common experiences. The result is a remarkable *esprit de corps.* In the United States, on the other hand, it is easier to invigorate the administrative establishment by providing new recruits from private life, and also to make use of talented individuals who may not have distinguished themselves as college undergraduates.

Traditionally "bureaucracy" has been viewed as an instrument of enforcement and execution of the law. Impartial and neutral—at least in theory—it was also remote, incarnating the authority and majesty of the state. It emphasized legality rather than equity, application of rules rather than innovation, continuity rather than change. The civil servant (or "mandarin," as the French called him) remained aloof from everyday affairs, saw more files than citizens, and made decisions of a quasi-judicial character.

But in some respects modern bureaucracy has departed from the Weberian model of a legal-rational organization. The increase in sheer numbers and the expansion of functions produced profound changes. The civil servant became ubiquitous, and as a result, less aloof and remote from the society he governed. By taking on new responsibilities the bureaucrat was transformed from the guardian of the law into a quasi legislator. His powers became increasingly political, and had immediate consequences for those affected by his decisions and for the whole society. The bureaucrat's world was expanded, and he began to view his constituency not as a host of individual plaintiffs who sought redress in accordance with the law, but as groups and interests pressing for decisions affecting the very nature of social relations. He found himself confronted with conflicts among interests that called for political analysis and choice among alternatives. While still clinging to the tradition of statism and neutrality, the bureaucrat and the bureaucracy as a whole became integral parts of the policy-making process.

The civil servant's mentality inevitably changed when he entered the realm of direct action in the world of commerce and industry. The skills required to set regulations for, let us say, credit, are different from those needed to apply laws in individual cases. The man responsible for the use of atomic energy to produce electricity, construction of new cities, settlement of labor disputes, or maintenance of full employment, no longer resembles his 19th-century counterpart. The requisites of bureaucratic decision making are knowledge, expertise, originality, inventiveness, and an ability to gain cooperation and support from the interests involved. The civil servant who participates in the drafting of an economic plan must not only know his job, but must be in touch with the interest groups that are affected by the plan.

Consultation with the organized interests and mutual interpenetration of interests and the civil service has become general. The old bureaucracy based on "imperative coordination" has become a "consultative" bureaucracy making decisions that affect the whole society, thoroughly permeated by the interests it serves. While links have always existed between organized interests and bureaucracy, the open consultative process is a central feature of modern political systems. Interest groups in the past have attempted to colonize, influence, or neutralize the bureaucracy, and usually tried to maintain anonymity while doing so. Now the dialogue is open, the anonymity has been shed, and decisions engage the responsibility of the civil servants who make them. The bureaucracy thus takes on some of the characteristics of political parties in seeking close ties with specific interests (like business or labor) and broad popular support from all consumers and citizens. The "mandarin" has become a manager and a politician, while the spokesmen of interest groups and executives of private corporations are directly involved in the decision-making process. A "new corporatism" seems to be emerging in all modern political systems.

ENFORCEMENT OF RESPONSIBILITY

The executive has become in all contemporary industrialized societies a huge bureaucracy in which millions of people work, performing thousands of interrelated tasks. A small group of persons are ultimately responsible for the policies made and the manner in which they are implemented. They alone have to confront the public in periodic elections and give an account of their activities. They have to answer questions raised in the representative assemblies and reply to criticism. They have the burden of political responsibility—and this applies to authoritarian and democratic systems alike, though the forms of enforcement may differ.

But political responsibility, even where enforced through periodic elections and accountability to legislative assemblies, is not enough. The magnitude and the complexity of modern government are so great that no legislature (not even through its committees) can take full cognizance of them. Legislative control has often proven inadequate for effective supervision of the operations of nationalized industries, the performance of regulatory actions, and many other technical decisions.

The crucial problem facing all democratic systems today is to devise other forms and techniques of executive accountability. One possibility is the development of a sense of "internal responsibility" within the civil service itself. This can be inculcated by education and the development of strict rules of performance and rules of accountability of subordinate to superior. Another technique often suggested is the creation of specialized legislative committees to deal with specific areas of executive activity—nationalized industries, delegated legislation, defense, and the budget. A third one is the establishment of advisory bodies in which the major interests affected by policy decisions may participate. Recently there has been considerable discussion concerning the parliamentary Ombudsman (or Grievance Man) in Scandinavia, and the possibility of transplanting this office in other parts of the world. None of these techniques, however, appear to be fully successful and the truth of the matter is that they cannot be. The notion of "political responsibility" appears to be increasingly anachronistic in an era of massive technological development. The leaders of any modern society—democratic or authoritarian—confront the challenge of implementing common aspirations. Success or failure depends mainly upon the technical competence and skill of the political leadership.

The growth of the executive and its assumption of policy-making functions, the tremendous expansion of public services coupled with the ineffectiveness of political controls over the bureaucracy, pose serious threats to individual freedom. A highly complex bureaucratized apparatus geared to performance is potentially an ever-present danger to the individual, even when it claims to serve his interests. To the old "reason of state" may be added a new, perhaps even more dangerous, "reason of service." Managerialism or *technocratie,* as the French call it, may finish by exalting efficiency, skill, and organization over criticism, freedom, and individualism. It may encourage conformity rather than eccentricity, unity rather than pluralism, action rather than thought, discipline rather than freedom. An astute author writing some 20 years ago predicted that managerialism would be the political form of the future in all contemporary industrialized societies—democratic or not. [1]

The rise of the large bureaucratized state as well as the example of totalitarianism have aroused widespread concern for the protection of individual rights and freedoms. In some post-World War II constitutions, higher courts were given power to scrutinize legislative acts and see to it that the legislative and executive branches remained strictly within the confines of the constitution. In Western Germany, Italy, Austria, and recently in France, constitutional courts were established for this purpose. In both Britain and the United States administrative courts have been created to try cases involving litigation between the state and individuals. "Administrative law," long misunderstood by American and British observers of the French scene, has developed slowly as a guarantee of the rights of individuals in their dealings with the administrative and regulatory agencies of the state.

Other safeguards have also been sought. Federalism, for instance, has as a major purpose internal limitation upon the omnicompetence of the state. Even in unitary states, like Britain and France, efforts have been made to revitalize local governments in order to stimulate experimentation and avert uniformity and rigidity of centralized control.

However, the techniques of judicial review, administrative courts and federalism have not proved capable of bringing central bureaucracies under effective political or legal control. Ordinary courts are even less qualified than legislative committees to evaluate the work of bureaucratic agencies. In the English-speaking countries, the common-law bias of the courts dispose them to favor property rights, which seriously interferes with the government's efforts to solve pressing social and national problems. The American Supreme Court's antipathy to social welfare legislation—up to about 1938—is a striking illustration of this tendency. Administrative courts are of limited utility. Federalism has been evolving, even in the United States, into a unitary system, for all practical

[1] J. Burnham, *The Managerial Revolution* (New York, 1941).

purposes. The problems of modern society are so complex and far ranging that local governments are simply incapable of meeting them. Only the central government has the financial resources, the administrative expertise, and the power to work out effective solutions. Administrative decentralization can reduce the burden somewhat, but is more than counterbalanced by the continual increase in the responsibilities of the central government. The difficulty of protecting the governed by enforcing responsibility of the governors remains a central political problem.

chapter IX

REPRESENTATIVE GOVERNMENT

There has been a shift in all parliamentary systems from "democracy by delegation" to "democracy by consent." That is, the 19th-century idea according to which public opinion, through voluntary associations and political parties, delegated to the government power to carry out specific policies has been gradually abandoned. Democratic government now acts on the basis of overall consent, rather than a clearly defined popular mandate. Initiation and policy making is increasingly in the hands of an elite composed of political leaders, civil servants, top military personnel, and industrial managers.

The threat of manipulation of the public by this elite is ever present. Perhaps the major function of the legislature and the political parties is to present different points of view, to mobilize the public in favor of alternative schemes and policies, thus providing safeguards against the possibility that consent will be manufactured, as in authoritarian systems. In the "new nations" the trend is distinctly in favor of a government by manipulation in which public opinion is created and directed by a small core of political leaders.

Whatever the nature of the regime, there is always a constitution—a written document or a set of traditions, customs, and understandings incorporating the general agreement of a community as to the manner in which it is to be governed. The effectiveness of a constitution depends upon the manner in which it is accepted and implemented, that is, upon its "legitimacy." In some systems the constitution as a written document is so much at variance with political reality and the actual location of political power that it may be considered little more than a literary curiosity. In other political systems the constitution undergoes violent changes primarily because it is not widely accepted by the community. This has been notably the case in France, which in the course of the last generation has had four different constitutional arrangements. Constitutions may also be viewed as ordained role structures. The conditions under which actors perform within the roles defined by the constitution, or depart from them, is a central problem in comparative politics. The Declaration and Bill of

303

Rights of 1689, the American Constitutions of 1781 and 1787, the Swiss Federation of 1848, the Constitution of the Fifth French Republic were more than "superstructures." They had the effect of channeling social and political conflict in new directions, thereby affecting the attitudes of the major social groups themselves.

Among the numerous works on representative government may be mentioned: W. I. Jennings, *Parliament,* 2d ed. (1957); G. Loewenberg, *Parliament in the German Political System* (1967); P. Williams, *The French Parliament* (1968); K. C. Wheare, *Legislatures* (1963); J. C. Wahlke and H. Eulau, eds., *Legislative Behavior* (1959); and R. A. Dahl, ed., *Political Oppositions in Western Democracies* (1966). The growing importance of the political executive is stressed by C. Barnard, *The Functions of the Executive* (1938); L. J. Edinger, ed., *Political Leadership in Industrialized Societies* (1967); and J. Mackintosh, *The British Cabinet* (1962). On constitutions and constitutionalism (that is, responsible government and individual rights), see: C. J. Friedrich, *Constitutional Government and Democracy* (1950) and *Man and His Government* (1963); C. H. McIlwain, *Constitutionalism: Ancient and Modern* (1947); F. D. Wormuth, *The Origins of Modern Constitutionalism* (1949); K. C. Wheare, *Modern Constitutions* (1963); A. Zurcher, ed., *Constitutions and Constitutional Trends Since World War II* (1955); and G. Sartori, "Constitutionalism: A Preliminary Discussion," *American Political Science Review* (December 1962).

22. The Proper Functions of Representative Bodies*

JOHN STUART MILL

The meaning of representative government is, that the whole people, or some numerous portion of them, exercise through deputies periodically elected by themselves the ultimate controlling power, which in every constitution, must reside somewhere. This ultimate power they must possess in all its completeness. They must be masters, whenever they please, of all the operations of government. . . .

But while it is essential to representative government that the practical supremacy in the state should reside in the representatives of the people, it is an open question what actual functions, what precise part in the machinery of government, shall be directly and personally discharged by the representative body. Great varieties in this respect are compatible with the essence of

*From *Representative Government* (1861), chap. V.

representative government, provided the functions are such as secure to the representative body the control of everything in the last resort.

There is a radical distinction between controlling the business of government and actually doing it. The same person or body may be able to control everything, but cannot possibly do everything; and in many cases its control over everything will be more perfect the less it personally attempts to do. The commander of an army could not direct its movements effectually if he himself fought in the ranks, or led an assault. It is the same with bodies of men. Some things cannot be done except by bodies; other things cannot be well done by them. It is one question, therefore, what a popular assembly should control, another what it should itself do. It should, as we have already seen, control all the operations of government. But in order to determine through what channel this general control may most expediently be exercised, and what portion of the business of government the representative assembly should hold in its own hands, it is necessary to consider what kinds of business a numerous body is competent to perform properly. That alone which it can do well it ought to take personally upon itself. With regard to the rest, its proper province is not to do it, but to take means for having it well done by others.

For example, the duty which is considered as belonging more peculiarly than any other to an assembly representative of the people, is that of voting the taxes. Nevertheless, in no country does the representative body undertake, by itself or its delegated officers, to prepare the estimates. Though the supplies can only be voted by the House of Commons, and though the sanction of the House is also required for the appropriation of the revenues to the different items of the public expenditure, it is the maxim and the uniform practice of the Constitution that money can be granted only on the proposition of the Crown. It has, no doubt, been felt, that moderation as to the amount, and care and judgment in the detail of its application, can only be expected when the executive government, through whose hands it is to pass, is made responsible for the plans and calculations on which the disbursements are grounded. Parliament, accordingly, is not expected, nor even permitted, to originate directly either taxation or expenditure. All it is asked for is its consent, and the sole power it possesses is that of refusal.

The principles which are involved and recognized in this constitutional doctrine, if followed as far as they will go, are a guide to the limitation and definition of the general functions of representative assemblies. In the first place, it is admitted in all countries in which the representative system is practically understood, that numerous representative bodies ought not to administer. The maxim is grounded not only on the most essential principles of good government, but on those of the successful conduct of business of any description. No body of men, unless organised and under command, is fit for action, in the proper sense. Even a select board, composed of few members, and these specially conversant with the business to be done, is always an inferior instrument to some one individual who could be found among them, and would be improved in character if that one person were made the chief, and all the others reduced to subordinates. What can be done better by a body than by any individual is deliberation. When it is necessary or important to secure hearing and consideration to many conflicting opinions, a deliberative body is indispensable. Those bodies, therefore, are frequently useful, even for administrative business, but in general only as advisers, such business being, as a rule, better conducted under the responsibility of one. Even a joint-stock company has always in practice, if not in theory, a managing director; its good or bad management depends essentially on some one person's qualifications, and the remaining directors, when of any use, are so by their suggestions to him, or by the power they possess of watching him, and restraining or removing him in case of misconduct. That they are ostensibly equal sharers with him in the management is no advantage, but a considerable set-off against any good which they are capable of doing: it weakens greatly the sense in his own mind, and in those of other people, of that individual responsibility in which he should stand forth personally and undividedly.

But a popular assembly is still less fitted to administer, or to dictate in detail to those who have the charge of administration. Even when honestly meant, the interference is almost always injurious. Every branch of public administration is a skilled business, which has its own peculiar principles and traditional rules, many of them not even known, in any effectual way, except to those who have at some time had a hand in carrying on the business, and none of them likely to be duly appreciated by persons not practically acquainted with the department. I do not mean that the transaction of public business has esoteric mysteries, only to be understood by the initiated. Its principles are all intelligible to any person of good sense, who has in his mind a true picture of the circumstances and conditions to be dealt with: but to have this he must know those circumstances and conditions; and the knowledge does not come by intuition. There are many rules of the greatest importance in every branch of public business (as there are in every private occupation), of which a person fresh to the subject neither knows the reason or even suspects the existence, because they are intended to meet dangers or provide against inconveniences which never entered into his thoughts. I have known public men, ministers, of more than ordinary natural capacity, who on their first introduction to a department of business new to them, have excited the mirth of their inferiors by the air with which they announced as a truth hitherto set at nought, and brought to light by themselves, something which was probably the first thought of everybody who ever looked at the subject, given up as soon as he had got on to a second. It is true that a great statesman is he who knows when to depart from traditions as well as when to adhere to them. But it is a great mistake to suppose that he will do this better for being ignorant of the traditions. No one who does not thoroughly know the modes of action which common experience has sanctioned is capable of judging of the circumstances which require a departure from those ordinary modes of action. The interests dependent on the acts done by a public department, the consequences liable to follow from any particular mode of conducting it, require for weighing and estimating them a kind of knowledge, and of specially exercised judgment, almost as rarely found in those not bred to it, as the capacity to reform the law in those who have not professionally studied it. All these difficulties are sure to be ignored by a representative assembly which attempts to decide on special acts of administration. At its best, it is inexperience sitting in judgment on experience, ignorance on knowledge: ignorance which never suspecting the existence of what it does not know, is equally careless and supercilious, making light of, if not resenting, all pretensions to have a judgment better worth attending to than its own. Thus it is when no interested motives intervene; but when they do, the result is jobbery more unblushing and audacious than the worst corruption which can well take place in a public office under a government of publicity. It is not necessary that the interested bias should extend to the majority of the assembly. In any particular case it is often enough that it affects two or three of their number. Those two or three will have a greater interest in misleading the body, than any other of its members are likely to have in putting it right. The bulk of the assembly may keep their hands clean, but they cannot keep their minds vigilant or their judgments discerning in matters they know nothing about; and an indolent majority, like an indolent individual, belongs to the person who takes most pains with it. The bad measures or bad appointments of a minister may be checked by Parliament; and the interest of ministers in defending, and of rival partisans in attacking, secures a tolerably equal discussion: but *quis custodiet custodes?* who shall check the Parliament? A minister, a head of an office, feels himself under some responsibility. An assembly in such cases feels under no responsibility at all: for when did any member of Parliament lose his seat for the vote he gave on any detail of administration? To a minister, or the head of an office, it is of more importance what will be thought of his proceedings some time hence than what is thought of them at the instant: but an assembly, if the cry of the moment goes with it, however hastily raised or artificially stirred up, thinks itself and is thought by everybody to be completely exculpated however disastrous may be the consequences. Besides, an assembly never personally experiences the inconveniences of its bad measures until they have reached the dimensions of national evils. Minister and administrators see them approaching, and have to bear all the annoyance and trouble of attempting to ward them off.

The proper duty of a representative assembly in regard to matters of administration is not to decide them by its own vote, but to take care that the persons who have to decide them shall be the proper persons. Even this they cannot advantageously do by nominating the individuals. There is no act which more imperatively requires to be performed under a strong sense of individual responsibility than the nomination to employments. The experience of every person conversant with public affairs bears out the assertion, that there is scarcely any act respecting which the conscience of an average man is less sensitive; scarcely any case in which less consideration is paid to qualifications, partly because men do not know, and partly because they do not care for, the difference in qualifications between one person and another. When a minister makes what is meant to be an honest appointment, that is when he does not actually job it for his personal connections or his party, an ignorant person might suppose that he would try to give it to the person best qualified. No such thing. An ordinary minister thinks himself a miracle of virtue if he gives it to a person of merit, or who has a claim on the public on any account, though the claim or the merit may be of the most opposite description to that required. . . . Besides, the qualifications which fit special individuals for special duties can only be recognized by those who know the individuals, or who make it their business to examine and judge of persons from what they have done, or from the evidence of those who are in a position to judge. When these conscientious obligations are so little regarded by great public officers who can be made responsible for their appointments, how must it be with assemblies who cannot? Even now, the worst appointments are those which are made for the sake of gaining support or disarming opposition in the representative body: what might we expect if they were made by the body itself? Numerous bodies never regard special qualifications at all. Unless a man is fit for the gallows, he is thought to be about as fit as other people for almost anything for which he can offer himself as a candidate. When appointments made by a public body are not decided, as they almost always are, by party connection or private jobbing, a man is appointed either because he has a reputation, often quite undeserved, for *general* ability, or frequently for no better reason than that he is personally popular.

It has never been thought desirable that Parliament should itself nominate even the members of a Cabinet. It is enough that it virtually decides who shall be prime minister, or who shall be the two or three individuals from whom the prime minister shall be chosen. In doing this it merely recognises the fact that a certain person is the candidate of the party whose general policy commands its support. In reality, the only thing which Parliament decides is, which of two, or at most three, parties or bodies of men, shall furnish the executive government: the opinion of the party itself decides which of its members is fittest to be placed at the head. According to the existing practice of the British Constitution, these things seem to be on as good a footing as they can be. Parliament does not nominate any minister, but the Crown appoints the head of the administration in conformity to the general wishes and inclinations manifested by Parliament, and the other ministers on the recommendation of the chief; while every minister has the undivided moral responsibility of appointing fit persons to the other offices of administration which are not permanent. In a republic, some other arrangement would be necessary: but the nearer it approached in practice to that which has long existed in England, the more likely it would be to work well. Either, as in the American republic, the head of the Executive must be elected by some agency entirely independent of the representative body; or the body must content itself with naming the prime minister, and making him responsible for the choice of his associates and subordinates. To all these considerations, at least theoretically, I fully anticipate a general assent: though, practically, the tendency is strong in representative bodies to interfere more and more in the details of administration, by virtue of the general law, that whoever has the strongest power is more and more tempted to make an excessive use of it; and this is one of the practical dangers to which the futurity of representative governments will be exposed.

But it is equally true, though only of late and slowly beginning to be acknowledged, that a numerous assembly is as little fitted for the direct business of legislation as for that of administration. There is hardly any kind of intellectual work which so much needs to be done, not only by experienced and exercised minds, but by minds trained to the task through long and laborious study, as the business of making laws. This is a sufficient reason, were there no other, why they can never be well made but by a committee of very few persons. A reason no less conclusive is, that every provision of a law requires to be framed with the most accurate and long-sighted perception of its effect on all the other provisions; and the law when made should be capable of fitting into a consistent whole with the previously existing laws. It is impossible that these conditions should be in any degree fulfilled when laws are voted clause by clause in a miscellaneous assembly. The incongruity of such a mode of legislating would strike all minds, were it not that our laws are already, as to form and construction, such a chaos, that the confusion and contradiction seem incapable of being made greater by any addition to the mass. Yet even now, the utter unfitness of our legislative machinery for its purpose is making itself practically felt every year more and more. The mere time necessarily occupied in getting through Bills renders Parliament more and more incapable of passing any, except on detached and narrow points. If a Bill is prepared which even attempts to deal with the whole of any subject (and it is impossible to legislate properly on any part without having the whole present to the mind), it hangs over from session to session through sheer impossibility of finding time to dispose of it. It matters not though the Bill may have been deliberately drawn up by the authority deemed the best qualified, with all appliances and means to boot; or by a select commission, chosen for their conversancy with the subject, and having employed years in considering and digesting the particular measure; it cannot be passed, because the House of Commons will not forego the precious privilege of tinkering it with their clumsy hands. . . . It is one of the evils of the present mode of managing these things that the explaining and defending of a Bill, and of its various provisions, is scarcely ever performed by the person from whose mind they emanated, who probably has not a seat in the House. Their defense rests upon scme minister or member of Parliament who did not frame them, who is dependent on cramming for all his arguments but those which are perfectly obvious, who does not know the full strength of his case, nor the best reasons by which to support it, and is wholly incapable of meeting unforeseen objections. This evil, as far as Government bills are concerned, admits of remedy, and has been remedied in some representative constitutions, by allowing the Government to be represented in either House by persons in its confidence, having a right to speak, though not to vote. . . .

Instead of the function of governing, for which it is radically unfit, the proper office of a representative assembly is to watch and control the government: to throw the light of publicity on its acts: to compel a full exposition and justification of all of them which any one considers questionable; to censure them if found condemnable, and, if the men who compose the government abuse their trust, or fulfil it in a manner which conflicts with the deliberate sense of the nation, to expel them from office, and either expressly or virtually appoint their successors. This is surely ample power, and security enough for the liberty of the nation. In addition to this, the Parliament has an office, not inferior even to this in importance; to be at once the nation's Committee of Grievances, and its Congress of Opinions; an arena in which not only the general opinion of the nation, but that of every section of it, and as far as possible of every eminent individual whom it contains, can produce itself in full light and challenge discussion; where every person in the country may count upon finding somebody who speaks his mind, as well or better than he could speak it himself— not to friends and partisans exclusively, but in the face of opponents, to be tested by adverse controversy; where those whose opinion is overruled, feel satisfied that it is heard, and set aside not by a mere act of will, but for what are thought superior reasons, and commend themselves as such to the representatives of the majority of the nation; where every party or opinion in the country can muster its strength, and be cured of any illusion concerning the number or power of its adherents; where the opinion which prevails in the nation makes itself manifest as prevailing, and marshals its hosts in the presence of the government, which is thus enabled and compelled to give way to it on the mere manifestation, without the actual employment, of its strength; where statesmen can assure themselves, far more certainly than by any other signs, what elements of opinion and power are growing, and what declining, and are enabled to shape their measures with some regard not solely to present exigencies, but to tendencies in progress. Representative assemblies are often taunted by their enemies with being places of mere talk and *bavardage.* There has seldom been more misplaced derision. I know not how a representative assembly can more usefully employ itself than in talk, when the subject of talk is the great public interests of the country, and every sentence of it represents the opinion either of some important body of persons in the nation, or of an individual in whom some such body have reposed their confidence. A place where interest and shade of opinion in the country can have its cause even passionately pleaded, in the face of the government and of all other interests and opinions, can compel them to listen, and either comply, or state clearly why they do not, is in itself, if it answered no other purpose, one of the most important political institutions that can exist anywhere, and one of the foremost benefits of free government. Such "talking" would never be looked upon with disparagement if it were not allowed to stop "doing"; which it never would, if assemblies knew and acknowledged that talking and discussion are their proper business, while *doing,* as the result of discussion, is the task not of a miscellaneous body, but of individuals specially trained to it; that the fit office of an assembly is to see that those individuals are honestly and intelligently chosen, and to interfere no further with them, except by unlimited latitude of suggestion and criticism, and by applying or withholding the final seal of national assent. It is for want of this judicious reserve that popular assemblies attempt to do what they cannot do well—to govern and legislate—and provide no machinery but their own for much of it, when of course every hour spent in talk is an hour withdrawn from actual business. But the very fact which most unfits such bodies for a Council of Legislation qualifies them the more for their other office—namely, that they are not a selection of the greatest political minds in the country, from whose opinions little could with certainty be inferred concerning those of the nation, but are, when properly constituted, a fair sample of every grade of intellect among the people which is at all entitled to a voice in public affairs. Their part is to indicate wants, to be an organ for popular demands, and a place of adverse discussion for all opinions relating to public matters, both great and small; and, along with this, to check by criticism, and eventually by withdrawing their support, those high public officers who really conduct the public business, or who appoint those by whom it is conducted. Nothing but the restriction of the function of representative bodies within these rational limits will enable the benefits of popular control to be enjoyed in conjunction with the no less important requisites (growing ever more important as human affairs increase in scale and in complexity) of skilled legislation and administration. There are no means of combining these benefits except by separating the functions which guarantee the one from those which essentially require the other; by disjoining the office of control and criticism from the actual conduct of affairs, and devolving the former on the representatives of the Many, while securing for the latter, under strict responsibility to the nation, the acquired knowledge and practised intelligence of a specially trained and experienced Few.

23. The Crisis of Modern Parliaments*

KARL DIETRICH BRACHER

THE DILEMMA

The phrase "crisis of parliamentarism" is nearly as old as the phenomenon of modern parliamentary democracy. It is closely bound up with the deeply rooted social and intellectual transformations in which the process of emancipation—first with a liberal, then with a socialistic stamp—broke the framework of constitutional government based on privileged estates, and in which the principle of

*From "Problems of Parliamentary Democracy in Europe," *Daedalus* (Winter 1964), pp. 179–98. Reprinted by permission of the American Academy of Arts and Sciences, the editor of *Daedalus,* and the author.

full representation and participation of all citizens in a parliament chosen in a general and equal election was carried out. This development reached its critical peak after World War I. For the concept of parliamentary democracy the moment of apparently complete victory over the autocracies of old Europe signified at the same time the beginning of a structural crisis which particularly affected the newly created parliamentary democracies of Europe and which aided the strongly antiparliamentary dictatorial movements toward a quick rise.

With the exception of Czechoslovakia and Finland this crisis quickly displaced and destroyed all new parliamentary democracies: in Russia and the Baltic states; in Poland, Hungary and the Balkan countries; in Italy, Germany and Austria; in Spain and Portugal. Everywhere in this area the parliamentary system seemed to prove itself unworkable; almost nowhere did it seem capable of absorbing the political and social tensions of the "age of the masses" in a democratic order that was both stable and flexible. The transition from the old liberal parliamentarianism of well-to-do individuals (*Honoratiorenstaat*) to egalitarian party-state parliamentarianism led to serious functional disturbances even in the tradition-bound older democracies of Europe. In England, to be sure, it was possible to absorb the effects of these disturbances by thorough-going changes in the system of parliamentary rule; in France the Third Republic was able to sustain itself, but only with difficulty. Even in the Scandinavian countries, spared by the World War and apparently sheltered against the European crises, minority governments were often only provisionally able to contain the tensions; even they scarcely provided a proof of the workability of the parliamentary system.

The second postwar epoch of the European parliamentary democracies is of course significantly different from this first crisis period, which ended in the catastrophe of another world war. On the one hand it was still confronted with those basic problems of democratic structural change which the nineteenth century had laid in the cradle of European parliamentarianism. But on the other hand conditions had deeply changed, giving a new profile to the attempts at reconstruction or new construction of parliamentarianism in western Europe after 1945. On three levels these new perspectives were opened.

1. *Constitutional:* The experience of the twenties and thirties directed attention to possible precautionary measures and modifications in the parliamentary system for the protection of its substance and its efficiency. The West German "chancellor democracy" and even more the half-parliamentary presidential regime of the Fifth Republic in France are examples of this attempt at a limitation of parliamentarianism.

2. *Sociological:* At the same time the process of realignment and leveling of society—the product of the radical changes of the war and postwar period, a tendency away from ideologizing and toward pragmatizing of the parties— fostered the concentration of parties and finally the approach to a two- or three-party system, which was strengthened and hastened by constitutional and technical electoral provisions. West Germany was the most strongly affected by this process, in the course of the immigration and absorption of well over ten

million displaced persons. But the tendency characterized much too simply as "Americanization" of party and parliamentary life was strong in the rest of Europe as well. This development seemed to simplify the formation of an administration and an opposition, to clarify political alternatives and to allow the parliamentary process to become less hindered by the formation of ideological fronts.

3. *Foreign Affairs:* The decisive phase of European political change at the end of the forties was marked by an increasingly firm opposition to the dynamics of Soviet Russia's European politics. The American politics of restraint, the Marshall Plan, the establishment of NATO placed western Europe within the framework of a broader international cooperation. It opened aspects of a supranational integration which could have an incomparably more lasting effect on the internal politics and structure of the European states than the League of Nations had once had. The idea and the weight of a European and Atlantic community formed, first of all, a kind of protection for the new parliamentary democracies; insofar as they were still limited by powerful groups hostile to democracy—as in the case of France and Italy with their strong Communist parties—the growing interdependence meant a supplementary support.

The starting conditions for the "new Europe" thus seemed more favorable than in 1918. The attempt at a self-limitation of sovereignties had taken the place of a confusion of national ambitions, which at that time had made the rise and triumph of nationalistic dictatorial movements possible. The East-West conflict seemed to outweigh the internal explosive forces of national parliamentarianism. In the foreground stood the overlapping problems of political cooperation, economic and military networks, and the overcoming of the colonial age. In the face of such problems intrastate tensions tended to diminish in sharpness and importance or at least to recede to a deeper level of confrontations more specific and more suited to compromise. Such a prognosis seemed especially plausible from the German point of view. Had not Germany immediately after the occupation joined, as the Federal Republic, the European and Atlantic politics of alliance, within whose frame the West German parliament system could develop and stabilize itself almost without hindrance? Indeed, the experience of a parliamentary democracy operating with political and economic success was something entirely new in the history of German political thought, which had learned from the catastrophes of 1848, 1918 and 1933 to identify parliamentary politics with crisis and collapse.

But these positive perspectives reflect only the external, superficial image of the reconstruction period. They say nothing about the real stability and functional capability of the reconstituted parliamentary democracies of western Europe. Upon closer inspection it has quickly become apparent not only that the old problems of parliamentary politics continued to exist unsolved under the double protection mentioned, but also that the new conditions of the postwar period, with their revolutionizing consequences in the economic, social and intellectual areas, necessarily led to new crises of adjustment in the political system. It became a question whether and how, in the light of the changes cited, the individual parliaments would be able to carry out their role—which was still conceived in the classical sense of control and "decision-making"—in the actual practice of national politics. The increasingly complicated network of the modern industrial state confronted them with a dismaying array of new problems for which political common sense and the old parliamentary practice no longer seemed adequate. These problems threatened to undermine the competence and decision-making ability of the individual member of parliament, to strengthen at the cost of parliament the power of committees, experts and the bureaucracy of the executives and to lead toward an undermining of the parliamentary system of government from within.

As a result a series of surprisingly similar basic questions came to the fore in all of the western democracies. Is a parliament as such still capable, under such circumstances, of exercising an effective control of politics, not even to mention active participation in the formulation of political desires? Further, is it possible any longer to defend the submission of complicated economic, social and military decisions, which demand precise planning, to the tedious discussion procedure of technically incompetent large assemblies, considering that the deliberations of a small circle of committee experts are simply repeated in these sessions? And under these circumstances is it at all possible to continue upholding the classical basic principle of parliamentarianism—to combine democratic representation and the correct decision of all questions—or does not the parliamentary process become reduced to a formality in the face of the incompetence of the mass of the representatives?

A further consideration derives from the fact that precisely the supra- and international network of those technical decisions transcends the capacities of the national parliaments and at the same time must impose sensitive limitations upon them. The development of European institutions has demonstrated in recent years what a great effect this consideration has had in shifting politics from the parliamentary level to that of administration and bureaucracy. A European bureaucracy of a new character has gained a decisive advance upon the parliamentary organs in those institutions; the supernational formation of politics has been shifted extensively to an extra- or superparliamentary area of competence handled by experts and governments; in the face of this power the merely advisory function of the European "parliaments," which moreover have possessed only a derivative legitimation, not a direct one through direct European elections, has had little effect.

In view of these problems our diagnosis of parliamentarianism in western Europe will consider the following elements. We shall inquire about the model, the reality and the structural transformation of "classical" parliamentarianism, which has also been the point of departure for the parliamentary democracies of postwar Europe. We shall analyze the most important factors and arguments that form the basis of this structural change. What are their consequences: the transformation or the decline of parliamentary politics? Last, we shall endeavor to ascertain what efforts toward reform, substitute forms and future perspectives can be recognized within the national and supranational framework. Although the examination will proceed from Germany to the particular conditions of the various countries, attention will be devoted principally to the typical instances of those problems which today more than ever bear a general European character, both in positive and in negative regards.

STRUCTURAL TRANSFORMATION OF DEMOCRACY

The "crisis of parliamentarianism" figured, immediately following World War I, as the central theme of countless conferences of the Interparliamentary Union—in Washington, Ottawa, Geneva, Paris, Prague and Berlin. The discussion probed deeply into essentials. It dealt with the actual and necessary adjustment to the new European situation; it vacillated between a modernization or a limitation of parliamentarianism. At the same time it became increasingly clear that parliamentarianism had undergone an actual structural transformation which also needed to be put into effect constitutionally and institutionally.

Indeed the language of the constitutions and of their interpreters—insofar as it referred to the original model of the "classical" parliamentarianism, developed according to the idealistically elevated English pattern—was so far from reality that it appeared to be more and more fictitious. Whereas constitutional theory held to the concept of the independent member of parliament, responsible only to his conscience, in reality the representative found himself to be working within a network of social and political ties, a network which had become increasingly dense with the complication of modern industrial society and with the organizational consolidation and increase in importance of parties and organized interest groups. The result was that the member of parliament, contrary to the postulates of the constitutions, was subjected increasingly, whether consciously or unconsciously, to an "imperative mandate" by party interests and other joint interests. His role as representative of the people as a whole had thereby become unreal. The classical-liberal form of representative parliamentarianism gave way to a parliamentary democracy determined by plebiscite and party politics, a democracy which also brought about far-reaching changes in the process of forming political opinion and the function of the parliament as an organ for decision and control.

The interrelationship of this "structural transformation of democracy" (Leibholz) with modern party history has meanwhile been thoroughly analyzed. After World War II some of the European constitutions tried to give the new reality its due—though only in a makeshift way and rather incidentally—by dedicating a few articles to the role of the parties and their structure. Probably the most prominent instance of this was in the Basic Law of the Federal Republic of Germany, the West German constitution of 1949, in which (contrary to the Weimar Constitution) not only is the participation of the parties in determination of political policy emphasized, but their democratic structure and their agreement with the ordinances of the constitution are also specifically required. To be sure the old postulate of representative democracy was also preserved. The deputies are considered the "representatives of the people as a whole, not bound to specific commissions and directions, and subject only to their consciences" (Art. 38); thus they are supposed to be free of the "imperative mandate" to which they are in fact so thoroughly bound by the manner of nomination of candidates, electoral modes, parliamentary practice and party coercion.

The whole tension between theory and practice continues in these introverse stipulations. In other European countries the situation appears to be scarcely any different. In the merely laconic, usually meaningless reference to the parties there still prevails that "conspiracy of silence" (Loewenstein) with which the constitutions hold to the fiction of partyless parliamentarianism and the super-party parliament member. This is true of the Italian constitution (Art. 49) as well as of the French constitutions of the Fourth and Fifth Republics, even though the beginnings of a transformation are visible and in the practice of constitutional interpretation there is a growing attempt to give the political reality of party democracy its due. It is expected that this reality will be taken into account still more thoroughly by the new Swedish constitution, which has been in preparation for years with the authoritative participation of political science.

There is, however, a further aspect of that structural change which, although so far it has enjoyed less attention, has a more fundamental, comprehensive significance than the constitutional-political reform of the relationship between party, parliament and government. This is the expansion of the organized interest groups on the one hand and of public administration on the other hand. The consequence of both is that "unpolitical" experts and superparty planning confront the parliament's claim to power of decision and control with an increasing claim to primacy, attempting to undermine or even displace the parliament. The reasons for this development are as various as they are obvious. They lie in the need for continually improved, rational organization and planning in a complex, highly differentiated, sensitive society which can no more afford mere improvisation and dilettantism than can modern economics and industry.

But at the end of this development, which opposes to the political process of parliamentary democracy the greater effectiveness of the "unpolitical" experts, the objectively planning and rationally functioning, specialized bureaucracy in state and society, there appears the frightful image of a mere technocracy, a rule by the managers and functionaries, which would evade control and the entire realm of democratic-parliamentary decision-making. Thereby the balance of power would be seriously disturbed and a new form of dictatorship would be coldly brought into being. It is this opposition between highly specialized expertise and the principle of democratic participation that appears as the central structural problem of all western parliamentary democracies. To be sure this dilemma is also by no means new, however sharply it confronts us today on all sides.

Bureaucratization and specialization, no less than liberal and social emancipation movements, accompanied the development of parliamentary democracy at an early stage and continue to do so to an increasing degree. They have governed its forms and at the same time complicated them. The development of the apparatus of government has meant more than an expansion of its political functions. It has fostered the rise of the modern professional bureaucracy, which especially in nineteenth-century Germany was most closely tied to the continuation of absolutistic and authoritarian-official (*obrigkeitsstaatliche*) elements in the structure of state and society. This became especially apparent after the establishment of the Weimar Republic, which tried, with the army and the state bureaucracy, to incorporate the great, allegedly indispensable supports of political continuity into the new order of parliamentary democracy—an attempt which is known to have been a huge failure. The collapse of the first German democracy was to a considerable degree a result of the unsolved tension between parliamentary and bureaucratic-authoritarian elements of structure; this tension was already prepared for in the dualism of the Weimar Constitution; it finally ended with the victory of a bureaucratic presidial dictatorship and its pseudo-democratic manipulation and subjugation by Hitler.

To be sure, the cause for this was not simply a faulty construction of the constitution. Rather, the problems of the first German republic showed how unavoidable was a clarification of the relation between the conflicting elements. Max Weber had already recognized at the end of World War I the tendency toward bureaucratization and expertise in the leadership of the state as a dominating sign of the age; according to him there remained only the choice between bureaucratization and dilettantizing. Later Karl Mannheim saw our "period of social change" to be essentially determined by the fact that great "strains" arose "out of the contiguity of the principle of competition and the principle of regulation and planning," strains which could be solved only by a system of "planning for freedom."

This problem certainly did not apply exclusively to the democracies. The authoritarian and totalitarian regimes were also unable to solve the strain, even after eliminating the parliaments; it continued to exist almost undiminished in the dualism of state and party, especially visible in the "Third Reich." And finally it became apparent in postwar France and Germany how great an importance is possessed by the continuity and the growing weight of the elite of experts in organized interest groups or unions and in state bureaucracy as opposed to the politically-parliamentary dynamics. Only recently it was once more pointed out, by Maurice Duverger, that the bureaucracy of experts in France plays a stabilizing role that alone makes government possible. The Fifth Republic deduces from this fact the consequence—albeit a disputed one—of a restriction of parliament, which ultimately aims at a *gouvernement de législature* in which the parliamentary and the presidial systems would be merged. This, however, could be the end of real parliamentarianism and the victory of rule by executive mandate with a plebiscitary façade.

In West Germany, which with controversial arguments held to the continuity of the political apparatus beyond the period 1933–1945, the development proceeded somewhat differently. Here the "chancellor democracy" commanded a continually growing governing and steering apparatus whose complication and indispensability in the modern bureaucratic state works against a change of government. Now that it has outlasted several parliamentary periods this apparatus is far superior in technical knowledge to the parliamentary agencies of power, which in the Bonn system are curtailed anyway. In addition there is the fourteen-year duration of the political constellation, which is modified only by the federalistic structure. Here the danger of instability of the government is averted at the cost of disempowering the parliament, whose capability for control becomes inferior to the claim to expert knowledge and the stability of the political apparatus. The head of the government himself was able, thanks to his constitutionally assured position and to the special authority of Adenauer as Chancellor and party head, to extend the executive power far into the parliament, which then converts his will into laws prepared for him by the government bureaucracy.

In both cases, even though by different courses, the consequence of the unsolved strain is a tendency toward authoritative remodeling of parliamentary democracy. Of course in both cases the concrete form owes much to a personal element. It may not outlast de Gaulle and Adenauer. But the development itself would scarcely be thinkable without the factual and structural problems which lie at the basis of the crisis of parliamentarianism in the industrial and mass state of the twentieth century.

BETWEEN CRISIS AND REFORM

In the following survey we shall try therefore to summarize the most important points of view and arguments which characterize the critical discussion of parliamentarianism in Europe.

In the representative system the direct contact with the will of the people is lost, since in the large modern state the parties of rank have become mass parties, and elections based on personality have become impersonal, machine elections. One consequence is the stronger demand for plebiscitary arrangements, which correspond to a more general tendency toward "supraparty" ties. Just recently de Gaulle, who set the Fifth Republic on this course, criticized the lack of such arrangements in the Bonn democracy. All the recent experiences indicate, however, that they are feasible only in the smaller framework of a direct democracy (such as Switzerland still is), if the danger of uninformed demagogy or even of a new autocracy is to be avoided.

The prestige of the members of parliament has fallen precipitously since they no longer have to resist an autocratic principality and are enjoying a career that is almost without risks. To the public they seem to be dispensable: a constitutional state and a functioning government are already insured by good organization and efficient development of the political apparatus.

The organization of parliamentarianism, originally created for political problems, is not suited to deal with the penetration of economic and social problems into the concerns of government. Lawmaking has extended its boundaries considerably. It embraces almost all areas of social existence and it makes too great demands on the abilities of the members of parliament, both technically and temporally. The results are extended periods of session and necessary specialization. The participating citizen is replaced by the professional politician, who himself becomes a bureaucrat, a functionary, without having the experience and the specialized training of the state official.

Thus the continual broadening of functions of the state threatens traditional parliamentarianism, which is thereby alienated from its real function and fragmented in its effectiveness. On the other hand, a limitation of the extent of parliamentary control, especially in the economic area, has proved fatal, the more complicated the economic and social organism of the modern state has become and the more it has called for coordination and planning. But one is confronted with the facts that the state is seldom a capable entrepreneur and that the parliament is not a good organ of control for economic undertakings, especially since in this case it will transfer its prerogatives to a great extent back to the political bureaucracy. A system of decentralization scarcely offers the satisfying solution either. Federalism can of course unburden parliamentarianism, given the appropriate historical premises (as in Germany or Switzerland) by disseminating responsibility and control more broadly. But thereby coordination and planning become more difficult and complicated.

As the expansion of the state places too great demands on the abilities of the members of parliament, it at the same time lowers their position and the importance of their activity. An elected representative cannot, by the nature of the thing, be equal to the many-sided detailed problems with which society and bureaucracy confront him. The fact that he has to make pronouncements and decisions and exercise control in these matters, as if he were an expert, contributes to the lessening of the prestige of parliamentarianism in the eyes of the public and makes the member of parliament himself vulnerable, insecure and resigned in the face of the real or alleged specialists inside and outside of the political institutions. It also does not help to make his activity more attractive to the really suitable persons. At the same time that technical and political competence is concentrated in a minority within the parliamentary parties, the representative becomes dependent on an apparatus of reporters and specialists, and parliamentary debate is reduced to a mock struggle in the foreground behind which work those anonymous and nonresponsible apparatuses upon which the member of parliament is dependent to a great extent in technical matters.

The consequence is not only a weakening of the parliamentary debates but also the loss of substance and interest which has become characteristic for the greater part of parliamentary activity, with the exception of the few debates over matters of principle; this is also especially true of that domain particularly proper to parliament, which has become so complicated—household politics. The attendance in the parliament chamber is often meager; the parties function as mere voting machines; their activity seems to the critical public to be an expensive waste and complication; derogatory remarks against the conduct of parliament, whether they come from the government and the bureaucracy or from the interest groups, fall upon fruitful ground; finally, the institution itself is no longer taken seriously and it is overridden wherever possible and led into error. Overtaxed in its assignments, the parliament limits itself to topics that have an effect on the elections and abandons important decisions in practice to the planning and formulating bureaucracy. Thus their roles are often exactly reversed. Lawgiving is transferred to the apparatus of administration and parliament loses its authority to a quasi-dictatorship of the executives. Finally the will of the experts triumphs over the parliamentary art of submitting technical decisions to political decision and control; the decisions have already been made.

The structural transformation into the party state has sharpened these problems still more. The advance determination of decisions in the party committees so extensively binds the parliamentary member, whose parliamentary existence rests upon the party's favor, that even without express party coercion his parliamentary flexibility is extremely limited. Discussion, the basic element of democracy, no longer takes place chiefly on the parliamentary level but in the pre-parliamentary area of party politics, and largely to the exclusion of the public. Parliamentary decisions are prefabricated there and become a mere matter of form, since the voices are previously counted; the minority, that is usually the opposition, is left with mere resignation—until the next election—or with increasing anger, which can become intensified to enmity toward the regime itself, to a revolutionary mood. Old and new attempts to put an end to this development—for instance by prohibiting the "imperative mandate"—are of course condemned to failure. But the consequences can be lessened, above all under two conditions: by the loosening effect of decentralization and federalism and by greater flexibility and elasticity of the parties themselves if they are no longer strictly bound to certain classes and programs and if there is a continuation of the process of leveling and pragmatization, which is so characteristic for the postwar development, especially that of Germany. On the other hand, here as in Italy and other countries the phenomenon of the "Christian party" has been thwarting this process and has added a new chapter to the European history of the (ideological) "Weltanschauung" parties.

The selection and education of the members of parliament is not holding pace with the complication of political tasks. Even the process of selecting the candidates seems inadequate from this point of view. The central dilemma of modern parliamentarianism becomes apparent here. A strong influence of the central party leadership is the only guarantee for the nomination of objectively suited, specialized candidates for parliamentary and party work; but this method endangers precisely that immediate contact with the constituency which seems to be possible only by way of local electoral committees, through a decentralized party organization. The technical question of the electoral system is secondary to this. The point of view of the continental backers of the majority election, in so passionately supporting the reform of parliamentarianism by a "personality election," is still oriented to the older model of parliamentarianism. However, empirical observations in England have confirmed that with the change from prestige democracy to party democracy, the elections have also changed from personality elections to party elections regardless of the electoral system.

It is felt especially urgent, therefore, that the representatives to parliament be better informed and equipped. An advance technical examination of the candidates, such as has been called for again and again, can be neither politically justified nor technically realized; it seems impossible to set up suitable standards. On the other hand, an expansion of the apparatus for information and assistance is under way everywhere. Assistants, experts, forces of aid of all sorts are to see to it that the balance of power between the government apparatus and the parliament, which is supposed to control the government apparatus, does not become too unequal in the conduct of affairs. But precisely this may give rise to another problem. A second big apparatus is created which is scarcely less subject to the tendencies of bureaucratization than is the government apparatus. Such a bureaucratization of parliamentarianism once more calls up, only on a different level, the old danger that the member of parliament is overridden by or becomes dependent upon extraparliamentary, nonresponsible experts. The collaboration of government officials, experts and members of parliament in committees of experts does increase the possibilities for objective information and controls, but it also considerably complicates the course of government and committee activity and in addition confuses the executive and legislative competences. One way out is the formation of commissions of experts in the government, as they are used in England with some success; thereby the technical knowledge of the organized interest groups is drawn especially into economic and social planning. But that does not essentially foster either a solution of the control problem or the reactivation of parliamentarianism as a whole; it only shifts, and probably sharpens, the tendencies to "expertocracy."

In all of this it is the ponderousness of the parliamentary system that is especially exposed to criticism. The first principle of modern government and economy, the principle of rationality and effectiveness, is apparently contradicted by the existence and practice of the parliaments so strikingly that the critics question not only their ability to function but also their justification for existence. Important decisions—as in Germany a new penal law, the social reform or the party law expressly required in the constitution—and also a plethora of detailed tasks are often postponed over several periods of sessions or remain entirely unsettled. For the greater part of the representatives the sessions mean up to 90 per cent idle time; for the public they mean a waste of valuable working power. This too scares many a qualified person away from the parliamentary career. Therefore recommendations have been put forward again and again for the technical rationalization of parliamentary procedure, which is still in the state it was in the eighteenth and nineteenth centuries. For example, time-wasting sessions might well be curtailed by the exchange of opinion and voting in writing or by telephone, extensive use of electric brains and other methods. But there are still narrow limits set to the simplification and shortening of the procedure. It is precisely the nature of the parliamentary system, as distinct from and contrary to bureaucratic procedure, to achieve a more comprehensive basis and sharper control of political decision through more extensive proceedings.

The idea of a second chamber of experts to bridge the gap between expert knowledge and political power has been playing a significant role right up to the present. Made up on the basis of technical suitability and professional grouping from the various provinces of economic and social life, such a "parliament of experts" could contribute as an auxiliary organ of the parliament and government to the objectification of the political process. To be sure, it has proved an insolvable difficulty to decide in what way and according to what key such an institution could be recruited. All previous attempts have also either run aground in useless technical discussions, as in the economic council of the Weimar Republic, or have been misused for the purpose of deposing the parliamentary system by authoritarian regimes, as in Mussolini's *stato corporativo* and similar institutions in Greece, Poland, Austria and Portugal in the thirties. In France since 1945 and especially in the Fifth Republic the idea of an economic council has been institutionalized; but this coincides again with a threat to parliamentary democracy.

Theoretically the auxiliary function of such an agency, which makes it possible to incorporate technical-economic expertise into the political process, should be hailed as a support of parliamentarianism. But the practical realization of it appears to be incomparably more difficult than the formation of commissions and councils, which according to the English example of the royal commissions and committees would have to bridge expert knowledge and politics and simultaneously curb and channel the pressure of interest groups. A chamber of professionals and experts seems to be not only historically discredited but also a danger in the present. The interest groups' influence on politics, which is already almost too strong, would have in such a chamber an additional vehicle and instrument. Therefore as a guarantor of objectivity it would be scarcely better qualified—indeed, its members would be still more subjectively tied to particular interests than the members of parliament, who have to represent various interests at once and therefore are more predestined for a comprehensive manner of making decisions. The primacy of politics is also indispensable in all matters of technical decision.

An especially weighty argument of the critics is finally the lack of stability of parliamentary governments. This was especially true of the unbridled parliamentarianism of the period between the wars. The twenty-one administrations in the fourteen years of the Weimar Republic were a frightening example. Even after World War II the French Fourth Republic exhausted twenty-five administrations in the space of thirteen years. It is true that the rapid change of cabinets was mitigated by the fact that often there were only minor shifts in the personnel component. But without a doubt, not only the total triumph of Hitler (and the assent of broad circles in Germany) but also the more moderate victory of de Gaulle over parliamentary democracy are to be ascribed in no small way to discontent about the discontinuity of parliamentary state politics. This discontinuity has been particularly consequential in periods of economic and political crises, which have needed the more far-sighted objective planning and persistent execution of a course of consolidation to a greater extent. Parliamentarianism appears to be not only a particularly cumbersome but also an unreliable form of government which, because it is entirely bound up with the transitory present, is incapable of demanding unpopular sacrifices for more far-reaching politics from a short-sighted "will of the people."

Thus the tendency of European democracy is toward a modification of the parliamentary system of government. Its particular goal is to lengthen the duration of periods of government and to render more difficult the overthrow of cabinets and the dissolution of parliaments. This of course has always implied the danger of lessening or even blocking political dynamics, the flexibility and capability for decision of the political forces. The rigidifying chancellor democracy of Adenauer and the pseudo-presidential regime of de Gaulle are examples of this problem, which can result in the undermining and displacement of a lively parliamentarianism rather than in reform. There are various forms of this modification. The Fifth Republic has established a dualistic system, which runs on two tracks by placing representative and plebiscitary execution of the popular will in a parallel position and thus producing a peculiar system of balance in which finally the presidial-plebiscitary element dominates. From the German point of view this recalls all too vividly the faulty construction of the Weimar Republic; a decision for genuine presidential democracy or for the restitution of parliamentary democracy will not be avoidable when the present special form is no longer protected by the peculiar phenomenon of de Gaulle.

But the forms of modification in the Bonn democracy are also disputed. Undoubtedly an astonishing stability of the political constellation has been brought about by the elimination of splinter parties by the 5-per-cent clause, by the officially privileged position of the parliament parties by state financing, by hindrances put in the way of the overthrow of government by the "constructive vote of lack of confidence"; at the same time the dissolution of parliament is impeded, owing to a weakened position of the federal president. But the other weaknesses of parliamentarianism enumerated above have appeared all the more prominently. And more particularly the government, the bureaucracy and the interest groups, protected by the stable parliamentary conditions, have achieved such a great weight that many clear-sighted critics characterize the Bonn democracy as an actual government by bureaucracy and interest associations. This parliamentary democracy also will not have to stand its test until the moment of a change of administration; the end of the Adenauer era leaves many questions open, even though it seems to be less dramatic than the transition to the post-de Gaulle era.

This summary of the critical points in European parliamentarianism, as incomplete as it is, nevertheless indicates the central significance of the inquiry into the relation between politics and technical knowledge with regard to the future of European parliamentary democracy. This problem should now be pursued first in the national, then in the supranational, contexts.

PERSPECTIVES TOWARD A SOLUTION

Three main directions are taken in the attempts to solve—without a loss of democratic substance—the sharpened conflict between parliamentary politics and technical planning in the expanding industrial state of present-day Europe. The first direction is pursued especially in England and in the Scandinavian countries. It is the attempt to democratize the growing phenomenon of specialists and experts by making it useful and at the same time bringing it under control within the framework of, or in association with, the apparatus of government. This attempt proceeds from the insight that the activity of the interest groups cannot be separated from the political process and abandoned or consigned to a fictitious neutrality of the experts. In England the development of the royal commissions and similar institutions is significant in this line and at the same time poses a counterbalance to the rule of an isolated state bureaucracy. To be sure, new problems are created by the expansion of such commissions, which advise the government and administration in economic, social and cultural-political questions with technical competence, but also with their own interests prevailing. The importance of the experts has been fostered, the "anonymous empire" (S. Finer) of interest groups becomes institutionalized, but the parliaments' loss in substance has progressed further while the cabinet system, which is founded on parties and the administrations, has grown stronger.

A second course proceeds by way of the attempt *to submit parliamentarianism itself to the tendencies toward technology and rationalization* which have led to the advance of the expertise-and-planning system. This course has been pursued most decisively in France by means of the unburdening of the parliament (which of course also means its loss of importance), and by means of the institutionalizing of the system of expertise in large planning commissions. Another variation of this "rationalization" of parliamentarianism is the progressive shifting of technical decisions from the plenum to the commissions of the parliament, as is especially characteristic of the German development. The plenum retains little more than the sanctioning of the decisions that the members of the commissions bring before it. Therefore the selection and incorporation of the experts into the parliamentary party groups becomes the principal content of parliamentary activity. Here too the "rationalization" results in a loss of substance and significance of the actual parliamentary discussion. The system of *hearings,* which could steer this development, is lacking in the European parliamentary democracies with the exception of the Swiss democracy, which has a different form. Substitutes such as the interrogation hour of the Bonn system, in which the ministers must answer critical questions before parliament, are hardly sufficient, although in some cases (as the Spiegel affair) it proved quite important. But the basic principle remains in danger—the principle that decision is the prerogative of the politically responsible, elected officials of the parliament and of the government, and that it is not to be relegated to the bureaucracy or to the experts, with or without an interest-group slant.

All the more important are the efforts toward a new delimitation of the altered functions of parliament, government, administration and the organized interest groups which are undertaken in view of this dilemma. Their premise is that in view of the general tendency to bureaucratization the future of democracy depends upon whether objectivity and expertise can also be exercised outside of bureaucratic areas of organization. A clear separation of political decision (parliament) and technical planning (bureaucracy) is not possible; it would finally lead to the hypertrophy of the administrative state, to the victory of the hierarchy of officials over open democracy. To equate bureaucracy with expertocracy could appear as the tempting solution to the problems. But it contains serious dangers; it implies an evasion of democratic control and creates a new gap between the state and the citizens; it sharpens their dependence and helplessness in the face of the political-social process and degrades them to subjects facing a highly specialized, uncontrollable network of rule without comprehension. The result could be indifference and resignation; the political answer could become an erroneous reaction such as that of 1933 in Germany, if in place of a political solution to the problems a bureaucratic one were to prevail.

It is indisputable that the number of the actual decision-bearers in the modern state is becoming steadily smaller and the tendency toward rule by experts is becoming steadily harder to control. Thus the future of democracy depends all the more on whether it becomes possible to open up new ways for the citizens to participate in political and social affairs and thus to rise above the role of mere observers. Parties, organized interest groups and self-rule offer possibilities to create a counterweight against the threatening depolitization; an improved political education seems to be its precondition. This is true at the same time for the expert in the planning and steering committee. His "democratization" and control is most likely to become feasible if every kind of monopoly and hierarchy of the agencies of competence is avoided and if room is made for the principle of free competition in the sense of competition for achievement.

The basis for all attempts at solving the problem is therefore the insight that there must be no necessary opposition between expert knowledge and politics, between expertise and democracy. The primacy of politics must be maintained. The question is only what place parliamentarianism is to retain here, in what form it is to be brought into accord with the changed conditions of modern state, social, economic and military politics. The parliament and the parties which support it still have the double function of first working for contact and conjunction between the various areas of expertise, interests and politics, thereby guaranteeing the openness, readiness for compromise and competition; and second of control of technical counseling and technical planning, re-examining them in the discussions between administration and opposition and relating them to concrete political reality.

For both tasks—the uniting of political determination and technical planning on the one hand; the critical examination of the interest associations and also those of the experts on the other hand—the European democracies now as before need parliamentary institutions that are capable of functioning. We have indicated what possible modifications are being discussed and also to some extent realized to reduce the disadvantages and crises of parliamentarianism and to consider the structural changes of society and state. These modifications are resulting everywhere—not only in France—in a limitation of the "classical" parliamentary rule. But at the same time they aim at an intensification and rationalization of parliamentarianism in its indispensable functions. Improvement of the channels of information, expansion of the systems of commissions, more conscious policy in the selection of their own experts on the part of the parliamentary parties and incorporation of the specialists into the work of the parliament are the means of this rationalization. Its goal continues to be to work as a clearing house and counterweight to the technical claims of the bureaucracy of government as well as of interest groups, and to provide the comprehensive impetus for the primacy of political decision.

This is particularly applicable to the new problems that have been brought forward by the international network and the creation of *supranational* institutions. Today an isolated view of intrastate parliamentarianism is no longer possible. It is superseded by the comprehensive question as to how the separation of politics and planning, of democracy and expertocracy can be bridged in the sphere of the European network, and partly also in the Atlantic network. Here too only an inadequate political control by the governments confronts the forward-moving, expanding bureaucracy of administrators and specialists. Commissions and ministerial councils of the European economic community incorporate this tendency as do the other European administrative offices. And here too the parliamentary institutions have remained far behind. As qualified as some of their members are and as favorable as the supranational exchange of thought is, European and parliamentary institutions have little actual weight as long as they lack legitimation through direct European elections and as long as they carry out only insignificant advisory functions. Here too it must be recognized that technical planning needs political planning and control if it is to be both effective and democratic.

The danger of self-satisfied expertocracy is heightened still more by the economic and technical successes of cooperation on the level of bureaucracy. The collapse of negotiations between the Common Market and England fits into this complex. If England can be counted as a model of a parliamentary democracy that has succeeded in adjusting to the changed conditions without a breach of the basic principles, then England's inclusion would without doubt shift the politics of European unification from the bureaucratic level to the Parliamentary level. Therein—and not only in a French claim to leadership—lies one of the reasons for the resistance of de Gaulle, who may fear the disturbing effect of such tendencies on the economic-technical development of the European cooperation. But therein also lies the reason for the all too long hesitation of England, which regards with mistrust the reciprocal effect on the tested institutions of its own political system.

Not only in Italy and the Benelux countries but also in Germany these political aspects of the problem—along with the economic and military ones—have in the meanwhile come into such prominent awareness that the French standpoint appears considerably isolated. The Fifth Republic is considered a special case, not a model for the solution of the problems of European parliamentarianism. Precisely at a moment in which a Europe of reduced sovereignties is considering its strengthened role in the world, a retreat into national, or even regional, small-European isolation has become unthinkable. This is not only a question of economic and military potential. It is still more a political question. The danger that threatens the European democracies externally because of their geographical position, and internally still more because of the multifariously broken tradition of their parliamentarianism, also has not been averted by their rapid reconstruction. In the search for security and necessary reform the European states need not only close association among themselves but also with the Anglo-Saxon democracies, which command the strongest traditions and experiences in the art of the adjustment of a firmly established parliamentarianism to the new conditions of the industrial world.

CONCLUSION

While there are striking parallels and similarities in the appearance and problems of parliamentarianism in present-day Europe, the differences between the national forms of its realization still seem very great. In Germany, the experience of the Weimar Republic and the causes of its fall form the exit-point for all discussions about the relation of parliament, government and bureaucracy. The pseudo-presidential experiments of 1930–1933, which led to the dictatorship of Hitler, seem to justify the widespread mistrust against all attempts to minimize the position and function of parliament in favor of bureaucracy. In France, under the impact of the failure of classical parliamentarianism in the Fourth Republic, the experiences influencing public opinion and discussion support a very different view, almost contrary to the German version of a parliamentary party state. While in both of these cases, however, the main tendency goes toward a modification of parliamentary democracy, in Italy the older type of a multi-party system still prevails, confronted with the classical problems of a parliament which is split up in many political groups hardly able to form stable coalitions.

Such profound differences in the domestic scene of the European states must be considered if the prospects of coordination and integration of the national systems into a "new Europe" are examined. Besides strong remnants of the past—including very different experiences—it is a question of how to combine strong government and executive authority with effective control, which has led to individual solutions of the problems of parliamentarianism; decentralization and federalism—as traditional in Germany—are further elements of difference. The quest for European integration may as well complicate these problems as it tends to neglect them. It is also for such reasons that the position of a European parliament as a legislative body seems still very uncertain.

If the relation between parliament, government and bureaucracy demands new answers on the national as on the supranational level, this applies even more to the role of parties, interest groups and expert commissions within the institutional framework of parliamentary democracy. Beyond all national differences, two main tendencies are discernible: the growing importance of pressure groups, tending even to a *Verbände-Staat;* at the same time, the decline of ideological parties. This process, to be sure, is modified by the existence of strong Christian parties which may work as integration factors in a biconfessional society, as in Germany; but it may simultaneously block the tendency to open two-party systems, as does the unbroken strength of Communist parties in Italy and France.

In summing up, the development of democracy in western Europe, showing so many different traits and tendencies has posed many new questions. On the level of domestic politics, there are as yet no common answers in terms of a "new Europe." This will be the future task of interstate compromises which may result in the creation of a European parliament. In spite of the experiments of the French Fifth Republic, however, the substantial form of European governments has remained that of parliamentary democracy, though modified: a fundamental change in the direction of a presidential system seems outside of all possibilities. On this point, the difference between Europe and the United States, whose peculiar political system seems not fit for export, remains a reality which in its importance for European and Atlantic politics should not be overlooked.

24. National Constitutions: A Functional Approach*

IVO D. DUCHACEK

This is an era of new nations and new goals and consequently of new constitutions.[1] Both the old and new nations seem today exceedingly busy translating their ferment and ambitions into chapters, articles, subheadings, and paragraphs in their new or drastically revised constitutions. More than two-thirds of the existing 140-odd constitutions were drafted and adopted in the past two decades. Others are in the process of substantial rewriting or their fundamental revision is being clamored for.

*From *Comparative Politics,* vol. 1, no. 1 (October 1968), pp. 91–102. Reprinted by permission of the author and the journal. This article is a modified version of chapters 1 and 2 in the author's book *Comparative Politics of Constitutions* (New York: Holt, Rinehart and Winston, 1971). (Footnote abridged by the editors.)

[1] Constitutions referred to here are those collections of solemn declarations, ideological commitments, and codified as well as uncodified rules that identify the sources, goals, uses, and restraints on official power and are labeled by political authorities as national constitutions.

Even in the United States, whose seemingly rigid Constitution has allowed so many timely reinterpretations in response to environmental changes, one hears today strong pleas for a fundamental revision of the system, ranging from a reform of the electoral college and the establishment of new relations of the cities to the federal government to dealing with the problem of constitutional controls of modern technology and its human and social consequences. Recently one author drew attention to "the institutions dominating today's American scene which were not even dimly foreseen by the Founding Fathers . . . immense corporations and trade unions; media of communication that span continent and globe; political parties; a central government of stupendous size and world-shattering capabilities; and a very un-Jeffersonian kind of man at the center of it all."[2] We might perhaps add the potential constitutional consequences (such as possible communal representation) of the emerging concept of a bi-ethnic American nation.

The Communist world has been engaged in diligent redrafting of national constitutions for the past decade. This effort partly reflects the Communist world's search for new methods and new national purposes, as well as its socialist-bureaucratic tendency to translate all social and political problems into edicts, manifestos, or regulations. In 1963, for instance, Communist Yugoslavia adopted its third constitution since 1946. East Germany adopted its second constitution in 1968. This German constitution was inspired by other East European models, all of which reflect some aspects of the Stalin Constitution of 1936, whereas the "old" East German Constitution of 1949 deliberately imitated some of the concepts and terminology of the liberal Weimar text. This imitation was part of the earlier East German effort to compete with West Germany's claim to be the only rightful successor to the pre-Nazi German unity and democratic traditions. Today, on the contrary, East Germany advocates the concept of two permanently separate German states. And in 1968 Yugoslavia revised its constitution again: the rights of its six contituent units were strengthened.

It should be noted that originally during the liberalization process in Communist countries the demand was not to scrap the old constitutions but, on the contrary, to ensure that, at long last, they be implemented in practice. Communist constitutions that contain elaborate and seemingly liberal bills of rights have often been invoked by students and intellectuals either with tongue in cheek or simply to legitimize their charge that the drafters of Communist constitutions had proved to be their most callous and consistent violators.

In the wake of its liberalization process Communist Czechoslovakia announced a plan for a more frankly federal constitution in order to satisfy Slovak nationalism, so dramatically reasserted in March of 1968. It will be Czechoslovakia's third Communist constitution drafted by the party since its accession to

---

[2] Wilbur H. Ferry, "Must We Rewrite the Constitution to Control Technology?" *Saturday Review,* March 2, 1968, p. 54. The main theme of the article is the conclusion that the 1789 Constitution "has become outdated by technical advance and deals awkwardly and insufficiently with technology's results." The author is a vice-president of the Fund for the Republic.

power in 1948. In the Soviet Union a plan for a new constitution to replace the one proclaimed by Stalin in 1936 was announced during the 1967 celebrations of the Fiftieth Anniversary of the October Revolution. Not much has been heard since about the progress of its drafting; probably the contemplated change in the nature of Soviet polyethnic federalism, previously suggested by Khrushchev, and its replacement by a less national and a more rational form have delayed an early agreement on the new distribution of territorial authority. In China, during one of the most violent phases of its Great Cultural Socialist Revolution in 1966, several Red Guard posters urged an immediate revision of the Communist Constitution of 1954, "article by article," apparently in order to remove from its text any close parallels with the Soviet model. As may be noted, in the Communist world the major impetus for constitutional redrafting seems to be the reassertion of centrifugal nationalism within Communist states as well as vis-à-vis the Soviet Union.

In the case of the newly established or reestablished nations emerging from colonialism in the general area stretching from Korea to Senegal and the Caribbean, one of the very first steps taken by the victorious elites, understandably enough, has been the adoption of all the symbols and instruments of nationalism triumphant: a constitution (even short-lived Katanga proclaimed one), a flag, a national animal, flower, or bird, an emblem, an anthem, and, of course, a new uniform. Whether they were of continental size, such as India or China, or were microstates, such as Mauritius or Western Samoa, all these nations went through the process of conceiving, drafting, proclaiming, celebrating, and, we suspect, finally violating their new constitutions.

A MIRROR OF POLITICAL THOUGHT

With the somewhat controversial exceptions of Britain, Israel, and Saudi Arabia, all nations today have written constitutions, but only an infinitesimal fraction of them enjoy constitutional government of the sort in which the use of public power undergoes institutionalized and continuous (in contrast to occasional crisis-control) restraints by an independent judiciary, participation in rule-making, and controls of rule application.

The time has come perhaps to review what this veritable avalanche of new constitutional texts or invocations of the old ones means today.

National constitutions have often been studied in a dominantly legalistic framework. It may be suggested, however, that a comparative analysis of national constitutions could be treated not as comparative supreme law, but primarily as a part of comparative theory and practice. Every constitution combines into one body a declaration of political intent, a commitment to an ideology, and an assertion of national purpose combined with a blueprint for political action expressed in legal terms. As such it reflects, in a capsule form, the national elite's view of the nation and the world. Like all national documents written by mere human beings (and constitutional lawyers are only human, too), every constitution may be expected to contain a dose of erroneous interpretation of past experiences and of existing national and international realities (see, for instance, the emotional commitment of so many African constitutions to pan-Africanism, Arab unity, or the Maghreb—in some cases, to all three at the same time). We also find in them some amount of deliberate deception of others, as well as some self-deception, especially in the form of wishful thinking about men and society and their ability to direct their mutual conflicts into nonviolent constitutional channels. As digests of political autobiographies of the elites, constitutions offer a shorthand record of both their memories and their hopes. What André Malraux said about all autobiographies—including his own *Anti-mémoires*—seems to apply to constitutional texts as well: "Face to face with the unknown, some of our dreams are no less significant than our memories."[3]

Like all documents recording man's hopes and plans, constitutions cannot be immune from the test of time, especially the challenge of unexpected environmental and technological changes and the different concepts and orientation of subsequent elites. Very often new reality sneaks up on the constitutional dream and erodes it beyond recognition. Like men, all constitutions age. Some become senile and unusable; others may be rejuvenated by a few amendments or by new interpretation; and some, like men, die in civil and international wars.

If we view national constitutions as mirrors of the elite's political thought, then their declaratory and declamatory portions must be given weight equal, if not superior, to the organizational and purely legal chapters. In the traditional study of comparative constitutions, the interest in the structure and particular institutions was dominant; some authors actually eliminated from their studies the declaratory portions of the constitutions. It may, however, be argued that the examination of a constitution's tone and style and of the symbolic and verbal behavior of its drafters, as reflected in the nonlegal declaratory chapters, may yield important insights into the motives and goals of the drafting elites. Although the legal jargon of constitutional lawyers is nearly universal, political leaders have always had the last political as well as editorial word when it comes to expressing elite's value preferences in appropriate chapters and articles. Following the 1967 coup d'état in Greece, for instance, the military leaders quite dramatically refused to consider the draft of a new Greek constitution as prepared by a panel of constitutional experts, since in the view of the junta, the experts had prepared only a "rehash" of the old constitution.

FOUR BASIC COMPONENTS

If a constitution is viewed as a reflection of the elite's concept of the way in which the national community should be governed for its own and/or the elite's good, the text may be expected to contain either explicit or implicit indications of the following intertwined components:

1. All national constitutions begin with an affirmation of the major principles and characteristics of their communities as interpreted by the drafting

---

[3] "En face de l'inconnu, certains de nos rêves n'ont pas moins de signification que nos souvenirs." *Antimémoires* (Paris, 1967), p. 17.

elite. Constitutional preambles, bills of rights, and directives of welfare policy contain a clear indication of the elite's belief about what the people want and reject—or what the people should want and reject, if the drafters choose to see a constitution as reflecting a "mandate of ideological heaven" rather than one of the people. All constitutions contain some elements of a polemic against the immediate past. Preambles and introductory articles address themselves primarily to collective memories, passions, and goals and only to a lesser degree to the legal and rational sense of men. In their emotional message, however, lies their main significance. Like the national anthem or emblem, the preambles and the pledges contained in bills of rights or directive principles of welfare policy are supposed to strengthen the people's identification with their nation's past and future and with its present political system. What Carl J. Friedrich has said about constitutions in general applies particularly to their declaratory chapters: they are "symbolic expressions of the unifying forces in a community and they are supposed to strengthen them further."[4]

The preambles, in particular, record with pride the cost as well as the glory of great deeds in the past, and they pledge to do more in the future—a classical statement of nationalism like that expressed by Ernest Renan in 1882. The stylistic elegance and the tone of the constitutions in their role as manifestos of nationalism naturally vary. In contrast to that of the United States Constitution, modern preambles tend to be quite long. Some are truly inspiring; others are dry and matter-of-fact; a few read like a chapter on recent history in a junior high school textbook or like a hastily written editorial in the party press and include the vilification of the national enemy (e.g., China on the United States). Almost all of them indulge in emotional clichés; they could be described in the terms used by Congressman Adam Clayton Powell to refer to his own sermons as pastor of New York's Abyssinian Baptist Church: "The message is soul food, baby." Whatever the variety in their style and tone may be, constitutions as political manifestos address themselves primarily to the national, not the universal, man.

2. The second component of all constitutions is a description of the manner, specific means, and various agencies by which the community's goals, as set and understood by the elite, are to be achieved. This description may make for some dull reading, as in the case for all organizational charts issued by the management. In establishing specific agencies for the purpose of performing special, interconnected roles, nearly all national constitutions are divided into three parts: legislative, executive, and judicial. This is so not only in Western and democratic but also in non-Western or Communist constitutions; the Baron de Montesquieu would probably recognize some of his conclusions about the British system not only in the constitutions of India and Uganda, directly inspired by the British model, but also in those of De Gaulle's France, Salazar's Portugal, and Mao's China, and even in the newly adopted panchayat system of Hindu Nepal. Often he would find his model of a tripartite separation of powers grossly distorted in actual practice, but this would also have been so at the time

---

[4] In Arnold J. Zurcher, ed., *Constitutions and Constitutional Trends Since World War II*, rev. ed. (New York, 1955), p. 35.

of his somewhat inaccurate analysis of the working of the British system in the first half of the eighteenth century. In the majority of national constitutions today (the ratio is roughly six to five), the legislative branch of government enjoys, at least editorially, a preferential treatment; in the United States Constitution, for example, it is treated before the executive and judiciary. In reality, the former legislative monopoly of parliaments has been almost everywhere challenged and diluted by the legislative appetite of modern executives; nowhere in practice will we find today a real counterpart to the still important legislative and financial powers of the U.S. Congress. Everywhere else where legislators still play an important role, their dominant function is to check on the executive's performance and only to modify or reject, but not initiate, legislative proposals. The former constitutional terminology that differentiates between legislation and execution of laws has therefore long ceased to correspond to reality. This is why the newly coined, though not yet fully adopted, terminology—rule-making, rule application, and rule adjudication—appears to us, too, to be preferable to the traditional but outdated constitutional terms.[5]

3. The third component of a constitution's text is the elite's concept of the way in which individual and group interests (including territorial interests, in the case of federations) should be articulated and communicated—the general principles and the organs by which the conflicts of interests should be arbitrated and converted into binding decisions.

If articulating, aggregating, and communicating demands based on individual or group interests and pressing for their satisfaction are viewed as the heart of politics, then from the point of view of constitutional analysis, the blood vessels are the constitutional guarantees of the right to vote, the right to freedom of expression, and the right to assemble, form political parties and interest groups, and petition the government. Like all veins these may be clogged by age or a wrong political diet. The common denominator of all these rights of access to rule-making, rule enforcement, and rule adjudication (such as juries, lay assessors, or the selection of judges) is *communication,* the message to be transmitted to the system for authoritative action.

By including such rights of access to the political system, national constitutions commit the authority to responsiveness, that is, to a constant readiness to receive legitimate articulated demands and convert the aggregates of *some* of them into laws and policies. Many modern constitutions contain very specific and detailed lists of such rights of access to rule-making. Others (for instance, those of France and many African nations) express the general principle of the authority's responsiveness and responsibility to the people in the ten words borrowed from the Gettysburg Address, "government of the people, by the people, for the people." In terms of the Almond-Easton analysis, this may be called the input-output formula à la Lincoln.[6]

---

[5] The traditional term "legislation" seems to connote "some specialized structure and explicit process whereas in many political systems the rule-making function is diffuse, difficult to untangle and specify," as Gabriel A. Almond and G. Bingham Powell, Jr., express it in their *Comparative Politics: A Developmental Approach* (Boston, 1966), p. 132.

[6] The Algerian Constitution rephrased Lincoln by proclaiming as its guiding principle the following (in Article 3): "Sa devise est: Révolution par le peuple et pour le peuple."

4. Finally, all constitutions contain provisions for their legitimate revision if it is desired by a substantial majority of the legislators. Such provisions are usually found in combination with those for popular referendum, general elections, or ratification by the component units in a federation. No national constitution claims that every one of its provisions is meant for eternity. Communist constitutions, in particular, deliberately emphasize their impermanence as stations on their societies' dialectical way to Utopia, where states and constitutions may wither away. By adopting a new constitution and prescribing a legitimate procedure for its anticipated changes, all elites, however unconstitutional and revolutionary their past, hope to eliminate violent transformation of their system altogether and to legitimize its substance into near permanence. As the record shows, this has been, on the whole, a vain hope. Times and men change, and their constitutions change with them. Only a few constitutions have been adapted to new environmental realities by formal amendment; many more have been profoundly altered by the emergence of new, extraconstitutional forces (such as political parties or new technology), judicial interpretation, or revolutionary violence from which, in turn, new elites and new constitutions issue.

The four components described above have been placed in a framework that puts a deliberate emphasis on the drafting elite rather than on what is usually described as the people's mandate, which depicts a constitution as a record and expression of the people's will. It seems to us that in practice the contrast between the people's mandate and the elitist concept may become quite blurred, since all constitutions are necessarily products of the labor of a relatively small group of men. But even in the most totalitarian context the leaders do not wish to antagonize all the people all the time; the political elite feels or deceives itself into thinking that its aims are basically in tune with the dormant as well as the articulated aspirations of that interested and mobilized portion of the population that politically matters. And even in the most democratically responsive context the political elite pursues not only what it believes to be the general interest, but also what it knows, but rarely admits to knowing, is its own particular one. No elite, even one most dedicated to the will of the masses, can help but look at the people's aspirations through its own glasses, colored by its personal experiences, ideological commitment, or economic or class interests. Furthermore, leaders being leaders have the duty to lead, not merely to follow; and it is the duty of the leaders to anticipate that which has not yet been articulated, awaken that which is useful but dormant, and circumscribe that which is awake but explosive.

WHY?

The known record of frequent violations or excessively "creative" reinterpretations of national constitutions seems to illustrate the futility of an elite's attempts to translate the rapid tempo of changes affecting man and society into neatly grouped and numbered articles and chapters of its nation's supreme law. And yet the preparation of new constitutional texts goes on everywhere more intensively than ever. Many of the newer products are much longer and more detailed than the extraordinarily succinct United States Constitution.[7] Their preparation has often been marked by acrimonious controversies, international propagandizing (such as Stalin's in 1936), and mobilization of mass interests. In China, for instance, 150 million persons were officially reported in 1954 to have taken part in the second grass-roots round of discussion of the definitive draft of the new constitution.

In addition, constitutional lawyers have spent thousands of working hours preparing the texts and refining their language. They have not been engaged in a playful legalistic minuet for its own sake; they have been ordered to undertake their task, and their labors have been constantly supervised and corrected by an attentive political elite. It is true that constitutional lawyers may be suspected of having vested interests in the wording of national constitutions even though they may have quite a cynical view of their actual working in the future. But these occasionally narcissistic legal interests cannot by themselves explain either the persistence and intensity of constant constitution-making or the preoccupation of otherwise overworked political leaders with it.

The question now necessarily imposes itself as to why, then, so much time, money, research, energy, and skill are still being spent on preparing new constitutional texts. The political elites in most cases know in advance that they do not intend or, in view of the universal experience, will probably find it impossible to abide by their own constitutional and ideological prose. The search for answers to the questions concerning the reasons and expectations of the drafters and promoters of new constitutional texts forms the background of our present functional inquiry. Four possible explanations may be suggested: (1) deliberate deceit, (2) the need for a national birth certificate, (3) the need for an organizational map, and (4) an attempt at social engineering.

1. In some cases a constitution has been drafted and propagandized for, among other things, the deception of the credulous masses. A constitution in such a case is merely a legalistic opium for the masses. Despite the gap between the constitutional promise and actual practices, the word "constitution" has still retained much of the optimistic sound associated with the nineteenth-century expectation that a well-drafted constitution might codify a rational, democratic, and socially progressive system into existence. Today, it is still a

---

[7] Some of the longest constitutions in the world are those of India (395 articles, some extending over several pages), Nigeria (245 articles), Malaysia (181 articles), and Kenya (145 articles). Their length could be facetiously interpreted as a last postcolonial affirmation of independence from their countries' former, "constitutionless" British master. In reality, their length reflects their drafters' anxious desire to codify and so perpetuate all the aspects of the preliberation consensus and thus to protect the task of nation-building against disruptive improvisations. An attempt to codify into chapter and verse that which has taken Britain two centuries to develop may lead to disappointing results, as the cases of Nigeria, Burma, or Uganda amply demonstrate. "Centuries that have been missed must be caught up with," wrote a Czechoslovak Communist after his experiences as a director of Nkrumah's Ideological Institute at Accra, "but the effort is greater than in the case of missed history classes at school. A nation cannot say that it had a headache or played hooky when the nineteenth century was assigned." *Literární Noviny* (Prague), October 8, 1966.

good echo-word, as vague and also as appealing as "peace," "rule of law," "democracy," "socialism," "general welfare," "justice," "modernization," and so on. All these terms mean all things to all men and therefore mean nothing very much. But even so, a constitution as a symbol may satisfy the masses' craving for a fixed point amid the torrent of change and uncertainty.

2. In our world of quickly emerging and highly insecure nation-states a constitution is often viewed as a birth certificate—or, to change the metaphor, as a union card—necessary for admission to the society of sovereign nations. Elites consequently prepare a national constitution before their communities have become nations. The newly adopted and proclaimed constitutions are intended to help individuals as well as tribal, ethnic, or linguistic groups to feel that their own personal or group identities "are in part defined by their identification with their territorially [and constitutionally] delimited country."[8] As solemnly proclaimed certificates of birth, constitutions have a limited but not unimportant role in helping to achieve a common sense of identity and so to help solve the identity and legitimacy crises[9] characteristic of all traditional societies. A constitution is expected to create "a surrogate tradition, where no national tradition could yet exist."[10]

In the case of new or would-be nations there is also an element of metooism: a constitution is also something that every group claiming to be a nation must have and display—like a new flag or a new uniform—regardless of the actual need for it. Internationally, constitution-drafting is definitely habit-forming. We noted above that even in the middle of political turmoil and war the secessionist leader of the very short-lived nation of Katanga, Moïse Tshombe, found time to draft, proclaim, and print a new constitution. Among the new nations perhaps only Israel could afford to remain so long without a constitutional certificate of rebirth, although a resolution of the Knesset on June 13, 1950, asked for one. Being not really a new nation but an ancient one, Israel was able to fall back on a strong prestatehood consensus, fortified by its history, its religious codes, and its neighbors' enmity.

It should be mentioned that the solemnity of a constitution may also serve, at least partly, to compensate for the potential inferiority complex of the insecure elites, especially in the case of countries created by revolutionary upheavals, which are always followed by constitution-making to legitimize the new reality. Many a constitution has been drawn and adopted, as K. C. Wheare has suggested, "because people wished to make a fresh start . . . to begin again."[11] As the record indicates, a fresh start seems to be difficult in all matters, constitutional or not. No doubt, in many revolutionary situations the adoption of a new constitution is expected—rather foolishly—to act also as a barrier against a new

[8] Lucian W. Pye, *Aspects of Political Development* (Boston, 1966), p. 63.

[9] "The problem of achieving agreement about the legitimate nature of authority and the proper responsibilities of government. . . ." *Ibid.*

[10] Harry Eckstein and David E. Apter, "Constitutional Engineering and the Problem of Viable Representative Government," in their *Comparative Politics: A Reader*, p. 102.

[11] *Modern Constitutions* (London, 1965), p. 8.

revolution threatening the present-day revolutionaries, now in the process of legitimizing themselves as a status-quo group.

In their role as birth certificates of their countries, national constitutions also recognize their own legitimate or illegitimate parents, who more often than not are foreigners. Selective copying of foreign constitutional models is general, deliberate, and open. Modern founding fathers begin their work armed with scholarly manuals that contain digests or verbatim copies of selected national constitutions. A search for a radically new formula is very rare today; the founding fathers seem to be mostly constitutional copycats. Concepts, institutions, and slogans migrate from one national charter into another, and in the process they are, as it were, deprived of their original nationality and naturalized in the country of their adoption, sometimes with, often without, any modification in substance or style. The Irish bill of social and economic rights, based on the papal encyclicals *Rerum Novarum* and *Quadragesimo Anno,* for instance, has found its way into the constitutions of Buddhist Burma (where state protection and support for the study of Pali and Sanskrit have been added), Muslim Pakistan (where expression of the Islamic abhorrence of liquor has been incorporated), and Hindu India (where provisions concerning the Untouchables and the status of cows have been made part of the basic welfare commitment). The French-oriented African states have understandably adopted and only slightly modified the cabinet-president system of De Gaulle's Fifth Republic. A modified British cabinet system has been adopted in the overwhelming majority of national constitutions, including all the Communist ones. Communist states in Europe and in Asia have also incorporated, often verbatim, several basic principles or sentences from the Soviet Constitution of 1936. Not only institutions and organizing principles but also new interpretations and even the declamatory and symbolic portions of national constitutions migrate. The United States judicial review has wandered not only south of the border into Latin America, but, in a modified form, around the world. The French Declaration of the Rights of Man has been circling in the constitutional orbit for almost two centuries. We also find that the drafting elites have been inspired by the motto of the French Revolution, the Gettysburg Address, Marx's definition of socialism and communism, the United States Declaration of Independence, and, to a lesser extent, the Bible, the Koran, and the Communist Manifesto of 1848. A study of the origins of the Japanese Constitution shows that "a partial listing (of the allusions and literary sources of the language of the Japanese Preamble) would include the Declaration of Independence, the Constitution of the United States, the Gettysburg Address, the Atlantic Charter and General MacArthur. No analogous references to the Japanese literary heritage occur."[12]

3. There is also a purely pragmatic side to the birth of all constitutions: no modern system, however revolutionary in its origins, can do without establishing and officially describing various central and local agencies for the purpose of

---

[12] Robert E. Ward, "Origins of the Present Japanese Constitution," *American Political Science Review,* L (December 1956), p. 1007.

rule-making, rule-implementing, and rule-adjudicating. The names, rules, and structures of the most important governmental agencies are communicated in this basic form to officials and citizens alike so that they can understand, use, and obey them.

The organizational portion of a national constitution may be therefore viewed as a macroscopic map for political communication, interest articulation, and conversion of demands into enforceable rules, that is, in Herman Finer's words, an "autobiography of power distribution." Like all autobiographies it often commits the sins of omission and distortion. Since the description of the various organs of the government implies the authority's commitment to respond to present needs as well as its commitment to leadership, initiative, and the anticipation of future needs, the purpose of a constitution as a power map is not only to organize but also to elicit support for, and cooperation with, political authority.

4. If, as Herbert Wiener has stated, communication is the cement that makes organization, a constitution then appears as one of many means to make the national community think together, see together, and act together. Through the instrumentality of the constitution the elite's messages are addressed to subordinate policymakers as well as the general public. Also in this way the audience learns about major rules, the institutional arrangements, and the ideological commitment of the political elite. Those who inspire or draft national constitutions expect that their charter will prove able at least partly or occasionally to affect and mold political attitudes and action and, in particular, to induce cooperative behavior and positive feelings toward the system.

To serve the purpose of social engineering, the nonlegal, declamatory portions of a constitution often play as important a role as its legal and organizational chapters. The power of emotional appeals should never be underestimated. Edward R. Murrow once said about Winston Churchill that he was the man who marshaled the English language and sent it to battle when he had little else. Similarly, many a leader of a newly born or reborn nation sends his constitution into domestic and international battle when he has little else to fight with. A newly adopted and propagandized constitution that glorifies its nation's immediately preceding revolutionary past and commits the community to a common program in the future is expected to quicken the pace of nation-building. The national discussion concerning the new constitution may, and often does, represent a more powerful tool of political socialization than does the finished document. Through nationwide debate, the younger generation—and, in some countries, the potentially secessionist ethnic or tribal elites—may be inducted into national political roles. This certainly was in part the aim of China's nationwide discussion in 1954, referred to above. In new nations the proclamation and promotion of the new constitution is supposed to help the elite to reach down to the village level and to increase and regulate political participation as well as the relationship between officials and articulate citizens.

If we think of a national constitution as one of the ingredients in the process of political communication that involves a source generating a message that travels through a channel to an audience,[13] the constitution may conceivably transform itself from a message or a channel into a source with a life of its own, thus becoming an autonomous fountain of political inspiration or a yardstick of performance of the political system. It is indeed conceivable that a new constitution—produced, publicized, and launched by the elite into the political orbit—may develop, as it were, its own momentum, independent of and beyond the expectation and design of its source, the drafting elite. So, for instance, the Soviet, Indian, Yugoslav, and Nigerian constitutions, which give linguistic and tribal nationalisms a federal accolade, may have finally endowed with erosive virulence those centrifugal forces that the drafters originally had intended to weaken, regulate, control, or manipulate.

The role that a constitution plays as a fountain of inspiration or a measuring rod naturally varies from country to country. We can surmise, for instance, that references to the constitution as a yardstick for the working of a political system may be more frequent, on account of the judicial review, in the United States than in France. In the older, established Western countries, the nationalistic and emotional preambles will probably be less frequently invoked than in those countries in the process of a febrile nation-building.[14] In the Communist countries, on the other hand, we were able to witness a dramatic resurgence of references to long-forgotten bills of rights. In the era of liberalization, constitutions have been transformed from organizational charts, guideposts for governmental action, and instruments of mass deception into unintended standards of desired reforms and sources of inspiration for antigovernmental opposition.

In conclusion, it should be reemphasized that present-day expectations as to the planned or unplanned effects of national constitutions are exceedingly modest in comparison with the excessive hopes of the eighteenth and nineteenth centuries. At that earlier time, many people, assuming the perfectibility of man and society by means of constitutional texts, tended to view constitutions, in Eckstein's words, as "tickets to Utopia." The tragic fate of the Weimar Constitution, among others, demonstrates that a constitution, however well designed it may be, cannot protect a system against profound environmental changes or against usurpers. Constitutions today are no longer viewed as the centers of gravity of national political systems; they merely represent only one, though a useful one, of many elements that compose and characterize a political system. National constitutions are neither a starting nor a culminating point, only a midpoint, in the development of a political system. Along with many other instruments a national constitution may be expected, at best, to help to coordinate the people's activities and expectations. "Coordinated habits, rather than

[13] Richard R. Fagen, *Politics and Communication* (Boston, 1966), p. 17.

[14] Only logic points to these tentative conclusions. We have found no empirical data available to indicate the frequency, intensity, and context of references to national constitutions in different national environments.

threats, keep things moving,"[15] Karl W. Deutsch has noted. Those who draft and proclaim national constitutions evidently do not want to overlook anything, including the traditional form and content of a national constitution, that might help to move events and men in the desired direction.

[15] *The Nerves of Government* (New York, 1966), p. 123.

chapter X

ADMINISTRATION

In all complex industrialized societies the scope of state activity has broadened. Government in democratic and nondemocratic nations alike has assumed ever larger responsibility for transportation, full employment, research, higher education, atomic energy, urban redevelopment, health, medical care, and social security. In England and France railroads, aviation, the banking system, the production of coal, gas and electricity—amounting to over 20 percent of the economy—have come under the direct control of the state. The state also directs, in large part, capital investment for technological progress and modernization. In the United States and Western Germany, regulation and indirect controls rather than direct ownership and administration are the rule. In the Communist countries, almost every type of economic activity has been nationalized. Among the nations that have recently emerged from colonial rule, state ownership is widespread. The immense task of running nationalized industries and regulating the economy in all cases has been taken on by the executive.

The result has been the emergence of a huge apparatus—the bureaucracy—consisting of millions of men and women, often accounting for more than 10 percent of the total working force. In order to perform its manifold duties the bureaucracy, or civil service, must be well organized, competent, and efficient. Within its internal structure there must be a clear distinction between superiors and subordinates, and between staff and line (or operational) personnel. The recruitment of competent and motivated men and women raises a host of problems. Should an advantage be given to university graduates? Should emphasis be placed on general education, or on training for a specific job? Above all, should candidates be drawn from all segments of the population, or from one major social group? These questions are all related to a larger issue: whether the civil service can or should be a neutral instrument of policy made by others. The very bulk of the civil service makes it a formidable political force. Yet, civil servants are as likely as any other group to display varied political attitudes and aspirations. Students of administration have therefore been increasingly con-

341

cerned with the values and orientations of civil servants and their actual role in the formulation of policy.

On the theoretical problems of bureaucracy and organization, see: Robert K. Merton, ed., *Reader in Bureaucracy* (1952); and Herbert Simon, *Administrative Behavior* (1945). Problems of recruitment and control are dealt with in J. D. Kingsley, *Representative Bureaucracy* (1944), and B. Chapman, *The Profession of Government* (1961). See also, M. Crozier, *The Bureaucratic Phenomenon* (1964); W. J. Siffin, ed., *Toward the Comparative Study of Public Administration* (1957); and J. LaPalombara, ed., *Bureaucracy and Political Development* (1963).

25. Bureaucracy: The "Ideal Type"*

MAX WEBER

The effectiveness of legal authority rests on the acceptance of the validity of the following mutually inter-dependent ideas.

1. That any given legal norm may be established by agreement or by imposition, on grounds of expediency or rational values or both, with a claim to obedience at least on the part of the members of the corporate group. This is, however, usually extended to include all persons within the sphere of authority or of power in question—which in the case of territorial bodies is the territorial area—who stand in certain social relationships or carry out forms of social action which in the order governing the corporate group have been declared to be relevant.

2. That every body of law consists essentially in a consistent system of abstract rules which have normally been intentionally established. Furthermore, administration of law is held to consist in the application of these rules to particular cases; the administrative process is the rational pursuit of the interests which are specified in the order governing the corporate group within the limits laid down by legal precepts and following principles which are capable of generalized formulation and are approved in the order governing the group, or at least not disapproved in it.

3. That thus the typical person in authority occupies an 'office.' In the action associated with his status, including the commands he issues to others, he is subject to an impersonal order to which his actions are oriented. This is

*Reprinted from Talcott Parsons, ed., *The Theory of Social and Economic Organization*, trans. by A. M. Henderson and Talcott Parsons, pp. 329–40. By permission of Talcott Parsons and The Free Press.

true not only for persons exercising legal authority who are in the usual sense 'officials,' but, for instance, for the elected president of a state.

4. That the person who obeys authority does so, as it is usually stated, only in his capacity as a 'member' of the corporate group and what he obeys is only 'the law.' He may in this connexion be the member of an association, of a territorial commune, of a church, or a citizen of a state.

5. In conformity with point 3, it is held that the members of the corporate group, in so far as they obey a person in authority, do not owe this obedience to him as an individual, but to the impersonal order. Hence, it follows that there is an obligation to obedience only within the sphere of the rationally delimited authority which, in terms of the order, has been conferred upon him.

The following may thus be said to be the fundamental categories of rational legal authority:—

(1) A continuous organization of official functions bound by rules.

(2) A specified sphere of competence. This involves (a) a sphere of obligations to perform functions which has been marked off as part of a systematic division of labour. (b) The provision of the incumbent with the necessary authority to carry out these functions. (c) That the necessary means of compulsion are clearly defined and their use is subject to definite conditions. A unit exercising authority which is organized in this way will be called an 'administrative organ.'

There are administrative organs in this sense in large-scale private organizations, in parties and armies, as well as in the state and the church. An elected president, a cabinet of ministers, or a body of elected representatives also in this sense constitute administrative organs. This is not, however, the place to discuss these concepts. Not every administrative organ is provided with compulsory powers. But this distinction is not important for present purposes.

(3) The organization of offices follows the principle of hierarchy; that is, each lower office is under the control and supervision of a higher one. There is a right of appeal and of statement of grievances from the lower to the higher. Hierarchies differ in respect to whether and in what cases complaints can lead to a ruling from an authority at various points higher in the scale, and as to whether changes are imposed from higher up or the responsibility for such changes is left to the lower office, the conduct of which was the subject of complaint.

(4) The rules which regulate the conduct of an office may be technical rules or norms.[1] In both cases, if their application is to be fully rational, specialized training is necessary. It is thus normally true that only a person who has demonstrated an adequate technical training is qualified to be a member of the administrative staff of such an organized group, and hence only such persons are

---

[1] Weber does not explain this distinction. By a 'technical rule' he probably means a prescribed course of action which is dictated primarily on grounds touching efficiency of the performance of the immediate functions, while by 'norms' he probably means rules which limit conduct on grounds other than those of efficiency. Of course, in one sense all rules are norms in that they are prescriptions for conduct, conformity with which is problematical.—Ed. [Parsons.]

eligible for appointment to official positions. The administrative staff of a rational corporate group thus typically consists of 'officials,' whether the organization be devoted to political, religious, economic—in particular, capitalistic—or other ends.

(5) In the rational type it is a matter of principle that the members of the administrative staff should be completely separated from ownership of the means of production or administration. Officials, employees, and workers attached to the administrative staff do not themselves own the non-human means of production and administration. These are rather provided for their use in kind or in money, and the official is obligated to render an accounting of their use. There exists, furthermore, in principle complete separation of the property belonging to the organization, which is controlled within the sphere of office, and the personal property of the official, which is available for his own private use. There is a corresponding separation of the place in which official functions are carried out, the 'office' in the sense of premises, from living quarters.

(6) In the rational type case, there is also a complete absence of appropriation of his official position by the incumbent. Where 'rights' to an office exist, as in the case of judges, and recently of an increasing proportion of officials and even of workers, they do not normally serve the purpose of appropriation by the official, but of securing the purely objective and independent character of the conduct of the office so that it is oriented only to the relevant norms.

(7) Administrative acts, decisions, and rules are formulated and recorded in writing, even in cases where oral discussion is the rule or is even mandatory. This applies at least to preliminary discussions and proposals, to final decisions, and to all sorts of orders and rules. The combination of written documents and a continuous organization of official functions constitutes the 'office'[2] which is the central focus of all types of modern corporate action.

(8) Legal authority can be exercised in a wide variety of different forms which will be distinguished and discussed later. The following analysis will be deliberately confined for the most part to the aspect of imperative co-ordination in the structure of the administrative staff. It will consist in an analysis in terms of ideal types of officialdom or 'bureaucracy.'

In the above outline no mention has been made of the kind of supreme head appropriate to a system of legal authority. This is a consequence of certain considerations which can only be made entirely understandable at a later stage in the analysis. There are very important types of rational imperative co-ordination which, with respect to the ultimate source of authority, belong to other cate-

---

[2] *Bureau.* It has seemed necessary to use the English word 'office' in three different meanings, which are distinguished in Weber's discussion by at least two terms. The first is *Amt,* which means 'office' in the sense of the institutionally defined status of a person. The second is the 'work premises' as in the expression 'he spent the afternoon in his office.' For this Weber uses *Bureau* as also for the third meaning which he has just defined, the 'organized work process of a group.' In this last sense an office is a particular type of 'organization,' or *Betrieb* in Weber's sense. This use is established in English in such expressions as 'the District Attorney's Office has such and such functions.' Which of the three meanings is involved in a given case will generally be clear from the context.—Ed. [Parsons.]

gories. This is true of the hereditary charismatic type, as illustrated by hereditary monarchy and of the pure charismatic type of a president chosen by plebiscite. Other cases involve rational elements at important points, but are made up of a combination of bureaucratic and charismatic components, as is true of the cabinet form of government. Still others are subject to the authority of the chief of other corporate groups, whether this character be charismatic or bureaucratic; thus the formal head of a government department under a parliamentary regime may be a minister who occupies his position because of his authority in a party. The type of rational, legal administrative staff is capable of application in all kinds of situations and contexts. It is the most important mechanism for the administration of everyday profane affairs. For in that sphere, the exercise of authority and, more broadly, imperative co-ordination, consists precisely in administration.

The purest type of exercise of legal authority is that which employs a bureaucratic administrative staff. Only the supreme chief of the organization occupies his position of authority by virtue of appropriation, of election, or of having been designated for the succession. But even *his* authority consists in a sphere of legal 'competence.' The whole administrative staff under the supreme authority then consists, in the purest type, of individual officials who are appointed and function according to the following criteria: [3]

(1) They are personally free and subject to authority only with respect to their impersonal official obligations.

(2) They are organized in a clearly defined hierarchy of offices.

(3) Each office has a clearly defined sphere of competence in the legal sense.

(4) The office is filled by a free contractual relationship. Thus, in principle, there is free selection.

(5) Candidates are selected on the basis of technical qualifications. In the most rational case, this is tested by examination or guaranteed by diplomas certifying technical training, or both. They are *appointed,* not elected.

(6) They are remunerated by fixed salaries in money, for the most part with a right to pensions. Only under certain circumstances does the employing authority, especially in private organizations, have a right to terminate the appointment, but the official is always free to resign. The salary scale is primarily graded according to rank in the hierarchy; but in addition to this criterion, the responsibility of the position and the requirements of the incumbent's social status may be taken into account.

(7) The office is treated as the sole, or at least the primary, occupation of the incumbent.

(8) It constitutes a career. There is a system of 'promotion' according to seniority or to achievement, or both. Promotion is dependent on the judgment of superiors.

(9) The official works entirely separated from ownership of the means of administration and without appropriation of his position.

[3] This characterization applies to the 'monocratic' as opposed to the 'collegial' type, which will be discussed below.

(10) He is subject to strict and systematic discipline and control in the conduct of the office.

This type of organization is in principle applicable with equal facility to a wide variety of different fields. It may be applied in profit-making business or in charitable organizations, or in any number of other types of private enterprise serving ideal or material ends. It is equally applicable to political and to religious organizations. With varying degrees of approximation to a pure type, its historical existence can be demonstrated in all these fields.

1. For example, this type of bureaucracy is found in private clinics, as well as in endowed hospitals or the hospitals maintained by religious orders. Bureaucratic organization has played a major role in the Catholic Church. It is well illustrated by the administrative role of the priesthood in the modern church, which has expropriated almost all of the old church benefices, which were in former days to a large extent subject to private appropriations. It is also illustrated by the conception of the universal Episcopate, which is thought of as formally constituting a universal legal competence in religious matters. Similarly, the doctrine of Papal infallibility is thought of as in fact involving a universal competence, but only one which functions 'ex cathedra' in the sphere of the office, thus implying the typical distinction between the sphere of office and that of the private affairs of the incumbent. The same phenomena are found in the large-scale capitalistic enterprise; and the larger it is, the greater their role. And this is not less true of political parties, which will be discussed separately. Finally, the modern army is essentially a bureaucratic organization administered by that peculiar type of military functionary, the 'officer.'

2. Bureaucratic authority is carried out in its purest form where it is most clearly dominated by the principle of appointment. There is no such thing as a hierarchy of elected officials in the same sense as there is a hierarchical organization of appointed officials. In the first place, election makes it impossible to attain a stringency of discipline even approaching that in the appointed type. For it is open to a subordinate official to compete for elective honours on the same terms as his superiors, and his prospects are not dependent on the superior's judgment.

3. Appointment by free contract, which makes free selection possible, is essential to modern bureaucracy. Where there is a hierarchical organization with impersonal spheres of competence, but occupied by unfree officials—like slaves or dependents, who, however, function in a formally bureaucratic manner—the term 'patrimonial bureaucracy' will be used.

4. The role of technical qualifications in bureaucratic organizations is continually increasing. Even an official in a party or a trade-union organization is in need of specialized knowledge, though it is usually of an empirical character, developed by experience, rather than by formal training. In the modern state, the only 'offices' for which no technical qualifications are required are those of ministers and presidents. This only goes to prove that they are 'officials' only in a formal sense, and not substantively, as is true of the managing director or president of a large business corporation. There is no question but that the

'position' of the capitalist entrepreneur is as definitely appropriated as is that of a monarch. Thus at the top of a bureaucratic organization, there is necessarily an element which is at least not purely bureaucratic. The category of bureaucracy is one applying only to the exercise of control by means of a particular kind of administrative staff.

5. The bureaucratic official normally receives a fixed salary. By contrast, sources of income which are privately appropriated will be called 'benefices.' Bureaucratic salaries are also normally paid in money. Though this is not essential to the concept of bureaucracy, it is the arrangement which best fits the pure type. Payments in kind are apt to have the character of benefices, and the receipt of a benefice normally implies the appropriation of opportunities for earnings and of positions. There are, however, gradual transitions in this field with many intermediate types. Appropriation by virtue of leasing or sale of offices or the pledge of income from office are phenomena foreign to the pure type of bureaucracy.

6. 'Offices' which do not constitute the incumbent's principal occupation, in particular 'honorary' offices, belong in other categories. . . . The typical 'bureaucratic' official occupies the office as his principal occupation.

7. With respect to the separation of the official from ownership of the means of administration, the situation is essentially the same in the field of public administration and in private bureaucratic organizations, such as the large-scale capitalistic enterprise.

8. At present [collegial bodies] are rapidly decreasing in importance in favour of types of organization which are in fact, and for the most part formally as well, subject to the authority of a single head. For instance, the collegial 'governments' in Prussia have long since given way to the monocratic 'district president.' The decisive factor in this development has been the need for rapid, clear decisions, free of the necessity of compromise between different opinions and also free of shifting majorities.

9. The modern army officer is a type of appointed official who is clearly marked off by certain class distinctions. . . . In this respect such officers differ radically from elected military leaders, from charismatic condottieri, from the type of officers who recruit and lead mercenary armies as a capitalistic enterprise, and, finally, from the incumbents of commissions which have been purchased. There may be gradual transitions between these types. The patrimonial 'retainer,' who is separated from the means of carrying out his function, and the proprietor of a mercenary army for capitalistic purposes have, along with the private capitalistic entrepreneur, been pioneers in the organization of the modern type of bureaucracy. . . .

THE MONOCRATIC TYPE OF BUREAUCRATIC ADMINISTRATION

Experience tends universally to show that the purely bureaucratic type of administrative organization—that is, the monocratic variety of bureaucracy—is, from a purely technical point of view, capable of attaining the highest degree of efficiency and is in this sense formally the most rational known means of carrying out imperative control over human beings. It is superior to any other form in precision, in stability, in the stringency of its discipline, and in its reliability. It thus makes possible a particularly high degree of calculability of results for the heads of the organization and for those acting in relation to it. It is finally superior both in intensive efficiency and in the scope of its operations, and is formally capable of application to all kinds of administrative tasks.

The development of the modern form of the organization of corporate groups in all fields is nothing less than identical with the development and continual spread of bureaucratic administration. This is true of church and state, of armies, political parties, economic enterprise, organizations to promote all kinds of causes, private associations, clubs, and many others. Its development is, to take the most striking case, the most crucial phenomenon of the modern Western state. However many forms there may be which do not appear to fit this pattern, such as collegial representative bodies, parliamentary committees, soviets, honorary officers, lay judges, and what not, and however much people may complain about the 'evils of bureaucracy,' it would be sheer illusion to think for a moment that continuous administrative work can be carried out in any field except by means of officials working in offices. The whole pattern of everyday life is cut to fit this framework. For bureaucratic administration is, other things being equal, always, from a formal, technical point of view, the most rational type. For the needs of mass administration to-day, it is completely indispensable. The choice is only that between bureaucracy and dilettantism in the field of administration.

The primary source of the superiority of bureaucratic administration lies in the role of technical knowledge which, through the development of modern technology and business methods in the production of goods, has become completely indispensable. In this respect, it makes no difference whether the economic system is organized on a capitalistic or a socialistic basis. Indeed, if in the latter case a comparable level of technical efficiency were to be achieved, it would mean a tremendous increase in the importance of specialized bureaucracy.

When those subject to bureaucratic control seek to escape the influence of the existing bureaucratic apparatus, this is normally possible only by creating an organization of their own which is equally subject to the process of bureaucratization. Similarly the existing bureaucratic apparatus is driven to continue functioning by the most powerful interests which are material and objective, but also ideal in character. Without it, a society like our own—with a separation of officials, employees, and workers from ownership of the means of administration, dependent on discipline and on technical training—could no longer function. The only exception would be those groups, such as the peasantry, who are still in possession of their own means of subsistence. Even in the case of revolution by force or of occupation by an enemy, the bureaucratic machinery will normally continue to function just as it has for the previous legal government.

The question is always who controls the existing bureaucratic machinery. And such control is possible only in a very limited degree to persons who are not technical specialists. Generally speaking, the trained permanent official is more likely to get his way in the long run than his nominal superior, the Cabinet minister, who is not a specialist.

Though by no means alone, the capitalistic system has undeniably played a major role in the development of bureaucracy. Indeed, without it capitalistic production could not continue and any rational type of socialism would have simply to take it over and increase its importance. Its development, largely under capitalistic auspices, has created an urgent need for stable, strict, intensive, and calculable administration. It is this need which gives bureaucracy a crucial role in our society as the central element in any kind of large-scale administration. Only by reversion in every field—political, religious, economic, etc.—to small-scale organization would it be possible to any considerable extent to escape its influence. On the one hand, capitalism in its modern stages of development strongly tends to foster the development of bureaucracy, though both capitalism and bureaucracy have arisen from many different historical sources. Conversely, capitalism is the most rational economic basis for bureaucratic administration and enables it to develop in the most rational form, especially because, from a fiscal point of view, it supplies the necessary money resources.

Along with these fiscal conditions of efficient bureaucratic administration, there are certain extremely important conditions in the fields of communication and transportation. The precision of its functioning requires the services of the railway, the telegraph, and the telephone, and becomes increasingly dependent on them. A socialistic form of organization would not alter this fact. It would be a question whether in a socialistic system it would be possible to provide conditions for carrying out as stringent bureaucratic organization as has been possible in a capitalistic order. For socialism would, in fact, require a still higher degree of formal bureaucratization than capitalism. If this should prove not to be possible, it would demonstrate the existence of another of those fundamental elements of irrationality in social systems—a conflict between formal and substantive rationality of the sort which sociology so often encounters.

Bureaucratic administration means fundamentally the exercise of control on the basis of knowledge. This is the feature of it which makes it specifically rational. This consists on the one hand in technical knowledge which, by itself, is sufficient to ensure it a position of extraordinary power. But in addition to this, bureaucratic organizations, or the holders of power who make use of them, have the tendency to increase their power still further by the knowledge growing out of experience in the service. For they acquire through the conduct of office a special knowledge of facts and have available a store of documentary material peculiar to themselves. While not peculiar to bureaucratic organizations, the concept of 'official secrets' is certainly typical of them. It stands in relation to technical knowledge in somewhat the same position as commercial secrets do to technological training. It is a product of the striving for power.

Bureaucracy is superior in knowledge, including both technical knowledge and knowledge of the concrete fact within its own sphere of interest, which is usually confined to the interests of a private business—a capitalistic enterprise.

The capitalistic entrepreneur is, in our society, the only type who has been able to maintain at least relative immunity from subjection to the control of rational bureaucratic knowledge. All the rest of the population have tended to be organized in large-scale corporate groups which are inevitably subject to bureaucratic control. This is as inevitable as the dominance of precision machinery in the mass production of goods.

The following are the principal more general social consequences of bureaucratic control:—

(1) The tendency to 'levelling' in the interest of the broadest possible basis of recruitment in terms of technical competence.

(2) The tendency to plutocracy growing out of the interest in the greatest possible length of technical training. To-day this often lasts up to the age of thirty.

(3) The dominance of a spirit of formalistic impersonality, 'Sine ira et studio,' without hatred or passion, and hence without affection or enthusiasm. The dominant norms are concepts of straightforward duty without regard to personal considerations. Everyone is subject to formal equality of treatment; that is, everyone in the same empirical situation. This is the spirit in which the ideal official conducts his office.

26. Bureaucracies: Some Contrasts in Systems*

WALLACE S. SAYRE

I

In Western political systems there appear to be two important types of myths about bureaucracy. The first of these casts bureaucracy in the role of villain. Thus Harold Laski, writing thirty years ago on *bureaucracy* for the Encyclopaedia of the Social Sciences, described bureaucracy as representing a passion for the routine in administration, the sacrifice of flexibility to rule, delay in the making of decisions, and a refusal to embark upon experiment. Laski saw bureaucracy as a threat to democratic government. His argument ran briefly as follows: the scale of modern government makes administration by experts inescapable, yet the power of these experts as bureaucrats is not easily controlled by democratic institutions. The bureaucracies continuously push the boundaries of their power, Laski asserts, while control over them becomes increasingly difficult and costly. Describing the problem in terms of the British parliamentary

*From *The Indian Journal of Public Administration* (April–June 1964), pp. 219–29. By permission of the Indian Institute of National Administration and the author.

system, he says control takes the following form: (1) the legislature can only reject or accept the proposals of ministers, (2) the ministers are in turn dependent upon their bureaucracies, and (3) the bureaucrats urge the ministers toward caution, toward minimizing innovation. The net influences, then, are in the direction of reliance on precedent, of continuity, and of minimum risk or change. More recently Von Mises, too, in his book called *Bureaucracy*, has argued that bureaucracy cannot be efficient, primarily because the profit-and-loss criterion is absent from the work of governmental bureaucracies.

A second type of myth casts bureaucracy in the role of hero. Max Weber is perhaps the outstanding proponent of this view. Weber argues that bureaucracy is capable of attaining the highest degree of efficiency and the most rational form of administration. This is so, he believes, because it represents the exercise of control through knowledge. He presents an "ideal type" of bureaucracy in which activities are distributed in a fixed way, authority to command is distributed in a stable manner and is delimited by rules, the hierarchy of authority is monocratic, management is based on written documents, and membership in the bureaucracy is a vocation. In these terms bureaucracy is made virtually synonymous with rationality and objectivity in the administration of large-scale organizations.

We may describe these broad characterizations of bureaucracy as myths because they are persuasive mixtures of both fact and invention. As such they explain both too much and too little. A more modest version might simply assert that bureaucracy is necessarily neither villain nor hero, but rather a phenomenon found in all large-scale, complex organizations. This phenomenon has certain major characteristics: (1) specialization of tasks for the members of the organization, (2) a hierarchy of formal authority, (3) a body of rules, (4) a system of records, and (5) personnel with specialized skills and roles. In this view bureaucracy is a system for the administration of scale and complexity in human efforts to develop and accomplish purposes not otherwise attainable. In serving these purposes bureaucracy has both merits and liabilities. But we may assume that, within broad limits, these merits or liabilities are the result of choices made in constructing the bureaucratic system in a particular time and place. For bureaucracies are not all constructed in the same mould. Instead they vary greatly, one from the other, and they vary also over time. The American bureaucracies differ significantly from the British, and the British from the European, while presumably each of these Western bureaucracies differs importantly from the Eastern ones, which in turn must differ greatly from each other. And "new" bureaucracies apparently differ in many ways from "mature" bureaucracies.

It is with the choices about the forms and methods of bureaucracy that this essay will be concerned, not with the probably unanswerable and somewhat metaphysical question of whether bureaucracy is villain or hero. It will be assumed that it may, in some periods and some places, be either or a mixture of both. And the discussion will focus upon three specific questions about bureaucracies:

1. How are the bureaucrats to be chosen?

2. What is the role of bureaucrats in decision-making?
3. How are the bureaucrats to be governed?

II

How are bureaucrats—especially the higher-ranking bureaucrats—to be chosen? The full answer to this question involves several important choices in public policy, choices which have major consequences for the nature and behaviour of the bureaucracy which will be developed. That is, the ways in which the bureaucrats are selected from among the population will influence their representativeness, their skills and capacities, their responsiveness to democratic controls, and their attitudes toward change in public policy and in managerial methods. These influences are especially consequent in the case of the choices of those who are to hold the higher posts in the bureaucracy, for these higher bureaucrats usually set the tone and tempo of the whole bureaucracy.

The choices involved in the question of how the bureaucrats are to be selected may be concretely illustrated by describing the choices made in the building of the United States Civil Services, with some contrasts offered by the British system. The first choice may be described as *open* versus *closed* recruitment. The American option is for open recruitment; that is, to recruit from among all the talents available in the national labour market.[1] The British option, by contrast, is to recruit directly from the schools and universities, at the school-leaving or graduating age. The selection of those bureaucrats who are to hold the posts of higher responsibility in the bureaucracy presents an especially sharp contrast: in the American system these persons may be, and often are, recruited from outside the ranks of the bureaucracy at mid-career, or even later, stages. The American system has no counterpart of the British Administrative Class; the posts of the higher bureaucracy in the United States are filled by a wider system of recruitment that draws upon the talents available in the national pool of talent. These briefly described alternatives in deciding how the bureaucrats are to be chosen serve to illustrate that a deliberate and consequential choice can be made in determining the kind of bureaucracy a government wishes to have.

A second kind of choice can be made about the way in which bureaucrats are to be chosen. That choice is between the American preference for "programme staffing" and the British preference for "career staffing". The American practice is to recruit for particular programmes of the government, and secondarily for careers in the government generally. In the United States a new programme of the government usually means also a new agency and a new staff—a response often explained by asserting that "new ideas" require "new blood". The Tennessee Valley Authority may serve as an example. When the TVA was

[1] The term "labour market" may require some explanation. The American labour market is somewhat distinctive. Career mobility and job mobility are among its strong characteristics. Thus it is possible to recruit for the civil service experienced, highly trained, and successful persons from the general labour market, even though such persons are already well advanced in non-civil service careers. Other national labour markets may be less flexible in their response to such recruiting efforts.

established in the 1930's it was not staffed from the ranks of the national civil service; instead, it was staffed primarily by newly-recruited experts from the professions and other relevant occupations in the national labour market. Two tests were paramount in the selection process: that the person recruited should have the knowledge and skills needed by the TVA, and that he should have a positive commitment to the objectives of the TVA. Thus programme-commitment, not neutrality, was deliberately sought in the recruitment process. More recent examples—the Atomic Energy Commission, the foreign aid and information agencies, the space agency—serve to support the TVA pattern as a major tendency in the American preference for programme-staffing.

These two choices in recruitment patterns are closely related to a third choice: whether one of the criteria of selection shall emphasize general capacity or specialized capacity. The British pattern is to select the junior members of the administrative class on the basis of their general knowledge and intelligence, demonstrated in examinations that test their mastery of a liberal-arts university education. These juniors are chosen at a young and plastic age; their training for advancement is provided by a variety of experiences within the bureaucracy, an experience pattern which continues to stress generalist capacities—a kind of amateur versatility within the frame of the bureaucratic tradition. The American pattern is a striking contrast. Although a growing number (but perhaps not an increasing proportion) of the bureaucrats are recruited by general examinations not very different from the British, the stronger preference is for specialized personnel often recruited after substantial experience has been acquired outside the bureaucracy. An example is provided by the recent history of the U.S. Foreign Service. In the 1920's the British model was in a general sense adopted as the recruitment method. World War II brought severe tests to this system, and it was in fact drastically modified by the creation of new agencies staffed by specialists. The Foreign Service Act of 1946 was an attempt to restore the generalist pattern of the inter-war years, but the restored system turned out to be not viable. By the mid-1950's it was necessary to reorganize the foreign service personnel system drastically. A massive transfusion of "new blood" was accomplished by transferring into the foreign service corps practically all the specialized and professional personnel of the State Department, so that the U.S. Foreign Service again reflects the deep-seated American preference for the highly-trained and experienced specialist rather than for the generalist.

Yet a fourth choice also confronts the framers of bureaucracies: Shall the interchange of personnel between governmental careers and non-governmental careers be minimized or maximized? The British choice is to minimize the cross-flow of careers between the public and private sectors of employment. The American choice is to maximize the interchange, especially among members of the professions and among business executives and specialists. There are few high-ranking bureaucrats in the U.S. Civil Service who have not in their lifetime been both a bureaucrat and a non-bureaucrat. Exposure to the tests of success in a professional career or in some other private endeavour is more often than not one of the decisive standards in the recruitment of the higher civil service.

These exchanges of personnel between public and private careers are not systematically organized, and are not always consciously sought by the personnel systems, but they are nonetheless one of the durable and prominent character-istics of the American bureaucracy.

These sets of choices, it will be apparent, are closely interrelated, in high de-gree interdependent. It will be apparent, too, that both Britain and the United States have made choices that give each of them a consistent series of choices; each of the two patterns is internally coherent. In a very real sense, also, the British set of choices arises out of the structure of British society, as does the American pattern out of its society. That is to say, each system of choices is indigenous. It is, therefore, doubtful that either is a neat package ready for export to other societies. The two systems of choices are accordingly less a problem in deciding which represents a preferable ideal than a demonstration that these persistent questions about the bureaucracy (Who are to be the bureaucrats? How are the bureaucrats to be chosen?) must be answered for each country in the context of its own society. The British answers, it may be hazarded, produce a more orderly and symmetrical, a more prudent, a more articulate, a more cohesive and more powerful bureaucracy; the American choices, it may be further hazarded, produce a more internally competitive, a more experimental, a noisier and less coherent, a less powerful bureaucracy within its own governmental system, but a more dynamic one. The most per-plexing question remains: for other countries, what is the relevance of these differences for their purposes?

III

What is the role of bureaucrats in governmental decision-making? We are all aware that the actual process of decision-making in governmental systems differs in some marked degree from the formal description of the decision-process. We have often observed, also, that the twentieth century has been especially hard on legislatures everywhere. Thus in Great Britain many commentators refer to Cabinet Government, as a way of noting the decline of the House of Commons, while some go a step farther and speak of Prime Ministerial Government to emphasize an even greater distance between the House and the centre of decisions. Similarly in the United States observers often write of Presidential Supremacy to emphasize a trend away from Congress as a centre of power. In both countries these phrases are oversimplified descriptions of an important fact: there are trends and changes in the decision-making process in all govern-mental systems, and the reality of the process is not found merely in constitu-tional and other formal statements of the way in which power is distributed. The actual process is complex and subtle, and is not easily discovered or described.

In this actual and informal process of governing, it is worthwhile to ask: what is the role of bureaucracy? The formal and official answer in most countries is that the bureaucracy is an agent of the decision-makers, not itself one of the decision-makers but rather their instrument, not an autonomous brain in its own right but rather the neutral executor of plans made by others. This formal theory of the bureaucracy is of course a myth. It is a myth which serves several purposes, but it does not help in a realistic description of the decision-making process. The fact is that in all countries the bureaucracy is one of the important actors in the making of governmental decisions; in some systems the bureaucrats are the leading actors, and in most systems their power as decision-makers would seem to be increasing. Our concern, then, is not with the formal, and now transparent, myth, but with the question of the roles that bureaucrats do in fact have in the decision-making process.

In a decision system does the bureaucrat take the initiative in making policy proposals, or does he wait upon the proposals of others? The answer appears to be that bureaucrats are increasingly the source of initial policy proposals, but that in most systems care is taken to obscure and to make ambiguous their initiating role. That is, the formal theory is deferred to, and a ritual is observed which masks the fact that bureaucrats are actually the source of many initiatives. The British system especially serves to mute the role of the bureaucrat as initiator and framer of policy. The American system, by contrast, pays less deference to formal bureaucratic theory; the higher civil servant is expected to initiate policy proposals, to do so often in full view of the other decision-makers and the public, and to take the career risks associated with such activity. There seems little doubt that the British bureaucrat makes a higher proportion of initial policy proposals than does the American bureaucrat, while the differing style and etiquette of the two systems create the opposite impression. One pattern protects the elected official by inflating his initiating role; the other provides the elected official with competition. One system cloaks the bureaucrat with the safety of anonymity; the other exposes him to equal risks with other decision-makers. The consequences are thus more substantial than they first appear to be.

Beyond the stage of initiation, is the bureaucrat an adviser on, or a protagonist of, policy and programme? The British system emphasizes the advisory and analytical functions of the bureaucrats, but this public posture obscures the more active roles pursued by bureaucrats behind the screen of ministerial responsibility. The American system also demands the advisory and analytical roles for its bureaucrats, but it gives equal or greater emphasis to the bureaucrat as champion of his programme—before Congressional committees, interest groups, and not infrequently with the communication media. This more open and visible policy role for the American bureaucrat is not unchallenged by other actors in the decision-making process (for example, by Congressmen, political executives, interest group leaders, and the communication media), but the role is widely and skilfully managed by the bureaucrats. In a large degree this practice is related to the fact that a substantial proportion of American bureaucrats are more fully committed to policies and programmes than they are to uninterrupted careers in the bureaucracy; many of them move in and out of the public service several times in a life-time. The role of protagonist is a recognized and legitimate role for the American bureaucrat; risks attend it, but these are softened by the alternative careers open to the American civil servant and the genuine prospects of a return to the bureaucracy when the policy wheel has turned.

As one of the actors in the decision-making system is the bureaucrat cast as innovator and source of energy, or as guardian of continuity and stability? The British system emphasizes his role as prudent guardian; his task is to make the minister aware of risks and difficulties, of errors in fact and reason, of unantici-pated and undesirable probable consequences. His most proper role is seen as the firm but deferential vetoer of amateur though perhaps popular enthusiasms. The American system is not free of these tendencies (probably common to the permanent staffs of all large and complex organizations, whether in the public or private sector), but the dominant characteristics of the system encourage the American bureaucrat to be an innovator, a source of forward-moving energy. The controlling expectations of the system are that new ideas, energetically ex-pressed, will emerge from the bureaucracy. The system awards the rank of hero to these innovators, not to the guardians of continuity and stability.

These three aspects of the bureaucrat as policy-maker serve to underscore again the complexities and subtleties of the governing process, the gap between formal doctrine and structure and the realities of decision-making, as well as to emphasize the central role of the bureaucracy in governing. And this central role of the bureaucracy gives significance both to the question of how bureau-crats are to be chosen and to the question of the actual roles of the bureaucrats as initiators of proposals, protagonists of policy, and sources of innovation. These questions in turn lead to an even more crucial one: how are the bureau-crats to be governed?

IV

In any society that has as central institutions large scale, complex organiza-tions for the conduct of governmental business, the bureaucracy has perforce greater power. The bureaucrats thus become not merely a problem in administra-tion but also an important problem in governance. How are the boundaries of bureaucratic power to be set, and by whom? What restraining rules are to con-fine the power role of the bureaucracy? What arrangements in the decision-making apparatus serve to make the bureaucrats visible and responsible actors in the exercise of their power?

Some commentators on these questions answer that the main ingredient of bureaucratic responsibility to democratic norms is a code of behaviour for bureaucrats which emphasizes deference to elected officials and other aspects of the democratic system. This "inner check", a democratic self-restraint to be exercised by the bureaucrats themselves, is regarded by other observers as an insufficient guarantee against bureaucratic domination. These skeptical com-mentators offer alternative answers, the more important of which can be examined by continuing to compare the characteristics of the British and the American bureaucratic systems.

There is first the proposal that the bureaucracy be made representative in its composition. The British system has given small emphasis to this criterion, while the American system has made it a major characteristic. Both systems recruit an elite group in terms of intelligence and skill, although these two terms are given different definitions in the two societies, but the American system has also been concerned to recruit a bureaucracy that is essentially a mirror of the nation—in social and economic class characteristics, in geographic, educational, ethnic, religious, and racial characteristics. To a very large degree, the American system does succeed in its aim to build a bureaucracy which is "representative", not an exotic elite. In fact, some students of the system declare that the American bureaucracy is more representative of American society than is the elected Congress. This is a large claim, and is perhaps not wholly relevant to the problem of a responsible bureaucracy, but it does reflect the degree of the American commitment to an open, mobile and representative bureaucracy, linked closely in its main characteristics to the American society itself.

There is also the proposal that the bureaucracy be made more responsible by making it more internally competitive, to make certain that bureaucrats compete openly with other bureaucrats for the exercise of power. The British system does not have this preference for a bureaucracy that is pluralistic and internally competitive in its structure and operations; instead, it values symmetry and a tightly meshed bureaucracy, especially in the monolithic characteristics of the administrative class at the top of the bureaucratic structure. The American system, by contrast, produces a bureaucracy that is so competitively pluralistic that contesting elements in the bureaucracy are compelled to seek allies outside the bureaucracy—in the Congress, in the interest groups, in the communication media. The American system accordingly does not often pose bureaucratic power against non-bureaucratic power; most often the contest in decision-making power is between opposing alliances each of which contains bureaucratic and non-bureaucratic elements. The American bureaucracy is not, as a consequence, self-contained as a centre of power, nor can it be self-regarding in its goals or strategies; each significant segment of the bureaucracy must be more involved with forces in its non-bureaucratic context than with other bureaucrats. And, to add to the pluralism of the system, most bureaucratic-non-bureaucratic alliances are vulnerable and impermanent, so that there is a constant reshaping and realigning, emphasizing still further the internally competitive nature of the American bureaucracy. Thus, one kind of answer to the problem of bureaucratic power is the American design for producing an internally competitive bureaucracy, a system in which bureaucrats restrain the power of other bureaucrats and each major group of bureaucrats must share power with non-bureaucratic allies.

There is a third approach to the governance of bureaucrats: personal responsibility rather than anonymity for the bureaucrat. In this respect the British and American systems also present contrasts. The British system emphasizes anonymity; the minister not only is required to take full responsibility but the bureaucrat remains a faceless unknown. (The establishment of this convention represents one of the great strategic triumphs of the bureaucracy, since anonymity is a method of exercising power without being required to pay the costs of error.) The American bureaucrat is not an anonymous, invisible actor in the decision-making process. He is, without any important limitation, held responsible for what he does. Presidents may on occasion try to shield him, or department heads may also; but in the end the Congressional committees, the interest groups, the communication media, or other actors, will usually bring home to the bureaucrat his personal responsibility for his own actions. This is not always accomplished with a fine sense of abstract justice—whether the bureaucrat is being praised or blamed—for this is a competitive world of power in which no actor is regarded as either privileged or fragile. The American civil servant who earns high and lasting prestige in his society is usually one who most completely breaks the mask of anonymity and becomes a public figure. There are, of course, situations in which American bureaucrats would prefer the cloak of anonymity, and the convention is sometimes invoked by them or by allies on their behalf; there are also American observers who urge the adoption of the British model. But the system of personal responsibility prevails against these reservations, and appears likely to continue to do so. The visibility and personal responsibility of the bureaucrat is a characteristic built strongly into the American governmental system.

There is, finally, another aspect to the governance of bureaucracies: publicity *versus* secrecy. Here also the British and the American models stand in sharp contrast. In the United States there is a widely accepted code that the public is entitled to know everything about what the government is doing, even what the government is planning to do. The strongest exponents of this doctrine are the communication media, especially the newspapers, which have increasingly used their motto "the Right to Know" as if it were a part of the Bill of Rights. But every cross-section of American society tends to believe that there ought to be no governmental secrets except those which clearly affect national defence or the rights of individual persons to privacy. This general belief is encouraged and made effective by central features of the governmental system: the inquiry powers of the Congressional committees which open up executive branch secrets, the internally competitive bureaucracy which shares its secrets with its outside allies, and the zeal of the communication media in its daily probing to reduce the boundaries of secrecy. The bureaucracy is directly affected by this system of publicity because it is the custodian of most governmental secrets. In the American setting the bureaucrat's inherent preference for secrecy is sharply limited by the assumption of all the other actors that secrecy most often serves the convenience of those who hold the secrets, and that a strong case must be made against publication, the presumptions of the system being that publication is the norm. And, further, the operation of the actual decision-system compels the bureaucrats to share their secrets with non-bureaucratic allies; secrets thus shared are not secrets very long. The functioning of this system, with its strong preference for publicity over secrecy, is not devoid of difficulties. It is accompanied by complaints and counter-complaints, by rough exchanges between the contestants and by rough justice rather than mercy toward some participants, but the system does curtail the bureaucratic uses of secrecy and does make the American governing process one of the most highly visible in the world.

V

These brief and somewhat oversimplified observations on the contrasts between two important bureaucratic systems are intended mainly to suggest a few general hypotheses about bureaucracies. One of them is that in the building of bureaucratic systems there are many options, each choice having different consequences for the whole system; that is, these options are not merely technical issues in personnel management but more importantly choices affecting the nature of the governing process. Another implication is that the contrasting choices made in constructing these two bureaucratic systems were in the main determined by the matrix of the society in which they were each made; in other words, the nature of a particular bureaucracy is linked to the system of government and the society in which it operates. The options are thus limited by the social and political context of the particular bureaucracy, but this is not to suggest a rigid limitation—for example, the context of a parliamentary system does not dictate a particular set of choices. Instead, what is suggested is that the whole indigenous context—social and political and governmental—is the limiting factor. Bureaucratic models are not packages ready for export or import; they provide illustrations of options and styles for consideration in their separate parts, and for adaptation before acceptance in a different context.

chapter XI

RESPONSIBILITY AND CONTROL

In all democracies the expansion of the state domain has resulted in increasing use of *delegated legislation,* that is, rules, regulations, and orders having the force of law issued by the executive under express authorization of the legislature. The executive in effect is invited to legislate on many matters: to fix prices and rates; regulate production; reorganize the executive branch and the civil service; increase or decrease taxes, modify the tariff; supervise and control the manufacture of drugs, the transportation of goods, the administration of hospitals; allocate funds voted by the legislature; establish the conditions under which persons will be drafted into the armed forces or be exempted from service, and so on.

This reflects a profound transformation of the character of law. Diversification of groups and conditions in an industrialized society is so great that the only way to provide for equal opportunities and equal rights is to legislate not according to general rules, but with full realization that conditions call for differential treatment and regulation. Legislative assemblies may attempt to control, to criticize, and to engage the overall political responsibility of the executive, but they cannot cope with the technical problems that legislation involves. They are forced to delegate virtual lawmaking power to the executive.

Widely used devices for implementing state control over the economy in democratic nations are *public corporations.* These are administrative agencies enjoying autonomous status. They are generally free to develop their own personnel policies, and are exempt from the normal budgetary and auditory controls to which the regular departments of government are subject. Within certain limits they are allowed to conduct their operations in the manner considered most expeditious and efficient by the directors. Too much control entails the intervention of the minister or the legislature in technical matters of a managerial nature; too little allows the members of a board to refer only to considerations of managerial efficiency in making decisions—it would leave the nationalized industries in the hands of "technocrats." Too much control would involve too much politics. Too little control would eliminate all political considerations.

Thus, one of the pressing problems of moderate democracies, and of non-democratic systems as well, is to render the civil service responsible without undermining its efficiency. The readings reproduced below are addressed to this problem. How can the bureaucracy be brought under political control? What kind of internal controls may be devised? How can autonomous power to act on the basis of expert and specialized knowledge be reconciled with control by a political superior who does not possess this knowledge? Problems of responsibility are examined in Carl J. Friedrich, ed., *Responsibility* (1960). With reference to delegated legislation and the problems it poses, see: William A. Robson, *Justice and Administrative Law,* 3d ed. (1951) and C. K. Allen, *Law and Orders* (1950). See also, Clinton Rossiter, *Constitutional Dictatorship: Crisis or Government in the Modern Democracies* (1948).

Administrative law is a generalized expression of the administrative state and the existence of administrative, as distinct from ordinary, courts reflects the need of new rules and procedures in order to safeguard individual rights and interests. For a critical view of administrative law and delegated legislation: A. V. Dicey, *The Law and the Constitution* (1885); Lord Hewart, *The New Despotism* (1929); and Friedrich Hayek, *The Road to Serfdom* (1945). A balanced treatment may be found in Charles E. Freedeman, *The Conseil d'Etat in Modern France* (1961); Bernard Schwartz, *French Administrative Law and the Common Law World* (1954); and Arthur W. Macmahon, *Delegation and Autonomy* (1961).

Regular courts may also be used as instrumentalities for the control and review of administrative and even legislative acts. The leading example of judicial review in the name of the supremacy of the constitution is, of course, the United States. A classic statement is E. S. Corwin, *The Doctrine of Judicial Review* (1914). For a more recent assessment, see Robert G. McCloskey, *The American Supreme Court* (1960).

The American practice has not been widely copied. In Britain the supremacy of Parliament cannot be contested by any court of law. In France this was also the case until 1958. Under the Weimar Republic, a special court was empowered to scrutinize legislation and set it aside, but only under very restrictive conditions. Since World War II, on the other hand, there has been a revival of judicial review in Europe, mainly as a reaction to the disregard of individual rights in Nazi Germany. In France, under the constitution of the Fifth Republic, a special Constitutional Court has been set up, whose power, however, is limited to jurisdictional conflicts between the executive and the legislature, the standing orders of the Parliament, and the validity of electoral returns. For a survey of some recent trends, see G. Dietze, "America and Europe—Decline and Emergence of Judicial Review," *Virginia Law Review* (December 1958).

27. Complexity and Control*

C. B. MAC PHERSON

Recent technical change has made it easier to measure and compute many things, but not to measure or compute the political consequences of technical change. Nevertheless, the spectacular successes of technology, and the effects they are having on all ways of life and thought, impose an obligation on political scientists to attempt some assessment of the political effects of technical change.

The importance of such an inquiry is as obvious as are the difficulties. The apparently boundless possibilities of industrial advance through electronic computation and automation have caught the imagination of writers both popular and scientific, to a degree surpassed only by the possible future of atomic energy. Technical advances in the production of foodstuffs, and in the extraction and processing of materials for clothing and shelter, are somewhat less striking, but here too the possible rate of advance is seen as enabling a vast improvement in world standards of living in spite of the expected population increases. The transformation and control of nature which is, in the largest view, the productive process, has clearly reached a new stage. The productive, or physical, consequences of technical advance are direct and clear: so long as technical advance does not destroy civilization, it can scarcely be prevented from enhancing at least its physical basis.

The rate of actual advance in man's control over nature now depends, to an unprecedented extent, on political decisions. It is national and international political decisions about nuclear armaments that will determine whether, or for how long, there is to be any civilization at all. Given that these decisions do permit the continuance of civilization, it is again political decisions which will determine the rate of advance. For although it may be admitted that science and technology have their own momentum, it is evident that in both socialist and non-socialist countries political decisions as to the rate and direction of economic growth and as to the support to be given to technical and scientific education and research will be fundamental to the rate of technical advance.

Thus the central importance of political decision is clear. The question, then, is whether technical change itself is doing or can do anything to make political decisions more efficient—efficient in the ultimate democratic sense which would be accepted in both the Western and the communist concepts of democracy—or whether technical change is making democratic decision less easy or less possible. These questions cannot be answered with any precision. Indeed, even the data for answering them cannot be assembled with any precision. Technical change, of which, as we have said, one of the most striking features is the new ability to

*From "Technical Change and Political Decision," *International Social Science Journal*, no. 3 (1960), pp. 537–68. Reprinted by permission of the United Nations Educational, Scientific and Cultural Organization.

measure and assemble data and so to facilitate decision-making, may well have created more political problems than it can help to solve; but it has certainly not made it possible to say whether this is so or not. Much will depend on political man's adaptability and inventiveness, and we do not know any way to quantify the present level or predict the possible future level of these human qualities.

Another difficulty presents itself at the outset of any such inquiry. Technical change cannot easily be analytically separated from the economic and social changes which accompany it: each is to some extent both cause and effect of the others, and abstract debate about the primacy of one or the other is not very helpful here. Any inquiry into the political effects of technical change alone would be fruitless. One must take into account, along with specific technical changes, significant changes in social relations and ways of thinking and living, for these are limiting, directing, and propulsive forces acting on technical change, whether or not they are themselves thought to be resultants of technical change. An inquiry as broad as this constantly faces the difficulty of becoming an unmanageable inquiry into the political consequences of everything. We can, at most, hope to disentangle some threads of the whole complex question.

THE DEMOCRATIC QUALITY OF DECISIONS

An inquiry into the political effects of technical change must have as one of its central concerns the effects of technical change on the democratic quality of political decisions. By the democratic quality of decisions we mean not simply the degree to which they express the day-to-day and year-to-year demands of the citizens; we mean, rather, the degree to which the decisions do successfully compound those demands with that knowledge, both administrative and expert, which the decision-makers are supposed to possess or to have at their command.

If an inquiry into the effects of technical change on the democratic quality of political decisions is to have more than a very limited reference, it must take into account the existence of very different systems and concepts of democracy in the world today. Democracy, in any sense of the term, requires that the wills of the people shall enter into the making of political decisions in some effective way. This in turn requires more than the formal stipulation, which is found in every democratic state, that those who are authorized to make the political decisions shall directly or indirectly be chosen by the electorate. What further arrangements are supposed to be required varies with different concepts of democracy. In the liberal or Western concept of democracy the essential means of making the wills of the people prevail are (a) competition between political parties, such that an existing set of decision-makers can be periodically replaced by another set and so can be held accountable by the electorate, and (b) some mechanism, usually both formal and informal, by which the public, or more frequently particular publics, are sounded out or specifically consulted before decisions are made. In this view of democracy, while both accountability and consultation are held to be important, accountability is the more so; in the last analysis it is because the decision-makers are accountable that they must, as a matter of prudence, consult those on whose approval their continued authority will depend.

In the communist concept of democracy the order of importance of accountability and consultation may be said to be reversed. There is no competition between political parties to render the top decision-makers accountable to the electorate, and while administrative accountability at lower levels is provided for, it is as much accountability to those above as to those below. The reason why accountability is given little weight in the communist concept of democracy is well understood. In the communist concept, democracy is more a social goal, a form of social relations to be attained by a transformation of society, than a method of current decision-making. The transformation of society is held to require strong direction from the top for an uncertain period of time; hence, during that time, the idea of accountability can be given little weight. But since, in the communist concept, the move towards full communism (and full democracy) requires the active participation of the largest possible number of citizens (in their capacity as producers and in other capacities) the importance of what we have called consultation is very considerable. Consultation must be continuous and widespread, at least at the level of implementing and modifying the general economic plans, and since in the soviet type of government there is no sharp line between legislation and administration, such consultation can be an effective means by which the wills of the governed enter into the decisions of the governors.

We need not, in an introductory essay, pursue these distinctions any further. In any full comparative study of the effects of technical change on democratic political decisions, it would be necessary to examine the specific differences between systems which have such different emphases on accountability and consultation. Here we may content ourselves with considering the effects of technical change both on accountability and on consultation.

A PATTERN OF INQUIRY

Two leading questions suggest themselves at once, arising out of two of the most obvious implications of technical change. We may ask, first, whether the speed with which political decisions must be taken as a result of technical change has led to, or tends to lead to, a decline in the democratic quality of political decisions, that is, a decrease in accountability or in effective consultation. And secondly, does the complexity of the political decisions which now have to be made, or the amount of knowledge required to make those decisions intelligently, lead to a decline in the democratic quality of decision-making?

When we address ourselves to these questions, we soon find that it is convenient to make a further distinction: between decisions of the first order of importance, and those of the second and subsequent orders of importance. No one will dispute that decisions about war or peace now outrank in importance all other political decisions. The elevation of those decisions to first rank is itself the result of the outstanding technical change of our age. Decisions as to whether to continue the manufacture and export of nuclear armaments, decisions as to the circumstances in which they are or are not to be used, and decisions of foreign or international policy which may affect the possibility of their use or the demand for their use, are clearly in a class by themselves.

In the second order of importance we may put national economic policies, that is, the main decisions as to the rate of investment, the redistribution of income through taxation or pricing policies, and so on. These decisions must now be made by national governments of every kind, socialist and non-socialist. They have a profound effect on the pace and direction of a country's development and on the daily lives of the citizens. In the third order of importance— not to complicate our classification unnecessarily—we may put all other kinds of governmental decisions, including the many legislative decisions and the thousands of administrative decisions that must be made in working out the decisions of the second order of importance.

This crude classification is indeed somewhat arbitrary. It might well be argued that certain decisions, here relegated to the third order of importance, should have been put in the second order. But the contents of the orders could be varied to some extent without significantly affecting the analysis that would follow from the suggested classification. Hence this oversimple classification will serve. . . .

SPEED, ACCOUNTABILITY AND CONSULTATION

Let us look first at the question of the speed with which political decisions must now be made. It will be granted that if there is a significant increase in the speed with which any classes of political decision must be made as a result of technical change, the increase in speed will operate to decrease the degree of effective consultation between those authorized to make the decisions and those affected by them. The quicker the decision, the fewer (even of those within the government) can be consulted. To this, one proviso must be made: if, before the increase in speed, the degree of consultation in any class of decisions was close to zero, the change in the degree of consultation will be insignificant.

The effect of increased speed of decision-making on the accountability of the decision-makers is less obvious, but one would expect it also to be negative. For there is no reason to suppose that an increase in the speed of making decisions will be matched by an increase in the speed with which the reasons for the decisions can be explained to and judged by the people. Yet the people cannot effectively hold the decision-makers to account, consistently with any rational concept of democracy, except in the measure that they know enough to do so. The same proviso must be made here as in the case of the degree of consultation: if, before the increase in speed, the degree of accountability in any class of decisions was close to zero, the change in the degree of accountability will be insignificant.

Bearing in mind these general propositions, we must now ask whether the speed with which political decisions must now be made has been significantly increased as a result of technical change, in any of the classes of decisions we have distinguished. In decisions of the first order of importance, one such increase in required speed does indeed haunt us: the decision to push the button which would send nuclear ballistic missiles towards a supposed enemy country must be made within a few minutes of the moment of the appearance of supposedly hostile objects on radar screens. The human consequences of the decision, together with the chances of error and accident, are appalling. The decision must be made by very few people, and in the nature of the case they cannot be held accountable. We seem to have here a clear case of technical change having resulted directly in a diminution (indeed, a disappearance) of democratic consultation and accountability in a decision of the first order of importance. However, the decision whether or not to push the button in such circumstances is not a political but a technical decision. The political decision was, and is, whether or not to have the push-button.

This decision is a continuing one, both in the countries which have nuclear armament and those which have not, and with it, of course, a whole range of foreign policy decision is inextricably involved. Is the speed with which these decisions must be made, in country after country, any greater now than in the pre-nuclear age? In principle, yes. For it is admitted on all sides, including the governments which maintain nuclear armaments, that nuclear disarmament is necessary for the survival of civilization. And, although this is not so widely admitted, the time available for making the political decisions that are necessary to put this into practice grows steadily less, because the statistical probability of the totally destructive mechanism being set in motion through accident or error increases more rapidly the longer those decisions are delayed.

But how, if at all, does the logical necessity for greater speed in those decisions work out in practice? The necessary decisions have not yet been made. But governments now show a greater readiness than ever before to move more steadily towards the agreements that are needed for those decisions. International conferences are more frequent, more protracted, and more readily resumed in some other form, than in the pre-nuclear era. To what extent this limited change has been due to the pressure of public opinion, and to what extent to the decision-makers' understanding of the new logic of the situation and their new vulnerability, we do not know. Nor can we be sure to what extent the future course of decisions will be a response to public opinion and thus an evidence of the effectiveness of public opinion in the new circumstances. For the technical change in armament has set in motion two opposite tendencies in the democratic process. On the one hand, the immensity of the consequence of nuclear decisions seems to have produced in some parts of the public a fatalistic apathy. On the other hand, there is in some quarters a new sense of the urgency and importance of organizing new pressures on the decision-makers.

We can perhaps say that just because the nuclear revolution has made the political issues more stark, and in that sense simpler to understand, the pressure of public opinion should be capable of making itself felt more rapidly on these decisions in the future than in the past. It is possible, then, but not demonstrable, that the speed with which democratic pressure is formed and brought to bear on decisions of the first order of importance will increase in the same measure as, or in greater measure than, the required increase in the speed with which the decisions must be made; if so, there need be no diminution, and there may be an increase, in the democratic quality of the decision-making. And when, finally, we bring into the calculation an estimate of the earlier degree of democratic control of decisions of foreign policy, any diminution of their democratic quality as a result of the technical change in question seems unlikely. For in every nation, however democratic its system of government, foreign policy decisions and especially the decisions for war or peace have usually been the least democratically made. The degree of accountability and of consultation that characterized those decisions before the nuclear era was close enough to zero that no significant decrease in their democratic quality can be charted.

Turn now to decisions of the second and third orders of importance, in which there has normally been an appreciable amount of accountability and consultation. Has technical change brought any increase in the speed with which these decisions are made, and if so has it tended to reduce accountability and consultation? We pass very briefly over these questions, for there is little reason to think that technical change has brought any change in the speed of these decisions; the effects of technical change here are to be sought rather in the effects of increased complexity than of increased speed. It might of course be argued that in, for instance, decisions of national economic policy, changes in the techniques of economic and statistical analysis (notably with the development of electronic computation) have increased the speed with which material can be organized in usable form, and hence the speed with which decisions can be made, without there being any increase in the speed with which they must be made. If the speed with which decisions must be made does not increase, while the speed with which the material for decisions can be assembled does increase, the time available for democratic consultation appears to be greater. But this does not necessarily follow. Consultation on decisions of central economic policy is normally between the government and officers of the large organizations representing various economic interests. Anyone who has observed such consultations will have noticed that the more quickly statistics can be produced on both sides of the table, the more time is consumed in arguing about their validity and their interpretation. It cannot be concluded that the degree of effective consultation is increased.

COMPLEXITY, ACCOUNTABILITY AND CONSULTATION

It is apparent that the question of speed of decision-making merges into the question of complexity, and we may turn at once to the latter. In considering the effects of increased complexity of political decisions on the democratic quality of decision-making, we shall confine ourselves largely to decisions of the second and third orders of importance. Decisions of the first order can be neglected here for two reasons, both suggested earlier. First the degree of accountability and consultation in decisions for war and peace and in foreign policy decisions generally has always been sufficiently close to zero that no increase in their complexity would significantly reduce their democratic quality. Secondly, while in one sense these decisions share the growing complexity of political decisions generally, in another sense the possible finality of such decisions in the nuclear age simplifies them in the popular understanding; they cannot therefore be assumed to be automatically increasing in complexity.

Going on, then, to decisions of the second and third orders of importance, we have to consider whether technical change has increased their complexity, and whether any such change has reduced (a) the extent to which the decision-makers can be held accountable, and (b) the extent to which democratic consultation enters into the decisions. It is tempting to answer all these questions immediately in the affirmative. It is amply apparent that the number of decisions made by governments and governmental agencies is much greater now than it was 50 or even 20 years ago. All such decisions must, to some extent, be made in relation to each other, for each has some bearing on others at various levels, notably at the level of the national budget or national economic plan. Thus every increase in the number of decisions may be said to increase the complexity of each decision. And one would assume that the greater the complexity, the greater the distance between the decision-makers and the non-decision-makers, and so the less the accountability and the effective consultation.

But while it is tempting to argue that technical change thus leads to decline in the democratic quality of decisions, it is not valid to do so. For the increase in the number and complexity of governmental decisions is hardly at all due to technical change. It is the combined result of the rise of the socialist state and the rise of the welfare state. And however one may explain their rise, whether as the outcome of changes in the fundamental nature of society, changed relations of production, or changes in the degree of class or national consciousness, one can hardly explain it as the outcome of technical change, except in the remote sense that improvements in the techniques of production have been a necessary condition of the emergence of the socialist and the welfare state. In short, it is for reasons having little directly to do with technical change that the number and complexity of governmental decisions has increased.

This being so, we must restate our question. Acknowledging the increase in complexity (from causes other than technical change), and assuming that any increase in complexity tends by itself to reduce the degree of democratic accountability and consultation, we must ask whether technical changes have done or can do anything to counteract the tendency to reduced democratic accountability and consultation. The question so stated is still somewhat too simple. For while the main increase in complexity of decisions is not due to technical change, it is true that the number of governmental decisions into which technical expertise must enter has increased. And it may also be found that the amount of expertise that must enter into the average decision is steadily increasing. The special skills of the town-planner, the economist, the specialist in nutrition or in mental health, the civil aviation expert, the agronomist, and so on, must increasingly enter into political decisions. And as each of these skills becomes more refined, it becomes more difficult to convey the results of expert thinking to the politicians and the public in terms which they can understand.

Every increase in the special knowledge required to make political decisions may be considered an increase in the complexity of those decisions. Hence there is, after all, some increase in complexity of decisions as a result of technical change. Our question, then, should be restated again. We should ask whether technical changes have done or can do more to counteract the tendency to reduced accountability and consultation than to reinforce it.

The problem when stated in this way can be seen to be a problem of communication in the broadest sense of that term. The heart of the problem is whether the public, and particular publics, can know enough to hold the decision-makers responsible or to enter into effective consultation with them. With every increase in the complexity of political decisions and the special knowledge that is required to make them, the ability of the public, and of particular publics, to understand the factors in the decision must increase if the democratic quality of the decisions is not to diminish.

We have referred to the public and particular publics. Political scientists are no longer satisfied with the simple model of democracy in which detached, informed, citizens make their wishes felt through their elected representatives, and periodically choose rationally between two or more sets of policies by voting for one party or another in general elections. It is true that in democracies which operate by a system of competing parties, the periodic choosing of governing parties by the whole electorate remains of central importance; so therefore does the ability of the whole electorate (the public) to comprehend the issues. But the electorate as a whole can at best give only a very general verdict at elections. The democratic quality of decision-making in between elections has come to depend increasingly on the degree to which particular publics can make their demands enter into the decisions. It is easier for governments to deal with organized groups than with an amorphous general public. These organized groups may themselves be political parties, or they may be interest groups (*groupes de pression*) which seek to influence governments at either the administrative or political levels or both. Such interest or pressure groups can, in the theoretical model now widely favoured, do much to make up for the obvious deficiencies of democratic control by the general electorate.

In this view, it is the ability both of the general public and of these particular publics to keep pace with the increasing complexity of governmental decisions that will determine the democratic quality of the decisions. Their ability to keep pace is largely a function of communication. Between whom must communication be adequate in order to maintain the democratic quality of decisions? First, between the politicians and the public, in both directions. Secondly, between the politicians and particular publics, again in both directions. And thirdly, since many decisions, especially among those of the third order of importance, are now made not by ministers or parliaments but by administrative officials, between the officials and the publics. And one might add, fourthly, between the politicians and the administrative officials.

What must be communicated, in order to maintain the democratic quality of decisions? The decision-makers must be able to communicate to the publics an understanding of the numerous factors that must or should enter into a decision that is to be made or that has been made; this involves an understanding of the relations between the factors and of the consequences of attaching different weights to them. The publics must also be able to register their views and to make them felt. But more than this is required. For we should not assume that the initiative should always come from the government. Members of the public, or of particular publics, should be able to take the initiative and to make the government aware of new problems and new possibilities. If the democratic quality of decisions is not to be reduced, communication of all these kinds must keep pace with the increasing complexity of the decisions.

This is a formidable list of requirements. The tasks it sets for technical change are not easy. Have technical changes in communication, in the broadest sense, done anything, or can they do anything, to offset the growing complexity of what must be communicated? It will be convenient to include here, under the heading of technical changes in communication, modern developments in electronic computation and even in automation, so far as the latter may be found relevant. Although they could equally well be treated in their own right, they can be considered to be aspects of communication: electronic computation is a means by which information can be sorted and transmitted in usable form to decision-makers; automation is an extension of that process to include the automatic making and execution of decisions according to a pre-arranged pattern.

Is the electronic revolution at all relevant to our problem of the democratic quality of decision-making? Electronic computation devices enormously increase the amount of information that can be assembled and put into usable form for decision-makers within the time in which decisions must be made. Indeed, if all the criteria that are thought to be relevant, and the weights to be attached to them, can be decided beforehand, the machine can make the decision. In automation the decisions are not only made but automatically carried out. In both computation and automation, the decisions as to what factors are relevant and what weights are to be given to them must be made in advance. Now it is evident that a great many administrative and political decisions are made today on the basis of less than the desirable amount of up-to-date information. Any technical changes which could increase the amount of information gathered and sorted, and the speed with which this could be done, would be a welcome contribution to the efficiency of the decisions. There is no reason why electronic devices cannot be beneficially introduced into public administration as well as into commercial and military administration. But the possible extent of their usefulness in political decision-making is far more limited than in commercial or military decision-making.

No electronic devices can be expected to reach as far as the democratic element in decision-making. This can readily be seen when the essential characteristics of the different types of decision are compared. In commercial and military operations the criteria are simpler, in that they can more nearly be stated in terms of a single objective and a single measurement of gains and costs. In commercial operations, while there are problems of long-run versus short-run net advantages, profit is the single criterion and all the factors affecting it can be reduced to the same monetary unit of calculation. In military operations the object is equally a single one, to impose one's will on the enemy. And while military commanders will normally try to do this at the least cost in lives (that is, of the lives on their side), the final weighting of human losses against strategic gains is not a military but a political decision.

In short, political decisions differ from commercial and military ones precisely in the one respect that we are here concerned with. In political decisions, if they are to have any democratic quality, the objectives themselves are not given (as they are in the other kinds of operations). More accurately, in democratic political decisions the weights to be given to different possible gains and different possible costs cannot be reduced to a single measurable standard nor determined by a single universally acceptable criterion. For this reason the use of electronic devices by the authorized political decision-makers cannot be expected to improve the democratic quality of political decisions.

So far we have been considering electronic computation as a communications device in a rather special sense: we have been looking at the way it communicates information from the environment so to speak, to the decision-makers. What of its possible role in communication in the more usual sense? Might it improve the quality of communication between the decision-makers and at least the particular publics that we call interest groups, by enabling the data for consultations between them to be assembled more fully and accurately? It might be argued that in such a way electronic computation could offset the growing complexity of the material which must now enter into effective discussion, and so improve the democratic quality of the consultation. Some improvement in the effective relation between governmental agencies and interest groups might thus be possible. But we must not overlook one effect which any increased use of such devices would have within the interest group itself: it would tend to give more real power of decision to the officials and experts within the interest groups at the expense of their membership. Anything which renders the internal structure of the interest groups less democratic is unlikely to improve the democratic quality of consultation between them and the government.

We cannot leave the subject of electronic developments without noticing one indirect but pervasive political effect that may be attributed in part to automation. In many countries political apathy is becoming a serious threat to effective democracy. Individuals, especially the younger generation of the electorate, have lost confidence in the democratic process or have no confidence in themselves as elements in the democratic process. This is attributable in part at least to technical changes in industry, changes of which automation is merely the most recent instalment. Technical change in industry and commerce increases the size of the average unit, increases the degree of expertise required for control and decision-making, and brings more and more of the work under an automatic discipline which calls for little judgment and skill and is best done by apathetic workers, perhaps soothed and moderately diverted by piped-in music. The disinterest and sense of personal insignificance so engendered in men in their working time affects their whole personality, and easily spills over into their political life, the more so to the extent that they see the same sort of people in directing and managerial positions in politics as in industry.

The net effect, then, of the technical changes we have considered so far appears to be to diminish the democratic quality of political decisions. It need not be so. A realization of the new possibilities for human freedom and initiative that are being released by technical changes in the productive process could, if widespread enough, bring an upsurge of democratic feeling counteracting the trend towards withdrawal and apathy. We do not know at present which tendency will prevail.

We may also consider briefly one other technical development which can have a direct bearing on the democratic process, namely, television. We need only pass in review some of the more evident possible effects of its spread. The most direct political effect is to be expected from the fact that political leaders can now be seen and heard by the whole electorate at once. Here, surely, is a technical change of very great importance, an enormous improvement in the means of communication between politicians and the public.

But this is communication in one direction only. The public can sit back but cannot talk back; their part is a wholly passive one. The same could of course be said about the role of the public in relation to the other mass media of communication: the general public has never been able to use the radio or the press to talk back. But we must consider also the ability of particular publics (the political parties and pressure groups) to answer back in the same medium. Here we do find some difference between television and the other media. The access which particular publics have to television is likely to be somewhat less than their access to the older media. Access to television broadcasting tends to be more limited to the orthodox within and among parties and pressure groups, because television, even more than the other media, is subject to monopoly or oligopoly control. Yet unless minority movements both within and among parties and pressure groups can effectively present new views, new ways of seeing problems, and new ways to their solution, a necessary part of the democratic process is impaired. Competition between the orthodox is no doubt more democratic than no competition at all, but in the measure that competition is confined to the orthodox the democratic quality of political communication is diminished. Thus, to the extent that television supplants other media of communication, the effect of its oligopolistic control is to reduce the democratic quality of the political process.

Much else could be said, and has been said by many observers, about the apparent political effects of television. It enhances the role of personality in politics, to the detriment of democratic responsibility. It turns elections into plebiscites or into single combats between leaders. Its general impact on the public contributes powerfully to that trivialization of culture and pulverization of the mind which were already well advanced from other causes. All these charges would bear analysis; if true, the net effect of television on the democratic process would be disastrous. But even without extensive analysis one may suspect that while the effects are as stated, they are not effects of television but of the prevailing economic and social relations of our time.

PROSPECTS

We return thus to the point made in the beginning. The effects of technical change on the democratic process cannot readily be isolated from the effects of changes in economic relations, in class structures, in nationalist aspirations and other fundamental social changes, none of which can themselves be attributed (except very indirectly) to technical change. The technical changes which have, or can have, a direct part in democratic decision-making may hinder or hasten tendencies which existed independently of those changes. But the impact of technical changes seems in every case to be of slight force compared with the other changes. The increased complexity of the decisions that must be made by governmental agencies is due in much larger part to the increase in the tasks they must perform in the socialist and the welfare state, than to the greater degree of special knowledge required for the performance of these tasks. Technical changes in the processing and communication of data, while they may improve the efficiency of the decision-makers, seem unlikely to touch the democratic quality of the decisions. And technical changes in the media of public communication appear, so far, to be of little consequence beside the changes in attitude and behaviour of the electorate which must be ascribed to other causes.

But if the force of technical change is less than the force of other changes, the two may still combine to produce results more striking than simple addition would yield. The effect of technical change on the democratic process cannot be detached from the larger question of the effect of technical change on the chances of maintaining civilization. The critical point is whether a democratic decision (or rather, the necessary series of democratic decisions) between the disastrous and the beneficial effects of technical change can be made in time to permit the continuance of civilization, and with it a further unfolding of democracy. The same qualities of imagination and social inventiveness that are needed to make those decisions should be quite sufficient to deal with the continuing problems of democratic decision-making.

28. The Parliamentary Ombudsman*

DONALD C. ROWAT

Each of the Scandinavian countries—Sweden, Finland, Denmark and Norway—now has an officer of parliament commonly known as the Ombudsman, whose job is to investigate complaints from citizens about the way they have been treated by government officials and, when he finds it necessary, to recommend remedial action. Recently, this Ombudsman scheme has gained widespread attention in other countries, particularly in the English-speaking world, and much discussion has taken place about whether it should be adopted elsewhere. In this article, then, we consider the history and nature of the scheme, the reasons why it is thought to be desirable in the modern democratic state, and arguments that have been raised against its transplantation to other countries.

I

The office of Ombudsman was first created by the Swedish Constitution Act of 1809, over 150 years ago. It has an even earlier prototype, however, the King's Chancellor of Justice, which extends far back into Swedish history. The Chancellor of Justice was empowered by the King to supervise the application of the law by judges and other officials. With the rise of parliamentary democracy in Sweden it became clear that the Chancellor's status as part of the executive made him too dependent upon executive authority. As a result, Parliament wrested the office from the executive by gaining power over the appointment of the incumbent. But Parliament lost its control over the executive after a short period, in 1772. When it regained control, in 1809, it decided to appoint an additional officer, the Ombudsman, as its own defender of the law. Just as the British Parliament's struggle for financial control over the executive laid the groundwork for the appointment of an Auditor General, the Swedish Parliament's struggle for political control laid the basis for the appointment of an Ombudsman.

Finland, too, has long had a Chancellor of Justice with powers of supervising the courts and the administration. Unlike Sweden, however, Finland, under its 1919 Constitution, made the Chancellor partially independent of the executive. In addition it created a parallel office of parliamentary Ombudsman. Thus Finland, like Sweden, has two public defenders, each with the power to receive and investigate complaints. But because of the historic prestige and independence

*From "The Parliamentary Ombudsman: Should the Scandinavian Scheme Be Transplanted?" *International Review of the Administrative Sciences*, no. 4 (1962), pp. 399–405. Reprinted by permission of the Institut International des Sciences Administratives, Brussels. Footnotes abridged by the editors.

of the Finnish Chancellor, he is much more powerful than his Swedish counterpart, and is perhaps even more important than the Finnish Ombudsman as a defender of the law.

Impressed with the obvious advantages of the schemes in Sweden and Finland, Denmark decided to adopt the institution under its new Constitution of 1953, and its first Ombudsman was appointed in 1955. Although the Norwegian Committee on Administrative Procedure, headed by the Chief Justice, had recommended a civilian Ombudsman for Norway in 1958, it was not until 1961 that the Norwegian Government introduced a bill on the subject, and the Parliament did not actually adopt the institution until the summer of 1962. The new Norwegian scheme is patterned mainly upon its Danish counterpart.

As one might expect, there are some significant differences among the Nordic countries in the Ombudsman's powers and procedures. The jurisdiction of the Swedish and Finnish officers is more extensive than that of their Danish and Norwegian counterparts. In Sweden and Finland the Ombudsman supervises not only the administration but also the courts, and has the direct power to prosecute officials before the courts for illegal acts. In Denmark he may only order that a prosecution be initiated, while in Norway he may only recommend this. Finland used to be the only country in which the Ombudsman supervised local government officials, but Sweden extended his jurisdiction to include them in 1957, Denmark did likewise in 1961, and it is expected that Norway will do so too. In Sweden and Norway the Ombudsman's jurisdiction does not extend to the armed services, because these countries have a special Military Ombudsman, dating in Sweden from 1915 and in Norway from 1952.

Another significant difference is that in cases where administrative authorities have been given discretionary power, in Sweden the Ombudsman has no specific right to criticize the wisdom of a decision and rarely does so, while in Denmark he has been given the right to do so if he considers the decision to be unreasonable. The Norwegian Committee proposed a similar power for the Ombudsman. The Norwegian Government at first refused this recommendation, but then accepted the wording "clearly unreasonable." The importance of these differences should not be exaggerated, however, because the Danish Ombudsman has used this power sparingly, while the Swedish Ombudsman has usually managed to intervene on grounds of illegality where a decision was patently unreasonable. He may conclude, for example, that a decision not based on the facts should be considered illegal. Moreover, the Nordic countries provide opportunities for appealing discretionary decisions that are wider than in the common-law countries. Both Finland and Sweden have a system of administrative appeal courts, which in Sweden may deal specifically with the reasonableness of decisions, and the courts in all four countries may hear appeals on grounds of both law and fact.

In other respects the competence and practices of the Nordic Ombudsmen are much the same. All of them can receive and investigate any written complaint, which can be submitted in a sealed envelope without reference to any superior authority. All can initiate investigations and make inspections, without

without first having received a specific complaint. All can call upon government agencies to give reports and all have the power to demand departmental records. All are appointed by Parliament, are entirely independent of the executive, and report annually to a special committee of the House. All can comment critically on official actions in their annual reports, and all can make a report on an urgent matter at any time. In the Commonwealth countries, the position of the Auditor General as an officer of Parliament is a close parallel, except of course that the Auditor General checks financial transactions rather than administrative decisions.

When the Ombudsmen find that a complaint is justified, in the less serious cases they make critical comments directly to the officers of the department or agency concerned. Many cases involve no more than explaining fully to the bewildered citizen the reasons for the decision of which he has complained, and warning the government office in question that in future it should give adequate reasons for its decisions. But the Ombudsmen's conclusions on important cases are given wide publicity and exert a profound influence on future administrative practice. Moreover, on questions of principle arising from cases investigated, the Ombudsmen can propose amendments in the regulations or the law.

The matters they investigate range all the way from official misbehaviour and outright illegality to less serious complaints of tardiness, inefficiency, or negligence. It is in the latter type of case that the Ombudsman comes into his own, for it is here that the biggest gap occurs in our systems of administrative control. Examples range from complaints about getting no answer to an application, leisureliness in replying to mail, tardiness or bias in making decisions, to giving insufficient information on a decision or right of appeal. Nevertheless, some of the Ombudsmen's most valuable work has been done on serious cases of illegality involving the liberty of the subject. Here are some recent examples from Sweden and Denmark: a mental patient complained that a male nurse had assaulted him; inadequate consent was given for mental patients to undergo shock treatment and brain operations; police unjustifiably recorded telephone conversations; a prison warden barred a magazine from his prison simply because one issue had criticized prison authorities; handcuffs were used unjustifiably; and the police refused to remove an acquitted person's photograph and fingerprints from police files. Nearly all of these are cases in which redress might have been given had they been taken to the courts, but in most of them the citizen could not be expected to know his rights, would not know what to do about it if he did, and very likely could not afford expensive aid. In several such cases the Ombudsmen have secured court action and free legal aid for the complainants. In others, they have simply demanded direct redress for the action and assurance that similar actions will not occur again. Where the authority refuses this redress, the Ombudsmen will of course report critically on the case to Parliament.

Some idea of the nature and extent of the Ombudsmen's work may be gained by considering the number and disposition of the cases with which they deal. Each handles about 1,000 cases per year (not counting about 1,000 handled by the Military Ombudsman and the Chancellor of Justice in Sweden, and 1,500 by the Chancellor in Finland). Most of them arise out of complaints from the public, but cases initiated by the Ombudsman himself, as a result of inspections or reports in the press, account for a large proportion of the criticisms and prosecutions. In Finland and Denmark only 10 to 15 per cent of all cases require criticism, recommendations, disciplinary action or prosecution, but in Sweden the proportion is above 20 per cent. Probably the reason for the higher percentage in Sweden is the greater number of cases that arise from inspections, nearly all of which require criticism or remedial action. Another reason may be the long experience with the institution in Sweden and the public's better knowledge of which actions are likely to be condemned by the Ombudsman.

The total number of cases per year requiring criticism or remedial action is about 70 in Denmark, and in Finland is nearly 100 (not counting about 200 handled by the Chancellor of Justice). In Sweden, a country of about eight million, the total was close to 300 in 1960 (not counting about 200 handled by the Military Ombudsman and a few by the Chancellor). This will give the reader some idea of the number of cases of maladministration and injustice that may be going unnoticed in other countries each year. The number may even be proportionately greater in the common-law countries, because of the weaker role played by the courts and administrative appeal bodies, and also because the mere existence of the Ombudsman scheme is a powerful preventive influence. Yet a democracy should be ashamed of even one substantial case of unremedied injustice per year.

II

The success of the new Ombudsman scheme in Denmark, and the discussion and recent adoption of it in Norway have caused other countries to become interested in the idea. In 1957, Western Germany adopted the institution of the Military Ombudsman, patterned to some extent on the systems in Sweden and Norway, and it is reported to be working successfully there. Partly as a result of the Danish Ombudsman's willingness to write and lecture in English about his new office, the United Kingdom and New Zealand took up the idea. Widespread discussion has ensued in the United Kingdom, and in 1961 the British Section of the International Commission of Jurists, *Justice,* issued a report, the so-called Whyatt Report, recommending the scheme.[1] So far, however, the British Government has made no favourable pronouncement on the matter. The New Zealand Government, on the other hand, has pursued the idea enthusiastically, and in 1961 introduced a bill on the subject. This bill was re-introduced and passed in the summer of 1962, and Sir Guy Powles, former High Commissioner to India, has been appointed as Ombudsman. In Canada, too, the scheme is now being discussed widely, and in the United States several articles have appeared

[1] *The Citizen and the Administration* (London, 1961); Director of Research, Sir John Whyatt.

favouring its adoption, with suitable adjustments, at least by the state and local governments.[2] In 1961, a Committee appointed by the Mayor of Philadelphia and chaired by the Dean of Law at the University of Pennsylvania recommended the system for Philadelphia, and the Administrative Conference of the United States is now considering the idea for the national government. In the summer of 1962 the United Nations held a European seminar in Stockholm on protections against the abuse of administrative authority, at which the scheme was fully discussed. Several Western European countries are now becoming more interested. In the Netherlands, for example, a semi-official committee under the chairmanship of A. D. Belinfante, Professor of Constitutional Law at the University of Amsterdam, is considering the scheme. Since the war, other countries of the world, such as Indonesia and the Philippines, have set up related schemes with similar functions. In the Philippines, for example, President Magsaysay appointed a complaints committee to receive and investigate complaints about official action.

The reason for this widespread interest in the Ombudsman type of institution is not far to seek: there is need for additional protection against administrative arbitrariness in the modern democratic state. All democratic countries in the twentieth century have experienced a shift from the laissez-faire to the positive stage. The accompanying tremendous growth in the range and complexity of government activities has brought with it the need to grant increasing powers of discretion to the executive side of government. As one of Britain's great constitutional lawyers, A. V. Dicey, has warned, "Wherever there is discretion, there is room for arbitrariness." In other words, it is quite possible nowadays for a citizen's rights to be accidentally crushed by the vast juggernaut of the government's administrative machine. In this age of the welfare state, thousands of administrative decisions are made each year, many of them by minor officials, which affect the lives of every citizen. If some of these decisions are arbitrary or unjustified, there is no easy way for the ordinary citizen to gain redress. In the preface to the recent Whyatt Report, Lord Shawcross expressed the situation in these words (p. xiii):

> The general standards of administration in this country are high, probably indeed higher than in any other. But with the existence of a great bureaucracy there are inevitably occasions, not insignificant in number, when through error or indifference, injustice is done—or appears to be done. The man of substance can deal with these situations. He is near to the establishment; he enjoys the status or possesses the influence which will ensure him the ear of those in authority. He can afford to pursue such legal remedies as may be available. He knows his way around. But too often the little man, the ordinary humble citizen, is incapable of asserting himself. . . . The little man has become too used to being pushed around: it rarely occurs to him that there is

---

[2] See, for example, H. J. Abraham, "People's Watchdog against Abuse of Power," *Public Administration Review*, vol. XX, no. 3 (Summer 1960), pp. 152–57, and K. C. Davis, "Ombudsmen in America," *Public Law* (Spring 1962), pp. 34–42.

any appeal from what "they" have decided. And as this Report shows, too often in fact there is not.

In the past the courts were the bulwark of individual rights. But the ordinary courts have lost their flexibility and are no longer an effective instrument for remedying the wrongs of modern administrative action. The courts are too costly, cumbersome and slow, and in the English-speaking world the extent of their power to review is not at all clear, though certainly severely limited. Generally, they will review a decision only on a question of legality and refuse to review its content, wisdom, or even reasonableness. For these reasons, in most common-law countries special administrative appeal bodies have been created, to which an aggrieved citizen may take his case. But these bodies cover only a small portion of the total field of administrative action, and the vast majority of administrative decisions carry no formal right of appeal. The situation is better, of course, in those European countries that have developed a comprehensive system of administrative courts, where appeal is easy and cheap. But even administrative courts can be imperfect. Many of them are cumbersome and slow, so that the delay in deciding cases results in a denial of justice. It is significant that though Sweden and Finland have administrative courts, in recent years their Ombudsmen have found it increasingly necessary to extend their supervision over administrative agencies.

The right to complain to one's Member of Parliament does not meet the problem. Citizens often do not know of this avenue of appeal, and it is usually unsuitable anyway. In countries with a parliamentary system of government, especially where there are only two major parties, the executive tends to dominate the legislature and to maintain a tradition of secrecy. Hence it is difficult to bring cases of maladministration to light. The Member's usual method of dealing with a complaint is to send an inquiry to the department concerned. Naturally the department is likely to put the best light on its own case, and the Member has no impartial source of information. If he is dissatisfied with the department's reply, about all he can do is ask a question of the Minister in the House. Even though the Minister may have had nothing to do with the original decision, he will naturally consider himself a party to the decision and will defend it as his own. About the only further recourse is for the Member, still with inadequate information, to debate the complaint in the House—in which case it will turn into a political battle with the dice loaded in favour of the Minister. The opposition party can of course demand a formal inquiry, but an inquiry is costly and cumbersome, and is accepted by a government only after enough public outcry has been raised. Clearly it is not an adequate device for remedying the average administrative wrong done to the little man. Even in countries where there is a multi-party situation and the executive is not quite so dominant, there is usually no adequate parliamentary procedure for handling complaints, sifting evidence or making recommendations.

In view of the shortcomings of all of these traditional protections against administrative arbitrariness, we may conclude that the office of Ombudsman has a number of desirable characteristics which argue for its adoption. In the words of the Whyatt Report (p. 52):

First, there is the principle of impartial investigation. If a citizen makes a complaint against the conduct of a civil servant, the matter is investigated and reported upon by the Ombudsman, who is an impartial authority entirely independent of the Administration. Secondly, the impartial authority acts on behalf of Parliament although he is also protecting the interests of the individual complainant. Thirdly, the investigation is conducted openly . . . Fourthly, the method of submitting complaints and the investigation of complaints is very informal.

And one might add that, fifthly, since the great weapon of the Ombudsman is criticism, he does not interfere with day-to-day administration. Unlike appeal bodies, he does not substitute his judgment for that of the official, nor does he, like the courts, quash decisions.

III

Let us now consider some of the arguments that have been raised against transplanting the Ombudsman scheme. One reason the English-speaking world took so little interest in the institution before it was adopted in Denmark is that nothing was known of the Finnish plan, and of the Swedish scheme it was argued that the systems of government and law in Sweden were too different for the scheme to be applicable. Sweden has administrative appeal courts, a different system of court review, and a unique tradition of publicity whereby the press and the citizens may have access to departmental files at any time. More important, Sweden has an administrative system radically different from most others; Swedish departments resemble public corporations in their independence, and are not subject to detailed day-to-day control by the Ministers responsible to Parliament. Because of these differences, it was said that the scheme would not work elsewhere. However, its successful adoption in Denmark and its proposal for Norway exploded these claims. For the systems of law and cabinet government in these countries resemble those of the Commonwealth much more closely; neither country has a system of administrative courts, neither has a strong tradition of administrative publicity, and both have the system of ministerial responsibility for administration characteristic of parliamentary government elsewhere.

Too much has been made of the dangers of administrative publicity, in any case. Even in Sweden there are laws against revealing state secrets or information that would be injurious to private persons or commercial firms. The names of complainants and officials involved in cases are not ordinarily revealed, and the amount of publicity given to cases is partly at the discretion of the Ombudsman and is voluntarily controlled by the press. In the nature of things no publicity is given to minor cases of no news interest, and of course important cases *should* be discussed publicly.

A closely related argument against transplanting the office is that, in view of the revelations of the Ombudsmen, the need for a check on officialdom must be greater in the Nordic countries than elsewhere. The Nordic countries, however, are among the best-governed democracies in the world. The standards of their public services are extremely high, and their provisions for appeal of administrative decisions are certainly more ample than in the English-speaking countries. In adopting the Ombudsman system, Denmark and Norway have simply recognized that in the age of the welfare state, traditional controls are not good enough. . . .

Curiously, the opposite argument has also been raised—that the need is greater in the English-speaking countries, and is in fact so great that an Ombudsman would be overwhelmed with complaints. *The Times* warned (January 13, 1960) that in a large country like Britain the office might burgeon into something like the Chinese Control Yuan during the Han dynasty (206 B.C.–A.D. 220), which became a parallel branch of government constantly looking over the shoulder of the harried official. Instead of a public watchdog over the official's acts, the Ombudsman might become a bloodhound sniffing after his every decision. But as the *Economist* replied (January 31, 1960), this argument is to stand logic on its head. It is tantamount to saying that because the demand would be overwhelming the need should not be met at all. In any case, the fear is false. The Ombudsman performs his task in the Nordic countries with only five or six legal officers and a few office assistants, and he is certainly no super-administrator with power to substitute his judgment for that of other officials. In fact, he rarely comments on the content of a discretionary decision but rather on the *way* in which the decision has been made, to ensure its legality and fairness. That the bloodhound theory arises from a false fear is shown by the reversal in the attitude of civil servants in Denmark. Before the scheme was introduced they opposed it, but after its adoption they soon realized that the office was an aid rather than a hindrance. For in nine cases out of ten the Ombudsman vindicated their decisions and hence increased public confidence in the civil service. The scheme also shifted much of the task of handling the public's complaints from the civil service to the Ombudsman. Furthermore, minor officials soon found that the Ombudsman was an ally in their own dealings with arbitrary superiors. It is true, of course, that in the absence of a comprehensive system of administrative appeals, the work of an Ombudsman would be greater, but this problem must be attacked at its source.

It is frequently argued that to be the little man's defender the Ombudsman's office must be a highly personal one, while in large countries the size of the office would cause it to lose this personal touch. This argument has also been inverted: it is said that the office is *too* personal, too dependent upon one man's integrity, understanding and daily time; and that the nature of the office demands for its success a virtual impossibility—finding exactly the right man for the job, in particular one who combines a profound knowledge of the law with wide experience in various types of administration. These arguments, too, can be easily challenged. In the first place, there has been a lot of sentimental twaddle about the Ombudsman's personal touch. The principle of impartiality is far more important than the personal touch. Certainly citizens need to know that there is an independent authority to which they can turn for an impartial investigation, but this objective can be achieved without the paternalism inherent in a personalized office. Moreover, there are good grounds for the view that important and complex cases of a judicial nature should *not* be decided by a single person. (In fact, they are not so decided under the Ombudsman scheme. Although the Ombudsman deals with all important cases personally, naturally he and his expert staff discuss all such cases before he reaches a final conclusion, so that in effect they work as a group.) The old adage applied to the higher courts that two heads are better than one also applies here. For this reason I would recommend for populous countries a commission of three members, which might be called the Parliamentary or Administrative Complaints Commission. Commissioners would decide important cases together, but could decide minor cases individually. Each could specialize in a particular area or type of administration. The commission could include a judge and an experienced administrator (and perhaps also a representative of the public). In this way the proposal by-passes the argument that it is virtually impossible to find in a single man the qualities demanded by the office.

Having seen that most of the arguments that have been raised against transplanting the Ombudsman scheme may be effectively demolished, we should at the same time keep in mind that it cannot be a panacea. A number of people in Britain seem to regard "Ombudsman" as a kind of magic word that will cure all their administrative ills. But the age-old problem of the relation between the state and the individual is far too complex to be solved by one simple scheme. We need a whole variety of controls over administrative action and the Ombudsman scheme must be accompanied by a number of other reforms that are needed to plug the gaps in our systems of control. Otherwise, the scheme may fail because we are trying to make it do too much. We must remember that in the Nordic countries the scheme only supplements a battery of other effective controls, and that New Zealand is adding this scheme to an already well-developed parliamentary grievance system.

On the other hand, the danger in setting up a network of controls is that if the administration is surrounded with too many controls it will be unable to move. This is the danger in extending court review too far or in judicializing the administrative process too much. The United States has already gone too far in this direction, and recent British changes and proposals seem to point to the same danger. What we need is a fence along the administrative road, not a gate across it. The great virtue of the Ombudsman scheme is that its weapons are publicity and persuasion rather than cumbersome controls; it is in the category of the fence rather than the gate.

part FIVE
Political Change

One of the most important historical developments of the 20th century has been the achievement of independence by peoples who had been brought under the political control of European states in the course of the preceding two centuries. At least one third of the population of the world is involved in this surge toward national independence. The Europeans were able to conquer and administer vast areas of Asia, Africa, and the Middle East because of their crushing superiority in military technology, in turn based on a vastly more developed economy. The Indonesians, Indochinese, Indians, and Africans simply were unable to resist the comparatively small but modern armed forces of the European powers intent upon expanding their influence in the world. The epoch of imperialism registered European advance and domination in all areas of human activity—economic, military, and even cultural. During the era of imperialism, political analysts confined their attention mainly to Europe and North America. Little attention was paid to other parts of the world, except by students of colonial administration.

The virtual monopoly of military and economic superiority, on which European domination depended, began to erode in the 20th century. Japan showed the way by rapidly assimilating European technology and creating a new power center in Asia within 50 years of Commodore Perry's voyage. Economic and industrial development took place in all colonial areas, along with an awakening of the political consciousness of the masses. The European powers in effect were busily creating the instruments which would inevitably be used by the colonial peoples to achieve their independence. Arsenals, factories, hospitals, roads, schools, newspapers, and radio stations all served to strengthen the local economy and develop the political awareness of the people.

Colonialism collapsed in the wake of World War II. The chief colonial powers—Great Britain, France, and Holland—were exhausted by the conflict and unable to engage in any new military ventures. Their rule over possessions in Asia and southeast Asia had been shattered by Japanese armies, which demonstrated to the world that the Europeans were not invincible. In order to gain the loyalty of India in the face of a threatened Japanese invasion, the British were compelled to promise independence. France and Holland were unable to re-impose their sovereignty in Indochina and Indonesia by arms. The countries of western Europe lost their predominant position in 1945. Power shifted to two non-European states: the United States and the Soviet Union, both of whom began to court the support of former colonial peoples. The European powers were thus at a severe disadvantage in relation to their former colonies. They were not permitted by the new dominant world powers to attempt reconquest, and in any case they were no longer capable of doing so.

The new relationship among the principal areas of the world is comparable in importance to the French Revolution, the industrialization of Europe and North America, and the triumph of Communism in Russia. Each of these historical events changed the social and cultural environment, and led to new forms of political power and organization. The resurgence of the formerly subjugated peoples of Asia and Africa symbolizes a new kind of world crisis and requires a new focus of interest in our study of comparative politics.

But political change is not confined to the developing nations. All political systems are undergoing a rapid evolution, including those of the advanced industrial societies. Change is inherent in the political process. We have already seen that in all political systems there must be institutions through which claims and demands are translated into decisions. Existing conditions are then inevitably modified. New groups assume a position of power and influence while others lose their prerogatives; new rights are proclaimed and new services provided. Throughout the 19th century, for example, there was a continuing struggle for the attainment of political rights on the part of the social groups brought into being by the industrial revolution. The 20th century is witnessing a similar struggle for political emancipation in the rest of the world and assumption of collective responsibility for economic development and social welfare.

The nature of change, the rate at which change takes place and the specific correlates of change are not yet fully understood. Nor is it easy to tell in advance the direction change is likely to take. According to the Marxists, societies evolve through clearly defined stages, from feudalism through capitalism to socialism, as a result of economic pressures. Under certain conditions change is wrought by violence and revolution since the groups and classes that wield power are un-willing or unable to adapt to new conditions. Innovation may also bring about sweeping changes in social and political institutions. All societies which have undergone the technological and scientific revolutions of the past two centuries have been transformed, regardless of their particular cultures and political sys-tems. At the present time economic, social, and political change is occurring at an accelerated rate throughout the world. Political leaders almost everywhere are now committed to a drastic overhaul of their societies. They are attempting to popularize new values and norms, and create new attitudes in order to achieve industrialization, prosperity, and equality. There is an unparalleled urgency in this movement, which is taking place in a variety of ways and through a number of political forms. A major challenge before students of comparative politics is the development of analytic categories in terms of which the component elements of change can be understood and societies undergoing rapid change fruitfully compared.

TRADITIONAL AND MODERN SOCIETIES

It will be useful for analytic purposes to distinguish between two "ideal-types" or "models" of societies: the *traditional* and the *modern*. These terms do not imply any value judgment. A traditional society may include a large number of highly educated persons whose level of culture and social grace is higher than that of the mass of inhabitants of any modern society. Furthermore, these terms refer only to abstract "constructs"; they do not describe any existing societies. For example, the United States is a predominantly modern society, but one with many traditionally oriented groups in its population.

The distinction here suggested is a familiar one in the literature of the social sciences. Similar classificatory schemes have been suggested by such eminent theoreticians as Sir Henry Maine, Ferdinand Tönnies, and especially Max Weber. Thus, Weber suggested that claims to legitimacy may be based on:

1. Rational grounds—resting on a belief in the "legality" of patterns of normative rules and the right of those elevated to authority under such rules to issue commands (legal authority).

2. Traditional grounds—resting on an established belief in the sanctity of immemorial traditions and the legitimacy of the status of those exercising authority under them (traditional authority); or finally,

3. Charismatic grounds—resting on devotion to the specific and exceptional sanctity, heroism or exemplary character of an individual person, and of the normative patterns or order revealed or ordained by him (charismatic authority).[1]

One implication which may be drawn from Weber's scheme is that the three types correspond to historical development from simple to more complex societies. In the former, obedience is to the person of the chief, and the values of the family permeate the whole social system. A society breaks out of this stage usually under the leadership of a charismatic chief, who is obeyed because of his personal or heroic qualities. In modern societies obedience is to the legal order. It is associated with the office more than with the person who occupies it.

In both traditional and modern societies the individual participates in the political process through groups or associations, but there are fundamental differences as regards their nature and importance. Traditional societies are characterized by the predominance of the family and family-type groups (that is, "primary organizations") in which the members are in a "face-to-face" relationship. An individual's status in the society is determined by his family's status. He

[1] Max Weber, *The Theory of Social and Economic Organization* (New York: Oxford University Press, 1947), p. 328.

is nurtured, cared for, educated, and protected by the family, which tends to be a self-sufficient economic as well as social unit. The dominant economic activity is agriculture, which requires the participation of the family as a cohesive group. Virtually the entire population (and not 1 in 10, as in modern societies) is engaged in agriculture, the hunt, or fishing in order to provide their sustenance. There is little knowledge of science or technology, no opportunity to accumulate reserves of food, no leisure class able to devote itself to the arts and culture. The people live close to nature, even as part of nature. They are almost completely at the mercy of the seasons, storms, droughts, and rains. Superstition and magic permeate the society. Men seek to relate events in their own lives with external occurrences, the stars, or the seasons.

Family values—personal loyalty, authority, reverence—pervade the whole social structure. The state tends to resemble the family, with the king or chief of state in the role of father, whose paternal authority derives from a superhuman source. The various families gathered together in clans or tribes are his children, bound to obey for the same reason that each elder in the tribe is obeyed by the younger leaders. Insofar as a bureaucracy comes into existence to administer the will of the chief, it is like a huge household—with nepotism an expected practice.

Examples of traditional societies may be found throughout Africa. Anthropologists have distinguished two main types of social organization in Africa, based primarily on economic activities. *Pastoral societies* predominate in east, central, and southern Africa, and *agricultural societies* in west Africa.[2] In pastoral societies, status and wealth are measured in terms of animals (generally cattle). The tribes live entirely off the produce and meat of these animals. As a consequence of their self-sufficiency there is little exchange of produce among tribes, and there are no cities. Social organization is based on age grades, with rites marking passage from one grade to another. The Masai, a people numbering about 200,000, who live mainly in the high plains of Kenya, are pastoral. They own over two million head of cattle and an equal number of sheep and goats. The Masai literally live on the meat, milk, and blood of their herd.

The agricultural societies of west Africa are characterized by a settled population, producing enough for subsistence and frequently a surplus. Market places and towns have come into being, and there is some specialization of labor and class divisions. Large kingdoms and empires emerged in the past and were maintained for long periods. The Ashanti, of Ghana, are a typical agricultural people. Cultivation and ownership of land is the fundamental value of Ashanti culture. A complicated system of matrimonial bonds is the basis of property rights and political rule. Reverence for ancestors pervades the culture and serves to surround the land and the chiefs with an aura of mystery. The chiefs are named by a "Queen Mother," but the choice is actually determined beforehand

[2] See James S. Coleman, "The Politics of Sub-Saharan Africa," in Almond and Coleman, *The Politics of the Developing Areas* (1960), pp. 247–368; David Apter, *The Gold Coast in Transition* (Princeton, N.J.: Princeton University Press, 1957); and Melville J. Herskovits, "Peoples and Cultures of Sub-Saharan Africa," *The Annals* (March 1955), pp. 15–19.

by the tribal elders. All chiefs occupy a stool or throne, in which resides the spirit of the ancestors. The chiefs are supposed only to interpret this spirit and do not rule in their own name.

There have been, historically, a wide range of types *within* the general category of "traditional societies," from the subsistence agriculture and pastoral societies of primitive tribes in Africa, to the military structure of Egypt, the land empires of Asia Minor and China, the island civilization of the Aegean, Ancient Greece and Rome, and the feudal age. All of these societies, however, preceded the technological and industrial breakthrough of the 18th century.

Technical and scientific progress brought in their wake far-reaching change in social and political organization. The old agricultural subsistence economy was replaced by an industrial market-place economy. In the "model" modern society, an individual gains his livelihood not within the family but in a factory, commercial enterprise, or office. Population concentrates in the great urban centers, creating a host of administrative problems (sanitation, transportation, education, etc.). Modern societies are characterized by the predominance of *secondary organizations,* that is, large specialized and impersonal associations like labor unions, corporations, farm cooperatives, political parties, universities, and churches. Unlike the family, the secondary organizations have large numbers of members who need not be in a face-to-face relationship, are joined by a voluntary action of the prospective members, and carry on highly specialized activities. Most of the former functions of the family are assumed by the new associations (education by the schools, charity by the state, religious instruction by the church, and exchange of produce by the banks and market place). The state itself tends to take on the character of these secondary organizations. It becomes large, complex, impersonal, and increasingly rational. Old ideas of divine right fall into disrepute, and more rational themes of legitimacy (for example, popular sovereignty) come into vogue. The family itself is grievously weakened and is based more and more on consent and mutual interest.

After a period of evolution, the state expands to meet the needs of an industrialized economy. The civil service, for example, cannot fulfill its obligations as the closed preserve of a single family or clan, but must recruit able men from all layers of society. As Max Weber has pointed out, a modern bureaucracy is "rational," that is, recruits universally, boasts a system of tenure, grade classifications, and fixed salaries. Political conflict resembles the market place itself: each specialized group puts forth its offers and demands, with the state acting as a broker. Individuals express their interests primarily through the secondary organizations to which they belong.

Let us briefly summarize the differences between the two "ideal-types." *Traditional* societies are characterized by: subsistence economies; face-to-face social structures in which the family predominates; cultural systems that emphasize heredity, devotion, and mystery; and a highly personalized political system that is virtually an extension of the joint family. *Modern* societies are the exact opposite in all these respects. They are characterized by industrial economies; complex and impersonal social structures; a culture that emphasizes the values of science, knowledge, and achievement; and a highly bureaucratized political system, legitimized through rational processes, like elections.

Typological analysis is only a first step in the study of modernization. In effect, it constitutes a checklist for the observer, pointing to relationships among social, economic, cultural and political factors that might otherwise escape his attention. It also makes possible an assessment of the pace and extent of modernization in any given society. But the explanatory power of typologies is limited. The complexities of world history, the rise and decline of great powers and of civilizations, and the shifting balance of international power cannot be reduced to a handful of sociological concepts. Modernization provokes crises to which there are any number of possible reactions or solutions within a political system. It is perhaps most fruitful to consider modernization as a complex process that produces a series of challenges to both modern and traditional societies. How these challenges are met is the major concern of the student of political change.

COMPARATIVE ANALYSIS OF MODERN POLITICAL SYSTEMS

All nations on the modern side of the scale may be compared in terms of their distinctive experience of modernization. Each of these nations at one time was "traditional"; in each case the traditional society was undermined, and eventually displaced by new forms of organization. As we have pointed out in the earlier introductory essays, the process of modernization inevitably causes a series of political crises. Whatever the nature of the traditional society and whatever the nature of the modern political institutions (whether one-, two-, or multiparty, presidential or cabinet, democratic or authoritarian) at least three political crises must be surmounted in the course of modernization: the crises of legitimacy, participation, and conflict management. The way in which these crises occur and are dealt with is of great consequence for the functioning of modern political systems.

The crisis of legitimacy is inevitable because of the close link between political values and the systems they serve to justify. The kind of values that permeate a traditional society, such as divine right or rule by a hereditary aristocracy, must undergo modification as that society is transformed. Throughout Western Europe, for example, the breakup of feudalism was accompanied by a shift in the basis of political legitimacy. Everywhere the rights of monarchs were circumscribed and the power of parliaments increased. Whether monarchy continued to exist with reduced prerogatives or was replaced by a republic, the political systems of Europe sought to justify themselves in some way as the expression of popular will and national sovereignty. The crisis of legitimacy also involved the status of the church, which was generally a bulwark of the traditional ruling classes.

A new but related crisis comes into being with the rapid growth of industry.

Power continues to be wielded by a landed aristocracy, the church, and the wealthier strata. But new social groups, above all the industrial middle classes and the working class, enter upon the political scene. These classes are officially excluded from power in the traditional society; they demand entry into the political system; they gain this entry by organizing themselves behind and through political parties. How this is accomplished—through slow and successful integration, or with violence and grudging acceptance—makes a deep mark upon the political life of the country. In some cases the working class is never fully incorporated into the political system, and in countries like France and Italy large communist parties constitute a permanent opposition of principle. In communist systems the problem of integration is solved by eliminating the aristocracy, small peasantry, and middle classes as autonomous political forces.

Whether in stable parliamentary democracies, unstable parliamentary democracies, or authoritarian regimes, mature industrial societies pose grave problems for the political system. Specialized groups proliferate within both the middle and working classes; the scientists, managers, bureaucrats, military, and intellectuals compete with party leaders for a share of decision-making power. The state must organize itself so as to cope with these strong interest groups, integrate them into the political system, and satisfy their minimal demands. As the technology becomes more complex, the task of the political leaders requires more and more technical knowledge and competence, as well as the ability to manage the distinctive political tensions of highly industrialized societies.

Comparative analysis of modern political systems requires broad knowledge of their historical evolution. The student should compare the way in which each of the crises of modernization was handled in individual systems, and the extent of "carryover" from one crisis to another. Many observers have suggested that the *timing* of the crises of modernization is of critical importance. Did these crises occur one by one, with a considerable period elapsing between crises? In these cases the political system has a greater opportunity to resolve them singly and thus acquire stability. Or were the crises "telescoped"? Did the political system have to confront the crises of participation and conflict management while the controversy over its basic institutions and values continued? In such cases a much greater load is placed upon the system, and it requires an immense collective effort to create dynamic, effective, and stable government. Special attention should be paid to the problems of mature industrial societies. Are similar techniques being used in all modern political systems in dealing with massive technological development, urbanization, and the maintenance of individual creativity in mass societies? Or are there significant differences between democratic and authoritarian systems? Are there differences between such parliamentary democracies as the United States and the countries of Western Europe? Between the Soviet Union on the one hand and China and Cuba on the other? Modernization theory thus provides the student with a framework for inquiry; it is the starting point for the formulation of hypotheses concerning political life in all industrialized societies.

COMPARATIVE ANALYSIS OF DEVELOPING NATIONS

Modernization theory can also be used for a study of contemporary trends in the developing nations. There is a clear tendency for these societies to move from the traditional category into a *transitional period* during which they acquire many of the characteristics of modern society while retaining some traditional features. But it is impossible to foretell the exact development of any of these societies. For example, the so-called "uncommitted" nations are doubtless on the way to modernization. But there are two chief prototypes of advanced industrial states in the world: the Western countries (especially the United States) and the Communist nations (notably the Soviet Union). Developing countries could pattern themselves after either model of modernity.

Comparative study could usefully be focused on the decision-making or political elite: their social origin, position with respect to the masses, technical or educational qualifications for governing, and relationship with the important social groups within the nation (for example, landowners, army, church, civil service, and intellectuals), and their characteristic ideologies. At least four different leadership "types" can be distinguished in the developing nations: traditional, liberal, authoritarian, and radical.

The *traditional* leaders derive their authority from historical status and prestige, and from one predominant form of property—land. They constitute a self-perpetuating group in that recruitment comes from a small circle (either royalty or landowning nobility) by virtue of birth. Their values vary from one system to another, but generally reflect a family structure—the emphasis is on kinship, loyalty, devotion, duty, and courage. They are averse to changes which will endanger their economic and social position. They are apt to react unfavorably to any economic or technological innovations that might weaken the political system. They insist upon the preservation of prevailing modes of political recruitment and hence are hostile to popular participation in politics. They are opposed to industrialization and to its political and social implications.

The *liberal* leaders are in favor of "reforming out of existence" the traditionalist-oriented economy, society, and political system. They welcome industrialization and mass participation in political affairs. They accept both the goals and the methods of the Western constitutional democracies. Thus, the liberals desire political reforms, establishment of a constitutional order with guarantees of individual rights, the articulation of interests within an accepted legal order, and the gradual displacement of the traditionalist groups from positions of power. They wish to create the proper conditions within which meaningful political choices can be made by the whole people. Recruitment of the liberal elite is usually from the professional and middle classes, particularly among those who have attended European and American universities. The traditionalists and liberals tend to be allied in their respect for property rights but split over the question of democratic reforms and modernization.

"Authoritarian" leaders, like the liberals, tend to accept democracy as an ideal or goal. But they do not believe it can be achieved by indiscriminate adoption of all features of Western systems. They distinguish between "formal"

or "procedural" democracy (elections, parliaments, organized opposition, etc.) and "real" or "substantive" democracy (equal opportunity, economic development, moral regeneration). An active opposition only obstructs the efforts of the government to bring about "real" democracy, and hence must be suppressed. The emphasis is therefore on national unity and the direction of the efforts of the masses by an educated, informed, morally responsible elite. Frequently the hope is held out that the people, one day in the future, after rapid economic progress has been accomplished, will be ready for representative government of the Western type. Authoritarian leaders, like the liberals, come mainly from the professional and middle classes, and occasionally from the landed aristocracy.

The fourth "type" of leadership is *radical*. Inspired by a revolutionary ideology, the radicals are committed to drastic and rapid change of the economic and social structure. They organize their followers in a manner that will enable them to take the system by assault. The classic pattern is the single mass party led by professional revolutionaries, along lines laid down by Lenin. Radical leadership comes from the "alienated" groups, particularly the intelligentsia, and it appeals to the disaffected elements of the population—the peasants, the students, and the city workers. They are in favor of industrialization, but at the expense of the liberal values—individual rights, political freedoms, and private property. Above all they impose collective goals upon the total society, and discipline the masses in order to achieve those goals. The main differences between the authoritarians and radicals are of degree and social origin: the latter want more change more rapidly, with greater social control and discipline, and tend to be drawn from less favored social classes. The radicals are also much more suspicious of the Western powers, and tend to seek aid as well as ideological inspiration from the Communist camp.

The "benefits" of modernization have been felt throughout the world in the form of manufactured goods, moving pictures, radio broadcasts, and so on. All native populations have had their expectations aroused or modified as a consequence. The economic structure of traditional systems has been undermined. Landownership is no longer a secure base for a political elite. New economic activities have created new social groups and stimulated others who view the traditional elite as a stumbling block on the road to further economic development.

Industrialization, however, is viewed only as a means for the attainment of economic goals and the satisfaction of wants. Its prerequisites—the development of skills, the training of the masses, the establishment of an orderly pattern of social intercourse, and particularly discipline and regular work in the factory— are understood only by a small group of political leaders. Industrialization is often equated with a vision of plenty in the foreseeable future and as such it becomes a potent political force. The discipline required for industrialization, however, is appreciated by very few, and perhaps only by the "radicals".

As the conflict develops over demands for industrialization, the political position of the traditional elite becomes precarious. Their legitimacy is brought into question. There follows a period of instability, overt defiance of authority, and sporadic uprisings. The new political leaders—liberal, authoritarian, and radical—vie for control. A limited number of alternatives for future political development present themselves.

One alternative is the maintenance of traditional social organization and leadership. This alternative, though always possible, is becoming anachronistic. Most of the traditional forces are fighting a losing battle for survival. The independence movement is associated with an ideology calling for social and economic reforms which are inconsistent with the interests of the traditional forces. Mobilization of the masses in the struggle for independence brings with it profound modifications in the economic and social structure. Change may be held off by a temporary alliance between the traditional and new leaderships and groups for the realization of independence, by the inability of one particular group to impose its ideology, or by foreign intervention. But the will for change in a society generally indicates that the emerging political elites will use every means available to eliminate the traditional leaders who are still desperately clinging to the last vestiges of their rule.

At a certain stage, the liberal elements come into sharp conflict with the authoritarian and radical elements. The liberals advocate a relatively slow pace of structural modifications and industrialization, technological improvements, a rising standard of living, the gradual training of managerial and labor groups, progressive land reforms, and involvement of the masses in politics through the extension of literacy and education. But these demands are made with little urgency and the envisaged manner of their implementation is permissive rather than coercive. Liberal elites attempt to create the conditions within which the individual can become capable of choice—always considered in the best tradition of liberalism as an individual act. The system should provide opportunities for the individual and only "hinder the hindrances."

The authoritarians and radicals, on the other hand, urge coercive and authoritarian practices in order to bring about quickly the same overall goals. Suspicious of the continuing strength of the traditionalist elements (particularly among the peasants), they insist on rapid mobilization of the masses in a manner that will wrench them from their former way of life. Distrustful of the colonial powers, they seek to industrialize rapidly by using their own human resources and by accepting aid from the Communist countries. This political leadership, therefore, uses force and not persuasion, seeks the outright organization of the masses rather than a gradual process of political education, stresses social discipline rather than general legal rules, norms, and guaranties of individual freedom.

In the contest for power, the "liberal" leaders are at a severe disadvantage. In relatively backward economies, the application of liberal economic doctrine does not result in rapid industrialization or structural change. Development of a market economy favors the merchant class and production of consumer goods, and fails to satisfy the pent-up demand of large social groups. Subordination of social goals to individual choice only increases the feeling of social injustice on the part of the masses. All too often, it leads to "private wealth and public poverty." Politically, liberalism has no slogan which can activate and mobilize the masses. Most important, liberalism as a social force fails to inculcate new social incentives for the purpose of industrialization. In brief, liberal elites are generally unable to reach the people, to capture their imagination, and to lead them into the modern era. On the other hand, the great advantage enjoyed by the authoritarian and especially the radical leaders is that they create a system of controls under which industrialization may take place.

Of course, it is impossible to predict the exact evolution of events in the developing nations. New forces may come to the fore, perhaps slowing down the tempo of modernization and permitting the traditional elite to rally. Industrialization may follow the Western historical experience and lead to the establishment of a legal order within which individual freedoms are guaranteed. The technician and the manager may win out over the party boss and the commissar—perhaps even in existing totalitarian systems! Indications are, however, that the new nations are departing from the norms and institutions of Western democracies. Liberal elites are finding it exceptionally difficult to attract mass support. Communism and Fascism seem to be models for the most dynamic leadership groups in the new nations, even though they may follow "their own path."

Comparative study of change, revolution, and modernization obviously calls our attention to the dynamics of the political process. Are there any similarities in conditions which precede revolutions? Are the new nations in a "revolutionary" situation like that of France before 1789 or Russia before 1917? Comparative study may focus on specific social groups—the intellectuals, the working class, the peasantry—to see how they react to the traditional elite, and to what extent they are influenced by revolutionary ideas. Comparison should also be made of political evolution in the developing nations. Liberal elites are more successful in gaining mass support in such nations as the Philippines and the Ivory Coast than in Ceylon and Guinea. What factors account for these similarities and differences? Analysis of political change in both industrial and traditional societies is perhaps the most serious and challenging task of contemporary political science.

chapter XII
MODERNIZATION

One of the striking developments in the field of comparative politics at the present time is the use of "modernization" as an analytic concept. In the past few years a large number of books have appeared in which the central theme is modernization. These include Dankwart Rustow, *A World of Nations* (1967); C. E. Black, *Dynamics of Modernization: A Study in Comparative History* (1966); Marion J. Levy, Jr., *Modernization and the Structure of Society,* 2 vols. (1966); Robert T. Holt and John E. Turner, *The Political Basis of Economic Development* (1966); David E. Apter, *Politics of Modernization* (1965); A. F. K. Organski, *Stages of Political Development* (1965); and Lucian W. Pye, *Aspects of Political Development* (1966). Reference may also be made to the six volumes in the Princeton series on political development, including notably Joseph LaPalombara, ed., *Bureaucracy and Political Development* (1963); Lucian W. Pye and Sidney Verba, eds., *Political Culture and Political Development* (1965); and Joseph LaPalombara and Myron Weiner, eds., *Political Parties and Political Development* (1966).

We have already tried to present the major outlines of modernization theory in the introductory essay. Modernization is a complex process whereby "traditional" societies take on the characteristics of "modernity." The transformation affects a whole range of factors—economic, social, political, and cultural. A social system has an internal logic in that its various parts bear a *necessary* relationship to one another. Thus, a society infused by ancestor-spirit, and where authoritative decisions are made by witch doctors, is not capable of sustaining a massive industrial economy. Conversely, once an advanced industrial economy comes into being, the habits of thought of science and the discipline of the machine (to use Thorstein Veblen's phrase) are incompatible with a feudal social structure. Such assertions are broad; as Veblen pointed out in his *Theory of the Leisure Class,* changes in the level of technology do not immediately bring about corresponding social changes. There is a tendency for new social classes to emulate the values and life styles of their "betters," and this introduces a note of dissonance. Correlations among the economic, social, political, and cultural factors are loose, but they exist; otherwise there is no point in discussing modernization as a process.

But the nature of this correlation cannot be assumed. It must be investigated in the context of general historical situations and specific political systems. The readings below present analyses of such factors as technology and social mobilization, and their importance in political change. There is also an appraisal of contemporary trends in modernization theory by S. P. Huntington. Many questions may be raised about modernization theory. What is the difference between political change and modernization? Are there any specific developments that trigger modernization, insofar as it is a distinctive process? How many roads are there to modernization? For a general view of the nature of political and social change, see: Robert M. MacIver, *The Modern State* (1926) and *The Web of Government* (1947); Pitirim Sorokin, *Social and Cultural Dynamics,* 1 vol. ed. (1957); and W. E. Moore, *Social Change* (1963). See also the classic synthesis by Alexis de Tocqueville, *The Old Regime and the French Revolution.*

29. Modern Technology*

THORSTEIN VEBLEN

. . . The machine process pervades the modern life and dominates it in a mechanical sense. Its dominance is seen in the enforcement of precise mechanical measurements and adjustment and the reduction of all manner of things, purposes and acts, necessities, conveniences, and amenities of life, to standard units. The bearing of this sweeping mechanical standardization upon business traffic is a large part of the subject-matter of the foregoing chapters. The point of immediate interest here is the further bearing of the machine process upon the growth of culture,—the disciplinary effect which this movement for standardization and mechanical equivalence has upon the human material.

This discipline falls more immediately on the workmen engaged in the mechanical industries, and only less immediately on the rest of the community which lives in contact with this sweeping machine process. Wherever the machine process extends, it sets the pace for the workmen, great and small. The pace is set, not wholly by the particular processes in the details of which the given workman is immediately engaged, but in some degree by the more comprehensive process at large into which the given detail process fits. It is no longer simply that the individual workman makes use of one or more mechanical contrivances

*From *The Theory of Business Enterprise* (New York: Charles Scribner's Sons, 1904), pp. 306–14, 323–24, 372–73. By permission of the publisher.

for effecting certain results. Such used to be his office in the earlier phases of the use of machines, and the work which he now has in hand still has much of that character. But such a characterization of the workman's part in industry misses the peculiarly modern feature of the case. He now does this work as a factor involved in a mechanical process whose movement controls his motions. It remains true, of course, as it always has been true, that he is the intelligent agent concerned in the process, while the machine, furnace, roadway, or retort are inanimate structures devised by man and subject to the workman's supervision. But the process comprises him and his intelligent motions, and it is by virtue of his necessarily taking an intelligent part in what is going forward that the mechanical process has its chief effect upon him. The process standardizes his supervision and guidance of the machine. Mechanically speaking, the machine is not his to do with it as his fancy may suggest. His place is to take thought of the machine and its work in terms given him by the process that is going forward. His thinking in the premises is reduced to standard units of gauge and grade. If he fails of the precise measure, by more or less, the exigencies of the process check the aberration and drive home the absolute need of conformity.

There results a standardization of the workman's intellectual life in terms of mechanical process, which is more unmitigated and precise the more comprehensive and consummate the industrial process in which he plays a part. This must not be taken to mean that such work need lower the degree of intelligence of the workman. No doubt the contrary is nearer the truth. He is a more efficient workman the more intelligent he is, and the discipline of the machine process ordinarily increases his efficiency even for work in a different line from that by which the discipline is given. But the intelligence required and inculcated in the machine industry is of a peculiar character. The machine process is a severe and insistent disciplinarian in point of intelligence. It requires close and unremitting thought, but it is thought which runs in standard terms of quantitative precision. Broadly, other intelligence on the part of the workman is useless; or it is even worse than useless, for a habit of thinking in other quantitative terms blurs the workman's quantitative apprehension of the facts with which he has to do.[1]

In so far as he is a rightly gifted and fully disciplined workman, the final term of his *habitual* thinking is mechanical efficiency, understanding "mechanical" in the sense in which it is used above. But mechanical efficiency is a matter of precisely adjusted cause and effect. What the discipline of the machine industry inculcates, therefore, in the habits of life and of thought of the workman, is regularity of sequence and mechanical precision; and the intellectual outcome is an habitual resort to terms of measurable cause and effect, together with a relative neglect and disparagement of such exercise of the intellectual faculties as does not run on these lines.

---

[1] If, *e.g.,* he takes to myth-making and personifies the machine or the process and imputes purpose and benevolence to the mechanical appliances, after the manner of current nursery tales and pulpit oratory, he is sure to go wrong.

Of course, in no case and with no class does the discipline of the machine process mould the habits of life and of thought fully into its own image. There is present in the human nature of all classes too large a residue of the propensities and aptitudes carried over from the past and working to a different result. The machine's regime has been of too short duration, strict as its discipline may be, and the body of inherited traits and traditions is too comprehensive and consistent to admit of anything more than a remote approach to such a consummation.

The machine process compels a more or less unremitting attention to phenomena of an impersonal character and to sequences and correlations not dependent for their force upon human predilection nor created by habit and custom. The machine throws out anthropomorphic habits of thought. It compels the adaptation of the workman to his work, rather than the adaptation of the work to the workman. The machine technology rests on a knowledge of impersonal, material cause and effect, not on the dexterity, diligence, or personal force of the workman, still less on the habits and propensities of the workman's superiors. Within the range of this machine-guided work, and within the range of modern life so far as it is guided by the machine process, the course of things is given mechanically, impersonally, and the resultant discipline is a discipline in the handling of impersonal facts for mechanical effect. It inculcates thinking in terms of opaque, impersonal cause and effect, to the neglect of those norms of validity that rest on usage and on the conventional standards handed down by usage. Usage counts for little in shaping the processes of work of this kind or in shaping the modes of thought induced by work of this kind.

The machine process gives no insight into questions of good and evil, merit and demerit, except in point of material causation, nor into the foundations or the constraining force of law and order, except such mechanically enforced law and order as may be stated in terms of pressure, temperature, velocity, tensile strength, etc.[2] The machine technology takes no cognizance of conventionally established rules of precedence; it knows neither manners nor breeding and can make no use of any of the attributes of worth. Its scheme of knowledge and of inference is based on the laws of material causation, not on those of immemorial custom, authenticity, or authoritative enactment. Its metaphysical basis is the law of cause and effect, which in the thinking of its adepts has displaced even the law of sufficient reason.

The range of conventional truths, or of institutional legacies, which it traverses is very comprehensive, being, indeed, all-inclusive. It is but little more in accord with the newer, eighteenth-century conventional truths of natural rights, natural liberty, natural law, or natural religion, than with the older norms of the true, the beautiful, and the good which these displaced. Anthropomorphism, under whatever disguise, is of no use and of no force here.

---

[2] Such expressions as "good and ill," "merit and demerit," "law and order," when applied to technological facts or to the outcome of material science, are evidently only metaphorical expressions, borrowed from older usage and serviceable only as figures of speech.

The discipline exercised by the mechanical occupations, in so far as it is in question here, is a discipline of the habits of thought. It is, therefore, as processes of thought, methods of apperception, and sequences of reasoning, that these occupations are of interest for the present purpose; it is as such that they have whatever cultural value belongs to them. They have such a value, therefore, somewhat in proportion as they tax the mental faculties of those employed; and the largest effects are to be looked for among those industrial classes who are required to comprehend and guide the processes, rather than among those who serve merely as mechanical auxiliaries of the machine process. Not that the latter are exempt from the machine's discipline, but it falls upon them blindly and enforces an uncritical acceptance of opaque results, rather than a theoretical insight into the causal sequences which make up the machine process. The higher degree of training in such matter-of-fact habits of thought is accordingly to be looked for among the higher ranks of skilled mechanics, and perhaps still more decisively among those who stand in an engineering or supervisory relation to the processes. It counts more forcibly and farthest among those who are required to exercise what may be called a mechanical discretion in the guidance of the industrial processes, who, as one might say, are required to administer the laws of causal sequence that run through material phenomena, who therefore must learn to think in the terms in which the machine processes work.[3] The metaphysical ground, the assumptions, on which such thinking proceeds must be such as will hold good for the sequence of material phenomena; that is to say, it is the metaphysical assumptions of modern material science,—the law of cause and effect, cumulative causation, conservation of energy, persistence of quantity, or whatever phrase be chosen to cover the concept. The men occupied with the modern material sciences are, accordingly, for the purpose in hand, in somewhat the same case as the higher ranks of those employed in mechanical industry. . . .

The intellectual and spiritual training of the machine in modern life, therefore, is very far-reaching. It leaves but a small proportion of the community untouched; but while its constraint is ramified throughout the body of the population, and constrains virtually all classes at some points in their daily life, it falls with the most direct, intimate, and unmitigated impact upon the skilled

[3] For something more than a hundred years past this change in the habits of thought of the workman has been commonly spoken of as a deterioration or numbing of his intelligence. But that seems too sweeping a characterization of the change brought on by habituation to machine work. It is safe to say that such habituation brings a change in the workman's habits of thought,—in the direction, method, and content of his thinking,— heightening his intelligence for some purposes and lowering it for certain others. No doubt, on the whole, the machine's discipline lowers the intelligence of the workman for such purposes as were rated high as marks of intelligence before the coming of the machine, but it appears likewise to heighten his intelligence for such purposes as have been brought to the front by the machine. If he is by nature scantily endowed with the aptitudes that would make him think effectively in terms of the machine process, if he has intellectual capacity for other things and not for this, then the training of the machine may fairly be said to lower his intelligence, since it hinders the full development of the only capacities of which he is possessed. The resulting difference in intellectual training is a difference in kind and direction, not necessarily in degree.

mechanical classes, for these have no respite from its mastery, whether they are at work or at play.

The ubiquitous presence of the machine, with its spiritual concomitant— workday ideals and scepticism of what is only conventionally valid—is the unequivocal mark of the Western culture of today as contrasted with the culture of other times and places. It pervades all classes and strata in a varying degree, but on an average in a greater degree than at any time in the past, and most potently in the advanced industrial communities and in the classes immediately in contact with the mechanical occupations. As the comprehensive mechanical organization of the material side of life has gone on, a heightening of this cultural effect throughout the community has also supervened, and with a farther and faster movement in the same direction a farther accentuation of this "modern" complexion of culture is fairly to be looked for, unless some remedy be found. And as the concomitant differentiation and specialization of occupations goes on, a still more unmitigated discipline falls upon ever widening classes of the population, resulting in an ever weakening sense of conviction, allegiance, or piety toward the received institutions. . . .

In the nature of the case the cultural growth dominated by the machine industry is of a sceptical, matter-of-fact complexion, materialistic, unmoral, unpatriotic, undevout. The growth of habits of thought, in the industrial regions and centres particularly, runs in this direction; but hitherto there has enough of the ancient norms of Western Christendom remained intact to make a very respectable protest against that deterioration of the cultural tissues which the ferment of the machine industry unremittingly pushes on. The machine discipline, however, touches wider and wider circles of the population, and touches them in an increasingly intimate and coercive manner. In the nature of the case, therefore, the resistance opposed to this cultural trend given by the machine discipline on grounds of received conventions weakens with the passage of time. The spread of materialistic, matter-of-fact preconceptions takes place at a cumulatively accelerating rate, except in so far as some other cultural factor, alien to the machine discipline, comes in to inhibit its spread and keep its disintegrating influence within bounds.

30. Social Mobilization and Political Development*

KARL W. DEUTSCH

Social mobilization is a name given to an overall process of change, which happens to substantial parts of the population in the countries which are moving from traditional to modern ways of life. It denotes a concept which brackets together a number of more specific processes of change, such as changes of residence, of occupation, of social setting, of face-to-face associates, of institutions, roles, and ways of acting, of experiences and expectations, and finally of personal memories, habits and needs, including the need for new patterns of group affiliation and new images of personal identity. Singly, and even more in their cumulative impact, these changes tend to influence and sometimes to transform political behavior.

The concept of social mobilization is not merely a short way of referring to the collection of changes just listed, including any extensions of this list. It implies that these processes tend to go together in certain historical situations and stages of economic development; that these situations are identifiable and recurrent, in their essentials, from one country to another; and that they are relevant for politics. Each of these points will be taken up in the course of this paper.

Social mobilization, let us repeat, is something that happens to large numbers of people in areas which undergo modernization, *i.e.*, where advanced, non-traditional practices in culture, technology and economic life are introduced and accepted on a considerable scale. It is not identical, therefore, with this process of modernization as a whole, but it deals with one of its major aspects, or better, with a recurrent cluster among its consequences. These consequences, once they occur on a substantial scale, influence in turn the further process of modernization. Thus, what can be treated for a short time span as a consequence of the modernization process, appears over a longer period as one of its continuing aspects and as a significant cause, in the well known pattern of feedback or circular causation.

Viewed over a longer time perspective, such as several decades, the concept of social mobilization suggests that several of the changes subsumed under it will tend to go together in terms of recurrent association, well above anything to be expected from mere chance. Thus, any one of the forms of social mobilization, such as the entry into market relations and a money economy (and hence away

*From "Social Mobilization and Political Development," *American Political Science Review*, vol. LV, no. 3 (September 1961), pp. 493–502. Article and footnotes abridged by the editors. Reprinted by permission of The American Political Science Association and the author.

from subsistence and barter) should be expected to be accompanied or followed by a significant rise in the frequency of impersonal contacts, or in exposure to mass media of communication, or in changes of residence, or in political or quasi-political participation. The implication of the concept is thus to assert an empirical fact—that of significantly frequent association—and this assertion can be empirically tested.

This notion of social mobilization was perceived early in intuitive terms, as a historical recollection or a poetic image. It was based on the historical experiences of the French *levée en masse* in 1793 and of the German "total mobilization" of 1914–18, described dramatically in terms of its social and emotional impact by many German writers, including notably Ernst Jünger. A somewhat related image was that of the long-term and world-wide process of "fundamental democratization," discussed in some of the writings of Karl Mannheim.[1] All these images suggest a breaking away from old commitments to traditional ways of living, and a moving into new situations, where new patterns of behavior are relevant and needed, and where new commitments may have to be made.

Social mobilization can be defined, therefore, as the process in which major clusters of old social, economic and psychological commitments are eroded or broken and people become available for new patterns of socialization and behavior. As Edward Shils has rightly pointed out, the original images of "mobilization" and of Mannheim's "fundamental democratization" imply two distinct stages of the process: (1) the stage of uprooting or breaking away from old settings, habits and commitments; and (2) the induction of the mobilized persons into some relatively stable new patterns of group membership, organization and commitment. In this fashion, soldiers are mobilized *from* their homes and families and mobilized *into* the army in which they then serve. Similarly, Mannheim suggests an image of large numbers of people moving away *from* a life of local isolation, traditionalism and political apathy, and moving *into* a different life or broader and deeper involvement in the vast complexities of modern life, including potential and actual involvement in mass politics.

It is a task of political theory to make this image more specific; to bring it into a form in which it can be verified by evidence; and to develop the problem to a point where the question "how?" can be supplemented usefully by the question "how much?" In its intuitive form, the concept of social mobilization already carried with it some images of growing numbers and rising curves. In so far as the constituent processes of social mobilization can be measured and described quantitatively in terms of such curves, it may be interesting to learn how fast the curves rise, whether they show any turning points, or whether they cross any thresholds beyond which the processes they depict have different side effects from those that went before. Notably among these side effects are any that bear on the performance of political systems and upon the stability and capabilities of governments. . . .

[1] Karl Mannheim, *Man and Society in an Age of Reconstruction* (New York, 1940).

SOME IMPLICATIONS FOR THE POLITICS OF DEVELOPMENT

In whatever country it occurs, social mobilization brings with it an expansion of the politically relevant strata of the population. These politically relevant strata are a broader group than the elite: they include all those persons who must be taken into account in politics. Dock workers and trade union members in Ghana, Nigeria, or the United States, for instance, are not necessarily members of the elites of these countries, but they are quite likely to count for something in their political life. In the developing countries of Asia, Africa and parts of Latin America, the political process usually does not include the mass of isolated, subsistence-farming, tradition-bound and politically apathetic villagers, but it does include increasingly the growing numbers of city dwellers, market farmers, users of money, wage earners, radio listeners and literates in town and country. The growth in the numbers of these people produces mounting pressures for the transformation of political practices and institutions; and since this future growth can be estimated at least to some extent on the basis of trends and data from the recent past, some of the expectable growth in political pressures—we may call it the potential level of political tensions—can likewise be estimated.

Social mobilization also brings about a change in the quality of politics, by changing the range of human needs that impinge upon the political process. As people are uprooted from their physical and intellectual isolation in their immediate localities, from their old habits and traditions, and often from their old patterns of occupation and places of residence, they experience drastic changes in their needs. They may now come to need provisions for housing and employment, for social security against illness and old age, for medical care against the health hazards of their crowded new dwellings and places of work and the risk of accidents with unfamiliar machinery. They may need succor against the risks of cyclical or seasonal unemployment, against oppressive charges of rent or interest, and against sharp fluctuations in the prices of the main commodities which they must sell or buy. They need instruction for themselves and education for their children. They need, in short, a wide range and large amounts of new government services.

These needs ordinarily cannot be met by traditional types of government, inherited from a precommercial and preindustrial age. Maharajahs, sultans, sheikhs and chieftains are quite unlikely to cope with these new problems, and traditional rule by land-owning oligarchies or long established religious bodies most often is apt to prove equally disappointing in the face of the new needs. Most of the attempts to change the characteristics of the traditional ruling families—perhaps by supplying them with foreign advisers or by having their children study in some foreign country—are likely to remain superficial in their effects, overshadowed by mounting pressures for more thoroughgoing changes.

In developing countries of today, however, the increasingly ineffective and unpopular traditional authorities cannot be replaced successfully by their historic successors in the Western world, the classic institutions of 18th and 19th century liberalism and laissez-faire. For the uprooted, impoverished and disoriented masses produced by social mobilization, it is surely untrue that that government is best that governs least. They are far more likely to need a direct transition from traditional government to the essentials of a modern welfare state. The developing countries of Asia, Africa and parts of Latin America may have to accomplish, therefore, within a few decades a process of political change which in the history of Western Europe and North America took at least as many generations; and they may have to accomplish this accelerated change almost in the manner of a jump, omitting as impractical some of the historic stages of transition through a period of near laissez-faire that occurred in the West.

The growing need for new and old government services usually implies persistent political pressures for an increased scope of government and a greater relative size of the government sector in the national economy. In the mid-1950's, the total government budget—national, regional and local—tended to amount to roughly 10 per cent of the gross national product in the very poor and poorly mobilized countries with annual per capita gross national products at or below $100. For highly developed and highly mobilized countries, such as those with per capita gross national products at or above $900, the corresponding proportion of the total government sector was about 30 per cent. If one drew only the crudest and most provisional inference from these figures, one might expect something like a 2.5 per cent shift of national income into the government sector for every $100 gain in per capita gross national product in the course of economic development. It might be more plausible, however, to expect a somewhat more rapid expansion of the government sector during the earlier stages of economic development, but the elucidation of this entire problem—with all its obvious political implications—would require and reward a great deal more research.

The relationship between the total process of social mobilization and the growth of the national income, it should be recalled here, is by no means symmetrical. Sustained income growth is very unlikely without social mobilization, but a good deal of social mobilization may be going on even in the absence of per capita income growth, such as occurs in countries with poor resources or investment policies, and with rapid population growth. In such cases, social mobilization still would generate pressures for an expansion of government services and hence of the government sector, even in a relatively stagnant or conceivably retrograde economy. Stopping or reversing in such cases the expansion of government or the process of social mobilization behind it—even if this could be done—hardly would make matters much better. The more attractive course for such countries might rather be to use the capabilities of their expanding governments so as to bring about improvements in their resources and investment policies, and an eventual resumption of economic growth. To what extent this has been, or could be, brought about in cases of this kind, would make another fascinating topic for study.

The figures just given apply, of course, only to non-Communist countries; the inclusion of Communist states would make the average in each class of government sectors higher. It would be interesting to investigate, however, whether and to what extent the tendency toward the relative expansion of the government sector in the course of social mobilization applies also, *mutatis mutandis,* to the Communist countries.

A greater scope of governmental services and functions requires ordinarily an increase in the capabilities of government. Usually it requires an increase in the numbers and training of governmental personnel, an increase in governmental offices and institutions, and a significant improvement in administrative organization and efficiency. A rapid process of social mobilization thus tends to generate major pressures for political and administrative reform. Such reforms may include notably both a quantitative expansion of the bureaucracy and its qualitative improvement in the direction of a competent civil service—even though these two objectives at times may clash.

Similar to its impact on this specific area of government, social mobilization tends to generate also pressures for a more general transformation of the political elite. It tends to generate pressures for a broadening and partial transformation of elite functions, of elite recruitment, and of elite communications. On all these counts, the old elites of traditional chiefs, village headmen, and local notables are likely to prove ever more inadequate; and political leadership may tend to shift to the new political elite of party or quasi-party organizations, formal or informal, legal or illegal, but always led by the new "marginal men" who have been exposed more or less thoroughly to the impact of modern education and urban life.

Something similar applies to elite communications. The more broadly recruited elites must communicate among themselves, and they must do so more often impersonally and over greater distances. They must resort more often to writing and to paper work. At the same time they must direct a greater part of their communications output at the new political strata; this puts a premium on oratory and journalism, and on skill in the use of all mass media of communication. At the same time rapid social mobilization causes a critical problem in the communications intake of elites. It confronts them with the ever present risk of losing touch with the newly mobilized social strata which until recently still did not count in politics. Prime Minister Nehru's reluctance to take into account the strength and intensity of Mahratti sentiment in the language conflict of Bombay in the 1950s and his general tendency since the mid-1930s to underestimate the strength of communal and linguistic sentiment in India suggest the seriousness of this problem even for major democratic leaders.

The increasing numbers of the mobilized population, and the greater scope and urgency of their needs for political decisions and governmental services, tend to translate themselves, albeit with a time lag, into increased political participation. This may express itself informally through greater numbers of people taking part in crowds and riots, in meetings and demonstrations, in strikes and uprisings, or, less dramatically, as members of a growing audience for political communications, written or by radio, or finally as members of a growing host of organizations. While many of these organizations are ostensibly non-political, such as improvement societies, study circles, singing clubs, gymnastic societies, agricultural and commercial associations, fraternal orders, workmen's benefit societies, and the like, they nevertheless tend to acquire a political tinge, particularly in countries where more open outlets for political activities are not available. But even where there are established political parties and elections, a network of seemingly nonpolitical or marginally political organizations serves an important political function by providing a dependable social setting for the individuals who have been partly or wholly uprooted or alienated from their traditional communities. Such organizations may serve at the same time as marshalling grounds for the entry of these persons into political life.

Where people have the right to vote, the effects of social mobilization are likely to be reflected in the electoral statistics. This process finds its expression both through a tendency towards a higher voting participation of those already enfranchised and through an extension of the franchise itself to additional groups of the population. Often the increase in participation amongst those who already have the right to vote precedes the enfranchisement of new classes of voters, particularly in countries where the broadening of the franchise is occurring gradually. Thus in Norway between 1830 and 1860, voting participation remained near the level of about 10 per cent of the adult male population; in the 1870s and 1880s this participation rose rapidly among the enfranchised voters, followed by the extensions of the franchise, until by the year 1900, 40 per cent of the Norwegian men were actually voting. This process was accompanied by a transformation of Norwegian politics, the rise to power of the radical peasant party *Venstre,* and a shift from the earlier acceptance of the existing Swedish-Norwegian Union to rising demands for full Norwegian independence. These political changes had been preceded or accompanied by a rise in several of the usual indicators of social mobilization among the Norwegian people. . . .

As we have seen, the process of social mobilization generates strong pressures towards increasing the capabilities of government, by increasing the volume and range of demands made upon the government and administration, and by widening the scope of politics and the membership of the politically relevant strata. The same process increases the frequency and the critical importance of direct communications between government and governed. It thus necessarily increases the importance of the language, the media, and the channels through which these communications are carried on.

Other things assumed equal, the stage of rapid social mobilization may be expected, therefore, to promote the consolidation of states whose peoples already share the same language, culture, and major social institutions; while the same process may tend to strain or destroy the unity of states whose population is already divided into several groups with different languages or cultures or basic ways of life. By the same token, social mobilization may tend to promote the merging of several smaller states, or political units such as cantons, principalities, sultanates or tribal areas, whose populations already share substantially the same language, culture and social system; and it may tend to inhibit, or at least to make more difficult, the merging of states or political units whose populations or ruling personnel differ substantially in regard to any of these matters. Social mobilization may thus assist to some extent in the consolidation of the United Arab Republic, but raise increasing problems for the politics and administration of multilingual India—problems which the federal government of India may have to meet or overcome by a series of creative adjustments.

In the last analysis, however, the problem of the scale of states goes beyond the effects of language, culture, or institutions, important as all these are. In the period of rapid social mobilization, the acceptable scale of a political unit will tend to depend eventually upon its performance. If a government fails to meet the increasing burdens put upon it by the process of social mobilization, a growing proportion of the population is likely to become alienated and disaffected from the state, even if the same language, culture and basic social institutions were shared originally throughout the entire state territory by rulers and ruled alike. The secession of the United States and of Ireland from the British Empire, and of the Netherlands and of Switzerland from the German Empire may serve in part as examples. At bottom, the popular acceptance of a government in a period of social mobilization is most of all a matter of its capabilities and the manner in which they are used—that is, essentially a matter of its responsiveness to the felt needs of its population. If it proves persistently incapable or unresponsive, some or many of its subjects will cease to identify themselves with it psychologically; it will be reduced to ruling by force where it can no longer rule by display, example and persuasion; and if political alternatives to it appear, it will be replaced eventually by other political units, larger or smaller in extent, which at least promise to respond more effectively to the needs and expectations of their peoples.

In practice the results of social mobilization often have tended to increase the size of the state, well beyond the old tribal areas, petty principalities, or similar districts of the traditional era, while increasing the direct contact between government and governed far beyond the levels of the sociologically superficial and often half-shadowy empire of the past.

This growth in the size of modern states, capable of coping with the results of social mobilization, is counteracted and eventually inhibited, however, as their size increases, by their tendency to increasing preoccupation with their own internal affairs. There is considerable evidence for this trend toward a self-limitation in the growth of states through a decline in the attention, resources and responsiveness available for coping with the implicit needs and explicit messages of the next marginal unit of population and territory on the verge of being included in the expanding state.

The remarks in this section may have sufficed to illustrate, though by no means to exhaust, the significance of the process of social mobilization in the economic and political development of countries. The main usefulness of the concept, however, should lie in the possibility of quantitative study which it offers. How much social mobilization, as measured by our seven indicators, has been occurring in some country per year or per decade during some period of its history, or during recent times? And what is the meaning of the differences between the rates at which some of the constituent subprocesses of social mobilization may have been going on? Although specific data will have to be found separately for each country, it should be possible to sketch a general quantitative model to show some of the interrelations and their possible significance.* . . .

*Editors' note: The author's quantitative model has been omitted.

31. The Change to Change*

SAMUEL P. HUNTINGTON

I. POLITICAL SCIENCE AND POLITICAL CHANGE

Change is a problem for social science. Sociologists, for instance, have regularly bemoaned their lack of knowledge concerning social change. In 1951 Talcott Parsons flatly stated, in italics, that *"a general theory of the processes of change in social systems is not possible in the present state of knowledge."* Thirteen years later Don Martindale could see little improvement. Sociology, he argued, could account for structure but not for change: *"its theory of social change,"* said he, also in italics (!), *"is the weakest branch of sociological theory."* Other sociologists have expressed similar views.[1] Yet, as opposed to political scientists, the sociologists are relatively well off. Compared with past neglect of the theory of political change in political science, sociology is rich with works on the theory of social change. These more generalized treatments are supplemented by the extensive literature on group dynamics, planned change, organizational change, and the nature of innovation. Until very recently, in contrast, political theory in general has not attempted to deal directly with the problems of change. "Over the last seventy-five years," David Easton wrote in 1953, "political research has confined itself largely to the study of given conditions to the neglect of political change."[2]

Why did this happen? Several factors would seem to play a role. While the roots of political science go back to Aristotle (whose central concern was "to consider things in the process of their growth"), modern political science is a product of the late nineteenth and early twentieth centuries. It came into being in the stable political systems of Western Europe and North America, where

*From Samuel P. Huntington, "The Change to Change: Modernization, Development, and Politics," *Comparative Politics*, vol. 3, no. 3 (April 1971), pp. 283–322. Article and footnotes abridged by the editors. Reprinted by permission of the author and the journal.

[1] Talcott Parsons, *The Social System* (Glencoe, 1951), p. 486; Don Martindale, "Introduction," in George K. Zollschan and Walter Hirsch, eds., *Explorations in Social Change* (Boston, 1964), p. xii.

[2] David Easton, *The Political System* (New York, 1953), p. 42.

radical change could be viewed as a temporary deviation in, or extraordinary malfunctioning of, the political system. In Parsons' terminology, political scientists might study change *in* a system (such as the fluctuations in power of political parties or of Congress and president), but they did not concern themselves with change *of* the system.[3] Political scientists neglected change because they focused their primary attention on states where change did not seem to be much of a problem.

Reinforcing this tendency was the antihistorical temper of the more avant garde movements in political science. Born of history out of law, political science could establish itself as a discipline only by establishing its independence from its parents. Consequently, political scientists de-emphasized their ties with history and emphasized the similarities between their discipline and other social sciences. Political science evolved with the aid of periodic infusions of ideas, concepts, and methods from psychology (Harold Lasswell in the 1930s), social psychology, (David Truman and the group approach of the late 1940s), sociology (structural-functionalism of the 1950s), and economics (equilibrium, input-output, game theory, in the 1960s). The behavioral stress on survey data, interviewing, and participant-observation reinforced the rejection of history.

Political scientists attempt to explain political phenomena. They view politics as a dependent variable, and they naturally look for the explanations of politics in other social processes and institutions. This tendency was reinforced by the Marxian and Freudian intellectual atmosphere of the 1930s and 1940s. Political scientists were themselves concerned with the social, psychological, and economic roots of political behavior. Consequently, social change, personality change, and economic change were, in their view, more fundamental than political change. If one could understand and explain the former, one could easily account for the latter.

Finally, political change tended to be ignored because comparative politics tended to be ignored. With rare exceptions, such as the work of Carl Friedrich and a few others, political scientists did not attempt systematic comparative analyses of similar processes or functions in different political systems or general comparisons of political systems as systems. In book titles and course titles, comparative government meant foreign government. The study of political change is, however, intimately linked to the study of comparative politics. The study of change involves the comparison of similarities and differences through time; comparative politics involves the analysis of similarities and differences through space. In addition, the comparison of two political systems which exist simultaneously but which differ significantly in their major characteristics inevitably raises the questions: Is one system likely to evolve into a pattern similar to that of the other? Are the two systems related to each other in an evolutionary sense? Thus, the analysis of political change is not likely to progress unless the study of comparative politics is also booming.

Not until the mid-1950s did a renaissance in the study of comparative politics

[3] Parsons, *op. cit.,* pp. 480 ff.

get under way. That renaissance began with a concern with modernization and the comparison of modern and traditional political systems. It evolved in the early 1960s into a preoccupation with the concept of political development, approached by way of systems theory, statistical analysis, and comparative history. In the late 1960s, the focus on political development in turn yielded to broader efforts to generate more general theories of political change.

II. THE CONTEXT OF MODERNIZATION

General Theory of Modernization

The new developments in comparative politics in the 1950s involved extension of the geographical scope of concern from Western Europe and related areas to the non-Western "developing" countries. It was no longer true that political scientists ignored change. Indeed, they seemed almost overwhelmed with the immensity of the changes taking place in the modernizing societies of Asia, Africa, and Latin America. The theory of modernization was embraced by political scientists, and comparative politics was looked at in the context of modernization. The concepts of modernity and tradition bid fair to replace many of the other typologies which had been dear to the hearts of political analysts: democracy, oligarchy, and dictatorship; liberalism and conservatism; totalitarianism and constitutionalism; socialism, communism, and capitalism; nationalism and internationalism. Obviously, these categories were still used. But by the late 1960s, for every discussion among political scientists in which the categories "constitutional" and "totalitarian" were employed, there must have been ten others in which the categories "modern" and "traditional" were used.

These categories were, of course, the latest manifestation of a Great Dichotomy between more primitive and more advanced societies which has been a common feature of Western social thought for the past one hundred years. Their post-World War II incarnation dates from the elaboration by Parsons and Edward Shils of their pattern variables in the early 1950s and the subsequent extension of these from "choices" confronting an "actor" to characteristics of social systems undertaken by Frank Sutton in his 1955 paper on "Social Theory and Comparative Politics."[4] Sutton's summary of modern and traditional societies (or, in his terms, "industrial" and "agricultural" societies) encompasses most of the generally accepted distinguishing characteristics of these two types:

Agricultural Society

1. Predominance of ascriptive, particularistic, diffuse patterns
2. Stable local groups and limited spatial mobility
3. Relatively simple and stable "occupational" differentiation
4. A "deferential" stratification system of diffuse impact

[4] Frank X. Sutton, "Social Theory and Comparative Politics," in Harry Eckstein and David Apter, eds., *Comparative Politics: A Reader* (New York, 1963), pp. 67 ff.

Modern Industrial Society

1. Predominance of universalistic, specific, and achievement norms
2. High degree of social mobility (in a general—not necessarily "vertical"— sense)
3. Well-developed occupational system, insulated from other social structures
4. "Egalitarian" class system based on generalized patterns of occupational achievement
5. Prevalence of "associations," i.e., functionally specific, nonascriptive structures

The essential difference between modern and traditional society, most theorists of modernization contend, lies in the greater control which modern man has over his natural and social environment. This control, in turn, is based on the expansion of scientific and technological knowledge. To a sociologist such as Marion Levy, for instance, a society is "more or less modernized to the extent that its members use inanimate sources of power and/or use tools to multiply the effects of their efforts."[5] Cyril Black, an historian, argues that modern society results from adaptation of "historically evolved institutions . . . to the rapidly changing functions that reflect the unprecedented increase in man's knowledge, permitting control over his environment, that accompanied the scientific revolution."[6] Among political scientists, Dankwart A. Rustow holds that modernization involves a "rapidly widening control over nature through closer cooperation among men."[7] To virtually all theorists, these differences in the extent of man's control over his environment reflect differences in his fundamental attitudes toward and expectations from his environment. The contrast between modern man and traditional man is the source of the contrast between modern society and traditional society. Traditional man is passive and acquiescent; he expects continuity in nature and society and does not believe in the capacity of man to change or to control either. Modern man, in contrast, believes in both the possibility and the desirability of change, and has confidence in the ability of man to control change so as to accomplish his purposes.

At the intellectual level, modern society is characterized by the tremendous accumulation of knowledge about man's environment and by the diffusion of this knowledge through society by means of literacy, mass communications, and education. In contrast to traditional society, modern society also involves much better health, longer life expectancy, and higher rates of occupational and geographical mobility. It is predominantly urban rather than rural. Socially, the family and other primary groups having diffuse roles are supplanted or supplemented in modern society by consciously organized secondary associations having more specific functions. Economically, there is a diversification of activity as a few simple occupations give way to many complex ones; the level of occupational skill and the ratio of capital to labor are much higher than in

---

[5] Marion Levy, *Modernization and the Structure of Societies* (Princeton, 1966), I:11.

[6] Cyril E. Black, *The Dynamics of Modernization* (New York, 1966), p. 7.

[7] Dankwart A. Rustow, *A World of Nations* (Washington, 1967), p. 3.

traditional society. Agriculture declines in importance compared to commercial, industrial, and other nonagricultural activities, and commercial agriculture replaces subsistence agriculture. The geographical scope of economic activity is far greater in modern society than in traditional society, and there is a centralization of such activity at the national level, with the emergence of a national market, national sources of capital, and other national economic institutions.

The differences between a modern polity and a traditional one flow from these more general characteristics of modern and traditional societies. Political scientists have attempted various formulations of these differences. Perhaps the most succinct yet complete checklist is that furnished by Robert E. Ward and Rustow.[8] A modern polity, they argue, has the following characteristics which a traditional polity presumably lacks:

1. A highly differentiated and functionally specific system of governmental organization;
2. A high degree of integration within this governmental structure;
3. The prevalence of rational and secular procedures for the making of political decisions;
4. The large volume, wide range, and high efficacy of its political and administrative decisions;
5. A widespread and effective sense of popular identification with the history, territory, and national identity of the state;
6. Widespread popular interest and involvement in the political system, though not necessarily in the decision-making aspects thereof;
7. The allocation of political roles by achievement rather than ascription; and
8. Judicial and regulatory techniques based upon a predominantly secular and impersonal system of law.

More generally, a modern polity, in contrast to a traditional polity, is characterized by rationalized authority, differentiated structure, mass participation, and a consequent capability to accomplish a broad range of goals.[9]

The bridge across the Great Dichotomy between modern and traditional societies is the Grand Process of Modernization. The broad outlines and characteristics of this process are also generally agreed upon by scholars. Most writers on modernization implicitly or explicitly assign nine characteristics to the modernization process.

1. Modernization is a *revolutionary* process. This follows directly from the contrasts between modern and traditional society. The one differs fundamentally from the other, and the change from tradition to modernity consequently involves a radical and total change in patterns of human life. The shift from tradition to modernity, as Cyril Black says, is comparable to the changes from prehuman to human existence and from primitive to

---

[8] Dankwart A. Rustow and Robert E. Ward, "Introduction," in Ward and Rustow, eds., *Political Modernization in Japan and Turkey* (Princeton, 1964), pp. 6 and 7.

[9] See Samuel P. Huntington, *Political Order in Changing Societies* (New Haven, 1968), pp. 32–37.

civilized societies. The changes in the eighteenth century, Reinhard Bendix echoes, were "comparable in magnitude only to the transformation of nomadic peoples into settled agriculturalists some 10,000 years earlier."[10]

2. Modernization is a *complex* process. It cannot be easily reduced to a single factor or to a single dimension. It involves changes in virtually all areas of human thought and behavior. At a minimum, its components include: industrialization, urbanization, social mobilization, differentiation, secularization, media expansion, increasing literacy and education, expansion of political participation.

3. Modernization is a *systemic* process. Changes in one factor are related to and affect changes in the other factors. Modernization, as Daniel Lerner has expressed it in an oft-quoted phrase, is "a process with some distinctive *quality* of its own, which would explain why modernity is felt as a *consistent whole* among people who live by its rules." The various elements of modernization have been highly associated together "because, in some historic sense, they *had to* go together."[11]

4. Modernization is a *global* process. Modernization originated in fifteenth and sixteenth century Europe, but it has now become a worldwide phenomenon. This is brought about primarily through the diffusion of modern ideas and techniques from the European center, but also in part through the endogeneous development of non-Western societies. In any event, all societies were at one time traditional; all societies are now either modern or in the process of becoming modern.

5. Modernization is a *lengthy* process. The totality of the changes which modernization involves can only be worked out through time. Consequently, while modernization is revolutionary in the extent of the changes it brings about in traditional society, it is evolutionary in the amount of time required to bring about those changes. Western societies required several centuries to modernize. The contemporary modernizing societies will do it in less time. Rates of modernization are, in this sense, accelerating, but the time required to move from tradition to modernity will still be measured in generations.

6. Modernization is a *phased* process. It is possible to distinguish different levels or phases of modernization through which all societies will move. Societies obviously begin in the traditional stage and end in the modern stage. The intervening transitional phase, however, can also be broken down into subphases. Societies consequently can be compared and ranked in terms of the extent to which they have moved down the road from tradition to modernity. While the leadership in the process and the more detailed patterns of modernization will differ from one society to another, all societies will move through essentially the same stages.

7. Modernization is a *homogenizing* process. Many different types of tradi-

---

[10] Black, *op. cit.,* pp. 1–5; Reinhard Bendix, "Tradition and Modernity Reconsidered," *Comparative Studies in Society and History,* IX (April 1967), pp. 292–93.

[11] Daniel Lerner, *The Passing of Traditional Society* (Glencoe, 1958), p. 438.

tional societies exist; indeed, traditional societies, some argue, have little in common except their lack of modernity. Modern societies, on the other hand, share basic similarities. Modernization produces tendencies toward convergence among societies. Modernization involves movement "toward an interdependence among politically organized societies and toward an ultimate integration of societies." The "universal imperatives of modern ideas and institutions" may lead to a stage "at which the various societies are so homogeneous as to be capable of forming a world state. . . ."[12]

8. Modernization is an *irreversible* process. While there may be temporary breakdowns and occasional reversals in elements of the modernizing process, modernization as a whole is an essentially secular trend. A society which has reached certain levels of urbanization, literacy, industrialization in one decade will not decline to substantially lower levels in the next decade. The rates of change will vary significantly from one society to another, but the direction of change will not.

9. Modernization is a *progressive* process. The traumas of modernization are many and profound, but in the long run modernization is not only inevitable, it is also desirable. The costs and the pains of the period of transition, particularly its early phases, are great, but the achievement of a modern social, political, and economic order is worth them. Modernization in the long run enhances human well-being, culturally and materially.

. . . .

Modernization Revisionism

Modernization theory, like any social theory, . . . suffered from a limited perspective deriving from its particular temporal and social origins. In addition, however, there were some logical and inherent weaknesses in the theory itself. In the later 1960s a small-scale corrective reaction set in which tended to pinpoint some of the difficulties of mainstream modernization theory. Among the theorists associated with modernization revisionism were Joseph Gusfield, Milton Singer, Reinhard Bendix, Lloyd and Suzanne Rudolph, S. N. Eisenstadt, and F. C. Heesterman.[13] Perhaps significantly, the empirical work of many of these scholars focused on India, the twentieth century's most complex traditional society. The criticisms which these analysts made of the traditional theory of

---

[12] Black, *op. cit.,* pp. 155 and 174.

[13] See Joseph R. Gusfield, "Tradition and Modernity: Misplaced Polarities in the Study of Social Change," *American Journal of Sociology,* LXXII (January 1966), 351–62; Reinhard Bendix, *op. cit.,* 293–346; Lloyd and Suzanne Rudolph, *The Modernity of Tradition* (Chicago, 1967); S. N. Eisenstadt, "Breakdowns of Modernization," *Economic Development and Cultural Change,* XII (July 1964), 345–67, and "Tradition, Change, and Modernity," Eliezer Kaplan School of Economic and Social Sciences, Hebrew University; J. C. Heesterman, "Tradition in Modern India," *Bijdragen Tot de Taal-, Land- en Volkenkunde,* deel 119 (1963), 237–53; Milton Singer, ed., *Traditional India, Structure and Change* (Philadelphia, 1959); Rajni Kothari, "Tradition and Modernity Revisited," *Government and Opposition,* III (Summer 1968), 273–93; and C. S. Whitaker, Jr., *The Politics of Tradition: Continuity and Change in Northern Nigeria, 1946–1966* (Princeton, 1970).

modernization focused on: (a) the meaning and usefulness of the concepts of modernity and tradition; (b) the relationship between modernity and tradition; and (c) the ambiguities in the concept of modernization itself.

In the first place, as many modernization theorists themselves pointed out, modernity and tradition are essentially asymmetrical concepts. The modern ideal is set forth, and then everything which is not modern is labeled traditional. Modernity, as Rustow said, "can be affirmatively defined," while "tradition remains largely a residual concept."[14] Dichotomies which combine "positive" concepts and residual ones, however, are highly dangerous analytically. In point of fact, they are not properly dichotomies at all. They encourage the tendency to assume that the residual concept has all the coherence and precision of the positively defined concept. They obfuscate the diversity which may exist in the residual phenomenon and the fact that the differences between one manifestation of the residual concept and another manifestation of the same concept may be as great as or greater than the differences between either of the residual manifestations and the more precisely defined other pole of the polarity. This is a problem common to many dichotomies; the concept "civil-military relations," for instance, suffers from a similar disability and one which has had a serious impact upon the understanding of the relationship between the military and the multifarious nonmilitary groups in society, whose differences among themselves often exceed their differences from the military. Tradition is likewise simply too heterogeneous to be of much use as an analytical concept. The characteristics which are ascribed to traditional societies are the opposites of those ascribed to modern societies. Given the variety among nonmodern societies, however, obviously the "fit" of any particular society to the traditional ideal type will be haphazarded and inexact at best. Pigmy tribes, Tokugawa Japan, medieval Europe, the Hindu village are all traditional. Aside from that label, however, it is difficult to see what else they have in common. Traditional societies are diverse in values and heterogeneous in structures.[15] In addition, the concept of a tradition as essentially changeless came under attack. Traditional societies, it was argued, are not static. "The view that tradition and innovation are necessarily in conflict has begun to seem overly abstract and unreal."[16]

The concept of modernity also suffers some ambiguities. These stem from the tendency to identify modernity with virtue. All good things are modern, and modernity consequently becomes a mélange of incompatible virtues. In particular, there is a failure to distinguish between what is modern and what is Western. The one thing which modernization theory has not produced is a model of Western society—meaning late twentieth century Western European and North American society—which could be compared with, or even contrasted with, the model of modern society. Implicitly, the two are assumed to be virtually identical. Modern society has been Western society writ abstractly and polysyllabically. But to a nonmodern, non-Western society, the processes of moderni-

14 Rustow, *op. cit.*, p. 12.
15 See, especially, Singer, *op. cit.*, pp. x–xvii, and Heesterman, *op. cit.*, pp. 242–43.
16 Gusfield, *op. cit.*, p. 352.

zation and Westernization may appear to be very different indeed. This difficulty has been glossed over because the modern, non-Western box in the four-way breakdown of modern-nonmodern and Western-non-Western societies has, at least until the present, been empty. Presumably, however, Japan is either in or about to enter that box, and it is consequently not surprising that a Japanese scholar should take the lead in raising squarely the issue of how much of modernity is Western and how much of Western society is modern.[17] How do two modern societies, one of which is non-Western, resemble each other as compared to two Western societies, one of which is nonmodern? (It should also be noted that non-Western is, like nonmodern, a residual concept: the differences between two non-Western societies may well be greater than the differences between any one non-Western society and a Western society.)

Other questions have developed about the relations between tradition and modernity. The simpler theories of modernization implied a zero-sum relation between the two: the rise of modernity in society was accompanied by the fading of tradition. In many ways, however, modernity supplements but does not supplant tradition. Modern practices, beliefs, institutions are simply added to traditional ones. It is false to believe that tradition and modernity "are mutually exclusive."[18] Modern society is not simply modern; it is modern *and* traditional. The attitudes and behavior patterns may in some cases be fused; in others, they may comfortably coexist, one alongside the other, despite the apparent incongruity of it all. In addition, one can go further and argue not only that coexistence is possible but that modernization itself may strengthen tradition. It may give new life to important elements of the preexisting culture, such as religion. "Modern developments," as Heesterman has said, "more often than not go to strengthen tradition and give it a new dimension. To take a well-known example: modern means of mass communications, such as radio and film, give an unprecedented spread to traditional culture (broadcasting of Sanskrit mantras or of classical Indian music, films on mythological and devotional themes)." Tribal and other ascriptive "traditional" identities may be invigorated in a way which would never have happened in "traditional" society. Conversely, traditional attitudes and behavior may also help modernization: the extended family may become the entrepreneurial unit responsible for economic growth; the caste may be the group facilitating the operation of political democracy. "Traditional symbols and leadership forms can be vital parts of the value bases supporting modernizing frameworks."[19]

For all the ambiguities involved in the concepts of modernity and tradition, their rough outlines nonetheless appear possessed of comparative conceptual clarity when compared with the fuzziness which goes with the concept of

[17] See Hideo Kishimoto, "Modernization versus Westernization in the East," *Cahiers d'Histoire Mondiale*, VII (1963), 871–74, and also Heesterman, *op. cit.*, 238.

[18] Bendix, *op. cit.*, p. 326, and also Whitaker, *op. cit.*, pp. 3–15.

[19] Gusfield, *op. cit.*, p. 352; Heesterman, *op. cit.*, p. 243; Lloyd and Suzanne Hoeber Rudolph, "The Political Role of India's Caste Associations," *Pacific Affairs*, XXXIII (March 1960), 5–22.

modernization. In general, the writings on modernization were much more successful in delineating the characteristics of modern and traditional societies than they were in depicting the process by which movement occurs from one state to the other. They focused more on the direction of change, from "this" to "that," than on the scope, timing, methods, and rate of change. For this reason, they were more theories of "comparative statics" than they were theories of change.[20] The dichotomic developmental theories, moreover, were often ambiguous as to whether the phases which they posited were actual stages in historical evolution or whether they were Weberian ideal-types. As ideal-types, they were abstract models which could be used to analyze societies at any point in time. As historical concepts, however, the traditional category was presumably losing relevance and the modern category was gaining it. Inevitably, also, the dual character of the concepts undermined the conceptual dichotomy. Obviously all actual societies combine elements of both the traditional and modern ideal-types. Consequently, all actual societies are transitional or mixed. Viewed in terms of static ideal-types, this analysis presented no problems. One could still use the traditional and modern models to identify and relate the traditional and modern characteristics of any particular society. Viewed as a theory of history or change, however, the addition of a transitional category tended to exclude the traditional and modern stages from the historical process. Traditional society (like the state of nature) could only have existed as a hypothetical starting point in the distant past. A truly modern society would only exist if and when traditional remnants disappear in the distant future. Traditionalism and modernity thus cease to be stages in the historical process and become the beginning and ending points of history. But if all real societies are transitional societies, a theory is needed which will explain the forms and processes of change at work in transitional societies. This is just what the dichotomic theory failed to provide.

Beyond this, each of the assumptions which underlay the original, simple image of modernization could also be called into question. Contrary to the view that modernization is revolutionary, it could be argued that the differences between traditional and modern societies are really not that great. Not only do modern societies incorporate many traditional elements, but traditional societies often have many universalistic, achievement oriented, bureaucratic characteristics which are normally thought of as modern.[21] The cultural, psychological, and behavioral continuities existing within a society through both its traditional and modern phases, may be significantly greater than the dissimilarities between these phases. Similarly, the claim that modernization is a complex process could be challenged by the argument that modernization involves fundamental changes in only one dimension and that changes in other dimensions are only consequences of changes in that fundamental dimension. This was, of course, Marx's argument.

[20] See Wilbert Moore, "Social Change and Comparative Studies," *International Social Science Journal,* XV (1963), 523; J. A. Ponsioen, *The Analysis of Social Change Reconsidered* (The Hague, 1962), pp. 23–25.

[21] Bendix, *op. cit.,* pp. 313–314; Gusfield, *op. cit.,* pp. 352–53.

Contrary to Lerner's view of the systemic qualities of modernization, it can be argued that the various elements of the modernization process are historically discrete and that, while they have their roots in common causes, progress along one dimension has no necessary relationship to progress along another. Such a view is, indeed, implied by rejection of the mutually exclusive nature of modernity and tradition. If these concepts, moreover, are thought of simply as ideal types, and "If we are to avoid mistaking ideal types for accurate descriptions, we must take care to treat the clusters of attributes as *hypothetically,* not as actually, correlated." In addition, as Bendix went on to argue, a distinction ought to be maintained between modernization and modernity. "Many attributes of modernization, like widespread literacy or modern medicine, have appeared, or have been adopted, in isolation from other attributes of a modern society. Hence, modernization in some sphere of life *may* occur without resulting in 'modernity.' "[22] By extension, this argument also challenges the assumption that modernization is a global process. Modernization may be simply a peculiarity of Western culture; whatever changes are taking place in African and Asian cultures could be of a fundamentally different character and have very different results from those changes which occurred in Western societies.

The early assumptions about the timing and duration of modernization were also brought under criticism. The latecomers, it could be argued, can modernize rapidly through revolutionary means and by borrowing the experience and technology of the early modernizers. The entire process can thus be telescoped, and the assumption that there is a well-defined progression of phases—preconditions, takeoff, drive to maturity, and the like—through which all societies must move is likely to be invalid. Contrary to the common idea that modernization produces homogenization or convergence, it could be said that it may reinforce the distinctive characteristics of each society and thus broaden the differences between societies rather than narrow them. To the contrary of the idea that modernization is irreversible, it could be argued that it is a cyclical process with major ups and downs over time or that a turning point in the process will eventually be reached where the "upward" secular trend of modernization will be replaced by a sustained "downward" trend of disintegration or primitivization. Finally, contrary to the view that modernization is a progressive process, it may be argued, as earlier twentieth century thinkers asserted, that modernization destroys the more intimate communities in which alone man can realize his full personality; it sacrifices human, personal, and spiritual values to achieve mass production and mass society. This type of argument against change was very popular at times in the past. The relative absence of such a traditional, romantic opposition to modernization among theorists in modern societies and politicians in modernizing societies was some evidence of the extent to which the fever of modernization gripped the intellectually and politically conscious world of the 1950s. Nonetheless, by the late 1960s some opposition to and criticism of

[22] Bendix, *op. cit.,* pp. 315 and 329; Eisenstadt, "Tradition, Change, and Modernity," pp. 27 and 28.

modernization along these lines were beginning to appear among intellectuals in many developing societies.

[Professor Huntington's discussion of the concept of political development has been omitted.—Eds.]

III. THEORIES OF POLITICAL CHANGE

The study of modernization and political development thus generated concern for the formulation of more general theories of political change. In the late 1960s the analysis of political change became in itself a direct focus of political science work, quite apart from any relations it might have with the social-economic-cultural processes of modernization or the teleological preoccupations which underlay much of the work on political development. In the course of a decade the work of political scientists moved from a generalized focus on the political system to the comparative analysis of modern and traditional political systems, to a more concrete concern with the discrete historical process of modernization, to an elaboration of related concepts of political development, and then back to a higher level of abstraction oriented toward general theories of political change. The transition from the static theory to dynamic theory, in short, was made by way of the historical phenomenon of modernization.

These new theories of political change were distinguishable from earlier approaches because of several characteristics. First, the theoretical frameworks could be utilized for the study of political changes in societies at any level of development. Second, these frameworks were either unrelated to the process of modernization or, at best, indirectly related to that process. Third, the variables and relationships which were central to the theories were primarily political in character. Fourth, the frameworks were sufficiently flexible to encompass sources of change and patterns of change in both the domestic and the international environments of the political system. Fifth, in general the theories were relatively more complex than earlier theories of political modernization and political development: they encompassed more variables and looked at the more extensive relationships among those variables.

One transitional approach was presented by Huntington in his 1968 volume on *Political Order in Changing Societies*. In this volume, the central focus of political change is held to be the relationship between political participation and political institutionalization. The relationship between these determines the stability of the political system. The fundamental source of expansion of political participation is the nonpolitical socioeconomic processes identified with modernization. The impact of modernization on political stability is mediated through the interaction between social mobilization and economic development, social frustration and nonpolitical mobility opportunities, and political participation and political institutionalization. Huntington expresses these relationships in a series of equations:[23]

---

[23] Huntington, *op. cit.*, p. 55.

$$(1) \quad \frac{\text{Social mobilization}}{\text{Economic development}} = \text{Social frustration}$$

$$(2) \quad \frac{\text{Social frustration}}{\text{Mobility opportunities}} = \text{Political participation}$$

$$(3) \quad \frac{\text{Political participation}}{\text{Political institutionalization}} = \text{Political instability}$$

Starting with a central concern of the social-process approach to modernization, i.e., the relationship between socioeconomic changes (urbanization, industrialization), on the one hand, and the political participation, political instability, and violence, on the other, this approach thus attempts to introduce into the analysis elements of social (mobility opportunities) and political (political institutionalization) structure.

Huntington is concerned with the relationship between political participation and political institutionalization. The source of the former is ultimately in the processes of modernization. What about the sources of the latter? Here he is less explicit. Implicitly, however, he suggests that there are two principal sources. One is the political structure of the traditional society. Some traditional political systems are more highly institutionalized than others (i.e., more adaptable, complex, coherent, and autonomous); these presumably will be better able to survive modernization and accommodate broadened patterns of participation. In addition, Huntington suggests that at particular phases in the process of modernization certain types of political leadership (aristocratic, military, revolutionary) and certain types of conflict may also produce institutionalization.

The relationship between political institutionalization and political participation, however, is clearly one that can be abstracted from a concern with modernization. The latter may be one major historical source of changes in participation, but it need not be the only one. The problem of balancing participation and institutionalization, moreover, is one which occurs in societies at all levels of development. The disruptions involving Negroes and students in the United States during the late 1960s could be profitably analyzed from this framework. In central cities and in universities, existing structures were challenged to provide new channels through which these groups, in the cliché of the times, could "participate in the decisions which affect them."

This theoretical approach, originally focused on the relationship between two political variables, could be extended to include more or different ones. One of the striking characteristics of much of the work on political development was the predominance of concern with the *direction* of change over the concern with the *objects* of change. This, of course, reflected the origins of political development research in the study of the transition from traditional to modern society. The first step in analyzing political change, however, is simply, as William Mitchell put it, to identify "the objects that are susceptible to changes."[24] It is to

[24] William C. Mitchell, *The American Polity* (New York, 1962), pp. 369–70.

identify what are or may be the components of a political system and then to establish what, if any, relations exist in the changes among them. Such an approach focuses on *componential change.*

A political system can be thought of as an aggregate of components, all changing, some at rapid rates, some at slower ones. The questions to be investigated then become: What types of change in one component tend to be related to similar changes or the absence of change in other components? What are the consequences of different combinations of componential changes for the system as a whole? The study of political change can be said to involve: (1) focusing on what seem to be the major components of the political system; (2) determining the rate, scope, and direction of change in these components; and (3) analyzing the relations between changes in one component and changes in other components. The political system can be defined in a variety of ways and conceived of as having various components, as, for instance, the following five:

a) culture, that is, the values, attitudes, orientations, myths, and beliefs relevant to politics and dominant in the society;

b) structure, that is, the formal organizations through which the society makes authoritative decisions, such as political parties, legislatures, executives, and bureaucracies;

c) groups, that is, the social and economic formations, formal and informal, which participate in politics and make demands on the political structures;

d) leadership, that is, the individuals in political institutions and groups who exercise more influence than others on the allocation of values;

e) policies, that is, the patterns of governmental activity which are consciously designed to affect the distribution of benefits and penalties within the society.

The study of political change can fruitfully start with the analysis of changes in these five components and the relations between change in one component and change in another. How is change in the dominant values in a system related to change in its structures? What is the relation between mobilization of new groups into politics and institutional evolution? How is turnover in leadership related to changes in policy? The starting assumption would be that, in any political system, all five components are always changing, but that the rate, scope, and direction of change in the components vary greatly within a system and between systems. In some instances, the rate of change of a component may approach zero. The absence of change is simply one extreme rate of change, a rate rarely if ever approximated in practice. Each component, moreover, is itself an aggregate of various elements. The political culture, for instance, may include many subcultures; the political structures may represent a variety of institutions and procedures. Political change may be analyzed both in terms of changes among components and in terms of changes among the elements of each component.

Components and elements are the objects of change. But it is still necessary to indicate what types of changes in these are significant, to the study of *political* change. One type of change which is obviously relevant is change in the power of a component or element. Indeed, some might argue that changes in power are the only changes with which political analysis should be concerned.

But to focus on power alone is to take the meaning out of politics. Political analysis is concerned with the power of ideologies, institutions, groups, leaders, and policies. But it is also concerned with the content of these components and with the interrelation between changes in content and changes in power. "Power" here may have the usual meaning assigned to it in political analysis. The "content," on the other hand, has to be defined somewhat differently for each component. The content of a political culture is the substance of the ideas, values, attitudes, and expectations dominant in the society. The content of the political institutions of the society, on the other hand, consists of the patterns of interaction which characterize them and the interests and values associated with them. The content of political groups refers to their interests and purposes and the substance of the claims which they make on the political system. The content of the leadership refers to the social-economic-psychological characteristics of the leaders and the goals which they attempt to realize. And the content of policies, of course, involves the substance of the policies, their prescriptions of benefits and penalties.

The analysis of political change may in the first instance be directed to simple changes in the power of components and elements of the political system. More important, however, is the relation between changes in the power of individual components and elements and changes in their content. If political analysis were limited to changes in power, it could never come to grips with their causes and consequences. The recurring problems of politics involve the trade offs of power and content. To what extent do changes in the power of a political ideology (measured by the number of people who adhere to it and the intensity of their adherence) involve changes in the substance of the ideology? Under what circumstances do rapid changes in the power of political leaders require changes in their purposes and goals (the "moderating" effects of power) and under what circumstances may the power of leaders be enhanced without significant changes in their purposes? History suggests, for instance, that professional military officers can acquire political power in liberal, socialist, or totalitarian societies only at the expense of abandoning or modifying the conservative military values. In most systems, the enhancement of the power of an ideology, institution, group, leader, or policy is bought at the price of some modification of its content. But this is by no means an invariable rule, and a variety of propositions will be necessary to specify the trade offs between power and content for different components in different situations. One important distinction among political systems may indeed be the prices which must be paid in content for significant increases in the power of elements. Presumably the more highly institutionalized a political system is, the higher the price it exacts for power.

Political change may thus be analyzed at three levels. The rate, scope, and direction of change in one component may be compared with the rate, scope, and direction of change in other components. Such comparisons can shed light on the patterns of stability and instability in a political system and on the extent to which change in one component depends upon or is related to change or the absence of change in other components. The culture and institutions of a political system, for instance, may be thought of as more fundamental to the system than its groups, leaders, and policies. Consequently, stability might be defined as a particular set of relationships in which all components are changing gradually, but with the rates of change in culture and institutions slower than those in other components. Political stagnation, in turn, could be defined as a situation in which there is little or no change in the political culture and institutions but rapid changes in leadership and policies. Political instability may be a situation in which culture and institutions change more rapidly than leaders and policies, while political revolution involves simultaneous rapid change in all five components of the system.

As a second level of analysis, changes in the power and content of one element of one component of the system may be compared with changes in the power and content of other elements of the same component. This would involve, for instance, analysis of the rise and fall of ideologies and beliefs, of institutions and groups, and leaders and policies, and the changes in the content of these elements associated with their changing power relationships. Finally, at the most specific level of analysis, attention might be focused upon the relation between changes in power and changes in content for any one element, in an effort to identify the equations defining the price of power in terms of purposes, interests, and values.

A relatively simple set of assumptions and categories like this could be a starting point either for the comparative analysis of the more general problems of change found in many societies or for the analysis in depth of the change patterns of one particular society. It could furnish a way of bringing together the contributions which studies of attitudes, institutions, participation, groups, elites, and policies could make to the understanding of political change.

A somewhat different approach, suggested separately by both Gabriel Almond and Dankwart Rustow, focused on *crisis change* and also provided a general framework for analyzing political dynamics. Earlier theories of comparative politics and development, Almond argued, could be classified in terms of two dimensions.[25] To what extent did they involve an equilibrium or developmental models? To what extent were they predicated upon determinacy or choice? Reviewing many of the writers on these problems, Almond came up with the following classification:

Approaches to Comparative Politics

	Equilibrium	Developmental
Determinacy	I Parsons Easton	III Deutsch Moore Lipset
Choice	II Downs Dahl Riker	IV Harsanyi Leiserson

[25] Gabriel A. Almond, "Determinacy-Choice, Stability-Change: Some Thoughts on a Contemporary Polemic in Political Theory," (Center for Advanced Study in the Behavioral Sciences, Stanford University, August 1969).

He then went on to argue that each of these approaches has its appropriate place in the analysis of political change. Change from one state to another can be thought of as going through five phases. In the first phase, an antecedent equilibrium can be assumed to exist, and for the analysis of this phase Type I and Type II theories are most appropriate. Change can be assumed to begin with the impact on the equilibrium of exogenous variables from the nonpolitical domestic environment or from the international environment of the political system. These Phase 2 developments produce changes in the structure of political demand and in the distribution of political resources, and can be most appropriately analyzed by Type III theories. In the next phase, political factors—the changing structure of political demand and distribution of political resources— become the independent variables. Political leadership manipulates these variables so as to produce new political coalitions and policy outcomes. For this purpose, Type IV "coalition theory and leadership skill and personality theory" are most useful. In the next or fourth phase, these policy outcomes and political coalitions produce cultural and structural changes. The relations in this phase require analysis by all four types of theories. Finally, a new "consequent equilibrium" emerges in Phase 5, which again can be studied in terms of Type I and Type II theories.

In formulating this theoretical framework, Almond once again played a leading and a representative role in changing thinking on comparative politics. Unlike his earlier formulations, this framework was precisely designed to deal with the problem of change and it was also clearly independent of any particular historical context. It was not tied in with modernization. It was instead a general framework for the analysis of political change which could be applied to a primitive stateless tribe, a classical Greek city-state, or to a modern nation-state. It encompassed both political and nonpolitical variables and recognized that each could play both dependent and independent roles. Perhaps most significantly, it effectively incorporated leadership and choice into a model of political change. All in all, it nearly synthesized several conflicting approaches to development and change in such a way as to capitalize on the particular strengths of each. The model was especially relevant to the analysis of intense changes of limited duration. Hence, it is not surprising that Almond and his associates applied it to the study of clearly delimitable historical crises, such as the Reform Act of 1832, the creation of the Third Republic, the Meiji Restoration, the Bolshevik Revolution, and the Cárdenas reforms of the 1930s.

In a parallel endeavor, Rustow came up with a somewhat similar model.[26] Political change, he suggested, is the product of dissatisfaction with the existing situation. This dissatisfaction produces political action; political action, indeed, is *always* the result of dissatisfaction. This action either succeeds or fails. If it succeeds, the organization, movement, or other group responsible for the success

[26] Dankwart A. Rustow, "Change as the Theme of Political Science," pp. 6–8 (mimeo.). See also his "Communism and Change," in Chalmers Johnson, ed., *Change in Communist Systems* (Stanford, 1970), pp. 343–58, and "Transitions to Democracy: Toward a Dynamic Model," *Comparative Politics*, II (April 1970), 337–63.

either develops new goals or it withers and dies. If its effort for change fails, either the group responsible for the effort dissolves or it continues to pursue its old objective with decreasing expectation of ever achieving it. In addition, Rustow argues, the forces involved in the creation of a government or the conquest of power by a group or individual are very different from those which sustain the government or keep the individual or group in power over the long haul. A theory of political change has to account for and to systematize these differences. Thus Rustow, like Almond, puts a primary emphasis on the choices which have to be made by political leadership.

A third approach to the analysis of political change was developed by Ronald D. Brunner and Garry D. Brewer.[27] In their study of the political aspects of modernization, they developed a model of a *complex change* involving twenty-two variables and twenty parameters. Ten of the variables and eight of the parameters were disaggregated in terms of rural and urban sectors; three variables and three parameters constituted the demographic subsystem, nine variables and six parameters the economic subsystem, and ten variables and eleven parameters the political subsystem. The relations among these variables and parameters were expressed in twelve equations derived from general theories of modernization and from analysis of the evolution of Turkey and the Philippines from the 1940s to the 1960s. Their model included variables which could be directly influenced by governmental action and others not subject to such influence. Using the model it is possible to calculate the probable effects on support for the governments (measured by the proportion of the population voting for the government party) and on the standard of living (measured by per capita consumption) of governmental policy changes—such as birth control programs producing a 5 percent decrease in the rate of natural increase of population, increases or decreases of 5 percent in urban tax rates, and changes in the relative preference accorded the urban and rural sectors in governmental expenditures. Alternatively, one policy parameter—such as governmental preference for urban and rural sectors—can be intensively analyzed to demonstrate how various degrees of change within it might affect dependent variables such as government support and standard of living.

The Brunner-Brewer approach opened up new horizons in political analysis. Theoretically, it provided a highly simplified but highly precise model of a political system encompassing a significant number of demographic, economic, and political variables, the relations among which could be expressed by equations. Practically, it pointed scientific inquiry in a direction which could ultimately provide policymakers with a means of analyzing the probable consequences of policy choices for outcomes directly relevant to their purposes. In effect, this model building introduced into political science the type of complex analysis of relations among variables which has long prevailed in economics. On the other hand, the Brunner-Brewer approach was limited by its initial theoretical assumptions and the relevance of those assumptions to the actual political

[27] Ronald D. Brunner and Garry D. Brewer, *Organized Complexity: Empirical Theories of Political Development* (New York, 1971).

systems to which the model was oriented. The twelve-equation model furnished a reasonably good guide to the interaction of the variables and parameters in Turkey and the Philippines during the 1950s and 1960s. Its relevance to the future was based on the assumption that the structure of the model and the magnitude of the parameters did not vary over time. The model provided ways of testing the consequences of major changes in governmental policy or major changes in other variables brought about by other means. It did not provide means for predicting major changes of the system unless or until these changes were reflected in significant changes in some variables in the model. Thus, the model could not predict a military coup bringing to power a radical, nationalist junta of officers. Once such a junta came to power the model might be able to predict some of the consequences of new policies they introduced. Its ability to do this would depend upon the continued existence of the relationships among variables which had existed in the past. The first goals of the revolutionary junta might be to change those relationships. Thus, the usefulness of the Brunner-Brewer approach was limited by the degree of discontinuity in the political system.

These various theories of componential change, crisis change, and complex change all tended, in one way or another, to liberate political analysis from the static assumptions which had limited it in one earlier phase and from the teleological concerns with modernization and development which had preoccupied it in a later phase. They indicated increasing parallelism between the study of political change and the study of social change. Most important, they were the very modest and first steps toward the formulation of general theories of political dynamics, the initial response to Rustow's challenge: "Aside from the refinement of evolutionary models and the more sophisticated use of historical data, is it not time to introduce some notion of change into our very conception of politics itself?"[28]

[28] Dankwart A. Rustow, "Modernization and Comparative Politics: Prospects in Research and Theory," *Comparative Politics*, I (October 1968), 51.

chapter XIII

MODERNIZATION AND DEMOCRACY

The Western democracies, whose peoples uniformly enjoy a high standard of living, constitute one of the "models" on which the development of the newly emerging nations might be based. But under what conditions may democracy—historically the product of European culture—be transplanted in "non-Western" countries?

Democracy involves more than the existence of formal institutions. British cabinet government, for example, in itself is easily adaptable to the requirements of dictatorship—in the absence of a vigorous opposition, a free press, and above all, historical traditions of individual freedom. The institutions function within a specific social, historical, and cultural context. Democracy can work only when democratic norms and values, particularly those relating to free expression and political organization, are understood and accepted by all the people. John Stuart Mill pointed out, in a classic analysis of the social conditions of representative government:

> A people may be unwilling or unable to fulfill the duties which a particular form of government requires of them. A rude people, though in some degree alive to the benefits of civilized society, may be unable to practice the forebearance which it demands. . . . In such a case, a civilized government, to be really advantageous to them, will require to be in a considerable degree despotic: to be one over which they do not themselves exercise control, and which imposes a great amount of forcible restraint upon their actions.[1]

In any case, the social structures of the developing nations are so different from those of Europe and North America, that some adaptation or modification of democratic institutions appears inevitable. The precise form which this modification assumes in the various nations of Africa, Asia, and Latin America makes an exciting subject for comparative study.

[1] *On Representative Government,* chap. 1.

426

Some of the more comprehensive studies of institutional transfer, with all that it entails, are: Robert Scalapino, *Democracy and the Party Movement in Prewar Japan* (1956); Sir Ivor Jennings, *The Approach to Self-Government* (1956); David A. Apter, *Ghana in Transition* (1963); Henry L. Bretton, *Power and Stability in Nigeria* (1962); and B. P. Lamb, *India: A World in Transition* (1963). See also F. S. C. Northrop, *The Meeting of East and West* (1953), and Barbara Ward, *Five Ideas That Change the World* (1959).

The readings below also deal with the conditions under which democracy emerged in Europe and North America. Among the works that treat this topic are: R. R. Palmer, *The Age of the Democratic Revolution* (1959); S. M. Lipset, *The First New Nation* (1963); L. Hartz, ed., *The Founding of New Societies* (1964); and Barrington Moore, Jr., *Social Origins of Dictatorship and Democracy* (1966).

32. Modernization and Democracy in Japan*

ROBERT E. WARD

I

The term "political modernization" is of late encountered with increasing frequency in the literature of political science. Its antecedents are somewhat diffuse. In the most general sense, it seems to represent a specialized adaptation of scholars' long-standing concern with the question of whether the process of social change is determinate or variable, random or patterned, continuous or episodic, cyclic or evolutionary. Within this tradition "political modernization" is a concept opposed in tendency to the relativistic character of much modern scholarship in the field of politics. It would seem to be oriented more in the direction of a patterned and evolutionary—although not necessarily determinate or value-laden—interpretation of social change.

In a more restricted sense, this concept is perhaps more directly related to the search for new methodological principles which has been so notable an aspect of the discipline of political science for the past ten years. For at least this period, students of comparative politics have been systematically seeking analytic concepts and categories of inquiry broad enough in ambit and yet sufficiently sensitive and researchable to permit meaningful cross-national comparisons of political systems and their component parts. This concern has focused upon

*From "Political Modernization and Political Culture in Japan," *World Politics* (July 1963), pp. 569–96. Abridged by the editors. Reprinted by permission of *World Politics*.

problems of both cross-sectional and developmental comparison and it is in the latter context that the concept of "political modernization" has seemed promising.

Third, the concept also finds a more practical provenance in the expanding commitments of the United States government to the "development" of many so-called underdeveloped areas. While initial efforts in this campaign were largely confined to the economic and military spheres, it was rapidly discovered that durable economic development required a comparable degree of political development. This circumstance has reinforced general professional interest in the process and determinants of "political modernization," and provided unusual opportunities for both study and experimentation in actual field situations.

Finally, the concept of "political modernization" is to some degree indebted to recent theorizing and writing in the analogous field of "economic development." This new concern within the profession springs, therefore, from a variety of sources. Since it has not as yet, however, gained general acceptance, it might be well at this point to provide a working definition for it.[1]

The concept of "political modernization" assumes and is intelligible only in terms of the existence of a "modern" society as the essential environment for a modern political system. A modern society is here viewed as a massive and new type of social development which has come upon the scene in mature form only in the course of the last century. It is characterized by its far-reaching ability to control or influence the physical and social circumstances of its environment, and by a value system which is fundamentally optimistic about the desirability and consequences of this ability. More specifically, in its non-political sectors it is also characterized by low birth, death, and morbidity rates and by high ratios, degrees, or levels of: (1) inanimate to animate sources of energy; (2) tool technology, mechanization, and industrialization; (3) specialization and professionalization of labor; (4) gross and per capita national product of goods and services; (5) urbanization; (6) differentiation, achievement orientation, and mobility in social organization; and (7) literacy, mass education, and mass media circulation.

No society, of course, possesses all of these qualities in a complete or polar sense. Even the most "modern" society contains substantial admixtures of what might be described as pre-modern or traditional elements and is, in this sense, mixed or dualistic in character. Despite the measure of commonality which this fact ensures to all societies, there obviously exist profound differences in the proportion and pattern in which modern and pre-modern elements are distributed or "mixed" in various societies. In some cases, the "mix" is such as to yield almost purely traditional types such as Yemen or Afghanistan; in others, it produces something as innovational, as "modern" as the United States or the USSR. In this sense judgments of modernity are more concerned with the central tendency or thrust of societies than with any undiluted conception of uniformly modern or traditional social characteristics.

---

[1] This definition is adopted from Robert E. Ward and Roy C. Macridis, eds., *Modern Political Systems: Asia* (Englewood Cliffs, N.J., 1963), p. 445.

A "modern" polity is a subsystem of a "modern" society. As such it has separable characteristics, the most important of which are a high degree of both functional differentiation and integration of political structure and political roles; a rational, secular, and scientific system of political decision-making; and the volume, range, authority, and efficacy of its output of political decisions and administrative actions. More specifically, it is also characterized by: (1) a reasonably general and effective sense of popular identification with the history, territory, myths, and national identity of the state concerned; (2) widespread popular interest and involvement in the political system, though not necessarily in the decision-making aspects thereof; (3) an allocation of political roles in accordance with standards of achievement rather than ascription; and (4) judicial and regulatory techniques based upon a predominantly secular and impersonal system of law.

Other attributes of importance to a definition of the process of political modernization can doubtless be adduced but, for present purposes, this may serve as a working list of central tendencies possessed by all political systems generally regarded as being "modern." It should be added that while political modernization is, of course, a continuing process—unachieved and probably unachievable in the ideal-type sense—it is not necessarily open-ended or permanent. It is quite possible to conceive of the emergence of other types of political systems differing in important respects from that defined above as "modern." In this sense—bizarre though the semantics may be—there may be point in speculating about the characteristics of post-modern polities, as we already do about those of pre-modern polities. Such speculation aside, however, the present utility of the concept of "political modernization" rests upon the hope that it validly and objectively defines the essential features of the political developments which have occurred in all so-called advanced societies and that it also represents the pattern toward which politically underdeveloped societies are now evolving.

Two other aspects of the concept should be noted. First, no political system is completely modern in this sense. Even those regarded as being the most modern have substantial admixtures of what are by definition pre-modern or traditional elements. These seem capable of coexisting with the dominant modern component for very substantial periods of time, perhaps indefinitely. In fact, their role is sometimes supportive of the political modernization process in important respects. Second, the concept of political modernization in its present form is neutral with respect to the philosophic or ethical orientation and particular form of government of political systems. It regards all such systems— whether democratic, totalitarian, or intermediate in type—as either actually or potentially modern. The form of government is not a critical factor. Both the United States and the USSR represent politically modern societies in this sense.

II

This statement of the characteristics of a modern society and political system poses the question of Japan's current status. How modern are contemporary Japanese society and the Japanese political system? How do their performances compare with those of other Asian and Western states?

No single indicator can provide a satisfactory answer to this question, but by combining a variety of indices one can achieve helpful insights. For the present, let us confine ourselves to some of the more obvious statistical measures of modernity. In recent years Japan's birth and death rates per thousand of population (17.5 and 7.4 respectively in 1960) compare very favorably with those of the United States, the USSR, France, or Great Britain, as does her population's expectation of life at age 0 (65.2 for men and 69.8 for women in 1959). Approximately 98 per cent of her population is literate, a figure that places Japan among the world's leading societies in this respect. The school enrollment ratios at the primary and secondary level are fully the equal of those of the leading Western countries, while her college and university enrollment ratios are considerably higher than those of Great Britain or France. In circulation of daily newspapers per 1,000 of population, Japan's figure of 398 in 1958 was exceeded only by the United Kingdom, Sweden, Norway, and Luxembourg. Sixty-three per cent of her population is urban in residence, and secondary or tertiary in employment characteristics. In 1961 her steel output ranked fourth in the world, ahead of Great Britain's, while for the sixth straight year she led the world in shipbuilding. Her gross national product on a per capita basis, while still low by Western European standards ($399 in 1961), is the highest in Asia if one excepts Israel. And it is increasing rapidly as a consequence of an economy which has been expanding at a rate of 18 per cent in 1959, 14 per cent in 1960, and 10 per cent in 1961. These are among the world's highest rates of economic advancement where already developed societies are concerned.

Thus, judging by the common statistical measures of modernity, Japan's performance is outstanding. Viewed in terms both more qualitative and more specifically political, her record, while somewhat less unequivocal, is impressive. Her formal political structure is among the most modern, rational, and functionally differentiated in the world. Her decision-making system, while still displaying a considerable number of traditional characteristics, stands far in advance of the norms for Asia or the underdeveloped world in general. The same is true of her output of political decisions and administrative actions.

By any standards of modernity, therefore, Japan indubitably possesses developed and modern social and political systems. The distance which separates her from American or Western European performance in these spheres may still be appreciable, but it is far less impressive than the gulf which separates Japanese performance from that of practically all other parts of Asia.

Against this background, it is our purpose to examine in a quite general and selective way certain aspects of the political modernization process in Japan in an attempt to clarify at least some of the circumstances which contributed to a successful outcome in this one historical case. It is not claimed that Japan's path to political modernization can or should be the sole or complete model for Asian or other developing societies seeking a similar result. Some aspects of the

Japanese experience are doubtless unique. But since Japan is the only indigenous Asian society that has succeeded in achieving types and levels of political performance which practically all other Asian states either desire or consider necessary, the nature of the Japanese experience inevitably becomes of extraordinary interest. It may not point to the only or the most effective path of political modernization for other developing societies, but it does represent the only mature specimen available for analysis. As a specific and concrete case it also affords opportunities for checking and enriching the types of relatively abstract and theoretical speculation which necessarily bulk large in the early stages of investigation in fields such as this.

III

As one looks back upon the history of political modernization in Japan, one might well be impressed first by the neatness of the manner in which it is usually periodized. In gross terms, for example, one is accustomed to distinguishing periods called Tokugawa (1603–1868) and post-Restoration (1868–) in Japanese political history. For somewhat more specific purposes, many distinguish an overlapping Restoration Period (ca. 1850–1890) when considering the beginnings of modern Japanese political development. Over the years these convenient denominators for the categorization of historical data have assumed an authority and potential for distortion which were never intended. . . .

In the Japanese case, this emphasis upon the Restoration and its aftermath as a time of revolutionary, i.e., discontinuous, new developments—especially in the political and economic spheres—acquired added force from a subsequent episode in Japanese historiography. This was the widespread practice of interpreting pre-Restoration Japan—the Japan of the Tokugawa Period (1603–1868)—in terms of a "feudal" model. Indeed, at a later period, this was compounded by the addition of the notion that the Tokugawa shoguns had in effect intervened in the normal course of Japan's historical development and succeeded in refeudalizing the country in the early seventeenth century at a time when its immanent tendencies were modernizing. Thus, pre-Restoration Japan came to be viewed not only as "feudal," but, in Professor J. W. Hall's apt phrase, as a "feudal throwback."

One can readily appreciate the consequences attendant upon so dichotomous a treatment of post-sixteenth-century Japanese history. For many the Restoration tended to become a watershed more formidable than the Rockies. What lay behind it was normally viewed as "feudal": what lay on this side of it became either "modern" or a "feudal survival"—that is, an undesirable remnant of earlier practices or attitudes slated for eventual discard. This tendency was probably reinforced by real ignorance where the actual circumstances of life and society in Tokugawa times were concerned. It is only within the past few years that professional research in this period has become at all fashionable, and it is still seriously neglected in favor of more "glamorous" subjects drawn from the Restoration and later periods. As a consequence, the real beginnings of modernization in Japan have frequently been overlooked or attributed to much later periods than was actually the case.

The degree of literacy and of formal institutionalized education in pre-Restoration Japan provides a case in point. The educational preparation of at least sizable segments of a population is a basic factor in both the general and the political modernization process. Until recently it has been widely assumed that any really critical advances in this sphere waited upon the introduction of compulsory mass education in the 1870's. In fact, this was far from true. . . . Dore concludes that, despite the Confucian orientation of most of this pre-Restoration education, "the attitudes to popular education, the sense of the contingency of social institutions on the human will, the training in abstract analysis and the application of evaluating principles to policy, the development of a respect for merit rather than status, the stimulation of personal ambition and the strengthening of a collectivist ideology . . ."[2] represented important contributions to the modernizing process in Japan, and that all of these had undergone very considerable development long before the Restoration.

In a more specifically political sense, the same could be said of the origins and development of another major element in the modernizing process—the emergence of a professionally trained, rationally structured, and achievement-oriented bureaucracy. . . . In the light of insights such as these into what was actually taking place throughout the Tokugawa Period in Japan, one begins to appreciate the long, gradual process of institutional and attitudinal preparation for modernization which was well under way at least a century before the Restoration. Comparable "preparations" may readily be identified at the village level or in the economic sphere; there is nothing unduly selective about these examples. Japanese society during the Tokugawa Period may still be appropriately described by such terms as "centralized or nationalized feudalism" but, if so, it was feudalism with an important difference. Japan had come a long way from the hierarchic, personal, loyalty-focused relationships and the intricate structure of fiefs and practically enserfed villagers which had characterized the polity in the sixteenth and early seventeenth centuries. On balance the "feudal" attributes of the society perhaps still predominated. But mingled with and gradually subverting these were a number of the most salient and potent elements of "modern" society.

When evaluating the modernization of Japan, it is useful to keep in mind this long, complex history of covert preparation from which the society benefited. This still stands as a unique accomplishment in Asia, but its main roots are buried at least two hundred years deep in the country's social and political history. The florescence of national leadership during the early Meiji Period, combined with the international circumstances and opportunities of the times, had a great deal to do with the amazing speed at which Japan modernized, but in a more fundamental sense Japanese society seems to have been prepared for the experience to a degree still unmatched in some important respects among

2 Ronald P. Dore, "The Legacy of Tokugawa Education" (unpublished paper prepared for the first seminar of the Conference on Modern Japan, January 1962), pp. 1 and 2.

many contemporary Asian societies. In this context, the Japanese preparations for more modern forms of social, economic, and political organization may not be so completely different from their Western analogues as the apparent persistence of a "feudal" period until 1868 makes it seem.

IV

This extension in historical depth of the development of a modern society and polity in Japan also calls attention to what Professor Almond has termed the "dualism" of political institutions.[3] All modern polities contain substantial admixtures of traditional elements, and these are frequently not confined to isolated or backwater areas but may play a prominent and functionally important role in the modernization process.

In the Japanese case, this is well illustrated by our earlier account of the historical development of a professionally trained, rationally structured, and achievement-oriented bureaucracy in Japan. In this instance it was pointed out that what seemed to be a purely feudal institution performing functions of major importance in a predominantly feudal society was at the same time gradually acquiring more and more of the basic characteristics of a modern professional bureaucracy. In a historical sense, therefore, the late Tokugawa bureaucracy played a Janus-like role. It faced both backward toward the truly feudal institutions and times of the sixteenth century and forward toward the emergent modern society of the twentieth. It also served in gradually shifting proportions the purposes of both waning and emergent societies, and it continued to do this for upward of one hundred and fifty years. In other words, the capacity for peaceful coexistence—and even mutual supportiveness—of "feudal" or traditional with modern elements within a given institution, as well as within a society, is well demonstrated by the Japanese experience.

But the context has shifted since Tokugawa times. First, it was the existence of modern elements and tendencies within a feudal environment that seemed noteworthy. Now it is the "survival" of numerous so-called feudal or traditional traits within the predominantly modern context of present-day Japan which seems striking and gives rise to comments which are apt to be emotionally charged. To some these "survivals" represent the old, the "real," the quintessential Japan and are to be treasured and savored; to others they represent discreditable vestiges of an outmoded, or "Asian," or "feudal" past which should be given speedy burial.

The explanation of such reactions would seem to lie in the dichotomous way in which the terms "traditional" and "modern" are usually related in our thinking. They tend to be viewed as mutually exclusive or polar opposites. The institutions and attitudes associated with one come to be regarded as antipathetic to the other. From here, it is but a step to the conclusion that any given traditional "survival" is fated for elimination from a "modern" society

[3] Gabriel A. Almond and James S. Coleman, eds., *The Politics of the Developing Areas* (Princeton, 1960), pp. 20–25.

through some inexorable process of social purgation impelled by a drive toward institutional self-consistency.

The history of the modernization of Japan challenges the tenability of any such thesis. It demonstrates in many ways not only the ability of "modern" institutions and practices to coexist with "traditional" ones for very substantial periods of time, but also the manner in which "traditional" attitudes and practices can be of great positive value to the modernization process.

The modernizing experience is a strenuous one for any traditionally organized society. If successful, it demands sacrifice, discipline, initiative, and perseverance in quantities and for periods of time which are certain to place the people concerned under very severe strains. One of the greatest problems of leadership under these circumstances is to devise conditions and motivations which will both liberate and focus an appropriate amount of popular energy, initiative, and resources and at the same time minimize dysfunctional behavior on the part of all significant elements in the population. Consider briefly some of the techniques used in Japan to achieve these goals and note the role played therein by traditional elements.

Most obvious of all, perhaps, was the use made of the emperor. This is not to say that there was not some measure of sincerity and philosophic or ethical commitment in the movement to restore the emperor to at least the semblance of temporal power. But the subsequent revival and institutionalization of Shinto and the cultivation of mass loyalty, obedience, and reverence for the emperor were too systematic and innovational to be anything but a deliberate and very clever attempt by the Meiji leadership to channel popular attitudes and conduct along lines which they considered constructive. In this instance the appeal was to an institutional complex that not only was traditional in terms of the circumstances of the 1870's, but would have been equally so in terms of those of 1603. The tradition of imperial rule, with very few exceptions, had possessed little validity since approximately the ninth century, while Imperial Shinto as a national cult had been moribund for at least as long, if indeed it had ever before existed in comparable form.

Again, one of the real keystones to the successful modernization of Japan was the device of holding constant, i.e. traditional, the circumstances of life in rural and agricultural Japan while at the same time using and exploiting the countryside as a means of building and rapidly developing the urban, commercial, industrial, and military sectors of the society. Modernization is an expensive undertaking and the costs must be borne by some segment of the population. In Japan in the early and critical years, it was the peasantry who, through the land tax, bore the bulk of this burden. A docile and productive agrarian labor force was, therefore, an element of crucial importance to the leaders of a modernizing Japan. In a social engineering sense, they strove to ensure this result by altering the actual socio-political circumstances of the pre-Restoration countryside as little as possible. Land reform was assiduously avoided; the existing political, social, and economic elites of the villages were insofar as possible confirmed in their status and authority; the traditional community and family systems were not only maintained but in a number of ways were reinforced and given new legal status and sanctions.

A systematic endeavor was made to ensure the tranquility, obedience, and loyalty of the countryside, and the control devices utilized were almost without exception traditional. This not only assured the government of a maximal flow of food, revenue, recruits, and urban-bound emigrants from the countryside, but also left them free to concentrate their attention and resources on the building of the more critical urban aspects of the national economy and defense establishment. This was a strategy of enormous importance to the rapid development of Japan, and its success rested ultimately on the effective enlistment of traditional institutions and appeals in the service of the modernizing process.

If one looks to the contemporary rather than the historical scene in Japan, many examples of this type of "reinforcing dualism" may still be discerned. The most reliable and important element in the long political dominance of the Liberal-Democratic Party in the post war period has been its control of the rural vote. Below the surface of this phenomenon, one will find a political support system compounded of largely personalized allegiance and loyalties reaching downward through the prefectures to roots in every farm hamlet in Japan. The ultimate approach of this apparatus to the voter is based upon a very shrewd admixture of appeals to personal and local advantage phrased in terms of traditional values and relationships. Again, the primacy of personal and hierarchical relations and loyalties in Japanese politics is obvious and well-known. The persistence of *oyabun-kobun* and similar forms of traditional fictive family relationships is but an extreme form of this trait. It would probably also be proper to regard the national predilection for consensual rather than adversary forms of decision-making and the dualistic nature of the national economy as other examples of the continued vitality and real functional importance of traditional attitudes and practices in the Japan of 1963.

In short, post-Restoration Japan has continuously represented a very complex amalgam of traditional and modern elements, a sort of mutually supportive or "reinforcing dualism" in which the relationship between the two sectors has often been symbiotic rather than antagonistic. This has been true to such an extent that it is probably accurate to claim that Japan could not have been successful in modernizing so rapidly and effectively had it not been for the many planned and unplanned ways in which traditional values and behavior positively contributed to and supported the process. Furthermore, there is a good deal of evidence indicative of the continued vitality of some segments of the traditional sector. It is still too early to predict even their gradual displacement by what we regard logically as more modern traits. . . .

V

The course of political modernization in Japan raises some interesting questions with respect to the form and organization of authority in modernizing societies. It was pointed out earlier that states which have achieved modernity may have democratic, totalitarian, or some intermediate type of political organization. The form of government does not seem to be a defining factor in mature cases of political modernization. The experience of Japan, however, makes one wonder if the same judgment applies with respect to forms of political organization in all earlier stages of the political modernization process. Is the process neutral in this respect throughout, or can one identify stages which demand authoritarian forms of government and which are antipathetic on grounds of developmental efficiency and potentiality to the introduction of democratic institutions on more than a very restricted basis? The question is of great importance from the standpoint of those who would prefer to see "backward" political systems develop along lines which are both modern and democratic. These are compatible but not necessary consequences of the developmental process. This poses the problem of how one can maximize the probability that developing polities will become both modern and democratic.

The experience of Japan alone certainly cannot provide definitive answers to either of the above questions. But neither is it irrelevant, and in circumstances where it represents the sole mature non-Western exemplar of the modernization process in all of Asia, it should be examined with unusual care and attention. The Japanese experience seems to suggest: (1) that authoritarian forms of political organization can be extraordinarily effective in the early stages of the modernization process; (2) that they need not debar the gradual emergence of more democratic forms of political organization; and (3) that some such process of gradual transition from authoritarian to democratic forms may be essential to the emergence of politics that are both modern and durably democratic. It should be emphasized again that these are no more than highly tentative hypotheses based upon the experience of Japan, but they do possess at least this much historical sanction and support. Let us then consider in a general way selected aspects of Japan's experience with the political modernization process which relate to the above three propositions.

First, authoritarian forms of political organization can be extraordinarily effective in the early stages of the modernization process. It is implied—though not demonstrable on the basis of the Japanese experience—that democratic forms are significantly less effective and that their early introduction may in fact result in conditions that will seriously inhibit the prospects of long-term democratic development.

This contention rests primarily on observations with respect to the relationship between the political modernization process and the process of social modernization in a general or total sense. The former is not autonomous, not a goal in itself. It is instrumentally related to the larger process and goal and should serve and expedite its purposes. This larger process of modernization entails for the society concerned, especially in the critical early or "take-off" stages, a series of shocks and strains of major proportions. It equally creates emancipations and new opportunities for some, but for major segments of the population this is apt to be a lengthy period of adjustment to new economic, social, and political situations and demands. Large-scale material and psychological stresses are invariably involved. One of the routine consequences of such a situation—at least in the non-Western world of the late nineteenth and the twentieth centuries—seems to be a greatly expanded role for government. A certain and perhaps very important amount of the modernization process may still take place under private auspices, but in recent times the needs and expectations which set the standards of modernization have been so urgent and expensive that national governments have had to assume a leading and dominant role. Only power organized at this level seemed capable of massing the resources and taking and enforcing the wide-ranging and difficult decisions involved.

This primacy of government in the modernizing process is more or less taken for granted throughout the underdeveloped world today. The situation was doubtless historically different in the case of the modernization of certain Western European societies and their offshoots, but in present-day underdeveloped societies there simply are no plausible and politically viable alternatives to the primacy of government as an agent of modernization. This was also true in the Japanese case at the time of the Restoration.

The overriding problems and goals of the 1870's and 1880's in Japan were well expressed by the popular political slogan of the day—*fukoku kyōhei* (a strong and wealthy nation). This captures the essence of the complex of forces and aspirations which underlay the Restoration movement and motivated its leaders in the difficult days that followed the initial successes of 1868. The greatest and most urgent needs were for national unity and the creation of armed strength sufficient to guarantee the national security against both real and fancied dangers of foreign imperialist aggression and economic exploitation. Instrumental thereto, of course, was the creation of a strong and stable government to lead the nation along suitable paths. Fortunately for Japan, her leaders were wise enough to define these goals in broad and constructive terms. Military strength meant to them far more than a large army and navy well-equipped with Western armaments; it also meant the industrial plant to sustain and expand such a military establishment and appropriate training for the men who must staff it. National wealth came to mean a radical diversification of the predominantly agrarian economy, urbanization, systematic mass and higher education, planned industrialization, new commercial and financial institutions, and a variety of other commitments which were perceived as essential to survival and effective competitive status in a Western-dominated world. Not all of these commitments were either generally perceived or welcomed at the outset by the leadership group, but in their search for national unity, strength, and security they found themselves embarked upon a species of "modernization spiral" similar in some respects to the "inflationary spiral" of the economists. The most intelligent and able of them adapted to the general course set by the imperatives which these goals entailed; the others were eliminated from leadership circles.

The realization of national goals of this sort did not come easily to a society such as Japan's, even given the forms of covert preparation for modernization which had characterized the later Tokugawa Period. The really critical years between 1868 and 1890 must sometimes have seemed an unending series of crises. Civil war, the threat of international war and the fact of foreign economic exploitation, a series of economic crises, inflation and deflation, the recurrent threat of samurai conspiracies against the government, the embitterment of the peasantry at the failure of the government to improve their lot, the dearth of desperately needed technical knowledge and personnel, and all of the widespread fears and tensions which attend a time of new beginnings—these were merely some of the problems which constantly confronted the new political leadership. Yet, by 1890, policies capable of dealing with all of these problems had been developed and the country was firmly embarked on the path to modernization. The foreign threats had been faced and Japan's international position was secure; the menace of civil war had been permanently liquidated; the structural vestiges of feudalism had been eliminated and the country effectively unified; the position and authority of the government had been confirmed and regularized by constitutional arrangements; the economy had been stabilized and a promising start made upon its diversification and industrialization; a system of mass compulsory education had been inaugurated and mass media of communication established; in every critical category the strength of Japan showed remarkable and promising improvements.

Under such circumstances it may be that some measure of democratic participation could successfully have been introduced into the political system. There were those who advocated such changes. The *Jiyūminken Undō* (Freedom and Popular Rights Movement), for example, called for the establishment of a national parliament, a limited suffrage, and some dispersion of political authority. Had this been attempted during these years, the results need not have been fatal to the modernization of Japan. But under conditions of more or less constant political or economic crisis, widespread popular disaffection and lack of understanding of the necessity for the sacrifices entailed by many government programs, the unpredictable qualities and perils of the country's foreign relations, and what we have learned in general of the limitations of fledgling democratic institutions in largely unprepared contexts, it is difficult to envisage the feasibility or practicality of any very significant democratic innovations at this time.

These years from 1868 to 1890, or some similar period, would seem to be a time in Japan's modernization when an authoritarian form of political organization offered distinct advantages where rapidity of response, flexibility, planning, and effective action were concerned. This is said with full appreciation of the fumbling and shortcomings of authoritarian leadership groups and irresponsible bureaucracies—including the Japanese of this period—in all of these departments. It thus assumes the availability of some at least minimally competent and unified political leadership. If this is not available—and there are obviously cases where it is not—political modernization is not a practicable proposition for the countries concerned.

In the Japanese case, however, it seems on balance highly improbable that (1) the addition of any significant or effective democratic institutions to the decision-making apparatus at such a stage of national development could have had other than deleterious effects upon the speed and decisiveness with which urgent problems were handled; and that (2) this stage of the modernization process, beset as it inevitably was by so many and such desperate problems, would have been an appropriate time to launch so delicate an experiment as democratization.

Our second hypothesis was that the dominance of authoritarian forms of political organization in the initial stages of the political modernization process need not debar the gradual emergence of democratic forms of organization. This is not intended to imply any quality of inevitability in such a development, although in a secular sense some such tendency may exist.

In the Japanese case, no significant measures of democratization were introduced into the political system until the enactment of the Meiji Constitution in 1890, twenty-two years after the Restoration. Even then it is very doubtful if any of the authors of this document thought of their handiwork as an act of democratic innovation. It is certain that their so-called "liberal" opposition did not. Rather does it seem that the Meiji leadership group conceived of this constitution primarily as a means of regularizing the structure and operations of political authority—the absence of any rationalized or stable structure and the continual innovation and experimentation of the intervening years must have been very trying—and of further unifying and solidifying both the country and their own authority. As a consequence of this and a variety of later developments, there has been a tendency to undervalue both the degree of political change which the Meiji Constitution brought to Japan and the measure of democratic development which took place under it.

It is helpful to look at the Meiji Constitution and its attendant basic laws both in terms of the general political standards and practices of 1890 and in terms of its actual operations as well as its legal and political theory. If this is done, one will note that it makes public, explicit, and authoritative a particular theory of sovereignty and the state, and derives from this a functionally differentiated and rationally organized governmental structure; it establishes the legal status of citizens and specifies their political and civil rights and duties; it distinguishes legislative, executive, and judicial functions and, although establishing a dominant and protected position for the executive, does provide for their separate institutionalization; it specifies legal equality before the law and creates means for the assertion of popular against official rights; it establishes a restricted but expansible franchise and, in terms of this, a popularly elected house in the national legislature; it provides for some measure of decentralization in government, and renders inevitable the introduction of a much greater pluralism into both the Japanese oligarchy and the political system in general.

Against the background of Tokugawa and Restoration political practices, these are notable and democratic innovations. They did not, of course, put an end to the period of authoritarian political rule in Japan. But they certainly launched a process of democratization which has continued to play a major, although usually not dominant, part in Japanese politics ever since. In this sense the history of the democratization of Japan, viewed in the light of present circumstances, is a product of erosive and catalytic agents. Much of the story is told, until 1932 at least, in terms of the erosion of the authoritarian political forms and practices characteristic of the pre-constitutional period. This process never reached the point of establishing what the contemporary West would regard as an authentically democratic political system, but, by the 1920's, the degree of pluralism, responsibility, and popular participation characterizing Japanese politics would certainly have surprised, and probably appalled, the great leaders of the Restoration Period. Between the 1920's and the 1960's there intervened, of course, the resurgence of military and ultra-nationalist rule, the war, and the Allied Occupation of Japan. This last acted as a catalytic agent on the submerged but still vital forms of Japanese democracy and gave them institutional and legal advantages, authority, and prestige beyond what they could have hoped for on the basis of their own political position and strength. The consequence has been a great and apparently sudden florescence of Western-style democracy in Japan. In fact, however, the roots of this development lie deep in the political experience of post-1890 Japan.

There are two things about this gradual emergence of democratic politics from the authoritarian system of pre-1890 Japan which might have more general validity and interest. The first is that even the concession of a very carefully restricted and seemingly impotent governmental role to a popularly elected body can, over a period of time, have consequences well nigh fatal to sustained authoritarian rule. It would be hard to be optimistic about the influence or authority of the Japanese House of Representatives in terms of the provisions of the Meiji Constitution or the relevant basic laws. These faithfully reflect and implement the desire of the founders to make of the House an appealing but powerless sop to the demands of the opposition and public opinion. But the lessons to be learned from the subsequent history of the lower house are: (1) that it provides a means of institutionalizing and enlarging the role of political parties; (2) that, in modernizing circumstances, even vested powers of obstructing the smooth and effective flow of governmental decisions and actions can be critical—positive powers of initiation and control are not necessary; and (3) that in circumstances where a popularly chosen body can thus blackmail an authoritarian leadership, there is a fair possibility of forcing the latter into piecemeal but cumulative accommodations which are democratic in tendency.

The second generalization suggested by the history of democratic development in Japan relates to the conditions necessary to support an effectively authoritarian system of government. Japanese experience suggests the existence of a close relationship between effective authoritarian rule and the unity and solidarity of the oligarchy involved. The limits involved cannot be described with much precision, but authoritarian government in Japan began to disintegrate as the heretofore fairly solidary oligarchy began to split into competing cliques and factions. The probability of such rifts seems to be very high in modernizing societies. The development of role specialization and professionalization even at high levels is an essential part of the process of modernization, and this makes it hard for an oligarchy to maintain the degree of unity and cohesion feasible in revolutionary or in simpler times. Pluralism in this sense seems to be built into the process. And as an oligarchy breaks down into competing factions in this fashion, the terms of political competition in that society undergo an important change. Extra-oligarchic groups such as emergent political parties acquire new room for maneuver and new political leverages, and the ex-oligarchic cliques themselves acquire new incentives for broadening the basis of their support. Out of these altered political circumstances are apt to come new political alliances involving elements of the former oligarchy with elements of more popularly based bodies—in particular, with political parties. The total process is dilutive from the standpoint of authoritarian government and supportive of the gradual emergence of greater degrees of pluralism and democracy.

It is not intended to depict either of the foregoing generalizations on the basis of Japanese experience as controlling or inevitable. But they did occur within a fairly authoritarian context in Japan's case and there seem to be some reasons for regarding them as of more general validity. The conclusion would seem to be that an initial or early stage of authoritarian government on the path to modernization (1) does not commit a polity to long-term adherence to authoritarian forms; (2) does not necessarily make an authoritarian course of development probable; and (3) may even contain built-in elements calculated with time and development to break down and liberalize such authoritarian forms.

Our third hypothesis is even more tentatively stated and adds up to a feeling that some such process of gradual transition from authoritarian to democratic forms may be essential to the emergence of a political system which is both modern and durably democratic. In this connection Japan's experience suggests several notions of possible interest.

First, our commonly employed systems of periodization may involve serious distortions where the history of political modernization is concerned. Thus, in Japan's case, while the feudal-modern or Tokugawa-Restoration frameworks have a plausible amount of relevance to the emergence of a modern Japanese political system, they also serve to obscure important aspects of the process. They are calculated, as is the prewar-postwar framework, to produce an over-emphasis on the significance of certain dramatic and allegedly "revolutionary" events in a country's history—in this case, the Restoration or the 1945 defeat plus the Occupation. This is conducive to a dichotomous view of the political development process which seriously overstates the enduring importance of alleged discontinuities in a national history at the expense of the less dramatic but fundamentally more important continuities.

Second, if the history of the development of democracy in Japan is weighted for this distorting effect of the commonly employed categories and system of periodization, the differences in preparation, timing, and depth of democratic experience which are often held to distinguish a democratic political system in Japan from its Western analogues would perhaps seem appreciably less valid and important than is usually assumed. The two patterns of development probably have more in common than is generally recognized.

Third, if the foregoing assumptions are valid, one is tempted to conclude that all practicing and at least ostensibly solid and durable democracies today are the products of lengthy and multifaceted evolutionary processes. In the Japanese case, if one looks only to the direct antecedents, seventy-three years intervene between the Meiji Constitution and the present. But far longer periods of preparation are involved if one looks to the less direct consequences of the introduction of mass literacy or a rationalized bureaucratic structure. In this sense it is questionable whether history provides any very encouraging examples of short-cuts to the achievement of a democratic political system.

Finally, such a train of argument suggests the importance of the relationship existing between a "modern" political system and a "democratic" political system. One hesitates to claim that all or a specific proportion of the attributes of a modern polity must be achieved before a society becomes capable of durably democratic performance or achievement, but Japan's experience at least suggests an important correlation between the two. It is hard to specify the proportions involved, but, in a rough and approximate way, one might say that perhaps only modern societies with modern political cultures of the sort defined in Section I are practical candidates for democratization.

33. The French Experience of Modernization*

BERNARD E. BROWN

Few theorists today admit to a belief in the "idea of progress." But, if the literature in comparative politics in the past several years is any guide, virtually all political scientists now believe in the concept of "modernization." Modernization theory is being invoked to compare traditional and modern societies, to analyze the evolution of individual political systems, and to appraise the effectiveness of political institutions in one or several political systems. All of the problems and subjects of political science are now being reexamined in terms of some concept of modernization.

It is generally argued that the enormous development of science and technology since the early nineteenth century has brought about a fundamental transformation of all political systems. Most recent studies present a polar contrast between "traditional" and "modern" societies in terms of four major elements of any social system: the economy, social structure, political institutions, and the values that permeate the whole and justify coercion.

. . . .

(Note by the editors: The traditional and modern types are dealt with in the introductory essay, above.)

. . . .

*From World Politics, vol. 21, no. 3 (April 1969), pp. 366–91. Article and footnotes abridged by the editors. Reprinted by permission of the journal.

One problem is evident from any survey of the literature. In order to sharpen the contrast between the two types, the "traditional" model is made so primitive that it is relevant only to tribal societies and prehistoric Europe. The kind of traditional society that preceded the modern form in Western Europe and North America, for example, was quite complex by any standard, and probably closer to "modernity" than to the ideal type of traditionalism. These extreme typologies also blur the significant differences among traditional societies—the kind of differences so brilliantly illuminated by Alexis de Tocqueville in his works on France, England, and the United States. Ideal types based on polar contrasts may be analytically useful as a check-list for observers or as a means of directing attention to the relationships among factors in any social system. The disadvantage is that the typology may take on a life of its own. Instead of seeking to grasp the internal logic of a political system with the aid of typological schemes, the observer may spend all his energy working out the abstract logic of a typology that has no relation to reality.

Whatever the mathematical and logical beauty of typologies, political scientists presumably are interested in the payoff for research. Does modernization theory deepen our understanding of political life? What difference does it make in the organization of research and study? Does it have explanatory power? One way of answering these questions—perhaps the best way, in fact—is to apply modernization theory to an individual political system. In this paper we shall take as a case study the French political system. Surely no argument is needed to demonstrate the importance of France in the development of modern Europe, or the contribution of the French to the industrial and scientific revolutions of the nineteenth century. We shall first examine the specific application of modernization theory to France by three highly imaginative and skilled observers: C. E. Black, Samuel P. Huntington, and Stanley Hoffmann.[1] Taken together, their writings offer a comprehensive view of the French experience of modernization from nation-building through late industrialization. We shall then return to the larger question of the utility and relevance of modernization theory in comparative politics.

THREE VIEWS OF FRENCH MODERNIZATION

C. E. Black's *The Dynamics of Modernization* is probably the best single book on the subject yet to appear. Professor Black moves fluently and surely from theory to practice and back again. He identifies four stages of political modernization:

(1) *the challenge of modernity*—the initial confrontation of a society, within its traditional framework of knowledge, with modern ideas and institutions, and the emergence of advocates of modernity; (2) *the consoli-*

---

[1] C. E. Black, *The Dynamics of Modernization: A study in Comparative History* (New York 1966); Samuel P. Huntington, "Political Modernization: America vs. Europe," *World Politics* xvii (April 1966), pp. 378-414; and Stanley Hoffmann, "Paradoxes of the French Political Community," in Hoffmann, ed., *In Search of France* (Cambridge, Mass. 1963), pp. 1-117.

dation of modernizing leadership—the transfer of power from traditional to modernizing leaders in the course of a normally bitter revolutionary struggle often lasting several generations; (3) *economic and social transformation*—the development of economic growth and social change to a point where a society is transformed from a predominantly rural and agrarian way of life to one predominantly urban and industrial; and (4) *the integration of society*—the phase in which economic and social transformation produces a fundamental reorganization of the social structure throughout the society.[2]

Black's typology of political modernization is based on the timing of the consolidation of modern political leadership (whether early or late in relation to other countries), the nature of the challenge of modernity to traditional institutions (whether internal or external), the continuity of territory and population in the modern era, the independent or dependent status of the nation, and the solidity of political institutions when the nation entered the modern era. The first of seven patterns that make up the typology is formed by the experience of Great Britain and France. In both countries the revolution that consolidated political leadership came early as compared to that of other countries (1649–1832 in Britain and 1789–1848 in France), the major challenge of modernity was primarily internal, there was an unusual continuity of both territory and population in the modern era, and the political institutions were fairly stable as the country entered the modern era. Professor Black then cites 1832–1945 as the period of economic and social transformation in Britain, 1848–1945 in France; and since 1945 as the phase of social integration in both countries.

In this analysis the similarities between British and French modernization are emphasized. The major differences between the two nations are thus the earlier rise to power of a modern leadership and the somewhat earlier industrialization in Britain. Black recognizes that the French never achieved the same degree of political consensus as did the British. But he suggests that the basis for orderly development in France was laid by the modern institutional framework established by the Napoleonic Code in 1802. In spite of the apparent political instability, he concludes that "France has nevertheless undergone at the administrative level a relatively gradual and stable transformation under many generations of skilled civil servants trained in the *grandes écoles*."[3]

Professor Black's typology of seven patterns is a stimulating way of comparing and evaluating the general process of political modernization in the world. But its specific application to France raises several questions. Was modern leadership in France first consolidated in 1789? The implication in Black's analysis is that this stage occurred in Britain more than a century earlier. No one would deny the importance of the English Civil War or the French Revolution as decisive turning points in British and French political history, especially as regards the shaping of political institutions and the evolution of consensus. But that Britain and France, so closely related in all things, were a century apart in political

---

[2] Black, *op. cit.*, pp. 67–68.
[3] *Ibid.*, p. 109.

modernization is implausible. Britain and France were both presented with the same kind of challenge in the course of the seventeenth century—basically the inability or unwillingness of the country as a whole to sustain the burden of a greatly expanded monarchical apparatus. The French monarchy proved somewhat more flexible and adaptable at the time; it was thus able to weather the storm. In spite of the political turmoil in seventeenth-century Britain, and the success of reformers in France, it would appear that similar developments were taking place in the two societies during the seventeenth and eighteenth centuries. De Tocqueville pointed out, for example, in his classic study, *The Old Regime and the French Revolution,* that the entire political, administrative, and social structure of the nation was being transformed well before the Revolution. In a famous passage, he wrote, "Chance played no part whatever in the outbreak of the Revolution; though it took the world by surprise, it was the inevitable outcome of a long period of gestation, the abrupt and violent conclusion of a process in which six generations had played an intermittent part. Even if it had not taken place, the old social structure would nonetheless have been shattered everywhere sooner or later."[4] Undoubtedly, a new political leadership emerged in 1789. But new social forces came to the fore, and began to participate in the political system, long before that date.

On the other hand, Professor Black may be overstating the similarities between Britain and France when he argues that in both countries there was "a relatively orderly and peaceful adaptation of traditional institutions to modern functions." In one sense this was certainly the case; France today is roughly as "modern" as Britain, and presumably her traditional institutions (at least those dating from the Revolution and the Napoleonic Code) have proved adaptable. But how useful is this approach for an understanding of French development? Modernization there has been, yes; but its pace, the way in which new social groups created by modernization have entered into the political system, and the role played by the State in furthering modernization have all been quite distinctive in France.

The contention that the *grands corps* really run France, despite the political bickering on the surface, is a venerable thesis. Studies of decision-making suggest that in France, as in all complex parliamentary systems, the civil service is itself divided politically. Major interest groups develop special channels of access to the civil service as well as to parliament, thus creating "whirlpools" of influence and power throughout the political system. For example, with regard to the issue of state subsidies to beetgrowers and other producers of alcohol there is a split within the French civil service; the Ministry of Agriculture is generally in favor of subsidies and the Treasury is generally opposed. Alliances are thus formed that include civil servants, interest groups, deputies, and party leaders on both sides of issues. The French civil service has been fortunate in the past in recruiting exceptional talent; but it has not been a unified political force, nor has it been able to resolve the problem of political legitimacy. In this sense, the

[4] Alexis de Tocqueville, *The Old Regime and the French Revolution* (Garden City, N.Y., 1955), p. 20.

French experience provides us with a contrast to that of Britain and other nations where there is general agreement on fundamental political values and institutions.

Our attention is directed especially to the period preceding the Revolution by Samuel P. Huntington, in his study of political modernization in America and Europe. He argues that modernization involves three things: rationalization of authority (replacement of traditional political authority by a single, secular, national authority), the development of specialized political structures to perform specialized functions, and mass participation in the political system. "On the Continent," comments Huntington, "the rationalization of authority and the differentiation of structures were the dominant trends of the seventeenth century," and he cites Richelieu, Mazarin, Louis XIV, Colbert, and Louvois as "great simplifiers, centralizers, and modernizers."[5] In addition, the seventeenth century saw the growth and rationalization of state bureaucracies and standing armies. Thus, in two important respects, the process of modernization took place on the Continent by 1700. A new political leadership rose to power in 1789; yet the way had been prepared over a long period of time.

It seems strange that divine right and hereditary monarchy should be considered forces for modernization. But Huntington explains that a prime requisite of modernization is the belief that men can act purposefully and effect change. Traditional society is permeated by a belief in unchanging custom and fundamental law. The modernization that began in the sixteenth century on the Continent required a new concept of authority, namely, that there was a sovereign who could make decisions. "One formulation of this idea was the new theory, which developed in Europe in the late sixteenth century, of the divine right of kings. Here, in effect, religious and, in that sense, traditional forms were used for modern purposes." Since mass participation in politics was a later phenomenon, modernization in the seventeenth century meant the rise of the absolute monarchy. "In terms of modernization, the seventeenth century's absolute monarch was the functional equivalent of the twentieth century's monolithic party."[6]

Huntington's analysis of Continental developments is a useful and necessary corrective. Most observers are fascinated by the Revolution, and have neglected the modernizing reforms of the Old Regime. But to consider monarchy the spearhead of modernization is an oversimplification of the situation in France. The absolute monarchy both furthered the trend to modernization and slowed it. It contributed to modernization by breaking the power of the local lords; it slowed modernization by glorifying irrational values, sustaining an archaic social structure, and imposing a terrible financial load upon the people. The modernizers in France before the Revolution also included the social critics, some who demanded parliamentary control of the executive, and some who greeted the American Revolution as the harbinger of a new era in history.

[5] Huntington, op. cit., p. 379.
[6] Ibid., pp. 384 and 386.

Nor were the advocates of fundamental law all opponents of modernization. It is true that some traditionalists invoked fundamental law to protect the privileges of the corporations. On the other hand, some modernizers tried to secure popular participation in the political system by appealing to fundamental law above the will of the monarch. In France as in colonial America, the doctrine of higher law was used for several political purposes, among which was the promulgation of rational principles of legitimacy.

Stanley Hoffmann deals with the later stages of modernization in France in his essay, "Paradoxes of the French Political Community." He begins with the two familiar models of feudal-agrarian society and industrial society, and then places France on the continuum. He suggests that a "Republican synthesis" gradually emerged in the century after the French Revolution and flourished in the period 1878–1914. The basis of the Republican synthesis was a unique mixture of the two models, neither one nor the other, but rather a "halfway house between the old rural society and industrialization." The French economy was both static and modern at the same time. Industrialization took place, but without an industrial revolution. The business class adopted many of the attitudes of the aristocracy that it had replaced, particularly that of emphasizing family continuity and social prominence rather than efficient production. The agricultural sector remained massive and largely traditional in orientation. Slow industrial growth in turn made it difficult to grant concessions to the working class, which was consigned to a "social ghetto." Comments Hoffmann, "For more than a century the political problem of France was to devise a political system adapted to the stalemate society."[7]

The basic solution to this problem under the Third Republic was the combination of a centralized and efficient bureaucracy with a strictly limited state. Politics became a kind of game in which a divided parliament prevented the formation of effective political executives. "But this game, played in isolation from the nation-at-large by a self-perpetuating political class, saw to it that the fundamental equilibrium of society would not be changed by the state."[8] However, the foundations of the Republican synthesis were undermined by the crises of the 1930's. The depression and the rise of Nazi Germany produced tensions in French society that the regime could not overcome. The assailants of the Republic converged and overwhelmed it. Writing in 1962, Hoffmann concluded that "the stalemate society is dead"—though many of the old tensions remained. It was killed by the transformation of French society during and after World War II—by the emergence of fully industrial attitudes, the more active role of the state in planning economic development, a reorientation of the French business class, and structural changes in the working class.

But the use of ideal types as literary devices makes French society appear to be far more static than was the case under the Third and Fourth Republics, and more dynamic than it actually was under the Fifth Republic. For example, there

[7] Hoffman, *op. cit.*, p. 12.
[8] *Ibid.*, p. 16.

was a period of very rapid and impressive economic growth from 1896 to 1914, with important social and political consequences. The Third Republic created conditions in which the whole infrastructure of the modern economy was perfected—including the railroad network, canals, and modern communications. Its greatest contribution perhaps was to lay the foundation of a universal, free, and secular educational system. This may not be the most desirable way to bring about modernization, but it surely is one way to do so. The balance among social forces and economic sectors was shifting, more or less rapidly, under both the Third and Fourth Republics. French society was, and still is, a mix of traditional and modern elements; but this is hardly unique. All industrial societies are characterized by tension between traditional and modern sectors. Nor is the French political system the only one alleged by critics to be "incoherent." If there is a distinctive French experience of modernization it will be found in the timing of the crises of modernization and in the persistent alienation of large groups at all stages of modernization, up to and including the present.

Modernization theory obviously is not a magic wand that eliminates the need for research or produces universal agreement among observers. But it is a fruitful way of organizing study, and permits significant comparison among political systems. In order to further comparative study of modernization, we offer the following generalizations concerning the French experience.

1. The traditional phase in France that preceded modern society was feudalism. But feudal society in France was relatively advanced compared to, say, tribal societies. Feudalism contained important elements of "modernity." The process of modernization in France, therefore, has been long and complex, dating at least from the eleventh century, and perhaps from as far back as the Roman conquest.

2. In the century before the Revolution, the social structure of France was gradually transformed. A system in which privilege derived from heredity was at least partly replaced by a system based on wealth and individual effort. The Revolution was the culmination of a long period of social change, whose pace then was greatly accelerated.

3. The values justifying feudalism and absolute monarchy lost their popular base under the Old Regime. The trend toward rationalization of political authority, brought to a logical conclusion by the Revolution, was a development of centuries.

4. In spite of continuing political turmoil the economic and social foundations of modernity were laid during the nineteenth century. Far from being a stalemate society, France under both the Third and Fourth Republics took on the characteristics of all modern societies.

We shall now discuss each of these generalizations at length.

I. THE TRADITIONAL SOCIETY

Feudalism was a highly personal political relationship between man and man, between subordinate and superior. As one historian has put it: "It is the posses-

sion of rights of government by feudal lords and the performance of most functions of government through feudal lords which clearly distinguishes feudalism
from other types of organization."[9] Feudalism was a "model" traditional society
in every respect. The mass of the population was engaged in subsistence agriculture or animal husbandry, the primary social unit was the family, the basic values
of the society were those of personal loyalty, fealty, and courage, and the state
(in so far as it continued to exist) was a larger version of family organization and
power. The feudal system reposed on mutual duties and rights of people in a
direct personal relationship, with the enjoyment of land rights as the foundation
of the structure.

If typological analysis is a checklist of characteristics, the contrast between
feudalism and contemporary society in France is virtually total. But historical
processes are too complex to be reduced to these terms. When placed in the
context of French historical development, it may be seen that feudalism departed from the traditional model in a number of ways. First, feudalism throughout Western Europe was a response to the decay of the highly organized Roman
Empire. Until the tenth century, the Roman way of life prevailed in Gaul.
Citizens owned land and slaves, subject to restrictions imposed upon them by
the state. But the state then disintegrated. No central authority was able to
protect the inhabitants of Western Europe from the incessant incursions of
Saracens and Scandinavians. Under these new circumstances the Roman notion
of a centralized state became obsolete. Defense and security inevitably became
local responsibilities. Thus, feudalism was not comparable, to primitive tribal
societies; it rather should be viewed as a civilized society in decline or decay.
The difference is important. Under feudalism the memory of the centralized
authority of the past always remained alive. One leading French historian contends that in the Middle Ages in France there were, strictly speaking, no feudal
institutions. Only the monarchy was legitimate; the functions of administering
justice, raising armies, and levying taxes were generally recognized as attributes
of monarchy, conceded to or usurped by feudal powers.[10] When conditions and
the technology of warfare changed, it was possible for the Capetian kings to
revive the spirit of social and national unity. The reconstruction of authority
that has fallen into decay is quite different as a political process from the
creation of central authority where none has ever existed.

Most important, the rise of feudalism in the eleventh century coincided with
a resurgence of the cities, a development that eventually sapped the feudal
system. The period in France that most closely approximates the model
traditional economy was the five centuries that preceded feudalism, rather than

[9] Joseph R. Strayer, "Feudalism in Western Europe," in Rushton Coulborn, ed.,
Feudalism in History (Princeton, 1956), p. 16. On feudalism in France see also Marc Bloch,
Feudal Society (Chicago, 1961); A. Tilley, ed., *Medieval France* (New York, 1964); and for
an excellent synthesis, J. Touchard et al., *Histoire des idées politiques* (Paris, 1959), pp. 1,
155–63.

[10] See the seminal work by Ferdinand Lot with the collaboration of Robert Fawtier,
Histoire des institutions françaises au moyen âge (Paris, 1957), I, p. viii; and II, p. 9 for
the comment, "the only political regime France had in the Middle Ages was the monarchy."
Vol. II is an extraordinarily complete analysis of the rise of the royal power.

feudalism itself. It was from the sixth through the eleventh centuries, apparently, that the Franks became an almost wholly rural people engaged in subsistence agriculture. Artisans during this period abandoned the towns and retired to the countryside. Commerce declined abruptly, the cities were largely deserted, and municipal administration ceased to exist. By the eleventh century the process of urbanization resumed. The renaissance of town life was the result of many factors: a deliberate desire to create the conditions of a peaceful and secure existence within the confines of a commune; technological innovations in transport and manufacturing that made it economically feasible for merchants and artisans to congregate in towns; and a general desire on the part of merchants to terminate their nomadic existence and degrading dependence upon the goodwill of the local lords.

Everywhere, the city people sought to free themselves from the domination of feudal lords. This became easier as the cities prospered and could afford to recruit mercenaries. Nobles then found it necessary, in some cases profitable, to grant special charters to the towns, in effect exempting them from feudal obligations. Many communes were based on a clearly modern rather than traditional theory of governance. They were created by "common oath" on the part of the inhabitants, that is, an agreement among equals rather than between a superior and his subordinates. The "consular cities" enjoyed complete municipal liberty, with citizens electing representative councils invested with large financial and executive powers.

The inhabitants of the *bourgs* (or bourgeois) did not fit into the feudal structure. Merchants and artisans worked on their own, handled money, had no obligations to the lords, and were receptive to new ideas. The bourgeois became likewise a firm support for the royal power, which alone could integrate the resources of large domains and provide adequate security for the towns. The medieval towns were breeding grounds of new values and ideologies that challenged the traditional notions of religion, cultivated skepticism concerning the established order, and glorified the qualities of intelligence, liberty, and work.

There was no steady, ineluctable progression from traditional to modern. The balance among the rival forces shifted frequently—particularly during the period of economic stagnation in the fourteenth century which brought about a decline of the middle class and a corresponding increase in the power and prestige of the clergy and lords. The secular trend, however, was to transform military vassalage into nobility in the service of the crown, and to transfer the idea of contract to the level of people and monarch. In brief, the social structure, economy, political institutions, and cultural values of medieval France by the thirteenth century already contained major elements of "modernity."

II. THE BREAKUP OF THE TRADITIONAL SOCIETY

The dramatic events of the Revolution have tended to draw the attention of observers away from the rapid pace of social change in the seventeenth and eighteenth centuries. In each of the social orders of the Old Regime—the clergy, aristocracy, and third estate—structural transformations took place that eventually undermined the whole delicate balance of feudal privilege.[11]

As is natural in any pre-industrial society, religious values permeated medieval France. The clergy propagated and popularized the values that sustained the feudal regime, and enjoyed a privileged position as the "first estate." Church revenue from the tithe and other levies amounted to about 13 percent of the gross national income, to which must be added income from vast church-held lands. The church performed a number of vital functions within the society, including the maintenance of a network of welfare and educational institutions.

Yet the clergy's grip on power was shaken. The priestly life was subjected to serious criticism and satire by the intellectuals. That respect so necessary to the maintenance of any priestly class began to evaporate, and concern became general over the waste and irrationality of a system of tithes. Furthermore, the clergy was itself divided sharply into a small group of high-living and wealthy archbishops, and a mass of impoverished priests. When the great explosion took place, a divided priestly class was unable to rally mass support for the old regime.

The position of the nobility likewise was transformed in the century preceding the Revolution. It, too, was affected by the process of modernization. The very composition of the nobility underwent a change. It was not a completely closed caste, since new elements were admitted to noble rank by a variety of methods. The king had the right of conferring nobility upon deserving commoners (usually men of great wealth, civil servants, and military officers). Whatever their origins, the nobles enjoyed extensive feudal privileges, which they sought desperately to maintain against pressures from the peasantry, the rising middle classes, and from the king. After 1750 the power of the aristocracy increased along with that of the middle classes. As Gordon Wright has put it: "The eighteenth century nobility was increasingly inclined to attack and destroy the *status quo*. The revolutionary goal of the discontented nobles was a return to a semimythical medieval system, to an unwritten constitution that had allegedly been torn up by the absolutist kings and their bouregois ministers."[12]

All the rest of the population—some 98 percent—was the third estate. In the course of the eighteenth century the bourgeoisie rose in spectacular fashion within the social structure. Considerable fortunes were made in industry (by such entrepreneurs as Decretot, Van Robais, Oberkampf, Réveillon, and Dietrich), in trade (especially by the shipping interests of Havre, Bordeaux, and Marseilles) and in finance. Perhaps 10 percent of the bourgeoisie was enabled, through investments and loans, to live entirely on dividends, without engaging in any kind of work. As the bourgeois acquired wealth, he tended to buy up land and cultivate it, thereby reestablishing a link between the middle class and agriculture. It has been estimated that perhaps 25 to 30 percent of all arable land

[11] For an excellent social and political analysis of this period, see Georges Dupeux, *La société française, 1789-1960* (Paris, 1964), pp. 59–102, and Gordon Wright, *France in Modern Times* (Chicago, 1960), chaps. 1 and 2.

[12] Wright, *op. cit.,* p. 18.

in France by 1789 was in the hands of the bourgeoisie. Most of the *petite bourgeoisie* were engaged in trade or skilled work, and usually were organized in corporations.

There were stirrings within the peasantry, too. In 1779, serfdom was legally abolished in the last few places where it had survived. The peasants were juridically free, and altogether owned perhaps 40 to 45 percent of the land. However, the individual holdings were small, and relatively few peasants were well off. The number of landless peasants and seasonal workers in rural areas probably was greater than the number of individual landholders.

The implications of these social trends were very great. First, they contradicted the assumption on which the Old Regime was based—that society was a pyramid, with peasants and middle classes at the base, with aristocracy above them and a king above all. Says Cobban: "The division of the nation into *noblesse, noblesse de robe,* clergy, bourgeois and peasants was a simplification which concealed the real complexity of French society. Each class had in fact its own internal divisions, which prevented it from being a coherent unit." Basically, it was impossible for the old feudal political system to survive in this kind of society. The new standards of performance related to wealth, ability, talent, and occupational role; considerations of noble birth were less relevant, and in the long run, if taken seriously would have led to an impairment of the efficiency of the society. As R. R. Palmer has pointed out, "Western Europe in the eighteenth century was already a complicated society, with elaborate mechanisms operating in the fields of government, production, trade, finance, scientific research, church affairs, and education. The allocation of personnel to these enterprises on the basis of birth and social standing could not but hamper, and even pervert (one thinks of the established churches, some of the universities, and many branches of government), the achievement of the purposes for which such institutions were designed. The old feudal days were over. It was no longer enough for a lord to look locally after the needs of his people. The persistence and even the accentuation of an aristocratic outlook derived from earlier and simpler conditions presented problems for European society itself, as well as for the individuals and classes that made it up."[13]

The rise of the bourgeoisie did not have to mean a fight to the death between the middle class and the nobility. Several different solutions were conceivable: The middle class could have disdained aristocratic values altogether, in which case the nobility might have ceased to be a political power; or the nobility could have opened its ranks to the newcomers and gradually absorbed its leading elements, thereby creating a greatly expanded new ruling class. But time ran out for peaceful solutions. Relations among aristocracy, bourgeoisie, and peasantry became increasingly bitter. The nobility resisted the pretensions of the middle classes and tried to block the development of embryonic capitalism. Eighteenth-century France had all the characteristics of a political system unsettled by the process of modernization.

[13] Citations are from Alfred Cobban, "The Decline of Divine Right Monarchy in France," *New Cambridge Modern History* (Cambridge, 1957), VII, p. 235, and R. R. Palmer, *The Age of the Democratic Revolution* (Princeton, 1959), p. 68.

III. REASON AND REVOLUTION

One of the basic assumptions of modernization theory is that as a society becomes more complex, the values serving to legitimize political authority become more rational. Or, rather than imply any causal relationship, rationalization of authority proceeds along with industrialization and increasing complexity of social structure. This assumption is borne out in a striking manner by the French experience, because of the great divide marked by the Revolution of 1789. The pattern of legitimacy clearly underwent a radical transformation, and took a form of greater rationality. But closer examination makes it apparent that the rationalization of authority was accentuated, not created, by the Revolution. It was part and parcel of the secular trend of modernization in all spheres of French society under the Old Regime.

Huntington has emphasized the modernizing role of the monarchy in breaking up feudal society. Hence, the theory of divine right of kings was more rational, or more modern, than feudalism itself. He comments, "The modernization that began in the sixteenth century on the Continent and in the seventeenth century in England required new concepts of authority, the most significant of which was the simple idea of a sovereignty itself, the idea that there is, in the words of Bodin, a 'supreme power over citizens and subjects, unrestrained by law.' One formulation of this idea was the new theory, which developed in Europe in the late sixteenth century, of the divine right of kings. Here, in effect, religious and, in that sense, traditional forms were used for modern purposes."[14]

Huntington's view is a useful reminder that ideal types make little sense outside historical context. The notion that a ruler receives a mandate from a divine source is characteristic of traditional societies; yet in the Europe of the seventeenth century it was part of the breakthrough to modernity. But even here we must beware of historical oversimplification. Divine right of kings was not a new theory. The Franks, before the conquest, combined hereditary right with election; an Assembly of Warriors elected a king from among members of the Merovingian family, which presumably had divine connections. After the Frankish conquest, the Merovingians tried to free themselves of this dependence upon the assemblies, but were only partially successful. The rise of the Carolingian and Capetian dynasties brought a renewed emphasis upon election, since heredity could not be invoked as the overriding principle of legitimacy in an era of dynastic rivalries. Once their grip on power seemed secure, the Capetians sought to reestablish the principle of divine right, which gradually became accepted by the thirteenth century—though even in the fourteenth century there were several occasions when an Assembly of Barons played at least a subsidiary role in choosing a king. Divine right and religious consecration was the ancient theory of governance, was weakened under feudalism, and then revived as the centralizing forces in French society triumphed over feudalism. Under Louis XIV an absolute monarchy replaced a weak feudal monarchy; in a sense the monarchy reverted to the pre-feudal principle of divine right.

[14] Huntington, *op. cit.*, p. 384.

The thesis that the absolute monarch was the agent of modernization can also be reversed, with perhaps even more validity. H. R. Trevor-Roper has argued cogently that the general European crisis of the seventeenth century had its origins in the rise of absolute monarchy. The Renaissance state, he contends, grew up in the sixteenth century at the expense of the cities. One by one, the great cities fell under the control of assorted princes and kings, whose military and administrative machines were irresistible. Monarchy helped bring about national unity, but once the Renaissance court was created, it became a wholly uneconomic and parasitic agency. The tested principles of commerce and industry were replaced by ostentation and deliberate waste. The burden of monarchy became too great to be borne; the sensible course was to eliminate the whole parasitic crew and return to the productive way of life that had made the medieval cities great. In England the royal power resisted and was swept away; in France the king, perhaps out of luck and apathy, allowed Richelieu to reduce royal expenses and enforce a mercantilist policy. The old regime was given a reprieve. According to Trevor-Roper, "By the seventeenth century the Renaissance courts had grown so great, had consumed so much in 'waste,' and had sent their multiplying suckers so deep in the body of society, that they could only flourish for a limited time, and in a time, too, of expanding general prosperity. When that prosperity failed, the monstrous parasite was bound to falter."[15]

This is not to deny the importance of the monarchy, and especially of the royal administrations, as a channel for innovative practices. But the medieval monarchy cannot be understood through the simple use of ideal types, nor can it be considered the sole agency of modernization. The rise of absolute monarchy in France coincided with the general modernization of French society, but so did the rise of opposition to absolutism.

It is also misleading to contrast divine right of kings with the concept of fundamental law, as if the latter characterized static traditional societies and the former embodied the principle of change. In France the situation was more confused. There were actually two different trends in theorizing about the fundamental laws of the kingdom. One view can properly be called "traditional," in that the fundamental laws were considered the creation of history and of God, beyond the competence even of the king to change. But a second view also developed, according to which fundamental laws were made by the people, and could be modified by the people through the Estates General. This conception, derived from the doctrine of social contract, was clearly more compatible with the process of modernization than were theories of divine right and hereditary

---

[15] H. R. Trevor-Roper, "The General Crisis of the Seventeenth Century," in T. Aston, ed., *Crisis in Europe, 1560–1660* (New York, 1965), p. 95. See also the dissent by Roland Mousnier, arguing that the monarchy was a progressive force, *ibid.,* p. 102. The thesis that modernization of French society took place through the crown is also presented by Barrington Moore, Jr., in *Social Origins of Dictatorship and Democracy* (Boston, 1967). But note the strong statement by Alfred Cobban on the inherent incapacity of the French monarchy, as early as the reign of Louis XIV, to deal with changing conditions, in "The Decline of Divine Right Monarchy in France," p. 239.

monarchy. As Rushton Coulborn put it, the theory of divine right was a "clumsy idea," an "interim notion," and a "slogan, not an argument." And he concludes, "the return to serious thought about the relations between rulers and ruled is marked by the extraordinary doctrine of Original Compact, or Contract."[16]

The social contract is in one sense an extension of the doctrine of "fundamental laws" under the Old Regime. The political struggles of the eighteenth century revolved around the question of whether fundamental laws restrained the powers of the monarch. It was generally accepted under the Old Regime that the monarch could not change the rules concerning succession to the throne, or alienate the public domain, or be anything but a Catholic. An effort was made by a number of Estates General to establish the principle of parliamentary approval of all new taxes as a fundamental law, but the monarchy managed to defeat these efforts. This view of fundamental law led ultimately to the notion that the people originally possessed sovereign powers, and then delegated these powers to their governors.

Once again it is necessary to emphasize the length and complexity of the process of modernization. By the eighteenth century the view was general that man was a creature of unlimited possibilities, that he was basically rational, and that the major purpose of political institutions was to permit him to develop his creative abilities to the fullest. As Gordon Wright has commented: "Enlightenment concepts were far more subversive than its proponents knew; they could scarcely be reconciled with the dominant ideas on which the old regime rested. The institutions of eighteenth-century France were still based on authority and tradition, not on any rational or utilitarian test; the old ideal of an organic society could not be harmonized with the new concept of an atomistic one made up of autonomous individuals."[17]

The ideas of the Enlightenment undermined the positions of both of the main contenders for power in the two decades that preceded the Revolution. The *Parlements* tried, with some success, to check the monarch, basically in the interest of the hereditary aristocracy. The king replied by affirming that full sovereignty resided in his person only. "Public order in its entirety," Louis XV proclaimed in the *séance de la flagellation*, in 1766, "emanates from me, and the rights and interests of the Nation, which some dare to set up as a body distinct from the Monarch, are necessarily joined with mine, and rest only in my hands." Neither the claims of absolute monarchy nor the proposals to restore aristocratic privilege were consonant with the intellectual mood of the time. By the standards of reason and the Enlightenment, the assertion that all sovereignty reposed in the king was absurd; and the contention that hereditary officeholders of the *Parlements* represented the nation only a little less so. When the showdown came, both protagonists found themselves without popular support.

The new principles of political authority were rational in essence; they were

---

[16] Rushton Coulborn, ed., *Feudalism in History*, pp. 311–12. On the fundamental laws under the Old Regime and social contract theory, see M. Duverger, *Les constitutions de la France* (Paris, 1950), pp. 31–37.

[17] Wright, *op. cit.*, p. 31.

compatible with either constitutional monarchy or a parliamentary republic, but marked an irrevocable break with both absolutism and feudalism. The Tennis Court Oath, the August decrees abolishing feudalism, and the Declaration of the Rights of Man and Citizen signalled the emergence of a wholly new principle of political legitimacy. Contrast, for example, Louis XV's pronouncement at the *seance de la flagellation,* the remonstrance of the *Parlement* of Paris in March, 1776, (glorifying the inequalities of feudalism) with the clear, forceful language of 1789. The Declaration was drawn up, in its own terms, "so that this Declaration, constantly present before all members of the social body, shall recall to them ever their rights and their duties; so that the acts of the legislative and executive Powers, being compared at every instant with the goal of all political institutions, shall be more respected. . . ." And the Constitution of 3 September, 1791, "abolishes universally the institutions that infringe upon liberty and the equality of rights—there is no longer any nobility, nor peerage, nor hereditary distinctions, nor distinctions among orders, nor feudal regime. . . . There is no longer, for any part of the Nation, nor for any individual, any privilege, nor any exception to the common law of all Frenchmen."

The revolutionary principle of political legitimacy was not accepted by conservatives, and the revolutionaries were themselves divided; the result was a long period of constitutional instability. Although France was converted almost overnight into a modern state as regards the official principle of legitimacy, it did not thereby achieve a large popular consensus on its basic institutions. The transformation of French society continued. But the way in which the successive crises of modernization were surmounted was drastically affected by endemic constitutional instability. In turn, the nature of controversy over the regime evolved in response to the pressures of modernization.

IV. MODERNIZATION AND CONSENSUS

Science and technology shape the politics of all modern societies. The development of industry necessarily brings about a redistribution of the active population within the economy. The percentage of the population engaged in agriculture decreases, those remaining on farms are able greatly to expand production in spite of their reduced numbers, and the percentage of the population engaged in industry, services, and administration increases. New social groups form and make claims upon the political system. In terms of historical sequence, these groups are the capitalists and businessmen in general, the managerial class, and the working class. At a later stage of industrialization the scientists and intellectuals become so numerous and important in the society that they also become a distinct force. In France, as in all other nations that have gone or are going through the process of industrialization, the entry of each of these social groups into the political system has posed an acute problem.

The first task is to gain an overall view of the extent to which French society has been reshaped. In French census statistics the active population is classified on the basis of participation in three large sectors of the economy: the primary sector (agriculture, forestry, fishing), the secondary (industry, mining, construction, production of energy), and the tertiary (all other activities, including distribution, administration, and personal services). One century ago the agricultural sector was more important than the other two combined; there were slightly more than two farmers for one worker and one person in the tertiary sector. In 1964 the agricultural sector was the least important of the three; the number of persons engaged in farming had been reduced by almost two-thirds, with corresponding increases in the other two sectors. The accompanying table summarizes these trends.[18]

Years	1851	1881	1901	1921	1931	1936	1954	1962	1964
Primary sector (%)	53	48	42	43	37	37	28	21	18
Secondary sector (%)	25	27	31	29	33	30	36	38	42
Tertiary sector (%)	22	25	27	28	30	33	36	41	40

One striking feature of contemporary France is the swift pace of social change. In the ten-year period from 1954 to 1964 the number of people engaged in agriculture declined by almost 40 percent, while the number of those in the secondary and tertiary sectors increased by about 15 percent. The political implications of these trends are obvious. The peasantry is now the smallest of the major social groups. Given their minority position, the peasants must make their claims upon the political system mainly through interest groups rather than through political parties seeking to form a political majority. Although the industrial workers have become more numerous, they still do not constitute a majority by themselves. Only through alliance with either the peasantry or the middle classes can they form a majority. Not only are the middle classes—business, proprietary, managerial, and professional groups—important because of the functions they perform, they are also a massive political force, about as numerous as all workers engaged in industrial production.

France now resembles the other industrial nations of the world, with roughly the same kind of balance among the three major sectors of the economy. In 1964 the number of people in the agricultural sector in France amounted to 18 percent of the total—smaller than in Italy (25 percent), or Japan (26 percent) or the Soviet Union (34 percent), but larger than in Germany (12 percent), the United States (8 percent), or Britain (4 percent). The number of people engaged in the tertiary sector in France was about 41 percent of the total, as compared to 58 percent in the United States, 48 percent in Britain, 42 percent in Japan, 38 percent in Germany, 33 percent in Italy, and 32 percent in the Soviet Union.

In all other respects as well, French society is displaying the general characteristics of modernization. The movement of population toward urban centers has been massive, as is normal. In 1846 the number of people living in communes of two thousand inhabitants or more amounted to 24 percent of the population, and those living in communes of five thousand inhabitants or more to about

[18] Table based on Georges Dupeux, *La société française, 1789–1960*, p. 33 and *Tableux de l'économie française* (Paris, 1966), p. 48a; and *Atlas historique de la France contemporaine* (Paris, 1966), p. 45.

17 percent; the comparable figures in 1962 were 62 percent and 55 percent. Particularly striking has been the growth of the Paris metropolitan area as an industrial and administrative center. Almost 20 percent of the nation's population now lives and works in the Paris region, as compared to only about 3 percent a century ago.

Although the outlines of French social structure are like those of most other industrialized nations, the manner in which that social structure evolved was quite distinctive. Industrialization in France up to 1815 was slow, and generally a result of the application of English methods in the field of textile manufacture. The way to industrialization had been prepared by the Revolution, which eliminated feudal barriers and created a vast market. But French energies were then directed mainly toward defense of the Republic and the creation of the far-flung Napoleonic empire. The industrial revolution did not begin until about 1815, and even then development was sluggish.

Protected by high tariffs, French businessmen were more interested in financial speculation than in creating mass industries. Aristocratic values were amazingly resilient in France after the Revolution, when the successful bourgeois sought to adopt the life-style of the class that had been virtually wiped out as an economic force. David S. Landes has emphasized the contrast between the British and French entrepreneurial classes throughout the eighteenth century: "What distinguished the British economy . . . was an exceptional sensitivity and responsiveness to pecuniary opportunity. This was a people fascinated by wealth and commerce." The French business class was handicapped by its greater attentiveness to what was considered gracious living. Landes speaks of the development within the French body social of "psychological and institutional antibodies to the virus of modernization."[19]

French industrialization was delayed, not prevented. Production increased regularly in the period from 1815 to 1848. Coal production and pig iron output went up dramatically, and a start was made in the metallurgical and chemical industries and in the building of railways. In all spheres, economic development followed the English pattern, but at a slower pace and less energetically.

Another phase of economic development began under the Second Empire, when industrial production roughly doubled between 1852 and 1870. The government of Louis Napoleon tried deliberately to create favorable conditions for capitalist development, and succeeded rather well. The banking system was adapted to the needs of an industrializing economy, providing a channel from the public and its savings to the entrepreneurs. This was also a period of adventurous experimentation by French businessmen, who introduced many innovations in the merchandising field (including the department store) and thoroughly modernized the metallurgical and textile industries. In addition, an extensive

[19] Citations from David S. Landes, "Technological Change and Development in Western Europe, 1750–1914," in H. J. Habakkuk and M. Postan, *The Industrial Revolution and After*, vol. IV of *The Cambridge Economic History of Europe*, pp. 298 and 463. On early industrialization in France, see J. H. Clapham, *The Economic Development of France and Germany, 1815–1914* (Cambridge, 1955).

railway network was constructed. After a slow start, France seemed well on the way to catching up to and surpassing Great Britain. By 1870 France's industrial production exceeded the value of its agricultural production, and its economic growth in the preceding fifty years had been second only to that of Britain.

After the defeat by Prussia in 1870 and the establishment of the Third Republic, there was a period of relatively slow economic growth that lasted until the 1890's. In a sense this was an understandable consequence of losing the war. As J. H. Clapham has remarked, "But the war of 1870, even more the Parisian turmoil of 1871 and the long years of national gloom and self-distrust which followed, chilled the confident ardor without which no nation ever did great work—even in factory building. France was doubting the value of her government and her Republican institutions, and doubting of her own destiny, for the best part of a generation after 1870. Contrast the self-confident, not to say self-satisfied, frame of mind in the England of 1860, in the Germany of 1875, in the United States of always."[20]

There followed, from 1895 to World War I, a period of economic development comparable to that under the Second Empire. From 1870 to 1914 industrial production tripled and real wages went up by some 50 percent. The discovery and exploitation of vast iron ore deposits in Lorraine gave a new impetus to French industrialization. At the same time, a protectionist agricultural policy largely shielded the peasants from the challenge of competition. It was during this period that the contrast between the "two Frances"—one modern and dynamic and the other pre-industrial and static—became significantly sharp. From 1924 to 1930 there was a brief period of rapid economic growth, averaging about 4 percent a year, and then the general decline of the depression. After the destruction of World War II, it took several years simply to regain the pre-war level. But beginning in 1950 there began a new era of rapid growth—about 6 percent a year, far larger than in any other period of French history. Between 1949 and 1965, for example, annual production of steel increased from 9 million tons to 20 million; of automobiles from 286,000 to 1.6 million; of agricultural tractors from 17,000 to 90,000; of housing units from 51,000 to 412,000. National revenue in this period more than doubled, and industrial production as a whole almost tripled.

From this brief survey, several points stand out. (1) Rapid economic growth took place from 1815 to 1848 (Restoration and July Monarchy), from 1851 to 1870 (Second Empire), from 1895 to 1914, from 1924 to 1930 (Third Republic), and from 1950 to the present (Fourth and Fifth Republics). There were thus periods of relative stagnation and of vitality under both monarchies and republics. (2) Until recently the size of the nonindustrial and even pre-industrial sector in the French economy was large compared to that of countries like Britain, Germany, and the United States. (3) Since 1950 there has been a real breakthrough in the attitude of businessmen and intellectuals toward modernization. The pre-industrial mentality glorified individuality and family enterprise

[20] Clapham, *op. cit.*, p. 233.

("mon verre est petit, mais je bois dans mon verre," etc.). This has largely given way to an affirmative view of science, technology, and industrial progress. But the political consequences of these developments are still obscure. The Fourth Republic was overthrown after eight years of impressive economic progress. The Fifth Republic has been beset periodically by grave crises, and its constitution has been under challenge by opposition parties from the day of its promulgation. Rapid modernization since 1950 has brought no discernible consensus concerning the basic values and institutions of the political system.

The French experience of modernization calls attention to the importance of the timing of crises, and the manner in which new social groups have entered upon the political scene. The brutal change of the Revolution produced a series of shock waves in public opinion that made it exceedingly difficult to establish solid political institutions. The aristocracy refused to accept the Republic, and the beneficiaries of the Revolution were restive under monarchy. Even after the establishment of a durable compromise in the form of the Third Republic, the rival forces continued to promulgate incompatible views concerning the way in which the Republic ought to be structured. In short, the French by an accident of timing had to confront the staggering problems of industrialization without the benefit of a stable political system. Industrialization took place anyway, and a series of regimes was able to help the process along.

Fitful industrialization created special problems for the leaders of the emergent social groups. In France, as elsewhere, the first great political crisis of modernization involved the relationship between the rising capitalist and managerial classes on the one hand, and the landed aristocracy on the other. These relations were marked by hostility on the part of the aristocracy and lack of firm purpose on the part of the business elements. Instead of fusing, the two social groups tended to distrust one another, even though the middle class emulated the life-style of their social "betters." The same pattern was repeated in the second great political crisis of modernization—the relationship between the established business class and the increasingly articulate and politically conscious proletariat. Once again there was hostility on the one side and distrust on the other. There was established a tradition, then, of alienation rather than participation, of rejection rather than acceptance.

France is now going through a period of rapid change comparable to that under the Second Empire and Third Republic. One novel aspect of this change is the spectacular rise of the intellectuals, managers, and highly skilled workers as a new kind of professional elite. Will the latest phase of modernization bring about a new spirit in politics, or will the rising social groups perpetuate the tradition of alienation, rejection, and hostility inherited from the earlier confrontations? It has long been the hope of Gaullists that politics would become more pragmatic and less ideological as modernization proceeds. But the Gaullist regime has not been able to provide for meaningful participation in the political system by the major social groups. Instead of being readily and willingly absorbed into the new industrial society, large numbers of university students and intellectuals have repudiated the regime, the educational system, and even the society itself. Modernization in France has always provoked movements of anarchistic and nihilistic protest. Like the Republic itself, modernization has enemies on both the Left and the Right. Whether a modern Republic can survive and advance in a divided society has been, and remains, the chief interest and potential tragedy of French politics.

The democratic or liberal prototype for modernization in Asia, Africa, and Latin America may prove to be France, rather than Britain or the United States. In most developing countries that aspire to parliamentary democracy today, as in France in the past, there is an absence of consensus over the basic institutions of the nation. At the same time there is a determination on the part of the political elites to modernize their nations as quickly as possible. But pre-industrial attitudes permeate the society; the business class is lacking in entre-preneurial vigor; the civil service and military are relatively well organized and are disposed to direct national purposes, and strong Communist and other revolutionary movements signal alienation of workers and intellectuals from the national community. Industrialization is now taking place under conditions of bitter social antagonism and unstable parliamentary institutions in many coun-tries of the "third world." For purposes of comparative analysis the most relevant model among the democratic industrial societies may well be the French experience of modernization.

34. Transitions to Democracy*

DANKWART A. RUSTOW

[Note by the editors: Professor Rustow's discussion of functional and genetic inquiry has been omitted.]

I

The methodological argument [here advanced] may be condensed into a number of succinct propositions.

1. The factors that keep a democracy stable may not be the ones that brought it into existence: explanations of democracy must distinguish between function and genesis.
2. Correlation is not the same as causation: a genetic theory must concentrate on the latter.
3. Not all causal links run from social and economic to political factors.

*From "Transitions to Democracy: Toward a Dynamic Model," *Comparative Politics*, vol. 2, no. 3 (April 1970), pp. 337–63. Article and footnotes abridged by the editors. Reprinted by permission of the author and the journal.

4. Not all causal links run from beliefs and attitudes to actions.
5. The genesis of democracy need not be geographically uniform: there may be many roads to democracy.
6. The genesis of democracy need not be temporally uniform: different factors may become crucial during successive phases.
7. The genesis of democracy need not be socially uniform: even in the same place and time the attitudes that promote it may not be the same for politicians and for common citizens.

My refrain, like Sportin' Life's, has been, "It ain't necessarily so." Each proposition pleads for the lifting of some conventional restriction, for the dropping of some simplifying assumption made in the previous literature, for the introduction of complicating, diversifying factors. If the argument were to conclude on this sceptical note, it would set the researcher completely adrift and make the task of constructing a theory of democratic genesis well-nigh unmanageable.

Fortunately, the genetic perspective requires or makes possible a number of new restrictions that more than compensate for the loss of the seven others. We may continue the listing of summary propositions before elaborating this second part of the methodological argument.

8. Empirical data in support of a genetic theory must cover, for any given country, a time period from just before until just after the advent of democracy.
9. To examine the logic of transformation *within* political systems, we may leave aside countries where a major impetus came from abroad.
10. A model or ideal type of the transition may be derived from a close examination of two or three empirical cases and tested by application to the rest.

That diachronic data, covering more than a single point in time, are essential to any genetic theory should be obvious. Such a theory, moreover, must be based on cases where the process is substantially complete. Although control data on nondemocracies and on abortive and incipient cases may become important at a later stage of theorizing, it is more convenient to start out by studying a phenomenon where it actually has come into existence. The "advent" of democracy must not, of course, be understood as occurring in a single year. Since the emergence of new social groups and the formation of new habits are involved, one generation is probably the minimum period of transition. In countries that had no earlier models to emulate, the transition is likely to have come even more slowly. In Britain, for example, it may be argued that it began before 1640 and was not accomplished until 1918. For an initial set of hypotheses, however, it may be best to turn to countries where the process occurred relatively rapidly.

The study of democratic transitions will take the political scientist deeper into history than he has commonly been willing to go. This implies many changes in method—beginning with suitable substitutions for survey data and for interviews. Even reliable statistics are harder to come by early in any democratic experiment. The United States Constitution (Article 1, Section 2) reminds us that our decennial census was introduced at that very time so that we might begin to govern ourselves by an accurate count of noses.

Whatever the difficulties in the vastly increased use of historical data by social scientists, at least three arguments can be made in extenuation and encouragement. Man did not become a political animal in 1960 or in 1945, as much of our recent literature pretends to suppose. History, to paraphrase Georges Clemenceau, is far too important a topic to be left just to historians. And recently scholars in comparative politics have turned with increasing zest to historical themes. The list includes Almond, Leonard Binder, Dahl, Samuel P. Huntington, Lipset, Robert E. Ward, and Myron Weiner—not to speak of those like Friedrich and Deutsch to whom a political-historical perspective was natural to start with.[1]

The next restriction—the omission early in the inquiry of cases where the major impulse to democratization came from the outside—is in accord with the conventional division of labor between the subfields of comparative politics and international relations. There are topics such as the theory of modernization where that division should be transcended from the start.[2] In tracing the origins of democracy, too, both perspectives may be applied at once, as witness the suggestive work of Louis Hartz, the masterly synthesis by Robert Palmer, and the current research by Robert Ward on Japanese-American interaction in the shaping of the 1947 constitution.[3] But for a first attempt at a general theory it may be preferable to stick to countries where the transition occurred mainly within a single system.

To speak of "major impulses from outside" or transitions "mainly within the system" acknowledges that foreign influences are almost always present. Throughout history, warfare has been a major democratizing force, because it has made necessary the marshalling of additional human resources. Democratic ideas, moreover, have proved infectious whether in the days of Rousseau or of John F. Kennedy. And the violent overthrow of one oligarchy (e.g., France in 1830, Germany in 1918) has often frightened another into peaceful surrender

[1] Almond, current study on nineteenth-century Britain; Leonard Binder, ed., *Politics in Lebanon* (New York, 1966); Dahl, see nn. 4, 7, and 8; Karl W. Deutsch, *Nationalism and Social Communication* (New York, 1953) and Deutsch et al., *Political Community and the North Atlantic Area* (Princeton, 1957); Carl J. Friedrich, *Constitutional Government and Democracy* (Boston, 1950); Samuel P. Huntington, "Political Modernization: America vs. Europe," *World Politics*, XVIII (April 1966); S. M. Lipset, *The First New Nation* (New York, 1963), and Lipset and Stein Rokkan, eds., *Party Systems and Voter Alignments* (New York, 1967); Robert E. Ward and D. A. Rustow, eds., *Political Modernization in Japan and Turkey* (Princeton, 1964); and Myron Weiner, current study on nineteenth-century social history of the Balkans.

[2] In this combination lies the strength of Cyril E. Black's *Dynamics of Modernization* (New York, 1966) compared to most of the other literature on the subject.

[3] Louis Hartz et al., *The Founding of New Societies* (New York, 1964); and R. R. Palmer, *The Age of the Democratic Revolution,* 2 vols. (Princeton, 1959–64).

(e.g., Britain in 1832, Sweden in 1918). From such ever present international influences we may distinguish situations where people arriving from abroad took an active part in the internal political process of democratization. A theory of democratic origins, that is to say, should leave aside at the beginning those countries where military occupation played a major role (postwar Germany and Japan), where democratic institutions or attitudes were brought along by immigrants (Australia and New Zealand), or where in these and other ways immigration played a major role (Canada, the United States, and Israel).

The preference expressed earlier for relatively rapid instances of transition and the omission of immigrant countries amount to a very serious restriction, for they leave out of account, at this first stage of theorizing, all the English-speaking democracies. The reasons, however, seem cogent. Indeed, it may well be that American social scientists have added to their difficulties in understanding transitions to democracy by paying undue attention to Britain and the United States, which for the reasons just suggested prove to be among the hardest instances to analyze in genetic terms. The total of eight provisional exclusions still leaves (among extant democracies) about twenty-three cases on which to base a comparative analysis, thirteen of which are in Europe: Austria, Belgium, Ceylon, Chile, Colombia, Costa Rica, Denmark, Finland, France, Iceland, Ireland, India, Italy, Lebanon, Luxembourg, Netherlands, Norway, Philippines, Sweden, Switzerland, Turkey, Uruguay, Venezuela.[4]

Among these twenty-odd democracies, the last methodological proposition urges an even narrower selection at this preliminary stage of theorizing. What is here involved is a choice between three research strategies: inclusion of all relevant cases, concentration on a single country, or some intermediate course.

Completeness is of course desirable, and all the more so where the "universe" consists of no more than twenty or thirty cases. But the more nearly complete the coverage, the shallower it will have to be. The number of possible variables is so enormous (economic conditions, social cleavages, political alignments, psychological attitudes) that they could be handled only by means of the kind of simplifying assumptions that we rejected earlier on logical grounds. A test, no matter how complete, of a fallacious set of propositions would hardly yield convincing results.

The country monograph would avoid this danger. Nor does it deliberately have to be antitheoretical or "merely descriptive." Any country study nevertheless sacrifices the advantages of comparison, the social scientist's nearest substitute for a laboratory. No such study can tell us which strands in a tangle of empirical factors represent the development of democracy and which the national idiosyncrasies of Monographistan.

The middle course avoids the twin dangers of inconclusive scholasticism and

---

[4] This list, together with the eight omissions noted (Australia, Canada, Germany, Israel, Japan, New Zealand, United Kingdom, United States), corresponds to the one I gave in *A World of Nations* (Washington, D.C., 1967), pp. 290ff., with the following exceptions: Greece has been omitted because democracy was superseded by a military coup in 1967; Mexico was omitted because, on second thought, I do not believe that it meets the criterion of a government based on "three or more consecutive, popular, and competitive elections"— the problems of course being the severe de facto restrictions on competition; Turkey and Venezuela have been added because they now have begun to meet the criterion.

of fact-grubbing. Instead, it can offer a more balanced and hence more fruitful blend of theory and empiricism. The many possible variables that can affect the origins of democracy and the even more complex relations among them can best be sorted out by looking at their total configuration in a limited number of cases—perhaps no more than two or three at the start. What will emerge from this exercise is a model, or as Weber used to call it, an "ideal type," of the transition from oligarchy to democracy. Being an ideal type, it deliberately highlights certain features of empirical reality and deliberately distorts, simplifies, or omits others. Like any such construct, it must be judged initially by its internal coherence and plausibility but ultimately by its fruitfulness in suggesting hypotheses applicable to a wide variety of other empirical cases. It is at this further stage of testing that the demand for completeness comes once again into its own.

The model I should like to sketch in the next few pages is based in large part on my studies of Sweden, a Western country that made the transition to democracy in the period from 1890 to 1920, and of Turkey, a Westernizing country where that process began about 1945 and is still underway. The choice of these two is accidental—except in terms of an autobiographical account for which this is not the occasion. I am now in the early stages of a study that will seek to refine the same set of hypotheses in the light of materials from a slightly larger and less arbitrary selection of countries.

II

A. BACKGROUND CONDITION

The model starts with a single background condition—national unity. This implies nothing mysterious about *Blut und Boden* or daily pledges of allegiance, about personal identity in the psychoanalyst's sense, or about a grand political purpose pursued by the citizenry as a whole. It simply means that the vast majority of citizens in a democracy-to-be must have no doubt or mental reservations as to which political community they belong to. This excludes situations of latent secession, as in the late Habsburg and Ottoman Empires or in many African states today, and, conversely, situations of serious aspirations for merger as in many Arab states. Democracy is a system of rule by temporary majorities. In order that rulers and policies may freely change, the boundaries must endure, the composition of the citizenry be continuous. As Ivor Jennings phrased it tersely, "the people cannot decide until somebody decides who are the people."[5]

National unity is listed as a background condition in the sense that it must precede all the other phases of democratization but that otherwise its timing is irrelevant. It may have been achieved in prehistoric times, as in Japan or Sweden; or it may have preceded the other phases by centuries, as in France, or by decades, as in Turkey.

Nor does it matter by what means national unity has been established. The

---

[5] Ivor Jennings, *The Approach to Self-Government* (Cambridge, 1956), p. 56.

geographic situation may be such that no serious alternative has ever arisen—Japan once again being the best example. Or a sense of nationality may be the product of a sudden intensification of social communication in a new idiom developed for the purpose. On the other hand, it may be the legacy of some dynastic or administrative process of unification. The various hypotheses proposed by Deutsch clearly become relevant here.[6]

I have argued elsewhere that in an age of modernization men are unlikely to feel a preponderant sense of loyalty except to a political community large enough to achieve some considerable degree of modernity in its social and economic life.[7] This sort of hypothesis must be examined as part of a theory of nationhood, not of one of democratic development. What matters in the present context is only the result.

I hesitate to call this result a consensus, for at least two reasons. First, national unity, as Deutsch argues, is the product less of shared attitudes and opinions than of responsiveness and complementarity. Second, "consensus" connotes consciously held opinion and deliberate agreement. The background condition, however, is best fulfilled when national unity is accepted unthinkingly, is silently taken for granted. Any vocal consensus about national unity, in fact, should make us wary. Most of the rhetoric of nationalism has poured from the lips of people who felt least secure in their sense of national identity—Germans and Italians in the past century and Arabs and Africans in the present, never Englishmen, Swedes, or Japanese.

To single out national unity as the sole background condition implies that no minimal level of economic development or social differentiation is necessary as a prerequisite to democracy. These social and economic factors enter the model only indirectly as one of several alternative bases for national unity or for entrenched conflict (see B below). Those social and economic indicators that authors are fond of citing as "background conditions" seem somewhat implausible at any rate. There are always nondemocracies that rank suspiciously high, such as Kuwait, Nazi Germany, Cuba, or Congo-Kinshasa. Conversely, the United States in 1820, France in 1870, and Sweden in 1890 would have been sure to fail one or another of the proposed tests of urbanization or per capita income—not to speak of newspaper copies in circulation, or doctors, movies, and telephones available to each one thousand inhabitants.

The model thus deliberately leaves open the possibility of democracies (properly so called) in premodern, prenationalist times and at low levels of economic development. To find a meaningful definition of democracy that would cover modern parliamentary systems along with medieval forest cantons, ancient city states (the ones where slavery and metics were absent), and some of the pre-Colombian Indians may prove difficult. It is not a task that forms part of the present project; still, I should not like to foreclose the attempt.

---

[6] Deutsch, *op. cit.;* Deutsch et al., *op. cit.*

[7] Rustow, *A World of Nations* (1967), pp. 30 ff., and *International Encyclopedia of the Social Sciences,* s.v. "Nation."

B. PREPARATORY PHASE

I hypothesize that, against this single background condition, the dynamic process of democratization itself is set off by a prolonged and inconclusive political struggle. To give it those qualities, the protagonists must represent well-entrenched forces (typically social classes), and the issues must have profound meaning to them. Such a struggle is likely to begin as the result of the emergence of a new elite that arouses a depressed and previously leaderless social group into concerted action. Yet the particular social composition of the contending forces, both leaders and followers, and the specific nature of the issues will vary widely from one country to the next and in the same country from period to period.

In Sweden at the turn of the century, it was a struggle first of farmers and then of an urban lower-middle and working class against a conservative alliance of bureaucrats, large landowners, and industrialists; and the issues were tariffs, taxation, military service, and suffrage. In Turkey in the last twenty years it has mainly been a contest of countryside versus city, more precisely of large and middling-size farmers (supported by most of the peasant electorate) against the heirs of the Kemalist bureaucratic-military establishment; the central issue has been industrialization versus agricultural development. In both these examples, economic factors have been of prime importance, yet the direction of causality has varied. In Sweden, it was a period of intense economic development that created new political tensions; at one crucial point, rising wages enabled the Stockholm workers to overcome the existing tax barrier for the franchise. In Turkey, conversely, the demand for rural development was the consequence, not the cause, of beginning democratization.[8]

There may be situations where economic factors have played a much lesser role. In India and in the Philippines the prolonged contest between nationalist forces and an imperial bureaucracy over the issue of self-government may have served the same preparatory function as did class conflict elsewhere. In Lebanon the continuing struggle is mainly between denominational groups and the stakes are mainly government offices. Although political struggles of this sort naturally have their economic dimensions, only a doctrinaire economic determinist would derive colonialism or religious divisions from solely economic causes.

James Bryce found in his classic comparative study that, "One road only has

<hr/>

[8] For developments in Sweden see Rustow, *The Politics of Compromise: A Study of Parties and Cabinet Government in Sweden* (Princeton, 1955), chaps. 1–3, and Douglas A. Verney, *Parliamentary Reform in Sweden, 1866–1921* (Oxford, 1957). On Turkey see Ward and Rustow, *op. cit.,* and the following essays by Rustow: "Politics and Islam in Turkey," in R. N. Frye, ed., *Islam and the West* (The Hague, 1957), pp. 69–107; "Turkey: The Tradition of Modernity," in Lucian W. Pye and Verba, eds., *Political Culture and Political Development* (Princeton, 1965), pp. 171–198; "The Development of Parties in Turkey," in Joseph LaPalombara and Myron Weiner, eds., *Political Parties and Political Development* (Princeton, 1966), pp. 107–133; and "Politics and Development Policy," in F. C. Shorter, ed., *Four Studies in the Economic Development of Turkey* (London, 1967), pp. 5–31.

in the past led into democracy, viz., the wish to be rid of tangible evils."[9] Democracy was not the original or primary aim; it was sought as a means to some other end or it came as a fortuitous byproduct of the struggle. But, since the tangible evils that befall human societies are legion, Bryce's single road dissolves into many separate paths. No two existing democracies have gone through a struggle between the very same forces over the same issues and with the same institutional outcome. Hence, it seems unlikely that any future democracy will follow in the precise footsteps of any of its predecessors. As Albert Hirschman has warned in his discussion of economic development, the search for ever more numerous preconditions or prerequisites may end up by proving conclusively that development always will be impossible—and always has been.[10]

More positively, Hirschman and other economists have argued that a country can best launch into a phase of growth not by slavishly imitating the example of nations already industrialized, but rather by making the most of its particular natural and human resources and by fitting these accurately into the international division of labor.[11] Similarly, a country is likely to attain democracy not by copying the constitutional laws or parliamentary practices of some previous democracy, but rather by honestly facing up to its particular conflicts and by devising or adapting effective procedures for their accommodation.

The serious and prolonged nature of the struggle is likely to force the protagonists to rally around two banners. Hence polarization, rather than pluralism, is the hallmark of this preparatory phase. Yet there are limitations implicit in the requirement of national unity—which, of course, must not only preexist but also continue. If the division is on sharply regional lines, secession rather than democracy is likely to result. Even among contestants geographically interspersed there must be some sense of community or some even balance of forces that makes wholesale expulsion or genocide impossible. The Turks are beginning to develop a set of democratic practices among themselves, but fifty years ago they did not deal democratically with Armenians or Greeks. Crosscutting cleavages have their place in this preparatory phase as a possible means of strengthening or preserving that sense of community.

Dahl notes wistfully that "one perennial problem of opposition is that there is either too much or too little."[12] The first two elements of the model between them will ensure that there is the right amount. But struggle and national unity cannot simply be averaged out, since they cannot be measured along the same scale. Strong doses of both must be combined, just as it may be possible to combine sharp polarization with crosscutting cleavages. Furthermore, as Mary

---

[9] James Bryce, *Modern Democracies* (London, 1921), vol. 2, p. 602.

[10] Albert O. Hirschman, *Journeys Toward Progress* (New York, 1963), pp. 6ff.

[11] *Ibid.*, and Hirschman, *The Strategy of Economic Development* (New Haven, 1958), and Hirschman, "Obstacles to Development: A Classification and a Quasi-Vanishing Act," *Economic Development and Cultural Change*, XIII (July 1965), 385–393.

[12] Dahl et al., *Political Oppositions in Western Democracies* (Yale University Press, 1966) p. 397.

Parker Follett, Lewis A. Coser, and others have insisted, certain types of conflict in themselves constitute creative processes of integration.[13] What infant democracy requires is not a lukewarm struggle but a hot family feud.

This delicate combination implies, of course, that many things can go wrong during the preparatory phase. The fight may go on and on till the protagonists weary and the issues fade away without the emergence of any democratic solution along the way. Or one group may find a way of crushing the opponents after all. In these and other ways an apparent evolution toward democracy may be deflected, and at no time more easily than during the preparatory phase.

C. DECISION PHASE

Robert Dahl has written that, "Legal party opposition . . . is a recent and unplanned invention."[14] This accords with Bryce's emphasis on the redress of specific grievances as democracy's vehicle and with the assumption here that the transition to democracy is a complex process stretching over many decades. But it does not rule out suffrage or freedom of opposition as conscious goals in the preparatory struggle. Nor does it suggest that a country ever becomes a democracy in a fit of absentmindedness. On the contrary, what concludes the preparatory phase is a deliberate decision on the part of political leaders to accept the existence of diversity in unity and, to that end, to institutionalize some crucial aspect of democratic procedure. Such was the decision in 1907, which I have called the "Great Compromise" of Swedish politics, to adopt universal suffrage combined with proportional representation. Instead of a single decision there may be several. In Britain, as is well-known, the principle of limited government was laid down in the compromise of 1688, cabinet government evolved in the eighteenth century, and suffrage reform was launched as late as 1832. Even in Sweden, the dramatic change of 1907 was followed by the further suffrage reform of 1918 which also confirmed the principle of cabinet government.

Whether democracy is purchased wholesale as in Sweden in 1907 or on the installment plan as in Britain, it is acquired by a process of conscious decision at least on the part of the top political leadership. Politicians are specialists in power, and a fundamental power shift such as that from oligarchy to democracy will not escape their notice.

Decision means choice, and while the choice of democracy does not arise until the background and preparatory conditions are in hand, it is a genuine choice and does not flow automatically from those two conditions. The history

[13] Mary Parker Follett, *The New State* (New York, 1918), and *Creative Experience* (New York, 1924); Lewis A. Coser, *The Function of Social Conflict* (Glencoe, 1956), p. 121 and passim. A widespread contrary position has recently been restated by Edward Shils, who writes in reference to Lebanon: "Civility will not be strengthened by crisis. It can only grow slowly and in a calm atmosphere. The growth of civility is a necessary condition for Lebanon's development . . . into a genuinely democratic system" (in Binder et al., *Politics in Lebanon*, p. 10). I find it hard to think of situations where there have been any notable advances in either civility or democracy except as the result of crisis.

[14] Dahl et al., *op. cit.,* p. xi.

of Lebanon illustrates the possibilities of benevolent autocracy or of foreign rule as alternative solutions to entrenched struggles within a political community. And of course a decision in favor of democracy, or some crucial ingredient of it, may be proposed and rejected—thus leading to a continuation of the preparatory phase or to some sort of abortive outcome.

The decision in favor of democracy results from the interplay of a number of forces. Since precise terms must be negotiated and heavy risks with regard to the future taken, a small circle of leaders is likely to play a disproportionate role. Among the negotiating groups and their leaders may be the protagonists of the preparatory struggle. Other participants may include groups that split off from one or the other side or new arrivals on the political stage. In Sweden these new and intermediate groups played a crucial role. Conservatives and Radicals (led by industrialists on one side and intellectuals on the other) had sharpened and crystallized the issues throughout the 1890s. Then came a period of stalemate when discipline in all the recently formed parliamentary parties broke down— a sort of randomization process in which many compromises, combinations, and permutations were devised and explored. The formula that carried the day in 1907 included crucial contributions from a moderately conservative bishop and a moderately liberal farmer, neither of whom played a very prominent role in politics before or after this decision phase.

Just as there can be different types of sponsors and different contents of the decision, so the motives from which it is proposed and accepted will vary from case to case. The forces of conservatism may yield from fear that continued resistance may lose them even more ground in the end. (Such thoughts were on the minds of British Whigs in 1832 and of Swedish conservatives in 1907.) Or they may belatedly wish to live up to principles long proclaimed; such was the Turkish transition to a multiparty system announced by President Inönü in 1945. The radicals may accept the compromise as a first installment, confident that time is on their side and that future installments are bound to follow. Both conservatives and radicals may feel exhausted from a long struggle or fearful of a civil war. This consideration is likely to loom large if they have been through such a war in recent memory. As Barrington Moore has aptly proposed, the English civil war was a crucial "contribution of early violence to later gradualism." [15] In short, democracy, like any collective human action, is likely to stem from a large variety of mixed motives.

The decision phase may well be considered an act of deliberate, explicit consensus. But, once again, this somewhat nebulous term should be carefully considered and perhaps replaced with less ambiguous synonyms. First of all, as Bryce suggests, the democratic content of the decision may be incidental to other substantive issues. Second, in so far as it is a genuine compromise it will seem second-best to all major parties involved—it certainly will not represent any agreement on fundamentals. Third, even on procedures there are likely to be continuing differences of preference. Universal suffrage with proportional repre-

[15] Barrington Moore, Jr., *Social Origins of Dictatorship and Democracy* (Boston, 1966), p. 3.

sentation, the content of the Swedish compromise of 1907, was about equally distasteful to the conservatives (who would rather have continued the old plutocratic voting system) and to the liberals and socialists (who wanted majority rule undiluted by proportional representation). What matters at the decision stage is not what values the leaders hold dear in the abstract, but what concrete steps they are willing to take. Fourth, the agreement worked out by the leaders is far from universal. It must be transmitted to the professional politicians and to the citizenry at large. These are two aspects of the final, or habituation, phase of the model.

D. HABITUATION PHASE

A distasteful decision, once made, is likely to seem more palatable as one is forced to live with it. Everyday experience can supply concrete illustrations of this probability for each of us. Festinger's theory of "cognitive dissonance" supplies a technical explanation and experimental support.[16] Democracy, moreover, is by definition a competitive process, and this competition gives an edge to those who can rationalize their commitment to it, and an even greater edge to those who sincerely believe in it. The transformation of the Swedish Conservative Party from 1918 to 1936 vividly illustrates the point. After two decades those leaders who grudgingly put up with democracy or pragmatically accepted it retired or died and were replaced by others who sincerely believed in it. Similarly, in Turkey there is a remarkable change from the leadership of Ismet Inönü, who promoted democracy out of a sense of duty, and Adnan Menderes, who saw in it an unprecedented vehicle for his ambition, to younger leaders in each of their parties who understand democracy more fully and embrace it wholeheartedly. In short, the very process of democracy institutes a double process of Darwinian selectivity in favor of convinced democrats: one among parties in general elections and the other among politicians vying for leadership within these parties.

But politics consists not only of competition for office. It is, above all, a process for resolving conflicts within human groups—whether these arise from the clash of interests or from uncertainty about the future. A new political regime is a novel prescription for taking joint chances on the unknown. With its basic practice of multilateral debate, democracy in particular involves a process of trial and error, a joint learning experience. The first grand compromise that establishes democracy, if it proves at all viable, is in itself a proof of the efficacy of the principle of conciliation and accommodation. The first success, therefore, may encourage contending political forces and their leaders to submit other major questions to resolution by democratic procedures.

In Sweden, for instance, there had been a general political stalemate in the last third of the nineteenth century over the prime issues of the day—the taxation and conscription systems inherited from the sixteenth century. But in

[16] Festinger, *A Theory of Cognitive Dissonance* (Stanford University Press, 1967).

the two decades after 1918, when democracy was fully adopted by the Swedes, a whole host of thorny questions was wittingly or unwittingly resolved. The Social Democrats surrendered their earlier pacifism, anticlericalism, and republicanism, as well as the demand for nationalization of industry (although they found it hard to admit this last point). The conservatives, once staunchly nationalist, endorsed Swedish participation in international organizations. Above all, conservatives and liberals fully accepted government intervention in the economy and the social welfare state.

Of course, the spiral that in Sweden went upward to greater and greater successes for the democratic process may also go downward. A conspicuous failure to resolve some urgent political question will damage the prospects of democracy; if such a failure comes early in the habituation phase, it may prove fatal.

Surveying the evolution of political debate and conflict in the Western democracies over the last century, it is striking to observe the difference between social and economic issues, which democracies handled with comparative ease, and issues of community, which have proved far more troublesome. With the advantage of a century's hindsight, it is easy to see that Marx's estimate was wrong at crucial points. In nationality he saw a cloak for bourgeois class interests. He denounced religion as the opiate of the masses. In economics, by contrast, he foresaw very real and increasingly bitter struggles that would end by bringing bourgeois democracy crashing down. But in fact democracy has proved most effective in resolving political questions where the major divisions have been social and economic, as in Britain, Australia, New Zealand, and the Scandinavian countries. It has been the fight among religious, national, and racial groups, instead, that has proved most tenacious and has caused recurrent bitterness, as in Belgium, Holland, Canada, and the United States.

The reasons are not hard to find. On the socioeconomic front Marxism itself became a sufficient force in Europe to serve to some extent as a self-disconfirming prophecy. But beyond this there is a fundamental difference in the nature of the issues. On matters of economic policy and social expenditures you can always split the difference. In an expanding economy, you can even have it both ways: the contest for higher wages, profits, consumer savings, and social welfare payments can be turned into a positive-sum game. But there is no middle position between Flemish and French as official languages, or between Calvinism, Catholicism, and secularism as principles of education. The best you can get here is an "inclusive compromise"—a log-rolling deal whereby some government offices speak French and some Flemish, or some children are taught according to Aquinas, some, Calvin, and some, Voltaire. Such a solution may partly depoliticize the question. Yet it also entrenches the differences instead of removing them, and accordingly it may convert political conflict into a form of trench warfare.

The difficulty that democracy finds in resolving issues of community emphasizes the importance of national unity as the background condition of the democratization process. The hardest struggles in a democracy are those against the birth defects of the political community.

The transition to democracy, it was suggested earlier, may require some common attitudes and some distinct attitudes on the part of the politician and of the common citizen. The distinction is already apparent during the decision phase when the leaders search for compromise while their followers wearily uphold the banners of the old struggle. It becomes even more readily apparent during the habituation phase, when three sorts of process are at work. First, both politicians and citizens learn from the successful resolution of some issues to place their faith in the new rules and to apply them to new issues. Their trust will grow more quickly if, in the early decades of the new regime, a wide variety of political tendencies can participate in the conduct of affairs, either by joining various coalitions or by taking turns as government and opposition. Second, as we just saw, experience with democratic techniques and competitive recruitment will confirm the politicians in their democratic practices and beliefs. Third, the population at large will become firmly fitted into the new structure by the forging of effective links of party organization that connect the politicians in the capital with the mass electorate throughout the country.

These party organizations may be a direct continuation of those that were active during the preparatory, or conflict, phase of democratization, and a suffrage extension at the time of the democratic "decision" may now have given them a free field. It is possible, on the other hand, that no parties with a broad popular base emerged during the conflict phase and that the suffrage extension was very limited. Even under such conditions of partial democratization of the political structure, a competitive dynamic that completes the process may have been set off. The parliamentary parties will seek support from constituency organizations to insure a steady supply of members for their group in future parliaments. Now this and now that political group may see a chance to steal a march on its opponents by enlarging the electorate or by removing other obstacles to majority control. This, roughly, would seem to have been the nature of British developments between 1832 and 1918. Complete democratization, of course, is the only logical stopping point for such a dynamic.

III

The model here presented makes three broad assertions. First, it says that certain ingredients are indispensable to the genesis of democracy. For one thing, there must be a sense of national unity. For another, there must be entrenched and serious conflict. For a third, there must be a conscious adoption of democratic rules. And, finally, both politicians and electorate must be habituated to these rules.

Secondly, the model asserts that these ingredients must be assembled one at a time. Each task has its own logic and each has its natural protagonists—a network of administrators or a group of nationalist literati for the task of unification, a mass movement of the lower class, perhaps led by upper class dissidents, for the task of preparatory struggle, a small circle of political leaders skilled at negotiation and compromise for the formulation of democratic rules, and a variety of organization men and their organizations for the task of habituation.

The model thus abandons the quest for "functional requisites" of democracy; for such a quest heaps all these tasks together and thus makes the total job of democratization quite unmanageable. The argument here is analogous to that which has been made by Hirschman and others against the theory of balanced economic growth. These economists do not deny that the transition from a primitive subsistence economy to a mature industrial society involves changes on all fronts—in working skills, in capital formation, in the distribution system, in consumption habits, in the monetary system, and so forth. But they insist that any country that attempted all these tasks at once would in practice find itself totally paralysed—that the stablest balance is that of stagnation. Hence the economic developer's problem, in their view, becomes one of finding backward and forward "linkages," that is, of devising a manageable sequence of tasks.

Thirdly, the model does suggest one such sequence from national unity as background, through struggle, compromise, and habituation, to democracy. The cogency of this sequence is brought home by a deviant development in Turkey in the years after 1945. The Turkish commitment to democracy was made in the absence of prior overt conflict between major social groups or their leading elites. In 1950 there was the first change of government as the result of a new electoral majority, but in the next decade there was a drift back into authoritarian practices on the part of this newly elected party, and in 1960–1961 the democratic experiment was interrupted by a military coup. These developments are not unconnected: Turkey paid the price in 1960 for having received its first democratic regime as a free gift from the hands of a dictator. But after 1961 there was a further evolution in the more appropriate sequence. The crisis of 1960–1961 had made social and political conflict far more acceptable, and a full range of social and economic issues was debated for the first time. The conflict that shaped up was between the military on one side and the spokesmen of the agrarian majority on the other—and the compromise between these two allowed the resumption of the democratic experiment on a more secure basis by 1965.

In the interests of parsimony, the basic ingredients of the model have been kept to four, and the social circumstances or psychological motivations that may furnish each of them have been left wide open. Specifically, the model rejects what are sometimes proposed as preconditions of democracy, e.g., high levels of economic and social development or a prior consensus either on fundamentals or on the rules. Economic growth may be one of the circumstances that produces the tensions essential to the preparatory or conflict phase—but there are other circumstances that might also serve. Mass education and social welfare services are more likely to be the result of democratization.

Consensus on fundamentals is an implausible precondition. A people who were not in conflict about some rather fundamental matters would have little need to devise democracy's elaborate rules for conflict resolution. And the acceptance of those rules is logically a part of the transition process rather than its prerequisite. The present model transfers various aspects of consensus from the quiescent state of preconditions to that of active elements in the process. I here follow the lead of Bernard Crick, who has strikingly written:

. . . It is often thought that for this "master science" [i.e., democratic politics] to function, there must already be in existence some shared idea of a "common good," some "consensus" or *consensus juris.* But this common good is itself the process of practical reconciliation of the interests of the various . . . aggregates, or groups which compose a state; it is not some external and intangible spiritual adhesive. . . . Diverse groups hold together, firstly, because they have a common interest in sheer survival, and, secondly, because they practise politics—not because they agree about 'fundamentals,' or some such concept too vague, too personal, or too divine ever to do the job of politics for it. The moral consensus of a free state is not something mysteriously prior to or above politics: it is the activity (the civilizing activity) of politics itself.[17]

The basis of democracy is not maximum consensus. It is the tenuous middle ground between imposed uniformity (such as would lead to some sort of tyranny) and implacable hostility (of a kind that would disrupt the community in civil war or secession). In the process of genesis of democracy, an element of what might be termed consensus enters at three points at least. There must be a prior sense of community, preferably a sense of community quietly taken for granted that is above mere opinion and mere agreement. There must be a conscious adoption of democratic rules, but they must not be so much believed in as applied, first perhaps from necessity and gradually from habit. The very operation of these rules will enlarge the area of consensus step-by-step as democracy moves down its crowded agenda.

But new issues will always emerge and new conflicts threaten the newly won agreements. The characteristic procedures of democracy include campaign oratory, the election of candidates, parliamentary divisions, votes of confidence and of censure—a host of devices, in short, for expressing conflict and thereby resolving it. The essence of democracy is the habit of dissension and conciliation over ever-changing issues and amidst ever-changing alignments. Totalitarian rulers must enforce unanimity on fundamentals and on procedures before they can get down to other business. By contrast, democracy is that form of government that derives its just powers from the dissent of up to one half of the governed.

[17] Crick, *In Defence of Politics,* rev. ed. (Penguin Books, 1964), p. 24.

chapter XIV
REVOLUTION

The pattern of beliefs which justify a given system is subject to constant strain. When these beliefs are no longer accepted by the population, that is, when the legitimacy of the state is widely questioned, a revolutionary situation comes into being. Economic specialization gives rise to social groups whose interests may conflict with those of the existing ruling elite. Technological developments may undermine the economic position of the groups in power. Capitalists, workers, engineers, and merchants no longer may see the reason for continued rule by the aristocracy. Each social group generates its own ideology, and the political system as a whole is faced with the challenge of adjusting conflicting claims and integrating diverse views.

Among the social groups who play a key role in the processes of change and revolution are the intellectuals, the "keepers of the myths." The intellectuals manipulate the ideological symbols of a given society. The teachers, writers, editors, and priests transform power into legitimacy and link the governors with the governed. They are also the first group to reflect doubts and uncertainty about the ideology of the regime and, as such, are sensitive indicators of the stability or instability of a system. Intellectuals furnish the masses with a "consciousness" of injustice which is an indispensable element in any revolutionary situation. Comparative study could usefully be made of the social status of intellectuals, the degree and extent to which they are valued in their society, their political and economic status, and the responsibility they have for the performance and maintenance of the system.

The student should attempt to think of revolution in terms of some unifying concepts. Perhaps the most influential theory of revolution is the one put forth by Karl Marx. Modern capitalism, according to Marx, encounters a basic contradiction between its mode of production and the social relations engendered. In order to secure a return on their investments, capitalists require the workers to produce "surplus value" (over and above what is required for mere subsistence). The social environment congenial to the continued functioning of capitalism is one in which the workers are divided and weak, and therefore unable to resist the demands of the capitalist.

When the workers come together in factories, they inevitably discuss their grievances; their revolutionary consciousness grows sharper. Eventually, capitalists find themselves confronted with a proletariat that is organized and militant, not dispersed and pliable. The productive forces (drive for profits under capitalism) come into conflict with productive relationships (development of a revolutionary proletariat that will no longer tolerate exploitation) and, at a certain point, a readjustment of forces and relationships takes place. Since the state represents the capitalists and controls all instruments of force, the change will have to take place by a workers' revolution.

Does the Marxist theory explain revolutionary developments in Russia, eastern Europe, China, and the "non-Western" nations? Have these revolutions all followed the same course? If not, what accounts for the variations? How has it happened that some countries have escaped these revolutionary upheavals, and managed to satisfy the demands of disaffected groups without recourse to violence? It may be suggested that revolutions are one among many manifestations of social change, which may also come about in other ways.

In addition to Crane Brinton's book (excerpted below), the reader is referred to P. A. Sorokin, *The Sociology of Revolution* (1925); C. E. Black and T. P. Thornton, eds., *Communism and Revolution* (1964); Chalmers Johnson, *Revolutionary Change* (1966); Carl J. Friedrich, ed., *Revolution* (1966); Hannah Arendt, *On Revolution* (1963); and Harry Eckstein, ed., *Internal War, Problems and Approaches* (1964). There are important reflections on revolution in Arnold J. Toynbee's *Study of History,* 6 vols. (1934–39).

35. The Historical Tendency of Capitalist Accumulation*

KARL MARX

What does the primitive accumulation of capital, *i.e.,* its historical genesis, resolve itself into? In so far as it is not immediate transformation of slaves and serfs into wage-labourers, and therefore a mere change of form, it only means the expropriation of the immediate producers, *i.e.,* the dissolution of private property based on the labour of its owners. Private property, as the antithesis to social, collective property, exists only where the means of labour and the external conditions of labour belong to private individuals. But according as

*From *Capital: A Critical Analysis of Capitalist Production* (Moscow: Progress Publishers, 1965), vol. I, chap. 32.

these private individuals are labourers or not labourers, private property has a different character. The numberless shades, that it at first sight presents, correspond to the intermediate stages lying between these two extremes. The private property of the labourer in his means of production is the foundation of petty industry, whether agricultural, manufacturing, or both; petty industry, again, is an essential condition for the development of social production and of the free individuality of the labourer himself. Of course, this petty mode of production exists also under slavery, serfdom, and other states of dependence. But it flourishes, it lets loose its whole energy, it attains its adequate classical form, only where the labourer is the private owner of his own means of labour set in action by himself: the peasant of the land which he cultivates, the artisan of the tool which he handles as a virtuoso. This mode of production pre-supposes parcelling of the soil, and scattering of the other means of production. As it excludes the concentration of these means of production, so also it excludes co-operation, division of labour within each separate process of production, the control over, and the productive application of the forces of Nature by society, and the free development of the social productive powers. It is compatible only with a system of production, and a society, moving within narrow and more or less primitive bounds. To perpetuate it would be, as Pecqueur rightly says, "to decree universal mediocrity." At a certain stage of development it brings forth the material agencies for its own dissolution. From that moment new forces and new passions spring up in the bosom of society; but the old social organisation fetters them and keeps them down. It must be annihilated; it is annihilated. Its annihilation, the transformation of the individualised and scattered means of production into socially concentrated ones, of the pigmy property of the many into the huge property of the few, the expropriation of the great mass of the people from the soil, from the means of subsistence, and from the means of labour, this fearful and painful expropriation of the mass of the people forms the prelude to the history of capital. It comprises a series of forcible methods, of which we have passed in review only those that have been epoch-making as methods of the primitive accumulation of capital. The expropriation of the immediate producers was accomplished with merciless Vandalism, and under the stimulus of passions the most infamous, the most sordid, the pettiest, the most meanly odious. Self-earned private property, that is based, so to say, on the fusing together of the isolated, independent labouring-individual with the conditions of his labour, is supplanted by capitalistic private property, which rests on exploitation of the nominally free labour of others, i.e., on wage-labour.

As soon as this process of transformation has sufficiently decomposed the old society from top to bottom, as soon as the labourers are turned into proletarians, their means of labour into capital, as soon as the capitalist mode of production stands on its own feet, then the further socialisation of labour and further transformation of the land and other means of production into socially exploited and, therefore, common means of production, as well as the further expropriation of private proprietors, takes a new form. That which is now to be expropriated is no longer the labourer working for himself, but the capitalist exploiting many labourers. This expropriation is accomplished by the action of the immanent laws of capitalistic production itself, by the centralisation of capital. One capitalist always kills many. Hand in hand with this centralisation, or this expropriation of many capitalists by few, develop, on an ever-extending scale, the co-operative form of the labour-process, the conscious technical application of science, the methodical cultivation of the soil, the transformation of the instruments of labour into instruments of labour only usable in common, the economising of all means of production by their use as the means of production of combined, socialised labour, the entanglement of all peoples in the net of the world-market, and with this, the international character of the capitalistic regime. Along with the constantly diminishing number of the magnates of capital, who usurp and monopolise all advantages of this process of transformation, grows the mass of misery, oppression, slavery, degradation, exploitation; but with this too grows the revolt of the working-class, a class always increasing in numbers, and disciplined, united, organised by the very mechanism of the process of capitalist production itself. The monopoly of capital becomes a fetter upon the mode of production, which has sprung up and flourished along with, and under it. Centralisation of the means of production and socialisation of labour at last reach a point where they become incompatible with their capitalist integument. Thus integument is burst asunder. The knell of capitalist private property sounds. The expropriators are expropriated.

The capitalist mode of appropriation, the result of the capitalist mode of production, produces capitalist private property. This is the first negation of individual private property, as founded on the labour of the proprietor. But capitalist production begets, with the inexorability of a law of Nature, its own negation. It is the negation of negation. This does not re-establish private property for the producer, but gives him individual property based on the acquisitions of the capitalist era: *i.e.,* on co-operation and the possession in common of the land and of the means of production. The transformation of scattered private property, arising from individual labour, into capitalist private property is, naturally, a process, incomparably more protracted, violent, and difficult, than the transformation of capitalistic private property, already practically resting on socialised production, into socialised property. In the former case, we had the expropriation of the mass of the people by a few usurpers; in the latter, we have the expropriation of a few usurpers by the mass of the people.

36. The Anatomy of Revolution*

CRANE BRINTON

THE DESERTION OF THE INTELLECTUALS

We come to a symptom of revolution well brought out in Lyford P. Edward's *Natural History of Revolution,* and there described as the "transfer of the allegiance of the intellectuals." Although the word "desertion" has perhaps unfortunate moral overtones, the shorter phrase "desertion of the intellectuals" is so much more convenient that we propose to use it, rather than the longer one, in this study.

We must, however, be clear as to what we are talking about before we attempt to use the desertion of the intellectuals as a symptom. Intellectuals we may define without undue worry over preciseness as the writers, artists, musicians, actors, teachers, and preachers. Further subdivision into the small group of leaders who initiate, or at least stand prominently in the public eye, and the larger group who grind out material they get from the leaders, is not of major importance here. What is important, and somewhat puzzling, is the general position of the intellectuals in our Western society since the Middle Ages. Clearly we must not posit agreement among its intellectuals before we decide that a given society is reasonably stable. Even in the thirteenth century, in which so many of our contemporary thinkers find an enviable unanimity as to fundamentals of belief, the amount of bickering among the intellectuals was in reality very considerable. There were rebels and prophets aplenty throughout the Middle Ages. In modern times we expect the individuals to disagree among themselves, and certainly to disagree with the nonintellectuals, the vulgar, the Philistines, the Babbitts—or whatever other name the intellectuals may coin for them. Moreover, for a number of reasons, writers, teachers, and preachers are to a large degree committed by their function to take a critical attitude toward the daily routine of human affairs. Lacking experience of action under the burden of responsibility, they do not learn how little *new* action is usually possible or effective. An intellectual as satisfied with the world as with himself would simply not be an intellectual.

Here, as so often in the social sciences, and indeed in the natural sciences, we are dealing with a question where quantitative and qualitative differences shade most confusingly one into the other. Our distinction between the two is actually no more than a matter of convenience, a complex mental image of the investigating mind.

Quantitatively, we may say that in a society markedly unstable there seem to be absolutely more intellectuals, at any rate comparatively more intellectuals, bitterly attacking existing institutions, and desirous of a considerable alteration in society, business, and government. Purely metaphorically, we may compare intellectuals of this sort to the white corpuscles, guardians of the bloodstream; but there can be an excess of white corpuscles, and when this happens you have a diseased condition.

Qualitatively, we may discern a difference of attitude, partly, no doubt, produced by the numbers and unity of these intellectuals in attack, but partly produced by a subtler reality. Victorian England, for instance, was a society in equilibrium, an equilibrium that looks in retrospect a bit unstable, but still an equilibrium. Here Carlyle upbraided a generation addicted to Morison's Pills instead of to heroes, Mill worried uncomfortably over the tyranny of the majority, Matthew Arnold found England short of sweetness and light, Newman sought at Rome an antidote for the poison of English liberalism, Morris urged his countrymen to break up machines and return to the comforts of the Middle Ages, and even Tennyson was worried over his failure to attain to anything more useful than a high, vague, and philosophical discontent.

Many, though by no means all, Victorian intellectuals were in disagreement among themselves, united apparently in nothing but a profound dislike for their environment. If, however, you look at them carefully you will find a curious agreement that not too much is to be done right away to remedy matters. Moreover, as Mr. Alan Brown has pointed out significantly in his study of the Metaphysical Society, they could actually meet together in Victorian comfort to discuss their differences. It is not, as we are told so often of the scholastic intellectuals of the Middle Ages, that these Victorians were in agreement on fundamental metaphysical and theological assumptions. They weren't in any such agreement. It is rather that they were in agreement about the less dignified but in some ways more important routines and habits of daily life, and they did not expect the *government* to change such matters.

The difference between the intellectual atmosphere of a group like the Victorians, writers who cannot be said as a whole to have deserted, and a group which has deserted, will be clear in a moment if we look at that famous group in eighteenth-century France which stood at the center of the great Enlightenment. One has first the impression of immense numbers of intellectuals, great and small, all studying matters political and sociological, all convinced that the world, and especially France, needs making over from the tiniest and more insignificant details to the most general moral and legal principles. Any of the textbooks will give you the roll—Voltaire, Rousseau, Diderot, Raynal, d'Holbach, Volney, Helvétius, d'Alembert, Condorcet, Bernardin de St. Pierre, Beaumarchais—rebels all, men leveling their wit against Church and State or seeking in Nature a perfection that ought to be in France. You will hardly find active literary conservatives like Sam Johnson or Sir Walter Scott, or even literary neutrals, men pursuing in letters a beauty or an understanding quite outside politics. Even the now almost forgotten opponents of the *philosophes,* even the pessimists who deny the doctrine of progress, are doctrinaire intellectuals, as unreasonable devotees of *la raison* as the radicals.

Literature in late eighteenth-century France is overwhelmingly sociological. If you look in the yellowing remains of French eighteenth-century journalism, if you try to reconstruct the chatter of salons and clubs, you will find the same chorus of complaints and criticisms of existing institutions, the same search for Nature's simple plan of perfection in politics. There is both a bitterness and a completeness in this chorus of complaint that you will not find in Victorian complaints. Statistically, one might establish the fact that there were proportionately more intellectuals "against the government" in eighteenth-century France than in nineteenth-century England. But the difference goes beyond statistics, and into what we have called the qualitative difference. The French have a tone, at once more bitter and more hopeful, quite different from the Victorians. That this is not altogether a national difference will be clear to anyone reading the pamphlet literature of the age of Milton. Then the English intellectuals had deserted, as they had not under Victoria.

Russia, too, is a clear example of this desertion of the intellectuals. There is certainly much more than political propaganda in the series of novelists who have made Russian literature a part of the education of us all. But there is unmistakably political and social criticism of Czarist Russia even in the work of the most detached and Olympian of them, Turgenev. The impression one gets from even a cursory view of Russian intellectual life in the nineteenth and early twentieth centuries is unmistakable; to write or teach in those days meant being against the government. It did not in those days necessarily mean to be Marxist. Indeed, Marx bulked far less heavily in the lives of pre-revolutionary Russia intellectuals than did the writers of the Enlightenment and the nineteenth-century romantic philosophers.

America is not so neat an instance. In Boston, for instance, in the 1760's and 70's, a good many of the kind of people we are discussing—"intellectuals" will have to do—were as firmly as many such people are now against so un-Bostonian an activity as sedition. It is clear that Harvard was by no means unanimous against the Crown, let alone in favor of the democratic machinations of her distinguished alumnus, Sam Adams. But if the literary and journalistic output in the colonies between 1750 and 1775—and even if we include the sermons—could be statistically assigned as either for or against the actual policies of the imperial government, there seems little doubt as to the very considerable balance against these policies. The Enlightenment, especially through Locke and Montesquieu, had come to the American colonies. The natural and inalienable rights of man were in this country, as in Europe, concepts introduced by intellectuals.

England may seem at first sight an exception to the desertion of the intellectuals. Lovelace, Suckling, even Donne seem hardly preoccupied with sociology. Yet at a second glance it is quite clear that English literature under the first two Stuarts is far from being the chorus of loyal praise it was in the days of Elizabeth I. A glance into Professor Grierson's *Cross Currents in English Literature in the Seventeenth Century* will show how much that literature was a dissolvent of the merry England of the Renaissance. Even more important is the fact that in those days there were no real newspapers. The pamphlet took their place. Now the pamphlet literature of the early seventeenth century in England, quantitatively enormous, even by modern standards, is almost wholly preoccupied with religion or politics—better, religion *and* politics—and is about as good an example of the desertion of the intellectuals as could be found. Indeed, as Professor Gooch has written, in the reign of James I "proclamation followed proclamation against the sale of 'Seditious and Puritan books,' and there was 'much talk of libels and dangerous writing.' "

There is such talk now, in the United States, in the mid-twentieth century. This simple statement should remind us of the difficulties of diagnosis of impending revolutions, of the need of considering all aspects of the syndrome, and not a single aspect, not even that fascinating one we have called here "desertion of the intellectuals." For one can make a case for the statement that from about 1900 on there has been desertion of the intellectuals in the United States. Yet the United States does not seem in this century ripe for revolution, does not seem to be a society in marked disequilibrium. Perhaps twentieth-century American intellectuals, like the Victorians we have just considered, are protesting from a sound background of basic agreement with their own Babbitts. Yet there is a bitterness in many American writers, a sense of being out of things in a country run by nonintellectual businessmen, which one does not quite feel even in the Matthew Arnolds, the Morrises, the Carlyles. American intellectuals tend to cling together as a class against other classes, which perhaps is why they show no signs of being about to inspire a revolution. We must not, however, be here led astray into the difficult and still poorly understood problems of *Wissenssoziologie* involved in the behavior of the intellectual classes of contemporary America. Sufficient that from Dreiser and Lewis to Hemingway, Farrell, and Mailer most of our widely read writers have been hostile to things as they are in the United States, and yet things as they are have remained unthreatened by revolutionary overturn.

To what did our successfully revolutionary intellectuals desert? To another and better world than that of the corrupt and inefficient old regimes. From a thousand pens and voices there are built up in the years before the revolution actually breaks out what one must now fashionably call the foundations of the revolutionary myth—or folklore, or symbols, or ideology. Some such better world of the ideal is contrasted with this immediate and imperfect world in all the ethical and religious systems under which Western men have lived, and notably in Christianity. It is not quite accurate to assert that for medieval Christianity, the other, ideal world is safely put off to heaven. Yet it is clear that with the Reformation and the Renaissance men began to think more earnestly about bringing part of heaven, at any rate, to this earth. What differentiates this ideal world of our revolutionaries from the better world as conceived by more pedestrian persons is a flaming sense of the immediacy of the ideal, a feeling that there is something in all men better than their present fate, and a conviction that what is, not only ought not, but need not, be.

Perhaps, indeed, it is the lack of any such immediate better world in the minds of American intellectuals that explains why they are not playing now the kind of role the Voltaires and the Lockes played in the eighteenth century.

American intellectuals have never really shared the Marxian dream; their dream—witness Parrington—has been the old eighteenth-century dream, which nowadays cannot be really revolutionary.

We shall later meet these revolutionary ideals in their fully developed forms. Here we need only notice that in the writings and preachings of the English Puritans—and to a lesser extent the constitutional lawyers—in those of the eighteenth-century *philosophes,* in those of the nineteenth and twentieth-century Marxists, the evil, and indeed illegitimate, existing regime is very effectively contrasted with the good, and indeed inevitable, rule of right to come. In England, America, and in France, the essential principle to which men appealed against present conditions was nature, with its clear and simple laws. Ship Money in England, Stamp Act in America, patents of nobility in France, were all contrary to the law of nature. Even in England and America, where there was also much appeal to rights to be found in Magna Carta or the common law, the final appeal was always to a law of nature "engraved in the hearts of men." As the Puritan Henry Parker wrote in England, the common courts were "furnished only with rules of particular justice, which rules being too narrow for so capricious a subject [the relation of Crown to People] we must refer to those that the original laws of nature hold out to us." By the eighteenth century this kind of language had become almost universal among intellectuals. That nature always counseled what the intellectuals in revolt wanted is an observation we must in these days feel bound to make. It seems likely, however, that for most of those who appealed to her nature was as definite and explicit as God had once been, and as dialectical materialism was to be.

For the Russian writers and agitators of the Czarist regime, nature did not play quite so prominent a part. Not that nature is lacking in the pages of Tolstoy and his fellows, and the contrast between "artificial" society and "natural" instincts was not disdained even in Socialist propaganda. For the liberals, a rather heady mixture of advanced Western thought from the Renaissance to Darwin gave them enthusiasm rather than firm standards. But the official ideology of the successful radicals in Russia was Marxism, and Marxism finds that the existence of capitalists, the rule of the bourgeoisie, is altogether natural. Only, its destruction by the proletariat is also natural, and this destruction is determined by forces quite beyond capitalistic control. The inevitable march of economic forces would then for the Marxists accomplish what the English Puritan expected from God and the French *philosophe* from nature and reason. The essential thing all these prerevolutionary agitators have in common, the essential ingredient, intellectually at least, in the revolutionary myth, is this abstract, all-powerful force, this perfect ally.

One special point is here worth our attention for a moment. Not only does God, nature, or dialectical materialism make the victory of the present underdog certain. The present upperdog can be shown—perhaps for propaganda purposes *must* be shown—to have acquired his preponderance by an accident, or a particularly dirty trick, while God or nature was temporarily off duty. Thus in the English Revolution the royalists and indeed the gentry as a whole were labeled

"Normans," descendants of a group of foreign invaders with no right to English soil. John Lilburne, the Leveller, goes so far as to assert that the whole common law was a badge of slavery imposed upon the free people of England by the Norman Conquest. American hatred of absentee British government hardly needed such artificial fanning. The French were told by no less a person than Siéyès that all their trouble came from the usurpations of the Franks over a thousand years ago. French noblemen in 1789 were descendants of barbarous Germans, while French commoners were descendants of civilized Gauls and Romans. Revolution was but restoring the conditions of 450 A.D. Marxism explained the exploiting class without recourse to such pseudo-historical notions. And yet there is plenty of reference in Russian revolutionary agitation to the usurpation of land by the nobles, to their Varangian, or Tartar, or Western, or at any rate foreign origins. Present evil as well as future good needs the strengthening force of what Sorel called the "myth."

Finally, a great deal of energy has been expended on the question as to whether this revolutionary ideology "causes" revolutionary action, or whether it is merely a sort of superfluous decoration with which the revolutionists cover their real acts and real motives. Most of this discussion is in the highest degree futile, since it is based on crude notion of causation altogether untenable in fruitful scientific work beyond a very simple level. There is no more point disputing whether Rousseau made the French Revolution or whether the French Revolution made Rousseau than in disputing whether egg or chicken came first. We note that in our prerevolutionary societies the kind of discontents, the specific difficulties about economic, social, and political conditions that hardboiled moderns focus on are invariably accompanied by a very great deal of writing and talking about ideals, about a better world, about some very abstract forces tending to bring about that better world. It is, indeed the *expression* of ideas, rather than particular ideas—which may vary enormously in different revolutions—that makes the uniformity. We find that ideas are always a part of the prerevolutionary situation, and we are quite content to let it go at that. No ideas, no revolution. This does not mean that ideas *cause* revolutions, or that the best way to prevent revolutions is to censor ideas. It merely means that ideas form part of the mutually dependent variables we are studying. . . .

SOME TENTATIVE UNIFORMITIES

When all necessary concessions are made to those who insist that events in history are unique it remains true that the four revolutions we have studied [English, American, French, and Russian] do display some striking uniformities. Our conceptual scheme of the fever can be worked out so as to bring these uniformities clearly to mind. We shall find it worth while, in attempting to summarize the work of these revolutions, to recapitulate briefly the main points of comparison on which our uniformities are based.

We must be very tentative about the prodromal symptoms of revolution. Even retrospectively, diagnosis of the four societies we studied was very difficult, and there is little ground for belief that anyone today has enough knowledge and skill to apply formal methods of diagnosis to a contemporary society and say, in this case revolution will or will not occur shortly. But some uniformities do emerge from a study of the old regimes in England, America, France, and Russia.

First, these were all societies on the whole on the upgrade economically before the revolution came, and the revolutionary movements seem to originate in the discontents of not unprosperous people who feel restraint, cramp, annoyance, rather than downright crushing oppression. Certainly these revolutions are not started by down-and-outers, by starving, miserable people. These revolutionists are not worms turning, not children of despair. These revolutions are born of hope, and their philosophies are formally optimistic.

Second, we find in our prerevolutionary society definite and indeed very bitter class antagonisms, though these antagonisms seem rather more complicated than the cruder Marxists will allow. It is not a case of feudal nobility against bourgeoisie in 1640, 1776, and 1789, or of bourgeoisie against proletariat in 1917. The strongest feelings seem generated in the bosoms of men—and women— who have made money, or at least who have enough to live on, and who contemplate bitterly the imperfections of a socially privileged aristocracy. Revolutions seem more likely when social classes are fairly close together than when they are far apart. "Untouchables" very rarely revolt against a God-given aristocracy, and Haiti gives one of the few examples of successful slave revolutions. But rich merchants whose daughters can marry aristocrats are likely to feel that God is at least as interested in merchants as in aristocrats. It is difficult to say why the bitterness of feeling between classes *almost* equal socially seems so much stronger in some societies than others—why, for instance, a Marie Antoinette should be so much more hated in eighteenth-century France than a rich, idle, much publicized heiress in contemporary America; but at any rate the existence of such bitterness can be observed in our prerevolutionary societies, which is, clinically speaking, enough for the moment.

Third, there is what we have called the desertion of the intellectuals. This is in some respects the most reliable of the symptoms we are likely to meet. Here again we need not try to explain all the hows and whys, need not try to tie up the desertion of the intellectuals with a grand and complete sociology of revolutions. We need state simply that it can be observed in all four of our societies.

Fourth, the governmental machinery is clearly inefficient, partly through neglect, through a failure to make changes in old institutions, partly because new conditions—in the societies we have studied, pretty specifically conditions attendant on economic expansion and the growth of new monied classes, new ways of transportation, new business methods—these new conditions laid an intolerable strain on governmental machinery adapted to simpler, more primitive, conditions.

Fifth, the old ruling class—or rather, many individuals of the old ruling class —come to distrust themselves, or lose faith in the traditions and habits of their class, grow intellectual, humanitarian, or go over to the attacking groups. Perhaps a larger number of them than usual lead lives we shall have to call immoral, dissolute, though one cannot by any means be as sure about this as a symptom as about the loss of habits and traditions of command effective among a ruling class. At any rate, the ruling class becomes politically inept.

The dramatic events that start things moving, that bring on the fever of revolution, are in three of our four revolutions intimately connected with the financial administration of the state. In the fourth, Russia, the breakdown of administration under the burdens of an unsuccessful war is only in part financial. But in all our societies the inefficiency and inadequacy of the governmental structure of the society come out clearly in the very first stages of the revolution. There is a time—the first few weeks or months—when it looks as if a determined use of force on the part of the government might prevent the mounting excitement from culminating in an overthrow of the government. These governments attempted such a use of force in all four instances, and in all four their attempt was a failure. This failure indeed proved a turning point during the first stages, and set up the revolutionists in power.

Yet one is impressed in all four instances more with the ineptitude of the governments' use of force than with the skill of their opponents' use of force. We are here speaking of the situation wholly from a military and police point of view. It may be that the majority of the people are discontented, loathe the existing government, wish it overthrown. Nobody knows. They don't take plebiscites *before* revolutions. In the actual clash—even Bastille Day, Concord, or the February Days in Petrograd—only a minority of the people is actively engaged. But the government hold over its own troops is poor, its troops fight half-heartedly or desert, its commanders are stupid, its enemies acquire a nucleus of the deserting troops or of a previous militia, and the old gives place to the new. Yet, such is the conservative and routine-loving nature of the bulk of human beings, so strong are habits of obedience in most of them, that it is almost safe to say that no government is likely to be overthrown until it loses the ability to make adequate use of its military and police powers. That loss of ability may show itself in the actual desertion of soldiers and police to the revolutionists, or in the stupidity with which the government manages its soldiers and police, or in both ways.

The events we have grouped under the names of first stages do not of course unroll themselves in exactly the same order in time, or with exactly the same content, in all four of our revolutions. But we have listed the major elements— and they fall into a pattern of uniformities—financial breakdown, organization of the discontented to remedy this breakdown (or threatened breakdown), revolutionary demands on the part of these organized discontented, demands which if granted would mean the virtual abdication of those governing, attempted use of force by the government, its failure, and the attainment of power by the revolutionists. These revolutionists have hitherto been acting as an organized and nearly unanimous group, but with the attainment of power it is clear that they are not united. The group which dominates these first stages we call the moderates. They are not always in a numerical majority in this stage—indeed it is pretty clear that if you limit the moderates to the Kadets they were not in a majority in Russia in February, 1917. But they seem the natural heirs of the old government, and they have their chance. In three of our revolutions they are sooner or later driven from office to death or exile. Certainly there is to be seen in England, France, and Russia a process in which a series of crises—some involving violence, street fighting, and the like—deposes one set of men and puts in power another and more radical set. In these revolutions power passes by violent or at least extralegal methods from Right to Left, until at the crisis period the extreme radicals, the complete revolutionists, are in power. There are, as a matter of fact, usually a few even wilder and more lunatic fringes of the triumphant extremists—but these are not numerous or strong and are usually suppressed or otherwise made harmless by the dominant radicals. It is therefore approximately true to say that power passes on from Right to Left until it reaches the extreme Left.

The rule of the extremists we have called the crisis period. This period was not reached in the American Revolution, though in the treatment of Loyalists, in the pressure to support the army, in some of the phases of social life, you can discern in America many of the phenomena of the Terror as it is seen in our three other societies. We cannot here attempt to go into the complicated question as to why the American Revolution stopped short of a true crisis period, why the moderates were never ousted in this country. We must repeat that we are simply trying to establish certain uniformities of description, and are not attempting a complete sociology of revolutions.

The extremists are helped to power no doubt by the existence of a powerful pressure toward centralized strong government, something which in general the moderates are not capable of providing, while the extremists, with their discipline, their contempt for half measures, their willingness to make firm decisions, their freedom from libertarian qualms, are quite able and willing to centralize. Especially in France and Russia, where powerful foreign enemies threatened the very existence of the nation, the machinery of government during the crisis period was in part constructed to serve as a government of national defense. Yet though modern wars, as we know in this country, demand a centralization of authority, war alone does not seem to account for all that happened in the crisis period in those countries.

What does happen may be a bit oversimply summarized as follows: emergency centralization of power in an administration, usually a council or commission, and more or less dominated by a "strong man"—Cromwell, Robespierre, Lenin; government without any effective protection for the normal civil rights of the individual—or if this sounds unrealistic, especially for Russia, let us say the normal private life of the individual; setting up of extraordinary courts and a special revolutionary police to carry out the decrees of the government and to suppress all dissenting individuals or groups; all this machinery ultimately built up from a relatively small group—Independents, Jacobins, Bolsheviks—which has a monopoly on all governmental action. Finally, governmental action becomes a much greater part of all human action than in these societies in their normal condition: this apparatus of government is set to work indifferently on the mountains and molehills of human life—it is used to pry into and poke about corners normally reserved for priest or physician, or friend, and it is used to regulate, control, plan, the production and distribution of economic wealth on a national scale.

This pervasiveness of the Reign of Terror in the crisis period is partly explicable in terms of the pressure of war necessities and of economic struggles as well as of other variables; but it must probably also be explained as in part the manifestation of an effort to achieve intensely religious ends here on earth. The little band of violent revolutionists who form the nucleus of all action during the Terror behave as men have been observed to behave before when under the influence of active religious faith. Independents, Jacobins, Bolsheviks, all sought to make all human activity here on earth conform to an ideal pattern, which, like all such patterns, seems deeply rooted in their sentiments. A striking uniformity in all these patterns is their asceticism, or if you prefer, their condemnation of what we may call the minor as well as the major vices. Essentially, however, these patterns are a good deal alike, and all resemble closely what we may call conventional Christian ethics. Independents, Jacobins, and Bolsheviks, at least during the crisis period, really make an effort to enforce behavior in literal conformity with these codes or patterns. Such an effort means stern repression of much that many men have been used to regarding as normal; it means a kind of universal tension in which the ordinary individual can never feel protected by the humble routines to which he has been formed: it means that the intricate network of interactions among individuals—a network which is still to the few men devoted to its intelligent study almost a complete mystery—this network is temporarily all torn apart. John Jones, the man in the street, the ordinary man, is left floundering.

We are almost at the point of being carried away into the belief that our conceptual scheme is something more than a mere convenience, that it does somehow describe "reality." At the crisis, the collective patient does seem helpless, thrashing his way through a delirium. But we must try to avoid the emotional, metaphorical appeal, and concentrate on making clear what seems to be the really important point here. Most of us are familiar with the favorite old Tory metaphor: the violent revolutionist tears down the noble edifice society lives in, or burns it down, and then fails to build up another, and poor human beings are left naked to the skies. That is not a good metaphor, save perhaps for purposes of Tory propaganda. Even at the height of a revolutionary crisis period, more of the old building is left standing than is destroyed. But the whole metaphor of the building is bad. We may take instead an analogy from the human nervous system, or think of an immensely complicated gridwork of electrical communications. Society then appears as a kind of network of interactions among individuals, interactions for the most part fixed by habit, hardened and perhaps adorned as ritual, dignified into meaning and beauty by the elaborately interwoven strands of interaction we know as law, theology, metaphysics, and similar noble beliefs. Now sometimes many of these interwoven strands of noble beliefs, some even of those of habit and tradition, can be cut out, and others inserted. During the crisis period of our revolutions some such process seems to have taken place; but the whole network itself seems so far never to have been altered suddenly and radically, and even the noble beliefs tend to fit into the network in the same places. If you kill off *all* the people who live within the network you don't so much change the network of course as destroy it. And in spite of our prophets of doom, this type of destruction is rare in human history. Certainly in none of our revolutions was there even a very close approach to it.

What did happen, under the pressure of class struggle, war, religious idealism, and a lot more, was that the hidden and obscure courses which many of the interactions in the network follow were suddenly exposed, and passage along them made difficult in the unusual publicity and, so to speak, self-consciousness. The courses of other interactions were blocked, and the interactions went on with the greatest of difficulties by all sorts of detours. The courses of still other interactions were confused, short-circuited, paired off in strange ways. Finally, the pretensions of the fanatical leaders of the revolution involved the attempted creation of a vast number of new interactions. Now though for the most part these new interactions affected chiefly those strands we have called the noble beliefs—law, theology, metaphysics, mythology, folklore, high-power abstractions in general—still some of them did penetrate at an experimental level into the obscurer and less dignified part of the network of interactions among human beings and put a further strain on it. Surely it is no wonder that under these conditions men and women in the crisis period should behave as they would not normally behave, that in the crisis period nothing should seem as it used to seem. . . .

Certainly none of our revolutions quite ended in the death of civilization and culture. The network was stronger than the forces trying to destroy or alter it, and in all of our societies the crisis period was followed by a convalescence, by a return to most of the simpler and more fundamental courses taken by interactions in the old network. More especially, the religious lust for perfection, the crusade for the Republic of Virtue, died out, save among a tiny majority whose actions could no longer take place directly in politics. An active, proselyting, intolerant, ascetic, chiliastic faith became fairly rapidly an inactive, indifferent, worldly ritualistic faith.

The equilibrium has been restored and the revolution is over. But this does not mean that nothing has been changed. Some new and useful tracks or courses in the network of interactions that makes society have been established, some old and inconvenient ones—you may call them unjust if you like—have been eliminated. There is something heartless in saying that it took the French Revolution to produce the metric system and to destroy *lods et ventes* and similar feudal inconveniences, or the Russian Revolution to bring Russia to use the modern calendar and to eliminate a few useless letters in the Russian alphabet. These tangible and useful results look rather petty as measured by the brotherhood of man and the achievement of justice on this earth. The blood of the martyrs seems hardly necessary to establish decimal coinage.

Yet those who feel that revolution is heroic need not despair. The revolutionary tradition is an heroic one, and the noble beliefs which seem necessary to all societies are in our Western democracies in part a product of the revolutions we have been studying. Our revolutions made tremendous and valuable additions to those strands in the network of human interactions which can be isolated as law, theology, metaphysics and, in the abstract sense, ethics. Had these revolutions never occurred, you and I might still beat our wives or cheat at cards or avoid walking under ladders, but we might not be able to rejoice in our possession of certain inalienable rights to life, liberty, and the pursuit of happiness, or in the comforting assurance that one more push will bring the classless society.

When one compares the whole course of these revolutions, certain tentative uniformities suggest themselves. If the Russian Revolution at the end of our series is compared with the English at its beginning, there seems to be a development of conscious revolutionary technique. This is of course especially clear since Marx made the history of revolutionary movements of the past a necessary preparation for revolutionists of the present. Lenin and his collaborators had a training in the technique of insurrection which Independents and Jacobins lacked. Robespierre seems almost a political innocent when his revolutionary training is compared with that of any good Bolshevik leaders. Sam Adams, it must be admitted, seems a good deal less innocent. All in all, it is probable that this difference in the explicitness of self-conscious preparation for revolution, this growth of copious literature of revolution, this increasing familiarity of revolutionary ideas, is not one of the very important uniformities we have to record. It is a conspicuous uniformity, but not an important one. Revolutions are still not a form of logical action. The Bolsheviks do not seem to have guided their actions by the "scientific" study of revolutions to an appreciably greater degree than the Independents or the Jacobins. They simply adapted an old technique to the days of the telegraph and railroad trains.

This last suggests another conspicuous but not very important tendency in our four revolutions. They took place in societies increasingly influenced by the "Industrial Revolution," increasingly subject to those changes in scale which our modern conquests of time and space have brought to societies. Thus the Russian Revolution directly affected more people and more square miles of territory than any previous revolution; its sequence of events compresses into a few months what in England in the seventeenth century had taken years to achieve; in its use of the printing press, telegraph, radio, airplanes and the rest it seems, as compared with our other revolutions, definitely a streamlined affair. But again we may well doubt whether such changes of scale are in themselves really important factors. Men's desires are the same, whether they ride toward their achievement in airplanes or on horseback. Revolutions may be bigger nowadays, but surely not better. Our prophets of doom to the contrary, notwithstanding, the loudspeaker does not change the words.

Finally, at the risk of being tedious, we must come back to some of the problems of methods in the social sciences which were suggested in our first chapter. We must admit that the theorems, the uniformities, which we have been able to put forward in terms of our conceptual scheme, are vague and undramatic. They are by no means as interesting or as alarming as the ideas of revolution held by the late George Orwell, who really believed that totalitarian revolutionary leaders have learned how to change human beings into something wholly different from their immediate predecessors. They cannot be stated in quantitative terms, cannot be used for purposes of prediction or control. But at the very outset we warned the reader not to expect too much. Even such vague theorems as that of the desertion of the intellectuals, that of the role of force in the first stages of revolution, that of the part played by "religious" enthusiasm in the period of crisis, that of the pursuit of pleasure during Thermidor, are, one hopes, not without value for the study of men in society. In themselves they amount to little, but they suggest certain possibilities in further work.

In the first place, by their very inadequacies they point to the necessity for a more rigorous treatment of the problems involved, challenging those who find them incomplete and unsatisfactory to do a better job. In the second place, they will serve the purpose of all first approximations in scientific work—they will suggest further study of the *facts,* especially in those fields where the attempt to make first approximations has uncovered an insufficient supply of the necessary facts. Notably here the facts for a study of class antagonisms are woefully inadequate. So, too, are the facts for a study of the circulation of the elite in prerevolutionary societies. But there are a hundred such holes, some of which can surely be filled. Our first approximations will then lead the way to another's second approximations. No scientist should ask more, even though the public does.

A PARADOX OF REVOLUTION

Wider uniformities will, to judge by the past of science, someday emerge from more complex studies of the sociology of revolutions. Here we dare not hazard much that we have not already brought out in the course of our analysis of four specific revolutions. After all, these are but four revolutions of what seems to be the same type, revolutions in what may be not too uncritically called the democratic tradition. So precious a word is "revolution" to many in that tradition, and especially to Marxists, that they indignantly refused to apply it to such movements as the relatively bloodless but certainly violent and illegal assumption of power by Mussolini or Hitler. These movements, we are told, were not revolutions because they did not take power from one class and give it to another. Obviously with a word in some ways as imprecise as "revolution" you can play all sorts of tricks like this. But for the scientific study of social change it seems wise to apply the word revolution to the overthrow of an established and legal parliamentary government by Fascists. If this is so, then our four revolutions are but one kind of revolution, and we must not attempt to make them bear the strain of generalizations meant to apply to all revolutions.

It is even more tempting to try to fit these revolutions into something like a philosophy of history. But the philosophy of history is almost bound to lead into the kind of prophetic activity we have already firmly forsworn. It may be that mankind is now in the midst of a universal "time of troubles" from which it will emerge into some kind of universal authoritarian order. It may be that the democratic revolutionary tradition is no longer a living and effective one. It may be that the revolutions we have studied could only have taken place in societies in which "progress" was made a concrete thing by opportunities for economic expansion which cannot recur in our contemporary world, with no more frontiers and no more big families. It may even be that Marxists are right, and that imperialist capitalism is now digging its own grave, preparing the inevitable if long-delayed world revolution of the proletariat. There are many possibilities, as to which it is almost true that one man's guess is as good as another's. Certainly a conscientious effort to study four great revolutions in the modern world as a scientist might cannot end in anything as ambitious and as unscientific as social prognosis.

We need not, however, end on a note of blank skepticism. It would seem that there are, from the study of these revolutions, three major conclusions to be drawn: first, that, in spite of their undeniable and dramatic differences, they do present certain simple uniformities of the kind we have tried to bring together under our conceptual scheme of the fever; second, that they point sharply to the necessity of studying men's deeds and men's words without assuming that there is always a simple and logical connection between the two, since throughout their courses, and especially at their crises, they frequently exhibit men saying one thing and doing another; third, that they indicate that in general many things men do, many human habits, sentiments, dispositions, cannot be changed at all rapidly, that the attempt made by the extremists to change them by law, terror, and exhortation fails, that the convalescence brings them back not greatly altered.

Yet one hesitant major generalization binding all four of these revolutions together may here be made from many anticipations earlier in this book. These four revolutions exhibit an increasing scale of promises to the "common man"— promises as vague as that of complete "happiness" and as concrete as that of full satisfaction of all material wants, with all sorts of pleasant revenges on the way. Communism is but the present limit of this increasing set of promises. It is not for us here to rail or protest, but simply to record. So far, these promises in their extreme form have been fulfilled nowhere. That they are made at all offends the traditional Christian, the humanist, perhaps even the man of common sense. But they are made, more vigorously perhaps today in China, in Southeast Asia, in the Near East, wherever Communism is still a young, fresh, and active faith. It is not enough for us Americans to repeat that the promises are impossible of fulfillment, and ought not to be made. It would be folly for us to tell the world that we Americans can fill these promises, especially since we have not filled them at home. Revolution is not a fever that will yield to such innocent and deceptive remedies. For a time, at least, we must accept it as being as incurable as cancer.

As to what the experience of a great revolution does to the society that experiences it, we cannot conclude here too widely without trespassing on wider fields of history and sociology. Yet it does seem that the patient emerges stronger in some respects from the conquered fever, immunized in this way and that from attacks that might be more serious. It is an observable fact that in all our societies there was a flourishing, a peak of varied cultural achievements, after the revolutions. Certainly we may not moralize too much about the stupidities and cruelties of revolutions, may not lift up our hands in horror. It is quite possible that wider study would show that feeble and decadent societies do not undergo revolutions, that revolutions are, perversely, a sign of strength and youth in societies.

One quiet person emerges from his study, not indeed untouched by a good deal of horror and disgust but moved also with admiration for a deep and unfathomable strength in men which, because of the softer connotations of the word, he is reluctant to call spiritual. Montaigne saw and felt it long ago:

> I see not one action, or three, or a hundred, but a commonly accepted state of morality so unnatural, especially as regards inhumanity and treachery, which are to me the worst of all sins, that I have not the heart to think of them without horror; and they excite my wonder almost as much as my detestation. *The practice of these egregious villanies has as much the mark of strength and vigor of soul as of error and disorder.*

Berkman the anarchist, who loathed the Russian Revolution, tells a story which may represent merely his own bias, but which may nonetheless serve as a brief symbolical epilogue to this study. Berkman says he asked a good Bolshevik acquaintance during the period of attempted complete communization under Lenin why the famous Moscow cabmen, the *izvoschiks,* who continued in diminished numbers to flit about Moscow and to get enormous sums in paper roubles for their services, were not nationalized like practically everyone else. The Bolshevik replied, "We found that if you don't feed human beings they continue to live somehow. But if you don't feed the horses, the stupid beasts die. That's why we don't nationalize the cabmen." That is not an altogether cheerful story, and in some ways one may regret the human capacity to live without eating. But clearly if we were as stupid—or as sensible—as horses we should have no revolutions.

37. On Peasant Rebellions*

ERIC R. WOLF

Six major social and political upheavals, fought with peasant support, have shaken the world of the twentieth century: the Mexican revolution of 1910, the Russian revolutions of 1905 and 1917, the Chinese revolution which metamorphosed through various phases from 1921 onwards, the Vietnamese revolution which has its roots in the Second World War, the Algerian rebellion of 1954 and the Cuban revolution of 1958. All of these were to some extent based on the participation of rural populations. It is to the analysis of this participation that the present article directs its attention.

Romantics to the contrary, it is not easy for a peasantry to engage in sustained rebellion. Peasants are especially handicapped in passing from passive recognition of wrongs to political participation as a means for setting them right. First, a peasant's work is more often done alone, on his own land, than in conjunction with his fellows. Moreover, all peasants are to some extent competitors, for available resources within the community as for sources of credit from without. Secondly, the tyranny of work weighs heavily upon peasants: their life is geared to an annual routine and to planning for the year to come. Momentary alterations of routine threaten their ability to take up the routine later. Thirdly, control of land enables them, more often than not, to retreat into subsistence production should adverse conditions affect their market crop. Fourthly, ties of extended kinship and mutual aid within the community may cushion the shocks of dislocation. Fifthly, peasants' interests—especially among poor peasants—often cross-cut class alignments. Rich and poor peasant may be kinfolk, or a peasant may be at one and the same time owner, renter, share-cropper, labourer for his neighbours and seasonal hand on a near-by plantation. Each different involvement aligns him differently with his fellows and with the outside world. Finally, past exclusion of the peasant from participation in decision-making beyond the bamboo hedge of his village deprives him all too often of the knowledge needed to articulate his interests with appropriate forms of action. Hence peasants are often merely passive spectators of political struggles or long for the sudden advent of a millennium, without specifying for themselves and their neighbours the many rungs on the staircase to heaven.

If it is true that peasants are slow to rise, then peasant participation in the great rebellions of the twentieth century must obey some special factors which exacerbated the peasant condition. We will not understand that condition unless we keep in mind constantly that it has suffered greatly under the impact of three great crises: the demographic crisis, the ecological crisis and the crisis in power and authority. The demographic crisis is most easily depicted in bare figures, though its root causes remain ill understood. It may well be that its ultimate

*From the *International Social Science Journal*, vol. XXI, no. 2 (1969), pp. 286–93. Reprinted by permission of the author and the editor of the journal.

causes lie less in the reduction of mortality through spreading medical care, than in the diffusion of American food crops throughout the world which provided an existential minimum for numerous agricultural populations. Yet the bare numbers suffice to indicate the seriousness of the demographic problem. Mexico had a population of 5.8 million at the beginning of the nineteenth century; in 1910—at the outbreak of the revolution—it had 16.5 million. European Russia had a population of 20 million in 1725; at the turn of the twentieth century it had 87 million. China numbered 265 million in 1775, 430 million in 1850 and close to 600 million at the time of the revolution. Viet-Nam is estimated to have sustained a population of between 6 and 14 million in 1820; it had 30.5 million inhabitants in 1962. Algeria had an indigenous population of 10.5 million in 1963, representing a fourfold increase since the beginnings of French occupation in the first part of the nineteenth century. Cuba had 550,000 inhabitants in 1800; by 1953 it had 5.8 million. Population increases alone and by themselves would have placed a serious strain on inherited cultural arrangements.

The ecological crisis is in part related to the sheer increase in numbers; yet it is also in an important measure independent of it. Population increases of the magnitude just mentioned coincided with a period in history in which land and other resources were increasingly converted into commodities—in the capitalist sense of that word. As commodities they were subjected to the demands of a market which bore only a very indirect relation to the needs of the rural populations subjected to it. Where, in the past, market behaviour had been largely subsidiary to the existential problems of subsistence, now existence and its problems became subsidiary to the market. The alienation of peasant resources proceeded directly through outright seizure or through coercive purchase, as in Mexico, Algeria and Cuba; or it took the form—especially in China and Viet-Nam—of stepped-up capitalization of rent which resulted in the transfer of resources from those unable to keep up to those able to pay. In addition, capitalist mobilization of resources was reinforced through the pressure of taxation, of demands for redemption payments and through the increased needs for industrially produced commodities on the part of the peasantry itself. All together, however, these various pressures disrupted the precarious ecological balance of peasant society. Where the peasant had required a certain combination of resources to effect an adequate living, the separate and differential mobilization of these resources broke that ecological nexus. This is perhaps best seen in Russia where successive land reforms threatened continued peasant access to pasture, forest and ploughland. Yet it is equally evident in cases where commercialization threatened peasant access to communal lands (Algeria, Mexico, Viet-Nam), to unclaimed land (Cuba, Mexico), to public granaries (Algeria, China), or where it threatened the balance between pastoral and settled populations (Algeria). At the same time as commercialization disrupted rural life, moreover, it also created new and unsettled ecological niches in industry. Disruptive change in the rural area went hand in hand with the opening up of incipient but uncertain opportunities for numerous ex-industrial peasants. Many of these retained formal ties with their home villages (Algeria, China, Russia); others migrated between country and industry in continuous turnover (especially Viet-Nam). Increased instability in the rural area was thus accompanied by a still unstable commitment to industrial work.

Finally, both the demographic and the ecological crisis converged in the crisis of authority. The development of the market produced a rapid circulation of the *élite,* in which the manipulators of the new 'free-floating resources'— labour bosses, merchants, industrial *entrepreneurs*—challenged the inherited power of the controllers of fixed social resources, the tribal chief, the mandarin, the landed nobleman.[1] Undisputed and stable claims thus yielded to unstable and disputed claims. This rivalry between primarily political and primarily economic power-holders contained its own dialectic. The imposition of the market mechanism entailed a diminution of social responsibilities for the affected population: the economic *entrepreneur* did not concern himself with the social cost of his activities; the traditional power-holder was often too limited in his power to offer assistance or subject to co-optation by his successful rivals. The advent of the market thus not merely produced a crisis in peasant ecology; it deranged the numerous middle-level ties between centre and hinterland, between the urban and the rural sectors. Commercialization disrupted the hinterland; at the very same time it also lessened the ability of power-holders to perceive and predict changes in the rural area. The result was an ever-widening gap between the rulers and the ruled. That such a course is not inevitable is perhaps demonstrated by Barrington Moore,[2] who showed how traditional feudal forms were utilized in both Germany and Japan to prevent the formation of such a gap in power and communication during the crucial period of transition to a commercial and industrial order. Where this was not accomplished—precisely where an administrative militarized feudalism was absent—the continued widening of the power gap invited the formation of a counter-*élite* which could challenge both a disruptive leadership based on the operation of the market and the impotent heirs of traditional power, while forging a new consensus through communication with the peasantry. Such a counter-*élite* is most frequently made up of members of provincial *élites,* relegated to the margins of commercial mobilization and political office; of officials or professionals who stand midway between the rural area and the centre and are caught in the contradictions between the two; and of intellectuals who have access to a system of symbols which can guide the interaction between leadership and rural area.

Sustained mobilization of the peasantry is, however, no easy task. Such an effort will not find its allies in a rural mass which is completely subject to the imperious demands of necessity. Peasants cannot rebel successfully in a situation of complete impotence; the powerless are easy victims. Therefore only a peasantry in possession of some tactical control over its own resources can

[1] S. N. Eisenstadt, *Modernization: Protest and Change* (Englewood Cliffs, N.J.: Prentice-Hall, 1966).

[2] Barrington Moore, Jr., *Social Origins of Dictatorship and Democracy* (Boston: Beacon Press, 1966).

provide a secure basis for on-going political leverage. Power, as Richard Adams[3] has said, refers ultimately 'to an actual physical control that one party may have with respect to another. The reason that most relationships are not reduced to physical struggles is that parties to them can make rational decisions based on their estimates of tactical power and other factors. Power is usually exercised, therefore, through the common recognition by two parties of the tactical control each has, and through rational decision by one to do what the other wants. Each estimates his own tactical control, compares it to the other, and decides he may or may not be superior'.

The poor peasant or the landless labourer who depends on a landlord for the largest part of his livelihood, or the totality of it, has no tactical power: he is completely within the power domain of his employer, without sufficient resources of his own to serve him usefully in the power struggle. Poor peasants, and landless labourers, therefore, are unlikely to pursue the course of rebellion, unless they are able to rely on some external power to challenge the power which constrains them. Such external power is represented in the Mexican case by the action of the Constitutionalist army in Yucatan, which liberated the peons from debt bondage 'from above'; by the collapse of the Russian army in 1917 and the reflux of the peasant soldiery, arms in hand, into the villages; by the creation of the Chinese Red Army as an instrument designed to break up landlord power in the villages. Where such external power is present the poor peasant and landless labourer have latitude of movement; where it is absent, they are under near-complete constraint. The rich peasant, in turn, is unlikely to embark on the course of rebellion. As employer of the labour of others, as money-lender, as notable co-opted by the State machine, he exercises local power in alliance with external power-holders. His power domain with the village is derivative; it depends on the maintenance of the domains of these power-holders outside the village. Only when an external force, such as the Chinese Red Army, proves capable of destroying these other superior power domains, will the rich peasant lend his support to an uprising.

There are only two components of the peasantry which possess sufficient internal leverage to enter into sustained rebellion. These are (a) a landowning 'middle peasantry' or (b) a peasantry located in a peripheral area outside the domains of landlord control. Middle peasantry refers to a peasant population which has secure access to land of its own and cultivates it with family labour. Where these middle-peasant holdings lie within the power domain of a superior, possession of their own resources provides their holders with the minimal tactical freedom required to challenge their overlord. The same, however, holds for a peasantry, poor or 'middle', whose settlements are only under marginal control from the outside. Here landholdings may be insufficient for the support of the peasant household; but subsidiary activities such as casual labour, smuggling, live-stock raising—not under the direct constraint of an external power domain—supplement land in sufficient quantity to grant the peasantry some latitude of

[3] Richard N. Adams, 'Power and Power Domains', *Americana Latina*, Year 9, 1966, pp. 3–21.

movement. We mark the existence of such a tactically mobile peasantry: in the villages of Morelos in Mexico; in the communes of the central agricultural regions of Russia; in the northern bastion established by the Chinese Communists after the Long March; as a basis for rebellion in Vietnam; among the *fellaheen* of Algeria; and among the squatters of Oriente Province in Cuba.

Yet this recruitment of a 'tactically mobile peasantry' among the middle peasants and the 'free' peasants of peripheral areas poses a curious paradox. This is also the peasantry in whom anthropologists and rural sociologists have tended to see the main bearers of peasant tradition. If our account is correct, then— strange to say—it is precisely this culturally conservative stratum which is the most instrumental in dynamiting the peasant social order. This paradox dissolves, however, when we consider that it is also the middle peasant who is relatively the most vulnerable to economic changes wrought by commercialism, while his social relations remain encased within the traditional design. His is a balancing act in which his equilibrium is continuously threatened by population growth; by the encroachment of rival landlords; by the loss of rights to grazing, forest and water: by falling prices and unfavourable conditions of the market: by interest payments and foreclosures. Moreover, it is precisely this stratum which most depends on traditional social relations of kin and mutual aid between neighbours; middle peasants suffer most when these are abrogated, just as they are least able to withstand the depredations of tax collectors or landlords.

Finally—and this is again paradoxical—middle peasants are also the most exposed to influences from the developing proletariat. The poor peasant or landless labourer, in going to the city or the factory, also usually cuts his tie with the land. The middle peasant, however, stays on the land and sends his children to work in town; he is caught in a situation in which one part of the family retains a footing in agriculture, while the other undergoes 'the training of the cities'.[4] This makes the middle peasant a transmitter also of urban unrest and political ideas. The point bears elaboration. It is probably not so much the growth of an industrial proletariat as such which produces revolutionary activity, as the development of an industrial work force still closely geared to life in the villages.

Thus it is the very attempt of the middle and free peasant to remain traditional which makes him revolutionary.

If we now follow through the hypothesis that it is middle peasants and poor but 'free' peasants, not constrained by any power domain, who constitute the pivotal groupings for peasant uprisings, then it follows that any factor which serves to increase the latitude granted by that tactical mobility reinforces their revolutionary potential. One of these factors is peripheral location with regard to the centre of State control. In fact, frontier areas quite often show a tendency to rebel against the central authorities, regardless of whether they are inhabited by peasants or not. South China has constituted a hearth of rebellion within the Chinese State, partly because it was first a frontier area in the southward march

[4] Germaine Tillion, *France and Algeria: Complementary Enemies* (New York: Knopf, 1961), pp. 120–21.

of the Han people, and later because it provided the main zone of contact between Western and Chinese civilization. The Mexican north has similarly been a zone of dissidence from the centre in Mexico City, partly because its economy was based on mining and cattle-raising rather than maize agriculture, partly because it was open to influences from the United States to the north. In the Chinese south it was dissident gentry with a peasant following which frequently made trouble for the centre; in the Mexican north it was provincial business men, ranchers and cowboys. Yet where there exists a poor peasantry located in such a peripheral area beyond the normal control of the central power, the tactical mobility of such a peasantry is 'doubled' by its location. This has been the case with Morelos, in Mexico; Nghe An province in Viet-Nam; Kabylia in Algeria; and Oriente in Cuba. The tactical effectiveness of such areas is 'tripled' if they also contain defensible mountainous redoubts: this has been true of Morelos, Kabylia and Oriente. The effect is 'quadrupled' where the population of these redoubts differs ethnically or linguistically from the surrounding population. Thus we find that the villagers of Morelos were Nahuatl-speakers, the inhabitants of Kabylia Berber-speakers. Oriente province showed no linguistic differences from the Spanish spoken in Cuba, but it did contain a significant Afro-Cuban element. Ethnic distinctions enhance the solidarity of the rebels; possession of a special linguistic code provides for an autonomous system of communication.

It is important, however, to recognize that separation from the State or the surrounding populace need not only be physical or cultural. The Russian and the Mexican cases both demonstrate that it is possible to develop a solid enclave population of peasantry through State reliance on a combination of communal autonomy with the provision of community services to the State. The organization of the peasantry into self-administering communes with stipulated responsibilities to State and landlords created in both cases veritable fortresses of peasant tradition within the body of the country itself. Held fast by the surrounding structure, they acted as sizzling pressure-cookers of unrest which, at the moment of explosion, vented their force outward to secure more living-space for their customary corporate way of life. Thus we can add a further multiplier effect to the others just cited. The presence of any one of these will raise the peasant potential for rebellion.

But what of the transition from peasant rebellion to revolution, from a movement aimed at the redress of wrongs, to the attempted overthrow of society itself? Marxists in general have long argued that peasants without outside leadership cannot make a revolution; and our case material would bear them out. Where the peasantry has successfully rebelled against the established order—under its own banner and with its own leaders—it was sometimes able to reshape the social structure of the country-side closer to its heart's desires; but it did not lay hold of the State, of the cities which house the centres of control, of the strategic non-agricultural resources of the society. Zapata stayed in his Morelos; the 'folk migration' of Pancho Villa simply receded after the defeat at Torreon; the Ukrainian rebel Nestor Makhno stopped short of the cities; and the Russian peasants of the Central Agricultural Region simply burrowed more deeply into their local communes. Thus a peasant rebellion which takes place in a complex society already caught up in commercialization and industrialization tends to be self-limiting, and hence anachronistic.

The peasant Utopia is the free village, untrammelled by tax collectors, labour recruiters, large landowners, officials. Ruled over, but never ruling, peasants also lack any acquaintance with the operation of the State as a complex machinery, experiencing it only as a 'cold monster'. Against this hostile force, they had learned, even their traditional power-holders provided but a weak shield, though they were on occasion willing to defend them if it proved to their own interest. Thus, for peasants, the State is a negative quantity, an evil, to be replaced in short shrift by their own 'home-made' social order. That order, they believe, can run without the State; hence peasants in rebellion are natural anarchists.

Often this political perspective is reinforced still further by a wider ideological vision. The peasant's experience tends to be dualistic, in that he is caught between his understanding of how the world ought properly to be ordered and the realities of a mundane existence, beset by disorder. Against this disorder, the peasant has always set his dreams of deliverance, the vision of a *mahdi* who would deliver the world from tyranny, of a Son of Heaven who would truly embody the mandate of Heaven, of a 'white' Tsar as against the 'black' Tsar of the disordered present. Under conditions of modern dislocation, the disordered present is all too frequently experienced as world order reversed, and hence evil. The dualism of the past easily fuses with the dualism of the present. The true order is yet to come, whether through miraculous intervention, through rebellion, or both. Peasant anarchism and an apocalyptic vision of the world, together, provide the ideological fuel that drives the rebellious peasantry.

The peasant rebellions of the twentieth century are no longer simple responses to local problems, if indeed they ever were. They are but the parochial reactions to major social dislocations, set in motion by overwhelming societal change. The spread of the market has torn men up by their roots, and shaken them loose from the social relationships into which they were born. Industrialization and expanded communication have given rise to new social clusters, as yet unsure of their own social positions and interests, but forced by the very imbalance of their lives to seek a new adjustment. Traditional political authority has eroded or collapsed; new contenders for power are seeking new constituencies for entry into the vacant political arena. Thus when the peasant protagonist lights the torch of rebellion, the edifice of society is already smouldering and ready to take fire. When the battle is over, the structure will not be the same.

No cultural system—no complex of economy, society, polity and ideology— is ever static; all of its component parts are in constant change. Yet as long as these changes remain within tolerable limits, the over-all system persists. If they begin to exceed these limits, however, or if other components are suddenly introduced from outside, the system will be thrown out of kilter. The parts of the system are rendered inconsistent with each other; the system grows incoherent. Men in such a situation are caught painfully between various old solutions to problems which have suddenly shifted shape and meaning, and new solutions to problems they often cannot comprehend. Since incoherence rarely appears all at once, in all parts of the system, they may for some time follow now one alternative, now another and contradictory one; but in the end a breach, a major disjuncture will make its appearance somewhere in the system. A peasant uprising under such circumstances, for any of the reasons we have sketched, can—without conscious intent—bring the entire society to the state of collapse.

chapter XV
BEYOND MODERNIZATION

The student should not expect to find in modernization theory the solution to all, or indeed, any of the persistent issues of political philosophy. Modernization implies an evolution from the simple to the more complex, but it does not necessarily mean "progress" or a better life for humanity. The problems faced by modern political systems are frequently more acute and less amenable to peaceful resolution than in traditional systems. In most cases modernization has been accompanied by violence.

One problem is created by the uneven pace of modernization. No society ever develops at a perfectly even rate; certain geographic regions and social or ethnic groups take the lead, and others fall behind. The more rapid the trend toward modernization, the greater may be the gap between the advanced and the less advanced sections of the society. A point may be reached where the contrast between wealth and poverty, and the consciousness of injustice, create widespread resentment and grave political crisis. Protest may take the form of reactionary political movements that seek to preserve the privileges of groups at a disadvantage in the modern economy (such as aristocrats or small shop-keepers); or of racial unrest wherever poverty coincides with race; or separatism wherever ethnic, religious, or linguistic groups that feel themselves exploited inhabit a specific geographic area.

Even in the absence of these problems, modern societies tend to display an element of "anomie," to use the term popularized by Emile Durkheim. In the process of modernization the values and norms of the traditional society are first called into question, then challenged, and finally repudiated. At the same time the family as a social unit loses its primordial importance, and parental authority is weakened. The old discipline is eroded, but the new discipline is not yet accepted. In the transitional period many individuals become utterly rootless, not knowing what to believe, not accepting the authority of either the traditional family and church or of the modern school and state. Under such conditions there may be an increase in crime, civil disorder, and other acts of individual and collective violence.

503

Protest against modernization is not limited to reactionaries who wish, instinctively, to revert to more traditional conditions. Many aspects of modern life are carefully appraised, especially by intellectuals, and then decisively rejected. Modernization is characterized by the proliferation of highly organized and specialized associations whose bureaucratic structure may stamp out individuality and eccentricity. Individuals may feel themselves reduced to component parts of a machine process and thus dehumanized. Expansion of the industrial base also leads to an absolute increase in military power, which is based more and more on science and technology. This in turn makes possible extension of national influence in the world. Since all modernizing societies are engaged in the same kind of rivalry, the end result is heightened international tension and constant intervention in the political affairs of other countries. Thus, bureaucratization, impersonality, violence, and imperialism (of which there are several varieties) may well produce apathy or alienation. An extreme manifestation of this alienation from the central values of modern society is withdrawal into the dream world of drugs and alcohol. Modernization is not universally perceived, to use Hegelian terms, as "the march of Reason on earth." Comparative analysis of modern political systems would deal with the impact of bureaucratic structures upon individual behavior, the extent of unrest generated by rapid social change, and the conditions under which certain groups are particularly susceptible to feelings of apathy or alienation. Mass societies vary in the degree of unrest and extremism they produce.

Among the books on the distinctive problems of modern societies are: William Kornhauser, *The Politics of Mass Society* (1959); Ortega y Gassett, *Revolt of the Masses* (1932); Erich Fromm, *Escape From Freedom* (1945); David Riesman, *The Lonely Crowd* (1950); Daniel Bell, ed., *The New American Right* (1955); Ralf Dahrendorf, *Class and Class Conflict in Industrial Society* (1958); Herbert Marcuse, *One Dimensional Man* (1964); and Zbigniew Brzezinski, *Between Two Ages: America's Role in the Technetronic Era* (1970).

38. Anomie*

EMILE DURKHEIM

No living being can be happy or even exist unless his needs are sufficiently proportioned to his means. In other words, if his needs require more than can be granted, or even merely something of a different sort, they will be under continual friction and can only function painfully. Movements incapable of

*Reprinted with permission of The Macmillan Company from *Suicide: A Study in Sociology* by Emile Durkheim. Translated by George Simpson. Copyright 1951 by The Free Press, a Corporation.

production without pain tend not to be reproduced. Unsatisfied tendencies atrophy, and as the impulse to live is merely the result of all the rest, it is bound to weaken as the others relax.

In the animal, at least in a normal condition, this equilibrium is established with automatic spontaneity because the animal depends on purely material conditions. All the organism needs is that the supplies of substance and energy constantly employed in the vital process should be periodically renewed by equivalent quantities; that replacement be equivalent to use. When the void created by existence in its own resources is filled, the animal, satisfied, asks nothing further. Its power of reflection is not sufficiently developed to imagine other ends than those implicit in its physical nature. On the other hand, as the work demanded of each organ itself depends on the general state of vital energy and the needs of organic equilibrium, use is regulated in turn by replacement and the balance is automatic. The limits of one are those of the other; both are fundamental to the constitution of the existence in question, which cannot exceed them.

This is not the case with man, because most of his needs are not dependent on his body or not to the same degree. Strictly speaking, we may consider that the quantity of material supplies necessary to the physical maintenance of a human life is subject to computation, though this be less exact than in the preceding case and a wider margin left for the free combinations of the will; for beyond the indispensable minimum which satisfies nature when instinctive, a more awakened reflection suggests better conditions, seemingly desirable ends craving fulfillment. Such appetites, however, admittedly sooner or later reach a limit which they cannot pass. But how determine the quantity of well-being, comfort or luxury legitimately to be craved by a human being? Nothing appears in man's organic nor in his psychological constitution which sets a limit to such tendencies. The functioning of individual life does not require them to cease at one point rather than at another; the proof being that they have constantly increased since the beginnings of history, receiving more and more complete satisfaction, yet with no weakening of average health. Above all, how establish their proper variation with different conditions of life, occupations, relative importance of services, etc.? In no society are they equally satisfied in the different stages of the social hierarchy. Yet human nature is substantially the same among all men, in its essential qualities. It is not human nature which can assign the variable limits necessary to our needs. They are thus unlimited so far as they depend on the individual alone. Irrespective of any external regulatory force, our capacity for feeling is in itself an insatiable and bottomless abyss.

But if nothing external can restrain this capacity, it can only be a source of torment to itself. Unlimited desires are insatiable by definition and insatiability is rightly considered a sign of morbidity. Being unlimited, they constantly and infinitely surpass the means at their command; they cannot be quenched. Inextinguishable thirst is constantly renewed torture. It has been claimed, indeed, that human activity naturally aspires beyond assignable limits and sets itself unattainable goals. But how can such an undetermined state be any more reconciled with the conditions of mental life than with the demands of physical life? All man's pleasure in acting, moving and exerting himself implies the sense that his efforts are not in vain and that by walking he has advanced. However, one does not advance when one walks toward no goal, or—which is the same thing—when his goal is infinity. Since the distance between us and it is always the same, whatever road we take, we might as well have made the motions without progress from the spot. Even our glances behind and our feeling of pride at the distance covered can cause only deceptive satisfaction, since the remaining distance is not proportionately reduced. To pursue a goal which is by definition unattainable is to condemn oneself to a state of perpetual unhappiness. Of course, man may hope contrary to all reason, and hope has its pleasures even when unreasonable. It may sustain him for a time; but it cannot survive the repeated disappointments of experience indefinitely. What more can the future offer him than the past, since he can never reach a tenable condition nor even approach the glimpsed ideal? Thus, the more one has, the more one wants, since satisfactions received only stimulate instead of filling needs. Shall action as such be considered agreeable? First, only on condition of blindness to its uselessness. Secondly, for this pleasure to be felt and to temper and half veil the accompanying painful unrest, such unending motion must at least always be easy and unhampered. If it is interfered with only restlessness is left, with the lack of ease which it, itself, entails. But it would be a miracle if no insurmountable obstacle were ever encountered. Our thread of life on these conditions is pretty thin, breakable at any instant.

To achieve any other result, the passions first must be limited. Only then can they be harmonized with the faculties and satisfied. But since the individual has no way of limiting them, this must be done by some force exterior to him. A regulative force must play the same role for moral needs which the organism plays for physical needs. This means that the force can only be moral. The awakening of conscience interrupted the state of equilibrium of the animal's dormant existence; only conscience, therefore, can furnish the means to re-establish it. Physical restraint would be ineffective; hearts cannot be touched by physio-chemical forces. So far as the appetites are not automatically restrained by physiological mechanisms, they can be halted only by a limit that they recognize as just. Men would never consent to restrict their desires if they felt justified in passing the assigned limit. But, for reasons given above, they cannot assign themselves this law of justice. So they must receive it from an authority which they respect, to which they yield spontaneously. Either directly and as a whole, or through the agency of one of its organs, society alone can play this moderating role; for it is the only moral power superior to the individual, the authority of which he accepts. It alone has the power necessary to stipulate law and to set the point beyond which the passions must not go. Finally, it alone can estimate the reward to be prospectively offered to every class of human functionary, in the name of the common interest.

As a matter of fact, at every moment of history there is a dim perception, in the moral consciousness of societies, of the respective value of different social services, the relative reward due to each, and the consequent degree of comfort appropriate on the average to workers in each occupation. The different functions are graded in public opinion and a certain coefficient of well-being assigned to each, according to its place in the hierarchy. According to accepted ideas, for example, a certain way of living is considered the upper limit to which a workman may aspire in his efforts to improve his existence, and there is another limit below which he is not willingly permitted to fall unless he has seriously bemeaned himself. Both differ for city and country workers, for the domestic servant and the day-laborer, for the business clerk and the official, etc. Likewise the man of wealth is reproved if he lives the life of a poor man, but also if he seeks the refinements of luxury overmuch. Economists may protest in vain; public feeling will always be scandalized if an individual spends too much wealth for wholly superfluous use, and it even seems that this severity relaxes only in times of moral disturbance.[1] A genuine regimen exists, therefore, although not always legally formulated, which fixes with relative precision the maximum degree of ease of living to which each social class may legitimately aspire. However, there is nothing immutable about such a scale. It changes with the increase or decrease of collective revenue and the changes occurring in the moral ideas of society. Thus what appears luxury to one period no longer does so to another; and the well-being which for long periods was granted to a class only by exception and supererogation, finally appears strictly necessary and equitable.

Under this pressure, each in his sphere vaguely realizes the extreme limit set to his ambitions and aspires to nothing beyond. At least if he respects regulations and is docile to collective authority, that is, has a wholesome moral constitution, he feels that it is not well to ask more. Thus, an end and goal are set to the passions. Truly, there is nothing rigid nor absolute about such determination. The economic ideal assigned each class of citizens is itself confined to certain limits, within which the desires have free range. But it is not infinite. This relative limitation and the moderation it involves, make men contented with their lot while stimulating them moderately to improve it; and this average contentment causes the feeling of calm, active happiness, the pleasure in existing and living which characterizes health for societies as well as for individuals. Each person is then at least, generally speaking, in harmony with his condition, and desires only what he may legitimately hope for as the normal reward of his activity. Besides, this does not condemn man to a sort of immobility. He may seek to give beauty to his life; but his attempts in this direction may fail without causing him to despair. For, loving what he has and not fixing his desire solely on what he lacks, his wishes and hopes may fail of what he has happened to aspire to, without his being wholly destitute. He has the essentials. The equilibrium of his happiness is secure because it is defined, and a few mishaps cannot disconcert him.

But it would be of little use for everyone to recognize the justice of the hierarchy of functions established by public opinion, if he did not also consider

[1] Actually, this is a purely moral reprobation and can hardly be judicially implemented. We do not consider any reestablishment of sumptuary laws desirable or even possible.

the distribution of these functions just. The workman is not in harmony with his social position if he is not convinced that he has his deserts. If he feels justified in occupying another, what he has would not satisfy him. So it is not enough for the average level of needs for each social condition to be regulated by public opinion, but another, more precise rule, must fix the way in which these conditions are open to individuals. There is no society in which such regulation does not exist. It varies with times and places. Once it regarded birth as the almost exclusive principle of social classification; today it recognizes no other inherent inequality than hereditary fortune and merit. But in all these various forms its object is unchanged. It is also only possible, everywhere, as a restriction upon individuals imposed by superior authority, that is, by collective authority. For it can be established only by requiring of one or another group of men, usually of all, sacrifices and concessions in the name of the public interest.

Some, to be sure, have thought that this moral pressure would become unnecessary if men's economic circumstances were only no longer determined by heredity. If inheritance were abolished, the argument runs, if everyone began life with equal resources and if the competitive struggle were fought out on a basis of perfect equality, no one could think its results unjust. Each would instinctively feel that things are as they should be.

Truly, the nearer this ideal equality were approached, the less social restraint will be necessary. But it is only a matter of degree. One sort of heredity will always exist, that of natural talent. Intelligence, taste, scientific, artistic, literary or industrial ability, courage and manual dexterity are gifts received by each of us at birth, as the heir to wealth receives his capital or as the nobleman formerly received his title and function. A moral discipline will therefore still be required to make those less favored by nature accept the lesser advantages which they owe to the chance of birth. Shall it be demanded that all have an equal share and that no advantage be given those more useful and deserving? But then there would have to be a discipline far stronger to make these accept a treatment merely equal to that of the mediocre and incapable.

But like the one first mentioned, this discipline can be useful only if considered just by the peoples subject to it. When it is maintained only by custom and force, peace and harmony are illusory; the spirit of unrest and discontent are latent; appetites superficially restrained are ready to revolt. This happened in Rome and Greece when the faiths underlying the old organization of the patricians and plebeians were shaken, and in our modern societies when aristocratic prejudices began to lose their old ascendancy. But this state of upheaval is exceptional; it occurs only when society is passing through some abnormal crisis. In normal conditions the collective order is regarded as just by the great majority of persons. Therefore, when we say that an authority is necessary to impose this order on individuals, we certainly do not mean that violence is the only means of establishing it. Since this regulation is meant to restrain individual passions, it must come from a power which dominates individuals; but this power must also be obeyed through respect, not fear.

It is not true, then, that human activity can be released from all restraint.

Nothing in the world can enjoy such a privilege. All existence being a part of the universe is relative to the remainder; its nature and method of manifestation accordingly depend not only on itself but on other beings, who consequently restrain and regulate it. Here there are only differences of degree and form between the mineral realm and the thinking person. Man's characteristic privilege is that the bond he accepts is not physical but moral; that is, social. He is governed not by a material environment brutally imposed on him, but by a conscience superior to his own, the superiority of which he feels. Because the greater, better part of his existence transcends the body, he escapes the body's yoke, but is subject to that of society.

But when society is disturbed by some painful crisis or by beneficent but abrupt transitions, it is momentarily incapable of exercising this influence; thence come the sudden rises in the curve of suicides. . . .

In the case of economic disasters, indeed, something like a declassification occurs which suddenly casts certain individuals into a lower state than their previous one. Then they must reduce their requirements, restrain their needs, learn greater self-control. All the advantages of social influence are lost so far as they are concerned; their moral education has to be recommenced. But society cannot adjust them instantaneously to this new life and teach them to practice the increased self-repression to which they are unaccustomed. So they are not adjusted to the condition forced on them, and its very prospect is intolerable; hence the suffering which detaches them from a reduced existence even before they have made trial of it.

It is the same if the source of the crisis is an abrupt growth of power and wealth. Then, truly, as the conditions of life are changed, the standard according to which needs were regulated can no longer remain the same; for it varies with social resources, since it largely determines the share of each class of producers. The scale is upset; but a new scale cannot be immediately improvised. Time is required for the public conscience to reclassify men and things. So long as the social forces thus freed have not regained equilibrium, their respective values are unknown and so all regulation is lacking for a time. The limits are unknown between the possible and the impossible, what is just and what is unjust, legitimate claims and hopes and those which are immoderate. Consequently, there is no restraint upon aspirations. If the disturbance is profound, it affects even the principles controlling the distribution of men among various occupations. Since the relations between various parts of society are necessarily modified, the ideas expressing these relations must change. Some particular class especially favored by the crisis is no longer resigned to its former lot, and, on the other hand, the example of its greater good fortune arouses all sorts of jealousy below and about it. Appetites, not being controlled by a public opinion become disoriented, no longer recognize the limits proper to them. Besides, they are at the same time seized by a sort of natural erethism simply by the greater intensity of public life. With increased prosperity desires increase. At the very moment when traditional rules have lost their authority, the richer prize offered these appetites stimulates them and makes them more exigent and impatient of control. The state of de-regulation or anomy is thus further heightened by passions being less disciplined, precisely when they need more disciplining.

But then their very demands make fulfillment impossible. Overweening ambition always exceeds the results obtained, great as they may be, since there is no warning to pause here. Nothing gives satisfaction and all this agitation is uninterruptedly maintained without appeasement. Above all, since this race for an unattainable goal can give no other pleasure but that of the race itself, if it is one, once it is interrupted the participants are left empty-handed. At the same time the struggle grows more violent and painful, both from being less controlled and because competition is greater. All classes contend among themselves because no established classification any longer exists. Effort grows, just when it becomes less productive. How could the desire to live not be weakened under such conditions?

This explanation is confirmed by the remarkable immunity of poor countries. Poverty protects against suicide because it is a restraint in itself. No matter how one acts, desires have to depend upon resources to some extent; actual possessions are partly the criterion of those aspired to. So the less one has the less he is tempted to extend the range of his needs indefinitely. Lack of power, compelling moderation, accustoms men to it, while nothing excites envy if no one has superfluity. Wealth, on the other hand, by the power it bestows, deceives us into believing that we depend on ourselves only. Reducing the resistance we encounter from objects, it suggests the possibility of unlimited success against them. The less limited one feels, the more intolerable all limitation appears. Not without reason, therefore, have so many religions dwelt on the advantages and moral value of poverty. It is actually the best school for teaching self-restraint. Forcing us to constant self-discipline, it prepares us to accept collective discipline with equanimity, while wealth, exalting the individual, may always arouse the spirit of rebellion which is the very source of immorality. This, of course, is no reason why humanity should not improve its material condition. But though the moral danger involved in every growth of prosperity is not irremediable, it should not be forgotten. . . .

For a whole century, economic progress has mainly consisted in freeing industrial relations from all regulation. Until very recently, it was the function of a whole system of moral forces to exert this discipline. First, the influence of religion was felt alike by workers and masters, the poor and the rich. It consoled the former and taught them contentment with their lot by informing them of the providential nature of the social order, that the share of each class was assigned by God himself, and by holding out the hope for just compensation in a world to come in return for the inequalities of this world. It governed the latter, recalling that worldly interests are not man's entire lot, that they must be subordinate to other and higher interests, and that they should therefore not be pursued without rule or measure. Temporal power, in turn, restrained the scope of economic functions by its supremacy over them and by the relatively subordinate role it assigned them. Finally, within the business world proper, the occupational groups by regulating salaries, the price of products and production itself, indirectly fixed the average level of income on which needs are partially based by the very force of circumstances. However, we do not mean to propose this organization as a model. Clearly it would be inadequate to existing societies without great changes. What we stress is its existence, the fact of its useful influence, and that nothing today has come to take its place.

Actually, religion has lost most of its power. And government, instead of regulating economic life, has become its tool and servant. The most opposite schools, orthodox economists and extreme socialists, unite to reduce government to the role of a more or less passive intermediary among the various social functions. The former wish to make it simply the guardian of individual contracts; the latter leave it the task of doing the collective bookkeeping, that is, of recording the demands of consumers, transmitting them to producers, inventorying the total revenue and distributing it according to a fixed formula. But both refuse it any power to subordinate other social organs to itself and to make them converge toward one dominant aim. On both sides nations are declared to have the single or chief purpose of achieving industrial prosperity; such is the implication of the dogma of economic materialism, the basis of both apparently opposed systems. And as these theories merely express the state of opinion, industry, instead of being still regarded as a means to an end transcending itself, has become the supreme end of ir. dividuals and societies alike. Thereupon the appetites thus excited have become freed of any limiting authority. By sanctifying them, so to speak, this apotheosis of well-being has placed them above all human law. Their restraint seems like a sort of sacrilege. For this reason, even the purely utilitarian regulation of them exercised by the industrial world itself through the medium of occupational groups has been unable to persist. Ultimately, this liberation of desires has been made worse by the very development of industry and the almost infinite extension of the market. So long as the producer could gain his profits only in his immediate neighborhood, the restricted amount of possible gain could not much overexcite ambition. Now that he may assume to have almost the entire world as his customer, how could passions accept their former confinement in the face of such limitless prospects?

Such is the source of the excitement predominating in this part of society, and which has thence extended to the other parts. There, the state of crisis and anomy is constant and, so to speak, normal. From top to bottom of the ladder, greed is aroused without knowing where to find ultimate foothold. Nothing can calm it, since its goal is far beyond all it can attain. Reality seems valueless by comparison with the dreams of fevered imaginations; reality is therefore abandoned, but so too is possibility abandoned when it in turn becomes reality. A thirst arises for novelties, unfamiliar pleasures, nameless sensations, all of which lose their savor once known. Henceforth one has no strength to endure the least reverse. The whole fever subsides and the sterility of all the tumult is apparent, and it is seen that all these new sensations in their infinite quantity cannot form a solid foundation of happiness to support one during days of trial. The wise man, knowing how to enjoy achieved results without having constantly to replace them with others, finds in them an attachment to life in the hour of difficulty. But the man who has always pinned all his hopes on the future and lived with his eyes fixed upon it, has nothing in the past as a comfort against the present's afflictions, for the past was nothing to him but a series of hastily experienced stages. What blinded him to himself was his expectation always to find further on the happiness he had so far missed. Now he is stopped in his tracks; from now on nothing remains behind or ahead of him to fix his gaze upon. Weariness alone, moreover, is enough to bring disillusionment, for he cannot in the end escape the futility of an endless pursuit. . . .

39. The End of Utopia*

HERBERT MARCUSE

Today any form of the concrete world, of human life, any transformation of the technical and natural environment is a possibility, and the locus of this possibility is historical. Today we have the capacity to turn the world into hell, and we are well on the way to doing so. We also have the capacity to turn it into the opposite of hell. This would mean the end of utopia, that is, the refutation of those ideas and theories that use the concept of utopia to denounce certain socio-historical possibilities. It can also be understood as the "end of history" in the very precise sense that the new possibilities for a human society and its environment can no longer be thought of as continuations of the old, nor even as existing in the same historical continuum with them. Rather, they presuppose a break with the historical continuum; they presuppose the qualitative difference between a free society and societies that are still unfree, which, according to Marx, makes all previous history only the prehistory of mankind.

But I believe that even Marx was still too tied to the notion of a continuum of progress, that even his idea of socialism may not yet represent, or no longer represent, the determinate negation of capitalism it was supposed to. That is, today the notion of the end of utopia implies the necessity of at least discussing a new definition of socialism. The discussion would be based on the question whether decisive elements of the Marxian concept of socialism do not belong to a now obsolete stage in the development of the forces of production. This obsolescence is expressed most clearly, in my opinion, in the distinction between the realm of freedom and the realm of necessity according to which the realm of freedom can be conceived of and can exist only beyond the realm of necessity.

*From Herbert Marcuse, *Five Lectures: Psychoanalysis, Politics, and Utopia* (Boston: Beacon Press, 1970), pp. 62–69. Translation from the German by Jeremy J. Shapiro and Shierry M. Weber. Reprinted by permission of the Beacon Press. Copyright © 1970 by Herbert Marcuse. [Note by the editors: The lecture presented here was delivered at the Free University in Berlin in July 1967.]

This division implies that the realm of necessity remains so in the sense of a realm of alienated labor, which means, as Marx says, that the only thing that can happen within it is for labor to be organized as rationally as possible and reduced as much as possible. But it remains labor in and of the realm of necessity and thereby unfree. I believe that one of the new possibilities, which gives an indication of the qualitative difference between the free and the unfree society, is that of letting the realm of freedom appear within the realm of necessity—in labor and not only beyond labor. To put this speculative idea in a provocative form, I would say that we must face the possibility that the path to socialism may proceed from science to utopia and not from utopia to science.

Utopia is a historical concept. It refers to projects for social change that are considered impossible. Impossible for what reasons? In the usual discussion of utopia the impossibility of realizing the project of a new society exists when the subjective and objective factors of a given social situation stand in the way of the transformation—the so-called immaturity of the social situation. Communistic projects during the French Revolution and, perhaps, socialism in the most highly developed capitalist countries are both examples of a real or alleged absence of the subjective and objective factors that seem to make realization impossible.

The project of a social transformation, however, can also be considered unfeasible because it contradicts certain scientifically established laws, biological laws, physical laws; for example, such projects as the age-old idea of eternal youth or the idea of a return to an alleged golden age. I believe that we can now speak of utopia only in this latter sense, namely when a project for social change contradicts real laws of nature. Only such a project is utopian in the strict sense, that is, beyond history—but even this "ahistoricity" has a historical limit.

The other group of projects, where the impossibility is due to the absence of subjective and objective factors, can at best be designated only as "provisionally" unfeasible. Karl Mannheim's criteria for the unfeasibility of such projects, for instance, are inadequate for the very simple reason, to begin with, that unfeasibility shows itself only after the fact. And it is not surprising that a project for social transformation is designated unfeasible because it has shown itself unrealized in history. Secondly, however, the criterion of unfeasibility in this sense is inadequate because it may very well be the case that the realization of a revolutionary project is hindered by counterforces and countertendencies that can be and are overcome precisely in the process of revolution. For this reason it is questionable to set up the absence of specific subjective and objective factors as an objection to the feasibility of radical transformation. Especially— and this is the question with which we are concerned here—the fact that no revolutionary class can be defined in the capitalist countries that are technically most highly developed does not mean that Marxism is utopian. The social agents of revolution—and this is orthodox Marx—are formed only in the process of the transformation itself, and one cannot count on a situation in which the revolutionary forces are there ready-made, so to speak, when the revolutionary movement begins. But in my opinion there is one valid criterion for possible realization, namely, when the material and intellectual forces for the transformation are technically at hand although their rational application is prevented by the existing organization of the forces of production. And in this sense, I believe, we can today actually speak of an end of utopia.

All the material and intellectual forces which could be put to work for the realization of a free society are at hand. That they are not used for that purpose is to be attributed to the total mobilization of existing society against its own potential for liberation. But this situation in no way makes the idea of radical transformation itself a utopia.

The abolition of poverty and misery is possible in the sense I have described, as are the abolition of alienated labor and the abolition of what I have called "surplus repression." Even in bourgeois economics there is scarcely a serious scientist or investigator who would deny that the abolition of hunger and of misery is possible with the productive forces that already exist technically and that what is happening today must be attributed to the global politics of a repressive society. But although we are in agreement on this we are still not sufficiently clear about the implication of this technical possibility for the abolition of poverty, of misery, and of labor. The implication is that these historical possibilities must be conceived in forms that signify a break rather than a continuity with previous history, its negation rather than its positive continuation, difference rather than progress. They signify the liberation of a dimension of human existence this side of the material basis, the transformation of needs.

What is at stake is the idea of a new theory of man, not only as theory but as a way of existence: the genesis and development of a vital need for freedom and of the vital needs of freedom—of a freedom no longer based on and limited by scarcity and the necessity of alienated labor. The development of qualitatively new human needs appears as a biological necessity; they are needs in a very biological sense. For among a great part of the manipulated population in the developed capitalist countries the need for freedom does not or no longer exists as a vital, necessary need. Along with these vital needs the new theory of man also implies the genesis of a new morality as the heir and the negation of the Judeo-Christian morality which up to now has characterized the history of Western civilization. It is precisely the continuity of the needs developed and satisfied in a repressive society that reproduces this repressive society over and over again within the individuals themselves. Individuals reproduce repressive society in their needs, which persist even through revolution, and it is precisely this continuity which up to now has stood in the way of the leap from quantity into the quality of a free society. This idea implies that human needs have a historical character. All human needs, including sexuality, lie beyond the animal world. They are historically determined and historically mutable. And the break with the continuity of those needs that already carry repression within them, the leap into qualitative difference, is not a mere invention but inheres in the development of the productive forces themselves. That development has reached a level where it actually demands new vital needs in order to do justice to its own potentialities.

What are the tendencies of the productive forces that make this leap from quantity into quality possible? Above all, the technification of domination undermines the foundation of domination. The progressive reduction of physical labor power in the production process (the process of material production) and its replacement to an increasing degree by mental labor concentrate socially necessary labor in the class of technicians, scientists, engineers, etc. This suggests possible liberation from alienated labor. It is of course a question only of tendencies, but of tendencies that are grounded in the development and the continuing existence of capitalist society. If capitalism does not succeed in exploiting these new possibilities of the productive forces and their organization, the productivity of labor will fall beneath the level required by the rate of profit. And if capitalism heeds this requirement and continues automation regardless, it will come up against its own inner limit: the sources of surplus value for the maintenance of exchange society will dwindle away.

In the *Grundrisse* Marx showed that complete automation of socially necessary labor is incompatible with the preservation of capitalism. Automation is only a catchword for this tendency, through which necessary physical labor, alienated labor, is withdrawn to an ever greater extent from the material process of production. This tendency, if freed from the fetters of capitalist production, would lead to a creative experimentation with the productive forces. With the abolition of poverty this tendency would mean that play with the potentialities of human and nonhuman nature would become the content of social labor. The productive imagination would become the concretely structured productive force that freely sketches out the possibilities for a free human existence on the basis of the corresponding development of material productive forces. In order for these technical possibilities not to become possibilities for repression, however, in order for them to be able to fulfill their liberating function, they must be sustained and directed by liberating and gratifying needs.

When no vital need to abolish (alienated) labor exists, when on the contrary there exists a need to continue and extend labor, even when it is no longer socially necessary; when the vital need for joy, for happiness with a good conscience, does not exist, but rather the need to have to earn everything in a life that is as miserable as can be; when these vital needs do not exist or are suffocated by repressive ones, it is only to be expected that new technical possibilities actually become new possibilities for repression by domination.

We already know what cybernetics and computers can contribute to the total control of human existence. The new needs, which are really the determinate negation of existing needs, first make their appearance as the negation of the needs that sustain the present system of domination and the negation of the values on which they are based: for example, the negation of the need for the struggle for existence (the latter is supposedly necessary and all the ideas or fantasies that speak of the possible abolition of the struggle for existence thereby contradict the supposedly natural and social conditions of human existence); the negation of the need to earn one's living; the negation of the performance principle, of competition; the negation of the need for wasteful, ruinous productivity, which is inseparably bound up with destruction; and the negation of the vital need for deceitful repression of the instincts. These needs would be negated in the vital biological need for peace, which today is not a vital need of the majority, the need for calm, the need to be alone, with oneself or with others whom one has chosen oneself, the need for the beautiful, the need for "undeserved" happiness—all this not simply in the form of individual needs but as a social productive force, as social needs that can be activated through the direction and disposition of productive forces.

In the form of a social productive force, these new vital needs would make possible a total technical reorganization of the concrete world of human life, and I believe that new human relations, new relations between men, would be possible only in such a reorganized world. When I say technical reorganization I again speak with reference to the capitalist countries that are most highly developed, where such a restructuring would mean the abolition of the terrors of capitalist industrialization and commercialization, the total reconstruction of the cities and the restoration of nature after the horrors of capitalist industrialization have been done away with. I hope that when I speak of doing away with the horrors of capitalist industrialization it is clear I am not advocating a romantic regression behind technology. On the contrary, I believe that the potential liberating blessings of technology and industrialization will not even begin to be real and visible until capitalist industrialization and capitalist technology have been done away with.

The qualities of freedom that I have mentioned here are qualities which until now have not received adequate attention in recent thinking about socialism. Even on the left the notion of socialism has been taken too much within the framework of the development of productive forces, of increasing the productivity of labor, something which was not only justified but necessary at the level of productivity at which the idea of scientific socialism was developed but which today is at least subject to discussion. Today we must try to discuss and define—without any inhibitions, even when it may seem ridiculous—the qualitative difference between socialist society as a free society and the existing society. And it is precisely here that, if we are looking for a concept that can perhaps indicate the qualitative difference in socialist society, the aesthetic-erotic dimension comes to mind almost spontaneously, at least to me. Here the notion "aesthetic" is taken in its original sense, namely as the form of sensitivity of the senses and as the form of the concrete world of human life. Taken in this way, the notion projects the convergence of technology and art and the convergence of work and play. It is no accident that the work of Fourier is becoming topical again among the avant-garde left-wing intelligentsia. As Marx and Engels themselves acknowledged, Fourier was the only one to have made clear this qualitative difference between free and unfree society. And he did not shrink back in fear, as Marx still did, from speaking of a possible society in which work becomes play, a society in which even socially necessary labor can be organized in harmony with the liberated, genuine needs of men.

Let me make one further observation in conclusion. I have already indicated that if critical theory, which remains indebted to Marx, does not wish to stop at merely improving the existing state of affairs, it must accommodate within itself the extreme possibilities for freedom that have been only crudely indicated here, the scandal of the qualitative difference. Marxism must risk defining freedom in such a way that people become conscious of and recognize it as something that is nowhere already in existence. And precisely because the so-called utopian possibilities are not at all utopian but rather the determinate socio-historical negation of what exists, a very real and very pragmatic opposition is required of us if we are to make ourselves and others conscious of these possibilities and the forces that hinder and deny them. An opposition is required that is free of all illusion but also of all defeatism, for through its mere existence defeatism betrays the possibility of freedom to the status quo.

40. Unreason and Revolution*

RICHARD LOWENTHAL

This is a tentative exploration of what I believe to be a major phenomenon of our time—the rise of a new type of revolutionary movement. Hitherto, we have been familiar with two broad classes of revolutions and revolutionary movements. First, there are the movements which may be understood as resulting when the normal growth, the spontaneous evolution of a society, meets an obstacle in the form of rigid political institutions that are increasingly felt as oppressive. In such cases, sooner or later an acute political crisis occurs in which the obstacle is swept away by revolutionary action. That is, broadly speaking, the formula fitting the great democratic revolutions of modern Western history; it may also be applied to a number of the national movements for independence from colonial rule that have occurred in our time.

In the last fifty years we have learnt, to our cost, to distinguish a second type of revolution and revolutionary movements—those which I, for want of a better name, would still describe as "totalitarian revolutions." It seems to be characteristic of them that they do not occur because of the clash between a growing, dynamic society and a static political framework tending to shackle its growth, but because of some elements of stagnation, some major lopsidedness of development *within* the society itself, leading to a deadlock which a dynamic state is then called upon to resolve by the massive use of political force. This appeal from a deadlock in society to the "saviour state" has been the background to the rise of German National Socialism as a mass movement and to the long-lasting reign of violence which its victorious régime inflicted on the prostrate body of

*From "Unreason and Revolution: On the Dissociation of Practice from Theory," *Encounter*, vol. 33, no. 5 (November 1969), pp. 22-34. Article and footnotes abridged by the editors. Reprinted by permission of the author and the journal.

society. But the overcoming of social stagnation in the midst of change and of lopsided development has also been underlying the rise of Communist régimes in a number of underdeveloped countries—the only ones that have come to power by the victory of indigenous revolutionary movements—and has given them the opportunity for their repeated, forcible transformations of the social structure.

Now it seems to me that in recent years, we have begun to be confronted by yet another kind of revolutionary movement. These new movements, both within our Western world and in the so-called underdeveloped countries, have much of the familiar language of Communist ideology, and actually have taken over much of the substance of the Marxist-Leninist critique of Western capitalism and imperialism as well as the Marxist Utopia of a society without classes or domination. Nevertheless they are radically different from the Communist movements that had been created in the image of Lenin's Bolshevik party—different in their forms of organisation, their strategies of political action, and indeed in the rank order of values that gives operative meaning to their vision of the goal. In fact, one of the preconditions for the rise of these new movements has been the increasingly obvious disintegration of the "Marxist-Leninist" doctrinal synthesis; they grow out of an ideological soil that has been fertilised by its decomposition. But some of the products of the decay appear to be as virulently destructive as any Leninist movements have been in the past—without, so far, offering any tangible prospect of comparable constructive achievements.

A preliminary survey of these new movements may perhaps best start by marking them off with two negative statements. On one side, they are not the democratic expressions of stable, productive sectors of the societies in which they arise; in other words, they do not originate in class movements, as interest groups or coalitions of interest groups. On the other hand, they are not disciplined parties of the Communist type organised from the top downward as instruments of a single will, with a systematic strategic concept of what they want and how to get there given in advance. On the contrary, it is typical for them that action often precedes thought. Despite the verbal echoes of the Marxist pathos of rationality that may still be heard from the ideological spokesmen of the Western "New Left," in practice the urge for violent action increasingly outruns consideration of any precise short-term objectives and of the rational tactical and organisational means for achieving them. It is the style of action and the utopian goal that define the movement, while all other ideas and organisational forms remain very much in flux. The goal itself, though it remains a powerful motivating force, never takes the form of a political programme with precise institutional content. That, on the contrary, is increasingly rejected: the tendency is to say that the new institutions, if any, will have to emerge from the process of struggle and from the destruction of the old order.

While the "New Left" in the West thus replaces Communist programmes, strategies and organisational forms by a faith in Utopia and a cult of violent action, a number of revolutionary movements in the underdeveloped world show a parallel trend—away from the elaborations of Communist doctrine and the organisational discipline based on ideological authority, and towards the primacy of violent action over social analysis and of military over political and ideological leadership. We may observe this tendency in the practice first of Castro's Cuban revolution and then of the guerrilla actions started in other Latin-American countries under the influence of the Cuban model; and we find its ideological justification sketched out by Che Guevara and elaborated by Régis Debray. A parallel, if delayed, breakthrough of immediate utopianism and immediate violence seems to have occurred in the transformation of Chinese Communism in the course of the last decade, beginning with the "Great Leap Forward" and the creation of the People's Communes and culminating in the recent "Cultural Revolution." Finally, analogous processes seem to be at work in some of those revolutionary nationalist movements which, without ever having become formally Communist, are developing as passionately an anti-Western, anti-modernistic, and anti-rational outlook as the last-named products of the disintegration of world Communism.

This, then, is our theme. Why do those phenomena arise in various parts of the world at this time? What are the intellectual roots of their beliefs and the social roots of their strength? And what are their significance and possible prospects?

FROM MARX TO LENIN AND MAO

Let us begin with a subject we know fairly well—the role of Marxism and Leninism in the development of revolutionary ideas. If we cast our minds back to the 1840s when Marxism was born, and if we recall Engels' proud phrase about the development of socialism from a Utopia into a science, it is evident to us today that the real difference between Marx and many of his socialist precursors was not that Karl Marx was no utopian: his goals were just as utopian, just as rooted in a profound need to discover a road to salvation on earth, as theirs had been. The difference was that Marx turned his back on *romantic* and *immediate* utopianism in favour of a historical and forward-looking version. The birth of utopian socialism in the early 19th century had been part of the romantic revolt of the new-born European intelligentsia against the beginning of industrialisation and the transformation of human relations by an increasingly specialised division of labour and an increasingly pervasive cash nexus. The new turn which Marx gave to those ideas was that he rejected the romantic element in them, the resistance to modernisation based on an idealisation of the past, and proclaimed instead that, thanks to the logic of history, Utopia would be achieved by ruthlessly carrying through the painful process of industrialisation to the end. To quote Raymond Aron, Marx put forward the thesis that the only way to achieve the goals of Rousseau was to follow the precepts of St.-Simon.

This was a highly original idea at the time, one might even say a rather absurd idea. But it also proved an extremely powerful idea: for it enabled Marx to forge a link between the belief in Utopia and the belief in the logic of History. As a result, he was able to inspire a movement that combined the religious fervour of utopianism with a historical and rational element. Utopia, and the violent revolution that was to precede it, were not to be achieved by mere enthusiasm and an act of will. They depended on well-defined economic and social conditions; but the laws of history guaranteed that these conditions would be achieved in the fullness of time. Moreover, one effect of this analysis was to inspire the followers of Marx with a conviction of the vital importance of material progress; for together with the growth of the organisation and consciousness of the working class, the rise of productivity was the most important of the conditions that must mature before mankind could enter the realm of freedom. Increasing productivity would eventually lead to abundance, and only abundance would permit the creation of a social order without classes or domination. Thus the utopian goal and the violent overthrow of the old order were not the objectives of immediate action: their possibility was mediated by the laws of the historical process, by Reason as manifested in History—their achievement by a rational strategy based on the insight into that process.

In a sense, the disintegration of this rationalist and historic concept of the road to Revolution and Utopia may be said to have started with Lenin—as well as with the early "revisionists" at the opposite pole. For while the latter sought to retain the evolutionary optimism of Marx yet to eliminate the revolutionary and utopian perspective, Lenin was the first pupil of Marx deliberately to separate the task of "organising the revolution" from some of its economic and social preconditions as formulated by the teacher. He argued, under the impact of World War I, that it was the duty of the socialist party to seize power in backward Russia without waiting for the maturing of the economic conditions for a socialist society. He had even earlier "emancipated" this party from dependence on the actual support of the working class by giving it a highly centralistic, instrumental structure. Implicitly, Lenin had thus attempted to replace the missing "objective" preconditions of socialism by the creation of his new vanguard party as an instrument for the seizure of power and for the subsequent transformation of the immature society, and to that extent had begun to turn Marxism upside down. But even while doing so, Lenin still clung to the Marxist analysis in believing that *some* objective conditions were needed for the victory of the revolution—not indeed the condition of economic abundance, of objective maturity for socialism, but certainly the condition of a profound and acute crisis of capitalist society, and of a mass mood of bitter discontent enabling the revolutionary party to gain a mass following. Only once the crisis had reached that stage, he taught to the end, only once the revolutionary party had won a strategically decisive following among the masses—only then could the violent seizure of power take place. As a result, the role of the party never consisted for Lenin *primarily* in the organisation of violence. Violence might play a crucial part in its action at the critical moment, but the primary task of the party was to win over the masses *before* that moment by a policy based on a correct analysis of the crisis of society.

Some of the strategic changes introduced by Mao Tse-tung in transferring revolutionary Marxism to Asian soil and deliberately "adapting" it to Asian conditions may still be interpreted as mere developments along the road shown by Lenin. Striving to conquer power in a country where economic and social conditions were incomparably more backward—and correspondingly more remote from "objective" maturity for socialism in the Marxist sense—than in the Russia of 1917, Mao became the first pupil of Lenin to make use of the structural flexibility of the centralised vanguard party by seeking the necessary mass support among the peasants rather than the urban working class, and that for many years. He thus completed the effective emancipation of a "Marxist" party from working-class support that had been implied as a potentiality in Lenin's separation of the seizure of power from conditions of economic maturity and of the party organisation from working-class democracy. Moreover, Mao recognised at an early stage that the role of armed force in the struggle for power was likely to be far more continuous and decisive in China than it had been in Russia—that here, power would "grow out of the barrel of a gun." But this greatly expanded role of violence in Mao's revolutionary strategy was still tied to objective political and social conditions in two important ways.

1. In the first place, it was in Mao's own view only made possible by the special conditions of a semi-colonial country, in which neither a single native government nor a single colonial power enjoyed an effective monopoly of armed force. That, at least, was Mao's view at the time of his own struggle for power, though after his victory he came to persuade himself that similar "protracted war" strategies would prove appropriate for *all* the colonial and underdeveloped countries of the world.

2. In the second place, Mao never ceased to insist that the success of the strategy of armed struggle depended not only on developing the correct military tactics for guerrilla warfare, but on winning and retaining the support of the peasant population in the regions concerned by correct policies and effective forms of political and economic organisation. Only a policy based on a realistic analysis of the conditions and needs of the people in the area, and a type of organisation that maintained communication with them, could enable the guerrillas "to live among the population like a fish in water," preventing their isolation by the militarily superior enemy and assuring them of intelligence, of supplies and of a reservoir for new recruitment. This insistence on maintaining mass support by policies based on a study of the concrete social situation constitutes the indispensable corollary to the Maoist emphasis on armed struggle and its link with the Marxist-Leninist tradition: it is the foundation for Mao's dictum that while power grows out of the barrel of a gun, the party must command the gun. For, though the party no longer represents (as with Marx) the actual evolving consciousness of a working-class increasingly aware of its true historical interests, it still represents (as with Lenin) the leaders' "scientific," analytical consciousness of the total social situation, its contradictions and tendencies, and hence of the objective possibilities for action which any successful political strategy must take into account. To that extent, Mao's concept of

the leading role of the party preserves, like Lenin's concept, the Marxian idea of a rational strategy based on perception of the rational laws of history.

Yet there is in Mao's emphasis on the decisive role of armed struggle also the germ of a different, more basically "voluntaristic" approach to social reality. This is to be found in his view that the use of violent action by itself may be one of the most effective means for changing the relation of forces between revolution and reaction, because the right technique of armed struggle may enable an initially much inferior, revolutionary force to whittle down step by step the initial superiority of its enemy—to tire him out by exhaustion, cause splits in his ranks, and finally wear down his will to fight. In a sense, the art of ensuring the survival and regeneration of inferior forces resisting a stronger and better-armed enemy is, of course, the essence of *all* guerrilla tactics, and the hope that this will enable the guerrillas to outlast the enemy's determination has always been their rationale. But the fulfillment of that hope depends clearly not on the dedication and skill of the guerrillas alone, but on a number of independent factors—such as the enemy's fighting commitments outside the theatre of guerrilla warfare, the importance of that theatre in relation to his general policy objectives, and the cohesion of his political system as reflected in the support for the anti-guerrilla campaign and the loyalty of his troops.

In the Chinese case, the evidence does not show that the Communists were effectively wearing down the Kuomintang régime (or even substantially increasing its divisions) before the attack of Japan, nor that they had any chance to defeat Japanese occupants (who regarded control of China as vital to their purposes), until their will to fight was broken by defeat on other fronts. Similarly, nobody has ever suggested that the Yugoslav Communists could have evicted the armies of Hitler Germany independent of the outcome of World War II. Conversely, guerrilla "wars of liberation" in Viet Nam and Algeria could achieve political victory by military means because neither area was truly vital for the French republic; and Mao's own final civil war defeated a nationalist régime whose political and moral cohesion had been gravely undermined by the disastrous effects of the long-lasting Japanese invasion.

Mao's original doctrine of protracted warfare, so far from neglecting the crucial importance of these "objective conditions," took them into account by laying down what conditions must be fulfilled for passing from guerrilla tactics proper to the stage of decisive battles, and thus implying that these conditions cannot be created at will but must be patiently waited for. (There have been echoes of that realistic approach even in fairly recent Chinese advice to the Vietnamese Communists.) Yet, on the other hand, the attempts of the victorious Chinese Communists to recommend the Maoist strategy of armed struggle as a model for colonial revolutions in general (which became prevalent since about 1959, in the context of their ideological rivalry with the Soviet Communists), have increasingly treated the revolutionary faith and tactical military skill of the guerrillas as universal and sufficient prescriptions for victory in "wars of liberation" that would achieve their magic effects *independent* of the objective conditions in any particular case.

CASTRO, GUEVARA, DEBRAY

This growing tendency to separate the use of armed revolutionary force from any analysis of political and social conditions, implicit in the transformation of Maoist doctrine under the impact of the ideological rivalry with Russia for leadership of the revolutionary movements of the underdeveloped world, has become quite explicit with the leaders of the Cuban revolution and its would-be imitators in Latin America—with Fidel Castro, Che Guevara, and Régis Debray.

Long before Fidel Castro ever dreamt of calling himself a "Marxist-Leninist," and presumably before he read any serious Marxist literature, he acted on the assumption that armed minority action would by itself be sufficient to *create* a revolutionary situation. After this prescription had proved successful in Cuba, Guevara spelt out his new doctrine in so many words as early as 1960. Guevara, of course, did have a background of Marxist knowledge, and in 1960 he still made the validity of the new strategy dependent on one objective condition: the existence of a—presumably unpopular—dictatorial régime. Armed minority up-risings, he then suggested, would not be effective against a government which enjoyed some degree of democratic legitimacy. However, this qualification was dropped by the *Fidelistas* a few years later, when the democratic government of Venezuela became the main target of their effort to export the strategy—and to some extent the leading personnel—of guerrilla insurrection.[1] Since then it has become an official dogma of "Castroism" that a small but determined and well-led *foco* of professional guerrillas is in principle sufficient to shake the stability of *any* political system in Latin America, and thus to create eventually, by its own action alone, the conditions for the seizure of power.

The consequences of this separation of armed violence from any analysis of social and political preconditions, and hence from any rational political strategy, have been most fully developed in Régis Debray's book *Revolution in the Revolution.* The political significance of this statement of the new doctrine lies in the fact that it represents more than its author's individual opinion. It was written on the basis of long conversations with Castro and other Cuban leaders, who had made the diaries and other documents of their struggle for power accessible to the author, and it was published for mass circulation and used as training material by the ruling party in Cuba. Hence it must be regarded as an authorised summary of Castro's and Guevara's own views of the "Cuban model" for the conquest of power. Now Debray has become the first to state plainly that it is positively harmful for the chances of armed struggle if it arises from the defence of the interests of a particular productive group; for such a struggle by people who are tied to their place of production—like the miners in Bolivia

[1] In 1960, Guevara wrote: "Where a government has come to power by popular vote, of whatever kind, whether falsified or not, and preserves at least the appearance of constitu-tional legality, guerrilla warfare cannot be started because the possibilities of peaceful struggle have not yet been exhausted." *La guerra de guerrillas* (Havana, 1960), p. 13. But in September 1963 he wrote that *all* Latin-American régimes were oligarchic dictatorships, and that the struggle could be successfully intensified by forcing them to drop their legalistic mask. "Guerra de guerrillas: un método" in *Cuba socialista*, no. 25 (1963).

or the peasants of the most impoverished region of Columbia—tends to take the form of "armed self-defence" also in military tactics. People who lead normal working lives, however poor and oppressed, have something to lose—their working place, their houses with their families—which they want to defend; hence they are militarily too vulnerable and are bound to be defeated in the end by the government's regular forces. In order to have a chance of success, the revolutionary struggle must be conducted by perfectly rootless, and therefore perfectly mobile, professional guerrillas alone!

In the context of this complete dissociation of the "revolution" from any concrete social basis, it is only logical that Debray goes so far as to give his own, arbitrary new meaning to the familiar Marxist terms of "bourgeois" and "proletarian." According to him, only the uprooted guerrilla is the true "proletarian," because he has chosen a life of extreme deprivation and constant danger; he has nothing more to lose but his life, and is willing to sacrifice that. Conversely, the industrial worker in the towns of Latin America is in the eyes of Debray a "bourgeois," simply because he has a regular job and values it. Now any writer is, of course, free to choose and define his own terminology. But an ideologist who uses the terms of "bourgeois" and "proletarian" in this purely moralistic and emotional way, and defines his "proletarian" as a figure wholly divorced from the productive process, has evidently completely abandoned the method of social analysis which Karl Marx inaugurated by *his* use of those terms in the *Communist Manifesto.*

Finally, the cutting of all ties between the revolutionary movement and any defined social basis leads Debray with equal logic to a reversal of the relation between military and political leadership and to a new view of the role and formation of the revolutionary party. He argues that it is futile to concentrate first on creating a Marxist-Leninist party which would then organise a guerrilla movement in due course, because the party could only develop in the towns and its leaders might then be afraid to leave the towns. Instead, the only promising way in Latin-America will be to begin by recruiting a band of armed volunteers who will form a guerrilla focus. The volunteers may have little or no previous political experience; they should be attracted on no narrower basis than their willingness to risk their lives in fighting Yankee imperialism and its ruling native stooges. As their ideas become more clearly defined due to the experience of the common struggle, a party will eventually arise—usually only after victory— with the proven guerrilla leaders at its head. Thus military leadership precedes political leadership both in time and as a source of authority.

It is no longer the party that commands the gun—it is the gun that creates the party.

. . . .

REVOLUTION AGAINST HISTORY

The dissociation of revolutionary passion and action from the Marxist belief in the rationality of history is not confined to the particular examples I have analysed. On the contrary, it appears to be a universal process, in which movements and régimes that remain strongly influenced by a Marxist outlook are ceasing to be revolutionary, while those that remain revolutionary renounce essential parts of the Marxist analysis.

Thus we observe that the Communist party régime in the Soviet Union—as it comes increasingly to regard the development of its productive capacity as the only decisive factor for its advance towards the "higher stage" of communism and as its principal contribution to the victory of its cause on a world scale— is becoming less concerned with either forcibly imposing "revolutions from above" on its own people or actively fostering revolutionary movements elsewhere. It has retained the belief that the final, world-wide achievement of communism is guaranteed by the laws of History—but it interprets those laws in an increasingly revisionist spirit as working mainly through the logic of economic development, so that the eventual attainment of Utopia will not require further revolutionary action on its part. Even more explicitly, Communist parties in some advanced Western countries, particularly those with a strong following in a modern, industrial working class, are proposing revisionist strategies for the socialist transformation of their countries by peaceful, democratic methods, based on the expectation that the inherent trends of modern industrial societies will enable them to join the governments and carry out their programme with majority support, and preferably without violence.

Conversely, those "New Left" movements in the same countries, recruited chiefly from students and other adolescents divorced from production, that are preoccupied with the need for violent action and the revolutionary overthrow of the social order, have come increasingly to reject the Marxist belief in the rationality of history and the link between the progress of industrialisation, the growth of the working class, and the utopian goal. Instead, they are looking for support to the peoples of the underdeveloped "countryside of the world" whose revolutionary ardour has not yet been damped by material comfort, and for guidance to Mao and Castro who promise to solve the economic problems of their poor countries through an upsurge of collective effort called forth by an appeal to solidarity rather than to egoistic self-interest. Nor is their choice difficult to understand in view of the fact that the working class in the industrially advanced countries has become less and less revolutionary, and that the successful industrialisation of Russia has evidently not created a society without classes and domination, but a bureaucratic class society still ruled by a harsh party dictatorship after 50 years.

To return to the remark of Raymond Aron's that I quoted earlier, it has become obvious that the world has not come the least bit closer to the goals of Rousseau after following the precepts of St.-Simon for more than a century. Hence those who will not abandon utopianism have at long last decided to try and approach those goals directly. The intellectual importance of Herbert Marcuse for the development of the Western "New Left" is that he has classically formulated this disappointment of the Marxist Utopian who feels betrayed by the logic of History. The author of *Reason and Revolution* still put his trust in that Goddess; to the author of *One-Dimensional Man,* the Devil is the Prince of the Modern World. But once the assurance is gone that justice will triumph when the millennium comes in the fullness of time, the only alternative left to the believer is to try and bring it about by storming the heavens here and now. We are faced with a regression to a more primitive kind of secular religion—as different from that of Marx as was the faith of the Bohemian Taborites and the Muenster Anabaptists from the main stream of Western Christianity.

A ROMANTIC "LEFT"

As the term "regression" implies, the breakdown of the rationalist and historical constructs by which Marx had "mediated" the revolutionary struggle for Utopia, and the consequent return to immediate utopianism and immediate violence links the contemporary "New Left" to an earlier type of revolutionary tradition. It is a tradition which, in contrast to Marx, directly expressed the romantic resistance to the growth of mechanised industry and to the destruction of "natural" communities by the process of modernisation, and exalted the values of "life," community feeling, and spontaneous, violent action in opposition to "calculating" reason. There are, in fact, two distinct but frequently entangled strands of this romantic-revolutionary tradition, which we may provisionally designate by the names of two friends who were together involved in the Dresden insurrection of 1849: Michael Bakunin and Richard Wagner.

It is hardly accidental that Bakunin has lately been rediscovered by sections of the "New Left" in a number of countries. What seems to attract them is not just his anarchist vision, the goal of a stateless society of free associations of producers (which others have developed more fully both before and after him), but his passionate opposition to the bureaucratic rationality of the rising industrial age; his readiness to assign priority to the "creative passion for destruction" over any programme for what was to come afterwards; his hatred and contempt for liberalism, reform, and all representative institutions, not only in Russia but everywhere; his belief that a cumulation of uncoordinated, spontaneous acts of local violence could bring down both the Tsarist régime and the ruling economic and social system (alternating with fantasies of a super-centralistic, conspirative organisation which were never put into practice); and his tendency to rely on the uprooted peasant (the "bandit") as the true revolutionary, and on the backward regions on the Eastern and Southern periphery of Europe—on Russia, Spain, Southern Italy—for the ultimate revolutionary assault on the modern core that was already corrupted by capitalism and bureaucracy. Yet Bakunin's Pan-slavism, his hatred of Germans and Jews, and his abiding hostility to liberalism (which he did not disdain to use as arguments in the *"Confession"* he sent to the Tsar from prison in the hope of being reprieved) constitute a bond with other ideologies of anti-modern violence directed not to the goal of egalitarian anarchy, but to that of the dictatorship of an élite in the name of nationalism. Richard Wagner, who was to become one of the intellectual ancestors of Nazism, already dreamt—and spoke and wrote—of the destruction of the bankers' rule by a popular Emperor and of the replacement of Westernised, liberal pseudo-culture by a truly national German folk culture at the time of his youthful friendship with Bakunin. The kinship between the more violent and irrational forms of anarchism and fascist tendencies has since been repeatedly demonstrated in other countries and later generations.

Thus Georges Sorel, whose special contribution to the syndicalist movement has been to give it an irrationalist turn and to exalt the role of violence as the test of social vitality, came for a time to support the extreme Right-wing *Action Française* and influenced the élitism of Pareto and Mussolini. Again, if one asks to what historical model Fidel Castro's early intellectual background, his style of governing Cuba by harangues and his reliance on a mixture of nationalist and social appeals resembles most strikingly, the picture that comes to mind is not that of any victorious Communist leader, but of Gabriele d'Annunzio, his "Republic of Fiume," and his highly original witches' brew of nationalist passion, anarchist ideals, and plebiscitary techniques of government (though Castro, no doubt, has shown less poetical and more political ability than his illustrious predecessor). And d'Annunzio's movement, by its ideological prestige and its practical failure, helped to recruit many of the cadres for Italian Fascism.

Finally, the semi-anarchist violence of Benito Mussolini's anti-militarist agitation during the Libyan war of 1911, when he was at the height of his "New Left" period as editor of the Socialist party daily, fed on the same emotional and partly on the same ideological sources which enabled him in 1914–15 to break with the Socialist workers' movement as a violent advocate of a "revolutionary" war for nationalist objectives on the side of the Entente, and later to become the founder of Fascism and lead it to victory through terror. I might also mention as belonging to the same spiritual family those German ideologues of the 1920s—the period preceding the victory of National Socialism—who were then known as "National Bolsheviks" or *"Linke Leute von Rechts."* They sought to combine an anti-capitalist social radicalism (which in their case was much more genuine than with the Nazi party) with an anti-Western, but often explicitly pro-Russian nationalism and with a cult of heroic violence based on the memory of the "front-line experience"—of the true community of those who had been ready to die (and to kill) for the fatherland.

In short, those ardent believers in salvation on earth by political revolution who rejected the historical and rationalist "mediation" of their goal in favour of irrational passion and immediate violence have always tended to rely on romantic ideologies using varying mixtures of arguments of the Bakunist and the nationalist-fascist type. It is typical that in the later writings of Marcuse, his earlier Hegelian-Marxist rationalism is getting increasingly overlaid by the élitist anti-Western cultural pessimism of Martin Heidegger—his first teacher.

THE REVOLT AGAINST THE WEST

The revival of both strands of the romantic ideological tradition in the irrational revolt of the Western "New Left" indicates a revival of the basic emotional attitude underlying them both. The rebels reject the modern industrial world in both its Western-capitalist and Soviet-Communist forms—the crude materialism of its values, the pervasive bureaucratism of its organisation, the purely instrumental character of its rationality. Indeed, their despair is a reaction to the discovery that the process of "rationalisation" in the instrumental sense, which Max Weber recognised as a universal law of the modern world, does not assure the triumph of "Reason" in the sense of the achievement of Utopia. It is the same rejection of the industrial order that also constitutes the fundamental link between the Western "New Left" and some of the revolutionary movements of the poor nations. To the new romantics, Mao Tse-tung and Castro embody the promise of a spontaneous community without conflict, hence without need for rational rules and institutions—just as to Frantz Fanon, Sorel has revealed the liberating dignity of irrational violence.

But this means that in some of the revolutionary movements of the ex-colonial and semi-colonial peoples, we are now facing a "revolt against the West" in a new and different sense. The classical nationalist movements for colonial liberation and for the independent development of the underdeveloped countries have always been, and many of them still are, characterised by ambivalence towards the West. They have been fighting for political independence from the Western powers, for economic independence from Western capital, to some extent also for the chance to preserve their cultural identity, to keep their own soul. But they have also wished to learn from the West in order to imitate it successfully in the techniques of production and power, to catch up with it in science and material development. For the classical movements of national liberation from colonialism or semi-colonialism, one essential goal has been to make their country as rich and powerful as its former Western masters, though this goal could only be achieved by a struggle for independence which often required prolonged conflicts with the Western powers. This was an ambivalent attitude in that it was *not* inspired by a total rejection of Western models and values, but in part by a desire to emulate Western achievements—even though the road there led through a struggle against Western domination.

The new attitude which we encounter in Mao's cultural revolution, in Castro's Cuba, and potentially in other movements influenced by them (whether formally Communist or not) *is* a total rejection of some Western values. It is a determination to stay poor-but-honest rather than imitate the West in promoting the development of economic man (as the Soviets have done), to accept some of the consequences of non-development (though not all) rather than assimilate to Western civilisation. Indeed, we observe for the first time since the decline of the early nativistic movements in those countries, for the first time in movements that claim to be not traditionalist but modern, nationalist, and revolutionary, a fundamental resistance not just to Western power and Western capital, but to the pull of Western civilisation that had hitherto been inseparable from any effort at the modernisation of non-Western countries.

This in turn throws further light also on the revolt of part of the young generation in the West; for that revolt, too, is directed against important aspects of Western civilisation.

This is often denied by well-meaning liberals who, in trying to understand the young rebels, argue that the latter "really" share our liberal values—that they merely take them more seriously than their hypocritical elders and want to *act* on principles which the establishment merely *talks* about. If that were all, we should be faced with a political and social movement of a familiar type, for that is indeed the classical role of revolutionary (and also of reformist) movements within a growing civilisation—to regenerate the traditional values of that civilisation by giving them a new institutional content corresponding to changed social conditions. Thus the basic Western idea of the rights of the human person has been reinterpreted in course of time from referring to "the rights of each according to his station" to meaning "equal political rights for all," and more recently to imply the rights of each to equal opportunity and social security. But this, it seems to me, no longer applies to many of either the politically active or the passive and non-political young rebels of our time.

For while it is true that they generally accept the familiar values of love and individual freedom, of truth and social justice, merely seeking to turn these values into an indictment of the older generation, it is also true that they have increasingly come to reject the values of material and in part even of intellectual achievement and of the effort and discipline needed to accomplish it, including the discipline of reason—values which are equally essential parts of the cultural heritage of the West. The same is apparent in their rejection of any time perspective in the name of a cult of immediacy; for the sense of measured time and the gearing of action to foresight have been basic for all Western civilisation from the age when Western church-towers were first endowed with clocks to the latest achievements of science and industry. In other words, we are witnessing a major failure to transmit an important part of our basic values to a significant part of the young generation.

Indeed it seems to me that the rebellion of the young which is taking place in all advanced Western countries, and which is assuming both politically revolutionary forms and the form of a passive non-political refusal to grow into roles within the industrial society and submit to its pressures, is not primarily a political phenomenon. It is, above all, a sign of a crisis in our civilisation.

SECULAR SAINTS AND NOBLE SAVAGES

For there are, I believe, two basic tests for the vitality of a civilisation. One is the ability to transmit to the young generation its essential values even while adapting their concrete, practical meaning to changing conditions. The other is its capacity to attract and assimilate outsiders, "barbarians," who come within range of its material influence—and not only subject them and disrupt their traditional forms of life.

As recently as the last generation, this vitality of Western civilisation was subjected to extremely serious strain, for the destructive outbreak of Nazism constituted a radical, nihilistic revolt against that civilisation from within. Yet following its military defeat, the reassimilation of Germany by the West has been extremely successful, and even the Soviet Union, for all the rigidity of its political structure and all the seriousness of its continuing conflicts with the Western powers, shows unmistakable signs of a progressive *cultural* "convergence" with the West. Now for the first time, the West is faced simultaneously with growing evidence of a crisis both in its capacity to assimilate its "external proletariat" (in the sense given to this term in Toynbee's *Study of History*), the poor, underdeveloped, non-Western peoples, and in its ability to transmit its heritage to its own youth.

This diagnosis is confirmed by the fact that the quasi-religious character of some of the new movements is manifested not only in their commitment to chiliastic goals, but in their cult of saviour-leaders and in their search for a new code of conduct. Thus the asceticism and heroic self-sacrifice of Che Guevara have permitted the growth of a legend around him that combines Christ-like features with those of a militant secular leader. The official cult of Mao Tse-tung no longer describes him as a mere creative continuator of the Marxist-Leninist revolutionary tradition, not even merely as the unique architect of the political rebirth of the Chinese nation and state: he is presented as the author of a totally new system of thought and action—a system that will enable all those to work miracles who believe in Mao and live by his rules. Many of the "Quotations from Chairman Mao" in the little *Red Book,* from which hundreds of millions of Chinese are taught to recite several times a day, stand in competition not with any Western or Soviet political document, but with the Analects of Confucius and the Bible.

Yet while the new movements are largely united in their rejection of the Western way of life (or, at any rate, of major aspects of it), they diverge widely in seeking to define their alternatives. Castro and Mao reject Western materialism, and at least Mao also Western individualism. But both believe in the need for collective effort and discipline which are rejected by large parts of the Western "New Left" as well as by the non-political Western hippies, drop-outs, and drug-takers. Conversely, many of the would-be revolutionaries of the "New Left" retain an anarchist type of individualism; but "petty bourgeois anarchism" remains a term of abuse in Cuba and China as much as in Russia, while the prophets of a non-political drug-culture clearly believe that community can only be established by escaping from individuality.

There is, thus, no unity of values among the new movements except in their common target of attack—their negation of the modern industrial society. Beyond that the "New Left's" admiration for Castro and Mao is based on a romantic misunderstanding that sees those hard-striving, hard-driving taskmasters of their peoples as the Noble Savages of our time.

A CRISIS OF CIVILISATION

This, then, is the tentative conclusion at which we have arrived. The new type of revolutionary movements, both on the outer fringes of our Western-centred world and in the advanced Western countries, as well as some phenomena within the latter that are not "revolutionary" in the conventional, political sense of the term, can best be understood as symptoms of a crisis of Western civilisation. It is this which explains their increasing turning-away from the Marxist type of analysis and strategy: for Marxism, in its origin, its values and its commitment to rationality, is indissolubly linked to its Western heritage.

I am conscious that while that conclusion may help us to grasp the historical significance, intellectual background and spiritual character of the new movements, it does not answer the further questions about their concrete social roots, the reasons for their appearance at this time, and their prospects of political success. Nor can I even attempt to deal seriously with those questions in the framework of the present essay. All that is possible here is to sketch out some of the directions in which the answers may be looked for.

The main point I should like to make here is that the crisis in our civilisation has followed an unprecedented acceleration both of the external expansion of its influence and of the pace of its internal change.

Externally, Western expansion over the last two centuries has effectively disrupted the traditional societies created by other civilisations all over the globe. The political reflux of that expansion, the extrusion of Western dominance from the former colonial areas in the last few decades, has not reversed its disruptive effects and has left the new nations with problems of "modernisation" which in most cases are proving far more difficult than anticipated.

As I have already suggested, the goal of modernisation was at first generally conceived as implying at least a partial imitation of the West, even if often by different institutional means—for instance, industrialisation not by free enterprise but by state planning, or political mobilisation by single-party rule rather than by multi-party competition. But it now looks as if in countries where "development" in this sense proves particularly difficult—owing to the pressure of population, or to the extreme shortage of cadres with modern training, or simply to the strength of traditionalist cultural resistance, or to any combination of those factors—important aspects of the goal itself are coming to be doubted. Total rejection of the Western model is proclaimed in the accents of revolt in order to avoid the confession of failure and the disappointment of the expectations aroused. As the West can always be blamed for having started the whole agonising process by its intrusion, and for either having refused to help the development of the latecomers or at any rate having failed to give enough aid to be effective, the rejection of the unattainable model is accompanied by a deepening of resentment against its possessors.

Internally, the acceleration of change in technology, and with it in social structures and habits of living, has in the last few decades created intense moral uncertainty in many Western countries. That moral uncertainty of a generation of parents who on many issues are no longer sure what is right or wrong is probably at the root of their failure to transmit their values effectively, and of the consequent revolt among the young. What appears today as a widespread rebellion of youth against authority is, I suspect, largely born of frustration caused by the absence of authority—in the sense of a lack not of severity, but of convinced and therefore convincing models of conduct. For a growing civilisation to survive in a climate of unending social change, as is the fate of ours, the central problem is to combine a belief in the absolute validity of its fundamental values with flexibility in the practical rules derived from them. As the pace of change accelerates, the difficulty of solving this problem increases, and the tendency towards a polarisation of attitudes between a combination of firm belief with impractical rigidity on one side and of pragmatic flexibility with fundamental relativism on the other becomes stronger.

In the Western industrial societies of today, this basic problem of preserving a continuity of values in the flux of changing conditions and rules appears in a variety of concrete shapes. Probably the most important of those is the loss of a sense of common purpose in the midst of enormous, accelerating material progress. While that progress has not abolished scarcity and made effort and discipline superfluous (as the new utopians believe), it has indeed created an unprecedented degree of relative affluence, solved the crucial problem of steadiness of employment, and permitted improvements in the standards of living, leisure and social security on so broad a front as to deprive traditional class conflicts of their revolutionary potential.

Yet this tremendous progress has been achieved at the price of a concentration on individual material advantage and been accompanied by the loss of a sense of common purpose, as first the traditional certainties of religious faith and then the substitutes offered by national loyalties were undermined. The moral sensitivity of the young is shocked by the contrast between the intense effort devoted by their elders to the pursuit of minor individual advantages or to expenditure for national military power on one side, and their lack of concern for the suffering of the marginal poor inside and the under-nourished majority of mankind outside the industrial world on the other. The young are all the more assured of the righteousness of their criticism because they have experienced the moral uncertainty of their elders from an early age. As a result, many of them perceive an acute moral conflict between the ideals they have been taught and the competitive conformism into which they are expected to grow—a conflict all the more insoluble because the society which they reject as "empty" is technically well-functioning and is apparently accepted without question by the large majority of adults. Now where intolerable moral conflict is not confined to individuals but expresses a crisis of civilisation, the response has always been an upsurge of utopian beliefs—a collective escape into the dream of a perfect society where every conflict would be solved in advance. The difference this time is that we are dealing with a utopianism inspired not by hope, but by despair. That is the ultimate reason for its lack of a time perspective, its irrationality and its violence.

As for the social locus of the revolt, just as a turn towards total rejection of the Western model is most likely to occur among those non-Western nations which experience the most discouraging difficulties in their effort at modernisation, so a radical denial of the need for material effort and discipline appears to prove most attractive to those strata of Western youth that have remained longest and furthest removed from the productive process—be it as students from upper- and middle-class families or as under-educated members of minority groups who find themselves virtually unemployable through no fault of their own.

Indulgence in pipe-dreams about the effortless abundance possible in the "post-industrial society" is most natural for those who have either been preserved from any contact with the productive sources of our relative affluence by the economic security of their parents, or have been barred from both those sources and their benefits by the underprivileged position of theirs. Karl Marx once pointed out that while the (non-productive) proletariat of ancient Rome lived on society, modern capitalist society lived on its (industrial) proletariat. But the "internal proletariat" that is coming to be as disaffected from Western civilisation as some parts of its "external proletariat" does not consist of the industrial workers for whom Marx reserved the term. It is a "proletariat" in the ancient Roman sense, divorced from production but convinced that society owes it a living, and willing only to supplement the publicly supplied bread by providing its own circuses. For today as in Rome, the only forms of separate collective action open to a group that cannot withdraw its productive contribution, because it makes none, are highly emotional and violent. The neo-Bakuninism of the "New Left" appears to be the ideological expression of this transfer of the revolutionary mission from the industrial working class to the neo-Roman proletariat of our time. As its purely destructive forms of action repel all productive sectors of society but attract its marginal and semi-criminal elements, the danger of its degeneration into a movement of the *Lumpenproletariat* becomes manifest.

THE REAL THREAT

There remains the question of the political prospects of these new movements. In terms of "power politics," I do not rate their chances of success very high; that is indeed implied in what I have described as their lack of rationality. Because of Maoist irrationality, China seems to have made very little progress in the last decade, except on the narrowest sector of nuclear weapons; and it will not become an effective model of development so long as it remains Maoist in this sense. Nor has the model of Castroism, and the strategy of small guerrilla bands starting operations regardless of social and political conditions, gained much influence in Latin America or shown much promise of doing so in the foreseeable future—unless widespread failures of development give them a chance. Finally, today's campus rebels are not, like the student movements of Tsarist Russia or Weimar Germany or British India, the forerunners of a political revolution. They do not operate in stagnant or politically oppressed societies and are not the articulate expression of the inarticulate mood of large masses of people. Moreover, for all the traits of kinship we have mentioned, the "New Left" students are not fascist—and Bakuninists have never and nowhere taken power: indeed they would not know what to do with it.

Nevertheless, the danger to Western society from these new movements is serious. It is not the danger of a "Third World bloc" abroad or "revolution" at home; it is the prospect of destruction, decay, and barbarisation. The real threat is not that Mao will be able to overrun Asia or that Castro will revolutionise Latin America. It is that overpopulation and hunger, indigenous governmental incompetence and Western self-satisfied indifference will cause the festering sores of despair, political instability, and violence to spread. Again, the real menace within the West is not that young extremists will "take over"; they cannot even take over the universities. But they can paralyse and, in some cases, destroy them by first destroying the climate of tolerance and rational discourse which is the breath of academic life. They can deprive our societies of an important part of the well-trained and loyal élites needed for the steady renewal of administration and economic management, of research and education. And they can create a backlash of police brutality and Right-wing extremism which will in effect help them to obstruct the working of democracy and the constructive solution of urgent problems.

I do not, of course, know any simple answer to these problems, any magic prescription for coping with them. All I should like to state in conclusion is that, in dealing with the danger constituted by the new type of revolutionary movements, it is wrong—even more wrong than it was with the old type of Communist movements—to be obsessed with "the enemy" as if he was a devil suddenly appearing out of nowhere, a *diabolus ex machina.* The forces of destruction have, of course, to be resisted; civilisation cannot be defended by surrendering to violence. But this is only the minor part of the task. Above all, civilisation must be defended by upholding and renewing its standards in action, by combining a faith in its values with the determination to apply them constructively in a changing world—and therefore to make sacrifices for them—inside and outside the West. Only if we can restore hope by doing that will the West survive. Otherwise it will succumb to barbarisation—and that means (as the whole of history is there to teach us) succumbing not to some particular barbarian ideology, movement, or tribe, but to its own failure.